MAGILL'S LITERARY ANNUAL
2009

MAGILL'S
LITERARY ANNUAL
2009

Essay-Reviews of 200 Outstanding Books
Published in the United States During 2008

With an Annotated List of Titles

Volume Two
Lib-Z

Edited by
JOHN D. WILSON
STEVEN G. KELLMAN

SALEM PRESS
Pasadena, California   Hackensack, New Jersey

LIBRARY OF CONGRESS CATALOG CARD NO.
ISBN (set): 978-1-58765-547-0
ISBN (vol. 1): 978-1-58765-548-7
ISBN (vol. 2): 978-1-58765-549-4

FIRST PRINTING

PRINTED IN CANADA

CONTENTS

CONTENTS

COMPLETE ANNOTATED LIST OF TITLES

VOLUME 1

Acedia and Me: A Marriage, Monks, and a Writer's Life—*Kathleen Norris* . . . 1
 Norris examines the concept of acedia from its ancient understanding in monastic spirituality through its more recent role in philosophy, psychology, literature, and American culture and also in her spiritual, marital, and writing life

The Age of Reagan: A History, 1974-2008—*Sean Wilentz*. 5
 A fast-paced, well-documented analysis of the rise of Ronald Reagan, his presidential administration, and his impact on American politics

Ajax—*Sophocles*. 10
 A fast-paced contemporary rendering of Sophocles' tragedy

Alfred Kazin: A Biography—*Richard M. Cook*. 14
 This first comprehensive literary biography of one of the most notable literary critics of his age chronicles Kazin's emergence while still in his twenties as a critic of considerable note, and it relates this emergence to the intellectualism that abounded in New York during the 1930's

Algeria: Anger of the Dispossessed—*Martin Evans and John Phillips*. 19
 A thoughtful and well-researched study that explains clearly why Algerian governments, since independence from France in 1962, have failed to meet the expectations and needs of the vast majority of Algerian Muslims

All of It Singing: New and Selected Poems—*Linda Gregg*. 24
 This collection of Gregg's older and new poems incorporates elements of classicism, nature, and contemporary life

All Shall Be Well; and All Shall Be Well; and All Manner of Things
  Shall Be Well—*Tod Wodicka*. 28
 Burt Hecker, a widower who has lived his entire life out of step with his family and his surroundings, attempts to find peace as he journeys across Europe in search of his lost son

COMPLETE ANNOTATED LIST OF TITLES

Goldblatt's comprehensive book intertwines the history of soccer with the general political and social history of the countries around the world where soccer has been an important popular sport

This biography of Quaker saint and social reformer Woolman traces his spiritual development, analyzes the roots of his activism, documents the changes he helped bring about, and recognizes his continuing relevance to issues such as racism, economic justice, cruelty to animals, and simple living

A profound and haunting collection that touches on isolation, love, loss, and spiritual growth

Coll illuminates the life of Osama Bin Laden by setting it against the rise to unimaginable wealth of his family, builders to the Saudi royal family at a time of unprecedented development

Moore explores her complex relationship with her father, the revered Episcopal bishop of New York, Paul Moore, Jr., and the impact that his hidden homosexual life had on his priesthood and his family

A partly historical, partly autobiographical account of a recent controversy in theoretical physics by one of the physicists involved

Le's first book offers seven short stories that cover the globe and feature an amazingly varied cast of central characters; his plots include assassinations in Colombia, a failed family reunion in New York City, religious festivals in Iran, and escape from Communist Vietnam

A semiautobiographical account of the author's life as a bookman, providing glimpses into the arcane and complex trade of bookseller and highlighting interesting books, characters, and personages he has known

COMPLETE ANNOTATED LIST OF TITLES

COMPLETE ANNOTATED LIST OF TITLES

VOLUME 2

COMPLETE ANNOTATED LIST OF TITLES

A large and comprehensive narrative account of the cultural, economic, and diplomatic relations between Americans and the British, from John Cabot's explorations
of North America of 1497 until the Iraq War of the early twenty-first century

The title character, a prickly, outspoken woman, plays a major role in this collection, which deals with the lives and the relationships of the people who live in a small
Maine town

Krasikov's first collection of short stories depicts experiences and travails of immigrants from Georgia and Russia, torn between their native country and the new one

Iyer traces the Fourteenth Dalai Lama's life from their first meeting in 1974, describing the exiled spiritual leader of Tibetan Buddhism's activities in Dharamsala,
India, and in his worldwide travels

The author samples beliefs about the origins and nature of sin in cultures from the
ancients to contemporary sages

A life of Riis, whose articles, books, and photographs taught the American public
about abysmal immigrant living conditions, helping spur urban reform in the Progressive Era

A selection of stories from Wolff's previous collections, along with ten previously
uncollected new stories

A definitive new biography of one of the United States' foremost naturalists, conservationists, and environmentalists

A valuable Jewish manuscript, dating from medieval Spain, has been preserved at
the National Museum in Sarajevo, Bosnia; this fictional story imagines how the book
might have survived through five hundred years of historical turmoil

COMPLETE ANNOTATED LIST OF TITLES

MAGILL'S
LITERARY ANNUAL
2009

THE LIBRARY AT NIGHT

Author: Alberto Manguel (1948-   )
First published: 2006, in Canada
Publisher: Yale University Press (New Haven, Conn.).
Illustrated. 376 pp. $27.50
Type of work: Essays, literary history

In this collection of bookish essays, Manguel explores the fascinating life of libraries from antiquity to the present

In 2002 Alberto Manguel, son of the former Argentine ambassador to Israel and longtime bibliophile, moved to a French village south of the Loire. Here, adjacent to his fifteenth century rectory, Le Presbytère, he rebuilt a dilapidated stone barn into a proper home for his thirty thousand books gathered throughout his life. During the day, he works in his library; at night he reads and listens to the ghosts whispering from the shelves. The fifteen essays in *The Library at Night* reflect on his personal collection and on libraries in general.

Much of the opening chapter, "The Library as Myth," discusses the greatest library in antiquity, that of Alexandria. Here Ptolemy I created an institution that he and his successors hoped would embody the memory of humanity. Whenever a ship docked at the port, agents of the ruler would search for manuscripts, which would be seized and copied. The copy, likely to contain scribal errors, would then be returned to the owner and the original kept. Ptolemy III Euergetes borrowed from Athens the official texts of the city's tragedians, including the works of Aeschylus, Sophocles, and Euripides. To secure these, he gave the large security of fifteen gold talents. He then made copies of these plays, kept the originals, and returned the transcriptions, gladly forfeiting his deposit. However, as Manguel notes, of this attempt to enshrine the thoughts of the world, nothing remains: not a single manuscript, not even a sense of what the building that housed them looked like.

Judging from the fragmentary remains of the *Pinakes* of Callimachus, that library probably was organized by genre, such as epic or tragedy or philosophy. In "The Library as Order" Manguel discusses his own various efforts to sort his collection. As a child he owned about a hundred volumes, which he repeatedly rearranged: by height, by subject, by language, by color, and, most logical of all, by the degree of his affection for them. All these methods, except perhaps the last, have historical antecedents. The author Valéry Larbaud had his books bound in different colors to indicate the language in which they were written. In the third century C.E., the Chinese Imperial Library used a similar color-coded scheme: green bindings for canonical or classical texts, red for history, blue for philosophy, and gray for literature. In the seventeenth and eighteenth centuries, Harvard University's library and the three thousand volumes of the seventeenth century diarist Samuel Pepys were organized by height. Nov-

~

*Alberto Manguel was born in
Argentina and lived in Canada for
twenty years before moving to France
in 2002. His books include* A
Dictionary of Imaginary Places *(1980),
with Guadalupi Gianni, and* A History
of Reading *(1996).*

~

elist George Perec listed a dozen ways to arrange books, including by alphabet, by date of purchase, by date of publication, by language, and by the owner's reading preferences.

As Manguel points out in "The Library as Space," regardless of the order one chooses, books always outgrow their allotted boundaries and so require new arrangements. To cope with this problem, the poet Lionel Johnson suspended shelves from his ceiling like chandeliers. Manguel tells of a friend who devised four-sided rotating bookcases. Even the largest tax-funded institutions confront "biblio-congestion" and have turned to technology for a solution that Manguel, along with Nicholson Baker in his book *Double Fold: Libraries and the Assault on Paper* (2001), reveals as sadly unsatisfactory. The Library of Congress and the British Library have tranferred to microfilm long runs of old newspapers and then discarded the originals, only to discover that the copies are incomplete. Moreover, the shelf life of microfilm is questionable. Even more problematic are computer files. Manguel points out with grim satisfaction that the 1986 computerized copy of the eleventh century Domesday Book was unreadable by 2002, whereas the thousand-year-old original can still be consulted without difficulty.

Another way to cope with the question of space is to restrict holdings, a method Manguel considers in "The Library as Power." He tells of the seventeenth century mathematician, philosopher, and librarian Gottfried Wilhelm Leibnitz, coinventor of calculus, who argued for the collecting of only scientific books. Leibnitz also favored small books because they required less shelf space. Callimachus had expressed the same sentiment two thousand years earlier, writing *Mega biblion, mega kakon,* (a great book is a great evil), reflecting his dislike of unwieldy scrolls. In the next chapter, "The Library as Shadow," Manguel examines examples of biblioclasm, such as the destruction of the texts of the Incas and Aztecs by the proselytizing Europeans. He includes pictures of book-burnings in Nazi Germany and in Warsaw, Indiana.

He returns to this subject later in "The Library as Oblivion." He describes the destruction of the Turgenev Library, established in Paris in 1875 by the Russian expatriate novelist Ivan Turgenev for émigré students from his homeland. According to the novelist Nina Berberova, it was the finest Russian library outside Russia; it has vanished. In 2003, in the aftermath of the American invasion of Iraq, that country's national library was looted as American troops stood by idly. Lost were clay tablets dating back millennia, medieval manuscripts, and later examples of Arabic calligraphy.

Still, as Manguel discusses in "The Library as Survival," some works escape even the most determined efforts to destroy them. He tells of a Jewish prayer book for the Sabbath that he owns; the work was printed in Berlin in 1908. On May 10, 1933, the Nazis held the first of their many book-burnings that targeted Jewish authors and Jewish books, though not limited to them. Nevertheless, somehow this prayer book survived. So did the volumes of the Sholem Aleichem Library in Biała Podlaska, Poland.

Manguel tells of its librarian, who hid its holdings in an attic, where they were found after World War II. These books serve as witnesses to the atrocities perpetrated on their readers.

For all the books that have been written and survived, many others exist only in the realm of the imagination. Manguel discusses these in his thirteenth chapter. Manguel used to read to Jorge Luis Borges, the blind Argentine author who served as head of the Buenos Aires National Library and who wrote about imaginary works such as the romances by the fictional Herbert Quain, the eleventh volume of the *First Encyclopedia of Tlön*, or a play by Jaromir Hladik called *The Enemies*. One of Borges's best-known tales concerns the fictional "Library of Babel," which contains all books. A less comprehensive but no less imaginary collection appears in the seventh chapter of *Pantagruel* (1532) by François Rabelais. Here the eponymous hero visits the actual Library of St. Victor in Paris, which contained theological works of no interest to humanists such as Rabelais. He therefore satirized the holdings by creating his own catalog. Entries include *Bragueta juris* (the codpiece of the law), *Ars honeste petandi in societate* (the art of farting decently in public), and *The Knavish Tricks of Ecclesiastical Judges*. The seventeenth century English writer Sir Thomas Browne published a list of imaginary books in 1653. Included here were Greek poems by Ovid, composed while he was in exile on the shore of the Black Sea, and a Spanish translation of the works of Confucius. Manguel relates that at Gad's Hill, the novelist Charles Dickens created a trompe l'oeil collection with such titles as *Hansard's Guide to Refreshing Sleep* and a ten-volume *Catalogue of the Statues to the Duke of Wellington*. Paul Masson, who worked at the Bibliothèque Nationale, supplemented its limited holdings in fifteenth century Latin and Italian books by adding fictional entries to the catalog. Some fictional libraries contain real books. Such is the collection of Captain Nemo in Jules Verne's *Vingt mille lieues sous les mers* (1869-1870; *Twenty Thousand Leagues Under the Sea*, 1873) or the one destroyed early in the first part of Miguel de Cervantes' *Don Quixote* (1605, 1615).

Manguel keeps a list of imaginary books that he would like to own should they ever be written. As he points out in "The Library as Identity," one's holdings and wish lists reveal much about a person. One looks over the shelves of a personal library not only to find unfamiliar titles but also to learn about the owner. Jay Gatsby, from F. Scott Fitzgerald's *The Great Gatsby* (1925), understood that a library was essential for anyone pretending to gentility, though he did not feel obliged to read any of the books he owned and so left the pages uncut. Petronius's Trimalchio similarly sought prestige and the appearance of learning by declaring that he owned three libraries, one Greek and the others Latin. These fictional characters differ from Gordian II, the third century Roman emperor whom Edward Gibbon describes as having had twenty-two concubines and sixty-two thousand volumes and whose productions show that both were intended for use rather than for show.

Manguel's wide-ranging survey of books and libraries provides delightful reading and demonstrates that, like the younger Gordian, Manguel has gathered his books for use rather than for ostentation. Into such a work, the occasional error is bound to creep. Manguel celebrates the endurance of the Domesday Book, written, he says, with ink on paper. In fact, the Domesday Book was written on parchment. The caption of a picture of a bookcase once owned by Samuel Pepys locates the diarist's library at Oxford; his collection and bookcases are at Magdalene College, Cambridge. Seventy of Pepys's manuscripts are, however, at the Bodleian. Manguel places the Codex Sinaiticus among the manuscripts owned by the English renaissance bibliophile Robert Cotton. This early manuscript of the Bible in Greek remained at the monastery of St. Catherine until 1859 and came to England only in 1933. The caption to the reproduction of the 1644 title page of Gabriel Naudé's *Advis pour dresser une bibliothèque* (*Advice on Establishing a Library*, 1950) describes it as belonging to the first edition of the publication, even though the title page states "Seconde Edition"; the first edition had appeared seventeen years earlier. These are cavils, but Yale had more than a year to correct these errors after the first edition appeared in 2006 in Canada. Still, all bibliophiles will enjoy dipping into Manguel's work in their libraries at night.

Joseph Rosenblum

Review Sources

Canadian Literature, no. 193 (Summer, 2007): 163-164.
The Daily Telegraph, May 24, 2008, p. 28.
The Globe and Mail, October 7, 2006, p. F10.
Library Journal 133, no. 12 (July 1, 2008): 112.
Los Angeles Times, March 25, 2008, p. E1.
National Review 60, no. 15 (August 18, 2008): 52-53.
New Statesman 137 (May 19, 2008): 55-56.
The Spectator 308 (November 22, 2008): 43.
The Times Literary Supplement, November 14, 2008, p. 29.
The Toronto Star, November 12, 2006, p. D6.
The Virginia Quarterly Review 84, no. 4 (Fall, 2008): 271.
The Washington Post Book World, April 6, 2008, p. 10
The Wilson Quarterly 32, no. 2 (Spring, 2008): 94-96.

LIFE CLASS

Author: Pat Barker (1943-   )
Publisher: Doubleday (New York). 311 pp. $23.95
Type of work: Novel
Time: 1914-1915
Locale: London, England, and Ypres, Belgium

Novelist Barker returns to a World War I setting in this story of a small group of art students in London who have their assumptions about art and life called into question by the arrival of the Great War

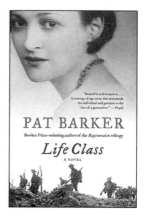

> "Beautiful and evocative.... A coming-of-age story that transcends the individual and gestures to the fate of a generation." —*People*

PAT BARKER
Booker Prize-winning author of the *Regeneration* trilogy

Life Class
A NOVEL

Principal characters:
> PAUL TARRANT, an art student and later a
>   Red Cross hospital orderly
> ELINOR BROOKE, an art student
> CHRISTOPHER "KIT" NEVILLE, an artist and later a Red Cross ambulance
>   driver
> TERESA HALLIDAY, an artists' model

Though trained as a historian, Pat Barker began writing novels in 1982, but she first gained wide readership and critical acclaim with the 1991 release of her fifth novel, *Regeneration*. That book and the two that followed, collectively referred to as the Regeneration Trilogy, were set against the backdrop of World War I and chronicled the horrors of the war as well as the seismic shifts that it brought to English society. Most readers associate Barker with this war, and she returns to it with *Life Class*, after more than a decade during which she published novels on more contemporary subjects.

Life Class is divided into two sections, the first of which opens with a scene in a life drawing class at the famous Slade School of Art in London. Readers are introduced to Paul Tarrant, a young student who apparently has some talent but is not progressing with his art at the rate that he or his teacher, the stern and overbearing Henry Tonks, would like. Paul has a friendship with, as well as some romantic interest in, his fellow student Elinor Brooke, who is also being wooed by recent Slade graduate and rising artistic star Kit Neville. The three, along with others from London's art scene, frequent the Café Royal, where Paul meets and becomes involved with Teresa Halliday, an artists' model whose physical charms and sexual frankness captivate him, despite his haunting sense that she is hiding something and despite the fact that her estranged husband stalks and threatens the lovers.

The world in which Paul and his compatriots move is filled, as he thinks, with "the sense of witty, significant things being said by interesting people," but it has a certain shallow, self-involved quality. It is also not without its worries or its serious side. Sexual and romantic tensions boil between Paul and Teresa, Paul and Elinor, and Kit and Elinor. Kit worries that Paul is a rival for Elinor's affection, though both are uncertain

~

Pat Barker's first novel, Union Street,
*was published in 1982, and her trilogy
of World War I novels—*Regeneration
(1991), The Eye in the Door *(1993),
and* The Ghost Road *(1995)—earned
her numerous literary accolades,
including the prestigious Man Booker
Prize for the final volume. Her work
draws heavily on her early training as
a historian.*

~

if her commitment to her art and to her independence precludes romantic involvement.
Her virginal detachment from all suitors suggests either an unlikely puritanical ethic or a
complete lack of interest in sex. Meanwhile
Paul, with his working-class northern roots, is
intimidated by much in the gentrified world
of art, notably Kit, who outstrips Paul with his
class privilege, his apparent (though illusory)
confidence, his sexual conquests, and particularly his artistic success. Throughout the
novel's early chapters, Paul struggles with the
question of whether or not to continue his
studies at the Slade or to accept that he is unlikely ever to succeed as an artist. Meanwhile, he is plagued with nightmares about the loss of his mother at an early age.

Behind these personal tensions, though, rumbles a far greater concern. All of Europe waits in anxiety as the once-distant possibility of war begins to resolve into a
near certainty. The rumblings can be heard even in the fairly sheltered circles in which
the characters travel. Near the end of the book's first half, Paul, Kit, and Elinor are
visiting her family's country home when the news comes that war has finally broken
out. Immediately discussions ensue as to how deeply and how soon England will become involved, who will enlist, and what all of this will mean to the future. The two
parts of the novel, then, hinge neatly on the moment when World War I begins, the
moment when Europe and the world are forever changed.

When the second part begins, Elinor is back in London, continuing her studies at
the Slade, while Paul is away at war. After attempting to enlist, he was rejected because of his weak lungs, so he joins the Red Cross and soon finds himself working as
an orderly at a Belgian field hospital a mere two miles from the front. After this point
in the novel, Paul and Elinor begin to embody opposing attitudes toward art. Paul is
strangely given new impetus to create by his hospital work, where he attends the
maimed and dying, bearing witness to unspeakable miseries. Though this work leaves
him physically exhausted and emotionally drained, he nonetheless rents himself a studio and finds the time and energy to paint and draw in his off hours, choosing as subjects the scarred land and the human misery that surround him every day. These are
subjects that he knows have no commercial viability, yet for the first time he is satisfied with his own work. He comes to see his own and his friends' relatively sheltered
lives before the war as "contemptible." It is only here that the irony of the novel's title
becomes clear, for his art school life class could never have taught Paul the life lessons he needs finally to create art of lasting value.

Elinor, meanwhile, remains in London and continues to attend the Slade, largely
depopulated since most of the male students have enlisted or otherwise committed
themselves to the war effort. Her social circle, now that her male friends are serving
overseas, comes to include pacifist society hostess Lady Ottoline Morrell, and though
she does not go so far as to denounce the war, Elinor does all she can to ignore its in-

fluence. She continues to study and to paint, holding firmly and defiantly to her belief that art is the highest human endeavor. She insists that war and suffering are unfit subjects for art, which should be about "the things we choose to love." Barker thus invites the reader to ponder the question of whether, and to what degree, art continues to matter in a world torn apart by irrational violence and unbearable suffering.

Unexpectedly, every separation in space and ideology that divides Paul and Elinor allows their former friendship to blossom into something more. Once Paul is stationed near the front, he and Elinor begin to write frequent and increasingly emotional letters, until it becomes clear they are, or at least imagine themselves to be, in love. The novel at this point alternates conventional narrative chapters with epistolary chapters made up of these letters. Elinor even manages, by pretending to be a volunteer nurse, to cross over into "the forbidden zone" and visit Paul for several days in Ypres, where they consummate their sexual relationship and argue about the role of art in the world. Even the bombing of the town, though, and firsthand exposure to the death and destruction it brings are not enough to shake Elinor's faith in the rightness of her belief that art is a thing apart, unassailable by the horrors of war.

Suffering a leg wound, Paul is sent home, but the man who returns to London is not the one who used to live there. At the end of the book, readers are left to wonder if Paul and Elinor have any hope of surviving as a couple or whether the war and their differing reactions to it have placed them too far apart to ever bridge the gap. Has Elinor really managed to escape the war and its consequences to the degree she believes? Will Paul's newfound confidence and skill as a painter be enough to sustain a career, and will he find suitable and compelling subjects now that he has left behind the horrors that inspired him in the first place? The war has irrevocably swept away the world of cafés and painting scholarships and glittering surfaces, leaving behind only a series of questions.

On a philosophical level, *Life Class* touches on many subjects, not the least among them issues of class and gender. Paul's early insecurities as an artist arise at least partly from class anxieties and the knowledge that his family does not regard art as real work. By contrast, it is Kit's easy upper-middle-class manner that allows him to appear supremely confident to those around him despite his deep insecurities. Elinor, meanwhile, is sheltered by both class privilege and gender from the expectations the men face to participate in the war effort. Ironically, it is her gender as well that makes it so difficult for her to be taken seriously as an artist or as an independent person and for her friends and family to believe she has aspirations beyond marriage and motherhood. In addition, the novel is about the nature of art, and whether art, love, or anything else, for that matter, should be immune from the ravages of war. As she has in previous novels, Barker brings the real world of 1914 London to the pages of her fiction in part by the inclusion of minor characters—anatomist and art teacher Tonks, socialite Lady Ottoline Morrell, artist Augustus John—drawn from history. The principal characters are based on composites of real artists as well. This and the gritty, nightmarish realism of the war and hospital scenes remind readers that the larger philosophical questions are not mere intellectual gymnastics but genuine problems, the answers to which go a long way toward helping people figure out how to live their lives. Barker's novels, then, ask her readers to contemplate many of the same questions that her characters do.

Critical reception of *Life Class* was mixed, certainly nowhere near as positive as that lavished upon Barker's earlier World War I novels, in part because it lacks the tight narrative structure that guided those books. The perspective in the first part of the novel drifts a bit, making it unclear at times whether Paul, Elinor, or Kit is meant to attract the reader's main focus. Characters and subplots—such as Paul and Teresa being stalked and harassed by her violent, estranged husband, or the story of a French soldier at the Red Cross hospital suffering from a self-inflicted gunshot—become central for a time, only to be dropped without a further mention. Many critics also found the conclusion too open-ended to be ultimately satisfying. Nonetheless, as a portrait of believable people struggling to answer complicated questions and living through a dark and difficult moment in history, *Life Class* has much to offer a reader.

Janet E. Gardner

Review Sources

Booklist 104, no. 3 (October 1, 2007): 5-6.
Commonweal 135, no. 9 (May 9, 2008): 28-29.
Kirkus Reviews 75, no. 20 (October 15, 2007): 1064.
Library Journal 132, no. 19 (November 15, 2007): 48.
New Statesman 136 (July 16, 2007): 64.
The New York Times, February 29, 2008, p. 31.
People 69, no. 4 (February 4, 2008): 47.
Publishers Weekly 254, no. 42 (October 22, 2007): 34.
The Spectator 304 (August 4, 2007): 33.
The Times (London), July 7, 2007, p. 5.
The Times Literary Supplement, July 6, 2007, p. 23.
The Wall Street Journal 251, no. 20 (January 25, 2008): W2.

THE LIFE OF THE SKIES
Birding at the End of Nature

Author: Jonathan Rosen (1963-   )
Publisher: Farrar, Straus and Giroux (New York).
   326 pp. $24.00
Type of work: Environment, history of science, natural
   history, nature

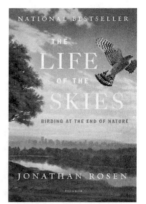

*In his exploration of bird watching and its interaction
with and impact on everything else in life, Rosen explores
many aspects of his life, putting them into a perspective obtained from watching birds*

Principal personages:
> JONATHAN ROSEN, American author and
> bird watcher
> EDWARD O. WILSON, American ant expert,
> sociobiologist, and conservationist
> ALFRED RUSSELL WALLACE and CHARLES DARWIN, English explorers
> and naturalists, cofounders of the principle of natural selection, the
> mechanism of evolutionary change
> WALT WHITMAN and ROBERT FROST, American poets who wrote poems
> about birds
> HENRY DAVID THOREAU, American naturalist and author of *Walden*
> JOHN JAMES AUDUBON, naturalized American who set out to paint every
> bird in North America
> DAVID KULLIVAN and GENE SPARLING, American outdoorsmen who
> believe they saw ivory-billed woodpeckers, long after they were
> thought to be extinct

Jonathan Rosen, an avid bird watcher, introduces the pastime in a never-before-seen way. In *The Life of the Skies*, he connects birds and bird watching to almost everything in his life, including the life of the United States and the problems of the world. In the process, he explores the history of ornithology and bird watching (though he denies that the book is such a history). He also contemplates aspects of the literature of North America, Jewish culture in North America and Israel, the creation-evolution debate, and the broader question of the existence of a spirit world. He considers human abuse of the natural world, and he argues for the preservation of that world. These and other topics are invariably connected to bird watching. Reader credulity is strained by some of these connections, but for Rosen they work in interesting ways.

The most poignant of those connections is his habit of walking in New York City's Central Park after visits with his dementia-stricken father. While bird watching in the park, he simultaneously loses himself in the birds and consciously attempts to stave off his father's fate by exercising his brain to remember bird names and bird songs. In this context, too, Rosen recalls the discovery that new nerve cells are formed in the

~

Jonathan Rosen lives in New York and works as the editorial director of the Web site Nextbook. He has written two novels, the memoir The Talmud and the Internet *(2000), and a number of articles for* The New Yorker *and* The New York Times.

~

brains of adult birds. Before that discovery, adult vertebrate brains were thought to be incapable of regenerating nerve cells and so incapable of repair. The discovery brings hope to victims of Alzheimer's, Parkinson's, and other diseases caused by brain-cell death, and it connects birds (and bird watching) to Rosen and his father even more firmly.

Though it would be incomplete as such, the book is a better history of bird watching, ornithology, and conservation than Rosen's denial suggests. He outlines Alexander Wilson's career, calling him the father of North American ornithology. He identifies John James Audubon as the father of North American bird watching. Both murdered birds with wild abandon so that they would have models to describe and paint. He finds it interesting that the Audubon Society, from its inception a bird-preservation organization, chose Audubon's name for its namesake. Rosen reasons that Wilson and Audubon were acting out of love for the birds, but that the expression of that love differed because of the times in which they lived. For Audubon, Wilson, and other early naturalists, nature seemed to afford endless resources in need of study, and the key to understanding them was, at first, a specimen at hand for study. The Audubon Societies formed later, at a time when the finite nature of all natural resources was becoming evident. To them, nature was a treasure to be preserved from impending decimation. Undoubtedly, Audubon's name was chosen for the organization because of his paintings, not his marksmanship. Rosen recognizes the important contribution hunters have made to conservation, paying considerable homage to U.S. president Theodore Roosevelt's role in this regard. However, the destruction of birds by the eighteenth and nineteenth century collectors and hunters may have been the beginning of the "end of nature" scenario Rosen warns about in the book.

Judging from the book's subtitle, a primary purpose of this work is to present the troubled state of nature and its birds and to encourage action to bring about their preservation. However, it is not always easy to identify this goal in the myriad subplots. Each subplot is interesting and informative in its own right, and losing the book's theme (if the subtitle does reflect it) from time to time is probably harmless. The "Epilogue" brings the subtitle's point into focus, and a look back through the book after reading the "Epilogue" illuminates the other chapters' contribution to that point. Several of the subplots become themes and are revisited throughout the book.

One of the most persistent of these is the ivory-billed woodpecker story. The book contains a brief history of the ivory-bill's presumed extinction and rediscovery in North America. Last seen there (at least last documented scientifically) in 1944, the bird was declared extinct, and that conviction was so profound that the ivory-bill is not included in some of the field guides to North American birds. It does appear in other field guides, but always with a note about its probable extinction. Rosen explores the claims of ivory-billed woodpecker sightings in Southern swamp forests in 1999 (by David Kullivan) and in 2004 (by Gene Sparling). He describes his own trips to those Southern swamps to get a good look at the big woodpecker, but he was unsuccessful in sighting one. Although the evidence gathered since the Kullivan and Sparling presumed sightings has not been definitive (despite a paper in *Science*, the premier North American research journal, declaring the woodpecker's rediscovery), Rosen expresses a belief (or at least a hope) that the ivory-billed woodpecker still lives in the swamps of the southeastern United States. In addition to the decimation of the ivory-billed population, he describes the extinctions of the passenger pigeon and the Carolina parakeet and considers their causes (overhunting and overcollecting by people such as Audubon and Alexander Wilson). He ponders the situation facing the birds he is writing about, those facing "the end of nature," likely to be caused by habitat destruction, the atmospheric greenhouse, and other less direct human impacts.

Other themes or subplots woven into the book involve literary efforts about birds. Walt Whitman chooses poetry for his life's work on the basis of a male mockingbird who sings all night, night after night, after losing his mate. As a boy, Whitman went out at night to listen and later addressed a poem to the bird. Whitman, the mockingbird, and the poem, "Out of the Cradle Endlessly Rocking," from Whitman's *Leaves of Grass* (1855), make recurrent appearances in *The Life of the Sky* to support the central nature of bird watching as a human activity.

Robert Frost's ovenbird asks "what to make of a diminished thing" in a poem named for the bird. The ovenbird seems to be asking the central question of Rosen's book. In Rosen's interpretation, the "diminished thing" is nature. Frost and the ovenbird are repeatedly called upon to remind the reader of Rosen's concern about the decimation of the natural world.

Henry David Thoreau's move to escape civilization at Walden Pond is almost belittled in the book. According to Rosen, Thoreau made frequent trips to his mother's for supplies, and the pond he lived near and cabin he lived in were at the edge of the town and near civilization. According to Rosen, Thoreau was escaping, but he was not isolated, and Rosen considers it dishonest of Thoreau to write of a wilderness experience while living adjacent to town. Nevertheless, Thoreau's *Walden* (1854) is held up as an exemplary piece of nature writing. He considers other examples of dishonesty among naturalists and nature writers. According to him, Audubon fabricated parts of his personal history. Rosen even apologizes for his past indiscretion in this regard: not including his Jewish heritage in the story of his introduction to bird watching. He is probably being too hard on himself, because the story does not inherently demand such a disclosure. Thoreau, on the other hand, may deserve the castigation: After all, he was writing of the evils of civilization and the freedom he gained in escaping to Walden Pond, when, if Rosen has it right, Thoreau maintained intimate contact with civilization throughout the Walden experience. The most dangerous dishonesty that Rosen observes in some nature writers is their attempt to separate humans from nature. Some had to get away from people to feel they were in communication with nature. Rosen argues that the separation is unnatural, that humans are a part of nature and the preservation of nature must include the presence of humans. However, in other parts of the book he warns that humans can no longer afford to dominate the natural world as they have tended to do in the past.

In another recurring theme, Rosen outlines the saga surrounding the discovery of natural selection, the mechanism driving the evolutionary process, and explains the role birds and bird watching played in that discovery. Charles Darwin's version was inspired, to a great extent, by the Galapagos finches, a group of bird species descended from one or a few original colonizers of the island group. Alfred Russell Wallace formed his ideas, in part, while seeking and studying birds of paradise. Rosen contrasts the two founders' behavior in sorting out and claiming credit for the idea, and in Rosen's mind Wallace fares better. He contrasts Darwin's loss of faith and rejection of spiritualism with Wallace, who also lost faith but embraced spiritualism. In this context, Rosen discusses Edward O. Wilson's books that explore evolution, conservation of nature, and religion. Rosen expresses admiration for the work of Edward O. Wilson, Darwin, and Wallace, but he tends to disagree with them on the question of faith, explaining his own convictions in this context.

These episodes are rarely covered in a single block of print, although most are introduced in a thorough discussion that seems to close the topic. However, many topics return in other contexts, to which they provide support, frequently adding substance to their original context as well.

Rosen lives in New York City, near Central Park, which is his favorite local bird-watching spot, and to which he returns repeatedly, in person and in the book. He outlines the history of Central Park, including the eviction of a colony of African Americans from the area when the park was created; the introduction of starlings to the park and thus to North America (where they became a classic example of the unfortunate consequences of introducing nonnative, especially invasive, species); and the planting of large numbers of trees in the new park (which leads him to ask if the park is natural). He expresses his concern for the Central Park birds, for which he has a special affinity. He also describes bird-watching trips to wilder places—in Israel, in the southeastern United States, and in other locations—and he discusses the national parks. His appreciation of these larger pieces of nature suggests that, despite his love for Central Park, it would bother him if natural areas were reduced to a collection of Central Parks, one possible "birding at the end of nature" scenario.

Although it might seem these revisited subplots would fragment the book, as Rosen fears civilization will fragment (and perhaps end) nature, the author always recovers continuity. In the "Epilogue" he brings many of the threads together in his most direct plea for an effort to preserve an appreciable part of nature, rather than letting it continue drifting, or even pushing it, toward the end alluded to in the subtitle. He concludes, on a hopeful but tenuous note, that there is still time to make the required adjustments in human behavior in order to preserve the functional remnants of the natural world.

The book is well written and carefully edited. Only two harmless errors were noticed in this reading. The illustrations and "Sources" section are helpful. Regrettably, there is no index. Reviewers have been appropriately kind to the book.

Carl W. Hoagstrom

Review Sources

Booklist 104, no. 8 (December 15, 2007): 11.
Kirkus Reviews 75, no. 22 (November 15, 2007): 1195.
Library Journal 133, no. 1 (January 1, 2008): 129.
Los Angeles Times, February 17, 2008, p. R2.
The National Post, March 8, 2008, p. WP17.
The New York Times Book Review, March 9, 2008, p. 12.
Publishers Weekly 254, no. 44 (November 5, 2007): 56.
The Wall Street Journal 251, no. 50 (March 1, 2008): W8.

LINCOLN AND DOUGLAS
The Debates That Defined America

Author: Allen C. Guelzo (1953-   )
Publisher: Simon & Schuster (New York). 383 pp.
    $26.00
Type of work: History
Time: August-October, 1858
Locale: Illinois

In a series of seven debates over a period of four months, Abraham Lincoln and Stephen Douglas, candidates for an Illinois seat in Congress, defined the issues which in less than three years would result in civil war, with Lincoln taking the first steps which would lead to his becoming a national figure

Principal personages:
> ABRAHAM LINCOLN, Illinois lawyer and congressman who challenged the expansion of slavery
> STEPHEN DOUGLAS, U.S. senator from Illinois and advocate of "popular sovereignty" on the issue of slavery
> HENRY CLAY, U.S. senator from Kentucky whose advocacy of compromise on the slavery issue was carried on by Douglas

As recounted in *Lincoln and Douglas* by Allen C. Guelzo, the Missouri Compromise of 1820 had seemingly settled, at least for a time, the issue of the expansion of slavery in the western territories of the United States. Crafted by Kentucky senator Henry Clay, the compromise had provided for the establishment of slave territory south of the southern boundary of the newly established state of Missouri. Clay's compromise only bought time. As settlers moved into new territories west of the Mississippi River, they brought with them the issue of slavery. The annexation of the Republic of Texas as a slave state in the 1840's brought the issue again to a head.

Democratic senator Lewis Cass of Michigan, the party's 1848 candidate for president, inserted into the argument the concept of "popular sovereignty," the idea that the decision of whether a future state should be "free" or legalize slavery should be left to a vote of the citizens within the territory rather than to a decision of Congress. Clay once again attempted to craft a compromise that would avert possible secession and war. However, elderly and in poor health, Clay was limited in what he could accomplish. Clay died in 1852, and the leadership for the issue of popular sovereignty fell to Stephen Douglas.

In this manner, Guelzo, a leading Lincoln historian, provides the background to the issues that undergirded what were arguably the most important debates in American political history. Judge Douglas, the incumbent senator from Illinois in 1858, had taken a strict constitutional interpretation on the issue of slavery: Only the people directly affected could decide the issue. As long as only Texas or the Southwest was affected, desert lands largely uninhabitable, the North was willing to ignore the issue. However, when slavery threatened to expand into the Nebraska Territory, potentially leaving Congress under the control of slave states, the issue again became one of national importance. Division of the Nebraska Territory into the future states of Nebraska and Kansas in 1854, the bill for which was shepherded by Douglas, resulted in an explosion of blood. What became known as "Bleeding Kansas" was the answer to popular sovereignty as settlers, both for and against slavery, moved into the territories and created a de facto civil war.

Allen C. Guelzo is the Henry R. Luce Professor of the Civil War Era at Gettysburg College in Gettysburg, Pennsylvania. He is the author or coauthor of numerous books and articles on the intellectual history of the church as well as those publications for which he is most noted, Abraham Lincoln: Redeemer President *(1999) and* Lincoln's Emancipation Proclamation: The End of Slavery in America *(2004), receiving the Lincoln Prize for each.*

Making the issue even more volatile as a national issue was the *Dred Scott* decision, in a portion of which the Supreme Court ruled that the "right" of slavery could not be legally outlawed.

In 1858 Abraham Lincoln was still a relatively unknown politician outside of his adopted state of Illinois. Elected to the state legislature as a Whig in the 1830's, Lincoln first came into conflict with Douglas when he campaigned on behalf of his law partner, John Stuart, running against Douglas for a congressional seat in 1838; allegedly Lincoln and Douglas were also competitors for the hand of Mary Todd, Lincoln's future wife. In 1846 Lincoln was elected to a single term in Congress, where, except for an ill-conceived opposition to President James Polk, he generated minimal notice.

Lincoln began his vocal opposition to Douglas's support for popular sovereignty at Douglas rallies throughout Illinois in 1854. As Guelzo points out, the effect was to galvanize antislavery elements in the state, but it accomplished little in uniting the Whig Party. At the same time, the strength (and growing popularity) of Lincoln's arguments brought him to the notice of the newly established abolitionist Republican Party. The seat held by Senator Douglas became available in 1858, and Lincoln was the primary opposition to Douglas for that seat.

In describing the background to Lincoln's candidacy for the Senate, Guelzo notes the two major problems Lincoln faced. First, the Republicans' chances in any election required the support of other disaffected voters, principally disaffected Whigs. Second was the question of whether Douglas was strongly committed to the Democratic Party, or whether he was willing to join the Republicans in exchange for their support of candidates allied with Douglas's position on the issue of slavery. To most, the idea of Republican support for Douglas was anathema. There is evidence Douglas may have been serious about such proposals.

At this point early in the election year of 1858, Lincoln's job was to convince the state Republican Party that Douglas was no supporter of its position. One method to carry this out was to hold a series of state conventions or "mass meetings," preferably in each of the nine federal congressional districts, in which the Republican candidate would address such concerns. The first business for the party would be to decide on its candidate, and in mid-June the state Republicans met in the statehouse in Springfield for that purpose. A resolution introduced by Charles Wilson nominated Lincoln as the party's candidate; the nomination was accepted unanimously.

Lincoln's speech in which he accepted the nomination ranks among the most important in American history. Although his phraseology is often linked with the Douglas debates, it was not directly associated. Rather it outlined the primary difference between the view of Douglas and the Democratic Party on the issue of the existence as well as the expansion of slavery and the view of the new Republican Party. Its prediction that the issue would have to be settled sooner rather than later was prescient:

> We are now far into the fifth year, since a policy [popular sovereignty] was initiated, with the avowed object . . . of putting an end to slavery agitation. Under the operation of that policy, that agitation has not only, not ceased, but has constantly augmented. In my opinion, it will not cease, until a crisis shall have been reached, and passed. A house divided against itself cannot stand. I believe this government cannot endure, permanently half slave and half free.

Guelzo continues with his analysis of the implication of these paragraphs. As the most prominent advocate of popular sovereignty, Douglas had argued that this solution had never been given a chance, given the near insurrections that had taken place in the Nebraska Territory. Using the imagery of the New Testament (Matthew 12:25), Lincoln argued that neither a government nor a nation could survive under such circumstances: that one way or another, the issue of slavery would be resolved.

Much of Lincoln's "house divided" speech reviewed the recent history of the arguments and attempted compromises over slavery. Finally, he addressed the candidacy of Douglas himself. Lincoln made clear that Douglas's views were not those of the Republican Party, and to believe so was merely a delusion. The response to Lincoln's speech, unlike that of history, was mixed. Though Lincoln disagreed, the Republican leadership's interpretation was that Lincoln had presented an abolitionist tract, one certain to divide both the party and the country. The state Democrats were overjoyed, but, as Guelzo points out, there was no question as to whom, and to what policy, any vote for the Republicans in that year's election would represent.

During the nineteenth century, U.S. senators were elected not by popular vote but by the respective state legislators. Therefore, the candidates were campaigning not just for themselves but for the election by the people of legislators supportive of their positions. The goal of the state Republicans was to create a state legislature that would in turn select Lincoln for the Senate seat. Guelzo summarizes the upcoming Republican strategy by addressing the demographics of the state. The northern portion of Illinois consisted primarily of antislavery or outright abolitionist voters who would vote solid Republican. The southern portion of the state comprised just the opposite: former Southerners who still retained strong Southern, and therefore proslavery, sympathies. It was in the central portion of the state that the election would be decided.

Lincoln's reference to a "house divided" was problematic. As Guelzo points out several times, some interpreted Lincoln's meaning as an invitation for war, and Lincoln suggested at times that the prediction might have been foolish. There was also the issue of the intent of the nation's founders—Douglas's interpretation being that these men accepted division on the issue, while Lincoln firmly believed they "tolerated division over slavery in order to finish building the house in the first place." Lincoln's speech at Cooper Union in New York during the 1860 election would lay out his views on this issue in significantly greater detail. Lincoln had preferred not to enter into a series of debates with Douglas, a renowned orator. It was, however, the decision of the state Republican Committee to move forward. In that way, the background for the debates was set.

The immediate decision as to where the debates would be held centered on each of the nine congressional districts. Nevertheless, in July Lincoln and Douglas each addressed crowds in Chicago and Springfield in a preliminary for the upcoming electioneering. It was decided the official debates would be held in towns from each of the other seven districts, beginning with Ottawa, seat of La Salle County, on August 21.

The sole issue of contention was slavery, specifically whether the doctrine of popular sovereignty as argued by Douglas should be accepted, and Lincoln's view that to do so would result in the perpetuation of this evil. However, what of Nebraska and Kansas? Douglas began the first debate by quoting the resolution of the Republican Party at its first Illinois convention in 1854: "to exclude slavery from all the territories . . . and to resist acquirement of more territories, unless the practice of slavery therein forever shall have been abolished." It was a trap to see if Lincoln would endorse the resolution of his party, in effect inviting war, or to hesitate and be exposed as a hypocrite, the thesis of his one-hour speech. Worse, in Douglas's view, Lincoln wanted black equality. Lincoln was equally adept in defending his position. He was not present when the resolution was passed, but he stated that "even if the black man was not my equal in many respects, it was also true that a great many white people were not each other's equals. So long as the black man is a man, he has a natural right to eat the bread . . . which his own hand earns. And in that respect he is my equal and the equal of Judge Douglas, and the equal of every living man." The applause signaled he had defended himself well.

Guelzo follows Lincoln and Douglas through the election season, providing an analysis for each of the six ensuing debates. History indicates that in the election on November 2, Douglas came out ahead. It was, however, a short-lived triumph, and the vote was significantly closer than initially apparent. Guelzo's last chapter contains an extensive analysis and breakdown of the vote. First, the turnout was substantial even for the times. Pro-Lincoln House votes probably exceeded those for Douglas by twenty-four thousand, but because of the apportionment in the state legislature, pro-Douglas districts had greater representation and the ultimate decision on the Senate race. The text of the debates was later published, providing an annoyance to Douglas and national recognition to Lincoln. Two years later, the two men faced off again. Lincoln won, and the war came.

Richard Adler

Review Sources

America 199, no. 5 (September 1, 2008): 26-27.

The Atlantic Monthly 301, no. 3 (April, 2008): 106.

Booklist 104, no. 12 (February 15, 2008): 25.

Christianity Today 52, no. 5 (May, 2008): 70.

Journal of American History 95, no. 2 (September, 2008): 540-541.

Kirkus Reviews 76, no. 1 (January 1, 2008): 23.

Publishers Weekly 254, no. 47 (November 26, 2007): 39.

Time 171, no. 6 (February 11, 2008): 84.

The Wall Street Journal 251, no. 37 (February 14, 2008): D7.

THE LINE UPON A WIND
The Great War at Sea, 1793-1815

Author: Noel Mostert (1930-   )
Publisher: W. W. Norton (New York). 774 pp. $35.00
Type of work: History
Time: 1793-1815
Locale: Portsmouth and London, England; Paris, Boulogne, Brest, and Toulon, France; Cape St. Vincent, Portugal; Tripoli, Libya; Algiers, Algeria; Naples, Italy; Acre, Syria; Alexandria, Egypt; Copenhagen, Denmark; Cadiz, Cape Trafalgar, Tarragona, and Catalonia, Spain; Quebec, Canada; Detroit, Michigan; Washington, D.C; New Orleans, Louisiana

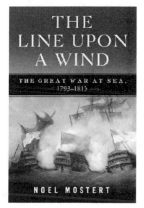

A naval history of Britain's wars with France and the United States during the Napoleonic period, with an emphasis on tactical developments

Principal personages:
> ADMIRAL HORATIO LORD NELSON, commander in chief of the Mediterranean fleet and Britain's greatest naval hero
> NAPOLEON BONAPARTE, emperor of France
> WILLIAM PITT, the Younger, prime minister of Britain
> CAPTAIN LORD THOMAS COCHRANE, a British naval officer who achieved notable success in opposing the French along the Spanish coast
> WILLIAM HOSTE, a Royal Navy captain renowned for his skills in close inshore fighting in the Adriatic Sea

In spite of its deadly consequences, war remains one of the principal driving forces of history, and the story of the victor and the vanquished often makes for enthralling reading. Never was this more applicable than in the Napoleonic wars, a twenty-two-year period of conflict that is the subject of Noel Mostert's *The Line upon a Wind: The Great War at Sea, 1793-1815.* As Mostert's engaging text makes clear, this was the first true world war, one that involved an ever-shifting series of coalitions that pitted the constitutional monarchy of Great Britain against revolutionary France. Since it was the first global conflict, it has inevitably generated a veritable library of historical studies, from the economic and political causes of the war to the resulting armed engagements. Books of the modern era that deal with the naval aspects of the war range from C. Nepean Longridge's *The Anatomy of Nelson's Ships* (1955) to N. A. M. Rodger's *The Command of the Ocean* (2004). However, these works are largely concerned with Britain's Royal Navy. With so much material already in print on this subject, it is a challenge for anyone to say anything new on the subject. Without significant new source material coming to light, Mostert is forced to mine such well-thumbed

~

A former U.N. correspondent for the
Montreal Star, *Noel Mostert won the*
National Magazine award in 1975 for
his articles in The New Yorker. *His*
nonfiction writing includes a book
about oil tankers, Supership *(1974),*
and a history of his native South Africa,
Frontiers: The Epic of South Africa's
Creation and the Tragedy of the Xhosa
People *(1992).*

~

publications as *The Naval Chronicle*, a British periodical written by maritime professionals that appeared throughout much of the war.

What distinguishes Mostert's work from that of his predecessors is the sheer comprehensiveness of his book. Although he opens with a description of the first naval action between the British and the French in 1793, the inital section, "The Tactical Evolution," is nothing less than a synopsis of the history of naval warfare. Beginning with the trireme of the ancient world, Mostert proceeds to the armed medieval cog, the galleon, the development of the modern concept of a navy in the seventeenth century, and what would prove to be the most important ship in the Napoleonic wars, the frigate: a fast, flush-decked craft that mounted a single row of cannons on each side. Mostert's approach to his subject is a curious one, and it says much about his background and his intended audience. Had this book been written by an academic historian, it is likely that it would have focused on a narrowly defined aspect of the naval war, perhaps a heavily researched monograph on a particular battle, or on a shorter span of years within the overall conflict. However, Mostert, a journalist by training, brings a reporter's sensibility to the subject matter. Rather than just assume the reader's familiarity with the Western naval tradition, he provides a synopsis of it. When he wants to convey the feeling of what it was like to experience naval warfare firsthand, he freely—and effectively—resorts to eyewitness accounts of battles. All of this suggests that *The Line upon a Wind* is designed with the armchair sailor in mind, someone who wants a fairly comprehensive one-volume history of Napoleonic naval warfare. It is probably no coincidence that W. W. Norton, the publisher of Mostert's book, is also responsible for the American edition of Patrick O'Brian's superb twenty-novel Aubrey/Maturin series about the Royal Navy of the same period. Given the book's wealth of detail, one could regard it as the ultimate gloss on O'Brian's fiction.

The development of naval tactics forms the subject of the first section of Mostert's work and constitutes an important thread that runs throughout this lengthy volume. By the last quarter of the eighteenth century, the concept of how a sea battle should be fought had reached a critical stage. Naval traditionalists held that the opposing forces should form two parallel lines and do battle broadside to broadside. The result was a ponderous danse macabre, a stalemate in which neither side could hope to achieve a decisive victory. It was not until the 1780's that a solution was proposed by John Clerk: This amateur tactical theoretician declared that, instead of matching battle line for battle line, the goal should be first to break the enemy line and then to capture or to destroy its vessels. It was a brilliant insight, and Mostert conveys both the effectiveness of the new tactic and the hidebound nature of naval tradition that resisted its implementation. This new, chaotic style of warfare was anathema to a culture obsessed with order. Instead of merely recounting the winners and losers in the numerous naval

engagements, Mostert characterizes battles in terms of tactical lessons learned or ignored. In describing the Battle of June the First in 1794, Mostert vividly makes clear
what a paradigm shift this new mode of fighting required of the participants. When
British commander Earl Howe signaled his order to break the French line and attack,
most failed to follow it—including the vessel that was supposedly leading the fight,
Anthony James Molloy's ship *Caesar*. Howe managed to bring the fleet to close action only by cutting through the enemy line himself. While this new style of fighting
exposed the attacking vessels to numerous broadsides, close engagement with the enemy deployed maximum destructive power at point-blank range. When the British
vessel *Queen Charlotte* caught the French ship *Montagne* off guard, the latter sustained three hundred casualties. With new short-range weapons, such as the carronade
and ammunition loads that included hundreds of musket balls or even metal pieces
and nails, close-range warfare dislodged showers of deadly splinters, shredded sails,
and dismasted ships in a matter of minutes.

Crucial to this new type of warfare was the man who would become Britain's most
famous sailor: Horatio Nelson. Rather than just laud him as the hero of the Battle of
Trafalgar, *The Line upon a Wind* demonstrates how Nelson's mastery of tactics enabled Britain, despite its inferiority in both ships and guns, to prevail against the
French, who allied with the Spanish. This is made apparent in Mostert's account of
the naval action that established Nelson's reputation, the Battle of Cape St. Vincent in
1797. Although British admiral Sir John Jervis had signaled for his ships to form a
line preparatory to battle, Nelson immediately realized that elements of the Spanish
fleet (headed for a French port) were attempting to square off their entire twenty-five-
ship force against Britain's tiny fifteen-ship squadron. Instead of taking his place in
battle order as most other commanders would have done, Nelson performed the audacious tactic recommended by Clerk: He took his seventy-four-gun ship *Captain* and
single-handedly attacked the most powerful warship in the world, the 130-gun
Santissima Trinidad. Displaying the visceral intensity of a war correspondent, Mostert exquisitely conveys the resulting shock and disarray that soon spread throughout
the Spanish fleet. With his seizure of the tactical initiative, Nelson became a model
for his fellow captains, many of whom proceeded to provide him assistance or follow
his own daring example. The result was a stunning and badly needed victory for the
British, although Mostert suggests that the true prize was the affirmation of their tactical superiority. This was Nelson's singular contribution to the war. If nothing else,
The Line upon a Wind proves that all of Nelson's subsequent naval victories were the
result of the intense tactical training he provided to his subordinates. When he commanded a fleet at the Battle of the Nile, Nelson prepared his captains by rigorously
schooling them in the tactical options open to them. Realizing that the smoke and
noise of battle renders communications with other ships difficult, if not impossible,
Nelson drilled his commanders in likely battle scenarios so that they could take independent action rather than needlessly wait for his approval. It was a strategy that resulted in decisive victories for the British at the Nile, at Copenhagen, and at Trafalgar,
the encounter that established British supremacy at sea for the next one hundred
years. These are oft-told tales, but Mostert deserves praise both for his mastery of the

minutia of naval life and for the narrative power with which he conveys the thrill and horror of sea battles.

As an island nation with a relatively small standing army, Britain was compelled to rely upon its navy not only for homeland defense but also as a partner to its land-based forces. More than any other book on the period, *The Line upon a Wind* demonstrates the fact that the nature of naval warfare changed after Trafalgar. With the majority of French ships destroyed or blockaded in port, naval engagements shifted from great fleet actions to single vessels providing support to land-based forces. Among the latter, the daring exploits of captains such as Thomas Lord Cochrane along the Spanish coast and William Hoste in the Adriatic ensured the ultimate victory of Britain and its allies over the French. Sailors were often called upon to seize fortresses or perform such Herculean tasks as hauling cannons up mountain peaks.

The only flaw in Mostert's approach to his material concerns the problem of what to include or exclude from such a rich era. On the one hand, his inclusion of the peninsular campaign is the pertinent due to the supporting role of the navy in the struggle for Spain. Then there is the problem of the War of 1812. The Second War for Independence, as it is also known, generated its own list of naval battles, both at sea and on the Great Lakes. Mostert is correct in stating that this was the conflict that established America as a rising naval power, and his vivid description of the Battle of New Orleans is undoubtedly one of the best in print. It is also to his credit that Mostert carefully interweaves this American war into the fabric of the larger world conflagration. However, one cannot help agreeing with Roger that this was really little more than a distraction in what was essentially a European contest. More serious is Mostert's failure to make more than a passing reference to the role of privateers in the Napoleonic wars. Although the notion may seem foreign to the modern concept of warfare, privateers were commercial raiders that were sanctioned by a government with a document known as a letter-of-marque. These privately owned vessels, which attacked and seized enemy commerce for profit, played a significant, if subordinate, role in harassing enemy shipping. These are small complaints regarding an otherwise enjoyable, informative book. *The Line upon a Wind* is one of the best one-volume histories of the zenith of the age of fighting sail.

Cliff Prewencki

Review Sources

Booklist 104, nos. 19/20 (June 1, 2008): 26
Contemporary Review 290 (Summer, 2008): 253.
Kirkus Reviews 76, no. 8 (April 15, 2008): 408.
Publishers Weekly 255, no. 18 (May 5, 2008): 54.

THE LODGER SHAKESPEARE
His Life on Silver Street

Author: Charles Nicholl (1950-   )
Publisher: Viking Penguin (New York). 378 pp. $26.95
Type of work: Literary biography, literary history
Time: 1603-1612
Locale: London

In his sixth book about the writers of Elizabethan and Jacobean England, journalist Nicholl explores the nuances of a legal deposition that William Shakespeare made at the end of his career, a record of the only words he is known to have spoken offstage

Principal personages:
    WILLIAM SHAKESPEARE (1564-1616),
        England's greatest playwright
    CHRISTOPHER MOUNTJOY (d. 1620), a maker of headdresses
    MARIE MOUNTJOY, his wife
    MARY MOUNTJOY, their daughter, later Mary Belott
    STEPHEN BELOTT (d. 1646), their apprentice, later their son-in-law
    SIMON FORMAN (1552-1611), astrologer consulted by the Mountjoys
    GEORGE WILKINS, brothel-keeper and playwright, Shakespeare's
        sometime collaborator

When he turned forty in 1604, William Shakespeare was lodging in the house of a London merchant who made "tires": decorative headwear for the aristocracy, members of the upper middle class, and, very likely, theater companies. According to *The Lodger Shakespeare* by Charles Nicholl, Shakespeare stayed for a season or two before moving. Eight years later, he gave a deposition in a lawsuit brought against his former landlord. Ironically, the playwright whose verbal memory has long amazed critics said he could not recall the terms of an agreement about which he was asked to testify.

The court papers were discovered a century ago, in the Public Records Office in London, and have been studied by biographers such as Samuel Schoenbaum, whose documentary life of Shakespeare is considered the standard study. The bare facts of the case seem unpromising. Christopher Mountjoy, tire-maker, had settled a dowry on his only child when she married his former apprentice Stephen Belott. Something went wrong between the two men, and Mountjoy refused to pay what Belott claimed he had promised. Belott took the matter to the Jacobean equivalent of small-claims court, naming Shakespeare as a witness to the contract. The famous playwright testified, though probably not as Belott anticipated. Shakespeare said that Belott was a fine young man but that he could not recall the promised sum. As Nicholl puts it, he weaseled out, displaying a memory more selective than defective.

∼

*Charles Nicholl has written books on
Elizabethan alchemy and portraiture as
well as on Shakespeare's
contemporaries Christopher Marlowe,
Thomas Nashe, and Sir Walter Ralegh.
He has also written lives of Leonardo
da Vinci and Arthur Rimbaud and
travel books and articles.*

∼

Nicholl has written about the legal ordeals of Shakespeare's contemporaries Thomas Nashe, the pamphleteer, and Christopher Marlowe, the author of *Doctor Faustus* (pr. 1588) and Shakespeare's early rival. Indeed, he has come close to writing the case for the prosecution of the shadowy figures responsible for Marlowe's early death, under suspicious circumstances, in a tavern brawl. The case of *Belott v. Mountjoy* is tamer by far, but Nicholl finds more interesting tidbits than one might reasonably expect. Following the first law of forensic science, that "every contact leaves traces," he discovers a world of detail concerning the people whose lives touched Shakespeare.

The case involves a good deal of bickering over household items to be included in the dowry and money to be settled on the bride. After hearing from the plaintiff and defendant, the court held three sessions to hear from witnesses. At each session, a set of interrogatories, or questions, was put to each witness. Shakespeare testified at the first session and seems to have signed his recorded account in haste: "Willm Shaks." Nine witnesses appeared in all, some of them more than once. (Shakespeare did not return.) Then the court took statements from the plaintiff and defendant on separate dates, including Belott's rejoinder to Mountjoy's final plea. Almost six months after the case opened, the court made a ruling of sorts. It ordered Mountjoy to pay Belott a small sum, representing only a fraction of the money in question, and sent the matter to arbitration.

Both Mountjoy and his former apprentice belonged to London's large community of Huguenots, French Protestants seeking refuge from religious persecution. Although each was formally affiliated with a different parish church near his place of residence, both were known to the larger body of the French Church, if only for nonattendance at Mass. The records of that body indicate that Mountjoy was summoned a year later to explain why he had not yet paid the amount awarded to Belott. He refused to recognize the church's authority, and he was excommunicated until such time as he repented the various scandals of his life, including two children born out of wedlock. By all appearances, he never settled the debt, for he wrote his will in such a way as to leave his daughter as little as was legally possible.

The Lodger Shakespeare has seven sections of roughly equal length. These sections move from Shakespeare at forty to the house where he lodged on Silver Street, the members of the household, and the business carried on in the house. Moving outward from Silver Street, they pass through the larger communities to which the Mountjoys belonged, including their French neighbors in London and their diverse clientele. The family's contacts include such colorful people as Simon Forman (the astrological physician whose casebooks have been studied by Shakespeareans such as A. L. Rowse) and George Wilkins, a caterer, or victualler, who served for a time as a playwright for Shakespeare's acting company. Following these contacts, Nicholl learns about problems in the Mountjoy marriage from notes taken by the astrologer and about Wilkins's criminal record as a brothel-keeper with a history of violence against women. A final section on marriage arrangements brings the story back to Shakespeare and his role in the legal dispute. The book ends, where it starts, with the elusive "Mr. Shakespeare."

Just before Shakespeare gave his testimony, another witness reported that Mountjoy asked his famous lodger to speak with Belott after marriage negotiations had broken down. The witness added that Shakespeare helped to settle the dowry and saw the agreement "Solempnized." Nicholl infers from this that Shakespeare performed the private ceremony known as troth-plighting or "handfasting"—in which the engaged join hands and promise to be true to each other for life. In Shakespeare's time, the ceremony had quasi-legal force; marriages were often consummated between the troth-plighting and the subsequent church wedding. The complications arising from such arrangements figure prominently in Shakespeare's *Measure for Measure*, first performed in 1604 and likely written under Mountjoy's roof. In that play, an interim ruler condemns a man to death for fornication while spurning his own fiancé and arranging to have premarital intercourse with another woman. Both men have in fact plighted their troth, but the one in power chooses to ignore the prior commitments, a sure sign of corruption in the state.

The years when Shakespeare lodged on Silver Street correspond to the period of his darker comedies or problem plays. Many of them involve domestic relations far closer to everyday experience than those in the great comedies of his earlier career— forced marriage, for example, and infidelity. Nicholl draws many parallels between events in the Mountjoy house and scenes from Shakespeare's plays of this period. For example, the character Parolles in *All's Well That Ends Well* (1623) is said to be a marriage counselor, albeit with a rather sour message. Partly because his name means something like "Mr. Words," Nicholl fancies that he may be "Shakespeare's own mocking self-portrait."

One play from this period, *Pericles, Prince of Tyre*, was not included in the first folio of Shakespeare's plays, published posthumously in 1623. One possible reason for the omission is Shakespeare only wrote parts of it, perhaps completing or improving the work of another playwright. Nicholl is not the first to suggest that other author was George Wilkins, but he adds details about Wilkins's life outside the theater and his connections with the newlywed Belotts, who took lodging in his tavern when they fled the house on Silver Street. Such detail helps readers appreciate the dilemmas that the play's heroine faces when she is sold to a brothel-keeper.

Nicholl makes a congenial guide to a vanished world, leading readers through the streets and alleys of Jacobean London. He estimates the annual rent that Mountjoy paid on the large house where he kept his shop and lived with his family, apprentices, servants, and lodgers (equivalent to between 2,000 and 2,500 British pounds today). He describes the shops of London's burgeoning costume trade, points out the equipment used there, and even speaks the argot of the different crafts. Such details could become tedious with a less knowledgeable and entertaining guide, but Nicholl is never boring. His credentials are those of a journalist, not an academic. He has written about the drug cartels of Colombia, the market for precious gems in Burma, and sex tourism in Thailand, among much else, and he makes the business of wigs and headwear just as interesting. He never seems to tire about what lies beneath the streets of London today.

The house on Silver Street was destroyed in the Great Fire of London in 1666. The entire area, just inside the old city wall near its northwest corner, was obliterated during the Blitz bombing of 1940. The street where silversmiths had congregated in the Middle Ages no longer exists. After pacing off the distance, Nicholl has determined that a large underground parking garage now occupies the space where the tiremaker's house once stood.

Throughout the long section on "Sex and the City," where Nicholl tells about Forman and Wilkins, he resists any temptation to guess about Shakespeare's sex life. Some gifted novelists have attempted to imagine what that life was like—notably James Joyce in *Ulysses* (1922) and Anthony Burgess in *Nothing Like the Sun* (1964). It would have been easy for Nicholl to draw implications about Shakespeare's forced marriage to the pregnant Anne Hathaway or his relations with London women such as Mrs. Mountjoy, who told Forman that her marriage was unhappy and that she had taken a lover. He has chosen instead to concentrate on the father-daughter relations that permeate plays such as *Pericles, Prince of Tyre* and *King Lear* (pr. 1605-1606).

Nicholl does engage in speculation, however, and readers with scholarly scruples may think he sometimes goes too far. He speculates, for example, that Shakespeare may have first encountered Wilkins when the Belotts lodged at his tavern. He wonders if Shakespeare may have thought of Mountjoy's daughter when he wrote in *Pericles, Prince of Tyre* of a woman who "weav'd the sleided silk/ With fingers long, small, white as milk." There is no evidence to support either conjecture. Wilkins worked for other acting companies before he came to Shakespeare's, and Shakespeare wrote about "sleided silk" in a poem published a decade before *Pericles, Prince of Tyre*. With such speculation Nicholl is reaching beyond the academic market to capture the popular imagination.

In addition to scholarly notes and a full bibliography, there are sixteen glossy pages of black-and-white illustrations and an appendix containing transcripts of all legal papers. Here as elsewhere, Nicholl preserves the original spelling for the historical "brogue" that it adds, but inserts letters missing from abbreviated words (thus "pl" becomes "p*laintiff*"). He also translates any statements made in French.

Reviewers on both sides of the Atlantic praised the ingenuity and perceptiveness of Nicholl's literary sleuthing. *The Spectator* remarked that his "unerring eye for telling circumstantial detail is as much poetic as forensic." *History Today* praised the reconstruction, remarking that it was highly evocative though necessarily conjectural rather than conclusive. In addition, the audiobook version distributed by Audible has won high praise and an award from *AudioFile* magazine. The young British actor Simon Vance cleverly modulates his voice to indicate the numerous quotations and the different voices in dramatic dialogues. He even reads the dull court documents with a zest that matches Nicholl's delight in presenting them.

The Lodger Shakespeare is detailed enough to be of value to scholars interested in the minutiae of the celebrated playwright's world. Its style is sufficiently engaging, and its contents are so arranged, that it should be of interest to anyone who values a good visit to a bygone world.

Thomas Willard

Review Sources

Booklist 104, no. 11 (February 1, 2008): 15.
The Christian Science Monitor, February 26, 2008, pp. 14-15.
History Today 58, no. 1 (January, 2008): 65.
Kirkus Reviews 75, no. 22 (November 15, 2007): 1193.
London Review of Books 30, no. 9 (May 8, 2008): 10-11.
The New York Times, February 8, 2008, p. 38.
The New Yorker 84, no. 2 (February 25, 2008): 74-76.
Publishers Weekly 254, no. 43 (October 29, 2007): 41.
The Spectator 305 (November 17, 2007): 52-53.
The Times Literary Supplement, December 14, 2007, p. 25.

THE LOST HISTORY OF CHRISTIANITY
The Thousand-Year Golden Age of the Church in the Middle East, Africa, and Asia—and How It Died

Author: Philip Jenkins (1952-   )
Publisher: HarperCollins (New York). 315 pp. $26.95
Type of work: Religion, history
Time: 300-2007
Locale: Syria, Iraq, Iran, and North and East Africa

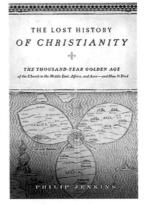

A history of the often-overlooked Eastern Christians, a third branch of Christianity as influential and pervasive during the first millennium of the faith as Orthodoxy and Roman Catholicism became in later Christian history

Principal personages:
> NESTORIUS, fifth century patriarch of the Assyrian Christian church in what is now Iraq and Iran
>
> JACOBUS BARADAEUS, sixth century patriarch of the Syrian Orthodox church
>
> TIMOTHY, patriarch of the late eighth and early ninth centuries who led the Church of the East, about a quarter of the Christians in the world at that time
>
> JACOB OF EDESSA, seventh century historian and biblical interpreter; the Jerome of the East
>
> GEORGE OF AKULA, Jacob's successor, commentator on Aristotle, and bishop to Arab nomads in Mesopotamia
>
> MICHAEL SYRUS, twelfth century Jacobite patriarch of Antioch and influential medieval historian
>
> GREGORY BAR-HEBRAEUS, thirteenth century Jacobite scholar of Mosul who authored a history of the world, a commentary on Aristotle, and works on logic, astronomy, and theology
>
> MARKOS, Nestorian monk born in China who, under the name of Yaballaha III, became patriarch of the Nestorian church from 1281 until 1317
>
> BAR SAUMA, Nestorian monk who returned from China with Markos, served as diplomat in Catholic Europe seeking military alliance between Kublai Khan's Mongol regime and Catholic forces for an assault on Muslim Egypt
>
> TIMUR, Muslim warlord of the 1360's whose custom was to pile the skulls of his victims into a pyramid outside the cities that resisted him

The world's first Christian state was not in Europe but in Osrhoene, Northern Mesopotamia. Its king converted around 200. Its capital, Edessa, was the center of the earliest Christian scholarship. Bordering Armenia, which converted around 300, remains Christian to this day. Armenia's capital, Ani, was known as the city of 1001 churches.

Nearby Georgia also converted around this time. Other ancient churches outside the purview of the West included the African churches of Nubia, which lasted from the sixth through the fifteenth centuries, and Ethiopia, once called Abyssinia, which converted early and remains strongly Christian after eighteen centuries.

Born in Wales and educated at Cambridge University, Philip Jenkins has been a professor in history and religious studies at Pennsylvania State University since 1980. He has written many books, including The Next Christendom *(2002) and* The New Anti-Catholicism *(2003).*

Philip Jenkins's *The Lost History of Christianity* reads initially like an alternative-history science fiction book. It supplies a bewildering number of unfamiliar names, covers thousands of miles of geography, and reviews a couple of thousand years of time. It even includes a map on its dust cover that looks more like a three-leaf clover than a map of the world. With Jerusalem in the center, surrounded by the three lobes of Europe, Africa, and Asia, this Middle Ages cartography asserted not geographic reality but an article of faith: the influence of Christ's sacrifice in Jerusalem extended throughout the entire world. It also underscored what has been largely forgotten: that two-thirds of early Christendom lay outside of Europe.

Jenkins's method is to force a reconsideration of the history of Christianity, putting its Eastern branch at the center of early development. After all, he argues, the Asian church lasted a thousand years, spread over a million square miles, and nourished hundreds of churches. Moreover, it was Semitic in flavor and language, like the earliest Christianity, and developed without either the hindrance or help of the powerful Roman Empire. It developed a church hierarchy not unlike Orthodoxy or Roman Catholicism, and its evangelical fervor propelled missionaries along trade routes, including the Silk Road that stretched from Syria to Northern Persia into Uzbekistan and Turkmenistan, Bukhara, Samarkand, and China: all told some 4,500 miles.

Asian Christianity, then, is a third branch of the faith that extended from the Holy Land, not westward as did the Orthodox and Catholic churches, but north and eastward. There is more heard about the latter two branches because they survived, and the Eastern church did not. Jenkins skillfully puts often strange new facts into perspective. Jerusalem, he notes, is an equal distance from Merv in the East and Rome in the West, and it is actually closer to central Asia than it is to France. Geography alone logically suggests that Christianity would have moved as far east as it did west. In fact, Jenkins shows that, in the first thousand years of Christendom, the Asian churches moved more quickly to evangelize the world, and their influence was without parallel. He argues persuasively that history is distorted when it forgets this Eastern faith.

Merv, in what is now Turkmenistan, is a dead city today, but in the Middle Ages it was, as Jenkins details, one of the largest cities on earth with some two hundred thousand people. Situated on the Silk Road, it was also one of the greatest centers of Christianity: Nestorian, or Eastern, Christianity, that is. By 420, it had a bishop; by 544, it had become a metropolitan see. It sent missionaries as far away as China. It had a school and translated Greek and Syriac texts—from Aristotle to the New Testament—into Asian languages. It flourished as a center of Christianity until the thirteenth century, much of that time under Muslim rule. Jenkins notes that Merv does not fit the Western paradigm of the spread of Christianity, developing much earlier than Western Christianity and lasting much longer than expected. It retained the Semitic roots of the faith long after they were thought to have been lost. Christianity in Merv developed without the aid of the Roman Empire or the sponsorship of a European king; it was a tolerated minority faith under Muslim rule.

The most influential ancient Christian groups in Asia were the Nestorians and Jacobites. They originated in the Near East and used the Syriac language, which was related to the Aramaic of Jesus. Although both dissented to some degree from the Orthodox Church, Jenkins is adamant that they not be considered fringe groups for three reasons: They agreed with the Western church on most essential points—the trinity, incarnation, baptism, the Eucharist, the two testaments, Resurrection, eternal life, the return of Christ, and the last judgment; they accepted the Council of Nicaea; and they accepted the faith as handed down from the apostles. If those are not sufficient reasons for taking them seriously as Christians then one must consider that they, very simply, outnumbered the Western churches.

The Nestorians took their name from the Patriarch Nestorius. They differed with the Orthodox Church on the nature of Christ. They agreed that He had two natures but did not agree that they were absolutely united in the mystical sense. The Jacobites took their name from Jacobus Baradaeus, who in the sixth century organized a group called Monophysites: those who asserted that Jesus had only one nature, a divine one. This group was declared heretical by the ecumenical council of Chalcedon and thus was split from the Orthodox Church. Egyptian Copts and Syrians (Suriani) were Monophysites, and Jacobus organized them into an underground church. They were dominant in what is now Syria, and Nestorians prevailed in the modern states of Iraq and Iran. The heirs of the Jacobites are called Syrian Orthodox, and the Nestorians became the Assyrian Church.

These two faiths, far away from Constantinople and the power of Orthodoxy, developed independently into powerful rivals of the Western church. The Nestorians were based in Seleucia-Ctesiphon, the capital of the Persian empire. The Jacobites were based in Edessa. However, these centers were not alone. Jenkins paints for his readers an Eastern landscape that, between 500 and 1200, was thick with churches and monasteries from Egypt and Syria to Iraq and Iran. Missionary ventures followed the trade routes as far as Sri Lanka and the western provinces of China as early as the sixth century. Compared to Western expansion into Europe, the Eastern churches moved more rapidly.

The Eastern churches had their own liturgies, monastic traditions, missionaries, and centers of learning. They also had their own particular brand of Christian teaching and heritage. Mysticism, familiar to modern readers because of interest in the gnostics, was a routine part of Eastern Christianity, but unlike heretical gnosticism, Eastern mysticism was folded into church teaching. To Eastern Christians, the notion of deification—that is, becoming like God—was a common goal of the spiritual life.

Tradition in the Eastern Church held that Christ Himself sent the disciple Addai (Thaddeus) to Edessa. Although it may only be legendary, it has at least some plausibility since Edessa was one of the earliest and therefore most closely connected churches to Christ and his followers. There was also a tradition of healing and miracles that set Eastern Christianity apart from more rationalistic Muslim contemporaries. Jacobite philosopher Yahya ibn 'Adi knew that "signs" were the most potent means of evangelizing.

Jenkins is particularly enthusiastic about the centers of learning associated with the Eastern churches. As in the West, they focused on translation, not only of Christian texts but also of Aristotle and other important works of the ancient world. Christianity was polyglot. In the East, the primary language of the faith was Syriac. By the second century, there was a Syriac Bible. Centers of Christian scholarship, such as Edessa and Nisibis, rivaled the great universities of the West. By 1300, texts by more than one hundred Christian Syriac authors were available. With names unfamiliar to most Western Christians, they were the great Christian thinkers of their time and place: from the seventh and eighth centuries, historians Jacob of Edessa and George of Akula; from the twelfth and thirteenth, Michael Syrus of Antioch, Jacob Bar Salibi of Amida, Abd Yeshua of Nisibis, and Gregory Bar-Hebraeus of Mosul.

Through much of his book, Jenkins addresses the relationship between Christians and Muslims in the East, and in the process, he is able to shed light on the ancient origins of twenty-first century controversies. First, he notes a significant difference between the Eastern and Western churches. While the West had to negotiate its way with the Roman Empire, the East coexisted for hundreds of years with Islam. The two religions influenced each other and had inextricable ties. Many Eastern Christian traditions, such as apocryphal texts, architecture (now associated with mosques), the raised pulpit, fasting, prostration during prayer, veiling and head covering, saints, shrines, and the importance of Jesus were adopted by Muslims. If Islam was built, sometimes literally, on the ruins of Christianity, it also philosophically developed in dialogue with the older faith. Jenkins finds evidence that Christian and Muslim leaders sometimes debated each other with mutual respect. Some Eastern Christians saw Islam as an advance over pagan polytheism and Zoroastrianism (a dualistic religion), and they found it more open-minded than hostile Orthodox Christianity. Even if critical of Islam, Eastern Christians saw it as more of a Christian heresy than a strange, hostile newcomer to the region. Accounting for this early amicability, Jenkins notes that it took centuries for Islam to define itself, and the many similarities with Judaism and Christianity created early common ground.

Unfortunately, as it did define itself, Islam became periodically more intolerant of Christianity, and the fourteenth century virtually ended the thousand-year flourishing of Eastern Christianity. Repressive measures by Muslim courts in the 1290's made minorities' lives more and more miserable. Non-Muslims were soon subject to *dhimma*, wherein they had to wear badges or clothing identifying themselves as outside the faith. *Dhimmis*, or outsiders, were tempting targets for discrimination and persecution. Many Christians converted to avoid this discrimination; if they continued to practice Christianity, it was covertly. By 1321, Muslim mobs were looting and destroying Coptic churches. Similar conditions prevailed between 1290 and 1330 in Syria and Mesopotamia. Mob violence, forcible conversions, and looting were common. The Turks spread their oppression to Armenia and Georgia. In 1354, the Muslim rulers under whom many Eastern Christians had lived peacefully began a campaign of persecution that over the period of a century wiped out their churches. By 1480, Jenkins illustrates through one account, fifty-one metropolitanates, eighteen archbishoprics, and 478 bishoprics were decimated, as were the three great patriarchs of Alexandria, Antioch, and Jerusalem.

Jenkins challenges recent efforts to portray Islam as a tolerant faith. The persecution, massacre, and general ethnic cleansing of the fourteenth century belie that characterization, he argues. On the other hand, he balances his account by pointing out the centuries in which Christians had lived relatively peacefully inside Muslim regimes. His conclusion is that persecution was not an integral part of Islam rule, but it became, at various points, and most fatally in the fourteenth century, aggravated for particular reasons. The Crusades, for example, begun in 1095 by the pope to recapture the Holy Land from the Turks, had the unfortunate side effect of increasing persecution of minority Christians who were viewed with increasing suspicion in Muslim areas. Jenkins analyzes many other, later examples of the effects of Muslim persecution on the Eastern Christians, such as Turkey's ethnic cleansing of 1.5 million Armenians and other Christian minorities in 1915. He notes that the term genocide itself was coined in response to the Muslim attacks on Nestorian Christians in Iraq in 1933.

The relative sudden destruction of these churches launches Jenkins into philosophical questions about why churches die, how they survive, and what implications such questions have for faith itself. Does such annihilation occur for providential reasons or by simple chance and brute force? He notes an assumption in Christian circles that the faith has been on a providentially patterned trajectory of ever-widening expansion, with modern inroads into China and Africa as miraculous examples. That view, however, as Jenkins persuasively argues, ignores the thorough destruction of the Eastern churches after a flourishing thousand-year history. As Jenkins notes, when a millennium of gospel expansion was virtually wiped out in one century and further remnants rooted out in a mere decade, it becomes clear to an objective historian that Christianization is neither inevitable nor a one-way road.

Jenkins balances his position, however, with an acknowledgment that, although churches end in one region, they spring up in another. European and American expansion of the faith occurred as, or not long after, the Eastern churches were disappearing. Jenkins plausibly notes that the "Church" continues even as individual "churches" die out. As the Jews' return to Palestine suggests, some exits are not terminal. Furthermore, as the Old Testament demonstrates, the chosen people of God suffered many reversals at the hands of neighboring enemies, sometimes being chastened and sometimes being triumphant and vindicated. Jenkins wonders whether positives such as these can arise from the ashes of the Eastern church's defeat. He cites the example of China, where Christianity had many false starts and was thought to be virtually dead at various points in history. Nevertheless, today, under a political system hostile to it, there are some fifty to ninety million Chinese Christians. Jenkins reminds his readers that Christians were never promised control of the governments that ruled them. Instead of marveling over the suppression and extermination of faith, he wonders if perhaps one should consider any peaceful coexistence with the world's rulers remarkable for its exceptionalism.

The Lost History of Christianity is an eye-opening survey of a history that until now has been largely confined to scholars. It both enlightens and stimulates further reading on an essential subject.

William L. Howard

Review Sources

America 200, no. 1 (May 5, 2009): 30-31.
Booklist 105, no. 3 (October 1, 2008): 16.
Kirkus Reviews 76, no. 16 (August 15, 2008): 69.
Library Journal 133, no. 11 (June 15, 2008): 73.
Publishers Weekly 255, no. 28 (July 14, 2008): 61-62.

LULU IN MARRAKECH

Author: Diane Johnson (1934-   )
Publisher: E. P. Dutton (New York). 307 pp. $25.95
Type of work: Novel
Time: The early 2000's
Locale: Marrakech, Morocco

In this novel, Johnson examines the cultural clashes among French, American, English, and Islamic residents and visitors in contemporary Morocco from the perspective of Lulu Sawyer, spy

Principal characters:
> LULU SAWYER, a novice intelligence
>> operative whose mission is to explore
>> money routes to Islamic extremists while
>> seemingly working for a literacy foundation
> IAN DRUMM, Lulu's lover and a person of interest to her employers
> SUMA BOURAD, a French Algerian who flees Paris because her family
>> wants to have her killed after she loses her purity
> AMID BOURAD, Suma's brother who is accidentally killed during a failed
>> kidnapping
> GAZI AL-SAYED, a Saudi wife who unexpectedly leaves her husband
> POSY CRUMLEY, an English woman who gives birth to her first child
>> while staying at Ian Drumm's house in Morocco.
> ROBIN CRUMLEY, Posy's husband, a famous English poet
> SEFTON TAFT, Lulu's case officer in Spain
> DESI, a young Moroccan girl who is implicated in a potential terrorist
>> bombing

Diane Johnson's *Lulu in Marrakech* is the first-person story of Lulu Sawyer, a newly recruited intelligence operative who is sent to Morocco to investigate how money given to charities there ends up in the hands of Islamic extremists elsewhere. Her sojourn in Marrakech is only her second espionage assignment in the organization, so she is, in effect, learning to be a spy on the job. The novel, however, does not always follow the typical trajectory of a spy thriller. Though Lulu does suggest that she knows how to wiretap rooms and make impressions of keys, her mission requires her to observe the people in her surroundings and send reports of their behavior back to her superiors—human intelligence, as she refers to it. Lulu does not fit the stereotype of an intelligence operative. Rather, Johnson depicts her as equal parts spy and romance novel heroine—part of her cover story for visiting Morocco is to stay with her lover, Ian Drumm, a man she had met and had begun a relationship with during her previous mission. Lulu also symbolizes the American abroad, thrown in with an unusual mixture of Europeans, Middle Easterners, and locals in Morocco. Though the novel works well as a story exploring cultural differences or as a spy text, Johnson's

intermix of these two genres creates some
problematic plot and character developments
that diminish the novel's effectiveness.

~

*Diane Johnson taught for many years
at the University of California at Davis.
She has written eleven novels, five
works of nonfiction, including a
biography of Dashiell Hammett, and
numerous reviews. Her collection of
essays and book reviews,* Terrorists and
Novelists *(1982), was nominated for a
Pulitzer Prize, as was her 1987 novel*
Persian Nights.

~

Several of Johnson's previous works explore the ramifications of this combining of
different lifestyles and mores in close quarters, most notably her 1987 Pulitzer Prize-
nominated *Persian Nights* and her French
trilogy—*L'Affaire* (2003), *Le Divorce* (1997),
and *Le Mariage* (2000). In all four of these
novels, Johnson juxtaposes a slightly adrift
American abroad with the more understated
and subtle culture of France, in the French tril-
ogy, and of Iran, in *Persian Nights*. Typically, the American character misreads cultural signs and symbols, is frequently criticized for her American qualities, but eventually learns to appreciate the foreign culture, eventually valuing her Americanisms and
the new aspects of her personality brought to life by immersion in the foreign climate.

Lulu in Marrakech follows many of these same patterns, as Lulu settles into the
Moroccan lifestyle. There, she must navigate through many different groups: the visiting French and English with their summer homes in Marrakech, the Algerian refugees, the Islamic cooks, the Islamic Americans, and the runaway Saudis. The cultural
melting pot allows Lulu a look into several cultures, but, unlike Johnson's previous
narrators who seem to gain in understanding the foreign culture, Lulu never seems to
come to terms with the Moroccan way of life. The odd mixing of cultures in
Marrakech highlights its diversity, but in the context of the novel, it creates a cultural
confusion that Lulu never quite masters.

As in *Persian Nights,* Johnson also tackles tough political issues, though the political climate of *Lulu in Marrakech* is a bit more extreme. Lulu becomes involved in the
rendition and torture of a perceived Islamic extremist, and this highlights the most
pressing concern of the novel: the general fear that the moderate Islamic culture's resistance to Islamic extremists is corroding. Thus, everyone is considered suspicious
and a potential terrorist. Johnson seems to ask: How does an intelligence operative infiltrate such an environment? Though *Persian Nights* looks at the naïveté of Chloe
Fowler, an American visiting a foreign culture and not really understanding the inherent danger, Lulu examines the culture of Marrakech from the opposite extreme.
Whereas the narrator in *Persian Nights* cannot imagine men shooting at a crowd in a
tourist area and believes that Americans and other foreigners in Iran will be safe because they are not natives, in Marrakech, no one is that naïve, particularly in the post-
9/11 world of the novel. Though Lulu acknowledges many of the potential dangers in
the area, she ignores the possibilities that her lover might be involved in espionage as
well. Thus, she is like some of Johnson's previous narrators in her naïveté, although,
ironically, her job title suggests that she should be more well informed. As the main
character, Lulu is a complex blend of an emotionally immature and insecure woman
who is also an intelligence agent, a person one would expect to be more decisive and

serious. Though Lulu will not ask her lover Ian how he feels about her, or question his romantic loyalty to her even when she spies him with another woman, she continues to seek information regarding money transfers and suspicious characters. Though the story is told from Lulu's perspective, her attitude about her business and her relationships seems clipped and emotionally sterile, thus distancing her from the other characters in the novel. Although this keeps her from becoming a likable heroine, such a temperament seems more suited to her profession. In addition, Lulu resembles other Johnson heroines in her decided inability to know what she wants and how to go about getting it.

Given the vast social and spiritual differences between the Western and the Eastern inhabitants of Marrakech, Johnson voices some of the feminist arguments against Islamic culture, but only in a cursory way, primarily focusing on Posy Crumley's declarations about the culture's violence against women and the Islamic male's fixation on a woman's virginity as a sign of purity. A subplot of the novel concerns Suma Bourad, who is pursued, perhaps, by her brother Amid, because of her lost virginity. Amid's threat to kill Suma as well as Gazi Al-Sayed's flight from her Islamic husband position the women in the novel to address issues of female autonomy within the Islamic culture. Though Posy and Lulu are outraged at the treatment of Islamic women, and Lulu expresses an interest in Islamic women and children being taught to read, somehow these feminist concerns are only tangentially referenced in the novel and neither of the women form close attachments to any of the Islamic women.

Despite the political and social dissonances that Johnson explores, much of the surface-level plot involves the romance between Ian and Lulu. Even here, Johnson does not seem to have the right formula. When Lulu first arrives in Marrakech and finds her situation with Ian a bit less romantic than she expected, she does not question him. Part of this reticence, she explains later in the novel, is that she is not "emotionally possessive," meaning that she does not need to know the motives for his actions. However, because Lulu never explores Ian's motivations, he remains a one-dimensional character whose presence is diminished by her lack of description. In fact, one could say that Lulu is a bad observer. The reader does not get the sense that she really sees beneath the surface of any of the concerns in the novel, leaving the reader to wonder if this is the nature of intelligence. In several conversations with her contact Taft, he indicates that he does not want Lulu to analyze anything; rather, she needs simply to report about the people she has befriended, her "pickets" and informants, and "storekeepers, waiters, and the like whose opinions would be useful." Since her job is merely to report, she is trained to avoid analysis. In the one instance when she does analyze actions—deducing that the young Moroccan girl Desi's heavy coat at a concert suggests that she is loaded with explosives—Lulu is chastised.

In keeping with the spy theme, the novel is filled with various cloak-and-dagger subplots, such as the one involving Gazi Al-Sayed, a Saudi wife attempting to leave her husband Khaled by first hiding out at Ian's house, then finding a way to get across the border into Spain. Lulu also meets operatives in the market who give her enigmatic messages containing code words and names. Johnson humorously references other popular culture spy favorites to highlight Lulu's locale and romantic situation.

By the end of the novel, when Gazi flees, the plot resembles that of the film *Casablanca* (1942): Like Ilsa, who needs letters of transit to be able to leave Morocco, Gazi needs her passport. In keeping with the spy plot, at two separate points of the novel, Lulu is compared to Ingrid Bergman's character Alicia Huberman in the film *Notorious* (1946), a spy who must sleep with a man in order to get information. Like Bergman, Lulu is recruited partially because of her sexual availability.

Johnson further focuses on spy culture by including a number of epigraphs from a book detailing intelligence plans, *Intelligence Requirements for the 1980's, Volumes 1-7* (1979-1986), which she acknowledges as a source for some of Lulu's references. In addition, the epigraphs about intelligence-related information that head several chapters hold the novel together. This use of epigraphs to begin chapters is a Johnson earmark, found in her last four novels, though their use in the previous works did not seem as critical a tool for understanding the plot. Ironically, focusing the attention on the background of spying allows Johnson to draw notice to the problems of the American spy system. In many ways, Lulu serves as an example of the inept spy whose actions, and those of her group, bungle matters in such a way that terrible things happen, such as the death of Amid Bourad, perhaps not an Islamic "person of interest" at all, but a French intelligence operator. Furthermore, the lack of continuity between what the intelligence texts suggest and what Lulu does in the novel underscores the difficulty of spying and the entrenched nature of the profession. Though many of Johnson's previous novels take bold, dramatic turns toward violence from the sometimes lighthearted romance or urbane discourse, the move in *Lulu in Marrakech* from her romance-infused sojourn with some lightweight spying to her involvement in rendition and torture seems odd in the midst of an otherwise engaging novel of manners. This disconnect showcases the limits of mixing the two genres, despite Johnson's efforts to make Lulu more cinematically palatable. Spying is ultimately nasty business and no amount of romantic whimsy or dinnertime banter can alter that central fact.

Rebecca Hendrick Flannagan

Review Sources

Booklist 104, no. 22 (August 1, 2008): 38.
Elle 24, no. 3 (November, 2008): 242.
Entertainment Weekly, October 3, 2008, p. 79.
Kirkus Reviews 76, no. 16 (August 15, 2008): 41.
Library Journal 133, no. 13 (August 1, 2008): 68.
The New York Review of Books 55, no. 19 (December 4, 2008): 41-43.
The New York Times, October 24, 2008, p. C32.
The New York Times Book Review, October 26, 2008, p. 8.
O, The Oprah Magazine 9, no. 10 (October, 2008): 220.
Publishers Weekly 255, no. 27 (July 7, 2008): 34.
Vogue 198, no. 10 (October, 2008): 278.

LUSH LIFE

Author: Richard Price (1949-   )
Publisher: Farrar, Straus and Giroux (New York).
  455 pp. $26.00
Type of work: Novel
Time: 2007
Locale: Lower East Side, New York City

The two worlds of contemporary urban life in Manhattan's Lower East side collide when a jumpy Latino teenager murders a young white would-be hipster during a mugging gone wrong

> *Principal characters:*
> IKE MARCUS, a young would-be writer and
>   murder victim
> BILLY MARCUS, Ike's father
> STEVEN BOULWARE, Ike's friend, a young, alcoholic would-be actor
> ERIC CASH, a would-be writer, ten years older than Ike and Steven
> MATTY CLARK, detective assigned to the murder case
> YOLONDA BELLO, Clark's partner
> HARRY STEELE, a successful businessman
> TRISTAN ACEVEDO, a teenager who kills Ike during an attempted robbery

Lush Life by Richard Price is not only an exploration of the diverse characters affected by a robbery-gone-wrong on New York City's Lower East Side but also an exploration of the contemporary nature of the area itself, in which upscale young people have been uneasily braided into the neighborhood's earlier identity as an urban ghetto. Price takes full advantage of the satiric potential for this social phenomenon, depicting new would-be artists in the neighborhood as living in a protected bubble that not only insulates them from the darker realities around them but also makes their very obliviousness one of the neighborhood's darkest realities. The bars and boutiques that cater to the privileged youngsters seem to blind them to the downmarket bodegas and housing projects that surround them; the surreal absurdity of this rich-man, poor-man setting is made more striking by the heartless arrogance of the young hipsters, demonstrated especially by Ike Marcus, the young would-be writer whose murder by a stressed-out young Latino sets the narrative in motion.

    The tragedy occurs in the early morning hours, when, after a night of drinking, Ike is helping home his inebriated friend, Steven Boulware. Along for the ride is Eric Cash, who had recently hired Ike as the new bartender for the trendy restaurant he manages for successful businessman Harry Steele. When the stumblebum trio are approached by two young Latinos, Ike's glib, high-handed manner does not shut the situation down, as perhaps it would in a Hollywood film in which he imagines he has been cast as the hero; instead, his response triggers the violence.

Ike's fatal arrogance is anticipated by an important previous episode, involving what appears to be the image of the Virgin Mary in the mist on a bodega's refrigerator door. When business at Steele's restaurant is threatened by the crowd attracted to this apparition, Eric and Ike are dispatched to take care of it. While Eric surprises himself by hanging back, Ike unhesitatingly allows a bit of warm air to dissolve the Madonna; an unbeliever himself, he has no respect for the tradition or the culture of those to whom this image mattered. This episode also suggests he has little respect for boundaries; he is never aware of when he is crossing the line. The devastation of this impromptu icon anticipates Ike's future run-in, and it is prefigured by the site of a recently collapsed synagogue Eric and Ike barely register on their way to the bodega. That Ike's grandparents once attended such a synagogue has no impact on Ike, who has no connection to his family's traditions or to the history of the immigrants who once populated the Lower East Side.

Richard Price was born and raised in the Bronx, New York. He is the author of seven novels, including Clockers *(1992),* Freedomland *(1998), and* Samaritan *(2003), and numerous screenplays. He won a 2007 Edgar Award for his writing on the HBO series* The Wire.

The endemic cluelessness of the privileged young is also demonstrated at Ike's memorial service, orchestrated by his media-savvy friend Steven. After a medley of pop songs, the service allows Ike's friends to unwittingly reveal in their eulogies both their own narcissism as well as that of the deceased. Steven ends the service by dancing in the streets in a state of near-ecstasy, making an impression that is less sacred than profane or perhaps simply hollow and meretricious.

While Ike and his friends appear largely free of guilt and anguish, there are those in the novel who do undergo crises of conscience. The primary soul-searcher is Eric Cash, an older and more jaded version of the younger artistic types around him. Eric is at first suspected of murdering Ike, not only because of misleading circumstantial evidence but also because of the self-loathing that has overtaken him as a result of his feeling that he has done nothing of value in his life.

The turning point for Eric comes after the murder of Ike, when he is briefly a suspect and is subjected to a searing, lengthy interrogation by detective Matty Clark and his partner Yolonda, an experience that breaks down every illusion by which Eric had been able to continue to live on the Lower East Side. When Matty describes Eric as little more than a selfish, self-pitying, envious, and cowardly failure, who would not be above an enraged and resentful murder of chance acquaintance Ike, Eric is devastated. Now thirty-five, Eric realizes he must accept the end of his youth and the promise of his literary ambitions; furthermore, he sees the hipster downtown life as one that simply allows him to lie to himself about who he is and what he has become.

Overwhelmed by the realization that the future he had anticipated for himself will never come to pass, Eric begins to steal the tips owed his coworkers to fund his getaway from a world he now finds alienating and even frightening. As he slides weakly into the criminality Clark has suspected in him all along, Eric is rescued by his conscience. Along with his growing fear is a deepening sense of guilt so powerful that it is only when a group of thugs rob and brutally beat him that Eric begins to feel a satisfactory sense of expiation. Eric's active conscience is something that appears to distinguish him from his friends and coworkers; in addition, unlike the others, Eric has always felt that the Lower East Side in which he has been living for eight years is haunted by the ghosts of the past, of those who were part of the old traditions brought over from Europe. The posh apartment of his boss Harry Steele is a desanctified synagogue and clearly a triumph of gentrification, and Eric is as uneasy in this contemporary tribute to the good life as he was when confronting the refrigerator Madonna. His reserve suggests that he is sensitive to issues of presumption and disrespect in a way that distinguishes him from those around him. The morally ambiguous Steele does, however, come close to being a much-needed father figure in Eric's life, and it is Steele who gives the penitent Eric if not a second chance than at least a way out of the Lower East Side.

Steele references the issue of fathers, which is one of this novel's important subjects. Like the fathers and father figures in this novel, Steele lives a life at a distance from that of his confused surrogate son Eric; similarly, Ike's father, Billy Marcus, divorced from his son's mother, is overcome by the realization that he has selfishly distanced himself from his son. The childish Billy ironically demonstrates even more adult dereliction after Ike's death by drinking too much, abandoning his second wife and stepdaughter, and making a perfect pest of himself with the police force. The death of Ike, however, has forced Billy to own up to his faults, even as his determined downward spiral seems to be yet another bad move. Billy finds something of a soul mate in the investigating detective, Matty Clark. In pursuing this case, Matty, whose name echoes Billy's, must face the fact that he has been wrong to distance himself from his two sons, who are about to become callow criminals; he understands that he must do something about it before it is too late.

Although by the end of this novel pervasive guilt has been established, the story does specify the orphaned Tristan Acevedo as the teenager who pulled the trigger on the gun. With his mother dead and his father absent, Tristan is living in a housing project with a callous stepfather and his new wife, who seem to retain him only because of his value as an unpaid caretaker for their small children. Tristan is given an opportunity to demonstrate some street "cred" when he is asked to join an older friend in a prowl of the neighborhood in search of likely prey, who turn out to be Ike and his buddies. The usual social pattern had ensured that Tristan and Ike are virtually invisible to each other, divided as they were along class, cultural, ethnic, and racial lines; it is only as a victim of crime that Ike finds himself face-to-face with Tristan. However, like Ike, Acevedo is unlucky in his choice of friends; it is his bullying pal who provides the inexperienced Tristan with the handgun with which he shoots Ike. In the aftermath, as was the case with Steven and Ike, the friendship is also tested and found empty. In addition, Tristan, like Ike, has artistic aspirations. He is a would-be writer of hip-hop lyrics, his voice and the voices of those like him mix in a jazzy way with the novel's cop lingo and its patois of privileged youth. In fact, it is Price's special talent to allow his characters to exist within their various voices, which blend and clash in a way that brings to life the entire spectrum of urban life, its low life, its high life, and its "lush life," the last a phenomenon that suggests that the high life is never very far from its opposite.

The final major urban tribe in Price's novel functions in a way that is both very near and quite far from such small-time criminals as Tristan. This tribe consists of the police, who keep an eye on the kids from the projects and run them to ground when necessary. The police see Ike and his friends as essentially well-to-do children on a protracted spring break, on occasion becoming the victims of the edgy teenagers from the housing projects. The job of the police is the surveillance and control of this latter group—the novel begins, in fact, with something called the Quality of Life Task Force, who patrol the Lower East Side in an unmarked car looking for likely black and Hispanic perpetrators. It is the perspective of the police, in fact, that supplies this story with its tension and structure; this novel is on the face of it a police procedural, and there is considerable time spent seeing this world through the eyes of the troubled detective Matty and his more grounded and empathic partner, Yolonda.

Although an exciting, expertly executed crime novel on the surface, *Lush Life* is also a novel of conscience, both social and psychological. As a moralist, Price shows that, while the young people of any race or class have yet to develop a sense of consequence, older voices recognize that, with age and time, the wrong life will call down suffering and remorse. As a novelist with a social conscience, Price is sensitive and satiric, and at times he seems a stern Old Testament prophet, warning of numbered days. In *Lush Life* the police are hardly on top of very much, and even the detective of record is living a life that he must put into turnaround. In fact, each story suggests that this time in everyone's life is about to be over or that time is running out. When the hip, downtown-Manhattan neighborhood depicted has been transplanted by novel's end to Atlantic City as part of a new theme park, it suggests not a definitive end of days but a final, irreverent evaluation of a cultural landscape that has broken many hearts and has already lost its soul. Its shining hour seems to have lasted little longer than a New York minute.

Margaret Boe Birns

Review Sources

Booklist 104, no. 7 (December 1, 2007): 5.
Chicago Tribune, March 15, 2008, p. 4.
Entertainment Weekly, March 7, 2008, p. 94.
Kirkus Reviews 76, no. 1 (January 1, 2008): 12.
Library Journal 133, no. 4 (March 1, 2008): 75-76.

Los Angeles Times, March 2, 2008, p. R1.
The Nation 286, no. 22 (June 9, 2008): 48-52.
New York 41, no. 9 (March 10, 2008): 144-145.
The New York Review of Books 55, no. 7 (May 1, 2008): 28-31.
The New York Times, March 4, 2008, p. E1.
The New York Times Book Review, March 16, 2008, p. 1.
The New Yorker 84, no. 8 (April 7, 2008): 79-81.
Newsweek 151, no. 10 (March 10, 2008): 50-52.
Publishers Weekly 255, no. 3 (January 21, 2008): 151.
World Literature Today 82, no. 6 (November/December, 2008): 64-65.

McMAFIA
A Journey Through the Global Criminal Underworld

Author: Misha Glenny (1958-   )
Publisher: Alfred A. Knopf (New York). 375 pp. $27.95
Type of work: Current affairs
Time: 1985-2007
Locale: Worldwide

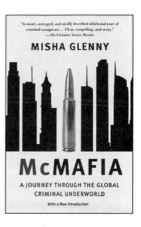

Glenny describes the operations of organized crime elements throughout all parts of the world and examines the causes and consequences of their activities and their impact on governments and law-abiding citizens

Misha Glenny begins *McMafia* with the story of a young British woman gunned down in 1994 at her front door in a London suburb. A subsequent investigation revealed that the real target of this seemingly senseless crime had been her sister, who was married to an Armenian embroiled in the illegal arms trade. In the previous five years, that business had grown exponentially to supply groups in Eastern Europe, where civil wars raged incessantly. Apparently the Armenian had fallen out with his partners in crime, and apparently the traffickers had decided that murdering his wife would be an effective way to express their displeasure. Unfortunately, his sister-in-law was the one who ended up dead. The circumstances leading to this unfortunate woman's death are indicative of the kinds of activities happening around the world in what Glenny describes as an exponential rise in the global shadow economy. Managing this vast enterprise of illegal businesses is a network of organized crime groups whose reach extends across the continents and whose annual net profits run into the billions. This new generation of criminals is the subject of Glenny's extensive, well researched, and at times provocative study.

As Glenny is quick to point out, however, there have been underworld elements in virtually every country for decades, even centuries. These have ranged from bands of hoodlums to more sophisticated groups with well-defined hierarchies and elaborate mechanisms for handling their illicit income. What has changed during the last decades of the twentieth century is the propensity for regional or national groups to establish ties with organized crime elements in other countries, creating in effect international cartels for the production, distribution, and sale of illegal goods and services—and for the equally important task of "laundering" money, transferring funds into legitimate businesses or investments to erase any trace of the activity from which they were originally obtained. The activities of organized crime have been aided—unintentionally, perhaps—by the worldwide trend toward globalization. Liberalized rules in international financial markets have made it possible for criminal groups to operate around the world, banking their ill-gained profits with little fear of discovery by law-enforcement agencies.

~

Misha Glenny is the author of The
Rebirth of History *(1990);* The Fall of
Yugoslavia *(1992), for which he won
the Overseas Press Club award for best
book on foreign affairs; and* The
Balkans: Nationalism, War, and the
Great Powers, 1804-1999 *(1999). He
has covered Central Europe for the
British Broadcasting Corporation and
served as a consultant to various
governments on Balkan issues.*

~

Glenny finds the seeds for the rise of this new criminal class in the collapse of the Soviet Union, which he says ushered in this wave of transnational organized crime. Criminal enterprises sprang up in Bulgaria, in the countries that once made up Yugoslavia, in the Ukraine, in Moldova and its rebellious Transnistria province, and inside Russia itself, where a handful of new oligarchs robbed the state of its assets and made personal fortunes taking advantage of the vacuum created by the absence of strong law-enforcement agencies. Having explained in broad terms how these new international networks have emerged to capitalize on political instability, Glenny then takes his readers on a worldwide tour of countries where organized crime has set down roots and prospered: India, Dubai and other sovereignties in the United Arab Emirates (a favorite place for criminals to bank their earnings), Nigeria, South Africa, Colombia, Brazil, and a number of African nations, including Angola and Nigeria. One seemingly unlikely place is Israel, where recent Russian immigrants have brought with them the dubious skills they learned in the lawless environment that existed in their home land for more than a decade after the Soviet Union fell apart. Another is western Canada, which Glenny identifies as a center of drug operations in North America. The variety of activities in which criminal organizations have become involved is truly mind-numbing, ranging far beyond the more sensational and obviously reprehensible activities such as extortion, robbery, drug trafficking, prostitution, and gambling. Glenny provides example after example of ways enterprising criminals have made fortunes in smuggling legal goods such as cigarettes and caviar into countries where tariffs are high or quantities available through legal means are low. He also explains in some detail the newest form of illegal activity, cybercrime—identity theft, bank fraud, and numerous scams aimed at separating unsuspecting citizens (especially in America and Europe) from their cash. The expansion of the Internet to all corners of the world, considered by many as a great boon, has made it possible for crime elements to communicate more effectively and avoid detection by law-enforcement agencies that have neither the staff nor the expertise to deal effectively with this new phenomenon.

An accomplished journalist able to get people on both sides of the law to speak freely with him, Glenny displays an unusual ability to ferret out the criminal infrastructure in countries as widely different as Bulgaria and western Canada and to explain with exceptional facility and clarity the machinations involved in laundering money in an international financial market. Always interested in putting a human face on his tale, he provides brief biographical sketches of a rogue's gallery of criminals whose brazen disregard for the law seems to strain the limits of readers' credulity. He also relates the stories of some of the more notable or pitiable victims whose lives have been ruined by the reckless behavior of overlords and underlings in the business of organized crime. There are portraits, too, of some of the people who have dedicated their lives to fighting these criminals, truly brave men and women whose efforts have occasionally resulted in the elimination of a major figure on the world's "Most Wanted" list. Unfortunately, Glenny points out, because most modern organized crime networks are carefully structured to limit the group's dependence on any one individual, taking down a crime boss frequently results in only a temporary setback for the organization.

Glenny is insistent that international organized crime presents a serious threat to the stability of governments and individual citizens everywhere. This shadow economy siphons off billions of dollars from legitimate businesses and deprives governments of taxes on goods and services. Criminal activity poses a real threat to those who get caught up in the web being spun by individuals whose rapacity for ever-increasing sums of money drives them to consider harm to innocent victims as mere collateral damage. Glenny insists, too, that virtually everyone on the planet is touched in some way by organized crime. Some are apparent: A portion of everyone's taxes must go to support law-enforcement efforts, and some neighborhoods become unsafe when members of organized crime groups set up business there. What may not be so obvious is the way people rely on organized crime to supply their needs or to support their lifestyles. It is not just those dependent on drugs or in search of illicit sexual encounters who make payments to these Mafiosi. Everyone who uses a cell phone may have been contributing, albeit indirectly, to the continued success of organized crime—because every cell phone requires coltan, a mineral obtained almost exclusively in Africa, where mining and trading have been controlled by criminal elements. Only recently have serious efforts been undertaken to delink the mining of this precious mineral from the unsavory characters that have profited for decades from sales to legitimate businesses for legitimate purposes.

Glenny's analysis of organized-crime activities suggests that historically the ability of organized crime networks to become established and to prosper is almost always linked directly to some action by government, whether that has been prohibiting the sale of certain commodities or failing to provide certain services or an acceptable level of security for its citizens. While he has little good to say about the hoodlums who profit from others' misery, Glenny is equally harsh in his critique of established governments, especially those in the First World, that seem to be doing all the wrong things in managing their economies or combating crime. Nowhere is this more apparent than in his excoriation of the United States for what he considers an ill-conceived policy regarding drug use and abuse. By criminalizing substances such as marijuana and cocaine, the United States is providing a reason for the establishment of criminal groups that see a way to make a substantial profit by supplying banned narcotics to a population whose demand for drugs is growing. Even worse, measures employed by U.S. officials to coerce cooperation in its worldwide effort to stamp out illegal drugs from countries where drugs are produced, specifically those in Latin America, have actually been counterproductive—and sometimes ludicrous. In one stinging example, Glenny points out that the United States built a library in a Colombian village as a reward for the government's efforts to drive out the drug cartels. Unfortunately, illiteracy is rampant in that area—as is poverty—and the building remains locked and empty. Meanwhile, drug cartels have continued operating with impunity throughout the country, often supported by a population that sees its own government doing little to alleviate harsh living conditions.

The European Union is no better. Glenny blames those countries (along with the United States) for policies that deprived states in the Balkans from generating revenues through exports during the Balkan conflicts of the 1990's, giving crime groups a golden opportunity to solidify their operations in the area by bribing local governments to ignore what they were doing. Smuggling is an epidemic in Europe because criminals are supplying Western Europeans what they are willing to purchase: drugs, prostitutes, cheap cigarettes, caviar, ivory, even human body parts. What may be even worse, countries in Western Europe want cheap labor but do not want to ease their restrictions on immigration, so mob bosses arrange to bring in labor illegally, at a great profit to them but at great personal cost to the unfortunate men and women who frequently end up being little more than slaves. On this topic Glenny abandons all pretense of journalistic objectivity, insisting that the West's attempt to support "globalism" will work only when labor is allowed to move freely across borders and people are compensated appropriately for the work they perform.

McMafia is an extended effort in advocacy journalism, the effort of a highly respected and often personally brave writer to expose the problems transnational organized crime has created and offer some suggestions on what might be done to curb its influence. Glenny's proposals are certain to provoke controversy, primarily because he argues from an economic rather than a moralistic (he would say falsely moralistic) position on many of these matters. For example, he believes the influence of the Mafia in drug trafficking has grown in direct proportion to the efforts of the United States and numerous other countries to regulate drugs and go after those who manufacture or distribute substances classified as illegal. Glenny's recommendation is to legalize most of these narcotics, thereby taking away the need for people to obtain them from organized crime groups. On the other hand, noting how easy it is for Mafia outfits to launder money and play fast and loose in the financial arena, he calls for much tighter global regulation on financial markets. Making financial markets more transparent, especially banking operations in places such as Dubai and Switzerland, would make it much more difficult for organized crime groups to disguise their financial transactions.

Recommendations such as these are sure to annoy people who believe that many of the activities in which organized crime is active are morally reprehensible. They will also not sit well with more conservative politicians who have joined forces with the moralists in fighting crimes such as prostitution, gambling, and drug abuse, but who retain a strong sense that there is already too much regulation in financial matters. Hence, it is unlikely that Glenny's proposals will get a fair hearing in any Western nation any time soon. Nevertheless, it is hard to discount the persuasive argument he makes that current policies have failed to stem the tide of organized crime, and that only by looking for bold new ways of addressing the problems caused by the international Mafias can nations and individuals hope to rid themselves of this global scourge.

Laurence W. Mazzeno

Review Sources

The Christian Science Monitor, April 22, 2008, p. 13.
The Economist 382 (April 12, 2008): 92.
Kirkus Reviews 76, no. 3 (February 1, 2008): 129.
London Review of Books 30, no. 13 (July 3, 2008): 3-6.
The New York Review of Books 55, no. 16 (October 23, 2008): 52-55.
The New York Times Book Review, May 25, 2008, p. 12.
Publishers Weekly 255, no. 3 (January 21, 2008): 163.
The Spectator 307 (May 3, 2008): 40-41.
The Wall Street Journal 251, no. 86 (April 12, 2008): W9.
The Washington Post Book World, April 13, 2008, p. 15.

THE MAGICAL CHORUS
A History of Russian Culture from Tolstoy to Solzhenitsyn

Author: Solomon Volkov (1944-   )
Translated from the Russian by Antonina W. Bouis
Publisher: Alfred A. Knopf (New York). 333 pp. $30.00
Type of work: History
Time: 1900-2000
Locale: Russia and the Soviet Union

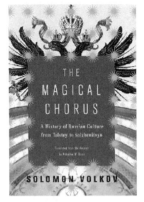

Volkov describes the often contentious relationship be-
tween government leaders and practitioners of the literary,
visual, and performing arts during the turbulent century in
which the Soviet Union rose and fell

Principal personages:
LEO TOLSTOY, Russian novelist
ANTON CHEKHOV, Russian playwright
VLADIMIR LENIN, born VLADIMIR ILYICH ULYANOV, leader of the
    Russian Revolution of 1916-1917 and leader of the Union of Soviet
    Socialist Republics (U.S.S.R.), 1922-1924
MAXIM GORKY, Russian poet and political activist
JOSEPH STALIN, born IOSIF VISSARIONOVICH JUGASHVILI, leader of the
    Soviet Union, 1927-1953
ANNA AKHMATOVA, Russian poet
MIKHAIL SHOLOKHOV, Russian novelist
NIKITA KHRUSHCHEV, leader of the Soviet Union, 1953-1964
BORIS PASTERNAK, Russian poet and novelist
MIKHAIL GORBACHEV, leader of the Soviet Union, 1985-1991
ALEKSANDR SOLZHENITSYN, Russian novelist and essayist

The Ukranian poet Anna Akhmatova once described the group of young poets living and working in Leningrad after World War II as a "magical chorus." Solomon
Volkov borrows the phrase for the title of his book on twentieth century Russian cultural history, a work in which the dissident Akhmatova figures prominently. Using
material from official records, personal memoirs, scholarly publications, newspaper
accounts, and interviews with many of the people whose stories he relates, Volkov
creates a lively and at times poignant narrative of struggle in which alienated artists
are constantly pitted against superior forces bound to make them conform or be silent.
In Volkov's estimation, the writers, performers, and visual artists living in Russia—
which for most of the century was the centerpiece of the Union of Soviet Socialist Re-
publics, or the Soviet Union—were somehow endowed with a kind of magic, allowing them to raise their voices against various forms of oppression that affected not
only the arts community but also the population as a whole. Hence *The Magical Chorus* is cultural history, but with a decidedly political slant.

When Volkov speaks of "culture," he means "high culture" in the sense it has been

defined in the West by writers such as the nineteenth century British critic Matthew Arnold
and the twentieth century American scholars Lionel Trilling, Allan Bloom, and E. D.
Hirsch. Although Volkov pays some attention to the genre in which individuals worked
and at times comments on individual works
or performances, he is interested principally
in the relationship between individual artists
and the state—or, more appropriately, the various dictators in charge of Russia's government. Whether writing about Nicholas II, the
last czar to rule before Vladimir Lenin and his
supporters ousted the monarchy and set up
their Communist utopia, or about the men

*Born in the Soviet Union during World
War II, Solomon Volkov emigrated to
the United States in 1976. An
accomplished musicologist and
aesthetician, he is the author of* St.
Petersburg: A Cultural History *(1995)
and* Shostakovich and Stalin *(2006). He
also published* Testimony *(1979), a
controversial book purported to be the
memoirs of Russian composer Dmitri
Shostakovich but which some claim to
be Volkov's original work.*

who succeeded Lenin as head of state—Joseph Stalin, Nikita Khrushchev, and
Mikhail Gorbachev the most prominent among them—Volkov stresses the important
role these leaders had in shaping the direction of the arts in Russia and determining
the fate of individual artists.

Like their counterparts in other countries, Russian artists began the twentieth century struggling to define the nature of art. There were clashes within the various communities of writers and performers as proponents of modernism, expressionism, and
abstract art challenged supporters of traditional realism, itself a tradition less than
three centuries old in fiction and even newer in the visual arts. In addition to battles
over aesthetics, however, Russian artists seem always to find themselves engaged in
conflict with the various forms of authority. In the early years of the century Leo Tolstoy, one of the world's most distinguished novelists and a figure revered throughout
his homeland, was excommunicated by the Russian Orthodox Church for his heretical views on religion. Unfazed, Tolstoy went on trying to tell anyone who would listen what Russia (and all humankind, for that matter) must do to achieve personal and
social salvation. Nicholas II ignored Tolstoy's advice on government, but the czar
took some interest in art being produced in the country. The czar seemed to favor realistic art that celebrated traditional (that is, monarchist) values, and he was averse to allowing subordinates to make life difficult for those who were experimenting with new
forms of expression.

Despite the crackdown by Nicholas's forces, avant-garde writers, dramatists, musicians, and painters seemed to be gaining the upper hand by the time Lenin's Red
Army defeated the czar's supporters. For a brief period, these artists held a privileged
place in society, seen by Communist leaders as harbingers of a new style that was re-
placing the moribund practices of traditionalists, whose ties to the old regime were
apparent in many ways. Eventually, however, these men and women came under suspicion for what Lenin and his followers described as subversive and decadent practices; it was not wise, leaders thought, to let people interpret art or anything else as
they might wish. By the time Stalin had firmly established his control over Soviet pol-

itics in the 1930's, "socialist realism" became the only approved form of art. Plays, novels, poetry, musical compositions, paintings, and sculptures all had to celebrate the achievements of the proletariat in order to receive public recognition and support. Concurrently, those who challenged the ideals of communism or protested the practices of Stalin or his successors often found themselves shuffled off to labor camps or, in the worst case, executed on trumped-up charges of crimes against the state.

Volkov provides insightful and sometimes heartwrenching sketches of dozens of writers whose careers rose and fell at the whim of Stalin. Even Stalin's trusted adviser Maxim Gorky came under a cloud of distrust, and only death may have prevented him from suffering further humiliation—or worse. While writers who had fled Russia for other countries in Europe or America before or shortly after the Bolsheviks came to power lamented the fate of their fellow artists suffering under Stalin's repressive regime, those who remained put up what Volkov describes as a heroic struggle to write or perform, even at the risk of personal safety.

Volkov also explains why some writers chose to adapt to the rules laid down by Communist leaders, and why works by these men and women have been underappreciated by those in the West who would dismiss "socialist realism" as inherently inferior art. Particularly interesting is Volkov's discussion of the Soviet government's attempts to have the Nobel Prize awarded to a Russian writer—specifically, to someone such as the novelist Mikhail Sholokov, of whom Stalin approved—and the political fallout when the first Russian to win the prize was the exiled Ivan Bunin. The government took little joy in several subsequent awards to Russian authors and went to great lengths to ensure that the poet and novelist Boris Pasternak did not go to Sweden to be honored upon being named the winner in 1958.

The artistic community took hope when Stalin died and there appeared to be some movement to release the stranglehold that government officials had on the production of art. It was during one of those brief moments of liberalization that Khruschev, working hard to paint Stalin in a bad light, in 1962 allowed the publication of Aleksandr Solzhenitsyn's *Odin den' Ivana Denisovicha* (*One Day in the Life of Ivan Denisovich*, 1963), a scathing account of the forced labor camps to which Stalin had exiled millions of Russians. That brief, halcyon period of détente between Khrushchev and Russian artists did not last, however, and the situation did not improve under Khrushchev's successors. Although Solzhenitsyn was awarded the Nobel Prize in 1970 for his efforts to reveal the horrors of the Soviet labor-camp system, authorities found his portrait of the government a bit too embarrassing, and by 1974 he was exiled. Even under the seemingly open and reform-minded Gorbachev, those whose work hinted at nonconformity suffered at the hands of state agents. Sadly, when the Soviet Union fell, Volkov notes, those who had suffered for the sake of their art found competition from an even more menacing foe: popular culture, and especially rock music, imported from the United States, which seemed to captivate the younger generation of Russians and make them oblivious to the art produced by those who clung to less commercial forms of expression.

Having begun with a discussion of Tolstoy's advice to the czar, Volkov deftly brings his narrative full circle by closing with a discussion of Solzhenitsyn's advice to

Russia's leaders as they tried to reorganize the country after the fall of communism. Once again, Volkov notes sadly, the writer of international reputation found himself unheeded at home. Having spent his entire writing life trying to point out the evils of the Soviet system, Solzhenitsyn seemed to modern Russians sadly out of touch with contemporary realities.

In this sweeping survey of Russian cultural history, no one writer dominates Volkov's landscape. Though some are discussed more extensively—Tolstoy and his contemporary Anton Chekhov, Gorky, Akhmatova, and Solzhenitsyn—Volkov weaves into his narrative stories of the careers of poets Alexander Blok, Osip Mandelstam, Joseph Brodsky, and Yevgeny Yevtushenko, poet and playwright Vladimir Mayakovsky, dramatist Konstantin Stanislavsky, and composers Sergei Prokofiev and Dmitri Shostakovich. They are, indeed, a magical chorus of artists who seemed to sing the same tune, a song of protest against authorities who would limit their creativity. Hence, on some meta-level, Volkov's book is a tale about repression versus freedom of expression. As he notes on more than one occasion, Soviet authorities frequently gave legitimacy to, and conferred status on, artists whose work might have otherwise gone unnoticed had government officials not chosen to harass them. There were some truly subversive works, but as Volkov notes in discussing a number of musical compositions and novels, it was sometimes hard for artists or their publics to distinguish what was actually seditious from work that simply displeased an official who had the power to censor it.

It is clear that Volkov likes some people—both artists and politicians—better than others, but throughout *The Magical Chorus* he strives for objectivity, saying to his readers: Here is what happened, make what you will of it. He does offer some controversial judgments about individuals whose reputation in the West is, in his opinion, unfairly distorted. At the top of that list is Stalin, whom Volkov portrays as a considerably more complex and thoughtful figure than others have made him out to be. Volkov insists that, unlike most other Soviet leaders, Stalin read voraciously and understood the propagandistic value of the arts. In some ways, these qualities make Stalin an even more menacing figure, as one can see him manipulating writers, painters, and performers often for no other reason than that he had power to do so. In these and other provocative assessments lies the particular strength of Volkov's portrait of twentieth century Russia. His well-researched, highly readable, and engaging account does much to expose for Western audiences some of the hidden wellsprings of the Russian character and culture and to make sense of its politics.

Laurence W. Mazzeno

Review Sources

America 198, no. 4 (April 28, 2008): 40-42.
Booklist 104, no. 14 (March 15, 2008): 23.
The Christian Science Monitor, March 11, 2008, p. 17.
Commentary 125, no. 5 (May, 2008): 50-52.
Kirkus Reviews 76, no. 2 (January 15, 2008): 84-85.
The New Leader 91, no. 2 (March/April, 2008): 21-22.
The New York Times Book Review, May 4, 2008, p. 18.
Russian Life 51, no. 3 (May/June, 2008): 62.

MAN IN THE DARK

Author: Paul Auster (1947-   )
Publisher: Henry Holt (New York). 182 pp. $23.00
Type of work: Novel
Time: 2007
Locale: A house in Vermont

A seventy-two-year-old widower, living with his daughter and granddaughter, suffers from insomnia and invents stories as he lies awake in the dark

> *Principal characters:*
> AUGUST BRILL, a seventy-two-year-old
>   book reviewer and critic
> MIRIAM, his forty-seven-year-old daughter
>   and a scholar
> KATYA, his twenty-three-year-old
>   granddaughter who grieves for a dead lover
> TITUS SMALL, Katya's former boyfriend
> OWEN BRICK, a character of Brill's imagination who finds himself a
>   central figure in a civil war

The novel *Man in the Dark* begins ominously: "I am alone in the dark, turning the world around in my head as I struggle through another bout of insomnia, another white night in the great American wilderness." That wilderness is Vermont, where August Brill has moved after a serious car accident has left him disabled. He resides with his divorced daughter, Miriam, and her college-aged daughter, Katya, who mourns a dead lover.

Brill is oppressed by a collection of personal sorrows, and to cope with those difficulties he seeks diversion through elaborate stories he concocts in his head. His most recent, and most compelling, concerns Owen Brick, a professional magician in Queens, New York, who works under the stage name of the Great Zavello. Brick is an otherwise unprepossessing figure, a quiet man, living a quiet life, married to a woman named Flora, who is expecting his first child and who frets over his humble means.

Inexplicably, though, he awakens suddenly to find himself in a deep hole, of which he has no memory of entering and no means of escape. When he is finally extricated, his commanding officer informs Brick that he is fighting in a civil war in America and that he has been chosen to assassinate the one man responsible for the conflict, "because he owns the war. He invented it, and everything that happens or is about to happen is in his head. Eliminate the head, and the war stops. It's that simple."

Brick seeks to avoid this responsibility, but after each attempt to escape or elude his superiors, he is beaten or dragged back into the conflict. When Brick protests that he does not recognize this war or this version of the United States, one that never endured 9/11 or the Iraq conflict, he is informed that he lives in different, parallel

With The New York Trilogy—City of Glass *(1985),* Ghosts *(1986), and* The Locked Room *(1986)—Paul Auster established his reputation as an experimental writer. His other novels include* In the Country of Last Things *(1987),* Moon Palace *(1989),* Leviathan *(1992),* Mr. Vertigo *(1994),* The Book of Illusions *(2002),* The Brooklyn Follies *(2005), and* Travels in the Scriptorium *(2007). He has published essay collections and screenplays.*

worlds, a condition postulated by a sixteenth century Italian philosopher who reasoned that because of God's infinitude there exists an infinite number of worlds.

Brick is allowed to return briefly to his former life, where he resumes his quotidian existence but also begins researching the writings of his putative victim, who is now revealed to be Brill himself. Brick is soon visited by his tormentors, as the two worlds collide, and he has a brief affair with a woman from his past who has been sent to persuade him to accept his mission. When he refuses yet again to participate in murder, he is eliminated.

At this point, a restless Katya visits her grandfather and insists he describe his marriage and explain why he once divorced his wife and then lived with her once again after leaving his second wife. During their late night colloquy, the reader also learns about Katya's grief and the guilt she feels over the murder of her boyfriend.

Paul Auster has a reputation for being one of American letters' premier metafictionists, a title that has led to criticism in some quarters and to praise in others. European readers have especially appreciated Auster's fictional experiments as evidenced by granting him the prestigious Prix Médicis Etranger and the Prince of Asturias Prize for Literature. *Man in the Dark* is in many ways a continuation of the self-reflexiveness established in the novels, published in 1985 and 1986, included in Auster's *New York Trilogy* and extending over his next ten novels.

This novel is located squarely in the creative consciousness of a writer, in this case a former book reviewer and critic. Unlike other writers, though, Brill does not create because of a vacancy he seeks to fill but rather from the press of heart-scalding losses that demand his attention. In short, Brill creates to divert or escape. Whereas metafictions typically revolve around the story of someone creating the story itself—its methods, its means, its shortcomings, its false starts—the narrative, though sometimes convoluted, remains focused on the story of the story.

Man in the Dark is similar, but with a significant difference. It presents an intricate nest of stories that parallel and compete with one another. Thus, one finds the narratives of a mother and daughter troubled by lovers lost and of a writer overwhelmed by his own personal loss and inability to assuage the sorrows of those he loves. Additionally, there is the invented protagonist—Brick—who wanders between two worlds and carries the burden of making peace for all those oppressed by war and death. Finally, there is Brill's failed memoir that comes to life only in a nightlong reminiscence for his granddaughter. Interspersed with these stories is a handful of brief anecdotes that Brill has acquired from relatives and friends as well as the synopses of films that he and Katya watch together in their home.

On the surface, these narratives seem to lack coherence, until one considers Brill's meditation on the possibility of multiple realities that Giordano Bruno postulated as issuing from the fecund imagination of the supreme creative consciousness. "There are many worlds [read also narratives], and they all run parallel to one another, worlds and antiworlds, worlds and shadow-worlds, and each is dreamed or imagined or written by someone in another world." These parallel experiences become a fitting metaphor for Brill's existence, both lived and invented.

Beneath the contortions of the stories sliding in and out of one another is the narrative of a post-George W. Bush United States. In Brick's invented United States, the Twin Towers remain intact, there are no wars in Afghanistan and Iraq, and Iran is a forgotten threat. However, there is still war, this time a second American civil war, a conflict precipitated by the Supreme Court decision to suspend the Florida vote count and award Bush the presidency. As a result, sixteen blue states have seceded, becoming the Independent States of America, an entity internationally recognized, and they do battle with the Federal States in a war resulting in the deaths of twelve million people.

Brill's America is hardly a salubrious alternative. Here people deal with daily suffering: Miriam's loss of a feckless husband, Brill's loss of his wife of thirty-nine years to cancer, and his incapacitation as a result of a traffic accident. There is, however, the chaos of 9/11 and the horrible specter of Iraq in the tragedy of Titus Small's execution, which will remind readers of *Wall Street Journal* reporter Daniel Pearl and various contract workers executed for being caught in a war zone.

Auster's title takes on further resonance in this context: Not only is Brill a man literally awake in the dark of night but also all humanity resides in the dark of bad behavior, callousness, and cruelty. As Brill says of his daughter's naïveté, "I wish to God she would learn that the rotten acts human beings commit against one another are not just aberrations—they're an essential part of who we are." Thus Auster's novel suggests that politics as a construct of order and justice is ultimately dubious; instead, politics is simply the mass representation of human venality and cruelty.

Throughout his career, Auster has revealed a strong existential concern with issues of alienation and personal identity in an absurd world. In this novel, Brill, his daughter, and granddaughter suffer from severe alienation, most obviously in their separation from spouses and lovers and in their vain attempts to evade memory and feeling. They find themselves living in "a house of grieving, wounded souls." Locked in their sorrow and in the house where they reside, they are furthermore alienated from the world around them, in the same way that Brick finds himself alienated in a deep hole that offers no exit. Perhaps the most striking embodiment of their alienation comes in Katya's theory about the way in which master directors convey profound human emotions: through inanimate objects. Each family member seeks some evasion from his or her emotions and would prefer forgetfulness or inanimate objects to feeling.

The search for identity is another longstanding concern of Auster that can be traced back to his earliest works. His characters are often confused about their identities, or their identities are confusing to others, and this shifting of identity is particularly evident in Brill and his alter ego, Brick. Brick exclaims at one point, "Someone's inside my head. Not even my dreams belong to me." The enduring existential question— Who am I?—bedevils Brick, and he is never able to settle the issue before his extinction. Similarly, Brill wonders who he is and what legacy he will leave after what he regards as a fractured, inconsequential life.

In his infamous essay "Stalking the Billion-Footed Beast" (1989), Tom Wolfe criticized his contemporaries by proclaiming they had renounced the true subject of the traditional American novel for solipsistic concerns and clever constructions. The essay presented a deeply flawed argument—that American novelists had renounced the importance of the historical moment—but if it did have any marginal validity, that position has been eroded in recent years by fictions such as Philip Roth's *The Plot Against America* (2004), Don DeLillo's *Falling Man* (2007), and even Cormac McCarthy's *The Road* (2006), to name just a few prominent examples. The criticism, in slightly different form, appeared again in 2008 when Horace Engdahl, permanent secretary of the Nobel Prize Committee, confidently declared that American writers were too insular and absorbed with issues of mass culture.

Man in the Dark, the work of one of the United States' supreme metafictionists, puts the lie to these glib assertions of fictional self-involvement. Auster's hall-of-mirrors narratives are not the novel's flash and filigree but integral components of a deeply humane vision. The strongest assertion of the novel's profound humanity comes at the end of Brill's late-night monologue when he proposes that he and Katya take her love of films and his dedication to language and create their own film, "something light—a frothy bagatelle, as frivolous and diverting as possible. If we really put our minds to it, we might have some fun . . . what I'm proposing is a cure, a remedy to ward off the blues."

David W. Madden

Review Sources

Booklist 104, no. 18 (May 15, 2008): 5.
The Guardian, September 19, 2008, p. 38.
International Herald Tribune, August 28, 2008, p. 20.
Kirkus Reviews 76, no. 9 (May 1, 2008): 447.
Library Journal 133, no. 10 (June 1, 2008): 89.
Los Angeles Times, August 24, 2008, p. F9.
New Statesman 137 (September 15, 2008): 58-59.
The New York Review of Books 55, no. 19 (December 4, 2008): 36-38.
The New York Times Book Review, September 21, 2008, p. 21.
The Observer, September 7, 2008, p. 24.

Publishers Weekly 255, no. 21 (May 26, 2008): 35.
The Times Literary Supplement, August 22, 2008, p. 21.
The Village Voice 53, no. 35 (August 27, 2008): 40.
The Washington Post, August 31, 2008, p. T2.

THE MAN WHO LOVED CHINA
The Fantastic Story of the Eccentric Scientist Who Unlocked the Mysteries of the Middle Kingdom

Author: Simon Winchester (1944-   )
Publisher: HarperCollins (New York). 316 pp. $27.95
Type of work: Biography
Time: 1900-1995
Locale: London and Cambridge, England; Chongqing
  (formerly Chungking), China

*A biography of Joseph Needham, the world's leading
figure in the historiography of Chinese science*

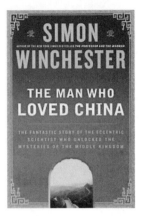

Principal personages:
  JOSEPH NEEDHAM, a scientist and historian
  LU GWEI-DJEN, his mistress and second
    wife

Joseph Needham's monumental *Science and Civilisation in China*, which continues to be published after his death in 1995, runs to twenty-four individual volumes, with more to come. Within a decade of the appearance of the initial volume in 1954, Needham's name teemed in China bibliographies. His reputation as the scientist-historian who brought to light the immense accomplishments of traditional Chinese technology and science grew steadily. While his name is widely known, however, the strange, often captivating, and at times morally problematic man behind it is not. Simon Winchester has done a signal service in bringing to light Needham's character and the saga behind his epic scholarship.

Needham was born in London at the dawn of the twentieth century, an only child of Scots lineage. His father was a physician, and his mother was a composer and a music teacher. His school years brought Needham's immense intellectual prowess to the fore. By the time he was seventeen, he was aware that science was his principal interest, and, thinking to follow his father in the field of medicine, he applied to Cambridge University. He entered Caius College in 1918, and three years later he took his first degree, followed in 1924 by a master's and a Ph.D.

As Winchester reveals, Needham was notorious for his eccentricities, which included nudism and the practice of Morris dance, a form of English folk dancing. By the 1930's, he was driving sports cars at breakneck speeds through the English countryside. He liked his morning toast burnt black, and he had a strict rule never to smoke before noon. Thereafter, he smoked constantly, nevertheless living to ninety-four. His politics ran to the far left. In 1917 he welcomed the Bolshevik coup in Russia and maintained far-left views throughout life, devoutly supporting socialism. At the same time, he was decidedly of a religious bent, belonging to a Catholic Brotherhood from 1922 to 1924. He balked at celibacy, however, and dropped out.

He was fluent in seven languages, including Polish.

Needham's initial academic field was chemistry, though his interest in biology was, if anything, greater. Eventually, he combined the two in biochemistry. For more than twenty years, he worked in embryology and morphogenesis, publishing distinguished works. His marriage in 1924 to fellow biochemist Dorothy Moyle was of a piece with his unconventionality. While still engaged, both announced to friends that their union would be of a thoroughly "modern" variety, excluding sexual fidelity. Needham later fulfilled this pronouncement at a key moment in his life.

That moment came in 1937, when several female Chinese scientists visited Cambridge. One of them, also a biochemist and four years his junior, was Lu Gwei-Djen, daughter of a Nanjing pharmacist. Lu, who had come to study with Needham's wife, attracted his am-

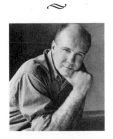

Simon Winchester studied geology at St. Catherine's College, University of Oxford, and spent twenty years as foreign correspondent for The Guardian, *before turning to independent full-time writing. He has written on such subjects as the 1906 San Francisco earthquake, the 1883 karate explosion, and conflict in the Balkans.*

orous attentions. The two became fast friends, then more than friends, even as Needham carried on as ("modern") husband. Lu stimulated in Needham a passion for all things Chinese, leading him to prodigious feats of learning in Chinese, both written and oral in Mandarin.

She also presented him with an enigma, known as "the Needham's Question," that preoccupied him for the rest of his life. Why, Lu asked, was China so successful in science and technology for so much of its history, only to fall hopelessly behind the West in recent centuries? In 1948 Needham put the question this way: "Why did science [in China] always remain empirical, and restricted to theories of primitive or mediaeval type?" He never found an answer.

Needham's consuming interest in China led him to plan, with the help of Chinese associates, a history of Chinese science, including medicine and technology. First, however, he had to get there. In late 1939 he and like-minded academics took up China's cause after Japan decimated more than fifty percent of the nation's colleges. How, Needham and others asked, could Chinese intellectual life, especially its science, be preserved in the midst of such destruction? Someone needed to travel to China, investigate the situation, and recommend to the British government how to preserve Chinese science. With linguistic ability and keen interest, Needham was a logical choice to lead such an inquiry.

It took eighteen months of persuading the Foreign Office and more months of waiting, but in the end Needham was sent to China's wartime capital, Chongqing, becoming director of a Sino-British Science Cooperation Office. From this vantage he was to survey the condition of Chinese science and make recommendations to prevent its collapse. Accordingly, early in 1943, he traversed the "air bridge" (provided by American Claire Chennault's Flying Tigers) over the "Hump" from India over the Himalayas, arriving first in Kunming, and then proceeded on to Chongqing in March, 1943.

Making Chongqing his base camp, Needham conducted a series of assaults on China's enormous geography. He was thrilled to be in China, whatever its wartime hardships. During his travels "he kept discovering again and again," Winchester reveals, that the Chinese "had the longest imaginable history of invention, creation, and the generation of new ideas." He came to believe he found pieces of the history of Chinese science unknown even to the Chinese. In the process of his travels and discoveries, he met a young Chinese man, Huang Hsing-tsung, who would become his secretary, confidant, and companion during years of travel in China.

Huang was an English-speaking college graduate who had arrived in China from Malaya during the war. Needham found him teaching at a Chengdu boys' school, not far from Chongqing. This association, invaluable to Needham in collecting the materials that formed the basis of his great work, resulted half a century later in Huang's production of an entire volume of *Science and Civilisation in China*.

Aided by his Man Friday, Needham undertook a series of expeditions, eleven in all, during which he encountered numerous human and documentary sources for a history of science in China and collected prodigious numbers of books, manuscripts, and other materials that became the foundation of his masterwork. These items were shipped back to Cambridge, sometimes in diplomatic pouches. Seven of his journeys were relatively short trips a few hundred miles from Chongqing.

Others were prodigious odysseys, involving thousands of miles and weeks or months of arduous trekking, some of it risky or even foolhardy during wartime. Needham and Huang managed to survive journeys that took them, for example, to the Silk Road, skirting the Gobi Desert, reaching Xinjiang, still occupied by the emperors' successors today. By the time he left for England in 1946, Needham had visited some 296 Chinese institutions of higher learning and had laid the foundations for a diplomatically sanctioned organization for the support of Chinese science.

Returning to England, Needham soon found himself involved in a United Nations organization to further education, science, and culture: UNESCO, the United Nations Educational, Scientific, and Cultural Organization. He spent two years in Paris heading its Natural Science division. His communist background alarmed Washington, D.C., where the Central Intelligence Agency informed President Harry Truman that communists were infiltrating UNESCO, though its director-general, Julian Huxley, pronounced Needham a "good communist."

Thus delayed, Needham returned to Cambridge in 1948 and went about the arduous business of shaping the volumes that would occupy the rest of his life and elevate his professional stature to a high level. He was fortunate to receive the assistance of Dr. Zhu Kezhen, a Chinese university president whom he had met during his travels and whom he informed of his intention to publish a history of Chinese science. Realizing that he was in a unique position to help, Zhu collected vast numbers of books and papers and shipped them to Cambridge, where they arrived unheralded, out of the blue. These included an 1888 distillation of the whole of Chinese knowledge, contained in some two thousand books.

Although in the early 1950's Needham experienced a temporary fall from grace among his Cambridge colleagues because of a sorry episode in his leftist politics, Needham's great project steadily took shape. The first volume was issued by Cambridge University Press in 1954. For thirty years Needham assumed sole authorship of successive volumes. As he aged, however, he needed increasing assistance, and in 1985 a volume by his friend Huang appeared with a note from Needham acknowledging that the era of his sole authorship had passed.

After his wife died in 1987, Needham and Lu Gwei-djen were at last free to wed. The marriage was cut short by Lu's death at age eighty-seven, two years after they wed. Needham himself lasted into his ninety-fifth year, passing away in March, 1995. He had the rare honor of being a Fellow of both the Royal Society and the British Academy. While his chef d'oeuvre was unfinished, its concluding parts progressively saw the light of day, overseen by Cambridge University's Needham Institute. In 2004 the twenty-fourth individual volume appeared, with more in preparation. Winchester's treatment of this remarkable life is sometimes troubling. Rather than writing a biography revolving around the serious issues of *Science and Civilisation in China* and the moral issues of Needham's fulsome acceptance of and support for Chinese communism under Mao Zedong and his chief lieutenant, Zhou En-lai, Needham's close personal friend, Winchester has written an entertaining, but seldom critical, description of the three-ring-circus that was Needham's life.

The consequences of such periods of Chinese communism as the Great Leap Forward, the famine that followed, and the Great Proletarian Cultural Revolution (CR) were deeply tragic: Tens of millions of lives were lost. Winchester relates that when Needham returned from travel to China in 1964 following the Great Leap famine, Needham's faith in Chinese communism was unshaken. He made no protest during the CR, when many of its horrors were known in England and the British Embassy in Beijing was burned to the ground. It took two years after Mao's death before Needham said anything critical about him, and then it was confined to Mao's effects on science. He denounced the repressive Gang of Four leaders, but only when all of China was doing the same. Winchester does not hide Needham's views, but the moral problems that arise from them are glossed over.

Worst of all was Needham's 1952 role in verifying evidence that supported Soviet and North Korean charges of American germ warfare in Korea. The "evidence," definitively proved in 1998 to be fabricated, was more than questionable, but that did not stop Needham from finding America guilty. He paid a price in temporary social ostracism and public derision. Winchester provides factual description but little critical commentary on his hero's central role in libeling the United States. The writer is far more interested in beating the dead horse of McCarthyism. What of Needham's failure to denounce Mao for crimes committed against the Chinese people in the name of "socialism"? In Winchester's hands, both Needham and China largely get a pass. Does Winchester suffer from some form of moral fatigue, or is it merely political bias?

A further problem is Winchester's frequent habit of gratuitously defending and aggrandizing China. Is it really necessary to state that "China is neither poor nor backward anymore," especially since it is no more than a half-truth? China has upward of five hundred million indigent rural people living on less than one dollar a day. Two hundred million more deeply impoverished internal immigrants live in cities. The arrogant, unrestrained embrace of Chinese communism (corrupt from the very outset) has wrecked much of the landscape and ecology of both China and Tibet. Human rights were and are a shambles. Winchester's gushing prose shows little of these facts. The author appends a list of Chinese inventions and discoveries, not all of which are necessarily Chinese in origin. Attribution of chess to China, for example, is questionable at best. China first used movable type for printing, but it was independently invented in Europe. Despite its flaws, *The Man Who Loved China* remains the absorbing saga of a prodigiously energetic scientist and historian who changed the West's view of traditional China and added immeasurably to respect for Chinese civilization prior to the nineteenth century.

Charles F. Bahmueller

Review Sources

Booklist 104, no. 14 (March 15, 2008): 4.
Christianity Today 52, no. 7 (July, 2008): 54.
The Economist 387 (June 7, 2008): 95.
The Humanist 69, no. 1 (January/February, 2009): 42-43.
Kirkus Reviews 76, no. 6 (March 15, 2008): 297.
Library Journal 133, no. 8 (May 1, 2008): 76.
Maclean's 121, no. 19 (May 19, 2008): 63.
New Scientist 199 (July 19, 2008): 47.
The New York Review of Books 55, no. 13 (August 14, 2008): 48-50.
Publishers Weekly 255, no. 10 (March 10, 2008): 68.
Scientific American 299, no. 2 (August, 2008): 106.

THE MAN WHO MADE LISTS
Love, Death, Madness, and the Creation of *Roget's Thesaurus*

Author: Joshua Kendall (1960-   )
Publisher: G. P. Putnam's Sons (New York). 304 pp.
   $25.95
Type of work: Biography
Time: 1779-1869
Locale: England, Europe

A biography of the physician who created the English-speaking world's most successful thesaurus by attempting to classify and quantify everything in the known world

Principal personages:
   PETER MARK ROGET, the physician who became famous for the publication of *Collection of English Synonyms Classified and Arranged* (1805), later known simply as *Roget's Thesaurus*
   CATHERINE (ROMILLY) ROGET, his mother
   ANN (ANNETTE) SUSANNE LOUISE ROGET, his sister
   MARY (HOBSON) ROGET, his wife
   JOHN LEWIS ROGET, his son
   CATHERINE MARY (KATE) ROGET, his daughter
   SAMUEL ROMILLY, his uncle
   CARL LINNAEUS, the Swedish botanist who developed the classification system for plants and animals still in use today
   GEORGES CUVIER, the French biologist whose work in comparative anatomy and paleontology helped later scholars classify animals by genus and species
   THOMAS BEDDOES, the English physician with whom Roget worked on early experiments testing ether's effectiveness as an anesthetic
   JEREMY BENTHAM, the English utilitarian philosopher who hired Roget in an unsuccessful attempt to develop prolonged techniques of refrigeration
   DUGALD STEWART, the Scottish philosopher and mathematician who became one of Roget's most influential professors
   PIERRE ÉTIENNE LOUIS DUMONT, the French political writer and longtime friend of Roget's uncle
   ANNE LOUISE GERMAINE (NECKER) DE STAËL-HOLSTEIN (MADAME DE STAËL), the Swiss author whose salons exchanged ideas among the most important intellectuals of her day

The Man Who Made Lists by Joshua Kendall is not only an account of the creation of *Roget's Thesaurus* (which occupies only a small section of the book) but also an exploration of the conditions that made such a book possible. Peter Mark Roget

∾

*Joshua Kendall is a freelance
journalist and author whose work has
appeared in publications such as*
Business Week, The Boston Globe, *and*
The Washington Post. *Kendall has also
served as coauthor on three academic
books dealing with psychology. For his
outstanding reporting on psychiatry, he
has received national journalism
awards from the National Mental
Health Association and the American
Psychoanalytic Association.*

∾

was born in London to a family with strong
Swiss roots. His uncle, Samuel Romilly, helped
shape Roget's personality but also nearly cost
his nephew his career. Throughout Roget's
youth, Romilly's fame as a legal reformer
helped provide access to new opportunities;
yet when Romilly, in despair at his wife's
death, committed suicide while under Roget's care, the fledgling physician found it all
but impossible to attract new patients. He
gave up his practice and directed his attention
to the academic side of medicine. Kendall's
treatment of Roget opens with this incident,
depicting this moment as the turning point in
Roget's life. Thus, out of a family tragedy
arose what would become a reference work found wherever English was spoken.

Even before Romilly's death, however, Roget was already viewing the world as a
perfectly ordered machine that simply needed human reason in order to be understood. His teachers, such as his uncle's close friend Dugald Stewart, encouraged him
in this direction, and a great deal of Enlightenment philosophy seemed to reinforce
Roget's outlook and temperament. For instance, the *Thesaurus* owes much to eighteenth century works such as the *Encyclopédie* of Denis Diderot, which similarly
sought to organize and classify the entire known world under the principles of reason.
Moreover, by Roget's day, earlier scholars such as Carl Linnaeus and Georges Cuvier
had already paved the way with a taxonomy of plants and animals that would soon
provide support for the evolutionary theory of Charles Darwin and lead eventually to
Dmitri Ivanovich Mendeleev's creation of the periodic table of the elements and the
development of historical linguistics. In creating his *Thesaurus*, therefore, Roget was
not seeking merely to provide a handbook of synonyms, but he was following the
common intellectual trend of the eighteenth and nineteenth centuries to classify everything in human experience. Try as Roget might to apply only pure reason to his efforts, however, elements of his final scheme owed much to his personal preference for
harmony and symmetry. Thus when Roget's original plan for the *Thesaurus* resulted
in an untidy 1,002 major concepts, Roget simply reorganized his system until it resulted in a more aesthetically pleasing 1,000 categories. As a way of immersing readers into Roget's philosophical system, Kendall uses several of these concepts, such as
"place of habitation," "weariness," and "scholar" as subheadings for his chapters and
sections.

Kendall's image of Roget is that of a man whose obsessions went far beyond
words alone. He insisted on cleanliness and order, losing respect for individuals such
as the philosopher Jeremy Bentham for failing to meet his standards for hygiene.
Most of all, Roget sought to bring order to his world by keeping lists. As a child, he
learned Latin by listing names for plants and animals, tabulating verbs related to reading or writing, and not so much reading texts as dissecting them. His lists included the

dates when important people in his life died. He was extremely parsimonious about this list, and few of even his closest relatives and friends made the cut. Kendall accounts for Roget's obsessive creation of lists and tables by seeing these efforts as the author's way of coping with life in a family in which his father died at an early age and several members demonstrated signs of severe depression. His mother, uncle, and eventually his daughter would be incapacitated by prolonged bouts of despair, and Roget may have viewed his lists as one part of his life that he could control.

Other family tragedies shaped Roget's personality. His sister had a form of neurosis, and Roget had to watch his thirty-eight-year-old wife Mary die painfully of cancer. Mary's father also died after a long and debilitating illness, and, late in Roget's life, his sister Annette died. By this time he was turning increasingly to religion for comfort in much the same way that he had earlier sought life's meaning in his work. Throughout his life, Roget, in Kendall's view, classified the world rather than allowed himself to be touched by it. Out of this personal approach to the world, he developed an educational philosophy that he passed on to his students. Hired in 1802 to provide "the grand tour" to fifteen-year-old Nathaniel and sixteen-year-old Burton Philips, Roget exposed them to what soon became a bookkeeper's exploration of France and Switzerland. He appears to have spent very little time encouraging his young charges to expand their horizons through conversations with local citizens or contemplating great works of art. Rather, they spent most of the journey measuring, recording, and counting everything they saw. Their letters home record the heights of monuments, the number of windows or spires seen on various buildings, attendance figures at parties (with a further breakdown of the number of people who danced), and the number of steps and organ pipes that could be found in places such as the Cathedral of Notre-Dame. Despite this unusual experience (or because of it), the Philips boys seem to have developed genuine affection for Roget, as did he for them. Their letters repeat with approval his judgments about which lodgings were clean and which cities were chaotic. The tour came to an abrupt end, however, when Napoleon's conflict with England led to the imprisonment of all adult Englishmen within French territory. The two young students were allowed to leave because of their age, and Roget narrowly escaped after he hastily secured evidence of Swiss ancestry because of his father's Huguenot lineage.

Roget published his *Thesaurus* only after his medical career was over, and his book became an unexpected success. In addition to bringing him a substantial income, it made Roget something of a celebrity late in life. Today Roget is so well known for the *Thesaurus* that his other important contributions—such as the log-log scale (which made the slide rule possible) and his discovery that the retina interprets rapid sequences of still images as continuous movement (which made films possible)—were all but forgotten. In his own day, Roget received a certain amount of acclaim for writing the fifth *Bridgewater Treatise* (1834). This work, officially titled *Animal and Vegetable Physiology, Considered with Reference to Natural Theology*, attempted to reconcile science and religion in a manner that greatly appealed to American writer and philosopher Ralph Waldo Emerson, and it used the phrase "intelligent design" in its argument that the universe demonstrates what appears to be an externally imposed order. Although the *Thesaurus* was not the first book of synonyms ever published in English, it proved to be so comprehensive and to reflect a philosophy so harmonious with its times that its predecessors have fallen into obscurity.

Kendall's style throughout *The Man Who Made Lists* is simple and direct, with relatively few flashbacks or forward glances. Kendall frequently draws parallels between aspects of Roget's personality and the content of his *Thesaurus*, such as when he notes that Roget, who was so obsessed with work that he never had time for hobbies, did not include "avocation" as either a major concept or even an acceptable synonym in his book. *The Man Who Made Lists* also includes numerous black-and-white illustrations and eight pages of index. The book does not, however, include notes of any kind, and so it is difficult to determine from precisely which source any particular piece of factual material has been derived. Moreover, for scholars wishing to pursue aspects of Roget's life further, the absence of notes makes it all but impossible to ascertain where the historical record ends and Kendall's imaginative reconstruction of events begins. Kendall's lengthy list of acknowledgments makes it clear, however, just how extensive was the research that made his book possible. As a result, while *The Man Who Made Lists* provides a valuable complement to D. L. Emblen's biography of Roget, *Peter Mark Roget: The Word and the Man* (1970), it does not completely supplant that earlier work.

One of the most intriguing parts of Kendall's biography comes in the epilogue, which deals with the history of Roget's *Thesaurus* since its original publication. To date there have been only six editors of the book, the first two of whom were the original author's son and grandson. Kendall observes, "Over the last century and a half, *Roget's* has lost ten concepts—it is down to 990—but it has gained a couple hundred thousand new words." Many of the words added to the *Thesaurus*, such as "Viagra" and "cybersex," did not even exist in Roget's day. As a result, each new addition continues to be a snapshot of the ideas, concepts, and values that characterize its generation. Moreover, each new word brings a potential challenge to Roget's original organization of his work by essential categories. If a new word does not appear to fit in well with the author's conceptual scheme, does the editor modify Roget's concepts or assume that the word is likely to be too transitory to merit inclusion? In the past, decisions have been made on each side of this alternative, and thus the editors of the *Thesaurus* continue both to reflect the world they encounter and to shape that world since the resource they are developing affects the writers and opinion makers in so many fields. In this way, the man who began making lists to avoid the painful realities of his own world continues to have a lasting influence on our own.

Jeffrey L. Buller

Review Sources

American Libraries 39, no. 7 (August, 2008): 84-85.
Booklist 104, no. 8 (December 15, 2007): 10.
Kirkus Reviews 75, no. 23 (December 1, 2007): 1232-1233.
Library Journal 132, no. 20 (December 15, 2007): 118.
The New York Times Book Review, March 16, 2008, p. 9.
Publishers Weekly 254, no. 45 (November 12, 2007): 43-44.
The Wall Street Journal 251, no. 68 (March 22, 2008): W10.
The Wilson Quarterly 32, no. 2 (Spring, 2008): 102-103.

MAPS AND LEGENDS

Author: Michael Chabon (1963-   )
Publisher: McSweeney's Books (San Francisco). 222 pp.
  $24.00
Type of work: Essays, literary history, literary criticism

A collection of essays examining different facets of genre fiction, sometimes presented as literary criticism and sometimes as autobiography

This collection by novelist Michael Chabon draws together sixteen nonfiction essays that explore the reading and writing of what is generally known as genre fiction. The book's title (sharing, but perhaps not taken from, a 1980's song by the rock band R.E.M.) evokes mythology and adventure—a sense strengthened by the unusual three-layer dust jacket with illustrations of sea monsters, giants, mystics, spies, and other characters. In essence, Chabon explores the geography and terrain of genre fiction through a piecemeal travelogue, taking time along the way to uncover various tales that spring from the landscape. Perhaps the legends are not so much stories as the cartographer's device of the same name, helping to explain the symbols on the literary map. Either way, the maps and legends promised in the book's title are delivered to the reader. (The acknowledgments page provides a literal example, employing a form of scatterplot map to show the relative contributions of "inspiration, opportunity, editing, and help" by twenty-two individuals.)

Collectively, the essays reveal the author's philosophy of writing, with particular attention to the relationship between the author and the reader. The pieces range from academic discourse to the somewhat more effective autobiographical narrative. Most of the essays were previously published, often in the pages of *The New York Review of Books* or as commissioned introductions to other volumes. As such, the collection lacks the degree of coherence and integration that one might assume from a book billed as Chabon's "first book of nonfiction." Nevertheless, the essays, which follow no clear ordering principle, make recurring visits to several broad literary themes.

The title's themes are most explicitly addressed in the first two essays. The first, "Trickster in a Suit of Lights: Thoughts on the Modern Short Story," is derived from an introduction Chabon wrote for a collection of short stories. In it, he holds up the short story as an especially effective category of maps for transporting ideas from the writer to the reader, but he protests that these maps are used too selectively and conventionally by readers and writers alike. He argues, then, against the strict compartmentalization of fiction into distinct territories, as most graphically revealed in the floor map of a modern bookstore. He celebrates instead writing that exists at "the boundary lines, the margins, the secret shelves between the sections in the bookstore." Above all, he defends genre fiction as a legitimate form of literature—a theme that is taken up in later essays as he celebrates horror stories, science fiction, detective fiction, comic books, and other genres.

The second essay, from which the book's title is drawn, describes how a map depicting the then-unbuilt housing development in Columbia, Maryland—an idealistic experiment that would contain Chabon's childhood home—could convey ideas and values and promises and dreams. On its surface, the essay is not explicitly about writing (except that the various neighborhoods of the housing development happened to be named after writers and poets). However, the underlying theme—about "the power of maps to fire the imagination"—clearly reinforces the idea of stories as maps and of maps as stories.

From there, the theme of maps becomes less prominent as the volume turns to an essay—part literary history, part appreciation—on the Victorian-era writer Arthur Conan Doyle and his famous literary creation, Sherlock Holmes. (In a subsequent essay, Chabon reveals his abiding affinity for Doyle and Holmes and his dedicated effort as a young man to copy Doyle's literary "voice.") The essay reveals an intimate familiarity with the Holmes stories, and it provides a brief but compelling assessment of why they have remained so well-loved more than 120 years after they first appeared in *Beeton's Christmas Annual*. The so-called detective fiction genre may have been invented a half-century earlier by Edgar Allan Poe, but it was Doyle who popularized it and outfitted it with the iconic persona of Holmes. Beyond this, Chabon credits Doyle with "completely reengineering" the short story's presentation of chronology, and with emboldening the coy, implicit assertion of verisimilitude that accompanies all fiction.

Michael Chabon received a B.A. from the University of Pittsburgh and an M.F.A. in creative writing from the University of California, Irvine. His thesis, subsequently published as The Mysteries of Pittsburgh *(1988), became a best seller and earned critical acclaim. His next novel,* Wonder Boys *(1995), was made into a motion picture. In 2001, his third novel,* The Amazing Adventures of Kavalier and Clay, *won the Pulitzer Prize in fiction.*

Another genre that Chabon both analyzes and celebrates is the comic book. Though not perhaps a conventional form of genre fiction, Chabon makes a compelling case for its rich storytelling potential. The topic featured prominently in Chabon's third novel, *The Amazing Adventures of Kavalier and Clay* (2000), which centered on a fictional pair of young cousins who conceived, wrote, and drew a number of commercially successful comic book series during the medium's heyday in the 1940's and 1950's. A quarter of the sixteen essays in this collection center on comic books. One is based on a keynote speech Chabon delivered at a comic books awards ceremony, urging practitioners of the craft to reorient comics in a way that recaptures children as readers. Another focuses on the comic book series *American Flagg* and its creator, Howard Chaykin. Another features a postmodern newspaper comic strip by Lawrence Weschler, and a fourth describes comic book impresario Will Eisner, whom Chabon studied and interviewed as part of his research for *The Amazing Adventures of Kavalier and Clay*. Together, these essays offer a warm, enthusiastic, nostalgic celebration of a medium that is seldom discussed alongside the likes of Doyle and F. Scott Fitzgerald (the latter figuring notably in Chabon's essay about authors who captured his imagination early on).

It is the autobiographical information Chabon provides that holds together the various essays into a partly coherent collection. Revelations by Chabon about himself, appearing here and there throughout the volume, help to connect disparate topics and moods. For example, the importance of Chabon's intimate familiarity with Doyle's Holmes stories (illustrated in the third essay) is illuminated a dozen essays later when Chabon explains that he was "born a second time [at age ten] in the opening pages of [Doyle's] 'A Scandal in Bohemia.'" This remark, in turn, is better understood when, in the final essay, Chabon reveals that at age ten he wrote his "first sustained work of fiction" that featured a meeting between Jules Verne's Captain Nemo and Doyle's Holmes, in which Chabon consciously tried to adopt Doyle's literary style and ended up virtually channeling the Victorian writer. Similarly, the genesis of the author's sixth novel, *The Yiddish Policeman's Union* (2007), is finally revealed in the penultimate essay, "Imaginary Homelands," which bemusedly speculates about the kind of nonexistent land that could justify the existence of a Yiddish phrase book he happened upon in a bookstore. In addition, the influence of Chabon's two marriages (one failed, one successful) becomes clearer with the cumulative information revealed by the autobiographical essays.

Jewishness is another theme that suffuses these essays. The motif of Chabon's and others' Jewish heritage—of the shared history of a lost promised land, of golems, of the Holocaust—is neither smug nor especially self-deprecating. Instead, the theme simply seems to exist, organically, in the soil of Chabon's literary world. At times this is used to especially powerful effect, as when Chabon uses the metaphor of the Jewish golem (a mystical being created from clay by man) to explain the process, joys, and risks of creating stories to be read by others.

Of particular interest is Chabon's repeated references to the boundary between truth and lies. He introduces this theme in the first essay, asserting "just because you have stopped believing in something you once were promised does not mean that the promise itself was a lie." The theme is explored implicitly and explicitly throughout the essays, and by the final essay Chabon, returning to the image of maps, concludes that "it is along the knife-narrow borderland between those two kingdoms, between the Empire of Lies and the Republic of Truth, more than along any other frontier on the map of existence, that Trickster makes his wandering way . . . ." Chabon frequently identifies with the Trickster, admitting in essence that his job as a novelist is to present fiction as fact, so that by the end of this "nonfiction" volume, when Chabon asserts that "naturally, I'm still telling lies," we are not sure what to believe. Perhaps that is the point. Perhaps Chabon's coyness in matters of separating fact from fiction is not merely impishness, but rather a manifestation of the belief (not unique to Chabon) that fiction holds its own kind of truth and facts their own kind of fiction.

Taken together, these essays reveal an author who is a highly literate and expressive master of the language; who is observant, insightful, and thoughtful; and who is remarkably self-aware. This last point, which is least evident simply from reading his novels, helps to explain much of Chabon's writing. He worries, for example, that readers will assume he shares the characteristics, such as homosexuality, of characters in his novels, and this might explain the extraordinary care that Chabon takes in describing such characters. As another example, he admits to worrying about employing the proper pronunciations of words that are typically mispronounced—that proper diction might result in being scorned as a pedant or, worse, being mocked by those who mistakenly think his is the wrong pronunciation. Such must be a common worry for one with a vocabulary as extensive as Chabon's. Evidently he tends to come down on the side of grammatical integrity, misguided critics be damned. The few times that he strays from his master-of-the-English-language approach to employ the occasional vulgarity or slang term comes across as an awkward, forced pose.

Taken as a whole, the collection serves best to illuminate the background, beliefs, experiences, philosophy, and purposes of the author, and only secondarily does it provide instruction on literary history and criticism. This will be of interest to readers who have enjoyed Chabon's novels. Those who approach this collection more for its insights into genre fiction may be less satisfied. In the end, however, this is an engaging and entertaining book about reading and writing by someone intimately familiar with both.

Steve D. Boilard

Review Sources

Booklist 104, no. 13 (March 1, 2008): 28.
Library Journal 133, no. 5 (March 15, 2008): 72.
The New York Times Book Review, June 29, 2008, p. 21.
O, The Oprah Magazine 9, no. 4 (April, 2008): 188.
Publishers Weekly 255, no. 3 (January 21, 2008): 163-164.

A MERCY

Author: Toni Morrison (1931-   )
Publisher: Alfred A. Knopf (New York). 167 pp. $23.95
Type of work: Novel
Time: 1682-1690
Locale: The mid-Atlantic region of the American colonies

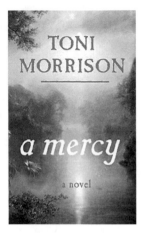

Morrison's ninth novel explores the lives of a range of women and men—some free, some enslaved—in the American colonies of the late seventeenth century

> *Principal characters:*
> FLORENS, a young female African slave
> LINA, a Native American woman
> SORROW, a servant girl
> REBEKAH VAARK, wife of Jacob and mistress of their farm
> JACOB VAARK, husband of Rebekah, master of the farm, trader in rum
> THE SMITH, a free black man who helps Jacob build his grand mansion

Throughout Toni Morrison's nine novels, certain key themes consistently appear, marking each book regardless of differences of setting, plot, character, and historical period. No issue is more significant to Morrison than the relationship between mother and daughter. Her most famous rendering of this remains *Beloved* (1987), in which a mother chooses to cut her daughter's throat rather than allow her to be returned to a life of slavery. Morrison's novel *A Mercy* has as its defining moment a similar horrible choice for a mother to make about her daughter's life. The novel asks "What is the cost and what is the measure of a mother's love?" *A Mercy* revisits many of the major concerns and motifs of Morrison's work and also many defining scenes. Morrison continues to imagine certain pivotal moments in her fictional world—the experience of the middle passage, the terror of being a hunted woman in the wild, the passion of men and women who give themselves wholly to each other—while re-visioning her past projections of these experiences. The result is a novel of impressive depth and great imaginative invention, not without its weaknesses, but offering fresh elements in Morrison's work.

The structure of *A Mercy* is intricate but not nearly as complicated or baffling as her novels *Beloved, Jazz* (1992), or *Paradise* (1998). The book consists of twelve chapters, five of which are directly narrated by one of the characters, Florens. The other chapters are each devoted to one of the other characters, narrated by an unnamed third person whose view is generally limited to the consciousness of that chapter's character. The Florens sections are shorter than the chapters devoted to others, serving as interludes to connect the different characters. By the novel's end, the reader learns that Florens is writing her "telling" with a nail on the floor of her dead master

Jacob Vaark's unfinished mansion. It is possible, then, to conceive of the entire novel as being told by Florens, and that the book is in some sense the very structure of Jacob's unfinished house, literally marked by the words of Florens.

Morrison has never before explored the historical period of *A Mercy,* which is late seventeenth century in colonial America. The novel is prefaced by an antiquarian map of what is now the long stretch from Connecticut to the Carolinas, marked throughout with the Native American place and river names. For *A Mercy* is also a cartography, an exploration of the land that is to some in the novel a brave new world and to others a very ancient and familiar landscape. For Jacob, English colonist, farmer, and now trader in rum and other goods, the land is an opportunity for great achievements, for establishing his posterity, and for creating a lasting domain. For Rebekah, his wife who answers his advertise-

Toni Morrison is the author of nine novels. She received the National Book Critics Circle Award for Song of Solomon *in 1977, the Pulitzer Prize for* Beloved *in 1988, and the Nobel Prize in Literature in 1993. She is the Robert Goheen Professor of the Humanities, Emerita, at Princeton University, a position that she has held since 1989.*

ment for "a healthy, chaste wife willing to travel abroad" and travels six weeks by ship from London to the colonies, the land is a chance for relative freedom, a different mastery: "her prospects were servant, prostitute, wife, and although horrible stories were told about each of those careers, the last one seemed safest. The one where she might have children and therefore be guaranteed some affection." Together, with a purchased Native American servant, Lina, a homeless orphan girl, Sorrow, and the slave girl, Florens, whom Jacob accepts in lieu of debt from a Spanish planter, they constitute for a time an idiosyncratic but functioning family unit.

Jacob is the prime mover of this family, a true patriarch as his forename suggests. The women revolve around him because in the economic and religious structure of the novel's time, they must. Jacob begins with the aspiration to be a farmer, but a growing restlessness compels him to seek other means to wealth. He begins trading in "goods and gold," and he is repelled by the commodity slave trade that he witnesses in Maryland. Nevertheless, he envies the plantation owner's ornate house and thus seeks greater riches, and thus he begins trafficking in rum. Jacob is thereby implicated in the barbaric molasses-rum-slaves triangle, deriving his wealth from precisely such a bloody business. Not long after he expands his business interests, his infant sons and his daughter die. In the midst of this, Jacob determines to build "a grand house of many rooms rising on a hill" that will rival the plantation demesne he envies. When Rebekah tells him they do not need such a house, he responds, "'Need is not the reason, wife . . . . What a man leaves behind is what a man is." This becomes a chilling epitaph for Jacob, for, like the literary predecessors he resembles—William Faulkner's Thomas Sutpen and F. Scott Fitzgerald's Jay Gatsby—Jacob leaves behind a shell, a mockery of the deathless house he envisioned.

In the novel's present, Jacob has recently died of smallpox, and his widow, Rebekah, has contracted the disease as well. Sorrow has survived the pox, cured by the remarkable free black man known only as The Smith. Consequently Rebekah sends Florens through the wilderness to find The Smith and bring him back to the farm, in the hopes that he can cure Rebekah, too. Florens's narrative interludes are told while she is journeying to find The Smith, a journey that in some ways mirrors young Sethe's desperate search for freedom in *Beloved*. Florens is on an archetypal quest, made more complicated because she is desperately in love with The Smith—a consuming, overwhelming passion reminiscent of Jadine and Son in *Tar Baby* (1981) and Hagar's adoration of Milkman in *Song of Solomon* (1977).

Florens travels through a series of portraits of the have-nots, the historical ciphers by and upon whom America was built: indentured servants, people who are the property of others, the poor and dispossessed or never-possessed, and Florens, a slave of African descent and first-generation African American (before America even existed). The result is a thicker concept of enslavement than Morrison has heretofore offered, even in her stunning portraits of American slavery, suggesting that America is precisely the product of a range of human enslavements.

Mastery and dominion constitute one of the novel's major themes, and Lina observes of The Smith: "He had rights, then, and privileges, like Sir. He could marry, own things, travel, sell his own labor." Such radical freedom is remarkable in this narrative of the enslaved, and he might well be the only character in the novel with such freedom. Hence the novel's nearly final words: "to be given dominion over another is a hard thing; to wrest dominion over another is a wrong thing; to give dominion of yourself to another is a wicked thing." The Smith constructs the magnificent and enigmatic iron gates to Jacob's unfinished mansion. These gates—"three-foot-high lines of vertical bars capped with a simple pyramid shape" and "crowned by a flourish of thick vines" that turn out to be serpents' mouths—function much like the powerful and elusive symbolism of the Oven in *Paradise*. The women of the novel oscillate between their founding figure, Jacob, and their salvation figure, the Smith, who is certainly one of the more compelling characters in Morrison's oeuvre. This, however, suggests one of the novel's weaknesses: One wants to hear more about the background and story of the Smith. Several elements in the novel suggest that other stories are lurking here, as if *A Mercy* is part of an unfinished epic. Indeed, the book certainly bears the major elements of epic, from its central quest to its concern with the founding of a nation to its flawed but magnificent heroes. It might have worked better had Morrison extended it, explored its unfinished elements. The result, then, might have been more akin to *Beloved* or *Song of Solomon*, whereas *A Mercy* in length is Morrison's shortest novel and its many intriguing vistas remain merely glimpses.

Like all of Morrison's work from *Beloved* onward, *A Mercy* is powerfully concerned with issues of religion, portraying an impressive array of late seventeenth century religious communities: Anglicans and Quakers in England, Anabaptists and Presbyterians in the colonies, Roman Catholicism in its most decadent and liberating

forms, and a blend of Native American, African, and European beliefs in the figure of
Lina. The portrayal of Christians is certainly dispiriting, as nearly all seem more concerned with who deserves punishment than with any question of salvific grace or
charity toward one's neighbor. Rebekah reflects that "Religion, as [she] experienced
it from her mother, was a flame fueled by a wondrous hatred." The radical Separatists
who live near Jacob left their original congregation "over the question of the Chosen
versus the universal nature of salvation"—a version of one of the great Morrison
questions, and the one that dominates *Paradise*, her most overtly religious novel. In
both novels, such discriminating theology reveals the hypocrisy of the believer. Morrison offers a memorable tableau of this drama when Florens happens upon a religious community that thinks some of its female members are "the Black Man's min-
ion," in a scene that recalls Nathaniel Hawthorne and Arthur Miller's portrayals of the
Salem communities. Ultimately, these experiences lead Rebekah to conclude that
God does not care about them: "We are not on his mind," she tells Lina.

This theological position underscores the novel's defining act, when Florens's
mother gives her to Jacob, rather than allow her to grow to womanhood in the nightmarish world of the tobacco plantation. Florens is haunted by this memory of "me
peering around my mother's dress hoping for her hand that is only for her little boy."
It impels her on her quest to find the Smith, which is also a quest for a sense of home
and belonging lost to her in this original "expel." The reasons for her mother's choice
are not revealed until the novel's closing chapter, when the reader receives her voice
and memory. "There is no protection," she communicates to Florens. "To be female
in this place is to be an open wound that cannot heal." The mother hopes that Jacob
will be a kinder master to his daughter than the Spanish planter: "One chance, I
thought. There is no protection but there is difference . . . . Because I saw the tall man
see you as a human child, not pieces of eight." To give her daughter away is the only
way to save her, and this becomes the mercy of the novel's title. Even this mercy,
however, is dispiriting in its insistence that God has abandoned these people: "It was
not a miracle. Bestowed by God. It was a mercy. Offered by a human." Morrison's vision, while it may redeem our view of the abandoning mother, suggests that in a world
without God, there is no protection.

Marc C. Conner

Review Sources

Booklist 105, no. 1 (September 1, 2008): 5.
The Boston Globe, November 9, 2008, p. K7.
Entertainment Weekly, November 14, 2008, p. 75.
Kirkus Reviews 76, no. 17 (September 1, 2008): 912.
Library Journal 133, no. 17 (October 15, 2008): 58.
Los Angeles Times, November 16, 2008, p. F1.
Ms. 18, no. 4 (Fall, 2008): 73-74.

The New Republic 239, no. 11 (December 24, 2008): 36-39.

The New York Times, November 4, 2008, p. C1.

The New York Times Book Review, November 30, 2008, p. 1.

The New Yorker 84, no. 35 (November 3, 2008): 112-113.

Newsweek 152, no. 24 (December 15, 2008): 8.

O, The Oprah Magazine 9, no. 11 (November, 2008): 190.

Publishers Weekly 255, no. 37 (September 15, 2008): 42.

THE MIRACLE AT SPEEDY MOTORS

Author: Alexander McCall Smith (1948-   )
Publisher: Pantheon Books (New York). 214 pp. $22.95
Type of work: Novel
Time: The first decade of the twenty-first century
Locale: Botswana, Africa

In this ninth novel in the series that began with McCall Smith's No. 1 Ladies' Detective Agency, Mma Ramotswe has several problems to contend with, including a woman who is looking for her family

Principal characters:
MMA PRECIOUS RAMOTSWE, founder of the detective agency
MR. J. L. B. MATEKOM, her husband, owner of Tlokweng Road Speedy Motors
MOTHOLELI, their adopted daughter
MMA GRACE MAKUTSI, assistant to Mma Ramotswe
PHUTI RADIPHUTI, son of the owner of the Double Comfort Furniture Shop, engaged to marry Mma Makutsi
MMA MANKA SEBINA, woman who comes to see if Mma Ramotswe can find her birthparents or other family members
MMA POTOKWANE, director of a home for orphaned children
CHARLIE, a young apprentice at the Speedy Motors garage
MR. POLOPETSI, a part-time worker in the garage and a part-time worker in the detective agency
VIOLET SEPHOTHO, a former student with Mma Makutsi at Botswana Secretarial College

Mma Precious Ramotswe is becoming recognized in her capital city Gaborone and other areas of Botswana as the founder of the No. 1 Ladies' Detective Agency and as someone who can solve problems for others. Such is the case with Mma Manka Sebina, who, in Alexander McCall Smith's *The Miracle at Speedy Motors*, comes to the detective agency to see if Mma Ramotswe can trace some family members for her. She starts by mentioning specific times and places she has seen Mma Ramotswe, and just as Mma Ramotswe is beginning to think of the word "stalker," Mma Sebina explains that some people just stand out, and that everybody knows about Mma Ramotswe, the only woman detective in Botswana. Mma Ramotswe silently agrees this is reasonable, especially since most people have an unreasonable idea of the glamour of what a private detective actually does.

When Mma Ramotswe asks who the relatives are that Mma Sebina wants located, there is some confusion when Mma Sebina says she does not know. Mma Ramotswe wisely asks her assistant, Mma Grace Makutsi, to put on the kettle to make some tea for the three of them. Tea almost always makes thing easier, she knows. Mma Sebina

Alexander McCall Smith is internationally acclaimed for his No. 1 Ladies' Detective Agency novels. He is the author of three other series, children's books, and academic works. He was a law professor at the University of Botswana and is professor emeritus of medical law at the University of Edinburgh in Scotland.

was adopted, and both of the parents who raised her are now "late," meaning dead. What she is seeking, then, is to find out who her birthparents are and to find any living relatives. Mma Ramotswe soon starts tracking down people who knew her adoptive parents in order to get leads on her birthparents. The persons she speaks to do not all tell the same story about the biological parents.

Mma Ramotswe then visits her old acquaintance, Mma Potokwane. It was from Mma Potokwane's farm for orphaned children that Mma Ramotswe's husband, Mr. J. L. B. Matekom (whom Mma Ramotswe always refers to and addresses by that full designation), had adopted two children, a boy, Puso, and a girl, Motholeli, before Mma Ramotswe agreed to marry him. When she did, she considered them her dear children, too. Mma Potokwane remembers Mma Sebina as a little four-year-old girl, and she tells Mma Ramotswe the name of an older brother, adopted by a different family. Mma Ramotswe locates him and introduces him to his long-lost sister, only to have Mma Potokwane tell her a few days later that she was wrong, and there was no brother.

This case, nearly the only client case in the novel, is complicated enough, but there are several other problems Mma Ramotswe has to deal with, one concerning her specifically and several concerning her family or the employees of the agency and the garage. The problem that relates directly to Mma Ramotswe is that someone is sending her anonymous threatening letters. Although she would prefer not to let this bother her, she is rightly disturbed, and she is not sure how to find the culprit. The letters are not sent through the mail but left at the building that houses both the detective agency and the Speedy Motors garage. It is even possible that they could be coming from her part-time helper, Mr. Polopetsi, who also works part time at the garage. She certainly does not want to believe that of him, since she was the one who hired him.

Mma Makutsi, ever mindful of her distinction of making the highest score in the history of the Botswana Secretarial School, consistently thinks she should be promoted to a higher rank in the detective agency, and she sometimes makes decisions without consulting Mma Ramotswe. She takes great pride in the fact she is engaged to a successful businessman, referring to him as the owner of the Double Comfort Furniture Shop, although his father is still the owner. Mma Makutsi thinks this engagement will show some of the others in her secretarial school class who had laughed at her, such as Violet Sephotho, that she is not someone to be considered beneath them socially. Currently, however, she has a problem concerning a fancy new bed that her fiancé, Phuti Radiphuti, has bought in anticipation of their still unscheduled wedding. Should she admit to Phuti what happened to the bed? How will he react? Why have they not agreed on a date for the wedding? When she does marry Phuti, will she still want to work at the agency?

Charlie, one of Mr. J. L. B. Matekom's apprentices, never seems willing to settle down and finish his apprenticeship. He tends to be lazy; he would rather tease and play tricks than to work and develop his skills as a mechanic. Mma Ramotswe is reluctantly admitting what everyone who rides with her says—that her tiny white van she loves to drive is making too many knocking noises and not providing the power it formerly had. Could Charlie be relied on to fix it, instead of Mma Ramotswe bothering Mr. J. L. B. Matekom, who has said the van needs to be replaced? That issue is not resolved, but it is in fact Charlie who is central in leading to the identification of the writer of the threatening letters.

Most serious and disturbing of the problems is Mr. J. L. B. Matekom's belief, based on the claims of a doctor whose car he had fixed, that his adopted daughter, Motholeli, could be given medical treatment for her paralyzed legs. The doctor believes that a new medical procedure offered by a particular clinic could repair her spinal cord and make it possible for her to walk instead of needing a wheelchair. Finding out if this is possible will mean Mr. J. L. B. Matekom going with Motholeli to the clinic the doctor has recommended and staying with her for at least two weeks of testing and treatment. The clinic is outside the country, in Johannesburg, South Africa, and the procedure is very expensive. The cost will be more than Mr. J. L. B. Matekom can afford, but he disregards that. He believes the doctor, and he also believes that if there is any chance Motholeli can walk again, it must be pursued. In addition to the cost, however, there is the problem of potentially unrealistic hope and what it will mean to Motholeli and to the rest of the family if, after all, nothing can be done, and she remains wheelchair bound for the rest of her life. Mma Ramotswe does not think the treatment can help.

It is clear that this would be a good time for some miracles around Speedy Motors, although miracles do not always appear just because they are wished for. Sometimes, almost playfully, they come when no one has even thought about them, or they come in disguise.

The same could be said of Mma Ramotswe. She knows that her success as a detective is often no more dramatic than checking the telephone directory or the public records about court cases. What it really takes, she repeatedly demonstrates, is a willingness to help people and to use her energy and her common sense to do so. She listens carefully to others and is always respectful of their sense of self and their pride. She is not always right in her initial assessments, but before acting rashly she is willing to enlist the aid of others, particularly her family and acquaintances, to gain more information and insight into the problem. She is also sensitive to the fact that while most issues can have satisfactory solutions, even if the solution is different from what might be anticipated, occasionally there must be only acceptance of the situation.

Mma Ramotswe also knows that one must make time for reflection and for one's own well-being. In addition to her trusty bush tea breaks, Mma Ramotswe likes to sit by herself outdoors in the garden of their home on Zebra Avenue, if not for a few minutes in the morning, then in the evening. Almost exactly halfway through the novel, when the series of crises has built up, she tells the others that she will be gone for the day, and she drives her tiny white van far outside the city to Mochudi, the area where she was born and had grown up. She stops along the edge of the road on a hill overlooking her village and gets out of the van. She sits looking at the plains below and the large sky above, and a sense of peace flows through her as she recognizes that, when viewed from above, human striving seems small. Worries could be allowed to float up into the sky. Some of the details may remain to be tended to, but general solutions to the problems she has been fretting over come to her: They require simplicity and the basics of love, truth, understanding, and respect for others.

It is this protagonist, Mma Ramotswe, and her basic philosophy of life, that has been enjoyed by literally millions of readers around the world. Throughout the series, she has been surrounded by a continuing and developing cast of characters: Mma Grace Makutsi, Phuti Radiphuti, Mma Potokwane, Mr. J. L. B. Matekom, the adopted children, the apprentices, and Mr. Polopetsi, all of whom are interesting and have their own distinct mixed characteristics. Added to this is the landscape of Botswana itself, often unfamiliar and amazing to those outside southern Africa. Mma Ramotswe loves her country and its people, and she is forever guided by the memory of her beloved and respected father, who raised cattle, taught sensible lessons, and always wished the best for his only child.

It is not the plots that readers tend to remember from the novels, but the characters and the country. Smith's simple style includes the rather formalized speech patterns of the characters and consistently entertains with light humor and the goodheartedness of Mma Ramotswe. He has three other series, mostly written and published concurrently with this series: the Portuguese Irregular Verbs series, the Sunday Philosophy Club series (better known as the Isabel Dalhousie series), and, most recently, the 44 Scotland Street series. All are popular, but none as immensely popular as the consistently best-selling series featuring the admirable, indomitable, life-affirming Mma Ramotswe.

Lois A. Marchino

Review Sources

Booklist 104, no. 13 (March 1, 2008): 30.
Kirkus Reviews 76, no. 6 (March 15, 2008): 274.
Library Journal 133, no. 6 (April 1, 2008): 78.
Publishers Weekly 225, no. 8 (February 25, 2008): 48.
The Washington Times, May 4, 2008, p. B7.

THE MODERN ELEMENT
Essays on Contemporary Poetry

Author: Adam Kirsch (1976-   )
Publisher: W. W. Norton (New York). 352 pp. $25.95
Type of work: Essays, literary criticism, literary history

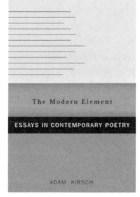

This collection of twenty-six previously published critical essays offers perceptive, hard-hitting commentary on poetry written in English during the postmodern period and on many of the leading poets

With *The Modern Element* and his previously published *The Wounded Surgeon: Confession and Transformation in Six American Poets* (2005), Adam Kirsch has established himself as a critical force on the American literary scene. He examines the leading, sometimes difficult poets of the postmodern period and sums them up with a youthful confidence grounded in a solid critical education, "the pragmatic tradition of Aristotle and Horace, Johnson and Arnold."

A student of scholar-critic Helen Vendler and a 1997 graduate of Harvard, Kirsch widened his impressive knowledge base and honed his critical skills by working as assistant literary editor of *The New Republic* and book critic of the now-defunct *New York Sun*. He combines a scholarly background with a general-audience style: The essays in *The Modern Element* originally appeared in such publications as *The New Republic*, *The New Yorker*, and *The Times Literary Supplement*. One advantage of this style is that it is accessible and readable rather than weighted down by scholarly vernacular and academic jargon. The style also allows Kirsch to express his opinions sharply and memorably.

Besides writing criticism, Kirsch writes poetry, in the tradition of poet-critics such as Matthew Arnold (1822-1888) and T. S. Eliot (1888-1965). He has published two collections of poetry: *The Thousand Wells* (2002), winner of the *New Criterion* Poetry Prize, and *Invasions* (2008). Both collections use traditional forms, including meter and rhyme, which is consistent with the traditional leanings in his criticism.

Kirsch takes his title *The Modern Element* from a lecture by Arnold, who, like Eliot later, defined "the modern element" in poetry as a response to the complexities of the modern age. Modernism and postmodernism are two phases of that response. Most of the postmodern poets about whom Kirsch writes in *The Modern Element* are either dead or aging, their careers often reflected in collected works. However, Kirsch seems to see contemporary poetry, which includes other, younger poets who in America are mostly graduates of creative writing programs, as a continuation of trends— not all good—noted in the postmodern poets whom he analyzes.

Although a collection of essays written at random over ten years, *The Modern Element* focuses on American poets and, together with *The Wounded Surgeon* (which

∼
Adam Kirsch is author of The
Wounded Surgeon: Confession and
Transformation in Six American Poets
(2005); two collections of poetry, The
Thousand Wells *(2002), winner of the*
New Criterion *Poetry Prize, and*
Invasions *(2008); and a biography,*
Benjamin Disraeli *(2008).*
∼

covers Robert Lowell, Elizabeth Bishop, John Berryman, Randall Jarrell, Delmore Schwartz, and Sylvia Plath) offers a fairly comprehensive introduction to postmodern American poetry. *The Modern Element* also looks at a number of postmodern English, Irish, Caribbean, and Australian poets plus (in English translations) émigré poets from Poland and Russia. The last essay is on a literary critic, Yvor Winters. Kirsch's analyses of individual poets enable him to form some conclusions about postmodern poetry in English that are scattered throughout his book but concentrated in the opening and closing sections.

Kirsch takes the common view that postmodern poetry is both a continuation of and a reaction to modernist poetry. However, he seems to agree with Lithuanian-Polish émigré poet Czesław Miłosz, whom he quotes at length, that modernism was not so much a startling new movement after World War I but instead a culmination of centuries of thought and tradition. Modernism, with its fractured techniques in the arts, was the broken phase of Western civilization that mourned the passing of old myths, beliefs, practices, institutions, and meanings. After modernism, what was a postmodernist poet to do except continue the mourning, use the new fractured techniques, and search for meaning among the shards? Kirsch further defines these two movements by juxtaposing two famous representative poems in one essay: modernism is represented by T. S. Eliot's *The Waste Land* (1922), which mourns the sterility of modern Western civilization, and postmodernism is represented by Allen Ginsberg's *Howl* (1956), which celebrates a wild counterculture of pleasure-seeking excesses.

Other postmodern poets in *The Modern Element* are shown seeking meaning in various ways, groping about in the darkness of a shattered, piecemeal world. One favorite way is retreating into the self, which is then spilled out in autobiographical and confessional poetry. Kirsch accuses Louise Glück of making poetry out of her self-dramatizing ego, Frederick Seidel of exposing his surreal inner consciousness, and Sharon Olds of obsessing about a religion of sex. He sees other poets cataloging the sufferings of their dull workplaces (Irish poet Dennis O'Driscoll) and loveless lives (English poet Philip Larkin). Still others, says Kirsch, unload on readers their prevailing temperament, joyous affirmation for Richard Wilbur and melancholy for Donald Justice.

Another way some poets deal with the splintered postmodern world is by grounding themselves in their provincial roots. Two of the poets Kirsch most admires do this: Caribbean poet Derek Walcott and Australian poet Les Murray. One might argue that poets of the New York School, represented in *The Modern Element* by Kenneth Koch, belong in this category: Kirsch characterizes Koch as a zany celebrant of cliquish New Yorker "Augustans" who make the "easy assumption of their own and their city's centrality."

Still another way some poets operate in the postmodern ambience is by reaching back and trying to connect with important cultural remains. For example, Kirsch notes that Billy Collins and English poet Geoffrey Hill build on the literary background they share with their educated audiences, Glück and A. E. Stallings draw on ancient Greek myth, Polish poet Adam Zagajewski (available in English translation) pursues mysticism, and James Merrill cultivates aestheticism, art for art's sake.

Finally, some poets such as Miłosz survive in the postmodern milieu by celebrating the ordinary. Kirsch places Collins with this group as well as Wilbur, who delights in life, simple pleasures, and the gifts of this world (maybe because as a fighting soldier in World War II, he saw the other side). However, Kirsch also calls Wilbur a "Transcendentalist" who senses a spiritual energy and beauty in the world similar to the secular holiness Miłosz finds and the mystical epiphanies Zagajewski seeks. Much less flattering is Kirsch's evaluation of Charles Simic, who over his career went from a "Kafkaesque childhood" in Yugoslavia to "a bourgeois appreciation of life's little pleasures" in America.

Kirsch is hard on some of these poets, but perhaps he is hardest on Collins, probably America's most popular poet. While acknowledging Collins's popularity, his educated audiences, and his wit, Kirsch describes Collins's "devotion to the ordinary" as "a peculiarly American form of mental laziness." Collins's "[r]elentless joking can be a way of discouraging curiosity, ambition, and endeavor, without which there is no greatness in art." Kirsch especially gets incensed at Collins for making fun of William Wordsworth's poem "Tintern Abbey" the same way he does of the Victoria's Secret catalog (thus targeting "not only mass culture but genuine culture"), and he accuses Collins, an apostle for accessible poetic style, of not knowing "there is a place for difficulty in poetry." As Kirsch notes in his introduction, Eliot argued that difficulty in poetry was necessary in response to the complex modern world.

When Kirsch is faced with a number of difficult poets, however, he condemns pretentiousness and obscurity as much as does Collins. Among the difficult poets are John Ashbery, Jorie Graham, and C. D. Wright. Kirsch feels that Ashbery's poetic epiphanies emerge from pages of playful triviality and nonsense. On the other hand, he claims that Graham and Wright have grown progressively more obscure over the course of their careers mainly by withholding information. Kirsch argues that all three poets push their techniques too far, sacrificing poetic communication and music, and that difficulty should be reserved for complex matters.

These poets and their many imitators might contend that their difficult techniques mirror postmodern reality and the workings of the poetic mind trying to grasp and communicate it. Here Kirsch draws on what Yvor Winters called "the fallacy of imitative form," blasting the idea that poets should load their confusion onto their readers. Kirsch opts for a return to music and form in poetry: Poetry should shape experience, not be mugged by it. Dividing poets into courteous and discourteous communicators, Kirsch notes that difficult techniques can go along with mundane matter, as he finds in the poetry of Wright. However, Wright has been a tremendous influence on younger poets, who might have even less to say but whose rush to be avant-garde betrays what Kirsch damns as a commodification of poetry.

The poets whom Kirsch admires tend to stand apart from the avant-garde, write poetry out of significant life experiences, and have an old-fashioned sense of form. His admiration for Walcott from the islands and Murray from the outback has already been noted: As provincials, colonials, and outsiders, Walcott and Murray seem to have developed well on their own. Murray is so far out of the mainstream that his masterpiece is a picaresque verse novel, *Fredy Neptune* (1998), a postmodern anomaly. Murray shares a working-class background with Theodore Roethke and James Wright, both of whom distrusted literary artifice and relied on intense feeling and the "deep image," a hit-or-miss approach that produced a number of poems admired by Kirsch (and the world).

Kirsch also admires Wilbur, whose joyous affirmation is another anomaly amid the gloom and doom of postmodernism. As noted earlier, Wilbur's appreciation for life might be in part a reaction to his battlefield experiences in World War II (he started writing poetry as therapy), but as a poet, like others whom Kirsch admires, he developed mastery of verse and metaphor. Another admired poet is Miłosz, who lived through World War II in Warsaw, Poland, and developed a postmodern humanism in which art serves life and poets are witnesses to history.

Nevertheless, while it seems to help, poets do not have to live through earth-shaking historical events in order to write important poetry. Two more whom Kirsch praises in *The Modern Element* are Irish poet Dennis O'Driscoll, the witty and dark chronicler of the office and middle-class existence, and English poet Philip Larkin, who, writing about similarly gloomy subjects, such as "provincial bachelordom," produced "some of the best English poems of the twentieth century." Both of these poets show superb mastery of the English language and poetic form.

Thus, with a messianic zeal, Kirsch identifies the virtues and vices of postmodern poetry and sorts out the sheep from the goats. At the same time, while not a complete survey of postmodern poetry in English, *The Modern Element* is a good introduction to the range of poets and techniques. Kirsch makes some excellent observations about individual poets and postmodern poetry as a whole, and he is fun to read. Besides offering readers a handle on this body of work, he also suggests some useful advice for beginning and would-be poets: Writers of poetry must begin with imagination, facility with language and metaphor, a sense of form, and something to say growing out of their life experiences. Then they need to practice a lot. Kirsch ends with this classical advice from Horace: "Of writing well, be sure, the secret lies/ In wisdom: therefore study to be wise."

Harold Branam

Review Sources

Booklist 104, nos. 9/10 (January 1, 2008): 36.
Library Journal 133, no. 4 (March 1, 2008): 82.
The New York Times Book Review, August 31, 2008, p. 15.
Poetry 192, no. 2 (May, 2008): 154-163.
The Times Literary Supplement, November 14, 2008, p. 33.

A MOST WANTED MAN

Author: John le Carré (1931-   )
Publisher: Charles Scribner's Sons (New York). 323 pp.
  $28.00
Type of work: Novel
Time: The present
Locale: Hamburg, Germany

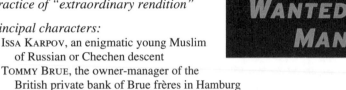

Le Carré's twenty-first novel of international intrigue and espionage, focusing on the human cost of the "war on terror" and the practice of "extraordinary rendition"

Principal characters:
  Issa Karpov, an enigmatic young Muslim
    of Russian or Chechen descent
  Tommy Brue, the owner-manager of the
    British private bank of Brue frères in Hamburg
  Annabel Richter, a young, attractive German lawyer who works for a
    German refugee support organization
  Günther Bachmann, head of the Foreign Acquisitions Unit of the
    Joint Steering Committee that coordinates German intelligence
    services
  Leyla Oktay, a Turkish widow who is a legal resident of Germany
    living in Hamburg with her son
  Melik Oktay, a top athlete who is torn between his Turkish heritage
    and his new country
  Dr. Faisal Abdullah, a well-known Muslim scholar living in
    Germany whose charities are suspected of funneling money to
    terrorist organizations.

If author John Updike was correct when he asserted wishfully in 1995 that the end of the Cold War would put an end to Cold War thrillers, John le Carré's career as a writer of international intrigue should have come to an end with the publication of his novel *Our Game* (1995). However, Updike's term "Cold War thriller" is not appropriate even for le Carré's early novels, from *Call for Dead* (1960) to *The Secret Pilgrim* (1991). The spy thriller dramatizes the conflict between "us" and "them" and operates in a clearly defined moral and ideological landscape, where the Western democratic forces clash with various "axes of evil," after World War II identified with the Communist Soviet Union and its satellites. This conflict tolerates no equivocation or indifference: 5 percent evil negates the other 95 percent of virtue or human weakness.

Even in his first novels but particularly in his first major success, *The Spy Who Came in from the Cold* (1963), as well as in his Karla trilogy (1974's *Tinker, Tailor, Soldier, Spy*, 1977's *The Honourable Schoolboy*, and 1980's *Smiley's People*), all set against the background of the Cold War, le Carré leaves the confines of genre fiction and elevates his novels of espionage into the realm of the mimetic. His protagonists

John le Carré has refused to enter his works into competitions for literary prizes and rejected a peerage in protest against his country's participation in the invasion of Iraq. He worked in the British Secret Service even after his first novel, Call for the Dead *(1961), was published.*

are not stereotypical superspies in the James Bond mold or demonic villains such as Dr. No. Instead, le Carré shows the world of espionage to be populated by foolish or misadvised politicians, ambitious and jealous spy masters motivated more by thoughts of advancement and internecine agency quarrels than by patriotism, willing to sacrifice their field agents and any innocent bystanders to pad their résumés. It is a world in which empathy, sentimentality, and ethical considerations not only have no place but also are cruelly punished in the end, with the protagonists either dead without having achieved anything or frustrated and disillusioned for having been deceived and thwarted by their superiors.

What Updike could not have known in 1995 was that, far from being dead, the Cold War thriller would be revived with a new set of "thems." The fall of the Berlin Wall and the subsequent rapprochement of the new Russia and the Western democracies left a brief vacuum during which both politicians and authors were looking for a new set of villains. After some brief excursions in the international arms trade and the machinations of large, multinational corporations, 9/11 and the "war on terror" provided the current set of villains—that is, Islamic terrorists—and authors of spy thrillers have begun to make full use of the subject. David Hagberg's *Soldier of God* (2005) and *Allah's Scorpion* (2006); Kenneth Floyd's *The Painted Man* (2006); and Brad Thor's Scott Harvath series, beginning with *The Lions of Lucerne* (2001), all are essentially carbon copies of the Cold War thriller with a different set of villains in a slightly changed physical environment.

A Most Wanted Man, in contrast, is not a thriller, but a masterfully crafted political novel in which le Carré convincingly expresses his anger and sadness at the sacrifice of humanity and civil liberty in the "war on terror," for which he lays the main blame on the United States, although the novel is set in Hamburg, Germany, the city where several of the 9/11 conspirators had gathered and prepared for the attack on U.S. targets. The fact that they were not discovered is considered a stain on the reputation of the city and German intelligence services. When Issa Karpov, a young Muslim with a connection to Chechen rebels, is discovered to have been smuggled into the city, after having escaped from a Turkish prison, the German authorities are doubly eager to apprehend him to avoid another disgraceful failure. Issa—his name is the Islamic form of Jesus—however, insinuates himself into the care of Leyla and Melik Oktay, who shelter him, in obedience to the commands of their religion, because he is ill and clearly has been tortured. Although he carries with him documents and a key that would entitle him to millions of dollars deposited at a private British bank in Hamburg, his avowed goal is to be allowed to stay in Germany and go to medical school. To this purpose, he seeks the help of Annabel Richter, a young lawyer working for Sanctuary North, a nonprofit agency dedicated to helping refugees and undocumented aliens gain residency in Germany. Annabel, in turn, gets in touch with Tommy Brue, the owner of the bank that holds Issa's money in a secret, passworded account.

As in many other le Carré's novels, a powerful motive for the main characters in *A Most Wanted Man* is the wish to escape from the clutches of a fraught relationship with a dominating father. Issa rejects his dead father, a former Soviet colonel who had worked for British intelligence in the waning years of the Soviet empire, and who had lavished his ill-gotten money on Issa to atone for his responsibility in the death of his Chechen mother. Annabel refutes her upper-class father and his elitist notions of the law to dedicate herself to the sort of clients for which her father would have felt contempt. In addition, she sees Issa as a chance to redeem herself for having failed a previous client whom she had to watch being taken away in shackles and deported to certain torture and death. Tommy Brue is trying to escape from yet another failed marriage and from the bank his father had turned into a money-laundering vehicle for British intelligence, in return for receiving an Order of the British Empire honor. In addition, he has fallen in love with Annabel. To a degree, this rejection of father figures—le Carré fictionalizes his own fraught relationship with his con man father in *A Perfect Spy* (1986)—also stands for a rejection of the older generation's confrontational Cold War mentality and its stereotyping of people and countries.

Apart from the enigmatic Issa—the reader is never conclusively told whether he has, indeed, engaged in terrorist activities or has been only falsely accused of them by the Russians—the most complex character of the novel is Günther Bachmann, the head of a German spy agency designed to recruit "human assets" in the fight against international terrorists. Bachmann genuinely wants to combat terrorism by going to the source: the big financiers. While he temporarily coerces and persuades minor villains or even innocent people into his service, he plans to let them go back to their normal lives after they have served their purpose. This gets him into conflict with his superiors in the Joint Steering Committee, the German equivalent of Homeland Security, whose main concern is revenge, body count, funding, and one-upmanship. Bachmann persuades Annabel to deliver Issa to him, in order to gain access to Dr. Faisal Abdullah, a Muslim scholar who runs charities to aid needy people in Islamic countries, but whom he also suspects of funneling money to terrorist organizations. Tommy has also been forced to assist British intelligence, which wants to cover up its past associations with his father in the laundering of funds paid to its spies, including Colonel Karpov, Issa's father. Bachmann's scheme, which would allow Issa to stay in Germany and go to medical school and release Dr. Abdullah after having discovered the destination for the 5 percent of his charitable funds that go to suspected terrorists, is approved by his superiors, in consultation with the U.S. Central Intelligence Agency (CIA).

At the climactic moment of the novel, however, everything goes terribly wrong.

Expecting them to be released shortly afterward, Tommy and Annabel accompany Issa and Dr. Abdullah to the bank, where Issa signs away his inheritance, around twelve million dollars, to Dr. Abdullah's charities, which they immediately transfer into the appropriate accounts, including fifty thousand dollars into the account of a shipping company in Cyprus that the CIA suspects of supporting terrorism. When they leave the bank, Bachmann must watch with Tommy and Annabel as Issa and Dr. Abdullah are apprehended, handcuffed, and thrown into a delivery van. If there is any doubt about their destination, it is dispelled by Newton, the CIA operative on the scene who explains to him that they are headed for "extraordinary rendition," in other words, they will be taken to another country—the agent refers to "some hole in the desert"—and tortured until they admit that they are terrorists. Newton calls this process with no lawyers around to pervert it "American" justice. Bachmann realizes impotently that he has been used in the destruction of the innocent Issa and the misguided Dr. Abdullah. Even Leyla and Melik, the good Samaritans, will suffer: Although they are legal residents, German immigration will not let them return from a family wedding in Turkey, because they have harbored a "known" terrorist.

Though *A Most Wanted Man* certainly makes for suspenseful reading and does not lack gripping plot development, it is above all a morality play, not a spy thriller. Its focus is not a battle between "us" and "them," but on the conflict in and between "us." It is an attempt to answer the question—much debated in the media and in academe—whether a noble goal, such as the defeat of international terrorism, justifies even the most abhorrent means, or whether in pursuit of this goal the moral high ground is lost. Le Carré poses this question sensitively and with great skill. The majority of his characters are complex, fallible humans whose instinct it is to come to the aid of their fellow humans, although they are not always clear about their own motives for doing so. Even though their own situation is precarious, Leyla and Melik take in Issa because he is confused and battered and because their religion commands them to do so. They choose to believe his story, although it is unlikely and contradictory. Annabel compromises her own safety and her career because, against her father's advice, she is willing to follow her feelings and instincts without always controlling them. Tommy wants to save himself from a disastrous marriage and from becoming an unprincipled social climber like his father. In this way, Issa has indeed become their redeemer, despite being crucified himself. The only less-than-human characters in the novel are the spy masters, especially the members of the CIA who are asked to play the role of the traditional villain, though maybe a little too stereotypically. Historical events may eventually relegate *A Most Wanted Man* to the back shelves, yet it is a sensitive and engaging dramatization of one of the great moral dilemmas of the early twenty-first century.

Franz G. Blaha

Review Sources

Booklist 104, no. 22 (August 1, 2008): 8.
Library Journal 133, no. 14 (September 1, 2008): 119.
New Statesman 137 (October 20, 2008): 53.
The New York Times, October 7, 2008, p. 1.
The New York Times Book Review, October 12, 2008, p. 1.
People 70, no. 16 (October 20, 2008): 51.
Publishers Weekly 255, no. 31 (August 4, 2008): 43.
The Times Literary Supplement, September 26, 2008, p. 22.
The Wall Street Journal 252, no. 88 (October 13, 2008): A17.

MY REVOLUTIONS

Author: Hari Kunzru (1969-)
Publisher: Dutton Penguin (New York). 288 pp. $25.95
Type of work: Novel
Time: The 1960's to 1998
Locale: London, England, and towns in surrounding areas; Thailand; South of France

A historically based novel whose major characters were centrally involved in the anti-Vietnam War protests in London in the late 1960's; the main action of the novel is set in the last decade of the twentieth century, with orchestrated flashbacks and updates

Principal characters:

CHRIS CARVER, the central character, a
former 1960's radical who for decades has lived under the assumed identity of Michael Frame
MIRANDA MARTIN, his enterprising capitalist wife, who does not know her husband's true identity or his history
SAMANTHA MARTIN, Miranda's daughter and Chris's adopted daughter
ANNA ADDISON, a former lover of Chris and a leader of the antiwar movement
MILES BRIDGEMAN, a journalist and photographer whose loyalty to the antiwar movement is not sincere
SEAN WARD, lover of Anna Addison and a leader of the antiwar protest movement
PAT ELLIS, a former antiwar radical now running for Home Secretary

Hari Kunzru's third novel, *My Revolutions*, is difficult to categorize, since it fits into several categories, none of which dominates the others. It is something of an historical novel, a political treatise, a coming-of-age work, and a pseudo-autobiography, all packaged in one work.

The main character is Michael Frame, something of a househusband living in the London suburbs, where he is married to the successful businesswoman Miranda Martin and where he also serves as father to her daughter Samantha. The opening event of the novel is preparation for Michael's fiftieth birthday. Slowly, readers learn that he is not Michael Frame, because this is an assumed identity, and that it is not really his fiftieth birthday. His real name and his previous life had been that of Chris Carver, a product of lower-middle-class English society who during the 1960's had been a student at the London School of Economics. While there, he became involved in protests against the Vietnam War, and, subsequently, he became more than a student radical; he became a political terrorist, robbing banks and blowing up the post office. He has been in hiding for most of three decades, and one day he is spotted by a former associate from those days in the 1960's. Time catches up with him at long last.

The narrative is unusually complicated and sometimes difficult to follow because the author intermingles the present—1998—with flashbacks and updates; moreover, he does not always cue the reader as to the changes in time, location, and event. The only consistency here is point of view, which is always that of Michael/Chris. This rather dysfunctionally organized plot is at first confusing, and it remains so. Still, it serves well to reflect the chaos of the times and the fractured nature of the main character's life.

Hari Kunzru, who is of mixed parentage (English and Kashmiri Pandit), is a British journalist and novelist who lives in East London. His work has received several awards, most noteworthy of which is from Granta *magazine, who identified him as one of the twenty best young British novelists in 2003. His first two novels,* The Impressionist *(2002) and* Transmission *(2004), were well received;* My Revolutions *is his third novel.*

As something of a historical novel, *My Revolutions* has at its base the 1971 bombing of the London Post Office by a group known as the Angry Brigade. Kunzru has also taken, very loosely, historical events surrounding the Stoke Newington Eight trial in 1972, for which several defendants received lengthy prison sentences for their politically motivated, yet highly illegal, activities. As a work about politics and the political system, the novel is full of characters who voice differing opinions and ideologies. They are concerned with the problems of the system, the best means for correcting it, and the most effective manner to get "the people" involved in this would-be "revolution." Michael is the character most torn: While he had given his youth to this revolution that never happened, he is now living a false life as a kept member of the capitalist society who is in no way doing his part to support himself or anyone else. His wife takes care of him financially; his part-time job at the bookstore is little more than a daily planned escape from the home. Chris never comes of age, even as he grows into his new identity as Michael; nor does he as Michael, the suburbanite househusband and father. Unable to accept himself as Michael, who is being "outed" by Miles Bridgeman, a slippery character from those days in the 1960's, and, similarly unable to acknowledge himself even as the ex-Chris, he fumbles along, running from both the past and the present. All of this is accomplished in a work that reads largely as an autobiography, though, clearly it is not: Kunzru was born only in 1969; this aspect of the story line, while completely manufactured, is done so successfully.

The first major flashback occurs during the preparations for Michael's fiftieth birthday party, when he recalls a recent vacation he and Miranda made to France. While walking along in a small town, looking at the architecture and enjoying the sunshine, he sees a woman he thinks is Anna Addison, his former lover and a leader of a radical and terroristic antiwar movement who was killed in 1975 while invading an embassy in Copenhagen. Michael is sure that it is she, and the conviction efficaciously and relentlessly propels the past into the present. This resurrection of a character from the past reflects the overall attempt of the novel to deal not only with historical and political matters but also with the dual identities of the main character.

The main thrust of the action (in the present of 1998) is for Michael to run from

Bridgeman, who is forcing a return of the Chris who will have to pay for terrorist crimes committed some thirty years earlier. Michael cannot bring himself to do this, so he steals his wife's car and takes their credit cards and escapes briefly to France where he believes he can find Anna and reunite with her, though it is not clear why he desires this. It is ironic that this run from reality, like his entire life as Michael, is funded by the business successes of his wife, who sells the ultimate of useless, bourgeois products: beauty creams.

This life Michael leaves behind forms one of the numerous "revolutions" referred to in the novel's title. Chris first revolts against his parents' middle-class, mindless existence and the standard upbringing they have given him. Next, as a college student at the London School of Economics, he revolts against the entire system, initially the institution of education. However, he comes to understand that education is only one institution abetting the causes of the paramount institutions of society, government, and politics. He takes on the cause of protesting against the Vietnam War, but this movement evolves into protesting about housing problems of the poor and other injustices caused by poverty and the inequitable distribution of wealth. He and his group occupy a tenement house, give out free food, organize rallies, and so on. During this time of the "peace movement," he and his group adopt a countercultural lifestyle, living in flats where walls are torn down and doors removed (including the door to the toilet) and where people come and go, sleeping and making love on mattresses that have been deliberately moved close to each other to avoid all pretense of privacy. This is done so that individual identities are subsumed into the identity of the group. Chris revolts against this method of protest and life when he realizes that all successes are only momentary and that only great acts will accomplish great deeds. He begins to rob banks and bomb the post office, persuading himself that if deaths occur, they are a necessary evil, the price to be paid for a greater good. On the run and about to be caught, he escapes for several months to Thailand, where Buddhist priests cure his drug addiction and help redefine his character. In the process, Chris redefines his identity, so he returns to England as Michael Frame.

This revolt is a success for two decades, as Michael falls in love with Miranda and marries her, and his past remains buried. However, Bridgeman discovers him and has need of him. Bridgeman wants to sink the political aspirations of Pat Ellis, a woman running for Home Secretary, and Michael must be "un-Framed" so that he can expose Ellis and derail her political campaign. The reasons for doing so are never known.

Michael revolts against Bridgeman's plot and flees to France, eventually to discover that the woman he saw was not Anna, who really had died in 1975, just as the newspapers had reported. Accordingly, he then commits his final revolt of the novel. He telephones Miranda, informing her that he will finally tell her his story and face the consequences of his radical crimes and of the problems wrought by his double life and his double identity.

Kunzru has written an undeniably intriguing story with an engaging plot and subject matter. However, at the end, it has moved only to irresolution: Michael's decision to return to England and face his past is not a moral act but rather one necessitated by desperation. There is no sense of rounding off to the narrative and the dilemmas depicted in the main character's life and being. Rather, the author provides well-crafted phrasing that dismisses Michael, rather than embraces or endorses him. At the end, his final thoughts go to the role and validity of love in his life, and he thinks of Miranda before calling her, presumably to return to England as Chris. The phone call to her and his return to England are credible, but not the shallow thoughts about love being the reason.

The politics of the novel are also left dangling in the air. Chris's youthful radicalism has got him nowhere in life and has simply denied him life: He has no identity that is real. The movement of which he was a part did perhaps contribute to the ending of the Vietnam War, but it did not further other causes, such as eliminating poverty and hunger. The world of 1998 is arguably worse than that of the late 1960's in a number of ways, specifically, the threat of terrorism, and Michael has done nothing but accept the situation and make no waves.

Finally, if this is a coming-of-age story, Chris never comes of age. He simply grows older and haunted by the problems of his past, but there is never any sense of dealing with them maturely and responsibly. The character is left hopelessly revolving and revolving, with never a stop at a final resolution.

Carl Singleton

Review Sources

Booklist 104, nos. 9/10 (January 1, 2008): 44-45.
Entertainment Weekly, January 25, 2008, p. 72.
Kirkus Reviews 75, no. 22 (November 15, 2007): 1172.
Library Journal 132, no. 20 (December 15, 2007): 101.
The Nation 286, no. 16 (April 28, 2008): 36-39.
New Statesman 137 (September 10, 2007): 55-56.
The New York Times Book Review, February 10, 2008, p. 12.
Publishers Weekly 255, no. 8 (February 25, 2008): 72.
The Times Literary Supplement, August 24, 2007, p. 24.
The Virginia Quarterly Review 84, no. 3 (Summer, 2008): 286.

MY SISTER, MY LOVE

Author: Joyce Carol Oates (1938-   )
Publisher: HarperCollins (New York). 562 pp. $25.95
Type of work: Novel
Time: 1990-2007
Locale: Northern New Jersey

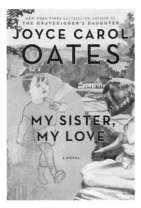

Oates weaves the story of an unsolved child murder into a portrait of modern American consumer culture and the families caught up in it

> *Principal characters:*
> SKYLER RAMPIKE, a teenager narrating the story of his sister's unsolved murder
> EDNA LOUISE "BLISS" RAMPIKE, his sister, murdered in 1997 when she was six and Skyler nine
> BETSEY RAMPIKE, their mother, a needy and ambitious suburban housewife
> BIX RAMPIKE, their father, a business executive who is often absent from home
> PASTOR BOB, a leader of an evangelical church who helps Skyler in his search for answers

In Joyce Carol Oates's *My Sister, My Love*, the central character Skyler Rampike is crippled in a number of ways. An accident in gymnastics when he was six has left him with a permanent limp, he has been through several treatment centers and schools for special needs kids, he has been a drug addict, and he now lives, at age nineteen, in a rundown rooming house in New Brunswick, New Jersey, in self-imposed exile from his parents and trying to write the story of *My Sister, My Love*. The novel is subtitled "The Intimate Story of Skyler Rampike," however, for while he is attempting to unlock the mystery of his sister's death—"One day, Skyler has to reveal all he knows of his sister Bliss's life/death. It is Skyler Rampike's responsibility"—he is also trying to decipher the meaning of his own life in order to save it. "Dysfunctional families are all alike," Skyler writes in the novel's first line. "Ditto 'survivors.'" In the process of trying to solve the decade-old crime, Skyler reveals the dysfunction of his family and exposes the pain of his childhood, including the social and familial forces that led to the murder of his sister and the disintegration of the Rampike family following that crime. The novel is painful to read, and at the same time its story is compelling.

My Sister, My Love shares many elements with the JonBenet Ramsey story, the six-year-old child beauty queen who was murdered in 1996 and whose death and murder investigation became front-page tabloid stories. Bliss Rampike is a six-year-old child ice skater who has been pushed into competition by her ambitious and needy mother. The Rampikes have moved after every promotion that Bix Rampike achieves in his corporate job, and they now live in a mansion in Fair Hills, New Jersey, where Betsey Rampike knows no one and her husband is away on business most of the time. Trying to win the love of her workaholic husband, she focuses all of her anxieties on her two children, especially training and outfitting Bliss as a child skater and leading her into the sordid world of preteen skating competitions, an arena inhabited by other needy, unhappy parents and an audience of obsessed fans. "Our daughter is our destiny," Betsey tells her husband, after changing Bliss's name from Edna Louise to make her even more glamorous. Bliss is almost illiterate, and, like her mother and brother, also heavily medicated, but for a few brief years she is famous, and her fame shines on her family as well. Mothers who have ignored Betsey in the past call to invite her to join their clubs, and schoolmates even start to talk to Skyler, whom they earlier called "weird," but only because of his

Joyce Carol Oates is the author of dozens of novels, story and poetry collections, dramas, and works of criticism. She is the Roger S. Berlind Distinguished Professor of the Humanities at Princeton University, and she has been a member of the American Academy of Arts and Letters since 1978.

sister. Soon after becoming the youngest "Little Miss Jersey Ice Princess" in 1996, however, Bliss is found dead in the furnace room of the basement. As in the Ramsey case, the police are unable to solve the brutal murder, even after repeated investigations, and the Rampike family rapidly dissolves into even deeper dysfunction.

The murder intensifies the pain Skyler has experienced since he was an infant. He was the first victim of his parents' ambitions; Skyler's father, a college football star, was embarrassed by his son's lack of athletic ability and pushed him into gymnastic training that ended in an accident that broke bones and left Skyler with a limp. Skyler's memoir traces his unhappy journey from childhood through a series of schools and then treatment centers, as the drugs he took as a child to mask his physical pain become the hard drugs he uses as a teenager to blunt the pain that fills his mind. In a sense, the novel is Skyler's therapy, for in it he works out his problems: his guilt as the "survivor" who abandoned his six-year-old sister to her "fate," his fear that he may have committed the murder himself, and his inability to understand why she died and he ended up in this condition. He has been estranged from his family for some years; after Bliss's death, his parents split up, his father remarried and started another family, and Betsey turned her grief into a series of popular books (such as *Pray for Mummy: A Mother's Pilgrimage from Grief to Joy*) and then into a line of beauty products aimed at what Skyler calls "the Christian-consumer community." Seeking to recover her youth and beauty, Betsey dies during the last of a series of cosmetic surgeries hours before Skyler rushes to her seeking reconciliation. This final trip to see his mother, however, leads to the beginning of Skyler's recovery, for at the funeral he sees his father for the first time in years, learning the truth about his sister's death and beginning the process of healing that starts with forgiveness.

My Sister, My Love is a fragmentary and nonlinear memoir or confession into which a novice writer pours his heart and his mind. The novel is made up of six books, each containing multiple chapters of varying length, and an epilogue. Often there is a hallucinatory tone to the work, for Skyler is deeply troubled ("And something in my brain is wrong," he admits) and a recovering junkie, subject to panic attacks and bouts of unconsciousness. Bright and at times self-aware, Skyler is also a beginning writer whose doubts often lead him to change direction in his writing or even cancel what he has written. He shifts his narrative point of view constantly from first person to third, he appends notes to his editor as well as to his reader, and his pages often contain footnotes that explain the text but also reveal his uncertainty about himself and his writing. He also misspells words, especially foreign phrases he is attempting to use: pince-nez, for example, becomes "pinch-ney" while gauche becomes "goosh." In Book V, Skyler inserts a fifty-five-page romance novella about his love for a schoolmate when he was sixteen: "First Love, Farewell: A Teen Memory of Lost Love." Heidi Harkness, the girl, is, like Skyler, a victim of a celebrity murder, and their brief idyll only highlights the hell they inhabited as children and will probably face as adults. Each of the books here starts as a journal page, and the novel is clearly a written therapeutic record in which Skyler is trying to unravel his multiple problems. It is also, however, a murder mystery, and the careful reader can follow the clues and solve the crime before Skyler does.

Oates has had her finger on the American pulse for more than forty years, and her stories and novels often dissect social follies and tragedies with surgical and satirical precision. While her novels sometimes contain violent and gothic strains, they also get to truths just beneath the surface of American life. She has also based some of her novels on real-life American tragedies; *Black Water* (1992), for example, followed the outline of Senator Ted Kennedy's Chappaquiddick story, while *Blonde* (2000) traced the tragic life of Marilyn Monroe. Similarly, *My Sister, My Love* has elements from the Ramsey story, but Oates uses them not to sensationalize but rather to uncover family patterns that led to what Skyler calls the "Tabloid Hell" that usually follow such incidents.

Oates has always written perceptively about family life and especially about children, about the unique way they experience life and how they view the adult world—often in fright or flight—and *My Sister, My Love* confirms this talent. The children here—not only Skyler and Bliss but also Skyler's schoolmates and play-date companions—are telling portrayals. Like Oates's previous portraits of troubled childhood and adolescence in novels such as *Foxfire: Confessions of a Girl Gang* (1993) or *The Gravedigger's Daughter* (2007) and in stories such as "In the Region of Ice" (1996), "Where Are You Going, Where Have You Been?" (1996), and "How I Contemplated the World from the Detroit House of Correction and Began My Life Over Again" (1969), Oates is particularly effective in dealing with teenagers like Skyler and picturing their world from the inside out, how they think and feel.

In spite of certain romantic elements in her plots, Oates's characters are usually realistic depictions of ordinary Americans, and this is certainly true of those in *My Sis-*

ter, My Love. Skyler is a tortured young man struggling, against enormous odds, to discover who he is and to find the strength to continue to live. The key to Skyler's identity is hidden in the tragedy of his sister's murder almost ten years before. Only by uncovering the truth surrounding that crime can Skyler begin to establish his own identity, free of the fears that followed it. Skyler's novel is the literary search for those answers. At the end, after a failed reunion with his parents, Skyler seeks help from the charismatic Reverend Bob, the leader of an urban evangelical church who helps addicts such as Skyler, but Bob has no simple answer either; Skyler must find his happiness in locating it for others. In the epilogue to the novel, readers watch Skyler as he takes his first stumbling steps in his journey toward redemption.

Some of the character traits or plot incidents here seem overblown because *My Sister, My Love* is also a satirical take on contemporary American life, especially families, and as such it exaggerates the faults Oates sees within it. Skyler suffers not only from attention-deficit disorder (ADD) but also from premature depression disorder (PDD), chronic anxiety disorder (CAS), repetitive compulsion disorder (RCD), and a host of other psychological conditions that child therapists have diagnosed, and he takes as many medications as he has diagnoses. By the end of Bliss's life, Betsey has spent hundreds of thousands of dollars on skating outfits, on trainers, on acupuncturists, on nutritionists, on therapists—the list is almost endless. Bix resists his wife's ambition only when she plans electrolysis to raise the hairline of their six-year-old daughter. Clearly, there is a large element of truth in Oates's portrait of upper-middleclass American ambition, but she is also having fun, through her narrator, pointing out the absurd extremes of this lifestyle, for example, lampooning the Rampikes' cars—a black Reaper and a Road Warrior SUV—and Skyler's elementary school, which has an H.I.P track, for "Higher Ivy Potential." The satire and the realism mesh easily in Oates's detailed and accurate account of life at the turn of twenty-first century America when parents turn their children's innocence and talent into a ladder for their own personal and social advancement.

David Peck

Review Sources

Booklist 104, no. 15 (April 1, 2008): 5.
The Boston Globe, June 23, 2008, p. 4.
Elle 23, no. 11 (July, 2008): 89.
Harper's Magazine 317 (July, 2008): 81.
Kirkus Reviews 76, no. 9 (May 1, 2008): 455.
Library Journal 133, no. 8 (May 1, 2008): 59.
The New York Times Book Review, August 10, 2008, p. 8.
Publishers Weekly 255, no. 14 (April 7, 2008): 40.
School Library Journal 54, no. 11 (November, 2008): 157.
The Times Literary Supplement, October 3, 2008, p. 20.

NAPOLEON
The Path to Power, 1769-1799

Author: Philip Dwyer (1957-   )
Publisher: Yale University Press (New Haven, Conn.).
   651 pp. $35.00
Type of work: Biography, history
Time: The 1760's to 1799
Locale: Corsica, France, Egypt, and Italy

   Dwyer presents a compelling picture of the young Napoleon Bonaparte, portraying him as an opportunist reacting to events and cleverly shaping his heroic image through the mass media

   Principal personages:
      NAPOLEON BONAPARTE, a successful
         general who seizes control of France in
         1799
      JOSEPH BONAPARTE, Bonaparte's older brother
      LUCIEN BONAPARTE, Bonaparte's younger brother
      JOSEPHINE BEAUHARNAIS, Bonaparte's wife
      CHRISTOFORO SALICETI, a government commissioner and political
         patron of the young Bonaparte
      PAUL BARRAS, a politician who promoted Bonaparte's military career

   Philip Dwyer's *Napoleon: The Path to Power*—the first volume of an extended biography of Napoleon Bonaparte—will be appreciated by readers familiar with the Napoleonic saga as well as by those encountering the life of the great conqueror for the first time. Although Dwyer is a distinguished scholar and an expert on the Napoleonic period, and the book, published by Yale University Press, is intensively researched and heavily footnoted, Dwyer's vigorous prose transcends the merely academic. He has managed the difficult feat of having something new to say about one of the most familiar stories in modern history.
   Bonaparte has been the subject of countless studies since his famous final defeat at Waterloo. The record of his spectacular rise and fall is inherently dramatic. In the midst of an age of revolution, when aristocracy was slowly being supplanted by liberalism and a rising bourgeoisie, Bonaparte was the ultimate self-made man. He came from obscurity to dominate the continent of Europe as the ruler of a new French Empire. Though a thoroughgoing tyrant, his ascendancy spread the French Revolution's ideal of equality before the law. While most of Europe eventually rebelled against his quest for power, he was for a time seen by many as a shining avatar of progress. Bonaparte achieved all this through a record of military success that earned him a place with the greatest leaders of history. He developed an unparalleled facility in maneuvering his troops, rapidly concentrating overwhelming force on a point of enemy

weakness. His speed and tactical aggressiveness seemed brilliantly innovative compared to the more stately rhythms of eighteenth century warfare. Building on the individual initiative and ideological fervor fostered in the citizen armies of the French Revolution, he cultivated a special bond with his soldiers, enabling him to demand more of them than could other commanders of his day. So superlative were Bonaparte's martial gifts that from early in his career he was universally regarded as a military genius.

Philip Dwyer teaches at the University of Newcastle in Australia. He is the editor of numerous books on the Napoleonic period, including The French Revolution and Napoleon: A Sourcebook *(2002), with Peter McPhee.*

Bonaparte was fortunate to win this reputation at the height of the Romantic movement. As a supremely gifted individualist, he fit the pattern of the Romantic hero, struggling to express his superior gifts in a sea of mediocrity. His final defeat ironically sealed his authenticity as a Romantic hero, leaving him unbowed and defiant despite rejection and misunderstanding. He is the very model of a "great man" attempting to bend history to his will. Bonaparte forced himself on the imagination of his contemporaries, and his life has never lost its fascination.

Dwyer's contribution to this vast Napoleonic literature provides a penetrating analysis of Bonaparte's evolving sense of self and his active contribution to the growth of his own legend. Dwyer does not see Bonaparte as the Romantic hero out of step with his inadequate times. Instead, he portrays Bonaparte as a work in progress: as a youth, torn between his Corsican homeland and an adoptive French identity; as a young man, trying to balance enthusiasm for the French Revolution with an innate desire for order. Bonaparte evolved through trial and error, and though his course was often diverted by personal disasters and sometimes propelled to success by strokes of luck, he displayed a growing adaptability and egotism. As he shed old enthusiasms and ideals, his interest and energies became increasingly focused on what was left: himself. Dwyer ends this first installment of his biography with the 1799 military coup through which Bonaparte seized power in France. By this point in his life, just past the age of thirty, the Bonaparte of legend was taking shape. Already an ambitious and cynical opportunist, he was confident enough in his abilities to challenge fate and grasp the reins of power. Facilitating his rise was an instinctive gift for self-promotion. The young Bonaparte was an indefatigable networker, ever on the alert for a connection that could prove useful. Early in his career as an army commander, he grasped the propagandistic power of the media, carefully managing his image. In his dispatches back to France, he shamelessly lied about his reverses and exaggerated his successes. Bonaparte skillfully manipulated the newspapers, even starting some of his own to sing his praises. He encouraged a proliferation of portraits and prints of himself and his exploits to reach a nonliterate audience and to help make him a hero in France. One of the strengths that Dwyer brings to his biography is a mastery of the organs of late eighteenth century French popular culture that helped lay the ideological foundations of Bonaparte's dictatorship.

Dwyer devotes a great deal of attention to Bonaparte's Corsican roots. Corsica was a Mediterranean island that had long been loosely governed by the Italian mercantile republic of Genoa. In the 1760's France established control over the island, and Bonaparte was born there on August 15, 1769, shortly after the French had decisively defeated a Corsican independence movement led by Pasquale Paoli. Bonaparte's father Carlo fought with Paoli, but after the French victory Carlo promptly accommodated himself to the new regime. The Bonapartes quickly acquired a collaborationist taint, and Bonaparte's mother Letizia may have even become the mistress of the French governor. Carlo worked assiduously to ingratiate himself with the French authorities in order to secure places for his eight children in the new system. Through his lobbying, he attained scholarships for the eldest to attend exclusive schools in France.

At the age of nine, Bonaparte was enrolled at the military academy of Brienne, a small school of 110 students that prepared young men for service as officers in the army. About half the pupils were scholarship students, most the sons of aristocratic families too poor to afford an education proper for their station in life. The young Bonaparte figured among these. According to the mythic narrative that Bonaparte later encouraged, he was an outcaste at Brienne, routinely persecuted because of his Italian accent. Dwyer is skeptical of these stories. There is no hard evidence that Bonaparte was singled out for mistreatment. What Dwyer finds more significant is the alienation from others that Bonaparte experienced from an early age. An inveterate loner, Bonaparte as a boy felt little loyalty to the monarchy that he was being trained to serve; instead, he identified himself with his Corsican heritage. He revered the freedom fighter Paoli and shed few tears when his hard-working father died young of stomach cancer. Ironically, Bonaparte came to resemble his father in his relentless efforts to advance the fortunes of his many siblings, usurping the role of head of the family that rightfully belonged to his elder brother Joseph. Bonaparte's devotion to his family, which continued into his days as the emperor of France, would be the last manifestation of the Corsican in him.

Bonaparte was a lieutenant in the artillery when France was engulfed in the revolution that began in 1789. He became an enthusiastic supporter of the revolutionary program, having no attachment to the old regime. In the early years of the revolution, Bonaparte embroiled himself in Corsican politics. He hoped that Corsica could achieve political autonomy in association with France. These hopes seemed within reach when Paoli was allowed to return to his homeland. Unfortunately, Paoli proved to be an autocratic ruler. He disapproved of the increasing radicalism of the French government, and he would never fully trust any member of Carlo's family. In the end, Bonaparte was forced to flee Corsica with his mother and his siblings. His disillusionment in Corsica helped prepare him for the political shoals that he would be forced to navigate in the coming years.

By the time Bonaparte and his family reached France in 1793, the country was in the grip of revolutionary terror. The king and queen had been executed, a republic declared, and the Jacobins who controlled the government were ruthlessly using the guillotine to consolidate power. In an effort to rally support for the revolution, the government had declared war on the hostile monarchies surrounding France. It also faced insurrections at home, as a large number of French people rose up against the

Jacobin ascendancy. Bonaparte went to war for the government, using his skills as an artilleryman to subdue the counterrevolutionary movement in the port of Toulon. Such was his identification with the radicals in Paris that he was briefly arrested when Maximilien Robespierre and his faction of Jacobin leaders were overthrown and guillotined. Bonaparte quickly bounced back, as the Directory, a less bloodthirsty regime, came to power. He benefited from the patronage of a fellow Corsican, Christoforo Saliceti, a government commissioner with the army, and Paul Barras, one of the Directors. He also strengthened his political position by helping thwart a royalist coup attempt in 1795. In March of the next year, he was appointed commander of the army of Italy, charged with bringing some energy to a desultory campaign against the Piedmontese and Austrians.

In Italy Bonaparte came into his own. Up to this point in his career, he had proven himself a capable soldier, but he had not yet demonstrated signs of military greatness. Now, with a significant command of his own, he stunned Europe with a brilliant campaign that over the course of a year and a half established France as the dominant power in Italy. Dwyer traces the course of these battles, but military history is not his chief concern. Instead, he explores the ways in which command and power shaped Bonaparte's personality. The young general discovered a taste for waging war. Repeated victories enhanced his self-confidence and revealed abilities and qualities in himself that he had not known before. He came to enjoy exercising the power that he had won, and he began wielding an authority in Italy greater than that normally accorded a general. He bought immunity for this by sending to Paris a stream of confiscated gold and art treasures that would later be the glories of French museums. Bonaparte also used the riches that he exacted from the conquered Italians to buy the publicity that made him a hero as well as a victor to the French. His experiences in Corsica and in the revolution had stripped him of idealism. Further souring his mood was the infidelity of his beloved wife Josephine Beauharnais. Bonaparte now saw the world through cold and self-centered eyes. From this point on, he would pursue the power that he treasured with singular determination and ruthlessness.

Bonaparte followed his exploits in Italy with an invasion of Egypt in 1798. This was the linchpin of a grandiose plan to disrupt the growth of the British Empire in India. Bonaparte's expedition included a large contingent of scholars and scientists, because he wanted to be seen as an apostle of enlightenment and progress as well as a conqueror. Bonaparte won control of Egypt through some initial victories, one glamorously fought in sight of the pyramids. Then his campaign fell apart. The British admiral Horatio Nelson destroyed Bonaparte's fleet at Aboukir Bay, and Bonaparte was checked in a foray into Syria, during which he displayed a cruelty to Turkish prisoners shocking even to a more rough-hewn age. Fortunately, he was able to defeat a Turkish landing at Aboukir Bay, and this enabled him to return to France as a hero, even though the army that he had abandoned in Egypt was doomed to certain defeat and capture. Perhaps recognizing the transient nature of his acclaim, Bonaparte threw himself into a plot with opponents of the corrupt Directory. With the crucial assistance of his politician brother Lucien, he seized control of the government on November 10, 1799. This was the first military coup in modern history, and it became the model of many to come. Bonaparte, a man who in eighteenth century terms had come from nowhere, was master of the most powerful nation in Europe. In the next volume of his biography, Dwyer will explore what Bonaparte made of this unexpected opportunity. Together with *Napoleon: The Path to Power*, it should provide contemporary readers a compelling and useful portrait of Bonaparte.

Daniel P. Murphy

Review Sources

Booklist 104, no. 14 (March 15, 2008): 23-24.
Library Journal 133, no. 7 (April 15, 2008): 92.

NATURAL ACTS
A Sidelong View of Science and Nature

Author: David Quammen (1948-   )
First published: 1985, in the United States
Publisher: W. W. Norton (New York). 350 pp. $24.95
Type of work: Essays, science, history of science, nature,
   natural history

A new edition of Quammen's 1985 collection of essays
on nature, scientists, the history of science, and human in-
teraction with the environment

This revised and expanded edition is a marriage of two
distinct and different collections of essays. The first half of
the book consists of nineteen essays, divided into three sections, taken, without revision, from the first edition of *Nat-
ural Acts*, which was published in 1985. The second half contains seven essays originally published within the last decade. The first half shows the young, exuberant
David Quammen, still learning his craft, but entertaining and educating his reader
with a different view of the natural world. The essays of the second half are those of a
mature, sure craftsman, still taking a sidelong view of science, but now a master of his
field. Confident in his skill to persuade, there is little of the showoff that is evident in
the earlier writing. Both sets of essays look at the same set of themes: nature, the place
of humans in nature, communities and relationships, and the life of the individual researcher in the history of science.

The early essays originally appeared between 1981 and 1985 and, with three exceptions, were first published as a column in the magazine *Outside.* Quammen's early
columns are characteristically short (limited by the format in *Outside*), informal, wander a bit, challenge prior preconceptions, and ask unusual questions. In the introduction to the original edition, he describes his point of view as "oblique" and "counter-
intuitive," which is a good way to put it. That is one of the chief attractions of these
early works: They force the reader to rethink his or her position on nature. For example, the essays collected in the section entitled "All God's Vermin" look sympatheti-
cally at creatures most of his audience probably had little love or appreciation for,
such as the mosquito and the black widow spider.

At the time of these early efforts, Quammen was conscious of what he perceives to
be his outsider's position in respect to one well-known and acknowledged community
of popular science writers, the scientist-essayists. He lacked, he pointed out in the
original introduction, the scientific training and research experience of the masters of
the genre, such as the anthropologist Loren Eisley, the paleontologist and evolutionary biologist Stephen J. Gould, and the biomedical researcher Lewis Thomas. To contrast himself with these practitioners of the craft, he emphasized, in his autobiographical introduction, the important roles of his personal curiosity and his love of nature

∼

The author of eleven books and numerous uncollected magazine articles, David Quammen has won the National Magazine Award three times. He is the Wallace Stegner Professor in Western American Studies at Montana State University.

∼

instead of literary research. His utilization of the published literature in these early essays was often limited to a handful of sources. His essay on the black widow spider, for example, relied, apparently, on only two sources, while that on the octopus used three. In addition, in what may have been an overreaction, he used language that emphasizes the distance between him, the lover of nature, and the researchers, with their technical knowledge and their efforts to reduce nature to numbers. A simple, extremely insightful algebraic expression used by ecologists becomes an "ugly cryptogram," highlighting and conveying both Quammen's lack of appreciation for the beauty of mathematics and its presumed impenetrability, while Robert J. Oppenheimer's team of atomic scientists and ingenious engineers become "a coven," invoking images of witchcraft and evil doing.

The essay on the mosquito, the earliest chronologically in the collection and the first in the book, captures, not unexpectedly, all of the early Quammen's strengths and weaknesses. His love of all nature, even aspects of nature that are commonly viewed negatively by most observers, is evident. So is his somewhat off-center point of view and his willingness to ask singular questions. Rather than limiting his account to the life history and feeding habits of the insect, or simply acknowledging or repeating the massive destruction that the mosquito has done to humans over recorded history, he asks what some readers may consider a ridiculous question. Is the insect truly just a horrible pest at best, and a conveyor of deadly diseases at worst, or are there any positive attributes of the mosquito? Does the mosquito have redeeming features? His insightful answer is that the mosquito is worthy of praise and defense, and it has been a true hero in the struggle for the protection of the environment. His argument is that this otherwise nasty insect helped ensure the survival of the tropical rainforests into the late twentieth century, long after other forest ecosystems were destroyed through economic exploitation, by limiting human activity in that ecosystem. As in his essay on the crow, which contends that the problem with crows is that they are highly intelligent birds who suffer from boredom, or the essay analyzing the rumors, never confirmed, of giant anaconda snakes in the Amazon River basin, Quammen thinks outside the box and forces his reader to do the same. It can be an exhilarating experience.

Evident in the mosquito essay is another of Quammen's traits in his early essays: his use of the unusual or questionable turn of phrase or analogy. In this case, he concludes his discussion by drawing an analogy between the mosquito and the Viet Cong, the Communist guerrilla force of the Vietnam War, and in doing so he seems to be making a strong political statement perhaps out of place in nature essays. The mosquito is presented as a jungle-loving, bloodthirsty anticolonialist, stopping Europeans and Americans from exploiting its habitat. Is that his picture of the Viet Cong? How does that fit in the historical debate over the nature of the Viet Cong? An analogy that conjures conflicting responses among readers is not the best.

The limitations of Quammen's early work come out clearly in his excursions into the history of science. His essay on Tycho Brahe, the sixteenth century Danish astronomer, is the weakest of the collection. It is underresearched, with only four sources cited, and shows a lack of understanding of the complexity of the man. When Quammen's portrait of Brahe is contrasted to the wonderful, multidimensional portraits he draws of living subjects that he has interviewed and has had the opportunity to interact with, such as George Ochenski, the Montana river-snorkeler, and John R. Horner, the paleontologist, who, despite a limited formal scientific education, has been a key actor in the development of a revolutionary view of dinosaurs, the difference is unquestionable. In the case of Brahe, Quammen had difficulty extracting the living person from the historical record.

There is such a great contrast between the early essays and the ones that follow in the final section of the book that at first glance one might wonder if they were the work of two different writers. In the introduction created for this edition, Quammen acknowledges his growth as a researcher and a writer during the more than two decades of essays collected in this book, touches upon all the major differences between his early and later writing, and admits that illustrating those differences was one of his motives in including both sets of essays. These later seven essays, originally published between 1998 and 2007 in a variety of magazines, are much longer, much more developed, more sophisticated, and better researched than their predecessors.

From comments in the introduction, Quammen appears to have identified "Planet of Weeds," his essay on species extinction that opens the second half of the book, as the most important of his later writings that appear in this collection. Based on extensive research in both the scientific and the popular literature (there are more than one hundred items in the list of sources, by far the most for any essay in the volume) as well as interviews with scientists, this essay explores the possibility of a mass extinction of species triggered by human action, resulting in a massive loss of biodiversity. As the result of such a mass extinction, the earth would be inhabited primarily by the so-called weedy species. These are the plant and animal species, including humans, that are survivor species, able to take advantage of whatever opportunities are presented and possessing a high tolerance for a broad range of habitat conditions. Pessimistically, Quammen warns that the coming of what he calls the "Planet of Weeds " may only be a few human generations away. The essay serves as a clarion call.

Three other essays in this section demonstrate the diversity of Quammen's later writing and his great skills. The longest piece, some fifty pages, and originally published in three parts in *National Geographic*, is an account of J. Michael Fay's one-thousand-mile trek across central Africa. Although Quammen does a fine job of explaining how Fay's expedition is a serious and important step in conservation studies in a relatively unstudied portion of Africa, by pinpointing the location of ecosystems, what makes the essay fantastic reading is how the author captures the spirit of a man who, in Quammen's words, "just loves to walk in the wilds."

The description of Fay's expedition, which focuses on a larger than life personality, can be contrasted with the shortest piece in this section, an account of Quammen's relationship with his wife's dog, Wiley. Through Wiley's life and death, Quammen explores how humans become, and recognize the fact that they are, part of a community. If the essay on Fay represents fascination with the stubborn individual who overcomes all obstacles through personal will, the essay on Wiley demonstrates the human need for the companionship and the support of others.

In his account of Carl Linnaeus, the eighteenth century Swedish naturalist who developed the most influential artificial system of biological classification, Quammen has distanced himself from the weaknesses demonstrated in his Brahe essay of two decades earlier. The historical essay is based on considerably more research, including eleven printed sources, correspondence, and a visit to Linnaeus's home. He takes the time to understand the historical actor in the same way he strives to understand contemporary scientists, and the result is an essay in which the long-dead scientist does come alive.

In the last twenty-five years, Quammen has evolved from an opinionated, somewhat atypical nature columnist to a significant and insightful commentator on American life, science, and the natural world. The essays collected in *Natural Acts* document that evolution. As Quammen states in his introduction, by collecting his work in book form, he has ensured the survival of the best of his otherwise ephemeral magazine writings.

Marc Rothenberg

Review Sources

Geographical 81, no. 1 (January, 2009): 63.
Publishers Weekly 255, no. 14 (April 7, 2008): 48.
Scientific American 298, no. 3 (March, 2008): 100.
SciTech Book News 32, no. 2 (June, 2008).

NAZI LITERATURE IN THE AMERICAS

Author: Roberto Bolaño (1953-2003)
First published: Historia de la literatura Nazi en
  America, 1996, in Spain
Translated from the Spanish by Chris Andrews
Publisher: New Directions (New York). 227 pp. $23.95
Type of Work: Novel
Time: 1900-2030
Locale: Latin America and the United States

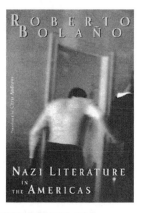

This fictional literary encyclopedia of invented North
and South American fascist authors includes the lives,
works, creative significance, and historical context of these
imaginary figures

Principal characters:

ROBERTO BOLAÑO, the narrative voice of the encyclopedia and a
  character in its final entry
EDELMIRA THOMPSON DE MENDILUCE, poet and patroness of
  Argentina's right-wing literary movement
LUZ MENDILUCE THOMPSON, daughter of Edelmira, bisexual fascist poet
  whose most cherished possession is a photograph of herself with
  Adolf Hitler
IRMA CARRASCO, a Mexican poet who flees her abusive Marxist husband
  to join the Falangist movement in Spain during its civil war
MAX MIREBALAIS, a Haitian author with many pseudonyms who
  attempts to merge black identity with Nazism in his writings
ARGENTINO SCHIAFFINO, Argentinine poet, novelist, and violent soccer
  fan with right-wing sympathies
CARLOS RAMÍREZ HOFFMAN, Chilean pilot and poet who participates in
  brutal assassinations and torture during the Pinochet regime

When Roberto Bolaño's *Los Detectives salvajes* (1998; *The Savage Detectives*,
2007) appeared, it made its author a literary celebrity in the Spanish-speaking world.
His readers declared him the leader of a new Latin American literary movement that
would replace the magic realism of Gabriel García Márquez, the author of *Cien años
de soledad* (1967; *One Hundred Years of Solitude*, 1970).

However, two years before, critics had already noted Bolaño's greatness when he
published *Nazi Literature in the Americas*, a biographical encyclopedia of thirty fictional fascist authors from North and South America. Whereas *The Savage Detectives*
is a decidedly Dionysian work with a strong Beat influence from Jack Kerouac, author of *On the Road* (1957), *Nazi Literature in the Americas* owes more to Apollonian
flights of intellectual imagination such as *Labyrinths* (1962) by Jorge Luis Borges and
Le città invisibili (1972; *Invisible Cities*, 1974) by Italo Calvino. However, *Savage
Detectives* and *Nazi Literature in the Americas* share Bolaño's concerns about the

Roberto Bolaño grew up in Mexico but returned to his Chilean homeland, where he was briefly imprisoned by the Pinochet government. While living in exile, he wrote seventeen books of poetry and prose, and he became one of the leading Latin American writers of his generation. He died in 2003.

relationship of the writer to society and history.

Nazi Literature in the Americas derives from the Latin American genre of literary encyclopedias that catalog a group of writers of one particular nationality or creative movement, but not in an objective fashion. Rather, the encyclopedia's author colors the entries with his or her own critical biases. The unique aspect of *Nazi Literature in the Americas* is that Bolaño does not catalog real authors; instead, he creates a menagerie of invented fascist authors. In essence, the entries in *Nazi Literature in the Americas* form a collection of thirty short stories. To give his work greater realism, Bolaño infuses it with references to real writers. So, for instance, the fictional, homophobic American poet Jim O'Bannon beats up Allen Ginsberg when Ginsberg, the author of *Howl* (1956), makes sexual advances. Bolaño's right-wing thug and detective author Amado Couto meets the real Brazilian mystery writer Don Rubem Fonseca and finds his "gaze was harder than his own." To complete his illusory reality, Bolaño includes three appendixes under the heading "Epilogue for Monsters": secondary figures, publishing houses, and books.

Bolaño creates this parallel realm of imaginary fascist authors in order to explore the nature of evil. Sometimes he finds it banal, even foolish, as with Luz Mendiluce Thompson's obsession over a photograph of herself as a baby held in the adoring arms of Adolf Hitler, a picture she would sacrifice everything to save, or Zach Sodenstern's novel *Candace*, which includes a character named Flip, "a mutant, stray German Shepherd with telepathic powers and Nazi tendencies." Sometimes evil can even evoke bravery, as when Jesús Fernández-Gómez stoically recovers in a Riga hospital from war wounds inflicted on the Eastern Front, or when Ignacio Zubieta dies in the streets defending Nazi Berlin against Soviet troops. Aways there is a deep horror lurking underneath the seemingly benign aspects, like a bloody gash hidden by a bandage. Couto ponders literature as he tortures enemies of a dictatorial Brazilian government. Poet John Lee Brook murders seven people—a poet, three pornographers, a shady art dealer, and the dealer's two bodyguards. Throughout *Nazi Literature in the Americas*, Bolaño reveals fascists whose lives are pathetic or even amusing, but they embrace chilling genocidal beliefs or commit dreadful atrocities. In this way, he demonstrates that, even in the most prosaic person, evil can be potent and dangerous.

What ultimately makes *Nazi Literature in the Americas* an important and troubling contemporary work is Bolaño's exploration of the intersection of art and evil, of how creative souls can accommodate or revel in a totalitarian philosophy. On one hand, Bolaño can identify with his characters, for in their striving to create literary art in the face of critical hostility, he mirrors his own youth in Mexico City, when he was a Trotskyite and the fiery leader of the Infrarealism poetry movement, sabotaging readings and writing diatribes against major mainstream authors such as Octavio Paz, author of *El laberinto de la soledad* (1950; *The Labyrinth of Solitude*, 1961). Bolaño probably feels sympathy for Luiz Fontaine Da Souza, who writes a dozen six-hundred-page works on philosophy, only to be met with a "sepulchral silence," or for Agentino Shiaffino, who has to self-publish his poems on Argentine soccer. He may even admire Edelmira Thompson de Mendiluce for building a replica of Edgar Allan Poe's concept of the perfect room, complete with crimson windowpanes, thick silver curtains, rosewood couches, and an octagonal table of gold-threaded marble.

Bolaño's comic empathy, however, goes only so far. While these characters may appeal with their heroic creative efforts and misbegotten lives, the darkness of their souls ultimately chills the reader's heart. Fernández-Gómez and Zubieta perform their acts of bravery for Francisco Franco and Adolf Hilter—two of the most bloody totalitarians in human history. Philosopher Da Souza's work includes tracts claiming that miscegenation will be the downfall of Brazil, and one of his works hints at his murder of a lover, an act concealed by his powerful family. In between writing soccer poetry, Shiaffino pens an essay titled "Jews Out," and he blows up a bus carrying fans of a rival soccer team. Just after de Mendiluce builds her Poe room, she helps Nazis fleeing the collapse of Germany to slip illegally into Argentina, and she starts the Fourth Reich Press, a major fascist publisher.

Even more disturbing are Bolaño's depictions of the active relationship between fascism and the literary arts. History provides many examples of Nazism seducing creative minds and hearts—most notably Albert Speer, Hitler's architect; Leni Riefenstahl, the filmmaker who directed *Triumph des Willens* (1935; *Triumph of the Will*), Richard Strauss, the composer of *Also sprach Zarathustra* (1896), and Ezra Pound, the American poet who broadcast pro-Mussolini propaganda from Italy throughout World War II. Bolaño's fictional encyclopedia allows him to generate new examples of creative artists pandering to fascism.

Thompson's most famous poem is "I Was Happy with Hitler." Fernández-Gómez writes a novel glorifying fascism and Franco's side of the Spanish Civil War titled *The Fighting Years of an American Falangist in Europe*. Silvio Salvático's books promote "the re-establishment of the Inquisition; corporal punishment in public; a permanent war against the Chileans, the Paraguayans, or the Bolivians as a kind of gymnastics for the nation; polygamy; the extermination of the Indians to prevent further contamination of the Argentinean race; curtailing the rights of any citizen with Jewish blood"; and many other extreme, far-right concepts. Science-fiction author Sodenstern writes the highly popular Fourth Reich saga, which includes *The Simbas*, "a surreptitious manifesto directed against African Americans, Jews, and Hispanics." Another science-fiction author, Harry Sibelius, writes a 1,333-page novel that describes a parallel history wherein the Third Reich conquers the United States and establishes a Nazi state. The entire piece precisely parallels Arnold J. Toynbee's *Hitler's Europe* (1954), and it includes chapter titles such as "The Political Structure of Hitler's America."

By the end of *Nazi Literature in the Americas*, the reader feels overwhelmed by all this creative energy turned toward such a malevolent cause. The literary community views writing as an almost sacred profession, and it tends to believe that creative artists lend their talents to only noble, democratic causes. In *Nazi Literature in the Amer-*

icas, Bolaño starkly shows that the literary arts can and have lent themselves to movements as darkly violent and destructive to democracy as Nazism and fascism.

The book's climax arrives with the final entry, "The Infamous Ramírez Hoffman." Here, Bolaño utilizes his own experiences during General Pinochet's coup, and in this section, the connection between poetry, fascism, and violence is at its most unsettling. Born in Chile, Bolaño moved with his family to Mexico, but he returned to his birth country in 1973 to help defend the democratic socialist Salvador Allende government. Arriving just as Pinochet seized the nation, Bolaño was briefly jailed, and he might have been executed, except for a guard who recognized him from childhood and ordered his release.

"The Infamous Ramírez Hoffman" begins just before the coup. Bolaño describes a poetry circle that includes María and Magdalena Venegas, girls in their late teens, and Ramírez Hoffman, who is María's lover. When the coup begins, the Venegas sisters, associated with the leftist poet Juan Cherniakovski, flee the city of Concepción for their aunt's home in the country. Two weeks later, Hoffman shows up, and the girls invite him to stay. They do not realize that Hoffman has become an informer for the Pinochet regime, and in the night, after Hoffman has made love to María, he slits the aunt's throat and then lets in two of Pinochet's agents who proceed to rape and slaughter the girls.

Meanwhile, Bolaño has been arrested and interred in a makeshift prison in Concepción. While Bolaño is out in the prison yard, Ramírez Hoffman, who has been studying to be a pilot, flies overhead and writes poetry in the sky, with lines that include "GOOD LUCK TO EVERYONE IN DEATH" and "LEARN FROM FIRE." With this grandiose form of public poetry, Hoffman becomes famous. One day, some of Pinochet's top generals ask Hoffman to present something truly astounding. He obliges, first with his skywriting poetry, but a thunderstorm rips apart the letters. Still, he manages to write a series of lines that begin, "Death is friendship." After the skywriting, Hoffman invites a select few to an apartment set up as a gallery, there to view photographs that he calls "the art of the future." While Bolaño does not describe the photographs, from the horrified reactions to the pictures, they are probably depictions of the Venegas girls' rape and murder. In this moment, Hoffman perfects the link between poetry, sadism, death, and fascism. In all of his horrifying glory, Hoffman is the supreme fascist artist.

Soon after, Hoffman is kicked out of the air force and wanders around Chile, writing for obscure literary magazines and staging various artistic and theatrical events. Eventually he leaves Chile for Europe, and by the early 1990's, when Chilean democracy had been restored, he is summoned to various trials. He never appears, and he cannot be found. Everyone assumes he is dead, until Abel Romero, a private detective who ferrets out torturers, assassins, and other criminals of the Pinochet regime, with Bolaño's help, finds Hoffman in France making sadomasochistic films. Romero assassinates Hoffman, and the most infamous fascist author discussed in *Nazi Literature in the Americas* dies, as it were, by his own sword, thus ending the book with the chilling reality beneath its thirty invented entries.

John Nizalowski

Review Sources

Entertainment Weekly, February 29, 2008, p. 65.
The Globe and Mail, March 8, 2008, p. D7.
The Nation 286, no. 12 (March 31, 2008): 29-32.
The New York Times Book Review, February 24, 2008, p. 9.
Publishers Weekly 254, no. 49 (December 10, 2007): 34-35.
Review of Contemporary Fiction 28, no. 2 (Summer, 2008): 166-167.
The Times Literary Supplement, February 22, 2008, p. 19.
The Village Voice 53, no. 50 (December 10, 2008): 44.
The Washington Post Book World, March 2, 2008, p. BW10.

NETHERLAND

Author: Joseph O'Neill (1964-   )
Publisher: Pantheon Books (New York). 272 pp. $23.95
Type of work: Novel
Time: 1999-2006
Locale: New York City and London

A Dutch banker struggles to move forward with his family in post-9/11 New York

> *Principal characters:*
> HANS VAN DEN BROEK, a Dutch banker
> RACHEL VAN DEN BROEK, Hans's wife,
>   who is a lawyer
> JAKE VAN DEN BROEK, Hans and Rachel's
>   young son
> CHUCK RAMKISSOON, an enterprising
>   immigrant from Trinidad
> ANNE RAMKISSOON, Chuck's wife
> ELIZA, Chuck's mistress
> MIKE ABELSKY, Chuck's shady Russian business partner

Joseph O'Neill's third novel, *Netherland*, delves into the immigrant experience, post-9/11 New York, and troubled personal relationships. The novel has rightfully drawn much critical attention. It was long-listed for the 2008 Man Booker Prize and won the PEN/Faulkner Award. In addition, *Netherland* was named by *The New York Times* as one of the top ten books of 2008.

O'Neill, born in Ireland, raised in Holland, and living in New York, draws on his immigrant experience, his crosscultural background, and his love of cricket to color the novel. In addition, he demonstrates a finely honed sense of post-traumatic stress, and the way such stress insidiously undermines individuals and relationships. Indeed, O'Neill seems to be saying, all who experienced such a cataclysm might find themselves as outsiders in their own lives.

O'Neill underscores the sense of isolation and paralysis that permeates the novel through every available means, including even his sentence structure. He uses long, perfectly crafted sentences, befitting his main character's penchant for thinking rather than acting. As a result, the book is dense, internal, and even sometimes claustrophobic. The main character, Hans van den Broek, tells the story almost entirely through his thoughts and memories, severely limiting the point of view. The technique, however, is highly effective, an example of craft and tone mirroring content. Hans's quiet adventure occurs entirely in flashback. Home with his family in London, years after the events of 2001, Hans learns of the death of Chuck Ramkissoon, a mysterious figure Hans knew during his time in New York City when he lived there without his family. From this point on, Hans reminisces about the time he calls "unbearable," in New

York, living at the Chelsea Hotel while his
family lives in London. Hans also recalls his
friendship with Chuck, the people who lived
at the Chelsea, and his time playing cricket in
New York. He also flashes back to earlier
times, as a child in The Hague, as a young
man in London, and as a man experiencing
his mother's death not long before September
11, 2001.

∽

*Joseph O'Neill was born in Ireland,
grew up in Holland, received his law
degree from Cambridge, and now
resides in New York. He also plays
cricket with the Staten Island Cricket
Club.* Netherland *is his third book and
the most widely acclaimed.*

∽

In flashback, Hans reveals himself to be a
Dutch banker, married to Rachel, an Englishwoman and attorney, living in New York
City prior to and immediately after the terrorist attacks of September 11, 2001. He
is profoundly affected by the collapse of the Twin Towers and finds himself lost,
floating above his world. His disconnection to his life may also trace back to the recent death of his mother, his only relative except for his wife and son. At the time of
the attack, his family lives in an apartment in TriBeCa, a neighborhood in lower
Manhattan. Forced out by the authorities, they live in fear at the Chelsea Hotel, unsure
of what will happen next. Hans acknowledges that he is unprepared for this new New
York, where everyone has an opinion about the world and current events, stating: "In
short, I was a political-ethical idiot. Normally, this deficiency might have been inconsequential, but these were abnormal times." He is insular, not unconcerned but overwhelmed, living primarily for his family and his work. His wife, finding herself unmoored as well, responds by withdrawing, as she regrets their move to New York and
becomes increasingly hysterical about world events and the role of the United States.
As a consequence, Rachel moves back to London, taking their young son Jake with
her, leaving Hans at the Chelsea, bereft and alone.

Being alone is nothing new to Hans, however, who has been an outsider since he
left The Hague, first for London and then for New York. O'Neill effectively develops
the theme of Hans's disconnection by placing Hans above the earth: He constantly
floats over his home, either through Google Earth, or the London Eye, or on a plane.
His sense of belonging exists only when he is with his family, which has been made
even smaller by the death of his mother. His relief at Rachel's statement to their thera-
pist that she "stayed married to me . . . because she felt a responsibility to see me
through life, and the responsibility felt like a happy one" illustrates not a passionate
love affair, but rather a familiar and comfortable companionship, one that speaks of
obligation, not abiding love.

In this way, O'Neill develops a common post-9/11 theme: the need for the familiar
during a time of great fearful change. Hans does not seek adventure or excitement but
rather sameness. He wants nothing more than his family, a job, and a home. As he says
after the attacks, he and Rachel must figure out whether they are in a "pre-apocalyptic
situation, like the European Jews in the '30's or the last citizens of Pompeii, or
whether our situation was merely near apocalyptic, like that of the cold war inhabitants of New York, London, Washington, and, for that matter, Moscow." For Hans and
Rachel, whether the world is really ending or whether it only feels like the world is

ending is a slim distinction and ultimately one that separates the couple due to their contradictory responses to the disaster: The only thing Hans wants is Rachel and Jake, and the only thing Rachel wants is to run away. Separated from his family, Hans essentially shuts down and wanders through the next year of his life.

However, while Hans pines for what he has lost, he meets Chuck, a Trinidadian immigrant who has a dream of opening a cricket arena in New York. They are drawn together by their love of cricket and Chuck's forceful personality. Hans speaks of cricket with a longing and love he usually reserves for his young son. He had played for a local club in The Hague from the time he was seven years old, and by chance he is invited by a cabdriver to play with a Staten Island team. Through cricket, Hans meets Chuck and the other side of New York, far from his Wall Street office. Usually the only white man on the team, Hans plays with primarily West Indians and Asians. They play a slightly different type of cricket, adapted to the inferior fields on which they are forced to play. Although Hans initially resists the change, soon he becomes more comfortable with his fellow cricket players than with his coworkers at his bank.

Chuck loves his adopted country and is given to long, unironic speeches about the United States and freedom. Hans has to check regularly to ascertain if Chuck is joking, though he usually is not. In response to a speech about the nobility of the eagle versus the turkey, Hans says, "From time to time, Chuck actually spoke like this." Chuck and Hans spend time together as Chuck teaches Hans to drive and lets Hans drive him to his various business locations. In addition, they spend time together tending the grounds on the field Chuck has purchased for his cricket arena.

Hans's emotional distance during this time becomes clear only later, when he describes some of his work for Chuck to Rachel. He explains a time when he dropped off Chuck at a location and later saw a man there beaten up and his office overturned. Rachel is appalled, and particularly so when she realizes Hans continued to spend time with Chuck after this potentially dangerous occurrence. Hans, however, cannot understand why Rachel finds this to be a problem as he experienced only minor uneasiness at the time.

Chuck also has wide-ranging business interests, including the running of a numbers game. He works with Mike Abelsky, a shady Russian immigrant. In both cases, it is difficult to tell if Chuck and Mike are truly involved in dangerous pursuits, or if they are relatively harmless. There are clues that others, and perhaps Hans, see Chuck as a ridiculous character with grand ideas not based in reality. However, since the book begins with the discovery of Chuck's body, a thread of tension about Chuck's "work" and his friends runs through the book, introducing an element of danger to Hans's world. Hans sees Chuck for the last time at the Macy's Thanksgiving Day Parade when Hans and Chuck's mistress, Eliza, lose him in the crowd. Two years later, when Hans hears of the discovery of Chuck's body, it becomes clear Chuck was murdered not long after this encounter. However, this tension dissipates with Hans's return to London and his inability to look into Chuck's death from abroad.

Hans's failure to act and his unwillingness to change his situation can be both frustrating and heartbreaking. "Night after night" Hans gets on the computer and uses Google Earth to fly from New York City to London to see his son's dormer window, but, he notes, with "no way to see more, or deeper. I was stuck." At the same time, his memories of his life with Rachel prior to 9/11 are of a cold wife who withheld love and emotional support, even at the time of the death of Hans's mother. Rachel's conflict, as reflected through Hans, seems to be of a woman who has fallen out of love with her husband. However, Rachel's character is also portrayed as somewhat condescending and cruel. While Hans claims to love her, he seems unsympathetic to her concerns and her reasons for withholding love. He acknowledges his own distance after the death of his mother, but he denies a link between that and the failure of his marriage. Their relationship, though repaired by the end of the novel, seems fragile and unstable. It is difficult to know what deep fissures remain in the structure of their marriage and whether the two will be able to regain a degree of normalcy in their lives.

Netherland is a beautifully written book with detailed descriptions of The Hague, New York, and cricket. O'Neill's contemplations on love and family are ultimately redeeming if difficult. The novel, however, is driven by character, not plot, and the main character is forever stuck, unable to move forward or backward, trapped within his consciousness and malaise. Indeed, this sense of paralysis ultimately and ironically makes the book compelling. It seems O'Neill's intent in *Netherland* is to illustrate how monumental catastrophe plays out in individual lives. In the postdisaster confusion, the characters are frozen in their incapacity to make right what has been irrevocably changed.

Kathryn E. Fort

Review Sources

Booklist 104, no. 16 (April 15, 2008): 26.
The Daily Telegraph, May 24, 2008, p. 26.
Kirkus Reviews 76, no. 6 (March 15, 2008): 265.
Library Journal 133, no. 9 (May 15, 2008): 93.
London Review of Books 30, no. 14 (July 17, 2008): 20-22.
Los Angeles Times, May 27, 2008, p. E1.
The New York Review of Books 55, no. 14 (September 25, 2008): 54-56.
The New York Times Book Review, May 18, 2008, p. 1.
The New Yorker 84, no. 15 (May 26, 2008): 78-81.
The Observer, June 1, 2008, p. 19.
Publishers Weekly 255, no. 9 (March 3, 2008): 28.
The Washington Post Book World, June 1, 2008, p. BW06.

NEW COLLECTED POEMS

Author: Eavan Boland (1944-   )
First published: 2006, in Great Britain
Publisher: W. W. Norton (New York). 320 pp. $27.95
Type of work: Poetry

An inclusive edition of Boland's poetry, containing all the poems in nine previous volumes, reversing exclusions from the Selected Poems, *adding two books that were not included in an earlier* Collected Poems, *and containing a brief excerpt from an unpublished verse play*

The title of Eavan Boland's *New Collected Poems* is particularly appropriate for a poet whose work has continued to evolve so that each edition as it was published was a commentary on previous work, as well as an expression of her most current sense of herself as an Irishwoman writing poetry. Boland was born in 1944; her mother was an artist, and her father was an Irish diplomat assigned to various locations outside their home country. Her education was essentially traditional, so that her initial idea of poetic form was built on the model of European and British writers. Her early work was admired for Boland's ability to use these forms with competence and to find subjects suitable for a poet working in a familiar tradition. One of her most celebrated poems from this time was "The War Horse," the title poem of a collection published in 1975. The poem is written in rhyming couplets, all the lines beginning with capital letters, the horse a symbol of mindless destruction:

> He stumbles on like a rumour of war, huge,
> Threatening; neighbours use the subterfuge
>
> Of curtains; he stumbles down our short street
> Thankfully passing us. I pause, wait,
>
> Then to breathe relief lean on the sill
> And for a second only my blood is still

The slant rhymes are small variants, acceptable alterations within a standard structure. The central image is of some uncontrollable force disturbing the community as sectarian violence in the United Kingdom casts Northern Ireland and England in tableaux of strife that the poet observes with a wary trepidation.

For Boland, this mode, which earned her considerable praise, became progressively unsatisfactory. "There was a nineteenth century shadow on the poetry world when I first knew it," she recalled, "a certain kind of well-structured poem was around me in the air." She understood the necessity for mastering the requirements of this kind of poem, and her early work was evidence of her skills. Then, in 1985, in a striking declaration of poetic purpose that she called "Writing the Political Poem in Ireland," she identified her problem with the kind of poetry she was writing by asserting, "For a long time Irish poetry kept an almost nineteenth century order" wherein "there was an apparent decorum about it all" that signified a consensus rarely challenged. Boland had reached a point where the idea of the feminine in Irish poetry, "the nationalization of the feminine, the feminization of the national," required the kind of scrutiny that would permit the "woman poet in Ireland" to move "from being the object of Irish poetry to being its author." This startling, unexpected reversal and expansion "had caused real disruption," she felt, and in spite of her previous successes, she was ready to employ it as the dominant element of her own poetic practice.

Eavan Boland is director of the Creative Writing Program at Stanford University and the author of ten volumes of poetry and a collection of essays. Her work has been chosen for a Lannan Foundation Poetry Award and an American Ireland Fund Literary Award.

From then on, her work continued to evolve in three specific areas—subject, style, and structure. In addition to an active engagement with the accelerating political transformation of Irish life in the latter decades of the twentieth century, Boland wanted to write from her location as a mother raising two young children in a suburb of Dublin, to "find a private history within the public one"—a direct echo of one of Virginia Woolf's notable intentions. This required the development of a voice that had no precedent in Irish poetry, but that was also beginning to emerge—given the individual qualities of her contemporaries Nuala Ní Dhomhnaill and Medbh McGuckian— as more than an isolated instance and as a part of a growing awareness of Ireland becoming an integral state in modern Europe. To register her "voice" as an authentic instrument of this culture, the measured rhetoric of her earlier poems was replaced by versions of the vernacular and by less conventional, more inventive structural arrangements. Boland anticipated this in "The Muse Mother" from *Night Feed* (1982), in which she sees from her window "a woman hunkering—/ her busy hand/ worrying a child's face." The poet is aware of her separation from something fundamental that she misses as "my mind stays fixed." She imagines a connection with the woman on "this rainy street" who "might teach me/ a new language" so that the poet would be "able to speak at last/ my mother tongue."

The multiple meaning implicit in the classic formulation "mother tongue" suggests the task she had set for herself: how to speak for and from a distinct cultural location, with a language that she must fashion capable of conveying her immediate, personal experience as an Irishwoman with two young children living at the turn to the twenty-first century. A crucial component of this undertaking was her understanding that language and form are linked in ways that demand attention to both simultaneously, the kind of composition that American poets since Charles Olson have regarded as basic to their craft. "I sought out American poetry because of that powerful, inclusive diversity," Boland observed, although this was complicated by her relationship to Irish history and its rendering in some powerful and memorable poetry, as indicated by her acknowledgement of W. B. Yeats in what might seem an almost compulsory quote preceding the early volume *New Territory* (1967). As one of Boland's most perceptive critics, Pilar Vellas-Argaiz, has put it, a central concern for Boland "has been to unearth the untold horrors of Irish history, to retell in a more accurate way the true stories of the famine, of suppression and suffering, without romanticizing them any further." Boland's recent volumes, according to Vellas-Argaiz, dwell "more on rootlessness and non-identity than on the formation of a centered grounded self" so that the poet's later work is characterized by "a context of fluidity and dissolution" that has become her way of expressing her Irishness, while also exploring the meaning of Irishness. Boland has said, "Poetry begins—as all art does—where certainties end," accounting for the shift from fixed forms and established tropes to a place where "imagination is rooted: in ambiguities and darkness." This position has enabled Boland to overcome an earlier concern that she was "doubly oppressed" as a woman writing poetry in Ireland, dealing with "a heroic tradition on which it was difficult to write your name" amid poems in which women were "passive objects or decorative emblems."

Boland's differing approaches to the river Liffey, its uses by James Joyce in *Finnegans Wake* (1939) looming over everything following, and its symbolic essence as feminine life force and emblem deeply embedded in Irish culture is indicative of her poetic development. Boland has "retrieved two poems from *23 Poems*, a chapbook which came out in 1962 when I was eighteen" for the *New Collected Poems*. The poems are "Liffeytown"—a local term for Dublin—and "The Liffey Beyond Islandbridge." The first is a lyric paen to homeground, with a wistful folkloric chorus, "O swan by swan my heart goes down/ Through Dublin town, through Dublin town," while the second is a young person's celebration of a cheerful riverscape, until a prospect for a future "Further beyond the river bend/ Are spaces teemed with cities which must/ Strike a destiny" arises and then recedes in the poet's view. The Liffey here is a comforting, placid presence, alive with inviting associations. The third section of *In a Time of Violence* (1994) is named "Anna Liffey," a longer poem covering pages 230 to 235. The river is no longer a mystic flow rife with historic implications. Now, the river-spirit is alive and addressable, recalled from legend:

> *Life*, the story goes,
> Was the daughter of Cannan,
> And came to the plain of Kildare.
> She loved the flat-lands and the ditches
> And the unreachable horizon.
> She asked that it be named for her.
> The river took its name from the land.
> The land took its name from a woman.

The poet, like the woman-river, is engaged in the process of naming, a basic of poetic functions reaching to the dawn of time. Boland makes the connection between the poet and the river-spirit tangible, asserting in the second stanza: "A woman in the doorway of a home./ A woman in the city of her birth./ There, in the hills above my house./ A river in the city of her birth." The image of the woman is a tonal complement to Adrienne Rich's poem about the astronomer Carolyn Herschel, "Planetarium," from *The Will to Change* (1971)—"A woman in the shape of a monster./ a monster in the shape of a woman"—which depicts a woman seen as a threat to male prerogatives, likened to mythical monsters as in male-drawn constellations. Boland is establishing an identity with other pioneers who were not confined to traditional boundaries restricting women scientists and artists, her fusion with the river-spirit like an invocation to the muses:

> Maker of
> Places, remembrances
> Narrate such fragments for me:
>
> One body. One spirit.
> One place. One name.
> The city where I was born.
> The river that runs through it.

Just as Yeats wrote himself into the history of a nation during its creation in "Easter, 1916," Boland is prepared to see herself "Becoming a figure in a poem," an audacious assertion that the poem itself must substantiate.

The last section of the poem is less a conclusion than a summarizing of circumstances. "In the end/ It will not matter/ That I was a woman," Boland states, implying that the poetry may endure, just as the image in the sky fixed by human mapping remains beyond its individual origins. In a paradoxical proposition, Boland says that "When language cannot do it for us," there are still "these phrases/ Of the ocean/ To console us." The limits of language are evident, and yet the entire universe for humans is apprehended through the means of language. Her conclusion, "I was a voice," is like an acceptance of restriction while proclaiming the value of intention.

Although it is not so dramatic a transposition as to describe Boland's poetry following "Anna Liffey" as radically different, there was a liberation that permits Boland to continue in modes that are not predictable from the early books. The last two books in *New Collected Poems*, *The Lost Land* (1998) and *Against Love Poetry* (2001) are marked by a continuing reduction of conventional rhetorical devices, by an inquiry about the lingering effects of a colonial condition, and by a further exploration of individual and national identity. Anna Liffey reappears at times, an "Emblem of this old,/ torn and traded city" in "The Scar" (from the first section, "Colony," of *The Lost Land*) whom the poet addresses almost as a sister, "One flawed head towards another." The idea of a mother tongue is explored in the title poem of *The Lost Land* and in "Mother Ireland" (on facing pages) where motherhood ("I have two daughters") implies caring, as well as a desire to be cared for as a child of the city. Her facility with a lyric is apparent in "The Proof That Plato Was Wrong," where a succession of images in a surge of rhythmic expression serves as a reminder for those who have "forgotten what/ song is":

> I have come here
> to find courage in
>   the way this dawn
> reaches slowly down
>   the canal and reveals
> a drowned summer
>   which is almost over.

The title *Against Love Poetry* is meant to be provocative, an "argument with traditional or conventional love poetry," Boland explained, saying she wanted to get at "the stoicism of dailyness." The eleven-poem sequence called "Marriage" includes the book's title poem, composed in the form of a compact paragraph, beginning "We were married in summer, thirty years ago. I have loved/ you deeply from that moment to this," and continuing in similarly direct, crisp "sentences" not set apart as "lines." The block of print enhances the intensity of the thought and feeling and poses as its central query the conundrum that the deep love for her husband does not contradict the fact that "marriage is not freedom." This sets the tone of the sequence, an investigation that does not diminish the value of her marriage. The final poem, "Lines for a Thirtieth Wedding Anniversary," regathers the sources of deep love epitomized as "All those years, all those years together," and concludes "through it all/ this constancy: what wears, what endures." It might stand as a motto for Boland as well as for her commitment to her craft, and it posits a direction for poems still to come. Due to publishing requirements, *New Collected Poems* does not include her volume *Domestic Violence* (2007), which shows Boland sustaining the strengths of her later work and offers a promise of the value of the next edition of collected poems that will continue to extend and expand what is already a distinguished and important achievement.

Leon Lewis

Review Sources

Booklist 104, no. 13 (March 1, 2008): 44.
Poetry 193, no. 2 (November, 2008): 149.
Publishers Weekly 255, no. 3 (January 21, 2008): 156.
The Times Literary Supplement, October 27, 2006, p. 24.

1948
The First Arab-Israeli War

Author: Benny Morris (1948-   )
Publisher: Yale University Press (New Haven, Conn.).
   524 pp. $32.50
Type of work: History
Time: 1947-1948
Locale: Middle East (Palestine/Israel)

Considered by some as a "revisionist" historian, Morris addresses both the military conflict that followed the declaration of the State of Israel and the underlying politics driving both the Jewish and Arab antagonists

Principal personages:
   DAVID BEN-GURION, first prime minister of
      the State of Israel
   YIGAL ALLON, one of the founders of Israeli forces and primary
      commander in 1948
   ABDULLAH IBN HUSSEIN, king of Transjordan
   JOHN GLUBB, British general and commander of the Arab Legion
   FAROUK I, king of Egypt
   YITZHAK RABIN, operations officer for Israeli forces
   MOSHE SHARETT, Israeli foreign minister
   YIGAEL YADIN, Israeli commander
   CHAIM WEIZMANN, first president of Israel

The end of World War II in Europe in May, 1945, brought the full extent of the Holocaust to the attention of the world. Some six million Jews had perished at the hands of the Nazis. In the aftermath, as Benny Morris relates in *1948*, the concept of a Jewish homeland in the Middle East, originating with the Balfour Declaration by British foreign secretary Arthur Balfour in 1917 and envisioned by a generation of European Jews, found international support with the United Nations Partition Resolution on November 29, 1947. Palestine was still under British control, the result of a post-World War I mandate, but as events unfolded the British increasingly desired to simply vacate the region.

Both Jews and Arabs had their own claims on Palestine. For the Jews the land represented their national homeland. More immediately, it represented the land to which survivors and displaced persons could emigrate after the war. Certainly no country, even the United States, showed any desire to incorporate hundreds of thousands of European Jews. Both the Franklin Roosevelt administration and that of Harry Truman initially avoided any strong support for the Jews. However, as the level of events in Europe became known, Truman modified his views to one of support for the resettling of displaced Jews into Palestine.

~

Benny Morris is a professor of history at Ben-Gurion University in Israel. In addition to contributions to numerous literary publications, Morris has written The Birth of the Palestinian Refugee Problem *(1989),* Israel's Border Wars, 1949-1956 *(1997),* Righteous Victims: A History of the Zionist-Arab Conflict, 1881-2001 *(2001),* The Birth of the Palestinian Refugee Problem Revisited *(2004), and* Making Israel *(2007).*

~

Arab support for the Allied armies had been minimal. At most, some six thousand had fought with the Allies, and many of those had deserted. Political support among the Arabs for the Allied cause grew only with the recognition of who the victors would be. In contrast, more than thirty thousand Palestinian Jews fought with the British army. The disparity in land was equally glaring. The five Arab countries in the Middle East encompassed more than one million square miles; the British mandate of Palestine included approximately 10,500 square miles and a population of approximately 1.6 million, two-thirds of whom were Arabs, at the end of the war.

Numerous books have been written on the subject of the 1948 Israeli War of Independence, or *nakba* (catastrophe) as it has been called by their Arabic adversaries. Most of this material has been written from the perspective of the victorious Israelis, with an obvious, if not unexpected, bias. In part this has been the result of the availability of primary sources: Israeli sources have been readily accessible, while Arabic sources have been limited. Those sources, which are believed to exist in Egypt or Syria, remain largely inaccessible.

Morris divides the period between the earliest Jewish settlements (circa 1915) and the war of independence into three parts. The first, titled "Staking Claims," provides the background to the conflict during the period from the end of the war until the U. N. vote on partition in November, 1947. The Israeli nascent defense forces consisted of the Haganah, the paramilitary defense force, and the Irgun Zvai Leumi, the National Military Organization that evolved into a more or less terrorist organization often at odds with the Haganah. For the Arabs, the British support for pan-Arab unity resulted in the formation of a League of Independent Arab States, signed in a seven-nation pact in March, 1945. Among the demands of the Arab League was the cessation of further Jewish immigration into Palestine and the establishment of an independent state of Palestine.

The second portion of Morris's account covers the civil war that ensued between the Arabs and Jews in the aftermath of the vote on partition in November, 1947, and lasting until the Israeli formal declaration of independence in May, 1948. Caught in the middle were the British occupying forces. The theoretical disparity in potential forces among the adversaries was most apparent during this period. The Arabs had a combined population of some forty million, while the nascent Jewish state had a population of fewer than seven hundred thousand. The numbers were misleading. Not least among the Arab difficulties was the lack of any central command structure. During this period of civil war, volunteers from a number of the Arab states formed the Arab Liberation Army (ALA), a force of between four and five thousand men led by a mix of retired officers from their respective states. Much of the Arab military, however, consisted of local militias raised by isolated villages. Weapons were often obsolete, and often these villages were as willing to help the Jews, in expectation of whom the victors would be, as they were to join their Arab brethren.

Israel declared its independence on May 14, 1948, the declaration being read at four in the afternoon by David Ben-Gurion, who would become the state's first prime minister. Minutes later Truman announced the recognition of the state. The Pan-Arab invasion that followed constitutes the third and largest portion of this book. Morris attempts to "read" the Arab mind through a combination of first-person Arab accounts in this period and his interpretation of policy and military decisions that subsequently took place. To his credit, Morris has attempted to be evenhanded, and he is in no small part handicapped by limited Arab sources.

For all of their bluster, the Arab armies were largely unprepared for the war that followed. As Morris points out, a portion of the dilemma lay in the roles played by the British and the French in the region. Arab armies were useful in maintaining internal order, but they were not meant to serve as a military force. This changed with the beginning of the Cold War, when both the British and the French began a modernization of those armies as a bulwark against Soviet forces.

The invasion in anticipation of declaration of the Jewish state was approved at the end of April. The initial plan was limited in scope: an attack in the eastern Galilee. However, as Morris points out, the greatest handicap to the Arab armies was a lack of central command or a semblance of unity. At the last moment, Lebanon in the north declined to participate, and both the Syrian and Egyptian invasion plans were changed. Abdullah, king of Transjordan, had little adherence to his Arab allies. The goal of his army was to take the western bank of the Jordan. As pointed out by Morris, Abdullah was arguably the most reasonable of the Arab leaders. In November, 1947, he met secretly with Golda Meir, future Israeli prime minister and at the time acting head of the Jewish Agency Political Department, and he met again with her the following May. Abdullah would likely have been satisfied with some form of de facto partition, similar to that agreed upon by the United Nations, for the region, and he had reluctantly participated in the war. Abdullah was certainly not "pro-Jewish," by any stretch of the imagination; he had been among the most vocal critics of any nascent Jewish state. However, Abdullah was also a realist who recognized the Jews could quickly evolve into an effective fighting force, while Arab armies would remain divided. His willingness to negotiate with representatives of the Jewish state would cost him his life several years later.

Morris attempts to provide a balanced account of the struggle that began with the Arab invasion of the new state. He begins with an assessment of the two sides: the Arabs holding the initiative and, at least in the beginning, the larger force as well as heavier weapons. Further, much of the high ground was Arab territory. The Haganah, the Jewish force, fighting largely on interior lines—albeit often surrounded—had greater motivation and, with a cadre of war veterans, was often better trained and led. The role played by Ben-Gurion is clearly pointed out in Morris's account. Unification and training of the army began well in advance of independence. Between the end of 1947 and independence in May, 1948, the number of full-time soldiers was expanded from two thousand to more than sixty thousand. By then known as the Israel Defense Forces (IDF), it incorporated not only the fighting force of the Palmach but also the Irgun, and, more important, it was organized under a unified general staff and a command structure of a modern army. At the same time, an effort was made on an international scale to obtain the weaponry, equipment, and airplanes necessary to defend Israel. The effort, obviously opposed by the Arab states, had to take place in the face of the British, who were opposed to the arming of the new state as well. As noted by Morris, by the end of the fighting, the Haganah outnumbered the Arab forces.

The vastly outnumbered forces fighting to establish a Jewish state is not the only historical myth addressed in this book. Each side has its own stories of the massacre of civilians as well as of captured fighters, the Arabs describing the killing at Deir Yassin near Jerusalem in April, 1947, as a massacre, and the Israelis likewise reporting the killing of Jewish prisoners and civilians during the course of the fighting. Morris is evenhanded in his approach to this sensitive topic. Events that took place at Deir Yassin continue to reverberate decades later. The British and Arab estimate that upward of 250 villagers had been murdered was significantly inflated; the actual number was probably around a hundred. Nonetheless, the incident remains an atrocity, even at the lower number. Morris notes the long-term significance of the murders was its effect on the Arab population at large. Arab villagers were panicked, fleeing from areas which in the partition were meant to remain in Arab hands. Further, the accounts of events at Deir Yassin resulted in similar reprisals from Arab forces; shortly afterward, a ten-vehicle convoy of Jewish nurses and doctors traveling to Hadassah Hospital was ambushed. The British refused to intervene, and nearly eighty people were murdered, many burned alive.

These events were more the exception than commonplace during the fighting. Morris suggests several reasons for this. First, the opportunity for indiscriminate killing on the part of the Arabs was probably limited, since most villages had been overrun by Jewish fighters early in the conflict; more Arabs were probably killed by Jewish fighters than the reverse. Second was the nature of the soldiers themselves. During the civil war portion of the fighting—pre-May, 1948—few prisoners were taken by either side. Morris notes only two "true" Arab massacres: forty workers at a Haifa oil refinery, and 150 unarmed Haganah fighters at Kfar Etzion. However, as Jewish militias were replaced by the IDF, and the Arab armies were being manned by regular, disciplined soldiers, killing of civilians and prisoners became less common.

Morris concludes *1948* with an extensive summary of the war. The Jewish fighters were indeed outnumbered, at least at the outset. However, their war aims were simpler: to survive. As the war progressed, the burgeoning Jewish state began to expand beyond the boundaries set by the United Nations in the vote for partition. The Arab armies, meanwhile, remained divided, with no true central command. Morris points out the failure of the Palestinians to acknowledge their defeat by this "ragtag Jewish militia." Could things have been different? For decades prior to 1948, Arab leaders refused any form of territorial compromise. Jewish settlements captured during the civil war were routinely destroyed, the Jewish inhabitants expelled. Whichever side one supports, and arguments can be made for both, the events of 1948 continue to have an impact generations later.

Richard Adler

Review Sources

The Chronicle of Higher Education 54 (May 16, 2008): B6.
Foreign Affairs 87, no. 5 (September/October, 2008): 148-156.
History Today 58, no. 7 (July, 2008): 64.
Journal of Military History 72 (July, 2008): 978.
Library Journal 133, no. 6 (April 1, 2008): 94.
The New York Times Book Review, May 4, 2008, p. 19.
The New Yorker 84, no. 12 (May 5, 2008): 72-77.
Publishers Weekly, May 9, 2008.
The Times Literary Supplement, June 20, 2008, p. 25.

NIXONLAND
The Rise of a President and the Fracturing of America

Author: Rick Perlstein (1969-   )
Publisher: Scribner (New York). 881 pp. $37.50
Type of work: History
Time: 1965-1972
Locale: The United States

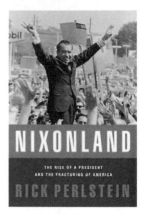

An insightful examination of forces that polarized America, commencing with the mid-1960's urban riots and the escalation of the war in Vietnam, making possible the amazing political comeback of cunning, tormented Richard M. Nixon and culminating in his 1972 landslide reelection victory

Principal personages:
RICHARD M. NIXON, thirty-seventh
    president of the United States
SPIRO T. AGNEW, Nixon's vice president
HUBERT H. HUMPHREY, Democratic candidate for president in 1968
GEORGE MCGOVERN, Democratic candidate for president in 1972
RONALD REAGAN, governor of California

"This country is going so far to the right you are not even going to recognize it," attorney general John Mitchell uttered in 1970 at a party while drunk. A sequel, in a sense, to the author's earlier book, *Before the Storm: Barry Goldwater and the Unmaking of the American Consensus* (2001), this harrowing tale examines the causes of the late-1960's conservative revival foreshadowing the "Reagan Revolution" of the 1980's. Perlstein focuses on so-called swing voters "who, in 1964, pulled the lever for the Democrat for president because to do anything else, at least that particular Tuesday in November, seemed to court civilized chaos, and who, eight years later, pulled the lever for the Republican for exactly the same reason." Few would have foreseen that the Watts ghetto in Los Angeles would go up in flames just days after Congress passed the 1965 Voting Rights Act, or that President Lyndon B. Johnson would escalate "that bitch of a war," as he called it, in the jungles of Southeast Asia. Poised to profit from the resultant "backlash" was an unlovable two-time loser (the presidency in 1960, the California governorship in 1962) nicknamed "Tricky Dick." Languishing in a New York law firm, Richard Milhous Nixon confided to partner Leonard Garment that he'd do anything to become president "except see a shrink."

The son of an Irishman who felt the world had it in for him, Nixon resented bluebloods and pretty boys who played by a different set of rules than outsiders such as himself. At Whittier College in California, the in-crowd belonged to the Franklins. Nixon started a rival club of strivers and commuter students, the Orthogonians (square shooters). He got elected student body president by promising to repeal a

campus ban on dancing. At Duke University
in North Carolina, the dogged law student,
nicknamed "Iron Butt" for putting in long,
uninterrupted hours at the library, graduated
third in his class. Even so, establishment law
firms spurned him. No connections. Ditto the
Federal Bureau of Investigation. In the Navy
his patience paid dividends in barracks poker
marathons. Running for Congress in 1946,
Nixon labeled the voting record of opponent
Horace J. "Jerry" Voorhis "more Socialistic and Communistic than Democratic." He
dogged the heels of former New Dealer and State Department official Alger Hiss during House Committee on Un-American Activities hearings until he tripped up the su-
percilious witness. Nixon employed "hardball" smear tactics his entire career. His
1950 Senate campaign literature included a pink-colored sheet that branded opponent
Helen Gahagan Douglas the "Pink Lady," right down to her underwear. Relishing the
role of hatchet man as Dwight D. "Ike" Eisenhower's 1952 running mate, he charged
Ike's rival Adlai E. Stevenson with being a graduate of the "College of Cowardly
Communist Containment." His aggrieved Orthogonian sensibility, an admixture of
rage and piety, carried him to within a heartbeat of the presidency by age forty.

A University of Chicago graduate and authority on how American politics came to be fractured in the 1960's, Rick Perlstein has written for The Village Voice *and* The New Republic *and is a Senior Fellow at the Campaign for America's Future.*

Liberal Harvard economist and Stevenson speechwriter John Kenneth Galbraith
coined the word "Nixonland" to describe "a land of slander and scare; the land of sly
innuendo, the poison pen, the anonymous phone call and hustling, pushing, shoving;
the land of smash and grab and anything to win." In 1960, however, it was the Democrats, particularly in the Windy City of Chicago and in Texas hill country, who used
fraudulent practices to deny Nixon the presidency. Two years later, blaming a loss to
California Governor Edmund "Pat" Brown on a biased fourth estate, he petulantly renounced elective politics. Not for long, however; it was too much in his blood. By
1964 he was maneuvering to accept a party draft in the event Goldwater's bid fizzled.
In 1966, after Reagan defeated Brown, Nixon advised the California governor-elect
to foreswear running for president two years hence. The former actor slyly demurred.
Leading up to the 1968 primary season, Nixon benefited from Michigan Governor
George Romney's naïve claim to have been brainwashed during a trip to South Vietnam and New York Governor Nelson Rockefeller's indecisiveness over throwing his
hat into the ring. To prevent Southern delegates from defecting to favorite son Rea-
gan, whom most preferred, Nixon promised racist Senator Strom Thurmond of South
Carolina that he'd tolerate all-white schools and place "strict constructionists" on the
Supreme Court. Enhancing Republican prospects exponentially were Robert F. Kennedy's violent death and Democratic convention turbulence in the streets of Mayor
Richard R. Daley's Chicago. Leaving nothing to chance, Nixon attempted to sabotage
the Paris peace talks through intermediary Anna Chennault. It wasn't necessary.
Johnson had no plans for an "October surprise" to end the war, having lost respect for
his vice president, who he said cried too much and whose pecker, he bragged, was in
his pocket. Johnson and Nixon, Perlstein writes, "shared a need to humiliate, but a

horror of being humiliated—and that nagging sense that the worst humiliations always, *always*, came at the hand of some damned Kennedy or another." This morbid insecurity festered even after Nixon reached the pinnacle of political success, as Watergate tapes attest.

Nixonland documents in chilling detail the widening racial rift that made the rest of the country more and more like the rebel South. Boston "Southies" defied the law, hoping to keep their schools all white. New York City Italian Americans formed SPONGE, the Society for the Prevention of Negroes Getting Everything. In New Mexico, vigilantes harassed "longhairs" and burned down hippie communes. Rogue cops in Newark and Detroit beat with impunity black people trapped in riot zones. The liberal press glamorized "Woodstock Nation" and the "New Morality"—*New York Times* film reviewer Renata Adler raved over *Wild in the Streets*, a 1968 farce about a rock star who becomes president and force-feeds everyone over thirty pills of LSD—but ignored the "blue collar" envy of privileged collegians and poked fun of "Decency" rallies attended by tens of thousands of "Middle Americans" in Miami, Cleveland, and Baltimore. Hundreds of New York City construction workers went on a rampage after Mayor John Lindsey ordered the flag lowered to half-staff in the wake of the Kent State killings. Nixon, who had recently called student protesters "bums," confided to an aide, "Thank God for the hard hats," and invited a delegation to the White House. Here was an opening to create a permanent Republican majority. Armed with the power of the Oval Office, he ordered aides, as he privately put it, to "get down to the nut-cutting."

In September, 1970, Vice President Spiro T. Agnew's alliterative-laced tirades charging media bias and questioning dissenters' patriotism signaled the most active White House off-year election since 1938, when Franklin D. Roosevelt had failed to purge Southern "Copperheads" from his party. Agnew told a partisan crowd: "We have more than our share of the nattering nabobs of negativism. They have formed their own 4-H Club—the hopeless, hysterical hypochondriacs of history." Utah's Frank Moss was "the Western regional champion of the Eastern establishment" and a friend of the "Spock-marked generation." Agnew compared liberal New York Senator Charles Goodell to sex-change celebrity Christine Jorgensen. Paid plants shouted obscenities at Republican rallies, red meat for the partisan faithful. Nixon passed the word: "If the vice president were slightly roughed up by those thugs, nothing better could happen for our cause. If anybody so much as brushes against Mrs. Agnew, tell her to fall down." In San Jose, California, the president leaped onto his limousine and flashed the "V" sign at protesters, afterward bragging, "That's what they hate to see." The only trouble was, with few exceptions (Tennessee's Albert Gore the most notable), Democrats targeted for defeat survived. The strategy backfired: "Mighty Spiro had struck out." Tired of overheated rhetoric, voters responded to chisel-faced Senator Edmund S. Muskie's telecast plea for reason and calm. Nixon became so paranoid about his reelection chances against Hubert Humphrey's 1968 running mate that he gave the green light to reckless criminal activities that derailed Muskie's subsequent presidential campaign but ultimately destroyed his own presidency and place in history.

Nixon took little interest in domestic policies—or, as he privately put it, "building outhouses in Peoria." Foreign affairs was the arena where he hoped to make his legacy. An advocate of secret diplomacy, he set out surreptitiously to normalize relations with China. As part of the complicated scenario to accomplish this laudable goal, Nixon cooperated with an autocratic Pakistani regime that slaughtered ten thousand civilians in Bangladesh. To his mind they were expendable. To facilitate the extrication of American troops from Vietnam, he authorized bombing missions into Laos, Cambodia, and North Vietnam that killed millions of civilians. An avid football fan who suggested plays to Washington Redskins coach George Allen, Nixon gloated after authorizing devastating air strikes code-named Operation Linebacker: "What distinguishes me from Johnson is that I have the will in spades." On election eve 1972, he declared: "The leaders in Hanoi will be watching . . . . Shall we have peace with honor or peace with surrender?" Earlier Nixon had persuaded Alabama demagogue George Wallace not to become a third party candidate by having federal tax fraud charges against his brother dropped. He successfully courted the crusty boss of the American Federation of Labor and Congress of Industrial Organizations, George Meany, who lamented that the Democratic Party had been taken over "by people named Jack who look like Jills and smell like johns." This comment is reminiscent of Reagan's definition of a hippie as someone "who dresses like Tarzan, has hair like Jane, and smells like Cheetah." Watergate operative G. Gordon Liddy even tried (unsuccessfully) to bug Democratic Party nominee George McGovern's campaign headquarters. After electronic expert James W. McCord was caught red-handed and provided Watergate Judge John Sirica with names of White House higher-ups as part of a plea bargain, Nixon railed that McCord must be a double agent. He always expected the worst from enemies. Though eschewing the GOP label during the campaign, he expressed amazement that "the coattail thing" hadn't worked. Republicans lost two Senate seats (down to forty-three) and only picked up a dozen in the House, where Democrats still dominated, 243 to 192. Gloomy despite carrying forty-nine states, Nixon would soon be facing scrutiny from hostile congressional investigative committees. The scandal known as Watergate encompassed multiple wrongdoings. Had it not been for a botched break-in at the Democratic National Headquarters, Nixon might have successfully covered up the crimes. His toxic legacy remains part of the American political landscape.

Perlstein's lively writing style brings to life an era that diminishing numbers of readers experienced firsthand. He acknowledges an intellectual debt to J. Anthony Lukas's *Nightmare: The Underside of the Nixon Years* (1976) and Paul Cowen's *Tribes of America: Journalistic Discoveries of Our People and Their Cultures* (1979). *Atlantic Monthly* reviewer Ross Douthat praised *Nixonland* for weaving social and political history into "a single seamless narrative, linking backroom political negotiations to suburban protests over sex education in schools to the premiere of *Bonnie and Clyde*" in 1967. *Commonweal*'s Melissa Mattes noted the "impressive knack for details—everything from the fire alarm set off by irate feminists at the 1972 Democratic convention that sent scantily clad *Playboy* bunnies onto the convention floor to the presidential commercials showing a blank page in Nixon's passport.

'There are still places to go,' it announced. 'Friends to be won. That's why we still need President Nixon. Now, more than ever.'"

James B. Lane

Review Sources

The American Spectator 41, no. 9 (November, 2008): 70-74.
The Atlantic Monthly 30, no. 4 (May, 2008): 83-86.
Booklist 104, no. 16 (April 15, 2008): 23.
Commonweal 135, no. 17 (October 10, 2008): 21-22.
The Economist 387 (May 10, 2008): 93-94.
Kirkus Reviews 76, no. 5 (March 1, 2008): 236.
The Nation 287, no. 6 (September 1-8, 2008): 39-44.
National Review 60, no. 11 (June 16, 2008): 49-53.
The New Republic 239, no. 4 (September 10, 2008): 16-23.
The New York Times Book Review, May 11, 2008, p. 1.
Newsweek 151, no. 20 (May 19, 2008): 48-50.
Publishers Weekly 255, no. 10 (March 10, 2008): 70.
The Wilson Quarterly 32, no. 3 (Summer, 2008): 98-99.

NOTHING TO BE FRIGHTENED OF

Author: Julian Barnes (1946-   )
Publisher: Alfred A. Knopf (New York). 244 pp. $24.95
Type of work: Memoir
Time: 1943 to the present
Locale: London and the United Kingdom

By embarking on a thoughtful journey through his family background and intellectual history, Barnes gradually zeroes in on the causes of his lifelong fear of what will happen when he dies

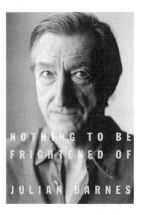

Principal personages:
    JULIAN BARNES, the author
    KATHLEEN MABEL BARNES, his mother, a
        vain, controlling woman
    ALBERT LEONARD BARNES, his father, a long-suffering schoolteacher
    JONATHAN BARNES, his older brother, a professional philosopher

Nothing to Be Frightened Of is a clever, learned, and at times somewhat repetitive exercise in whistling in the dark, as Julian Barnes gingerly creeps up on the fear of death that he admits provoked occasional anxiety in his younger years but has now become a serious preoccupation for this distinguished literary senior citizen. Born in 1946, Barnes has had a fruitful career as a writer of elegant fiction and ruminative essays, and he has not previously demonstrated any discernable tendency to balk at humanity's inexorable march toward the graveyard. Recently, however, his thoughts have turned to speculations as to what awaits on the other side of corporeal existence, and the result is a combination of essay and memoir that compulsively interrogates this question.

Barnes begins *Nothing to Be Frightened Of* jauntily enough by joking that "I don't believe in God, but I miss Him." This mildly flippant tone continues through the first of the book's several considerations of his family history, as he initially serves up a light, amusing sketch of his parents and their forebears that only occasionally foreshadows the darker reflections to come. His mother, an atheist, and his father, an agnostic, passed away in the modern, antiseptic surroundings of a residential home and a hospital, respectively, and as Barnes begins to think about how he will meet his death, it becomes clear that something about their manner of going deeply disturbs him.

The first step in what turns out to be an extended tour through Barnes's personal and intellectual history is an autobiographical reminiscence of his failure to develop any sort of religious faith, a perfectly understandable consequence of his parents' attitude toward religion. His mother, who claimed not to fear death, refused to have any of what she called "that mumbo-jumbo" at her completely secular funeral; his father, her henpecked and submissive husband, was so dominated by her that he seemed to

Julian Barnes has written ten novels, two short-story collections, and two collections of essays. He won the Somerset Maugham Award for his novel Metroland *(1981) and the Geoffrey Faber Memorial Prize for his novel* Flaubert's Parrot *(1984). In 2004, he won the Austrian State Prize for European Literature.*

have few views of any substance about anything, or at least none that his children could perceive. Even when Barnes went through his phase of adolescent rebellion, he had little against which to rebel, and so he came away with the impression that religion was a mildly foolish set of superstitions in which a few misguided people found consolation.

Although Barnes never puts it in quite such unequivocal terms, one senses that for the first time in his life he has begun to have doubts about being a doubter, and he is now troubled by the fact that, having never had faith, he can never return to it as a source of consolation. Deprived of confidence in a future life, he clearly feels a sense of urgency concerning the achievement of some sort of personal equilibrium—whether it be based on logic, conviction, or simply the opinions of respected authorities—that will enable him to conquer, or at least control, his anxiety regarding his existence after death.

Barnes's consequent search for peace of mind is conducted through a series of inquiries that, in an often repetitive manner that at times borders on the obsessive, engages with his favorite authors and his sole remaining close relative as the likeliest sources of meaningful answers to his queries. The relative in question is Barnes's brother Jonathan, an academic philosopher who, in the portrait on display here, impresses as a cold, unsympathetic, and on the whole extremely unsatisfactory source of spiritual comfort. His responses to his brother's requests for advice are unfailingly dismissive and at times contemptuous: Jonathan denies any knowledge of their parents' emotions, claims to be uninterested in (and therefore immune to) his own doctor's health warnings, and fobs Barnes off with injunctions to read Aristotle and David Hume when serious philosophical issues are raised. After several such interactions, one cannot help but wonder about the point of these humiliations. Is Barnes simply adding to the sense of dread that his inability to deal with death has engendered, or is he settling a fraternal score with a lifelong source of irritation? Whatever the answer, Jonathan is a strange and inexplicable presence in what purports to be a meditation on facing the threat of nonexistence—definitely "someone to be frightened of" rather than not.

Fortunately, for himself and his readers, Barnes's revisiting of the literary, philosophical, and religious texts that he has come to love offer a much more substantial gathering of advice to the lifelorn. His enjoyment and understanding of French literature, most prominently displayed in the wonderful fiction-based-on-fact *Flaubert's Parrot* (1984), is here enlisted in the service of his struggle against death. He finds particular solace in the writings of Jules Renard (1864-1910), a successful novelist whose journals chronicle a lifelong fascination with questions of mortality. Like Barnes, Renard was profoundly moved by the deaths of his parents; unlike Barnes, he seems to have achieved a stoic equilibrium that enabled him to consider nonexistence philosophically: "All I feel is a kind of anger at death and his imbecile tricks," he wrote, after his brother's sudden demise added to the catalog of the Renard family's sorrows.

A less prominent but still influential presence is that of the French novelist and short-story writer Alphonse Daudet (1840-1897), whose *La Doulou* (1930) Barnes translated in 2002 as *In the Land of Pain*. This book records Daudet's slow and, as noted by outside observers, agonizing death from tertiary syphilis, but it does so in an unemotional, objective, and at times even whimsical literary style that embraces death as a new territory to be explored with curiosity and wonder. Reflecting on Daudet's experience in *Nothing to Be Frightened Of*, Barnes admires the relative calm with which the French author passed away after fifteen years of excruciating suffering but finds himself unable to share such philosophical placidity. "I do not expect such luck, or such calmness," he concludes with regard to what he expects to undergo before death.

Such thoughts are repeated frequently throughout *Nothing to Be Frightened Of*, and one must admire Barnes for the honesty of his sentiments in a culture where narratives of heroic resistance to death and disease constitute the conventional wisdom as to how our extinction should be met. In acknowledging that from his point of view death certainly is something to be frightened of, he is performing a different sort of heroic act: showing the courage to confess feelings that the censorious and hypocritical will brand weak and cowardly, but which many others will welcome as an expression of solidarity with those who suspect that their body's demise marks the irreversible termination of their existence.

Nevertheless, Barnes is not one to accept such a gloomy prospect without exhausting all possible avenues of escape. Although *Nothing to Be Frightened Of* frequently cites, in addition to the authors already mentioned, relevant quotations from Gustave Flaubert, Michel de Montaigne, Somerset Maugham, and Émile Zola, this reliance on literary sources is punctuated with additional candid anecdotes drawn from Barnes's family history—for which his introductory sketches of his parents and brother have already prepared the reader—as well as personal reflections that meditate upon the meaning of it all. As far as the family-history passages are concerned, the circumstances under which his parents died return several times as part of the larger pattern of alternation and repetition that holds *Nothing to Be Frightened Of* together. Time and time again, Barnes adds new thoughts and observations as to the manner of their passing after intervals of concentrating upon the literary quotations and philosophical musings that constitute the other two main sources of the book's content, as he crafts a work whose unusual tripartite structure rejects the conventions of linear narrative.

As a result of this repetition and recycling, the sections of *Nothing to Be Frightened Of* that concern his parents are much more dramatically powerful than the literary and philosophical material that surrounds them, and so tend to cast the latter into the emotional shade. Almost halfway through the book, for example, Barnes describes in graphic detail the effects of the series of strokes that left his father, a French teacher, unable to communicate, and then he adds to the pathos of this account by depicting his mother's insensitive treatment of her husband as a kind of defective household appliance that had stopped working properly. Fifty pages later, after an intervening series of literary quotations and philosophical thoughts, he returns to the subject of his father's death in a harrowing passage that emphasizes both his mother's callousness and his father's frustration with his inexorable mental and physical breakdown; another fifty pages on, after more literary and philosophical interludes, Barnes relates his mother's death in a way that stresses his awkward inability to relate to her at the same time as it dwells on the bodily decline that turns a sentient human being into someone confused, frightened, and suspicious of even their loved ones.

It could be argued that the decision to present these moving accounts of parental decline and death separately makes sense in contrast to the opposing strategy of combining them into a longer and more coherent unit; they are, without question, the most affecting element in the tale Barnes has to tell, and dispersing them throughout the book provides the reader with periodic, and unpredictable, moments of compelling drama. On the other hand, this material is so much more engaging and absorbing than its literary and philosophical accompaniment that it emphasizes just how relatively ineffectual the latter is. It results in a narrative that offers occasional moments of riveting intensity parceled out among more distanced reflections that, although often elegantly written, must necessarily pale in comparison. There is a sense that Barnes has written three rather different books here, and there are quite a few moments when one wishes that his materials had been more coherently organized.

If *Nothing to Be Frightened Of* disappoints in terms of its consistency and its sometimes awkward transitions between different kinds of content, it still provides a frequently gripping and always fluently expressed collection of experiences and thoughts on a topic of presumably universal interest. Barnes has written an unusual, thoughtful, and often intriguing response to questions about death, and the reader hopes that he has sufficiently resolved his fears to return to the writing of fictions that engage with the entirety of the human spectrum.

Paul Stuewe

Review Sources

Booklist 104, no. 22 (August 1, 2008): 26.
The Boston Globe, August 31, 2008, p. C5.
The Guardian, March 8, 2008, p. 9.
Harper's Magazine 317 (October, 2008): 79.
JAMA: Journal of the American Medical Association 300, no. 12 (December 24, 2008): 2922-2923.
Kirkus Reviews 76, no. 12 (June 15, 2008): 93.

Los Angeles Times, September 29, p. E6.
New Statesman 137 (March 10, 2008): 56.
The New York Review of Books 55, no. 15 (October 9, 2008): 38-40.
The New York Times Book Review, October 5, 2008, p. 1.
Publishers Weekly 255, no. 28 (July 14, 2008): 56.
The Times Literary Supplement, March 28, 2008, p. 13.
The Washington Post Book World, August 31, 2008, p. BW10.

OLD WORLD, NEW WORLD
Great Britain and America from the Beginning

Author: Kathleen Burk (1946-   )
Publisher: Atlantic Monthly Press (New York). 797 pp.
   $35.00
Type of work: History
Time: 1497-2005
Locale: Mostly the area that is now the United States

A large and comprehensive narrative account of the cultural, economic, and diplomatic relations between Americans and the British, from John Cabot's explorations of North America of 1497 until the Iraq War of the early twenty-first century

With the contemporary emphasis on multiculturalism and on minority studies, it has become rather commonplace for academic historians and social scientists to denounce Eurocentric and Anglocentric perspectives. Increasingly, colleges and universities have replaced requirements in general American and European history with courses devoted to issues of race and ethnicity, often emphasizing the theme of "white privilege." This point of view has promoted a strong tendency to minimize, sometimes even to deny, the importance of the Anglo-American relationship and the influences of Britain on American civilization. In *Old World, New World*, Kathleen Burk reminds us that for hundreds of years Britain was the primary source of the nation's dominant culture and the model for its political institutions, as well as its most important trading partner and economic rival. Into the early twenty-first century, despite cultural differences and frequent disagreements, the two countries "were, nevertheless, more alike than any other two powers on the globe. And this instinctive feeling persists: there is a true love-hate Anglo-American special relationship."

Historical accounts of bilateral relations between two countries have often been rather dull, but this is certainly not true of Burk's lively written book. Based on fifteen years of teaching Anglo-American relations and more than seven years of research and writing, the book is filled with interesting details and hundreds of anecdotes. A partial list of notable topics includes the "lost colony" on Roanoke Island; the establishment of Virginia, Massachusetts, and other English colonies; the causes, battles, and outcome of the American Revolution; the War of 1812; disputes and agreements concerning the Canadian border; perceptions of British travelers in America; tensions that grew out of the U.S. Civil War; the Venezuelan Boundary Dispute; the Spanish-American War; the two world wars of the twentieth century; cooperation and conflict during the Cold War; and the various components of the contemporary war on terrorism. *Old World, New World* is a book that can be read with pleasure from cover to cover. In addition, it is also an excellent reference source for dependable and interesting summaries about particular topics.

When discussing the thirteen British colonies that became the United States, Burk emphasizes their great diversity in religion, economics, and geographical challenges. In spite of their diversity, however, she writes that they shared a number of things in common, including "an urgent and even reckless desire to own land." All the colonists, moreover, enjoyed the benefits of the British Constitution, which included the Bill of Rights of 1689, and they took pride in "being part of a liberal empire, one whose power and glory derived from those very liberties which the Americans claimed as part of their birthrights." Colonial charters typically promised that American settlers would "enjoy all liberties and immunities of free and natural Subjects . . . as if born within the Realm of England." The charters recognized their right to have elected assemblies with the power to enact their own laws and tax policies.

Born and raised in a California wine-making family, Kathleen Burk studied history at the University of California at Berkeley and at Oxford. Currently a professor of modern history at University College in London, she previously published several well-respected works, including Britain, America, and the Sinews of War, 1914-1918 *(1985) and* Troublemaker: The Life and History of A. J. P. Taylor *(2002).*

Readers might reasonably take issue with some of Burk's interpretations, such as her rather negative description of the Mayflower Compact of 1620. The Puritans affirmed that their purpose was the "advancement of the Christian faith" and "the honor of our King and country," and they promised to establish "just and equal laws, ordinances, acts, constitutions, and officers" that were to be "convenient for the general good of the colony." Burk denies that there was anything democratic about the Mayflower Compact. Rather, she writes that "the intention was to preserve authority in the hands of the self-chosen few. It was to be an oligarchy, not a democracy." Everyone will agree, no doubt, that the Puritans shared seventeenth century political notions, envisioning neither women's suffrage nor political participation by religious dissidents. Nevertheless, in view of the small number of voters in England at the time, it appears significant that forty-one of fifty-one male settlers signed the compact. Although vague about how the government would be organized, the wording of the compact appears to imply the idea of popular sovereignty, at least to some extent. There are, after all, degrees of democracy, and idealistic words, which are open to various interpretations, can have unexpected consequences for future generations.

Burk observes that the American Revolution has frequently served as an "American Foundation Myth," a story of bravery and a contest between tyranny and liberty. Like most contemporary historians, she acknowledges that the historical reality was "infinitely more complicated" than this. At the end of the Seven Years War in 1763, the British debt totaled 132.6 million pounds—requiring an annual interest of 5 million pounds—whereas the crown's annual income was only 8 million pounds. Since the burden on British taxpayers was already unacceptably high, it only seemed fair that the Americans "should contribute to their own defense." Following a series of conflicts over taxation, British officials were naturally angered by the destruction of property during the Boston Tea Party, and they were even more upset by their inability to find those responsible. The prime minister, Lord North, decided to use the event "to restore full authority in the colonies, because if they did not, this authority would continue to bleed away." Thus, he pushed Parliament to enact the so-called Coercive Acts of 1774, which were denounced as tyrannical measures in the Declaration of Independence.

Although Burk is careful not to express chauvinistic views, she acknowledges that there were democratic elements to the American Revolution. She points out, for instance, that the intent of parts of the Coercive Acts "was to curtail the more 'democratic' elements of New England government." An important difference between the British and the Americans, moreover, was the voting franchise. In eighteenth century Britain, only about 15 percent of adults were able to vote, compared with approximately 63 percent in America. Such structural differences in political systems were "fundamental to the growing conflict between the imperial center and its colonies." The greater opportunities of Americans to participate in government, no doubt, was one of the main reasons that the concept of "direct representation," reflected in the slogan "no taxation without representation," was taken so seriously by the colonists, whereas persons living in Britain were predisposed to be satisfied with the theory now called "virtual representation," meaning that the Parliament represented both voters and nonvoters alike. In summarizing why Americans declared independence, Burk succinctly writes: "Fundamentally, the war was fought over a constitutional issue: who was to control the American colonies, Parliament or the colonies' own legislative assembles?"

Following the war for independence, the Paris Treaty of 1783 "set the stage for a century of unfriendly and sometimes threatening relations." Although Jay's Treaty of 1794 was extremely unpopular, Burk defends U.S. negotiator John Jay for following instructions, for preventing an Anglo-American war in the short term, and for finally resolving the issues of the Western forts and the war debts. In interpreting the War of 1812, she asserts that U.S. leaders had two main objectives: first, to conquer Canada, and, second, to eliminate the power of the Indians to block western expansion. Although unable to take Canadian lands, the United States benefited from the Treaty of Ghent in 1814, "a remarkable achievement for the U.S., a country internally divided, militarily weak, and nearly bankrupt." Burk writes that the foreign minister at the time, Lord Castlereigh, was "the first British statesman to recognize that the friendship of the United States was a major asset to Britain." From the mid-1820's until the 1840's, the forces of Manifest Destiny resulted in considerable Anglo-American boundary disputes, but the two countries were eventually able to reach peaceful compromises on the Canadian boundaries as well as with Maine and the Western states.

Burk quotes David Reynolds's statement that Britain's "dominance of the world economy in the mid-nineteenth century was greater than that of the USA at its peak a century later." The country remained "the only true global power" until at least the 1890's. With 2 percent of world's population, it produced 20 percent of manufacturing output. However, the global balance of power was shifting westward. In 1895, when the United States supported Venezuela in its boundary dispute with British Guiana, Secretary of State Richard Olney sent a blistering note, asserting that "the United

States is practically sovereign on this continent," because "its infinite resources combined with its isolated position render it master of the situation and practically invulnerable as against any or all other powers." Like most historians, Burk believes that there never was an imminent threat of war in 1895. About this time, in fact, "the concept of the 'special relationship' was gradually developing, at least on the British side." American annexation of foreign colonies in the late nineteenth century helped popularize the concept of a common "Anglo-Saxon race," which sometimes was combined with the Social Darwinian concept of "survival of the fittest" to promote support for imperialism.

During many historical periods, the Anglo-American relationship has been influenced by the personal interactions of individual political leaders. During World War II, for instance, the close friendship between British prime minister Winston Churchill and U.S. president Franklin Roosevelt was significant to the formation of many important policies, including the wording of the Atlantic Charter, the creation of the Lend-Lease Act, and the founding of the United Nations. During the war, informed British leaders became conscious that their small country was no longer wealthy or powerful enough to defend its interests without allies. Part of their solution "was to try to co-opt American power, a policy which would continue after 1945." By the war's end, the United States had clearly emerged as "a global superpower of unparalleled wealth and strength."

Although Burk is moderately favorably toward Anglo-American policies during the Cold War, she writes that one unfortunate characteristic that the British passed on to the Americans was a sense of "self-righteousness," and that Americans' "conviction that they were the guardians of democracy entrenched the self-perception of righteousness." She views the Marshall Plan, nevertheless, as a success, allowing the United States to acquire "a reputation for a caring generosity which contributed substantially to its attractiveness for decades." During the difficult period of the 1950's, the British feared that U.S. policies in the Korean War could expand into a larger conflict, and they were also deeply offended by President Dwight Eisenhower's opposition to their use of force during the Suez Crisis. The Vietnam War was also a source of disagreement. In the 1980's, U.S. president Ronald Reagan and British prime minister Margaret Thatcher were "ideological soulmates," although the British public was generally hostile to Reagan's anti-Communist rhetoric and military buildup.

During the premiership of Anthony "Tony" Blair, from 1997 to 2007, the Anglo-American relationship was again at center stage in the international arena. Whereas his predecessor, John Major, wanted to stay out of the Balkan conflict, Blair formed a close alliance with U.S. president Bill Clinton and enthusiastically encouraged Clinton to bomb Kosovo and Serbia in the attempt to stop genocide against the Albanians of Kosovo. It was Blair who came up with a "doctrine of international community," holding that military intervention in other countries was justified when the goal was to stop genocide. Quoting several other writers, Burk argues, not entirely persuasively, that the bombing campaign was not decisive. More important than bombs, she asserts, the Anglo-American threats of sending ground troops into the region convinced Slobodan Milošević to negotiate a withdrawal from Kosovo.

Living in Britain during the presidency of George W. Bush, Burk saw firsthand the extent to which Blair's close relationship with Bush became extremely unpopular among the British public, resulting in his being ridiculed as "Bush's poodle." Although Blair's endorsement for the campaign against the radical Taliban and their allies in Afghanistan did not severely damage Blair's standing, his cooperation with Bush in the Iraq War was widely denounced in Britain as well as throughout Western Europe. Even though Blair remained loyal in his commitment to the war effort, Burk comments that the Bush-Blair "relationship was clouded by their differing approaches to foreign policy, in particular since Blair sometimes treated it as a moral issue."

Thomas Tandy Lewis

Review Sources

Booklist 105, no. 1 (September 1, 2008): 17.
Foreign Affairs 87, no. 6 (November/December, 2008): 164-165.
History Today 58, no. 9 (September, 2008): 66.
Kirkus Reviews 76, no. 15 (August 1, 2008): 118.
Library Journal 133, no. 15 (September 15, 2008): 67-68.
Political Quarterly 79 (July, 2008): 438-458.
Publishers Weekly 255, no. 29 (July 21, 2008): 153.
The Times Literary Supplement, March 21, 2008, p. 31.

OLIVE KITTERIDGE

Author: Elizabeth Strout (1956-   )
Publisher: Random House (New York). 288 pp. $25.00;
    paperback $14.00
Type of work: Novel, short fiction
Time: The late 1970's through the early 2000's
Locale: Crosby, Maine; New York City

*The title character, a prickly, outspoken woman, plays a
major role in this collection, which deals with the lives and
the relationships of the people who live in a small Maine
town*

Principal characters:
> OLIVE KITTERIDGE, a seventh-grade
>   mathematics teacher
> HENRY KITTERIDGE, her husband, a pharmacist
> CHRISTOPHER KITTERIDGE, their son, a podiatrist
> ANN KITTERIDGE, his second wife
> DENISE THIBODEAU, a cashier at Henry's pharmacy
> KEVIN COULSON, a young man formerly from Crosby
> ANGIE O'MEARA, a middle-aged woman and a piano player in a cocktail
>   lounge
> HARMON, the owner of a hardware store
> DAISY FOSTER, a widow and Harmon's mistress
> LOUISE LARKIN, a mentally ill woman and the mother of a murderer
> MARLENE BONNEY, the widow of a grocer
> JACK KENNISON, a widower and Olive's lover after Henry's death

The title character in Elizabeth Strout's novel *Olive Kitteridge* is not an altogether
likable person. As a widow in her seventies, Olive is just as difficult as she was three
decades earlier, when she terrorized her seventh-graders. During their long lifetime
together, she routinely opposed and criticized her kindly, long-suffering husband
Henry, and she effectively drove away their only child, Christopher. However, Olive
does elicit respect, if not always affection, from the other residents of Crosby, Maine,
for though she is tactless, she is incapable of pretense, and sometimes she can be surprisingly kind. In any case, Strout evidently realized that though Olive is a fascinating
character, a novel written entirely from her perspective would be difficult to read.
Wisely, the author chose to organize her work as a collection of connected short stories. In that way, she could avoid having the book dominated by Olive, and, by changing frequently from one point of view to another, she could present both the title character and the other people in her village from several different perspectives.

Thus the initial story, or chapter, is told not from Olive's point of view but from
that of Henry. As the title "Pharmacy" suggests, his work is of central importance
in Henry's life. As a pharmacist, he can help others, not only by carefully filling

~

Elizabeth Strout's first novel, Amy and Isabelle *(1999), won both the* Los Angeles Times *book award for first fiction and the* Chicago Tribune Heartland Prize. *Her second novel,* Abide with Me *(2006), was also a national best seller.*

~

their prescriptions but also by simply listening to them. Moreover, when he is at the pharmacy, he does not have to deal with Olive's fits of temperament or her gratuitous cruelty, which she displays in dozens of ways (for example, by stubbornly refusing to accompany him to church, despite the fact that he is embarrassed by her absence). Olive's comment about Henry's new clerk, Denise Thibodeau, is typical: The girl is unimpressive, Olive points out, and her posture is poor. When Henry invites Denise and her young husband over for dinner, Olive objects, and then, after Henry overrides her veto, she serves her guests nothing but a plateful of baked beans and a scoop of vanilla ice cream. However, Denise proves to be the bright spot in Henry's life. Though he is much too principled to be unfaithful to Olive, he commits a kind of adultery by letting thoughts of Denise occupy his mind, by having imaginary conversations with her, and even by pretending that it is Denise, not Olive, to whom he is making love. Then Denise's husband is accidentally killed, and she remarries and moves away. Over the next two decades, Henry continues to feel guilty about his feelings for her. When a note comes from Denise, suddenly Henry understands why Olive had been so inconsolable when a male colleague was killed: Obviously, she had loved him just as Henry had loved Denise. With that realization, Henry's long-standing guilt is replaced by a new understanding of Olive and new feelings of tenderness toward her.

Though the stories in *Olive Kitteridge* vary greatly in tone—some of them nostalgic, others sad, and others humorous—all of them end as "Pharmacy" did, with an epiphany. One of the saddest stories, "A Different Road," illustrates how little it takes to mar a relationship. When Olive and Henry are held hostage at the local hospital, they say things in front of their captor that they know they will never be able to forget. In the final story, "River," for the first time Olive admits her own shortcomings, especially in her treatment of Henry, and she regrets that she cannot go back and make amends. Nevertheless, old habits die hard. When Jack Kennison, a widower, happens along, Olive's inclination is to look for his flaws. With some amusement, Kennison recognizes the fact that as a well-to-do Republican, he represents everything that Olive loathes. However, after seventy years of finding fault with everyone but herself, Olive finally has to admit that she is not always right. When Jack phones and asks her to come over, she knows that she will end up in bed with him. Almost too late, she has realized that life is short and that love is too important to be wasted.

Nevertheless, love, or desire passing for love, accounts for a good deal of the misery in *Olive Kitteridge.* One of the funniest stories in the collection is "Ship in a Bottle." After the groom decides that he does not want to be married after all, the bride's mother takes after him with a rifle, only to discover that her daughter has run off with the man who jilted her. "The Piano Player" has a different tone. After twenty-two years as the mistress of Malcolm Moody, Angie O'Meara realizes that he no longer seems to care about her, and she telephones him to break off their affair. When she arrives at her house after work, Angie finds Malcolm waiting for her, furious because she called him at home, and his insults make it clear that he has never thought of her as anything but a convenient whore. By contrast, in "Starving," what begins as desire is transmuted into love. After his wife Bonnie announced that she was finished with sex, Harmon began stopping by every Sunday at the home of an attractive widow, Daisy Foster. Over time, they find that they cannot live without each other. Unless fate and his bad heart intervene, Harmon will divorce his wife and marry Daisy.

One of the points that Strout makes in *Olive Kitteridge* is that one cannot predict how someone will react to a particular situation. In "Winter Concert," Jane Houlton's discovery that her husband had spent a night with another woman while he was away on business somehow diminishes her marriage. She had believed that, whatever happened, they would at least have each other; now she realizes that what she believed was perfect relationship is something less. The wife in "Basket of Trips" has a different reaction. At her husband's funeral, Marlene Bonney is told by her drunken and disreputable cousin Kerry Monroe that she slept with Ed Bonney at least once. After Kerry passes out, Marlene puts her to bed, then sits beside her holding a paring knife, trying to decide whether or not to kill her. Fortunately, Olive happens along, and in this instance, she remains calm, quietly encouraging Marlene to put down the knife. Instead of stabbing Kerry, Marlene destroys the basket full of travel brochures that Ed had perused during his last days, as his wife helped him to pretend that he was not dying. What amazes Olive is that instead of being furious with her unfaithful husband, Marlene feels guilty because she was not honest with him about the impossibility of his recovering.

Olive's sympathy for Marlene is just one instance of her being genuinely kind to someone in trouble. In "Incoming Tide," sensing that there is something wrong with a former student, she insists on getting into his car and talking with him. She had no way of knowing that he had been contemplating suicide. Similarly, in "Starving," Olive arranges help for a young girl who is dying because she could not conquer her anorexia. In "Tulips," after Henry has had a stroke that leaves him blind and mute, Olive tries to escape from her own depression by paying a visit to Louise Larkin, whose son is in prison for murdering his wife. However, in this instance, Olive's kindly gesture has an unfortunate result: Though at first Louise is polite, the presence of a willing listener propels her into a rage so violent that Olive realizes she can be of no help to her.

Where Olive fails most miserably, however, is in her relationship with those she loves most. Although Olive has always thought she was a good mother, her irrational, violent outbursts during his childhood frightened Christopher so much that he became deathly afraid of her. In "Pharmacy," Christopher is shown as a troubled and bitter adolescent, one who might well have turned to drugs, run away, or committed suicide. In other stories, the reader learns that, after leaving home, he managed to make a life for himself, but he could maintain his equilibrium only by remaining at a distance from his mother. In "A Little Burst," Christopher, who is now middle-aged and a successful podiatrist, is marrying a gastroenterologist who is as opinionated as his mother. Naturally, Olive dislikes her, and the feeling is mutual. After she overhears the bride criticizing her home-made dress, Olive tampers with the young woman's clothing in a spiteful effort to make her doubt her sanity. The couple move to California, and, not surprisingly, they are soon divorced. However, every time Olive suggests that she visit him, Christopher finds an excuse to keep her away. In "Security," which appears near the end of the novel, Olive finally gets her invitation, and she goes to New York, where Christopher lives with his easygoing second wife, Ann, who is heavily pregnant, and their two children. Though she likes Ann, Olive gets tired, succumbs to self-pity, loses her self-control, screams at her son, and leaves ahead of schedule, thus destroying any chance of ever having a close relationship with him.

One might be tempted to see Olive's failure with Christopher as just another example of her destructive tendencies. However, in story after story, Strout has shown that Olive is not unique, for one of the flaws in human nature is the tendency to hurt those one loves most. Judged fairly, then, Olive is not an oddity but an Everywoman or, more appropriately, an Everyperson, often unthinking and unwise in action, frequently betrayed by her emotions, consistently guilty of the sin of pride, and far better at seeing the faults in others than her own flaws. The epiphanies that end the individual stories add up to a grim definition of human existence, for they include betrayal, spitefulness, broken relationships, and diminished expectations. However, *Olive Kitteridge* is not a pessimistic book. While, like Olive, the author insists on honesty, she also includes in her stories instances of compassion, forgiveness, and humility. The dominant theme of *Olive Kitteridge*, then, is what Olive realizes in her own epiphany: that personal happiness comes as the result of accepting and appreciating others just as they are.

Rosemary M. Canfield Reisman

Review Sources

The Atlantic Monthly 302, no. 1 (July/August, 2008): 140.
Booklist 104, nos. 9/10 (January 1, 2008): 46.
Kirkus Reviews 76, no. 3 (February 1, 2008): 113-114.
Library Journal 133, no. 2 (February 1, 2008): 65.
The New York Times Book Review, April 20, 2008, p. 13.
The New Yorker 84, no. 12 (May 5, 2008): 77.
People 69, no. 14 (April 14, 2008): 46.
Publishers Weekly 254, no. 49 (December 10, 2007): 31.
San Francisco Chronicle, April 9, 2008, p. E5.
USA Today, April 24, 2008, p. 7D.

ONE MORE YEAR
Stories

Author: Sana Krasikov (1979-   )
Publisher: Spiegel & Grau (New York). 196 pp. $21.95
Type of work: Short fiction
Time: The second half of the twentieth century
Locale: Ukraine, Georgia, and northeastern localities of
the United States, especially New York City and sub-
urbs

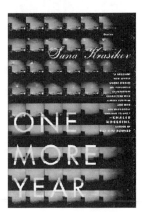

*Krasikov's first collection of short stories depicts expe-
riences and travails of immigrants from Georgia and Russia, torn between their native country and the new one*

Principal characters:
ILONA SIEGAL, a middle-aged immigrant
    from Tbilisi, Georgia
EARL, Ilona's seventy-year-old husband
MAYA, an immigrant from Tbilisi.
GOGI, her son on a visit from Tbilisi
GULIA, a woman in love with Rashid, a Muslim
RASHID, a New York carpet factory owner, Gulia's husband
NASRIN, a femme fatale in Rashid's life
ANYA, an immigrant from Russia, married to Rayan
RAYAN, an American drifter, difficult to live with
LEV, a successful businessman in New York who is from Tbilisi
SONYA, Lev's niece, visiting her uncle
DINA, Lev's suspicious wife
VICTOR, a computer expert, an immigrant from Russia
ALINA, an immigrant Victor meets in New York
GRISHA ARSENYEV, an IBM and Morgan Stanley employee, who prefers
    life in Russia
LERA, Grisha's wife, commiserating with him
LARISA LEBEDEVA, a good-hearted elderly woman, typical of her Slavic
    race
REGINA, an Americanized young Russian woman

The first book by Sana Krasikov, *One More Year*, consists of eight different stories that share something in common. In this sense, they evoke a collection of stories by the Russian author Ivan Turgenev, *Zapiski okhotnika* (1852; *A Sportsman's Sketches*, 1932). The main connecting feature is the fact that the main characters are females. The protagonist of the first story, "Companion," Ilona Siegal, is followed by leading characters in other stories: Maya ("Maya in Yonkers"), Gulia ("Asal"), Anya ("Better Half"), Sonya ("Debt"), Alina ("The Alternate"), Lera ("The Repatriates"), and Regina ("There Will Be No Fourth Rome"). Most of these women have left their native country—the Soviet Republic of Georgia, Russia, or Ukraine—and often their lovers

An Ashkenazi Jew, Sana Krasikov was born in Ukraine and raised in the former Soviet republic Georgia and the United States, where she immigrated when she was nine years old. She graduated from the Iowa Writers' Workshop. Her stories have appeared in The New Yorker, The Atlantic Monthly, *and other magazines. She received a Fulbright Scholarship to Moscow and the O. Henry Award.*

by immigrating to the United States. In their thoughts, however, they live on two continents, the one they came from and the one they are anxious to adjust to, no matter how difficult. Most of them belong to the middle class.

A former nurse in Tbilisi, Ilona Siegal works in America in a urologist's office, where she deals with older males, including her seventy-year-old husband Earl. Maya, a former accountant, has been unemployed for three years and now takes care of an elderly woman. Anya is working as a waitress in a diner while attending college. Sonya is helping her husband open a restaurant, where she would cook.

Another similar feature in the stories is conflicts the protagonists endure in adjusting to the new world. Among other things, they seem not to understand the ways of American business. As seen in "Debt," Sonya and her husband Meho visit her well-off uncle Lev and his wife Dina in New York, talking roundabout until Dina figures out the real reason for their visit—obtaining a loan to start a restaurant. When Sonya finally reveals the size of the needed loan, Lev tells her he is not a bank. He rightfully suspects they will never visit them again, let alone repay the loan.

Another common element is the conflict between generations. In "Maya in Yonkers," perhaps the best story in the collection, Maya, an immigrant from Georgia, brings her son Gogi from Tbilisi for a visit. Much of the story deals with Maya's attempts to find rapport with her son. She can tolerate the usual commotion, misunderstandings, and hassles with bureaucracy, but it disturbs her peace of mind that Gogi is unsatisfied with things in New York, expressing his displeasure with almost everything his mother suggests. In reality, he resents her leaving him behind in Tbilisi. For example, on a visit to the city, he begs her to buy him an expensive jacket, which she refuses. When his grandmother buys it for him, he returns to Tbilisi happy but still lacking an understanding of his mother, in a typical generational conflict.

By far the greatest problem in the stories is love affairs. Some of the women have left their lovers, even husbands, back in the old country. Not only do the women find it difficult to deal with American counterparts, they have trouble with their immigrant compatriots as well. In "Better Half," Anya's marriage to Rayan is filled with love, hate, and constant fighting. Even though Anya is Rayan's Russian Queen, his Pot of Gold, he treats her with jealous contempt. Anya is trying to stay legally in America on account of her marriage, but their constant fighting is making it more difficult. After he hurt her in a physical attack, she obtained a restraining order against him. He tries to heal the rift, but to no avail. Yet, Anya still feels attracted to him. Whenever she sees him at a distance, she thinks of what might have been. The love relationship between immigrants is also difficult, as Gulia experiences in "Asal." She struggles with accepting the fact that her husband Rashid is a Muslim, already married, and with being tormented by his other wife, Nasrin. Gulia tries relationships with other men, but she thinks of Rashid all the time. When Rashid finally divorces Nasrin, he and Gulia try to resume their marriage. For him she has always been his "Asal"—"honey darling." However, when Nasrin survives a suicidal self-immolation, Rashid refuses to leave her, which brings a definite end to the love affair between "Asal" and Rashid. A sudden romantic break-up followed by a lingering attraction is a recurrent motif in this collection, adding complexity to the love element in the stories.

At the same time, the protagonists sometimes show rather lax attitudes in their love affairs. Ilona has no qualms about having an extra lover or two. To be sure, her liaison with Earl is difficult, mainly because of the difference in their ages and his failing health. He is like "a dog" to her, as she explains to the landlady on the phone. Thus, the search for an acceptable companion turns out to be a problem rather than a solution. In "There Will Be No Fourth Rome," Regina has a troubled relationship with Conrad, who is married. Seeing similar relationships among her acquaintances in Russia, she realizes that such behavior is basically human. In this sense, she finds that the two cultures have something in common after all. "The Alternate" is a story about what has been but cannot be resurrected. After being guests at a wedding of friends, Victor and Vera return home, thinking but not talking about Victor's youthful relationship with Mila in St. Petersburg. The two almost got married, but he left for the United States to look for a better life and she was killed in an automobile accident back in the old country. Victor meets her daughter, Alina, who had also immigrated to the United States. At a dinner, they reminisce about Victor and Mila, and Victor wonders if, by meeting with Alina, he is trying to resurrect in some strange way his long-past affair with Mila. Alina, however, does not respond. They part amicably, and Victor continues to be burdened with his memories of his early love and with accepting his present wife Vera as an alternate. Again, love is a many-splendored thing, but not always with pleasant results.

The difference between the two cultures, American and Russian, is also a recurrent motif. In "The Repatriates," Grisha Arsenyev, who works for IBM and Morgan Stanley in the United States, considers his immigration to the United States to be the great anticlimax of his life. He believes that America has no culture or spirituality, and he refers to his life in Russia as being superior to American emptiness. He would like to work not only for his own wealth but to better American life where it is needed. After his return to Russia, he would like to use his American experiences in real estate and the mortgage business on the stock market. His wife Lera joins him in Russia, and they observe that the bureaucracy, inefficiency, rudeness, fraud, deceit, and other shortcomings remain. As one character says, there is no decency anymore. Lera realizes she has only two options: to leave Russia again or to pretend not to know. In his despair, Grisha invests most of his money in the restoration of an old church and leaves Lera, who returns to New York, hurt but still feeling compassion for Grisha.

The juxtaposition of the two cultures, Russian and American, is depicted again in "There Will Be No Fourth Rome." Regina, an accountant, visits the city of her childhood, Moscow. She relishes her impressions of changed Russia and the people she remembers. The people seem unable to live without human companionship, no matter what the circumstances. While Regina is appalled by some primitive aspects that still plague her native land, she feels deep sympathy for the basic goodness of its people and their love for each other, displayed especially by old Larisa.

Stylistically, the stories in *One More Year* mix straightforward realism with complex psychological elements. Krasikov holds on to the main sinews of the plot, although she gets away from it sporadically by change of locality or by flashbacks. The plot centers around the protagonist, although secondary characters often receive a fair share of attention. Sometimes the stories seem a bit too long, yet in many cases the length is justified with emphasis on the psychological probing that sheds more light on the character or on the nature of the conflict. The author shies away from tendentious or engaged writing. For example, when Meho ("Debt") complains about Home Depot's Jewish way of doing business, it is the only reference to anti-Semitism in the entire collection, although there are hints at other intolerances.

Reviews of *One More Year* have been almost entirely positive, with a few minor criticisms. For such a young author, Krasikov is hailed as a surprisingly mature story-teller, and her first book is a stunning accomplishment.

Vasa D. Mihailovich

Review Sources

Booklist 104, nos. 19/20 (June 1, 2008): 43.
Entertainment Weekly, August 15, 2008, p. 71.
Kirkus Reviews 76, no. 8 (April 15, 2008): 5-8.
Library Journal 133, no. 8 (May 1, 2008): 58.
The New Leader 88, no. 6 (2008): 54-55.
The New York Times Book Review, September 7, 2008, p. 15.
Publishers Weekly 255, no. 14 (April 7, 2008): 38.
The Village Voice 53, no. 33 (August 13, 2008): 48.

THE OPEN ROAD
The Global Journey of the Fourteenth Dalai Lama

Author: Pico Iyer (1957-   )
Publisher: Alfred A. Knopf (New York). 275 pp. $28.00
Type of work: Biography
Time: 1959-2008
Locale: Tibet, India, and the global community

Iyer traces the Fourteenth Dalai Lama's life from their first meeting in 1974, describing the exiled spiritual leader of Tibetan Buddhism's activities in Dharamsala, India, and in his worldwide travels

Principal personage:
        THE FOURTEENTH DALAI LAMA, born
        TENZIN GYATSO, the spiritual leader of
        Tibetan Buddhism

Pico Iyer has reported on Tibet and the Fourteenth Dalai Lama in major publications for twenty years. Iyer first met the spiritual leader of Tibetan Buddhism in India in 1974, when the author was seventeen. Iyer's father, Indian by birth, and the Tibetan shared an interest in Mohandas K. (Mahatma) Gandhi, one as a scholar, the other determined to employ nonviolence as a response to China's 1959 military takeover of Tibet. One result of their conversations was that the forward to Iyer's father's book about Gandhi was written by the Dalai Lama, and the book was dedicated to Pico Iyer and "those of his generation for whom there will be no curtain." A common desire to see artificial barriers between people and cultures come down became the bond of friendship for Iyer and the Fourteenth Dalai Lama.

During the next thirty years, as Iyer and the Dalai Lama watched the development of a world more and more connected economically and technologically, they dreamed of finding the emerging global community's spiritual and ethical foundation. Iyer traveled the world as a journalist and became increasingly dissatisfied with the media's constant reporting about the mechanics of human connections across the globe, looking for something more spiritual. Disturbed by that same lack, the Dalai Lama took to his message of spiritual interconnectedness outside of Dharamsala. As both journeyed the world, Iyer often met his friend in private, and when the Dalai Lama began his public mission, Iyer attended many lectures. Always the reporter assessed the impact of the spiritual leader's words on himself and on others. In *The Open Road*, the writer reports and critiques these conversations and lectures, concluding that the Dalai Lama's ever-larger audiences around the world seek, as Iyer does, a spirituality for the emerging global community,

The strength of Iyer's narrative lies partly in a tone that combines deep affection for his subject and continued questioning of the teacher's message. Callng himself a

~

Pico Iyer, a journalist, has published two novels and six works of nonfiction. He has reported on Tibet for Time, The New Yorker, The New York Times, *and* The New York Review of Books *for two decades.*

~

"skeptical journalist and non-belonger," Iyer relates his own spiritual journey, his walking alongside the Dalai Lama on an "open road." Although Iyer's view of the Dalai Lama is subjective, this quality and especially the many private conversations the author retells allow the reader to expand his or her own perceptions of Buddhism and global spirituality. The resulting narrative is very readable, as informal as its subject, whose gestures, words, and laughter break down any barriers between him and his listeners, whether one or many thousands.

Iyer divides his study into sections titled "In Public," "In Private," and "In Practice." In the first section he observes the Dalai Lama as an idealized, iconic, although puzzling figure who attracts followers from all over the world. In the second section, the writer brings the reader into his private conversations with the Dalai Lama and other Tibetan Buddhists, some of whom dispute what their leader is promoting. The third section recounts Iyer's final extended visit to Dharamsala; in this section, Iyer presents some of his conclusions. Most valuable to one seeking additional information on the Dalai Lama, Tibet, and Tibetan Buddhism is the final chapter of *The Open Road*, "Reading."

The Dalai Lama, who was born in 1935, was selected to be Tibet's spiritual leader when he was two years old. Leaving home and family, he moved to Lhasa, Tibet's capital, to begin a monastic life dedicated to long days of praying, studying, debating, and practicing Tibetan Buddhism. In 1950 he assumed leadership of his people. The country he ruled had been isolated from the world for centuries. Tibet was not part of the industrial age, and even in the first half of the twentieth century, the country by choice adapted almost nothing from the advances of modern science and technology. Indeed, to the outside world Tibet, which allowed few visitors, was a hidden and mysterious land of myth.

When the Chinese army invaded the country in 1949, Tibet lacked any defense against the well-armed invaders. As a result, an estimated ten million Tibetans died, and many more were imprisoned and tortured. The Chinese destroyed several thousand Tibetan monasteries and burned most of their treasured ancient Buddhist texts. In 1959, following many of his people, the Dalai Lama fled over the Himalayan mountains to India, where that country granted the Tibetans a new home in Dharamsala. Exile from Tibet and separation from ninety-eight percent of his people did not sever the Dalai Lama from his Buddhist roots, but it did, he believed, allow for some needed changes in the way he would lead his people.

In India he could more easily end any idea that he was a deity high above ordinary people. In doing this, he emphasized that despite his people's perception of him as their god, he was simply their spiritual leader for this time in their history. Further, rather than continue the hierarchical government structure that had existed in Tibet, he wanted to empower his people to move toward a democratic form of government in which they would take more responsibility for themselves and their future. He would use their exile to "set up whole settlements, with central monasteries and lay people around them" everywhere, but without Tibetan culture as it had been. The basics of that culture should go on, especially the Buddhist ethos of the interconnectedness of all things and compassion for all. The Dalai Lama also hoped that individuals practicing different kinds of Buddhism around the world would unite around their commonalities. Such changes, he believed, would not dilute Buddhism but strengthen its "original, classic, authentic" teachings of compassion for others, daily meditation, and responsibility for oneself and one's world.

The Dalai Lama saw clearly that the tragic events that had overtaken Tibet were caused in large part by Tibet's many centuries of self-imposed isolation from other countries and cultures, from the world outside and what it could have taught Tibet. He asked his people in exile not to waste time blaming others for their problems, but rather to look inward and realize that they had to become part of the world community. This did not mean that the Dalai Lama would forget his people still in Tibet. Rather, he had two complementary goals: first, reforming Tibetan Buddhism and "constructing a new more durable Tibet outside Tibet"; second, ensuring the rights of Tibetans in the homeland while respecting the rights of the Chinese who were occupying Tibet. The problem of China must be settled nonviolently, he insisted and continues to insist; and when that happened, he would immediately implant his reforms of Tibetan government and life there.

However, other effects of the exile, Iyer suggests, weakened the Tibetans' basic identity. Forty-five years after the Dalai Lama's exile began, Iyer notes, no progress has been made in freeing Tibet. Rather, Iyer observed when he visited Tibet, the Chinese were trying and in some cases succeeding in making Tibetans into Chinese. Also, he observed that in India some Tibetan refugees were losing their own culture and adapting their host country's ways. Further, because people from around the world could come freely on pilgrimage to Dharamsala to see the Dalai Lama, and came in large numbers, some settling there, the Tibetan refugees, especially the youngest who had never lived in their homeland, saw the possibility of other lifestyles and found ways to move away from their roots in body and sometimes in spiritual outlook. Thus some looked for opportunities to secure jobs in more economically developed parts of the world, competed for scholarships in other countries, and found various ways to connect with visitors who might assist their escape from Dharamsala.

Some refugees wanted to rescue Tibet from China's control and return. Paradoxically, their spiritual leader who disapproved of any violent action to save Tibet gave his approval to his people joining the Indian army to aid the host country in its war with Bangladesh to repay India's kindness. When Iyer attended in Dharamsala a meeting of the Tibetan Youth Congress (TYC), considered by many "the official voice of the unofficial Tibet in exile," that is, an organization separate from the government that is headed by the Dalai Lama, he discovered the rebellious thirty-thousand plus members wanted immediate Tibetan independence from China even by violent means. Still, Iyer learned, they revered the Dalai Lama—their source of spiritual strength, "their leader, their hero," and "the incarnation of a god it would be a sacrilege to go against." A further paradox that Iyer points out is that while the leader counsels his people to trust in themselves, he also wants them to accept his way of freeing Tibet.

Magill's Literary Annual 2009

Iyer also looks at the causes of the Dalai Lama's decision to travel the "open road" on a "global journey" of spiritual leadership. When he arrived in Dharamsala, lowering from his traditional high position, the Dalai Lama for the first time walked the streets and countryside, meeting people from all walks of life informally. As the years passed, Dharamsala became a pilgrimage site for visitors from all parts of the world, where those of all faiths and of all economic backgrounds, became, in Iyer's words, "as compressed and bittersweet an image of the global village as I have ever seen." At the same time, the Dalai Lama studied modern science, met with scientific experts, and heard daily about the growing economic and technological inventions that made human connections easier and faster each year. Thus he found the mission that started him on a journey to so many countries of the world. In his travels, Iyer writes, the Tibetan spiritual leader consistently spoke on behalf of his fellow Tibetans controlled by the Chinese invaders, saying to the world, "If you really think we inhabit a global universe, then your welfare depends on Tibet, as much as its welfare depends on you." This was but one example of the ethical system he taught. In the Dalai Lama's vision, if the world adopted a lifestyle that included the practices of compassion for all, deep meditation, and responsibility, this would become a better world.

Connectedness is the basic truth of Buddhism that the world needed, providing a foundation of a global ethics for the global city. The Dalai Lama did not say that the citizens of the global community must become Buddhists. Rather, everyone, no matter what his or her faith tradition, had within the possibility of taking the "open road" by practicing that stillness and meditation that leads to finding that "everything is linked in a pulsing network." Then all individuals would become compassionate and responsible.

How many of the Fourteenth Dalai Lama's listeners would follow his teaching? How long would it take for his teaching to bring about this transformation of the world? The readers of Iyer's book, like the audiences of his spiritual teacher, are invited to choose the "open road." Each time that path is chosen, the world is a better place.

Francine A. Dempsey

Review Sources

Booklist 104, no. 13 (March 1, 2008): 31.
The Economist 386 (March 22, 2008): 93-94.
Kirkus Reviews 76, no. 6 (March 15, 2008): 287-288.
Library Journal 133, no. 1 (January 1, 2008): 74-75.
The New York Review of Books 55, no. 9 (May 29, 2008): 46-49.
The New York Times Book Review, April 6, 2008, p. 12.
The New Yorker 84, no. 7 (March 31, 2008): 120-123.
Outside 33, no. 4 (April, 2008): 31.
Publishers Weekly 255, no. 2 (January 14, 2008): 53.

ORIGINAL SIN
A Cultural History

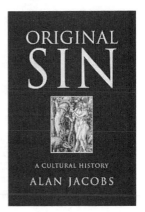

Author: Alan Jacobs (1958-   )
Publisher: HarperCollins (New York). 286 pp. $24.95
Type of work: Ethics, history

The author samples beliefs about the origins and nature of sin in cultures from the ancients to contemporary sages

Original Sin is a slippery concept. Is it some inherited and resistant stain on the soul of each person that must be washed carefully in baptism? Is it a quaint biblical notion, an artifact from the clueless behavior of the first lady and her partner, not to be taken seriously in a postmodern world? Is it a reality located within the person's nature or experience? Is it merely the influence of negative social context on behavior? Is it the result of some devil tempting a weak individual into immoral but alluring action? In *Original Sin*, Alan Jacobs considers these questions in his engaging and rich cultural study of the subject. He is clear in the introduction that his task is cultural rather than theological. His interest is in describing the serious wrestling with the question of sin's origins across the ages of human history.

The author begins his examination with six stories that deal with the origins of evil and the differences that various cultures play in interpreting and vanquishing it. They depict the potency of evil in historical contexts and in imagination as well as the need in some way to expiate that evil. They illustrate the hope for a better future even in the face of seemingly insurmountable evil.

Much of Christian thinking about Original Sin is saturated with the theological positions of Saint Augustine, the fourth century bishop of Hippo, in northern Africa. Often drawing his conclusions through the lens of Paul the apostle, Augustine conceives of Original Sin as a tangible reality "inherited" from the first sinful father, Adam. Augustine's theory damns unbaptized babies to hell, consistent with his idea that human beings are totally unable to achieve salvation without the intervention of God. He does not believe that human beings alone are capable of transcending the power of evil in their lives.

Augustine's position on Original Sin may very well have become polarized because of his dealings with certain contemporary heretical movements, notably those of the Donatists and the Pelagians. It is equally possible that Augustine's thinking is rooted in his personal negative views on sex. Sexual desire, when not regulated by the will, is a reminder of the shame of Adam and Eve's sin, in that it "reenacts Adam's disobedience." Predictably Augustine's frame of reference is his youthful firsthand experience of the difficulty controlling his sexual activity. Jacobs believes that Augustine's somewhat odd conclusions about the connections of sin and sex have en-

Alan Jacobs is professor of English at Wheaton College in Illinois. He is the author of several books, including The Narnian: The Life and Imagination of C. S. Lewis *(2005). Besides his longer works, he has written for* The Boston Globe, American Scholar, First Things, *and* The Oxford American.

dured in centuries of theology that postulates a conjugal relationship between sexual pleasure and seminal sin.

Besides ancient stories that grapple with the experience of sin, there exist many other attempts to describe and dissect this fundamental reality. Jacobs examines not only the biblical account found in the book of Genesis but also the accounts of such well-known writers as John Milton, in *Paradise Lost* (1667), and C. S. Lewis, particularly in his *Perelandra* (1943). Over the centuries, many authors have written about sin, evil, and the devil. Some of these had primarily literary concerns, while others wrote with heavy political or ideological agenda. Jacobs samples both, putting the works in their cultural contexts.

Often fundamental evil is personified in some sort of Satan or devil. From Milton's Lucifer to the modern comic-book fictional demon Hellboy, from the conniving snake that beguiled Eve to the diminutive but disastrous demon who perches on the shoulder of the confused agent and offers evil—a variety of representations that personify the human tendency to commit evil are examined. Is the Devil real, an entity with horns or cloven hooves or devoid of thumbs? Is the Devil, as psychoanalyst Sigmund Freud believed, a projected externalization of the inner conflicts that plague the human psyche? Jacobs points out that modern psychological takes on the Devil are not so different from the conclusions at which Paul or Augustine arrived. Both recognize the struggle between good and evil that human beings wage within themselves. Still not clear, however, is whether people have real choices to make. Can Hellboy undergo a change, a metanoia, to become a good person? Can Lucifer repent his break from God to reemerge as the angel of light? Is the struggle to be good truly under human domination, or is the person controlled by nature or by some external coercion ("the devil made me do it") with no real free will?

Another question concerns the essence of salvation and damnation. Jewish belief in the communal nature of humanity leads to the conclusion that all are ultimately saved (or damned). Accounts in the Hebrew scripture see God as saving the total people, no matter what the good behavioral titer in the population seems to be. Nevertheless, in some instances, the whole people are condemned (the "punishment" of the various biblical exiles, for example). The first conclusion fits nicely with the egalitarian notion of universal sin: All sin, but all are eventually saved. The collective consequence of universal redemption is not unreasonable, given that an inherited universal stain is not a Jewish idea. Rather it is a Christian interpretation of the ancient story found in Genesis. The Jewish position, however, leaves the difficulty of what to do with confirmed sinners, if they are considered apart from the whole. Should there be a punishment fitting to the serious crimes people commit? A sense of justice seems to indicate that evildoers should not get away with conscious malice. Later Jewish thought indicates that sinners can be separated from the saved and condemned to eternal damnation; or, alternatively, they are "retrained" in some kind of reincarnation (as the Jewish Kabbalistic tradition believes).

Jacobs sees a clear pattern in human history. In some periods human beings are believed to have great moral potential, even though the counterpoint of ubiquitous human bondage to Adam's sin is always lurking in the background. Pelagius argues for human potential to achieve the good; Jonathan Edwards argues that even infants are "young vipers" and infinitely more hateful because they are not in Christ. Even Augustine attributes infants with an "inborn sinfulness, " which is demonstrated in their inherent selfishness and willfulness.

A romantic picture of primitive people painted in the eighteenth and nineteenth centuries, largely the idea of Enlightenment philosopher Jean-Jacques Rousseau, is that of the "noble savage." An innate innocence and goodness, unstained by evil, characterizes those who live in harmony with nature. Perhaps children and primitive people are not worse than vipers after all. Perhaps this pristine innocence could be true of all citizens if a society were properly organized without private property. Perhaps there is no need for a universal religious doctrine of Original Sin, because people are by nature good. Perhaps it is religion itself that is responsible for human evil. To do away with religion is to do away with sin.

Jacobs makes an interesting observation about the persistence of the doctrine of Original Sin. It is the universal leveler, the "binding agent" that links all people one to another. Why not, the author suggests, take as fundamental and paramount the idea that humanity is made in the image of God? Is this not an equally strong assertion about humanity found in the scripture, and would it not work as well? Jacobs makes this almost poignant observation (is it a plea?) in his discussion of the work of Louis Agassiz, the Swiss naturalist, who was among the last major scientists to repudiate Charles Darwin. Agassiz rejects the idea that there was a universal primordial parent—a first sinner. His rejection, sadly, is rooted in his personal experience in a Philadelphia hotel, which left him unable to identify himself as a brother to all. The hotel staff were "men of color." Agassiz could not countenance the idea that these people, in his view so foreign and offputting in appearance, could be of the same human stock as he. They were members of a "lower race" who should not be allowed to have their blood "flow freely into that of our children." His position leads logically to a theory of polygenesis. The belief that there was more than one set of human parents destroys the belief that there exists a single "original" sin.

Jacobs believes that, in some ways, a theory that all human beings participate in a universal sinfulness is a uniquely democratic assertion. It is exquisitely egalitarian to think that everyone has the same stain or tendency or reality. As the Christian feast of All Souls implicitly proclaims: All sin, but all have the promise of salvation. Heaven is not reserved for the rich or the hyper holy (saints), but it is open to all sinners, that is, all people. The invitation is universal, based on the ubiquitous effect of sin on the human population. This equality under God, particularly in the strictly stratified society of most of Europe from Roman times until fairly recently, is acutely countercultural.

Ultimately the book eludes a definitive answer to the questions posed. As the sands of history shift, so do theories about Original Sin. Certain approaches come down on the side of some primordial episode whose result is an inherited stain or weakness. This real event makes people either unable to achieve salvation through human endeavor or so weakened by the father's flaw that they cannot perform good actions. Original Sin is the ticket to hell, unless it is washed away by an ecclesial action— baptism. Other approaches deny the Adam and Eve fall as definitive, yet persist in defining people as defective and impotent. Sin becomes the owned action of the individual, not some ancient legacy. Alternately, the imperfection is an environmental disposition toward evil that can be metaphorically breathed in and consequently compromising of the good in people.

While the whole book smells of Augustine, Jacobs takes pains to move beyond Augustine's theory of Original Sin. The work is chock-full of interesting tidbits of history and insight. The reader is delighted by the tantalizing yet accessible erudition of the material.

Jacobs does a fine job of summarizing difficult and disparate historical material. He informs the reader without overwhelming. His range of material—biblical stories, fiction, biology, and serious theological commentary—is extensive. Although he sometimes moves to material not quite on target, even this fascinates and informs. Happily, instead of cumbersome footnotes, the author has included a chapter-by-chapter bibliography.

In many ways the doctrine of Original Sin is one of anthropology rather than theology. Here the author is on the right track. The doctrine transcends political systems, all of which Jacobs asserts ultimately fall within its scope of judgment. What human beings are at root is a study of reality. Even without a definitive answer to the nature of Original Sin, Jacobs's look at the span of cultural interpretations of Original Sin offers much insight into the question.

Dolores L. Christie

Review Sources

America 199, no. 9 (September 29, 2008): 39.
Booklist 104, no. 17 (May 1, 2008): 57.
The Christian Century 125, no. 25 (December 16, 2008): 24.
Christianity Today 52, no. 7 (July, 2008): 53-54.
Library Journal 133, no. 3 (February 15, 2008): 109.
Publishers Weekly 255, no. 8 (February 25, 2008): 68-69.
The Wall Street Journal 251, no. 138 (June 13, 2008): A13.
The Wilson Quarterly 32, no. 3 (Summer, 2008): 107-108.

THE OTHER HALF
The Life of Jacob Riis and the World of Immigrant America

Author: Tom Buk-Swienty (1966-   )
First published: Den Ideelle Amerikaner: En Biografi om
   Journalisten, Reformisten og fotografen Jacob A. Riis,
   2008, in Denmark
Translated from the Danish by Annette Buk-Swienty
Publisher: W. W. Norton (New York). 331 pp. $27.95
Type of work: Biography, history
Time: 1849-1914
Locale: Denmark and the United States

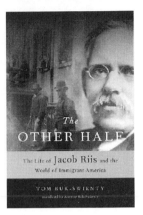

   A life of Riis, whose articles, books, and photographs
taught the American public about abysmal immigrant liv-
ing conditions, helping spur urban reform in the Progres-
sive Era

        Principal personages:
            JACOB RIIS (1849-1914), Danish American journalist and photographer
            ELISABETH GIØRTZ RIIS (1852-1905), his first wife
            MARY PHILIPS RIIS (1877-1967), his second wife
            THEODORE ROOSEVELT (1858-1919), president of the United States,
               1901-1909

    Tom Buk-Swienty first learned about Jacob Riis in a course on the Progressive Era when he was an exchange student at the University of California, Santa Barbara. Although a history major, Buk-Swienty had never heard of Riis, who was relatively unknown in Denmark. Intrigued by the idea that a Danish American strongly affected American social history, he found an old copy of Riis's *How the Other Half Lives* (1890) and was fascinated by the power of Riis's language and photographs depicting New York City's squalid slums. Seeing an exhibit of Riis's photographs in the 1990's stimulated Buk-Swienty to research and write *The Other Half.*

    Using diaries and letters, and stressing the historical context of Riis's activities, Buk-Swienty provides the reader with an informative narrative of Riis's life. He devotes the first fifty pages of his book to Riis's life in the stuffy, somnolent town of Ribe. Buk-Swienty notes that Riis later romanticized the town in his memoirs, contrasting life there to crowded city slums and ignoring how unhealthy Ribe actually was. Only three of his parents' fourteen children reached adulthood, most dying of tuberculosis. Riis rebelled against his father, a stern village schoolmaster, dropped out of school at fifteen, and apprenticed himself to a carpenter. That same year he fell in love with twelve-year-old Elisabeth Giørtz, the adopted daughter of the richest man in town.

    Buk-Swienty covers Riis's love affair in detail, through its various vicissitudes to a final happy ending. Upon completing his apprenticeship in October, 1869, Riis proposed to Elisabeth, who flatly rejected him. Since Riis had fantasized about her during his five-year apprenticeship in Copenhagen, he was totally unprepared for her refusal. He fell into a deep depression, and he decided to seek his fortune in the United States. On May 1, 1870, he left Ribe with forty American dollars, some clothing, and a locket containing a picture of Elisabeth and a lock of her hair given to him by a sympathetic friend.

The author narrates Riis's life in America as a rags-to-riches story, from deep poverty in the 1870's to affluence and fame in the 1890's. His first job at a mining company in Pennsylvania, working as a carpenter building miners' huts, paid only $10.63 for the month. He returned to New York City, where his money ran out. Riis wandered the streets, homeless, begging for food at the back door of restaurants and contemplating suicide. While he was sleeping at a police station sheltering homeless men, someone stole the locket with Elisabeth's hair. When Riis angrily protested the loss and fought with police, they subdued him and put him on a ferry to New Jersey.

Riis walked to Philadelphia, where a sympathetic Danish consul sent him to Jamestown, New York. Riis found temporary jobs, and he proved to be a successful traveling salesman. When paid less than the promised commission, Riis headed back to New York City in 1873, hoping to train as a telegraph operator, a well-paid occupation. Despite the deep depression following the Panic of 1873, Riis found a night job as a reporter at ten dollars a week to pay for his training, thereby stumbling on his true calling. In 1874, he became editor of a Brooklyn weekly, writing all four pages himself for twenty-four dollars a week. Buk-Swienty admiringly notes that, unlike most adult immigrants who rarely acquire more than rudimentary fluency in English, in four years Riis had become sufficiently at home in his new language to become a successful journalist.

In May, 1873, he heard that Elisabeth had become engaged to a war hero of the Danish-German War, which infuriated Riis, who still hoped she would change her mind once he had succeeded in America. He concentrated on his American career. When the owners of his paper agreed in January, 1875, to sell it to him for $675, payable in installments, he became owner of the *South Brooklyn News*. Late in 1874, Riis learned that Elisabeth's fiancé had died of tuberculosis before the marriage could take place, rekindling his hopes. In August, 1875, he wrote to Elisabeth, eliciting an angry rejection letter that she gave to Riis's mother, who decided not to forward it.

Elisabeth was estranged from her family and working as a governess to support herself, a position she disliked. In October, she reconsidered her rejection and wrote to Riis explaining that, although she was not in love with him, she appreciated his long devotion to her and would be willing to marry him and try to be a good wife. The two were married in the Ribe cathedral on March 5, 1876. When the couple arrived in

New York early in 1877, Elisabeth was already pregnant with their first son. The marriage became an affectionate union. Elisabeth ran the home and took responsibility for raising the children while Riis devoted long hours to journalism.

The paper proved so prosperous under Riis's management that the previous owners bought it back for three thousand dollars. In 1878, the *New York Tribune* assigned Riis to the police beat, where his hard work and investigative bent produced scoops that pleased his editors but made him unpopular with fellow reporters, who preferred to depend on police handouts. Spending his working hours at police headquarters in the heart of the slum district, going on raids with police that penetrated deep into the worst areas of the city, and following health inspectors on their rounds, Riis saw aspects of poverty and degradation more dire than he had before experienced.

The great Eastern and Southern European migration to the United States in the last decades of the nineteenth century poured millions of Italians, Poles, and Jews fleeing Russian pogroms into the city. Landlords provided minimal rents by crowding in as many people as possible. To Riis, the worst was the area he called Mulberry Bend, perhaps the most heavily populated area in the world—less than three acres in size, it held 2,047 people per acre (Buk-Swienty cites in contrast the twenty-first century population density of New York City as 104 per acre). When the district ceased to be desirable, landlords carved single-family homes into small apartments and built ramshackle houses in the back yards, creating a warren of noisome alleys. Even cellars were rented, with entire families living in an underground room without ventilation. Crime and disease flourished, and frequent epidemics ravaged the area, killing especially children and elderly.

Buk-Swienty asserts the tenement district both fascinated and repelled Riis. He determined to alert the public through lectures where he could reveal the true extent of the problem more completely than in daily news bulletins, hoping to stimulate immediate reform efforts. Riis was not alone in his endeavor. Settlement house workers aware of conditions in the blighted areas, architects appalled by what they saw, who produced plans to raze and rebuild the tenements, ministers and social workers active in the slums, all shared the same goal as Riis.

Buk-Swienty depicts these lectures as particularly powerful because Riis took advantage of a recent technological advance in photography, flash powder. Until then photographers had been limited to taking pictures in daylight or indoors at long exposures under lights. Igniting the powder while the camera lens was open permitted stop-action photography under the dimmest conditions. Amateur photographers interested in testing the new process accompanied Riis on night expeditions, taking pictures at Riis's direction in the darkest attics and cellars and in the murkiest alleys in the slums. The images were sensational, though of little interest to photographers who thought them ugly; satisfied with the results of their test after a few nights, they withdrew. Riis then trained himself as a photographer, continuing to record the people and living conditions in the slums. Riis never called himself a photographer, claiming he was not very good at taking pictures, but he made photographic history as a pioneer photojournalist. Buk-Swienty asserts this was the first use of photography designed to portray ugliness, dirt, and wretchedness rather than beauty.

For his lectures, Riis turned the photographs into lantern slides. Projected on a large screen, they provided powerful images that moved people more effectively than the written or spoken word. While continuing his job as a reporter, Riis lectured widely in New York, New Jersey, and Connecticut. In 1889, *Scribner's Magazine's* Christmas issue printed a twenty-page article based on his lectures, illustrated with woodcuts of his slides.

Scribner's then commissioned a book on the topic. In ten months, while working full time as a reporter, Riis produced *How the Other Half Lives: Studies of the Tenements of New York* (1890). He explained how previously healthy areas of New York City became slums and then took the reader on a tour of the tenement district, describing the area and introducing the reader to various slum inhabitants. Riis used narrative techniques he had learned from an admired author, Charles Dickens, to put a human face on the horrors he recorded. The impact of Riis's words was multiplied by forty-four searing photographs of slum living conditions that shocked reviewers and readers with images they had never seen nor even imagined. Photographs convinced viewers as drawings never could.

Buk-Swienty admits that *How the Other Half Lives* is disfigured by Riis's frequent use of racist group stereotypes, which make the book uncomfortable to read today. He ascribes the stereotypes to the conventions of the day, arguing that Riis's descriptions of individual slum residents are usually positive, carrying the message that people who might not look like the reader really shared much in common with the reader. The book became a best seller in 1891, launching Riis's national reputation as a social critic and reformer.

Theodore Roosevelt, then police commissioner of New York City, sought out Riis after reading his book and accompanied him on visits to the worst of the slums. The two teamed to improve police relations with slum dwellers and to call for tenement house reform and elimination of the worst areas. Riis was particularly proud of his role in achieving destruction of Mulberry Bend in 1897 and its transformation into a much-needed park. The two remained friends throughout Riis's life. In 1903, Riis published a laudatory campaign biography of Roosevelt and campaigned for him in 1912.

Riis produced many books and articles on urban problems in the 1890's and early twentieth century. His autobiography, *The Making of an American* (1901), was a major best seller, producing sufficient income for Riis to devote himself to his books and magazine articles. His wife died in 1905 of pneumonia. Two years later, at the age of fifty-eight, he married his thirty-year-old secretary, Mary Phillips. Riis was diagnosed with coronary artery disease in late 1912 and died almost two years later.

Buk-Swienty believes that although Riis actively participated in many reform organizations, his major contribution to social reform was as a writer of exposés. He was an early example of the Progressive Era journalists and authors called muckrakers. Although Riis thought of himself as a writer and not a photographer, the rediscovery of his original plates and prints has led to a reevaluation of his achievements and a recognition that he was an accomplished pioneer in that field as well.

Milton Berman

Review Sources

American History 43, no. 5 (December, 2008): 68-69.
Booklist 104, no. 22 (August 1, 2008): 30.
Houston Chronicle, September 7, 2008, p. 14.
Kirkus Reviews 76, no. 11 (June 1, 2008): 70.
Library Journal 133, no. 11 (June 15, 2008): 65.
The New York Sun, August 27, 2008, p. 11.
The New Yorker 84, no. 29 (September 22, 2008): 91.
Publishers Weekly 255, no. 21 (May 26, 2008): 48.
San Francisco Chronicle, September 21, 2009, p. M4.
The Wall Street Journal 252, no. 47 (August 25, 2008): A11.

OUR STORY BEGINS
New and Selected Stories

Author: Tobias Wolff (1945-   )
Publisher: Alfred A. Knopf (New York). 379 pp. $26.95
Type of work: Short fiction

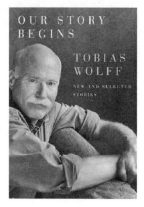

A selection of stories from Wolff's previous collections, along with ten previously uncollected new stories

Although Tobias Wolff is probably best known as the author of the memoir *This Boy's Life* (1989), an account of his youthful struggles with a brutal stepfather that was made into a 1993 film starring Robert De Niro and Leonardo DiCaprio, his critical reputation rests largely on his three collections of short stories. *Our Story Begins* includes stories from each of these books, as well as ten new ones.

His first collection, *In the Garden of the North American Martyrs* (1981), was well received by critics, several stories becoming favorite anthology pieces read widely by university students. The title story centers on a female history professor who goes for a job interview, only to find out that she has been invited merely to satisfy an affirmative-action requirement. When she presents a public lecture as part of the interview, she ignores her prepared paper and launches into a passionate account of how the Iroquois once captured two Jesuit priests in the area, graphically describing the tortures they suffered. She quotes one of the priests who, just before his agonizing death, tells his torturers to mend their lives. When the professorial audience tries to shout her down, she continues to exhort them to turn from power to love, to walk humbly. She even turns off her hearing aid so she will not be distracted. The story is an example of what Wolff has called "winging it," which he describes as a kind of "lifting off, letting go," listening to the voice within and speaking with the "magic of that voice."

Wolff's most famous example of "winging it" is the concluding story of *In the Garden of the North American Martyrs*, "The Liar," for it describes a sixteen-year-old boy who creates his own fictional world, precipitated by the death of his father, with whom the boy identifies because he coped with his fears by telling lies. The story ends with a poetic scene on a bus trip to Los Angeles, during which the boy tells his fellow passengers that he works with refugees from Tibet. When a woman asks him to speak some Tibetan, the others passengers lean back in their seats and close their eyes, while the boy, who knows no Tibetan, sings to them "in what was surely an ancient and holy tongue." The story is a fiction-writer's manifesto, a lyrical evocation about the human need to create an imaginative reality that bonds people together even as it asserts one's own unique identity.

"Hunters in the Snow," another favorite anthology piece from Wolff's first collection, is a caricature of the macho-male buddy story. Tubby is the butt of jokes that his name suggests, stumbling clumsily with hidden snacks falling out of his hunting garb. Kenny is the bullying, sadistic practical joker. Frank is the central consciousness, the philosophic one, who talks of "centering" and going with the "forces" in the natural world, but who has romantic illusions of escaping a loveless marriage by running off with the baby sitter. This comedy of errors culminates when Kenny says he hates a dog they encounter and then shoots it. When he turns to Tub and says he hates him, too, the frightened Tubby shoots Kenny in the stomach. As Tub and Frank make comically clumsy attempts to get Kenny to the hospital in the back of their pickup, they stop at a cafe for coffee and get into a satiric conversation about friendship and being "really

Tobias Wolff, the author of eight books, has won the PEN/Malamud Award and the Rea Award for his short fiction. In addition, he has won the Los Angeles Times *Book Prize and the PEN/ Faulkner Award.*

in love," while Kenny is freezing outside. They both get a big laugh when Frank reveals to Tub that the dog's owner asked Kenny to shoot it. Because of further comic mistakes and other stops, it seems clear that they will never get Kenny to the hospital in time to save him. However, that seems less important than Tub coming clean about his obsessive eating and Frank spouting still more clichés about love and friendship. The final joke is the last line, when, as Kenny mumbles he is going to the hospital, the reader discovers that he is wrong, for the two men had "taken a different turn a long way back."

In Wolff's second collection of stories, *Back in the World* (1985), "Soldier's Joy" focuses on the search for camaraderie in the army, as one character insists that the Vietnam War was a fulfilling experience for him because it provided a home where he was with friends. Being back in the States, or "back in the world," he says, lacks order and meaning. The final story in the collection, "The Rich Brother," another frequent anthology favorite, is, Wolff has said, the closest thing to a fable he has ever written. The prodigal brother Donald is humane, generous, and a financial failure; the older brother Pete is successful, unfeeling, and dissatisfied. In the story, Pete comes to rescue Donald as he has in the past, but Pete gives up on his brother when once more he throws away his money on foolish fantasies and the needs of others. Nevertheless, the story ends with a redemptive change of heart.

Wolff demonstrates his careful control of the short-story form best when he follows Anton Chekhov's famous dictum that it is better to say too little than too much. "Say Yes," also from Wolff's second collection, is a short, deceptively simple, piece. The initiating situation is a trivial, domestic one, and the characters, ordinary people, exist primarily to illustrate the points of view important to the story's conflict. The simple situation soon develops into a significant universal conflict for no other reason than the participants are husband and wife, and therefore, in the tenuousness of that relationship, they are always hovering on the edge of conflict and collapse. The story is not about a minor conflict in the life of a particular couple, but rather it is an exploration of the ultimate strangeness of others, no matter how confident an individual may be that he "knows" another individual. The story suggests that strangeness or difference is not skin-deep but profound and universal.

Wolff's third collection, *The Night in Question* (1996), received more positive reviews than *Back in the World*. It would seem that Wolff also likes these stories better than his earlier ones. He includes only four or five stories from each of the first two collections, but he includes twelve from the third one. Wolff continues to explore a favorite theme in this collection: the substitution of an imaginative reality for the unsatisfactory or unworthy real one. For example, in the story "Firelight," a boy and his mother play fantasy shopping games by trying on clothes they know they cannot afford. When the boy finds out that his mother once turned down a marriage proposal from an all-American football player, he scolds her, complaining that they could be rich now. Wolff also continues to focus on another favorite theme here—the importance of story itself. In "The Night in Question," the story is not a simple moral exemplum but a complex challenge to one's own reason for being.

However, some of the stories in Wolff's third collection suggest a slackening from his earlier work. Some are merely concept stories, clever and well told, but predictable and pat. "Mortals" is a "what if" story, based on the premise of "what if" an obituary writer, acting on misinformation, writes an obituary for a man who has not died? "What if" the misinformation came from the man himself? What would such a story reveal? Not a great deal, as it turns out, when the two men get together and reflect on the limits of their own lives.

Similarly, "The Chain" develops the implications of what would happen if a man committed an act of revenge for another man, who later feels compelled to commit an act of revenge in return. What if these acts set into motion other, unforeseen acts that continue in an unbroken chain of reverberations?

Another "what if" story in the third collection is "Bullet in the Brain," a sort of writer's revenge tale about a book critic, who, while waiting in line at a bank, cannot resist critiquing the dialogue of a bank robber, ridiculing his use of such language as "dead meat" and "capiche" as clichés, until the robber shoots him in the head. Wolff then explores in the moments before the critic dies all those things he did not remember, singling out one seemingly inconsequential incident in his youth, the kind of moment that only a writer would remember.

The ten new stories included here, which originally appeared in such publications as *The New Yorker*, *The Atlantic Monthly*, and *Playboy*, suggest a man who has accepted himself as a professional writer, who knows he can get well paid for publishing stories in such places, who is comfortably established in residence at Stanford University, who knows how to exploit the short-story form well, but who does not always challenge himself to go beyond his obvious competency.

For example, "A White Bible" is a conventional story that hooks the reader with pop-fiction suspense when a young female teacher is kidnapped by a man as she returns to her car after a night drinking with friends. However, the reader's anxiety that the woman is going to be brutally assaulted is defused when the story changes into a thematic tale of cultural conflict. The kidnapper is a Middle Eastern immigrant whose son has been flunked in the woman's class, and he is demanding that the teacher not have the boy expelled. She quickly takes control of the situation, even eliciting an apology from the contrite man.

The weakest story in this new set is "Her Dog," an inconsequential piece about a man whose wife has died and who now cares for her dog, a dog that he ignored when she was alive. Although the theme is potentially significant, Wolff's treatment, in which the reader is privy to the dog's thoughts about how faithful he has always been, is sentimental and a bit banal.

There is, nevertheless, still some of the old Wolff evident in these stories. "Awaiting Orders" is a complex story about a gay sergeant who tries to help a woman whose brother, recently sent to Iraq, has neglected his duties to his child. The sergeant's kindness and the woman's tough hillbilly strength create a memorable confrontation. Similarly, "A Mature Student," an encounter between a female ex-soldier and her art professor, an immigrant who betrayed her friends during the Russian invasion of Prague in the 1960's, is a subtle exploration of the nature of cowardice.

In the final story, "Deep Kiss," Wolff returns to his signature theme—the superiority of the imagined life over the merely real—as a man lives a "submerged life" parallel to his actual existence. This story's theme is one that Chekhov explored definitively in his classic "Lady with a Pet Dog," about a man who leads a double life—one in public, full of conventional truth, and another that "flowed in secret." Wolff's stories, like many great short stories, reflect the secret of the form that Chekhov knew well: "Every individual existence revolves around mystery."

Charles E. May

Review Sources

America 198, no. 14 (April 28, 2008): 31-33.
The Atlantic Monthly 301, no. 3 (April, 2008): 107.
Booklist 104, nos. 9/10 (January 1, 2008): 45.
Kirkus Reviews 76, no. 5 (March 1, 2008): 217-218.
Los Angeles Times, March 23, 2008, p. R1.
New Criterion 26, no. 10 (June, 2008): 87-89.
The New York Times, March 28, 2008, p. 29.
The New York Times Book Review, March 30, 2008, p. 10.
Publishers Weekly 254, no. 48 (December 3, 2007): 46-47.
Review of Contemporary Fiction 28, no. 2 (Summer, 2008): 170-171.
The Times Literary Supplement, August 1, 2008, p. 19.
The Washington Post Book World, April 13, 2008, p. BW06.

A PASSION FOR NATURE
The Life of John Muir

Author: Donald Worster (1941-   )
Publisher: Oxford University Press (New York). 533 pp.
   $34.95
Type of work: Biography
Time: 1838-1914
Locale: Scotland, Wisconsin, and California

   A definitive new biography of one of the United States'
foremost naturalists, conservationists, and environmental-
ists

A Passion for Nature
The Life of
JOHN MUIR
DONALD WORSTER

   Principal personages:
      JOHN MUIR, an American naturalist,
         conservationist, and environmentalist
      DANIEL MUIR, his father
      ANN MUIR, his mother
      LOUIE (STRENTZEL) MUIR, his wife
      JOHN BURROUGHS, a friend and fellow American naturalist
      THEODORE ROOSEVELT, the twenty-sixth U.S. president and a friend of
         John Muir

   One of the great figures in the nineteenth century American conservation movement, John Muir is most often identified with California, where he spent most of his
adult life and where he came to be identified so closely with the Sierra Nevada and
Yosemite Park that his formative years tend to be neglected. Now environmental historian Donald Worster has written *A Passion for Nature*, sure to become the definitive
Muir biography, in which he chronicles Muir's childhood and early years that helped
to shape his deep passion for the natural world. The first Muir biography to meet modern standards of scholarship, this book makes use of Muir's hitherto unavailable private correspondence. Worster describes how Muir's love of the outdoors grew out of
a rebellion against his strict, fundamentalist upbringing, his early interest in botany,
the natural beauty of the Wisconsin frontier, and his strong desire to explore exotic
places, including Florida and California.
   Muir was born in Dunbar, Scotland, on April 21, 1838, the third of eight children
of a zealous and restless Scotsman, a successful grain merchant who impulsively decided to immigrate to America in 1849 to enjoy greater freedom to practice his extremely fundamentalist Campbellite beliefs and try his hand at homesteading in the
Midwest. As the oldest son, Muir suffered from his father's heavy-handed patriarchal
rule, with its strict work ethic, harsh physical punishments, and many prohibitions,
based on his Calvinistic view of human nature. He later remembered the Scottish
countryside as his one escape from the oppressiveness of his home life.
   Arriving in the frontier of central Wisconsin, the Muir family homesteaded in

a sandy tract of land in Marquette County near the confluence of the Fox and Wisconsin Rivers. The eleven-year-old Muir was at first exhilarated by "that glorious Wisconsin wilderness," as he later called it, but he was soon worn down by the physical rigors of pioneer life and his father's expectation that his sons would bear the brunt of clearing the land and removing the stumps. The frequent whippings and sermons Muir endured as an adolescent strengthened his rebellion and his determination to leave home as soon as possible. Though the Muir children were obviously bright, they received little formal schooling beyond scriptural readings, so with his meager earnings Muir bought himself a small private library and developed an interest in travel narratives.

∽

Donald Worster is the Hall Distinguished Professor of American History at the University of Kansas and the author of many books, including A River Running West: The Life of John Wesley Powell *(2001);* The Wealth of Nature: Environmental History and the Ecological Imagination *(1993);* Dust Bowl: The Southern Plains in the 1930's *(1979), winner of the Bancroft Prize; and* Nature's Economy: A History of Ecological Ideas *(1977).*

∽

Muir showed an early mechanical aptitude that promised an escape from the drudgery of farm work. His exhibition of his homemade inventions at the Wisconsin State Fair led to an invitation to study at the University of Wisconsin at Madison, though he could not afford to stay to finish his degree. Instead, he left for Canada to avoid the Civil War draft and worked in Ontario for two years before returning to the United States.

An unfortunate industrial accident in an Indianapolis carriage factory left Muir temporarily blinded and in 1867 motivated him to embark on a thousand-mile botanizing walk through the South to Florida, where he stopped in Key West to recuperate after contracting malaria and then sailed for Cuba. He had hoped to follow Alexander Von Humboldt's footsteps and explore the Amazon, but instead he changed his plans and sailed to California in 1868. After arriving in San Francisco, Muir headed for Yosemite Valley and spent his first summer in the Sierras as a shepherd. That experience awakened in him a deep passion for the California mountains, and he recorded in his journals: "I am hopelessly and forever a mountaineer." Though he hated the destructiveness of the sheep, Muir appreciated the freedom to wander in and explore Yosemite Valley and its surroundings. He had enormous physical strength and vitality, and he could hike all day on nothing but bread and water. He often risked life and limb in scaling perilous cliff faces and glacier fields. Once he climbed a tall sugar pine to swing back and forth, experiencing the exhilaration of a Sierra windstorm. Muir settled in Yosemite and worked as a tour guide as he began to ponder the geology of these mountains and how they had been shaped. He took part in several scientific surveys and gradually became a knowledgeable, self-taught field geologist. An accomplished mountaineer, he climbed most of the high peaks in California, including Mount Ritter, Mount Whitney, and Mount Shasta. During his field excursions, Muir carefully noted the signs of recent glaciation and gradually developed his glacial theory of the formation of Yosemite Valley and the California Sierras, which was at odds with the conventional Uniformitarian theories of the time. He was later vindicated by other scientists. An abstract of his field studies of glaciers was published by the American Academy of Sciences. He collected alpine plant specimens for the distinguished Harvard botanist Asa Grey. After he returned to San Francisco, he began to publish travel and natural history essays about the California Nevadas in *The Overland Monthly, Harper's,* and *The Century.*

The spiritual influence of the mountains also gradually led him to abandon his orthodox fundamentalist Christianity and embrace a mystical pantheism. He felt a deep connection to the rest of nature. "Come to the mountains and get their glad tidings," he proclaimed. He believed that climbing mountains elicits intellectual and spiritual elevation. He came to "worship all of God's works" because, for him, "the laws of Nature were only another way of saying the laws of God." He began to write travel and natural history essays for California newspapers and magazines extolling his wilderness ethic. A fervent egalitarian, Muir linked democracy and nature in his mind. At Yosemite he discovered that "when we try to pick out anything by itself, we find it hitched to everything else in the universe." He became a firm Darwinist and rejected all biblical notions of Creation, though toward the end of his life he became more conventionally religious, more of a Deist than a pantheist. When Ralph Waldo Emerson traveled to California in 1871, he asked to meet Muir, who guided him through Yosemite Valley. Muir began to be viewed as the Transcendentalist successor to Emerson and Henry Thoreau.

Muir gradually became more active in California conservation efforts. He protested the destruction of California's forests and the hydraulic mining that ravaged forests and rivers. He spoke out to save the last groves of sequoias from cutting, including the largest, the General Sherman Tree. In addition, he protested against the burning of forests by sheep men and the destruction of mountain meadows and wildflowers by the ravening hordes of sheep.

In 1879, Muir made the first of his seven trips to Alaska, where he risked his life exploring the glaciers in Glacier Bay to find evidence of glacial activity. He returned with the famous story of Stickeen, the heroic dog who accompanied him on his explorations of the glaciers. About this time, Muir was introduced to his future wife, Louie Strentzel, the only child of parents who owned a large fruit and vineyard ranch in the central California valley. After their marriage in 1880, Muir took over the daily operation and management of Alhambra, the Strentzel estate, but that did not prevent him from making annual excursions, though his wife preferred to remain at home with their two daughters, Wanda and Helen. In 1881, he was invited to accompany an official American survey along the Alaska coast. Muir would spend the next twenty years alternating between his farming responsibilities and his desire to return to the wilderness. He became active in the Grange Movement and gradually assumed increasingly important leadership roles in the state and national conservation and parks movements. He was one of the founding members of the Sierra Club in 1886, and he used his influence to promote a public appreciation of the outdoors. Muir believed that "there is a love of wild nature in everybody."

In 1893, he was urged by his admirers to collect his magazine articles and essays into his first book, *The Mountains of California*, which was published in 1894. Despite his reputation as an eccentric loner, Muir was actually a warm, gregarious person and a great conversationalist who had many friends and admirers. His vitality and exuberant love of nature taught Americans of the Gilded Age to enjoy outdoor exercise and natural history. Wealthy businessmen and prominent leaders sought his company on their wilderness excursions, including the railroad baron Edward Harrison, as well as Emerson and Theodore Roosevelt, both of whom became close friends of Muir.

Muir's prominence as an author and naturalist gradually drew him into the controversies over the formation of Yosemite National Park and the fate of Hetch Hetchy Valley, which Muir believed should be preserved because it was as spectacular as Yosemite Valley. Despite his efforts, it was ultimately dammed in 1913 to create a reservoir for the city of San Francisco. Muir advocated public ownership of wilderness and spent the last decade of his life fighting to preserve the legacy of the parks and conservation movement after it split into the "wise use" and preservationist factions. He was one of the United States' first and best park naturalists and guides. Along with his friend John Burroughs, Muir became a prominent voice during the Progressive Era, developing a love of nature and the outdoors into a post-Calvinistic wilderness ethic. Muir split with his old friend Gifford Pinchot over the damming of Hetch Hetchy Valley and the extent of mining and logging that should be permitted on federal lands. Though Muir understood that some resource extraction was inevitable, he fought to protect national parks and forests from uncontrolled greed and avarice.

Muir saw the publication of four of his major books during his lifetime—*The Mountains of California*, *Our National Parks* (1901), *The Yosemite* (1912), and *The Story of My Boyhood and Youth* (1913)—and he left several other book manuscripts to be published posthumously, including *A Thousand-Mile Walk to the Gulf* (1916) and *My First Summer in the Sierras* (1916). Otherwise, his last years were marked by illness and loss. His wife Louie died of pneumonia in 1905, and Muir and his daughter Helen wintered in Arizona for health reasons. Muir's lung problems were persistent, and he eventually died of pneumonia in Los Angeles in 1913.

Despite this book's overall excellence, Worster does not present a literary biography. Instead, his *A Passion for Nature* presents Muir more as a public figure than as an author or natural history writer. Worster does not sufficiently evaluate Muir's literary reputation or importance as an American nature writer. After all, Muir was considered an important enough writer to be elected to the American Academy of Arts and Sciences in 1912, and he received honorary degrees from Harvard and University of California at Berkeley. The issues of how Muir developed the post-Transcendentalist tradition of American nature writing and the extent of his legacy as a nature writer still need to be addressed.

Andrew J. Angyal

Review Sources

American Scientist 96, no. 6 (November/December, 2008): 508-510.
Booklist 105, no. 14 (October 15, 2008): 7.
Library Journal 133, no. 16 (October 1, 2008): 91.
Science 322 (November 7, 2008): 859-860.

PEOPLE OF THE BOOK

Author: Geraldine Brooks (1955-   )
Publisher: Viking Penguin (New York). 372 pp. $25.95
Type of work: Novel
Time: 1480 and 1492; 1609; 1894; 1940, 1996, and 2002
Locale: Tarragona and Seville, Spain; Venice, Italy;
   Vienna, Austria; Sarajevo, Bosnia

A valuable Jewish manuscript, dating from medieval Spain, has been preserved at the National Museum in Sarajevo, Bosnia; this fictional story imagines how the book might have survived through five hundred years of historical turmoil

Principal characters:
   HANNA HEATH, a young woman from
      Australia, an expert on medieval manuscripts
   OZREN KARAMAN, librarian at the Sarajevo National Museum who
      rescued valuable artifacts during the Serbian siege
   LOLA, a Jewish girl who joins the partisans in fighting against the
      German occupation
   SERIF KAMAL, the chief librarian at the National Museum, a Muslim
   LELA KAMAL, his wife who befriends Lola
   GENERAL FABER, a German commandant who directs the ethnic
      cleansing of the city
   FRANZ HIRSCHFELDT, a Jewish physician who treats clients having
      venereal diseases
   FLORIEN MITTL, a bookbinder with advanced syphilis
   JUDAH ARYEH, a Jewish rabbi
   DOMENICO VISTORINI, a Catholic priest who censors books suspected of
      containing heresy
   REYNA DE SERENA, a wealthy Jewish woman who pretends to be a
      Catholic convert
   KING FERDINAND and QUEEN ISABELLA, rulers during the Spanish
      Inquisition
   DAVID BEN-SHOUSHAN, a Jewish scribe
   RUTI, his daughter
   REUBEN, his son, who converted in order to marry a Catholic girl
   ZAHRA, an African slave girl who has a talent for artwork
   THE EMIR, a tyrannical Muslim ruler with a harem of concubines and
      eunuchs
   NURA, a Catholic young woman in the harem, captured in war
   NETANEL HA-LEVI, a respected Jewish physician
   BENJAMIN, his son who is deaf and dumb

Geraldine Brooks is an accomplished writer with a broad repertoire. She wrote for *The Wall Street Journal* as a foreign correspondent, reporting from Bosnia, Somalia,

Geraldine Brooks, born and raised in Australia, was a correspondent for The Wall Street Journal *in Bosnia, Somalia, and other war zones. She has published two works of nonfiction:* Nine Parts of Desire: The Hidden World of Islamic Women *(1995) and* Foreign Correspondence: A Pen Pal's Journey from Down Under to All Over *(1998). Her Civil War novel, titled* March *(2005), won the Pulitzer Prize.*

and other locations of conflict. Her observations as a journalist formed the background for two books about current international issues. More recently, she made a name for herself with two novels of historical fiction. One of these, a Civil War novel entitled *March*, received the prestigious Pulitzer Prize in Fiction for 2006.

People of the Book is based on the remarkable survival of a fifteenth century Jewish haggadah, a manuscript that tells the story of the exodus from Egypt, to be used at the annual Passover celebration. This book, with its colorful illustrations, somehow survived the Spanish Inquisition, the Catholic Church's book burnings in Italy, looting by German troops during World War II, and the Serbian-Bosnian civil war in the 1990's. While Brooks was a correspondent in Sarajevo, Bosnia, she heard the dramatic, true story of the Muslim librarian who put himself into personal danger to rescue the book from destruction. She was inspired to write an imaginative account of the people who might have been involved in creating and preserving this cultural treasure through five centuries of human history.

The story begins in 1996 in Sarajevo, shortly after U.N. troops had brought an end to the three-year Serbian siege of the city. Hanna Heath, a feisty, young Australian woman who is an expert in preservation of medieval manuscripts, has been called in to prepare the haggadah for a public exposition. Hanna is picked up at the Sarajevo airport by a U.N. armored car and is driven to the bank where the manuscript was hidden in a vault when Serbians were shelling the city. Brooks gives a vivid description of the destruction of the once-beautiful city as seen through Hanna's eyes: "We passed an apartment block that looked like the dollhouse I'd had as a girl, where the entire front wall lifted off to reveal the rooms within. In this block, the wall had been peeled away by an explosion . . . . As we sped by, I realized that people were somehow still living there, their only protection a few sheets of plastic billowing in the wind."

At the bank, Hanna is introduced to Ozren Karaman, the chief librarian at the Bosnian National Museum. During the Serbian bombardment, he personally had carried various valuable objects, including the haggadah, from the museum to the bank for storage. Karaman symbolizes the human suffering of civilians in wartime, his wife having been killed by a sniper and his son left in a coma because of a brain injury. Hanna works for several days on the technical aspect of repairing the manuscript, but she becomes fascinated by several unusual clues that give hints where the book may have been during its five-hundred-year history. Among the pages she finds a white hair, an insect wing, a reddish stain, and the signature of an Italian book censor, and she notes that the clasp to hold the pages together is missing. Each clue leads to a fictional episode in the history of the book.

The first episode takes place in 1940 after German troops had marched into Sarajevo. General Faber, the Nazi commandant, had orders to cleanse the city of Jews and Serbs by deporting them to labor camps. Lola, a teenage Jewish girl who escapes by wearing a Muslim headscarf that hides her face, is rescued by Serif Kamal and his wife, who pretend that she is their family servant. Serif works at the National Museum, where the haggadah is one of its most valuable treasures. General Faber wants to confiscate the book for himself, but the museum director tricks him into thinking that the museum no longer has it. Serif then carries the manuscript to a nearby village, where a butterfly wing accidentally is caught between its pages. Serif finds a perfect hiding place for the haggadah in the library of the local mosque between two volumes of Islamic law. Lola survives the Nazi genocide and the manuscript survives confiscation only through the courageous efforts of a dedicated Muslim.

The next episode takes place in 1894 in Vienna, Austria, where the haggadah had been sent from the regional museum in Sarajevo for rebinding. Brooks gives a negative description of fashionable Vienna toward the end of the nineteenth century as a "capital of carnality," with frequent sexual scandals in the news. Franz Hirschfeldt is a Jewish doctor who treats wealthy, aristocratic clients for venereal disease. Florien Mittl is a bookbinder who is desperate for medical help to treat his advanced case of syphilis. The museum has given him the job of rebinding the haggadah. Since he does not have the money for a treatment, he gives Hirschfeldt in payment the ornate silver clasp of the manuscript. The clasp that was missing when Hanna inspected the manuscript a hundred years later was made into a beautiful set of earrings. As a participant in Vienna's casual morality, Hirschfeldt has both a wife and a mistress, putting him into a frivolous quandary as to which woman deserves the earrings more.

Going further back in time, the third episode in the history of the haggadah takes place at Venice, Italy, in 1609. Judah Aryeh is a Jewish rabbi who has formed a friendship with a Catholic priest, Domenico Vistorini, who was appointed by the Vatican as the official censor of heresy. (To create the character of Aryeh and his life in Venice, Brooks gives credit to a 1988 book titled *The Autobiography of a Seventeenth Century Venetian Rabbi*.) In the story, a wealthy woman, Reyna de Serena, makes a generous donation to Aryeh for support of Jews in the ghetto, and she also entrusts him with her haggadah in order to obtain the censor's approval for its content. During the Carnival season just before Lent, people can wear masks in public, which hides their identity. Aryeh, who has an unfortunate addiction to gambling, puts on a mask that enables him to leave the ghetto after curfew and to enter a Venetian gambling parlor where Jews are not permitted. Brooks gives a vivid description of Aryeh's emotions as he first doubles Serena's money but eventually loses everything. The haggadah then becomes the focus of an intense, theological argument between the rabbi and the priest in which both men reach a personal crisis.

The fourth fictional episode takes place in Spain in 1492, when the Spanish Inquisition was at its worst. King Ferdinand and Queen Isabella believed that the just completed defeat of the Muslim infidels at Granada was "a sign of divine will that Spain be a Christian country. It is then their intention to thank God for their victory by declaring Spain a land where no Jew may remain." The king signs a decree of expulsion, stating that all Jews either have to convert to Christianity or have to leave the country immediately. The family of an elderly Jewish scribe, David ben-Shoushan, is caught in this situation. David is preparing a haggadah in Hebrew script for his nephew's wedding. To accompany the text, he has purchased a set of biblical illustrations. His son, Reuben, who has converted to Catholicism in order to marry a Christian girl, has been arrested by the Inquisition. The explicit description of what his torturers do to him makes for gory reading. David's daughter, Ruti, is away from home when soldiers come and kill her father. Ruti survives the persecution by wearing a Christian woman's clothing. She carries the haggadah to the harbor at Tarragona, Spain, from where some of the more fortunate Jews were able to escape to Italy by ship.

In the final episode, Brooks imagines how the colorful illustrations that accompany the haggadah might have been created. Zahra is a young African girl who is captured by Berbers, taken to Spain, and sold as a slave. Her new owner instructs her how to draw, using a single white hair from a cat, tiny pictures on a grain of rice. Her talent as an artist brings her to the palace of a despotic Muslim emir who demands a painting of the current favorite concubine in his harem. When the emir is overthrown by a revolt, Zahra is taken in by a Jewish doctor's family, which includes a deaf-mute son, Benjamin. She hears Bible stories read from the Old Testament, some of which parallel those in the Qur'ān. Zahra makes it her mission to illustrate the biblical narratives so that Benjamin can understand and appreciate the history of his people.

The five episodes in *People of the Book* are independent short stories, tied together by the survival of a valuable manuscript. A similar format was used successfully in the popular novel *The Girl in Hyacinth Blue* (1999) by Susan Vreeland, in which fictional anecdotes were used to trace a painting back to the time of the seventeenth century Dutch artist Jan Vermeer. Brooks has created a series of memorable characters who struggle with problems of intolerance, persecution, and the social upheavals of their time. There is a subplot in the book that deals with the life and personality of Hanna, the Australian woman who had come to Sarajevo to examine the manuscript. As a teenager, she had rebelled against a domineering mother, and that conflict had never been resolved. Hanna's story seems extraneous to the historical episodes, which are the core of the novel. Brooks is a talented storyteller whose writing gives an engrossing view of the human drama in its historical settings.

Hans G. Graetzer

Review Sources

Booklist 104, no. 3 (October 1, 2007): 5.
The Christian Century 125, no. 25 (December 16, 2008): 26.
Elle 23, no. 5 (January, 2008): 77.
Kirkus Reviews 75, no. 21 (November 1, 2007): 1116.
Library Journal 132, no. 18 (November 1, 2007): 58.
New York 41, no. 3 (January 21, 2008): 94.
The New Yorker 84, no. 1 (February 11, 2008): 153.
Publishers Weekly 254, no. 39 (October 1, 2007): 34.
School Library Journal 54, no. 4 (April, 2008): 172.
The Times Literary Supplement, February 22, 2008, p. 120.
The Wall Street Journal 251, no. 9 (January 11, 2008): W2.

A PERSON OF INTEREST

Author: Susan Choi (1969-   )
Publisher: Viking Penguin (New York). 356 pp. $24.95
Type of work: Novel
Time: Unspecified year in the first decade of the twenty-
first century
Locale: A small college town in Midwest United States

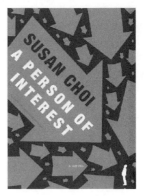

Choi's story of a professor, whose life changes dramati-
cally when a colleague is killed in the adjoining office and
he becomes a "person of interest" to the federal agents try-
ing to identify who mailed the deadly bomb

> *Principal characters:*
> LEE, an Asian-born professor of
>   mathematics in his late sixties
> RICK HENDLEY, a popular young mathematics professor, victim of a
>   bomb in his office
> LEWIS GAITHER, a graduate student with Lee decades earlier
> AILEEN, Gaither's wife, who married and divorced Lee prior to her death
> JOHN GAITHER, son of Lewis and Aileen born shortly after Aileen left
>   Lewis
> MICHIKO, Lee's second wife, long since divorced
> ESTHER, Lee and Aileen's daughter, estranged from Lee
> JIM MORRISON, Federal Bureau of Investigation (FBI) agent who tracks
>   Lee
> FRANK FANSO, a former colleague Lee had admired but was not close to
> THE BRAIN BOMBER, the media nickname for killer who writes
>   manifesto saying the smartest scientists should be destroyed

Lee, whose first name is never given, was born in an unspecified Asian country but
has been in the United States most of his life. He is in his late sixties, nearing the end
of a rather mundane career in the Department of Mathematics and Computer Science
at an undistinguished university in a small town in the Midwest. He lives alone, and
he is in general distanced from the community and the college. Not ready to retire
from teaching because he has nothing else to do, he foresees none of the upheavals
that will change his set routines and force him to reevaluate his entire life history.

As Susan Choi's novel *A Person of Interest* opens, Lee is realizing that he had
never liked the bomb victim, his colleague Professor Hendley, and that much of that
dislike was because, unlike himself, Hendley was young and popular with students.
Their offices were next to each other, and Lee jealously noticed that students seldom
came to see him, but there were often lines of students eager to talk with Hendley.
Both professors, however, are alone in their offices when Hendley opens a small
packet he has received through campus mail and it explodes in his face. Lee is
knocked over by the blast, and it is a student who first sees Hendley and calls for help.

Hendley is taken to intensive care at the local hospital, where he dies a few days later.

No culprit is immediately identified, and rumors abound. Lee is startled when it begins to appear that he is being singled out for more than routine questioning by the FBI agents who are pursuing the case. Lee does not attend the campuswide memorial ceremony for Hendley, and his absence is noticed. Soon, all the office staff, so important in every department, are avoiding him, and faculty and students in groups suddenly stop talking when he appears. Attendance in his classes dwindles. Although Lee has had tenure for more than twenty years, the chair of the department informs him that another faculty member will take over his classes for the remainder of the spring semester and will teach his summer class. Things become even worse when the FBI refers to him as "a person of interest," not necessarily a suspect but someone who has information about the case. Agent Jim Morrison believes Lee knows a lot more about the case than he has told them.

∼

Susan Choi has a B.A. in Literature from Yale University and an M.F.A. from Cornell University. In addition to three novels, she has published several short stories and coauthored with David Remnick an anthology of stories from The New Yorker. *She was named a Guggenheim Fellow in 2004.*

∼

Television and newspaper media pick up on this aspect, and Lee's name is always mentioned in conjunction with the fatal explosion. When major newspapers and journals across the country publish an anonymous manifesto by someone, now referred to as the Brain Bomber, who says that all the brightest scientists should be killed before they create more harm in the world (there would have been no atom bomb without an Albert Einstein, for example), Lee finds himself not just ostracized but constantly plagued by the media and the FBI agents. He is forced to take a polygraph test, which first seems to exonerate him but then is discarded because statistics suggest that the "lie detector" is not reliable when administered to people from certain groups, including Asians.

Complicating things for Lee and for the investigating agents is that immediately after the fatal bombing, Lee receives a long, unsigned letter, although Lee knows its source. The letter is from a disliked acquaintance from his past, Lewis Gaither, who says he has read about the bombing and wants to know if Lee is safe. Lee knows there is more to it than apparent concern; it is a taunting and an unwelcome reminder of long-ago events.

In an extended flashback, the reader learns that decades earlier Lee had been in graduate school with Gaither, and what started as a tentative friendship between them had ended badly. Gaither, less capable at math than Lee, was an ardent fundamentalist Christian who always wanted to convert people. He had insisted Lee accompany him and his wife to an evangelical gathering, but the result was unexpected. When Lee met Aileen, he learned she was equally antithetical to Gaither's religious fervor, and they soon began a secretive affair. When Lee learned that Aileen was pregnant with Gaither's child, he ended their relationahip. Aileen, however, had no wish to stay with Gaither, and soon she left him and wrote to Lee. They married, but Gaither insisted on having the baby boy, John, and tricked Aileen into signing a document that gave him full custody. Lee now remembers with shame that he was glad not to have Gaither's baby around, and, although he and Aileen eventually had a baby girl, Esther, he knows Aileen had wanted her son, too. Lee blames Gaither for the unhappiness of his marriage, though he eventually recognizes it was in large part because of Lee's resentment at having a wife who had been Gaither's. Aileen died when their daughter Esther was fourteen. Lee thinks his second marriage, to Michiko, a Japanese woman who, it turned out, primarily wanted a way to become an American citizen, was also tainted by his distrust in the idea of closeness as manifested in his relationship with Aileen.

Lee is guilt-ridden and angry at the letter from Lewis. He writes back, but his letter is returned, addressee unknown. The FBI agents, who have been checking all campus mail, ask Lee about the letter, and Lee lies and says he has thrown it away. The agents search his house. Jim Morrison becomes increasingly interested in what Lee might be hiding. Lee is certain now that Gaither is the bomber, and he tells this to Morrison. A few days later, Morrison claims that Gaither is dead, so Lee must still be withholding information.

Lee becomes increasingly disoriented, stressed, and insomniac as the FBI pursues him. He has no friends, and the only lawyer he knows is his divorce lawyer, who tells Lee this case is beyond his expertise. Lee would like to believe his daughter Esther would be among those who read about his situation and somehow come to rescue him, but for many years he has not even known her whereabouts. Frank Fanso, a former colleague who had left for a more prestigious university, does read about him and phones Lee, but there is little Frank can suggest to solve the case and thus remove Lee as a suspect.

Often operating only at the level of hallucination and panic, Lee knows he is the one who needs to find the Brain Bomber, but he has no idea how to do so. Another mail delivery brings further complications. Lee receives a brown envelope that contains a page from his dissertation—a page, not a duplicated copy. He surreptitiously sneaks into the university library to the section that contains one of only three copies of his dissertation, and he finds that indeed the page has been cut from his work. Why is Gaither or, if he is dead, someone else determined to stalk and frame him so thoroughly?

What the novel does brilliantly is to take the reader into the increasingly tortured mind of a fairly ordinary man when he is faced with the perilous unknown. At one point, Lee is hiding in his bedroom. From his bed, he looks in the mirror on the dresser, seeing the reflected images of part of the windows and beyond to the crowd of neighbors outside who are gathered to watch with glee the FBI agents and television reporters coming to the house of someone they do not know but are ready to consider guilty. What mathematician Lee sees in the mirror is, he thinks, "the simplest geometry, the angles of incidence and reflection," but clearly it is also symbolic of his entire situation at this point. The unexpected incidents that have occurred have forced him to reflect on what led to his being in his present miserable situation. Only by exhaustive examination of his past and of the kind of person he really is (apart from the idea of himself that he has created) does he have a chance to do anything to ameliorate the current predicament.

In addition to Lee's intense self-examination, which leads him to revise his view of himself and others when secrets he has buried even from himself are unexpectedly uncovered, another theme that resonates throughout the novel is the ease with which outsiders can garner information about anyone. The Brain Bomber clearly has access to intimate knowledge of Lee and his career as well as his current address and situation. The media, insatiable in the quest for sensational copy related to the case, are careless of truth in what they print and report. The FBI has no qualms about searching Lee's house, tailing him (sometimes as many as six cars follow him around), tapping his telephone, or intercepting his mail. His garbage containers are suddenly emptied on a day when the sanitation department is not due. He does not have a cell phone, but if he did his every location could be easily traced, and similarly if he used a computer his e-mail and all Internet activity could be tracked. Fingerprints on letters become an issue, and if there were DNA evidence that, too, would be under scrutiny. Even more glaring, concerning human rights, is the fact that Lee is essentially used as bait in the effort to capture the killer.

Susan Choi's first novel, *The Foreign Student* (1998), won the Asian-American Literary Award for fiction, and her second, *American Woman* (2003), loosely based on the life of Patty Hearst, was a finalist for the 2004 Pulitzer Prize. *A Person of Interest* has been widely reviewed and critically acclaimed and was a finalist for the PEN/Faulkner Award. Increasingly, her fiction is particularly noted for its literary style and for her often poetic use of language. In *A Person of Interest*, Choi repeatedly demonstrates that she knows how to use language to build tension and suspense, although the whodunit detective fiction aspect of the novel is less in the foreground than her creation of the main character, Lee, and her in-depth portrayal of his mental state as the plot unfolds.

Lois A. Marchino

Review Sources

Booklist 104, no. 8 (December 15, 2007): 24.
Kirkus Reviews 75, no. 21 (November 1, 2007): 1117.
Los Angeles Times, February 3, 2008, p. R3.
The New York Times Book Review, February 17, 2008, p. 9.
The New Yorker 84, no. 3 (March 3, 2008): 83.
Publishers Weekly 254, no. 44 (November 5, 2007): 41.
The Village Voice 53, no. 5 (January 30, 2008): 47.
Vogue 198, no. 2 (February, 2008): 25.
The Wall Street Journal 251, no. 15 (January 18, 2008): W2.
The Washington Post Book World, February 24, 2008, p. BW07.

PICTURES AT A REVOLUTION
Five Movies and the Birth of the New Hollywood

Author: Mark Harris (1963-   )
Publisher: Penguin Press (New York). 490 pp. $27.95
Type of work: Film
Time: 1963-1968
Locale: Los Angeles, New York City, Texas, Illinois,
    Tennessee, England, St. Lucia

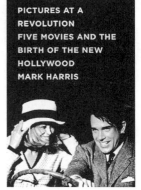

Five films released in 1967 reflect major changes in Hollywood

Principal personages:
WARREN BEATTY, actor and producer
ARTHUR PENN, director
ROBERT BENTON, screenwriter
DAVID NEWMAN, screenwriter
MIKE NICHOLS, director
BUCK HENRY, screenwriter and actor
DUSTIN HOFFMAN, actor
NORMAN JEWISON, director
STIRLING SILLIPHANT, screenwriter
HAL ASHBY, film editor
SIDNEY POITIER, actor
ROD STEIGER, actor
STANLEY KRAMER, director and producer
KATHARINE HEPBURN, actor
SPENCER TRACY, actor
ARTHUR P. JACOBS, producer
LESLIE BRICUSSE, screenwriter and composer
REX HARRISON, actor
JACK WARNER, studio executive
DARRYL F. ZANUCK, studio executive

Film scholars have long contended that 1967 represented a turning point for American films. Since the advent of television in the early 1950's, the Hollywood studios had been struggling to retain their audience, trying gimmicks such as 3-D, widescreen processes such as CinemaScope, and large-scale biblical epics, adventure films, and musicals, anything to make Americans think they were missing something bigger and better by staying at home and staring at the tiny, usually black-and-white box. American films remained aimed at the mythical average viewer, meaning white, middle class, and middle aged. As a result, the studios continued in the 1960's to turn out products that imitated each other, whether Doris Day sex comedies or James Bond spy thrillers. According to Mark Harris in *Pictures at a Revolution: Five Movies and the Birth of the New Hollywood*, "emotional ambiguity and grown-up sexuality were virtually black market items in American films of the time." When *The Sound of Music* (1965) became the all-time box-office champion, the studios rushed to make more big films based on Broadway musicals. Hollywood faced, writes Harris, "a creative low point in the sound era."

What the Hollywood executives refused to recognize was that there was not one audience but a cluster of audiences: men, women, children, teenagers, college students, African Americans, and others defined by age, ethnicity, sexuality, education, and income. Then along came two films that no one initially wanted to produce—*Bonnie and Clyde* and *The Graduate*, both released in 1967—to shake the foundations of the studio system. Harris examines these two films and contrasts them to the three other films nominated for Academy Awards as the best pictures of 1967: the interracial romance-family drama *Guess Who's Coming to Dinner*, the family musical *Doctor Doolittle*, and the murder mystery with racial overtones *In the Heat of the Night*.

For fifteen years, Mark Harris was a writer and editor covering films, television, and books at Entertainment Weekly, *where he now writes the Final Cut column.* Pictures at a Revolution *is his first book. A graduate of Yale University, Harris lives in New York City with his husband, playwright Tony Kushner.*

The heroes of Harris's engrossing tale are the *Bonnie and Clyde* contingent of screenwriters Robert Benton and David Newman, director Arthur Penn, and, especially, producer-star Warren Beatty; director Mike Nichols, screenwriter Buck Henry, and star Dustin Hoffman of *The Graduate*; and Sidney Poitier, star of both *In the Heat of the Night* and *Guess Who's Coming to Dinner*. The villain is Rex Harrison, the egotistical star of *Doctor Doolittle*. Harris also offers sympathetic portraits of Arthur P. Jacobs, bumbling producer of *Doctor Doolittle*, and the somewhat-out-of-touch Stanley Kramer, director-producer of *Guess Who's Coming to Dinner*. In his evenhanded, nonjudgmental manner, Harris shows how complicated film production is, a process too often marred by compromise, infighting, jealousy, insecurity, incompetence, and the unexpected, as with the unpredictable weather and uncooperative animal performers plaguing the already-over-budget *Doctor Doolittle*.

Harris provides a detailed production history for each film, from inception to financing to completion to public display and beyond. Benton and Newman took the mythical American story of 1930's bank robbers Bonnie Parker and Clyde Barrow and imbued it with such influences as the films of French Nouvelle Vague directors François Truffaut and Jean-Luc Godard to make it a completely different kind of crime film. The screenwriters wanted *Bonnie and Clyde* to be the first American film made in the New Wave style, with an elliptical narrative and strong sexual content, and they wanted to turn the protagonists into antiestablishment antiheroes. Truffaut and Godard were both initially interested in directing the film before abandoning the project for complicated reasons Harris painstakingly explains. Once Beatty joined the project as producer and star, he persuaded a reluctant Arthur Penn, with whom he had worked on *Mickey One* (1965), to take charge.

Comedian-turned-stage-director Nichols was committed to *The Graduate*, based on Charles Webb's 1963 novel, before making his first film, *Who's Afraid of Virginia Woolf?* (1966). The major problems facing Nichols, also influenced by European films, were coming up with a workable script (several screenwriters preceded Henry) and casting, especially the lead, a sensitive and confused recent college graduate. One of the highlights of *Pictures at a Revolution* is Harris's long account of how unlikely unknown Hoffman got the part, painting the actor as almost afraid of success.

While *Doctor Doolittle* is clearly inferior to the other nominees, Harris makes the story of how this lumbering musical, based on Hugh Lofting's children's books, came to be as fascinating as his accounts of *Bonnie and Clyde* and *The Graduate*. The film's budget slowly swelled into one of the biggest in history as Darryl F. Zanuck of Twentieth Century-Fox watched in horror. Leslie Bricusse, the screenwriter, composer, and lyricist, struggled to appease everyone in the production while a never-to-be-pleased Harrison threw tantrums.

The big story of *Guess Who's Coming to Dinner* was less its plot than the casting of Katharine Hepburn and Spencer Tracy as the supposedly liberal parents whose daughter, played by Hepburn's niece, Katharine Houghton, plans to marry an African American doctor, played by Poitier. The film was the ninth and final pairing of Hepburn and Tracy, whose casting was the main reason that Poitier agreed to an underwritten role. Kramer's challenge as director was to keep the film going despite the obviously serious illness of Tracy, who died shortly afterward.

The other problem with *Guess Who's Coming to Dinner* was the timid approach to the theme of interracial marriage taken by Kramer and screenwriter William Rose, an American expatriate long in England who knew nothing about American cultural changes since World War II. Harris shows how Kramer and Rose created a sanitized vision of racial relations that reviewers ridiculed, yet the film was Columbia Pictures' biggest hit ever, partly because of its star power and the growing black audience and perhaps even because of its inoffensiveness during the era of race riots in cities such as Detroit and Newark.

Harris's account of the making of *In the Heat of the Night* is less dramatic than those about the other four films. He recounts the changes screenwriter Stirling Silliphant made in John Ball's 1965 novel, the casting of Rod Steiger as the sheriff of a small Mississippi town, the efforts of Poitier, as a visiting Philadelphia policeman, to meet the challenge posed by Steiger's powerhouse performance, and the many contributions of film editor Hal Ashby, who took on extra duties, including casting and finding locations for director Norman Jewison. Though the film was shot in Sparta, Illinois, a few scenes involving a cotton plantation had to be shot in Tennessee, creating considerable uneasiness for Poitier, given the racial mood of the time.

While America was caught up in a period of vast social change and conflict, involving the restlessness of African Americans and women, the turmoil of the Vietnam War, and the protests against the war, Hollywood itself was also in a period of flux. Since the 1930's, American films had been restrained by the Motion Picture Production Code, which placed great restrictions on sexual activity, profanity, violence, and the depiction of criminal and antisocial behavior. Several films in the mid-1960's, particularly *Who's Afraid of Virginia Woolf?* and *Blow-Up* (1966), offered strong challenges to the code, weakening it so severely that it became obvious that the antiquated system was on its way out. Harris examines how the ongoing changes helped *Bonnie and Clyde* and *The Graduate* be more mature than they could have been just a couple of years earlier. These changes resulted in the film rating system, which began in the fall of 1968.

In 1967 and afterward, *Doctor Doolittle* and *Guess Who's Coming to Dinner* were seen as relics of a Hollywood resistant to change, while *Bonnie and Clyde* and *The Graduate* were at the other extreme. Except for having a black hero solve a crime in the South and showing some discreet nudity, *In the Heat of the Night* was somewhere in the middle, essentially a conventional murder mystery.

Jack Warner and other Warner Bros. executives hated *Bonnie and Clyde*, seeing it merely as an excessively violent B-film. When it opened in August, 1967, many of the film reviewers agreed, notably Bosley Crowther of *The New York Times*, who attacked it relentlessly, leading to his removal as the newspaper's primary film reviewer at the end of the year. Joseph Morgenstern of *Newsweek* gave the film a harsh review, had second thoughts, saw it again, and reviewed it again, this time enthusiastically. *Bonnie and Clyde* gradually became a cause célèbre, with *Time* offering a cover story to explain its wide appeal, and Pauline Kael publishing a lengthy rave in *The New Yorker*, after the essay was rejected by *The New Republic*. Despite critical support and good box office, Warner Bros. was reluctant to give the public a chance to see the film, opening it only in locales scattered about the country and closing it in places such as New York City where it was doing booming business. Not until the Academy Award nominations were announced in February, 1968, did *Bonnie and Clyde* finally receive wide distribution.

Nichols arranged screenings of *The Graduate* for friends who did not know what to make of it and who were puzzled by the casting of the ordinary-looking Hoffman. Few of its first viewers understood *The Graduate*, and many of its reviewers saw it as an attack upon "their standards, their notion of what a well-made picture should be, their ability to control a cultural conversation that they suddenly felt was slipping out of their grasp." The mainstream press that bemoaned hippies and antiwar demonstrators saw *Bonnie and Clyde* and *The Graduate* as further evidence of the decline of American values. One can imagine their horror when *The Graduate* became the third-highest-grossing film of all time, trailing only *The Sound of Music* and *Gone with the Wind* (1939).

When young audiences rushed to theaters and returned for multiple viewings of both *Bonnie and Clyde* and *The Graduate*, what the press termed "the film generation" was launched, and the studios began making more films, such as *Easy Rider* (1969) and *Five Easy Pieces* (1970), about the outsiders or antiestablishment types with whom the young could identify. *Pictures at a Revolution* has an outstanding companion piece in Peter Biskind's *Easy Riders, Raging Bull: How the Sex-Drugs-and-Rock 'n' Roll Generation Saved Hollywood* (1998), which chronicles what Harris calls "a second golden age of studio filmmaking."

The Academy Award voters, up to a point, recognized the quality of the two outsider films, bestowing ten nominations on *Bonnie and Clyde* and seven on *The Grad-*

uate. Even its makers were surprised when, despite unenthusiastic reviews and weak box office, *Doctor Doolittle* received nine nominations. This was still an era, soon to end, when studios were able to control large blocs of votes, and Twentieth Century-Fox employees showed their support despite the film's poor quality. The members of the Academy of Motion Picture Arts and Sciences finally voted with their hearts, however, giving *In the Heat of the Night* five Oscars, including Best Picture, and *Guess Who's Coming to Dinner* two. *Bonnie and Clyde* won two Oscars, for Burnett Guffey's cinematography and Estelle Parsons's supporting performance as Beatty's sister-in-law, and *The Graduate* won one, for Nichols's direction. The most unjust loss was seen to be the choice of Rose's clichéd script over the originality of Benton and Newman's.

Pictures at a Revolution is not just film history but a perceptive character study. Harris excels at describing Beatty's difficult personality, especially his constant battles with Penn; Hoffman's insecurities; Nichols's perfectionism; and the burden placed on Poitier as the main representative of his race for much of the world. Kramer was a mediocre director because he thought "like a producer, concentrating on the overall package rather than the shaping of individual scenes, performances, and moments." Harris does not just report the facts but interprets them, placing them within their historical context and making certain his readers understand what might seem inexplicable more than forty years after the events.

Michael Adams

Review Sources

Booklist 104, nos. 9/10 (January 1, 2008): 32.
Cineaste 33, no. 4 (Fall, 2008): 72-74.
Kirkus Reviews 75, no. 22 (November 15, 2007): 1188.
Library Journal 132, no. 19 (November 15, 2007): 61.
The New York Times, February 11, 2008, p. 9.
The New York Times Book Review, February 17, 2008, p. 13.
Newsweek 151, no. 8 (February 25, 2008): 50.
People 69, no. 8 (March 3, 2008): 46.
Publishers Weekly 254, no. 43 (October 29, 2007): 40.

THE PLAGUE OF DOVES

Author: Louise Erdrich (1954-   )
Publisher: HarperCollins (New York). 314 pp. $25.95
Type of work: Novel
Time: 1896-1980's
Locale: Pluto, North Dakota

The long-ago slaughter of a white family casts a shadow over the inhabitants of a small North Dakota town and the nearby Ojibwa reservation

Principal characters:
> EVELINA (EVEY) HARP, a young part-Ojibwa woman
> SERAPH MILK (MOOSHUM), her maternal grandfather
> SHAMENGWA MILK, Mooshum's crippled younger brother
> GERALDINE MILK, Evey's maternal aunt
> ANTONE BAZIL COUTTS, a judge, hopelessly in love with Geraldine
> CORWIN PEACE, Evey's ne'er-do-well boyfriend
> BILLY PEACE, Corwin's uncle, a powerful evangelist
> MARN WOLDE, the young white wife of Billy Peace
> SISTER MARY ANITA BUCKENDORF, Evey's sixth-grade teacher
> FATHER "HOP ALONG" CASSIDY, a Catholic priest
> HOLY TRACK, an Ojibwa youth who is hanged as a killer
> NEVE HARP, Evey's paternal aunt, the town historian
> CORDELIA LOCHREN, a physician

In *The Plague of Doves*, Louise Erdrich returns to the familiar plains of North Dakota, but with a completely new cast of characters who offer, as usual, a continual surprise. This time her setting is the small town of Pluto (named for the former planet, not for the god of the underworld), where the sparse population consists of Germans, Norwegians, and Metis, the descendants of French-Canadian settlers who intermarried with Ojibwa (also called Chippewa) from the neighboring reservation.

This is a story of connections, mixing regional and human history with fiction and elements of the supernatural. Typically for Erdrich, time is fluid; the present is filled with dizzying relationships, interspersed with tales from the past that reveal the origin and history of the community. The novel begins with a horrific glimpse of a 1911 bloodbath that only an infant survives, then immediately shifts back fifteen years to the time when a sudden plague occurs—brown doves blacken the skies like locusts and settle over the land, devouring everything. Ironically, these frequent emblems of peace are viewed as invaders, and desperate people attempt to drive them away. As the local Catholic priest organizes a procession of the mixed-blood population to pray for deliverance, his young half brother, Seraph Milk, then an altar boy, seizes the re-

Louise Erdrich, an enrolled member of
the Turtle Mountain Band of Ojibwa,
has authored twelve novels, including
Love Medicine *(1984), winner of the*
National Book Critics Circle Award,
and The Last Report on the Miracles at
Little No Horse *(2001), a finalist for*
the National Book Award for fiction.

sulting confusion to run off with his future wife and become the progenitor of the Milk-Harp family.

Erdrich employs three main story lines as well as several minor ones. The first belongs to Evelina (Evey) Harp, granddaughter of Seraph Milk, who is now known as Mooshum (Grandfather). Evey, who comes of age in the novel, is one of several narrators, revealing her childhood crushes on a mischievous classmate, Corwin Peace, and on her sixth-grade teacher, Sister Mary Anita Buckendorf, whom the children call Sister Godzilla. Both will figure in her later life. Evey, who reads Albert Camus's *La Chute* (1956; *The Fall*, 1957) and adores all things French, will attend college, become a psychiatric aide in the state mental hospital, have a brief relationship with one of the patients, and eventually sign herself in as a patient after a bad experience with the LSD that Corwin gives her. (In an Erdrich novel, someone is always slightly mad.)

Mooshum is another of Erdrich's delightful and rascally old men, as is his crippled brother Shamengwa, an untutored artist who plays a magical violin in spite of his "folded-up" arm, damaged by the kick of a cow. (As it was foretold in a dream, Shamengwa received that ancient instrument when it floated directly to him in an otherwise empty canoe, and when his cherished violin is finally stolen, Shamengwa suspects the culprit is Corwin, by then grown, good looking, and reckless.) The two elders delight in teasing Mooshum's strict daughter by sneaking forbidden whiskey past her, which they can manage whenever the unpopular white priest Father Cassidy comes calling in an attempt to save their souls. Shamengwa's conversion is hopeless, since he long ago left the church to return to traditional beliefs, but Mooshum enjoys sparring with the priest and watching his frustration. Later, Father Cassidy eulogizes the wrong brother at a funeral and earns the enmity of the whole family.

One of the tales that Mooshum relates to Evey is a shameful secret widely known in the community yet seldom spoken of—the story of a thirteen-year-old boy who was a distant relative of her grandmother. The youth's pious mother, who was dying of tuberculosis, nailed wooden crosses to her son's boot soles to protect him from the disease, so that his footprints revealed a cross, a holy track, which then became his nickname. Holy Track, whom Erdrich has modeled on a historical figure of the same name, was one of four innocent Ojibwa captured and lynched by an angry mob of Pluto's white citizens, who believed them to be responsible for the brutal murders of the baby's family. Descendants of the mob, as well as of their victims, still live side by side in the area; one of them is Sister Mary Anita. The unspoken bitterness between whites and Indians still remains in Pluto, but silence helps to preserve the amenities of everyday living.

A parallel story line, that of the family of Judge Antone Bazil Coutts, mirrors the history of this region in another way. He explains, "Nothing that happens, *nothing*, is not connected here by blood." In the past the judge's grandfather, Joseph Coutts, a classics teacher, joined a surveying party on a whim to explore town sites in Dakota for the projected railroad. (Elsewhere, Erdrich indicates that this doomed expedition actually took place in 1857.) This group was guided by two Ojibwa brothers, ancestors of Corwin. Unfortunately, both the real and the fictional expeditions chose to leave Minnesota in January to get a head start on other parties. Challenged by bone-chilling temperatures and insufficient provisions, most of which were lost in prairie blizzards, members of the surveying party barely survived. The two Peace guides saved the life of Joseph Coutts near the site that would become Pluto; he then turned to the practice of law, as did his son and grandson after him.

At present, Antone maintains tribal law on the tribal land, observing that "the entire reservation is rife with conflicting passions. We can't seem to keep our hands off one another." Neither can the judge, usually a deliberate man, keep his hands off Evey's unmarried aunt, Geraldine Milk, eagerly courting the tribal enrollment specialist in spite of his ongoing relationship with a married woman.

Still a third story line is narrated by Marn Wolde, the farmer's daughter who marries Corwin's uncle. Marn is only sixteen when she encounters the charismatic Billy Peace, who has already served in the Korean War and is now a minor traveling evangelist. He invites her to a camp meeting where he and others preach and where he prays in tongues over the main speaker's dying mother. Smitten, Marn admits she is "too young to stand against it" and soon marries Billy; they have two children. Eventually they and Billy's followers move back to her family farm, which abuts the reservation and where her parents live with her elderly great-uncle. Billy cajoles Marn's father into signing over his power of attorney to her and thereby to him.

After Billy is suddenly struck by lightning, he seems transformed into a kind of monster, physically expanding as his fame and appetites increase (he can eat a whole cake a day). He grows more inflexible as a healer and a prophet, while his burgeoning organization, known as the kindred, becomes a full-blown cult whose members live in a compound on the farm. He controls their behavior through his rigid Manual of Discipline, ultimately taking away even their names.

Marn herself has a bent toward the supernatural with what she calls her "pictures" or visions. As a form of solace, she has taken up beautiful but poisonous serpents, handling them as a test of faith. The snakes make her feel powerful for the first time, perhaps because Billy is afraid of them. After the copperhead bites her, thus warning her to leave her fanatical husband, Marn recognizes that her life has become a trap, and she plans an escape for herself and for her children. Her final retribution against her husband is melodramatic but nevertheless satisfying.

In terms of style, Erdrich exhibits effortless skill with language. For example, with the arrival of the doves, "the people woke . . . to the scraping and beating of wings, the murmurous susurration, the awful cooing babble, and the sight . . . of the curious and gentle faces of those creatures." In another section, Marn introduces her narrative with a lyrical paragraph as she awaits a storm: "The wind came off the dense-grassed slough, smelling like wet hair, and the hot ditch grass reached for it, butter yellow, . . . each stalk so dry it gave off a puff of smoke when snapped." The involvement of the reader's physical senses renders these images vividly and perfectly.

Having a faultless memory would be helpful in order to follow the frequent time shifts and muddled relationships of these various characters. There are so many diverse threads to the story that it is easy to get lost or confused, and the plot is so densely woven that at first a reader may have difficulty making connections. However, by the end of the book, Erdrich skillfully pulls these threads together. The novel follows Evey's observation: "When we are young, the words are scattered all around us. As they are assembled by experience, so also are we, sentence by sentence, until the story takes shape."

In the end, everything seems to come back to the tree that stands on the farm owned by Marn's parents and that also graces the dust jacket. This is the same tree that was filled with doves during the plague of 1896 and where birds continue to roost in the present—a Tree of Life. After a lengthy search in 1911, this tree was finally selected by the town vigilantes (even though the vote was never unanimous) as sturdy enough for the lynching of Holy Track and his three companions; thus, it is a Hanging Tree. It is also a Funeral Tree, for in its branches the cross-soled boots of Holy Track still dangle as a kind of memorial. While it symbolizes the interrelationships of the extended family tree that so many of these characters share, it remains a tree of bitter, even biblical, knowledge, an emblem of a great wrong and of a reconciliation.

Joanne McCarthy

Review Sources

Booklist 104, nos. 9/10 (January 1, 2008): 21.
Elle 23, no. 9 (May, 2008): 174.
Kirkus Reviews 76, no. 3 (February 1, 2008): 106.
Library Journal 133, no. 3 (February 15, 2008): 90.
Ms. 18, no. 2 (Spring, 2008): 71.
The New York Review of Books 55, no. 12 (July 17, 2008): 37-38.
The New York Times, April 29, 2008, p. E1.
The New York Times Book Review, May 11, 2008, p. 9.
People 69, no. 17 (May 5, 2008): 53.
Publishers Weekly 255, no. 2 (January 14, 2008): 36.
The Women's Review of Books 25, no. 5 (September/October, 2008): 12-13.

THE POST-AMERICAN WORLD

Author: Fareed Zakaria (1964-)
Publisher: W. W. Norton (New York). 292 pp. $25.95
Type of Work: History
Time: "Three tectonic shifts" in world geopolitical history over the last five hundred years—the rise of the Western world, beginning in the fifteenth century and accelerating in the late eighteenth; the rise of the United States at the close of the nineteenth century; "the rise of the rest" in the last years of the twentieth and first decade of the twenty-first centuries
Locale: The major nations of the West—the United States, England, Russia, Germany, and France; the emerging countries of Asia, South America, Africa—notably China, Japan, India, Iran, Iraq, Saudi Arabia, South Korea, North Korea, Brazil, and South Africa

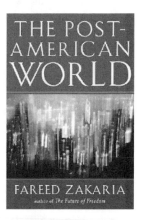

Newsweek *editor-columnist Zakaria presents a breathtaking picture of the emergence of the non-West to create a rich composite of the two hemispheres; his well-titled book envisages not the United States' decline but the gradual suspension of hegemony for accommodation to what he calls the global "stakeholders in the new order"*

Principal personages:
GEORGE W. BUSH, two-term U.S. president of whose foreign policy Zakaria is critical
WINSTON S. CHURCHILL, Britain's World War II prime minister, who possessed "superhuman energy and ambition"
BILL CLINTON, U.S. president during whose tenure American power became more apparent
INDIRA GANDHI, "combative" Indian prime minister, daughter of Jawaharlal Nehru
SADDAM HUSSEIN, long-time dictator of Iraq whose ouster Zakaria at first favored
RONALD REAGAN, U.S. president in 1982 when Zakaria immigrated to the United States and seen by the author as the "embodiment of a strikingly open and expansive country"
ZHENG HE, fifteenth century Chinese admiral who, eighty-seven years before Christopher Columbus, began the first of seven expeditions to the New World with 317 vessels and 28,000 men

In 2003, a young British historian posed an impertinent question for Americans. In his cocktail-table book *Empire: The Rise and Demise of the British World Order and the Lessons for Global Power*, Oxford's Niall Ferguson, who is also Herzog Professor of Financial History at New York University, asks, "Hasn't the time come for the U.S.

~

Fareed Zakaria is the editor of
Newsweek International *and writes a*
weekly column on international affairs.
Born in Mumbai, India, he moved to
the United States to attend college at
Yale. After receiving his Ph.D. from
Harvard, he became the managing
editor of Foreign Affairs. *His previous*
book was The New York Times *best*
seller The Future of Freedom *(2003). A*
naturalized U.S. citizen, Zakaria lives
in New York City.

~

to rethink its historic distaste for colonies and play an imperial role?" Less formally, Ferguson acts like the son-in-law from an eminent family who wishes to persuade his bride's lately powerful family to follow the long out-of-fashion traditions of his own people.

In 2008 came another scholar—an émigré to American shores—to answer the question in the emphatic negative. Writing in *The Post-American World*, India-born Fareed Zakaria, editor of *Newsweek International*, columnist for its parent magazine, and CNN commentator, presents convincing evidence that any "imperial role" for America or any other country is anachronistic in today's world; not even with its military missions in Iraq and Afghanistan ought the United States assume a presence like Great Britain's in its "empire" days that ended with World War II.

Zakaria begins his survey of the multipolar world with the undisputed hegemony ("multipolar" is Zakaria's favorite buzz word; "unipolar" and "hegemony" are his most pejorative words) that the United States enjoyed at the time of Soviet communism's meltdown. Since then, there has occurred the phenomenon that provides the title of chapter 1: "The Rise of the *Rest*," whose opening sentence is one Zakaria will never let readers forget: "This is a book not about the decline of America but rather the rise of everyone else."

However, this is not essentially a book about "declinism," whose heyday came about two decades ago with Paul Kennedy's *The Rise and Fall of the Great Powers* (1987), which concluded that the United States' dominance was fast eroding. A skilled journalist such as Zakaria has fascinating ways of raising the bars of distinction for emerging nations without explicitly lowering those of the United States. He notes the tallest building is now in Taipeh, the richest man is Mexican, the largest publicly traded corporation is Chinese, the biggest plane is built in Russia and Ukraine, the leading refinery is under construction in India, the largest factories are all in China, and the United Arab Emirates is home to the most richly endowed investment fund.

Often by deft positioning Zakaria will leave the reader applauding America after he seemingly has downgraded her. After devoting fifteen lines to Europe's "significant challenge" to U.S. superiority in the economic line, he accords more than double to the United States as the first to create a "universal nation, made up of all colors, races, and creeds, living and working together in considerable harmony."

In a previous book, *The Future of Freedom: Illiberal Democracy at Home and Abroad* (2003), Zakaria argued that too much democracy can be counterproductive. In his new book he is critical of the manner in which the Bush administration pushed its democracy agenda forward, relying on elections in Iraq, the Palestinian Authority, and Lebanon as the solution to these countries' problems and minimizing the building of the institutions of law, governance, and liberty. He bashes what he sees as Bush's fear-based policies on terrorism, immigration, and trade, arguing that beyond Bush the world needs an open and confident United States.

Today he observes a move away from American dominance in every dimension with the exception of military power. He defines this post-American world as one shaped by many people in many places—his prime mover, multipolarity, center stage, everywhere.

Zakaria finds success stories for globalized capitalism wherever he looks. In addition, he is at pains to add, this success is all the United States' doing because for the last sixty years it has been urging the world to open up to free markets and develop new industries and technologies, training their best and brightest in U.S. universities: "The natives have gotten good at capitalism." Rampant outsourcing, viewed as a plague by both of the most recent presidential hopefuls, is lightly mentioned in this book. Zakaria proudly notes that India has more billionaires than any other Asian country but does not mention the proportion of U.S.-trained Indian doctors who have become rich while remaining to practice medicine in the United States.

Zakaria concentrates on China and India as the world's current success stories. While India—handicapped by "messy" democracy—will have the third-largest economy by 2040, China's astonishing rise is already here, having compressed two hundred years of Western industrial development into thirty and still growing faster than any major economy in recorded history. It makes two-thirds of the world's photocopiers, microwave ovens, and shoes, with the average Chinese personal income rising 700 percent in the last thirty years. Thus has the world's largest country also become its largest manufacturer, second-largest consumer, biggest saver, and, probably, second-largest military spender. Development on such a scale adds "a wholly new element to the international system," he writes.

In outlining the rise of China, referred to as "the challenger," and India, whom he proudly calls "the ally" to honor its democratic traditions, Zakaria marshals his facts scrupulously and to dramatic effect. Of China, the reader learns that it manufactured two hundred air conditioners in 1978 and forty-eight million in 2005; that its exports to the United States have zoomed 1,600 percent in the last fifteen years; and that it had twenty-eight billion square feet of space under construction in 2005, five times the figure for America in the same year. In India, the revenue from auto parts went from under six billion dollars in 2003 to more than fifteen billion dollars in 2007.

Zakaria has no fear that China's challenge to the United States for world hegemony could lead to military aggression. He says that China, like India, wants "to gain power and status and respect, for sure, but by growing within the international system, not by overturning it. As long as these new countries feel they can be accommodated, they have every incentive to become 'responsible stakeholders' in this system." In a crucial dialectic, noted by Zakaria, the neoconservative writer Robert Kagan implicitly questions whether powerful autocratic regimes such as China's can really be accommodated in global economic institutions without undermining either its own autocratic powers or the liberal democracies. The author, instead of heeding Russia's recent incursions against several small democracies, takes refuge in such American efforts at international cooperation as the League of Nations, United Nations, and the Marshall Plan. "The chair of the board who can gently guide a group of independent directors is still a very powerful person," Zakaria observes.

This prophetic scenario has been attacked by some as an attempt to darken the United States' outlook for continuance as world leader. Nevertheless, a reader can only guess how much more dire Zakaria's prospectus might have been had it been published after the worldwide financial crisis began in autumn of 2008, rather than six months before. While charting the economic and soft-power rise of the European Union, India, and China, he also marks the seemingly enduring American advantages in productivity, demographics, research and development, and overall economic and cultural vibrancy that will keep the other comers, with dismal problems of their own, just that for a good half century at least.

Richard Hauer Costa

Review Sources

Booklist 104, no. 18 (May 15, 2008): 10.
Business Week, May 19, 2008, p. 80.
Commentary 126, no. 2 (September, 2008): 64-68.
Kirkus Reviews 76, no. 5 (March 1, 2008): 241-242.
Library Journal 133, no. 7 (April 15, 2008): 99-100.
National Review 60, no. 14 (August 4, 2008): 47-48.
The New York Review of Books 55, no. 16 (October 23, 2008): 59-62.
The New York Times Book Review, May 11, 2008, p. 31.
The New Yorker 84, no. 10 (April 21, 2008): 126-130.
Publishers Weekly 255, no. 8 (February 25, 2008): 63.
The Wall Street Journal 251, no. 106 (May 6, 2008): A21.

POSTHUMOUS KEATS
A Personal Biography

Author: Stanley Plumly (1939-   )
Publisher: W. W. Norton (New York). 392 pp. $27.95
Type of work: Literary biography, literary criticism
Time: 1818-1917
Locale: England and Italy

Plumly's meditation on the final eighteen months of John Keats's life and posthumous reputation brings the dying poet and his work to life

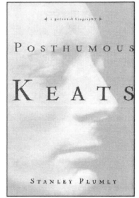

Principal personages:
 JOHN KEATS, an English poet
 TOM and GEORGE KEATS, his brothers
 ANNA ANGELETTI, his landlady in Rome
 FANNY BRAWNE, his fiancée
 JAMES CLARK, his doctor in Rome
 CHARLES ARMITAGE BROWN, his friend and neighbor, an artist
 CHARLES WENTWORTH DILKE, another friend and neighbor, a clerk and author
 ROBERT BENJAMIN HAYDON, an artist
 JOSEPH SEVERN, an artist
 JOHN TAYLOR, Keats's publisher

At a writers' conference in 1980, Stanley Plumly met Deborah Digges, a poet like himself, who had a passion for John Keats. The feeling soon became mutual; they would wake each other up in the middle of the night to share passages by the Romantic writer. In the early 1980's, Plumly wrote a poem, "Posthumous Keats," which takes its title from the last letter Keats wrote. It was addressed to Charles Armitage Brown, one of his closest friends, dated November 30, 1820, from Rome, when the poet had fewer than three months to live. Here Keats laments, "I have an habitual feeling of my real life having past, and that I am leading a posthumous existence." Plumly's poem describes the autumn journey that Keats and his companion, Joseph Severn, made from Naples to Rome. Keats rode in a carriage. Severn, to give his dying friend more space and to avoid the jolting of the vehicle, often walked alongside. The artist was enthralled with the wildflowers filling the countryside. He would pick armloads of them and then, having no place else to put them, deposit them in the carriage with the poet. By the time Keats reached Rome, his carriage resembled a flower-filled hearse.

Plumly then embarked on a book-length account of Keats's last eighteen months, after Keats had composed the great odes that would render him immortal, after he had stopped writing poetry and knew that he was dying. After some twenty-five years and much alteration, *Posthumous Keats* marks the fruition of Plumly's project, which

*Stanley Plumly has published nine
volumes of poetry, including* Old Heart,
*which was nominated for a National
Book Award in 2007. He also has
written a critical study of poetry,*
Argument & Song: Sources & Silences
in Poetry *(2003). He is a Distinguished
University Professor at the University
of Maryland.*

lasted about as many years as Keats lived (1795-1821). This book is not a biography of the poet, nor even a chronological account of his final months. Rather, in seven chapters, each divided into seven sections, Plumly reflects on various aspects of Keats's life and reputation.

Some chapters explore a single theme. The first examines various images of the poet. Plumly most likes those executed during Keats's life. Among Plumly's favorites is Benjamin Haydon's image that he included in his book *Christ's Entry into Jerusalem* (1817). Haydon placed some of his friends among the onlookers. A lively Keats stands next to the older Romantic poet William Wordsworth in this group portrait of historical and living figures. The year before, Haydon had made a life mask of Keats. Another picture that Plumly praises originated on the Isle of Wight. In July, 1819, Keats and Charles Brown were visiting there, the one to write, the other to draw. On July 31, 1819, Brown sketched his friend. The other drawing that Plumly admires is that by Severn; it is another quick sketch, executed by Severn a few weeks before Keats died.

After Keats's death, his portrait was painted more than a hundred times. The images became increasingly idealized, as artists sought to re-create not the lively young man or the individual dying of tuberculosis but instead the general idea of the poet. Even Severn became a victim to this tendency as he repeatedly reproduced his original drawing but in altered form. According to Plumly, artists in the nineteenth century fell into one of two errors. They presented either a Keats who was too effeminate and ethereal to live in the real world or one too solid for the world to affect. Plumly includes in his strictures the portrait by William Hilton that hangs in the National Portrait Gallery in London. This painting, based on an 1819 sketch, presents a reflective writer untouched by illness.

In his second chapter, aptly entitled "Cold Pastoral," the phrase Keats uses to describe a Grecian urn, Plumly looks at other unhappy attempts to immortalize the poet. Keats knew for about a year that he was dying of tuberculosis, the disease that had claimed his mother and his brother Tim and that would also kill his other brother, George. Keats asked Severn for a monument shaped like a Greek lyre with four broken strings. Shortly before his death, hearing the Roman fountain playing outside his window and thinking of Francis Beaumont and John Fletcher's line in *Philaster* (pr. 1620), "All your better deeds/ Shall be in water writ," Keats told Severn that the only inscription he wanted on the memorial was, "Here lies one whose name was writ in water." There were to be no name, no dates.

Severn and Charles Brown wanted a longer epitaph. In the winter of 1823 Keats's tombstone was erected in the Protestant cemetery in Rome. It includes a lyre, but atop a base resembling a Greek altar. The inscription reads:

This Grave
contains all that was Mortal
of a
YOUNG ENGLISH POET
Who
on his Death Bed
in the Bitterness of his Heart
at the Malicious Power of his Enemies
Desired
these Words to be engraven on his Tomb Stone
"Here lies One
Whose Name was writ in Water"
Feb 24th 1821

Brown and Severn, who devised the inscription, were using it to attack the Tory John Gibson Lockhart of *Blackwood's Edinburgh Magazine* and John Wilson Croker of the *Quarterly Review*, whose negative comments about Keats's poetry they blamed for the young man's death. Twenty years later, Brown conceded that the inscription had been a mistake, that Keats's wishes should have been heeded.

This same image of Keats as a spirit too frail to withstand the assaults of obtuse critics appears in Percy Bysshe Shelley's *Adonais* (1821) and Byron's semiserious lament for Keats in stanza sixty of canto eleven of *Don Juan* (1823). The latter reads:

> *John Keats, who was killed off by one critique,*
>   *Just as he really promised something great,*
> *If not intelligible, without Greek*
>   *Contrived to talk about the Gods of late,*
> *Much as they might have been supposed to speak.*
>   *Poor fellow! His was an untoward fate;*
> *'Tis strange the mind, that fiery particle,*
> *Should let itself be snuffed out by an article.*

Shelley in his elegy likened Keats to "a pale flower by some sad maiden cherished" and called him "a frail Form." William Hazlitt, another Romantic author with no love for Tories, referred to Keats as "the tender bloom" blighted by Tory criticism. In "the Advertisement" to the 1820 edition of Keats's *Lamia, Isabella, The Eve of St. Agnes, and Other Poems*, the publishers claimed that Keats had stopped work on *Hyperion* because of the negative reviews of *Endymion* (1818), even though Keats abandoned the poem because he was unhappy with it. Like some nineteenth century artists, these writers thus contributed to the image of the young poet as a sensitive plant.

In chapter 3 Plumly examines Keats's relationship with his bothers George and Tom. Plumly regards George as the practical brother, Tom the ethereal one, and argues that Keats is a combination of these traits. Plumly links the death of Tom (December 1, 1818) with Keats's poetic flowering in 1819, the year in which he wrote the great odes that ensured that his name would not be writ in water. This chapter also traces Keats's 1818 walking tour of northern England and Scotland, which the poet undertook with Brown. Keats hoped to gain experience and images that would aid his poetry; Plumly examines some of the sonnets Keats composed during this excursion.

Elsewhere Plumly discusses Keats's search for a paying profession (chapter 4) and his relationship with Fanny Brawne (chapter 5). These sections are less coherent than other chapters. They recall Keats's description of Samuel Taylor Coleridge's conversation when they walked together on Hampstead Heath on April 11, 1819: "In those two miles he broached a thousand things." Chapter 6 describes Keats's last months in Rome at 26 Piazza di Spagna, which in 1909 became the Keats-Shelley Memorial House. Keats was initially strong enough to walk and to ride. Then, on December 10, 1820, he suffered the first of many severe hemorrhages. Dr. James Clark, following the standard medical practice of the time, bled him further and prescribed a starvation diet: an anchovy and small piece of toast a day. Keats rallied, declined, rallied, and relapsed. On February 23, 1821, at about eleven at night, he died in Severn's arms. The final chapter returns to the subject of Keats's posthumous memorialization.

Interspersed among the chapters are discussions of Keats's poems; these analyses make the reader wish that Plumly had devoted more attention to the works. For example, he offers tantalizing comments about assonance and alliteration in "Ode to a Nightingale" and "To Autumn" and about the relationship between these two great poems. One also wishes for better proofreading. Still, this book will delight any lover of Keats and will turn any of its readers into an admirer of the poet.

Joseph Rosenblum

Review Sources

American Scholar 77, no. 3 (Summer, 2008): 152-153.

The Economist 388 (August 23, 2008): 72.

International Herald-Tribune, August 15, 2008, p. 22.

Kirkus Reviews 76, no. 5 (March 1, 2008): 236.

Library Journal 133, no. 7 (April 15, 2008): 85.

Literary Review 52, no. 1 (Fall, 2008): 192-194.

Los Angeles Times, June 1, 2008, p. R8.

The New York Times, August 8, 2008, p. 25.

The New Yorker 84, no. 20 (July 7, 2008): 92-95.

Publishers Weekly 255, no. 16 (April 21, 2008): 36.

The Times Literary Supplement, December 19, 2008, pp. 8-9.

The Washington Post Book World, April 20, 2008, p. BW7.

THE POWER MAKERS
Steam, Electricity, and the Men Who Invented Modern America

Author: Maury Klein (1939-   )
Publisher: Bloomsbury Press (New York). 543 pp.
    $29.99
Type of work: History, technology
Time: 1700-1939
Locale: Primarily the United States

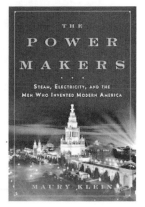

A panoramic history of the development and application of steam power and electric power, with biographic information on leading figures and attention to social, economic, financial, and technological dimensions

Principal personages:
   THOMAS ALVA EDISON (1847-1931), one of
      America's most famous inventors
   OLIVER EVANS (1755-1819), American inventor and automation pioneer
   SAMUEL INSULL (1859-1938), British-born American entrepreneur and
      holding-company organizer
   FRANK J. SPRAGUE (1857-1934), American engineer, inventor, and
      entrepreneur
   NIKOLA TESLA (1856-1943), Croatian-born American inventor
   ELIHU THOMSON (1853-1937), British-born American teacher, inventor,
      and entrepreneur
   JAMES WATT (1736-1819), Scottish machinist and inventor
   GEORGE WESTINGHOUSE, JR. (1846-1914), air-brake inventor, electrical
      pioneer, creator of eponymous company

Tracing the challenges and achievements of entrepreneurs and inventors is a noble enterprise. As our economy evolves toward increasing emphasis on services, it is well to be reminded of the material basis of modern civilization and the people who formed it.

In *The Power Makers*, Maury Klein does this very well: He is a superb storyteller, taking the time to delineate the personalities of the many principals, putting their activities in the context of their times, and making a painstaking effort to explain the various technological developments. Perhaps nonspecialist readers can't fully grasp the differences between direct current and alternating current, but they will readily follow the way in which the competition between these was personified in the careers of Thomas Edison and George Westinghouse, Jr., and what a landmark it was when the two systems were successfully blended.

Klein's decision to cover both steam power and electric power follows the logic that steam power is a major basis for generating electricity. It also makes for a long book and increases the likelihood that some people's favorite parts of the story may

*Maury Klein is professor emeritus at
the University of Rhode Island. He is
the author of fourteen other books,
including* The Life and Legend of Jay
Gould *(1986);* Days of Defiance:
Sumter, Secession, and the Coming of
the Civil War *(1999); and* Rainbow's
End: The Crash of 1929 *(2001).*

appear neglected. Improvements in iron metallurgy were critical to facilitating the upgrading of steam engines, and the problems encountered in moving from steamboats to locomotives probably warrant more attention. The tubular boiler and the steam blast receive only passing mention. Klein's integration of steam and electrical narrative does pay off when he analyzes the development of the steam turbine soon after 1900.

A large proportion of the book deals with the period between 1880 and 1920—the heyday of Edison and Westinghouse. The narrative is benchmarked with details on the Centennial Exposition in Philadelphia in 1876 and the Columbian Exposition in Chicago in 1893. We learn in detail about the evolution of central-station power generation, electric lighting, electric motors, and street railways. There is a titillating aside on the emergence of electrocution—but railroad fans might have enjoyed more on the impressive development of electric trains on intercity and commuter routes in the Northeast. The description of the development of Niagara Falls hydroelectric power properly salutes the rapid rise of electrochemical firms (notably Alcoa) at that site. The electrical industries largely created the modern emphasis on research and development as central elements in business strategy.

Naturally much of the narrative focuses on the career of Edison. Eccentric and compulsive, he determined at age twenty-two, after five years as a telegrapher, to devote himself to invention. In 1876, he established his laboratory in the "obscure hamlet" of Menlo Park, New Jersey, to which he attracted a team of talented associates. Successful inventions relating to the telegraph, the telephone, and the phonograph yielded revenue and prominence. By 1879, he successfully had addressed the problem of subdividing electric current to serve incandescent light bulbs. This led in 1882 to the vastly more important development of the central generating station at Pearl Street in New York. Edison was the central figure in a bewildering sequence of companies, many of which were brought together in Edison General Electric (GE) Company, incorporated in 1889.

Edison's work concentrated on direct current. His contemporary and rival, George Westinghouse, Jr., saw the potential for alternating current, which could allow high-voltage transmission facilitated by step-up transformers at the generating end and step-down transformers at the applications end.

Klein focuses heavily on the Edison-Westinghouse rivalry in developing electric lighting systems—systems that embraced generation, transmission, and final application. Though electric lighting spread rapidly, the process encountered vigorous competition from the gas industry, which was also innovating significantly. Inexpensive "water gas" was produced by blowing steam through red-hot coke, and the Welsbach mantle provided an incandescent reading light.

While working for Edison, Frank Sprague began experimenting with electric motors. Since Edison was preoccupied with lighting, Sprague left in 1884 to start his own company, which led the way in creating electric-powered street railways, beginning with Richmond in 1887. By 1889, there were 180 electric railway systems in the country. Sprague's electric railway company was merged into Edison General Electric in 1889. Sprague also pioneered the development of electric elevators, which facilitated the emergence of skyscraper architecture.

Elihu Thomson was a clever technician who was able to improve on many devices originated by Edison and others, and he developed a rival business installing dynamos and lighting systems. In 1883, he became part of Thomson-Houston (TH) Electric Company, which by 1891 had become highly profitable as a manufacturer. By then electrical manufacturing was dominated by TH, Edison GE, and Westinghouse. As part of a wave of mergers throughout American industry, TH and Edison GE merged in 1892 to form the modern General Electric Company, a combination motivated in part by the opportunity to combine conflicting patents. The merger shifted power to finance and marketing specialists, leaving the inventors with a diminished role. Edison, who opposed the combination, feared that innovation incentives would be weakened by the decrease in competition. GE and Westinghouse became a durable dominant duopoly. In 1896, GE and Westinghouse pooled their patents. The royalty arrangements reinforced a program of market sharing to limit competition.

One of the most exciting sections of the book comes toward the end, as Klein follows the career of Samuel Insull. An Englishman, Insull had become Edison's private secretary in 1881 at age twenty-one. Though not a scientist or engineer, he developed an extraordinary degree of insight into the economic and financial dimensions of electric power. In the process, he discovered the "public utility concept." Generation of electricity was subject to extreme economies of large-scale operation, so large operations had lower unit costs. Fixed capital and overhead costs were a large part of total costs. To Insull, the ideal form of organization would be for a monopoly of generating operations, in order to achieve minimum costs. Appropriate government regulation would grant long-term franchises, to restrict entry and to protect customers against exorbitant rates. As state governments adopted this model, it produced rich benefits for the franchised monopolies. Rates were based on historical costs, but because of the rapid technological improvements and rapid expansion of demand, costs were always lower than they had been when rates were set, yielding handsome profits. However, Klein does not develop the story of public-utility regulation.

Likewise, although patents figure prominently in much of the story, Klein does not reflect on the patent system. His narrative makes it clear that at many points technical innovations were being developed by numerous people, and that strategies of patenting that incorporated considerations other than pure technological progress were evolving.

Insull came to his insights about the public-utility concept after an audacious career move. Breaking away from Edison, he became president of the Chicago Edison Company, a generating operation, at age thirty-two. He proceeded aggressively to acquire rival companies, construct larger facilities, and drive down costs and rates. He discovered the importance of the "load factor": generating capacity had to accommodate the peak of production, but the marginal cost of producing during off-peak hours was very low. Pricing adjustments could be made to attract off-peak customers. Insull also developed a complex network of public-utility holding companies, ingeniously designed to transmute the modest profit-rate targets of regulated companies into much higher rates of return for the unregulated holding companies.

Insull's story occupies more than forty pages of the book, and it is easy to understand why. Insull had come early to the vision of an electrified America, and he had the energy and skills to make a huge contribution to creating it. In particular, he helped bring about the suburbanization of America. Fortunate cities such as New York, Philadelphia, and Chicago developed networks of electric transportation along which grew residential areas such as Westchester and the Main Line. Considering that Klein has written at least five books on railroads, they receive surprisingly little attention here.

The collapse of Insull's financial empire was one of the many dramatic aspects of the catastrophic economic downturn that followed 1929. He became a scapegoat and was the target of a series of criminal indictments. Although he was ultimately exonerated on all counts, he emerged from the process a broken man.

Klein's play-by-play tapers off with the 1920's. A brief final chapter uses the New York World's Fair of 1939 as a showcase for the nation's electrical achievements, contrasting the emphasis on household appliances with the earlier stress on generators and other equipment.

It is doubtful that any other period in American history brought about such profound and rapid change in the way Americans lived as the one between 1900 and 1930, when the electrical revolution proceeded at maximum intensity. To be sure, the coming of the automobile was a big contributor. While the internal-combustion engine depended on the electric spark, this was a relatively unsophisticated contribution. In combination, electric train, trolley, and car facilitated the separation of workplace and living place. Electric light reclaimed the nighttime hours for recreational reading and, perhaps more important, for homework for school and work. Well-lighted workplaces could operate around the clock, exemplified by the morning newspaper, with its inputs from telegraph and telephone, its electrically driven Linotypes and presses. By 1930, the up-to-date suburban home was not only lighted by electricity but furnished with an electric refrigerator, a radio, an electric stove, even thermostatically controlled heating.

According to Klein, "we have [largely] become what our technologies made us." Jill Leflore, reviewing Klein's book for *The New Yorker*, reminds us that "a long-standing tradition argues against the inescapability of our machine destiny" and implies that Klein is unaware of this fact. However, Klein does acknowledge that "the consequences of a new technology can never be predicted." In particular, one cannot predict the extent to which consumers will choose to adopt innovations—consider the electric toothbrush and electric slicing knife featured by GE in its advertising in the mid-1960's.

By implication, Leflore is challenging the proposition that economic "progress," economic growth, and rising real income—all facilitated by technological innovation—represent basic improvement in people's lives. The apologist economist points to longer and healthier life spans, wider choices in jobs and consumption, greater leisure. However, not everyone makes good choices—the debt-propelled consumption boom that began in the 1990's affirms that. In addition, the atomic bomb ended once and for all the illusion that all technological innovation makes the world a better place.

Klein's perspective is perhaps simple minded by Leflore's standards, but it is congruent with pervasive American values. He is less concerned with large ideas than with telling a good story.

Paul B. Trescott

Review Sources

Booklist 104, nos. 19/20 (June 1, 2008): 18.
Foreign Affairs 87, no. 6 (November/December, 2008): 165.
Kirkus Reviews 76, no. 7 (April 1, 2008): 346.
Library Journal 133, no. 6 (April 1, 2008): 94.
New Scientist 198 (May 31, 2008): 49.
The New Yorker 84, no. 13 (May 12, 2008): 118-122.
Publishers Weekly 255, no. 16 (April 21, 2008): 47-48.
The Wall Street Journal 251, no. 130 (June 4, 2008): A19.

THE PRIVATE PATIENT

Author: P. D. James (1920-   )
Publisher: Alfred A. Knopf (New York). 352 pp. $25.95
Type of work: Novel
Time: The present
Locale: London and Dorset, England

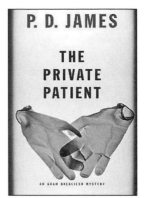

The eighteenth crime novel by the "Queen of Detective Fiction" features James's recurring detective team and includes the distinguished octogenerian author's insights into old age's redefinition of self, reflecting a continuing refinement of her elegant, restrained prose style that accords perfectly with the subject matter

Principal characters:

ADAM DALGLIESH, commander of the Metropolitan Police working out of New Scotland Yard on serious cases that might have political or social ramifications, a skillful detective and navigator of the police bureaucracy, and an admired poet

INSPECTOR KATE MISKIN, who is struggling with her relationship to former colleague Piers Tarrant and her yearning for Dalgliesh, an impossible romantic match

FRANCIS BENTON-SMITH, the junior member of Dalgliesh's team, ambitious like Kate but, unlike her, having had a privileged educational background

EMMA LAVENHAM, Dalgliesh's fiancé, a Cambridge Victorian Studies literature professor, as usual put off in every sense by his call to a murder investigation

RHODA GRADWYN, the first victim, a successful middle-aged investigative journalist whose decision to have a childhood facial scar removed at Cheverell Manor clinic triggers events

ROBIN BOYTON, a failed actor and black sheep of the wealthy Westhall family who has been excluded from an inheritance he felt he deserved

MR. GEORGE CHANDLER-POWELL, a renowned Harley Street plastic surgeon who operates a clinic at Cheverell Manor, a great house in Dorset, which he bought to fulfill his need for a country-squire identity

CANDACE WESTHALL, an academic pushed out of her university teaching position by supposed reforms who is now living in Stone Cottage on the Cheverell Manor grounds

MARCUS WESTHALL, Candace's brother, a surgeon who also resides on the grounds, assists Chandler-Powell, but desires meaningful medical service in Africa

HELENA HAVERLAND, née Cressett, whose family owned Cheverell Manor for nearly four hundred years but who now is a woman-of-all-work there

LETTIE FRENSHAM, Helena's old governess who now is in charge of the office

FLAVIA HOLLAND, head of nursing at Cheverell Manor and Chandler-Powell's mistress

DEAN and KIM BOSTOCK, cooks for Cheverell Manor but ambitious to be chefs

SHARON BATEMAN, née Shirley Beale, who killed her younger sister in an inexplicable childhood rage and now is working under a new name as a servant at Cheverell Manor

THE CHEVERELL STONES, a Neolithic circle of upright stones next to the Manor where Mary Keyte was burned as a witch in 1654 and a haunting presence for the contemporary characters

In the great crime story tradition of Agatha Christie, P. D. James's *The Private Patient* isolates a toxic mix of characters at a four-hundred-year-old manor house haunted by a mini-Stonehenge-like stone circle in an adjoining meadow. There a young girl was once sacrificed and burned alive. James kills off one character, then another, and provides credible-seeming alibis for most of the possible miscreants. The plot threading through the novel is ingenious and varied, involving anger over inheritances possibly tainted by fraud, sexual jealousy, long-distant but unresolved childhood violence, mysterious motives, and a looming sense of impending violence. As in the best of English detective fiction, setting acts as character, supplying motive and mood rather than simply backdrop scenery.

Cheverell Manor, named after the stone circle most of the characters visit almost obsessively throughout, has acquired a new identity as a cosmetic surgery clinic for the wealthy, a private great house in rural Dorset where Mr. George Chandler-Powell (British surgeons use Mr. rather than Dr.) can reinstate lost youthful appearances and repair the damage of accidents in complete privacy, while patients enjoy gourmet food prepared by Kim and Dean Bostock, chefs trained in London. Chandler-Powell has himself aspired to a new identity, finding solace in the Great Hall of the Manor as he escapes the pressures of his busy Harley Street London second practice. He plays country squire on his days off, buoyed by workers and servants, all deferential to his brilliance and his deserved reputation.

For all the apparent calm in this elegant setting, however, Chandler-Powell has surrounded himself with an unstable mix of helpers. His chief surgeon, Marcus Westhall, idolizes his mentor but also feels stifled; he has no future at Cheverell Manor and is pursuing more consequential work in Africa, where surgery saves lives rather than appearances. Marcus's sister Candace, a resident of Stone Cottage on the Manor premises, is marking time while the siblings await the resolution of probate in their father's inheritance. Candace cannot return to university teaching—her position has been dumbed-down by a heedless government bureaucracy—and she is emotionally worn after nursing her emotionally brutal father for two years as he lay dying in Stone Cottage. Chandler-Powell's head of nursing, Flavia Holland, is also his mistress, but, dissatisfied with her status, she pushes the divorced surgeon to marry her. Robin Boyton, a black sheep in the Westhall family, makes return visits to his cousins Marcus

Oxford-born P. D. James worked for the National Health Service and then the Home Office. A Fellow of the Royal Society of Literature and of the Royal Society of the Arts, a one-time chair of the Society of Authors, and a member of the Detection Club, she has received the Decorated Order of the British Empire (1983) and awards for crime writing from Britain, the United States, Italy, and Scandinavia.

and Candace, not out of love but in hopes of passive-aggressively gaining a financial settlement. Sharon Bateman, a nondescript servant girl working under an assumed name, horrifically murdered her sister at age twelve. Helena Haverland, a member of the Cressett family that originally owned Cheverell Manor, seems settled in her work as an administrator of the complex medical and residence operations, but the reasons for her satisfaction with this role are not readily apparent. Even the Bostocks, Kim and Dean, hopeful young married chefs from London, might well move on: He misses big-time cooking in London, and she wants a baby.

Rhoda Gradwyn's fateful decision to have Chandler-Powell repair her disfigured cheek at the Manor clinic—she asserts she no longer "needs" the scar, the result of a brutal swipe with a bottle by her drunken father—sets off an unpredictable cascade of events. It shakes the unstable social structure of the Manor's permanent staff and leads to wholesale changes in their lives. Boyton learns of Gradwyn's surgical intentions and turns up at the Manor in pursuit of his interests. Dalgliesh and Kate later speculate (no one is left alive to explain motives and intentions) that Boyton and perhaps Gradwyn were trying to ascertain if Candace Westhall had mimicked the plot of a real-life detective novelist, one not invented by James, Cyril Hare, whose *Untimely Death* (1980) hinges on the body of a wealthy man dead by natural causes being kept in a freezer to satisfy a quirk in inheritance law about date of death. Gradwyn may also have intended an exposé of wealthy plastic surgery patients and practices; the obscurity of motives becomes a theme at the end of the book. Whatever Gradwyn's reasons, her strangulation in her room after surgery brings in Dalgliesh's team and instigates the unraveling of the Manor's social fabric.

The Metro Police team is typically frustrated by the suspects' reluctance to cooperate fully and sometimes by their outright hostility. The police fan out, searching Gradwyn's London house and interviewing people who know the suspects' back stories. Emma Lavenham, Dalgliesh's fiancé, turns up unexpectedly, in distress about the rape and beating of a friend, but she realizes she cannot intrude on the investigation and leaves. Only after Boyton is found dead do personal histories and motives begin to converge, as Kate and Benton help Dalgliesh fill in possible scenarios for the killings. The ending to the murder mystery plot comes quickly, as the culprit tries to duplicate the burning of Mary Keyte and leaves an apparently complete confession.

Dalgliesh, however, is dissatisfied, and in a coda to Book Four he visits an elderly lawyer privy to secrets that throw a different light on the killer's motives. The point is not a new one in James: appearance and reality rarely jibe completely, but here human motive is purposely obscured, both by the murderer and by at least one other character. Dalgliesh speculates several times about the arrogance, even the impertinence of presuming to know the whole truth. He ends up resigned to his limited view, and there are intimations that he is considering retirement.

As if to drive home the point that one is able to see only incompletely, strenuous investigation notwithstanding, a short Book Five reprises the notion as Chandler-Powell, a figure epitomizing control, dominance, and even arrogance, submits docilely to Helena Haverland's plans for his future: He has quite possibly been manipulated from early on, and Helena appears in a different light. The remaining chapters of Book Five wrap up other loose ends. The reader learned earlier that Kate and Piers Tarrant are reuniting romantically. Lettie Frensham makes a decision to turn down the security offered by a permanent position at the Manor to engage risk through traveling the world. The last chapter is Dalgliesh's wedding as conveyed through the point of view of Clara, Emma's former student and friend, who quotes Jane Austen for her final word: In the end, all we can hope for is love.

As with all of James's novels, the sum is far greater than the resolution of plot lines and character prognoses. With each book, her prose style becomes more refined and lucid, and her economy of phrasing, always admirable, becomes in this novel a model for writers: Not a word is wasted. Like Dalgliesh, the prose is logical, orderly, inexorable, leading to definite but suitably restrained conclusions. As with Dalgliesh's worries about the arrogance and impertinence of presuming too much about the unknowable human animal, James keeps her prose on a short leash.

James's philosophical vision is similarly reserved and restrained. Nighttime strollers to the Cheverell Stones hear noises from the surrounding woods, screams of terror and pain as small predators feed on prey. This is not the cozy countryside of many British mysteries but nature tooth and claw, a metaphor for the human jungle in which James's characters compete for advantage. Civilized exteriors conceal a humankind still capable of terrible acts, which Dalgliesh and his team must witness and respond to. However, all is not gloom in this worldview, as the descriptions of the Manor's furnishings and architecture attest: Art, like love, can redeem human misery. There is comedy, too: Dalgliesh's interview with Emma's father about the detective's suitability as a son-in-law owes much to Oscar Wilde's Mrs. Bracknell in *The Importance of Being Earnest* (1895).

The most affecting episode in *The Private Patient* is Dalgliesh's questioning of an elderly lawyer, Philip Kershaw, who has information about Candace Westhall. Kershaw lives near Bournemouth in Huntingdon Lodge, an institution that James says is careful not to distress visitors with words such as "retirement," "elderly," "nursing," or "home." Huntingdon Lodge is single-minded in its anti-institutional layout and decor, but nevertheless cloyingly sentimental in ornamentation. It is clean and well intentioned but, for Dalgliesh, depressingly reminiscent of prep school. Kershaw is still sharp of mind, but frail and without a social role in this institution that separates "clients" from each another. The old are warehoused in such institutions, James implies, their identity only a shadow of their past. Kershaw's younger brother keeps him informed about the family firm, but he does no work. He and his fellow "guests" at Huntingdon Lodge (there are no "patients") have long since exhausted conversational topics and are out of reach of human life below them on the shore front. James spent much of her nonliterary working life supervising institutions; in her own old age, she casts a sharp discerning eye on how institutions for the old dehumanize and depress, robbing people of what means the most to them: their place in society.

Andrew Macdonald

Review Sources

Booklist 105, no. 2 (September 15, 2008): 5.
Kirkus Reviews 76, no. 18 (September 15, 2008): 979.
Library Journal 133, no. 17 (October 15, 2008): 63.
New Statesman 137 (August 25, 2008): 52-53.
The New York Times, November 20, 2008, p. 7.
The New York Times Book Review, December 14, 2008, p. 26.
People 70, no. 21 (November 24, 2008): 56.
The Times Literary Supplement, September 26, 2008, p. 22.
USA Today, November 13, 2008, p. 3D.
The Washington Times, December 14, 2008, p. M29.

THE PYRAMID

Author: Henning Mankell (1948-   )
First published: Pyramiden, 1999, in Sweden
Translated from the Swedish by Ebba Segerberg with
    Laurie Thompson
Publisher: New Press (New York). 392 pp. $26.95
Type of work: Short fiction
Time: 1969-1989
Locale: Ystad, Sweden

*Although the first Kurt Wallander mystery appeared in
1991, these five stories cover the years between 1969 and
1989 and present Wallander as a young policeman by illustrating some of the cases that made him into a master
detective*

Principal characters:
KURT WALLANDER, an alienated police investigator in Ystad, Sweden.
MONA WALLANDER, his wife
LINDA WALLANDER, his daughter
THE ELDER WALLANDER, his quirky artist father
HEMBERG, his boss
HANNSON, his colleague
RYDBERG, his mentor and colleague

When Swedish police detective Kurt Wallander first appeared in *Moerdare utan
ansikte (Faceless Killers,* 1996) in 1991, he was a well-seasoned police officer who
had just turned forty. However, his personal life was chaotic. His wife, Mona, had left
him. His grown daughter, Linda, was busy with her own life, and his quirky artist father barely talked to him. His poor eating habits and solitary drinking had caused him
to develop diabetes. Although he dreams of escaping from dark and dreary Ystad,
Wallander remains in the city year after year vigilantly solving cases that stump his
colleagues.

The Pyramid, a chronological series of five short works, serves as a prequel to author Henning Mankell's popular Wallander detective series. The book presents
Wallander as a young police officer intent on solving the crimes that will make him
into a master detective.

The first story, "Wallander's First Case," is set in 1969. It deals with the twenty-
one-year-old uniformed patrolman Wallander who is so intent upon solving his first
case that he disregards safety precautions. Indeed, as the story begins, Wallander is
fighting his way out of a coma, recalling the events of the past week when, after finding the body of his shadowy next-door neighbor named Hålén, he took it upon himself
to find the killer. Although his superiors announce Hålén's death as a suicide,
Wallander does not agree, especially after a fire is set in the man's apartment, as he

～

Swedish writer Henning Mankell worked as a dramatist before publisheing his first novel in 1973. He lives in both Sweden and Maputo, Mozambique, where he has worked as a director of Teatro Avenida since 1985. Mankell's Wallander series has sold more than 30 million copies worldwide, and the British Broadcasting Corporation began airing The Kurt Wallander Mysteries, *starring Kenneth Branagh, in 2008.*

～

sees it, to cover up evidence. Wallander becomes so involved in the case that he is late picking up his girlfriend Mona, and when he does manage to get to the ferry landing, he finds she has left him. He is devastated when she tells him later that evening that she wants to take a weeklong break. No matter how hard he tries, over and over again Wallander will forget about Mona when duty calls. Similarly, he will disregard his elderly father who has been feeling ignored and put aside. Wallander is amazed to find that his father has sold his childhood home and moved to a remote area in a house he has not even seen.

Eventually, Wallander discovers that the victim, Hålén, had been a sailor. In Brazil, he and a buddy named Rune had come across some jewels. However, after Rune was arrested, Hålén absconded with the jewels and hid out back home in Sweden, hoping that Rune would spend the rest of his life in a Brazilian prison. However, Rune returned to Sweden intent on revenge, and he stabs Wallander in an altercation. When Wallander comes out of the coma, Mona is smiling.

In the first story, Mankell cleverly foreshadows the Wallander couple's future. Their love is fragile and their marriage is doomed. In addition, the author begins a theme that will continue in the entire Wallander series: the encroachment of outside negative forces—in this case from Brazil—that affects all of Swedish society. Wallander's problems with his father illustrate how contemporary Sweden is forgetting its past.

In the next short story, "The Man with the Mask," Wallander is a new father on his way home from work to his wife, Mona, on Christmas Eve. When he stops at a grocery store—someone called earlier to report a suspicious stranger—he discovers the body of the elderly owner, Elma Hagman. Suddenly, he is hit from behind and, after he gains consciousness, discovers a silent young man wearing a mask standing over him holding a gun. Something has gone terribly wrong in a simple robbery, Wallander realizes, and he attempts to talk to the young man. He knows Mona will call the office to find out why he is late, the police will show up, and things could get out of hand. For a long time, the young man does not say a word, but finally he removes the mask and speaks. His name is Oliver, and he has fled South Africa after his father resisted the government and was executed. Wallander attempts to coax Oliver into putting the gun down, but when sirens are heard in the distance, the terrified young man raises the gun and, yet again, Wallander fears for his life. However, instead of shooting Wallander, the desperate man shoots himself. In this sad tale, Wallander continues to illustrate how violent outside forces moving into Sweden affect the previously peaceful country.

"The Man on the Beach," the third story in *The Pyramid*, concerns an elderly man named Alexandersson whose body was found in the back seat of a taxicab. On the surface, the death appears to be the result of an ordinary heart attack, but an autopsy reveals that the man, who was on vacation, died from ingesting poison. At first, Wallander is stumped, but eventually he traces the case to a very cold beach and the house of an elderly doctor named Stenholm. It seems Alexandersson has been taking a cab from Ystad to the same seaside spot every day and returning again in the evening. The doctor pleads ignorance; his wife is upstairs, he claims, in bed dying from cancer. Wallander continues to dig and learns that years ago the victim's only son died in a violent crime. The doctor's wife, it turns out, was the district attorney in charge of his son's case and Alexandersson believed she was at fault for not pressing harder to bring the killer to justice. For years the Stenholms have not known a moment of peace. They have been hounded continuously by the heartbroken father. In an effort to bring some peace to his dying wife, Stenholm poisons the old man simply to get him to stop stalking them. In this touching story, Mankell demonstrates that the rise of violent crime in Sweden in recent times has deeply affected the older generation, in this case two respectable families, who are left confused, angry, and ultimately helpless.

In the fourth story, "The Death of the Photographer," Wallander is newly separated from his wife, Mona, who has moved away to Malmö with their daughter, Linda. Sad and lonely, he has turned to food and solitary drinking for comfort. He investigates the death of mild-mannered photographer, Simon Lamberg, who takes studio portraits in a store on the main town square and who finds satisfaction in distorting and diminishing the faces of famous people at night. The photographer does this, it can be supposed, to make himself feel more important. Why, Wallander wonders, would anyone want to murder such a harmless man who was known to everyone? Lamberg had been married for years but lived with his wife in name only. The wife hardened toward him after he put their only child Matilda away in a home for the mentally challenged. When Wallander finds out that a mysterious woman has for years been visiting Matilda, he puts the facts together that Lamberg had been having an affair with a minister's wife whom he had he met on a bus tour of Continental Europe. In a fit of rage, the minister had entered Lamberg's studio late one night and killed him. In this story, Mankell poses the idea that leaving Sweden, such as on a bus tour in another country, leads to dangerous changes and influences that can damage Sweden's delicate social fabric.

"The Pyramid," the fifth and final story in the prequel series, is set in 1989 and leads Wallander to, of all places, Egypt. He follows his vacationing father who has been arrested there, incurring a steep fine after attempting to climb a pyramid, an act forbidden by Egyptian law. His father, an artist, has been living alone in the country, painting the same landscape motif over and over.

Deep into the investigation of two puzzling, seemingly unrelated cases, Wallander has to take a loan to pay for the trip to Egypt. One case involves a small plane crash and the other the murder of two old sisters who owned a small sewing store. There is no record of the flight and the plane is unmarked, and how, the dismayed Wallander wonders, could anyone kill the two old Eberhardsson sisters, the most innocent of victims?

After a grueling flight, Wallander is welcomed by an Egyptian police officer named Radwan who helps him untangle his father's mess. When Wallander considers that his father could have died in an Egyptian jail, he begins to soften toward him. He comes to appreciate his father a bit more, and after paying the fine in court, the two enjoy sharing an Egyptian adventure together. Since his wife Mona has left him, Wallander suffers from loneliness and physical neglect. He has taken up with another woman, named Emma Lundin, but he does not care for her that much and is too nice, or too cowardly, to end it.

After he returns to his solitary apartment in Ystad, Wallander dreams of a pyramid, and when he awakens he finds he is able to use the model of a pyramid to put the building blocks of both cases he has been working on together. Through this process, he discovers that the plane that crashed came in under the radar and was involved in drug smuggling, and that the two seemingly innocent old Eberhardsson sisters are really sharks with a safe full of loot and a villa in Marbella, Spain: They arrange the shipments of drugs into Sweden. In this brilliant story, Wallander again illustrates how forces outside Sweden, in this case drug smugglers, are infiltrating his country and destroying its once-wholesome society.

Although Wallander is not the best family man, he is a highly admirable, indeed a remarkable character. At times moody and irritable, he nevertheless is deeply troubled by the crimes he witnesses and feels an inner determination to solve them, not merely for self-satisfaction or to advance his career, but because he is concerned about contemporary Swedish society. Indeed, Wallander's marriage parallels Sweden's problems and the breakup of the traditionally solid Swedish family. This anxious concern deepens as Wallander becomes older and witnesses a Europe very different socially and culturally from the one in which he grew up. For thousands of years, Sweden has been more or less isolated geographically and socially from mainstream Europe. Not so any more. Wallander anxiously worries about how to control the criminal forces that continually penetrate his country's borders. Indeed, in the forward to *The Pyramid*, Mankell claims that the Wallander series should be subtitled "novels of Swedish anxiety."

M. Casey Diana

Review Sources

Booklist 104, no. 22 (August 1, 2008): 46.
Kirkus Reviews 76, no. 14 (July 15, 2008): 8.
Publishers Weekly 255, no. 30 (July 28, 2008): 56.
The Times Literary Supplement, October 24, 2008, p. 21.

QUIET, PLEASE
Dispatches from a Public Librarian

Author: Scott Douglas (1978-   )
Publisher: Da Capo Press (Cambridge, Mass.). 330 pp.
   $25.00
Type of work: Memoir
Time: 2001-2004
Locale: Anaheim, California

Douglas writes about his personal transition from aimless college student to professional librarian during a time when libraries and librarianship are also experiencing a critical transition

In *Quiet, Please: Dispatches from a Public Librarian,* author Scott Douglas chronicles his first three years working in a small Anaheim, California, public library. During this time Douglas earned a master's degree in Library and Information Science (MLIS) from San Jose State University and was promoted from library page, to technician, to librarian. Douglas had not planned to become a librarian; majoring in English literature at college, he had no specific plans for his future. By chance he saw a classified advertisement for a job as a library page, and he applied partly because of his love of books and reading and partly because he had nothing else in mind. During his first few months in the library, an older male library clerk suggested Douglas pursue a professional degree because he was more familiar with new technologies than many librarians and because the clerk felt outnumbered by women on the staff.

Promoted to library technician, Douglas applied to San Jose State's graduate program and began thinking more seriously about library work. Noting that he started in his new position on September 11, 2001, as the United States was attacked by terrorists, Douglas recounts how various regimes throughout history—the Germans in 1914 Belgium, the Nazis in Poland during World War II, the Taliban in Afghanistan—have destroyed libraries and other cultural artifacts in their attempts to conquer foreign cultures. As a library-school student, he began to notice how people searched for information about the September 11 attacks, and how critical they were (or were not) about what they found. He also noted that historically communities, not librarians, rebuild and reestablish destroyed libraries. This sequence is typical of Douglas's digressive but entertaining writing style, moving from the personal to a historical observation or extended factoid, then back again to his own story.

Douglas completed a two-year MLIS program, and he is fairly critical of the education he was offered in library school, raising an ongoing argument in librarianship about its professionalization and the value of theory versus practice. Typically, Douglas found much of his formal education would not help him with practical, day-to-day library work (his final project is to write a report about terrorism in Southeast

Scott Douglas has published articles in magazines, including School Library Journal *and* The Door Magazine, *and he blogs about his experiences as a public librarian in Anaheim, California.* Quiet, Please *is his first book.*

Asia); at the same time, on the job he began to appreciate the skills and knowledge of library workers who did not have professional degrees.

Beginning his career just as personal computers were becoming a staple of library service, Douglas worked with librarians and staff who were unable to make the transition to providing online service or to cope with an influx of young, unruly library patrons who came to use computers. At first library employees knew nothing about computers or the Internet and could only look on as patrons surfed the Internet, used e-mail, and launched programs unfamiliar to anyone on the staff. The library also encountered a new surly attitude on the part of younger patrons and the advent of Internet pornography (Douglas opens his first chapter with a remark about patrons masturbating while viewing Internet pornography, a common situation in libraries allowing public access).

Douglas entered the profession just as libraries were losing patrons to bookstores and Internet resources they could access at home, and he argues that libraries must change radically to compete with these threats. He suggests the classification systems used to arrange library materials should be jettisoned in favor of clearly labeled subject areas typical of bookstores, and he points out that many libraries have fallen behind in making online resources available and providing ways for users to plug in their own laptops and other electronic peripherals.

However, Douglas also believes public libraries serve their communities in ways that cannot be replaced by retail outlets or the Internet. He gives many examples showing how libraries are important in the lives of senior citizens, the mentally disabled, children, teens, the homeless, and immigrant families. Objecting when his library starts giving away free bags of popcorn, Douglas is told that for some children the popcorn will be the largest meal they have that day. Two years later he is ready to argue not only that patrons should be allowed to eat and drink in the library but also that libraries should sell food, claiming that the damage food and drink can cause to books, computers, and the physical environment is minimal compared to the comfort and convenience that might make the library more attractive to users. A library promotion for a fast-food restaurant, which disgusts him because the library is encouraging consumption of unhealthy food, shows him how desperate some families are to earn coupons for free hamburgers, filling out multiple reading logs to trade for coupons and even completing reading logs for infants. Library employees provide role models and emotional support to teenagers from troubled homes, companionship to the homeless and elderly, and social practice to the developmentally disabled.

Quiet, Please is characterized by its dual view of library workers and patrons. Douglas is ambivalent about most library users, who can be difficult—sometimes even frightening—to deal with, but at the same time they offer wisdom, amusement, and social interactions he values highly. His reactions to elderly patrons range from empathy and concern to dread and disgust. He loves to hear the stories older patrons can tell and appreciates the perspective they have on life, realizing they are often lonely and come to the library just to chat. At the same time, he notes that elderly patrons often refuse to learn skills for using the Internet, might ask the same question every day, and are the most likely to approach him with complaints. Douglas is brutal in describing his coworkers, who use library computers for personal projects and arrive for work reeking of pot—although even the most mean-tempered library clerk serves a valuable purpose in customer service by commiserating with elderly patrons who need someone to whom they can freely complain.

Douglas has doubts about becoming a professional librarian, linked to his ideals and sense of purpose, but more practically to the hazards of working in a public-access library. Douglas recounts several instances when patrons threatened him with physical harm. Teenagers become angry when asked to turn off blaring rap music; a homeless patron accuses Douglas of stealing his belongings; a man talking loudly on his cell phone in a public area threatens Douglas when asked to end the call.

Occasionally Douglas betrays a limited exposure to varieties of librarianship. Two or three years into his job, he is ready to assert that many librarians do not read, either because they do not have time or because at the end of the day, they are simply weary of dealing with books. Douglas also declares that cataloging (the creation of records that enable patrons and librarians to search for books) is obsolete, footnoting several "meaningless" cataloging terms he was expected to learn in library school (several of which are in daily use in libraries larger than his own).

Quiet, Please is refreshingly politically incorrect and irreverent, but sometimes jarring. Douglas uses "dick" liberally to describe patrons, coworkers, and himself. He is surprisingly open about the frustrations of customer service, often speaking the unspeakable: suggesting that older patrons would be less troublesome if they would just die, describing his initial discomfort with disabled patrons as a dislike for the handicapped, or calling one patron "a stupid old man in a wheelchair." His account of an obese patron's refusal to leave the men's room contains a bizarre footnote describing a fearful fantasy of being trapped with the patron and sexually assaulted: "I had dreams that one day I would go into the bathroom and he would . . . rape me," and it ended with him "killing and eating me."

Quiet, Please began as a more formal version of short essays Douglas wrote for an online magazine, and as a book developed from an Internet project it reflects a willingness to play with styles and formats as well as with a conviction that trivial personal information is worth posting. One chapter is presented as a screenplay, inexplicably introduced as an intermission during the film *Ben-Hur* (1959) while assuring the reader that the entire chapter serves no purpose and could be skipped. Douglas's account of his foray into MySpace.com, where he finds an online community of other young librarians, transcribes information from his MySpace page, including schools he attended from high school forward, lists of his favorite television programs, recording artists and books, and a personal profile listing his zodiac sign and telling whether he smokes.

The book is heavily and frivolously footnoted, usually with brief humorous comments that could have been incorporated into the text. In a few cases Douglas creates several back-and-forth interactions between his text and footnotes within a sentence or two, distracting the reader in an attempt to serve as his own straight man. A few footnotes provide factual information, which, again, might have been incorporated into the text, and are distinguishable from the sidebars only in their relative brevity.

Detachment from one's work is typical of contemporary humor, and Douglas frequently disparages his own text and suggests his readers are wasting their time. Numerous sidebars titled "For Shelving" allow Douglas, by nature an information scientist, to tell what he knows about history (of libraries, of children's literature, of eugenics, and of Anaheim and Disneyland), statistics (the economics of obtaining, then having, a college degree), and odd miscellany (evidence that the first moon landing was a hoax; the difference between a hobo and a bum; which country allows people to marry their pets; what scientists have discovered about boredom). In a footnote Douglas says these sidebars are pointless and are meant as little breaks from his main text, allowing the reader to "regroup and return to the pages with a fresh sense of interest."

Douglas learns that the purpose of the library is to support the community as well as to provide access to books. In many cases library purchases and policies are driven by economic considerations, as administrators decide how to satisfy the largest, most vocal, or most powerful community group. In his first years as a librarian, Douglas continually reviews his choice. Having joined the profession by default, he looks for the kernel of purpose in his job, always rediscovering where his responsibilities lie. His job is not to protect materials owned by the library, show people where to find titles, or even to like library patrons, but to serve the people who use the library in whatever way he can.

Maureen Puffer-Rothenberg

Review Sources

Booklist 104, no. 15 (April 1, 2008): 102.
Los Angeles Magazine 53, no. 4 (April, 2008): 92.

THE REAVERS

Author: George MacDonald Fraser (1925-2008)
Publisher: Alfred A. Knopf (New York). 268 pp. $24.00
Type of work: Novel
Time: The late sixteenth century
Locale: The border between England and Scotland

In a comic novel marked by wordplay, anachronisms, and outlandish events, the Scots and the English unite to defeat a vicious Spanish plot

Principal characters:
    ARCHIE NOBLE, an English secret agent
        masquerading as an outlaw
    EBENEEZER "BONNY" GILDEROY, a Scottish
        secret agent and a highwayman
    LADY GODIVA DACRE, a tall, red-haired, strong-willed young heiress and
        part-time secret agent
    MISTRESS KYLIE DELISHE, her pretty little companion
    THE WIZARD, later revealed to be La Infamosa, leader of the conspiracy
        against James VI
    DON COLLAPSO REGARDO BALUNA DEL LOBBY Y CORRIDOR, the Spanish
        ambassador to Scotland and a conspirator
    LORD ANGUISH, a Scottish traitor
    FREY BENTOS, a Spanish monk and conspirator, formerly Lord Waldo
        Dacre's chaplain
    CLNZH, an Amazon pygmy and a conspirator
    JAMES VI, the king of Scotland

George MacDonald Fraser begins his "Foreword" to *The Reavers* by asserting that "This book is nonsense," a "rebuke" to a society he insists is obsessed with doom. This work, he explains, is written in the same spirit as his previous novel, *The Pyrates* (1984). Certainly both books share some of the same elements that made Fraser's twelve Flashman novels so popular: historical settings, roguish heroes, voluptuous noblewomen, buxom barmaids, deep-dyed villains, and an assortment of outlaws. The Flashman novels also include plots, abductions, barroom brawls, and pitched battles, all staged to display the heroes' reckless courage and their magnificent swordsmanship. However, though the tone of the Flashman novels is satirical, they are essentially adventure stories with a historical setting; by contrast, *The Reavers* defies history and denies probability. It is indeed a romp of unreason.

However, this most irrational comic novel has a carefully reasoned structure. It is divided into twelve chapters of equal length, all but the first preceded by Fraser's commentaries on what has transpired or what is to come. These comments are designed to suggest that the action is not planned but improvised; for example, after chapter 1, Fraser discards several other ideas for the next segment before it strikes him

∼

*George MacDonald Fraser is best
known as the author of twelve comic
novels about Harry Flashman, a
fictional nineteenth century adventurer.
Fraser's script for* The Three
Musketeers *(1973) won him the 1974
Writers Guild of Great Britain award
for best comedy screenplay. Among his
other screenplays was the James Bond
film* Octopussy *(1983). The Reavers
was Fraser's final work.*

∼

that what he needs now is some glamorous women.

Fraser's success in making *The Reavers* appear to be a spur-of-the-moment lark is indicated by the fact that a number of reviewers insist that the book has no real plot. Admittedly, it is difficult to follow the story, in part because one incident follows another in a seemingly random fashion, and in part because the author introduces so many characters and describes them in such vivid detail that it is hard to tell which members of his cast are important. The direction of the plot does not become evident until the third chapter of the book, in which the author introduces his villains—a set of Spaniards and Spanish sympathizers who have met in a cave in order to fine-tune a vicious plot—and their plan to substitute an impostor for James VI, the reigning Scottish king, who after the death of Queen Elizabeth I will take her place as the ruler of England. The leader of the conspirators first appears as a wizard but is later revealed to be the malignant La Infamosa. Another member of the group is Don Collapso Regardo Baluna del Lobby y Corridor, the Spanish ambassador to Scotland. A Scottish traitor, Lord Anguish, and an Amazonian pygmy called Clnzh are also present at the meeting. One of the most important conspirators is Frey Bentos, a Spanish monk, who somehow managed to convince the late Lord Waldo Dacre that he was neither Spanish nor a monk, was appointed chaplain to that prominent aristocrat, and used his position to obtain information that would aid the cause of Spain.

In the third chapter, Fraser makes it clear that as rambunctious as *The Reavers* may be, its plot line has a solid foundation: the conflict between good (England, Scotland, and Protestantism) and evil (Spain and Catholicism). At this point, the author sets out to identify the heroes and heroines in this struggle. Though all of them appeared earlier, they are now shown as both more important and more complex than they seemed. Archie Noble, for example, was introduced as a man who had just been paroled after being imprisoned for vagrancy and was wandering about with no protector and no means of support. Only his dexterity in disposing of the fearsome Scottish gang leader Black Dod Pringle suggested that Noble might be more than a minor outlaw. As the plot progresses, Noble has to admit that he is in fact an English secret agent, and subsequently he is always in the forefront of the action. Another seemingly unlikely hero is the highwayman Ebeneezer "Bonny" Gilderoy, who, though an accomplished swordsman, is best known for being able to kiss any female into acquiescence. Now, however, he has to admit to Noble that he is a Scottish secret agent. The relationship between the two men is never easy. On a personal level, Noble clearly resents Gilderoy's unique gift, especially when the two heroes desire the same woman. Moreover, in the past their two countries have often been bitter enemies. However, Noble and Gilderoy realize that now they have a common cause: protecting James VI from the

Spanish conspiracy. They know that if a puppet of Spain replaced James on the Scottish throne and later became king of England, the results would be disastrous for both nations.

Not only does *The Reavers* have two heroes, but it also has two heroines. Lady Godiva Dacre, a tall, handsome, and wealthy young lady, first appears in the second chapter of the novel, as one of two passengers in a coach that is stuck in the mud on the road to Carlisle, Scotland. It seems that Lady Godiva was sent away from court because the queen viewed the red-haired beauty as a competitor. Though her own estates are in East Anglia, Lady Godiva is making her way north to see about the property of her grandfather, Lord Waldo Dacre, who has recently died. The other passenger is Lady Godiva's friend and companion Mistress Kylie Delishe, a small but well-endowed young woman with an overactive libido. While the coach is halted, some of the local bandits decide that it would be an ideal time to steal the horses and rob the passengers. However, the handsome, well-dressed highwayman Gilderoy comes to the rescue, drives off the bandits, retrieves the horses, and brings back Godiva's servants, who had fled from their attackers. Gilderoy swears his undying love to Godiva, favoring her with one of his famous kisses. However, while she is in ecstasy, Gilderoy is busy taking her jewels. When she discovers what he has done, she is furious, but Gilderoy refuses to give them back, arguing that his reputation as a highwayman would be ruined if he did so.

At this point in the novel, it is not clear that Godiva will emerge as a heroine, though she has demonstrated that she has the spirit, or at least the temper, to qualify her for the role. Later, however, she admits to being a part-time secret agent, reporting to Sir Francis Walsingham, Queen Elizabeth I's secretary of state (1573-1590) and one of the few historical personages in the novel. It later turns out that the jewels of which Gilderoy relieved Godiva were supposed to provide funds for Walsingham's agents and specifically for those who are attempting to outwit the Spaniards. These revelations make it evident that Godiva is more than the spoiled rich girl she at first appears to be. She is also much more than the passive heroine whom men must rescue. As the novel proceeds, she fights beside the heroes, thus proving herself to be both as clever and as courageous as they are.

Kylie Delishe, too, at first appears to be a superficial character, defined by her obsession with sex. Kylie's primary function seems to be that of the confidant in French drama: to enable the heroine, in this case, Godiva, to express herself. However, Kylie, too, proves to have heroic qualities. Late in the novel, she outwits Clnzh, seizes a knife, and frees Noble, along with one of his bandit allies, thus setting in motion the events that lead to the defeat of the Spanish conspiracy.

Though it has the plot structure of a traditional novel, with characters lined up on both sides of a clearly defined conflict between good and evil, in other respects *The Reavers* is truly extraordinary. The language alone qualifies it for that description. The book begins with the hackneyed phrase "It was a dark and stormy night," which proves to be the beginning of a sentence that goes on for some thirty lines, rambling from phrase to phrase like an Elizabethan gossip. From that point on, Fraser indulges in language, often mischievously piling up as many verbs or nouns as come to mind, and just as often inserting contemporary slang in the midst of the "forsooths" and "eftsoons" that one would find in a bad novel with an Elizabethan setting. The author switches at will from one dialect to another, then comes back to standard English just when his readers have begun to find their way through a dialect.

As a reviewer in *The New York Times* pointed out, in *The Reavers* Fraser also ignores the rules of punctuation. He keeps his sentences going long after any other writer would insert a period, and he scatters dashes and dots with wild abandon. There are enough sentence fragments to give a freshman English teacher apoplexy. What makes the difference is that unlike the student, the author knows exactly what he is doing.

Fraser takes particular pleasure in inserting contemporary slang, references to recent events, and even allusions to modern technological devices such as DVDs into his narrative. He seems to take special delight in introducing anachronistic references at the most dramatic moments. For example, just before the conspiracy is to come to fruition, he shows Lord Anguish and the Scottish Sir Prising hammering out a contract that will decide the distribution of the profits from James's memoirs as well as from commemorative souvenirs such as T-shirts, cups, and stickers.

The Reavers is not a novel that everyone will enjoy. It is exhausting to read; there are so many characters, so many twists in the plot, so much swordplay, and so much sexual innuendo, and such frequent interruptions for authorial comments that one may be tempted to put down the book and turn to a work that is less taxing. However, the reader who can suspend disbelief and join the author in simply having fun will find *The Reavers* truly delightful.

Rosemary M. Canfield Reisman

Review Sources

Booklist 104, no. 13 (March 1, 2008): 30.
Kirkus Reviews 76, no. 5 (March 1, 2008): 209-210.
Library Journal 133, no. 6 (April 1, 2008): 74-75.
The New York Times Book Review, June 8, 2008, p. 24.
Publishers Weekly 255, no. 8 (February 25, 2008): 48-49.
The Washington Times, April 20, 2008, p. B06.

RECONCILIATION
Islam, Democracy, and the West

Author: Benazir Bhutto (1953-2007)
Publisher: HarperCollins (New York). 328 pp. $27.95
Type of work: Current affairs, history

Bhutto's vision for reconciling differences within the Muslim world and between the Muslim world and the West was finished just days before her assassination in December, 2007

Principal personages:
BENAZIR BHUTTO, prime minister of
    Pakistan (1988-1990, 1993-1996), the
    first woman to lead an Islamic state
ZULFIKAR ALI BHUTTO, founder of the
    Pakistan People's Party in 1968,
    president of Pakistan (1971-1973), and first prime minister elected in
    Pakistan (served 1973-1977 and reelected in 1977)
PRESIDENT AYUB KHAN, president of Pakistan in the 1950's and 1960's
GENERAL YAHYA KHAN, commander-in-chief in 1969 and president and
    military dictator until 1971
GENERAL MUHAMMAD ZIA-UL-HAQ, general who imposed military rule
    in 1977, became president in 1978, and executed Zulfikar Ali Bhutto
    in 1979
GENERAL PERVEZ MUSHARRAF, Army chief of staff who seized power in
    Pakistan in 1999 and who was president (2001-2008)

According to her collaborator, Mark A. Siegel, Benazir Bhutto believed that two major world issues would dominate this millennium: the struggle between democracy and dictatorship and the struggle between moderation and extremism. *Reconciliation*, published after her death, explores these struggles from "a modern Muslim woman's view." It includes historical and contemporary perspectives that are critical to understanding the worldwide confrontation between Muslim extremists and the West.

Bhutto's avowed purpose in returning home to Pakistan in 2007 was to further democracy and moderation in that country. She describes in detail her dramatic return to Karachi on October 18, after a self-imposed exile of eight years, to a tumultuous welcome by three million supporters. Their enthusiastic support reminded her of her emotional return to Pakistan in 1986, after two years abroad, when she assumed the leadership of the Pakistan Peoples Party (PPP). Bhutto makes it clear that she understood the danger of returning to Pakistan. Her father, Zulfikar Ali Bhutto, the founder of the PPP and Pakistan's first elected prime minister, had been executed in 1979 by General Zia-ul-Haq, the military dictator who deposed him. Many of the same forces that ended democracy and conspired to kill her father and two brothers were still in power, and General Pervez Musharraf, Pakistan's military dictator in 2007, warned

~

Benazir Bhutto, the first woman to lead a Muslim state, was prime minister of Pakistan from 1988 to 1990. Reelected in 1993, she was forced to resign in 1996, when the military assumed control of the government. She returned to Pakistan in October, 2007, and was assassinated by extremists two months later. In 2008, she was one of seven winners of the United Nations Human Rights Prize.

~

that suicide squads threatened to assassinate her. Bhutto, anticipating elections scheduled for January, 2008, was willing to take a calculated risk. On October 19, 2007, the progress of her cavalcade was marked by two bomb blasts that killed almost two hundred people. She suspected that Musharraf was in collusion with her enemies, doing little to provide her security. Bhutto escaped this attempt on her life, but she was assassinated by extremists two months later, on December 27, 2007. Ironically, Siegel received the manuscript of *Reconciliation* on the day she died.

Bhutto devotes a chapter in *Reconciliation* to conflicts within the Muslim world. The Islamic world faces both internal and external crises. If the internal struggles in Muslim society are not resolved, conflicts will "degenerate into a collision course of values spilling into a clash between Islam and the West." The history of Islam and the differences between the beliefs of the Sunnis and Shias and their various sects are many, but overriding these differences are two major tensions within Islam: democracy versus dictatorship and moderation versus extremism. Bhutto finds it ironic that moderate Muslims, who were outraged by the U.S. invasion of Iraq, have little to say about Muslim-on-Muslim violence. Arguing for moderation and democracy, she debates the fundamentalists' interpretation of the Qurʾān . She argues that the Qurʾān must be interpreted from a modern understanding of Islam and related to its historical context or a given situation. Citing the Qurʾān, Islamic scholars, and historical precedent, she argues that extremists distort the message of Islam and enforce many restrictive traditions derived from ancient tribal values or medieval interpretations of Islam. They use the Qurʾān to suppress women and enforce strict dress codes, but women are equal to men; and men, as well as women, are admonished by the Qurʾān to guard their modesty. Although terrorists call their violence jihad (holy war), jihad literally means a struggle to follow the right path—either in an internal struggle or in an external struggle that is defensive or against persecution. Historically, in a region of constant warfare, Islam outlawed war except for jihad; violence was a last resort. "Holy war" was never intended to be used again monotheists (Christians and Jews or "the people of the Book"). Indeed, today some Muslims believe that the materialism, corruption, and hedonistic values promoted in the Western-dominated media require a jihad, but armed conflict must be constrained. Osama bin Laden and other terrorists equate suicide, which is prohibited by the Qurʾān, with dying for a just cause. They want to unite the Muslim world politically and to provoke a clash of values with the West. A clash between Muslim and Western civilizations, however, is not inevitable. Islam, unlike the caricature portrayed in the Western media, is not incompatible with democracy, which is a universal longing. Tolerance, justice, rationality, and gender equality are inherent in true Islam.

Although Muslim societies have contributed to their own problems because of internal strife and Muslim-on-Muslim violence, Bhutto lays responsibility for the failure of Muslim countries to develop democratic governments at the door of the Western powers, especially France, Britain, and the United States. In a concise and reasoned history of Western interference in Muslim countries, she shows, country by country, how Western governments have meddled in the affairs of Muslim societies and exploited them in their self-interests. By supporting dictators and failing to foster true economic and democratic development, they have created resentment and hostility, leading to the current instability and violence in the world.

Pakistan, a case in point, has been in turmoil for most of its sixty-year history. It is now "ground zero" in the world confrontation between radical Islamists and the West, due to its nuclear capability and its political and economic instability When the British pulled out of India in 1947, the country was hastily partitioned into two states, India and Pakistan, roughly along religious lines (Hindus and Muslims), with the disputed territory of Kashmir separating East and West Pakistan. Geography and serious ethnic and linguistic differences separated East and West Pakistan. Distrust over elections for the constituent assembly in 1969 and irreconcilable political differences with the PPP resulted in war in 1971. India entered the war on East Pakistan's side and defeated Pakistan in 1971. East Pakistan became Bangladesh in January, 1972.

From its beginning, Pakistan has been plagued by wars, poverty, a lack of educational and economic resources, religious extremism, and frequent military coups, dictatorships, and assassinations. The mind-boggling problems caused by the ethnic and linguistic diversity of the country have been exacerbated by the arrival of millions of Muslim immigrants (muhajirs) from India, uprooted in 1947, and by the concentration of Afghan refugees on its border with Afghanistan.

When Mohammad Ali Jinnah, the father of independence, died soon after the partition, General Ayub Kahn became president and was in power in the 1950's and 1960's. He imposed a state of emergency in 1965, when Pakistan went to war with India over Kashmir and there was widespread dissent and violence. In 1968, after an assassination attempt, he arrested opposition leaders, including Zulfikar Ali Bhutto, Benazir's father and founder of the PPP. Ayub Kahn resigned in 1969, handing over power to General Yahya Khan, the military commander-in-chief, who assumed the title of president and imposed martial law. Yahya Khan called for elections in December, 1970, and resigned in 1971 after his invasion of East Pakistan led to defeat by India. Benazir's father, Zulfikar Ali Bhutto, became the undisputed leader of Pakistan. He was president from 1971 to 1973 and became Pakistan's first elected prime minister in 1973. He instituted a policy of Islamic socialism. Zulfikar Ali Bhutto was reelected 1977, but his campaign had been marked by violence. Protests by the opposition—alleging discrimination, fraud, and corruption and demanding new elections—resulted in General Muhammad Zia-ul-Haq's deposing Zulfikar Ali Bhutto and imposing military rule. Zia-ul-Haq assumed the presidency in 1978, and Zulfikar Ali Bhutto was arrested on charges of attempted murder. His execution in 1979 was the turning point in his daughter Benazir's life. She felt compelled to assume her father's mantle. (She ignores accusations that he became very autocratic, suppressing criticism and jailing opponents. She claims that her father was falsely accused and executed because he was the only politician of mass appeal and there was no political alternative.) Bhutto became the leader of the PPP and became prime minister in 1988, serving until 1990, and again from 1993 to 1996. Her government was accused of massive corruption, and she was imprisoned and later exiled. Bhutto's political history is informative, but biased, fragmented, and self-justifying.

After the Soviet Union invaded Afghanistan in December, 1979, the United States began channeling massive arms supplies through Pakistan to the Afghan mujahideen (freedom fighters) who were waging guerrilla warfare. After the mujahideen established bases in northern Pakistan, thousands of refugees fled to Pakistan. The United States supported Zia-ul-Haq with massive aid programs between 1987 and 1992, in exchange for his cooperation. A zealous Muslim, Zia-ul-Haq increased the Islamization of Pakistan and aligned Pakistani intelligence agencies with radical elements of the mujahideen. He destroyed political parties, eliminated the independent judiciary, and suspended human rights.

In 1999, the army's chief of staff, Musharraf, seized power in a coup, naming himself president in 2001. He also accepted U.S. aid, but he was unable to control political extremists. The invasion of Afghanistan by the United States after 9/11 alienated Muslim tribal people and increased support for the Taliban and unrest in Pakistan. Political pressure forced Musharraf to resign as army chief in 2007, and he agreed to hold elections in 2008. Although he allowed Bhutto to return to Pakistan, he imposed martial law in 2007. Bhutto was hopeful he would relinquish power. He was forced to step down in 2008.

In "A Clash of Civilizations?" (an essay published in 1993), Samuel P. Huntington predicted an unalterable opposition between the West and the Muslim world. Bhutto reasons that such a clash is not inevitable. To believe Huntington's theory would make it a self-fulfilling prophecy. Both camps must seek reconciliation. The Muslim world must seek reform and learn to deal with modernity. The West must foster democracy and economic progress in Muslim countries. Bhutto proposes more cultural exchanges, based on the tenet that "the more you know about others, the less likely you are to fear them." Critics argue that this commonly accepted notion is debatable, citing the example of the suicide bombings of the World Trade Center and the Pentagon on 9/11 by terrorists who were educated in the United States.

This book could be a wonderful primer for Muslims and Westerners who seek to understand the historical, cultural, and theological tensions within the Muslim world. Most Westerners are ignorant of how their governments have contributed to the present world crisis by trying to control Muslim countries. Unfortunately, the historical and political complexity of the Muslim world and the numerous unfamiliar names, terms, and organizations present a challenge to the reader. There is no index, and there are no chapter headings at the tops of pages, which makes it difficult to access information. A map of the subcontinent of Asia would also have been helpful.

Despite these problems, Bhutto makes an informative and persuasive case for an urgent need to address problems and forge creative solutions in order to avoid a clash of civilizations. Given the problems in Pakistan and her failure to establish a truly democratic government in the past, Bhutto may not have been able to accomplish much, had she become prime minister again. This book may be her greatest legacy.

Edna B. Quinn

Review Sources

Booklist 104, no. 13 (March 1, 2008): 28.
Library Journal 133, no. 13 (August 15, 2008): 126.
Los Angeles Times, February 12, 2008, p. E1.
New Statesman 137 (March 3, 2008): 54-55.
The New York Times, January 7, 2008, p. 2.
The New York Times Book Review, April 6, 2008, p. 16.
The Times Literary Supplement, June 13, 2008, p. 27.
The Washington Post, February 12, 2008, p. C1.

RED BIRD

Author: Mary Oliver (1935-   )
Publisher: Beacon Press (Boston). 78 pp. $23.00.
Type of work: Poetry

In this collection of sixty-one new poems, well-known poet and nature writer Oliver observes the Cape Cod landscape from the perspective of her seventy years, encompassing love and loss, happiness, and grief

In her twelfth book of poetry, *Red Bird*, Oliver breaks new ground while still offering readers what they love best: the sharp image, the keen observation, and the near-mystical identification with the natural world. From the opening poem, "Red Bird," to the closing poem, "Red Bird Explains Himself," Oliver weaves together the journey of her life, through love, through sorrow, and back again to an embrace of the world.

In 2005 Oliver's beloved companion, Molly Malone Cook, died at the age of eighty. The two had shared an oceanside home on Cape Cod for more than forty years. Oliver's 2006 collection, *Thirst*, was heavy with the grief of that loss. In 2006, as a tribute to Cook, Oliver selected a representative sampling of Cook's photographs and published them along with her own prose in a book titled *Our World*. Now, through the words of *Red Bird*, Oliver emerges from her grief to once again open her arms, her vision, and her heart to all of the creatures of the natural world. Nonetheless, her vision is slightly shifted from her earlier work; the poems of *Red Bird* carry with them a subtle, dark undercurrent. It is as if her understanding of the world is being severely tested. While her earlier work demonstrates her connectedness to all living things, *Red Bird* lays bare a grief over the death of one particular person. Further, whereas in earlier work, Oliver has many times portrayed the deaths of creatures large and small, it is in this book that she integrates into her worldview the necessity of death. To do so, she must enlarge her scope, finding sympathy for the fox and the mouse, the bear and fish, paradoxically and equally. She must confront herself squarely as an aging woman who will surely experience her own death, more likely sooner than later. Despite these thematic concerns, it would be wrong, however, to depict *Red Bird* as a sad or sorrowful book, although there is surely both sorrow and sadness within the pages. The book is filled with wonder, some laughter, many sharp images, and evidence of the redemptive power of nature.

The red bird of the title signals Oliver's return to the land of the living, "firing up the landscape/ as nothing else could do." In the winter of the spirit and the heart, the passion that the red bird represents continues to call all creatures to life, even the poet herself. In "Self-Portrait," Oliver claims that she is "still/ in love with life. And still/ full of beans." Even at seventy, she finds the strength and the purpose to tramp the woods and hills. Her characteristic joy in life in all its varieties, including her own, is evident here and throughout the book.

Early in the collection, however, Oliver
strikes another, more somber note. In "Night
and the River," Oliver describes the scene of a
bear fishing along a river. Without first naming the bear, she creates his power: The bear
has "great feet leaping in the river," and she
sees "the sudden fire of his mouth" as he eats
a fish. It is as if the power of the bear exists
separately from his physical body. For Oliver,
this is a beautiful, yet terrifying, experience,
one that she is not sure how to explain or understand. "I could not tell/ which fit me/ more

Mary Oliver is one of the best-known
poets and essayists in the United States.
The winner of the 1998 Lannon
Literary Award, Oliver also won the
Pulitzer Prize for American Primitive
(1983) and the 1992 National Book
Award for New and Selected Poems.
Born in Ohio, Oliver lives in
Provincetown, Massachusetts.

comfortably, the power,/ or the powerlessness." Once the fish has been consumed and
the bear leaves, Oliver is left only with the story of the event, one that is "a difficult
guest" in her home. The story is like the river, never stopping, but continuing to sing
the same song, over and over and over. At the same time, however, the story "sounds
like a body falling apart." In this poem, Oliver addresses head on the theme she has
hinted at in previous volumes, such as *Owls and Other Fantasies* (2003): Death is a
gory but necessary business. It is as if Oliver has butted up against the hard truth that
no matter how much one revels in the natural world and in the abundance of life, all
life ends in death, and often the weak lose their lives to the strong. Even more unsettling, life requires death. Thus the difficulty of the story she brings home from the
river: The bear's life depends on the fish's death. The fish was a beautiful creature,
and the bear, too, will someday face death.

Oliver again returns to this theme in the poem "Another Everyday Poem." Oliver's
first stanza reads, "Every day/ I consider/ the lilies—/ how they are dressed—," a
graceful and clear response to Matthew 6:28-29: "And why are you so anxious about
clothing? Consider the lilies of the field, how they grow; they neither toil nor spin; yet
I tell you, even Solomon in all of his glory was not arrayed like one of these." Christians read this verse as an admonition to trust God in all things, and not to worry about
the necessities of life, since God will provide.

For Oliver, however, the consideration of the lilies of the field moves her not to a
greater trust in God but rather to a consideration of the ravens, and "how they are fed."
Scavengers of carrion, ravens feed off death. The juxtaposition of glorious lilies and
voracious ravens hungry for meat demonstrates two sides of the same coin, two examples from the natural world of the interdependence of life and death. For Oliver, the
mystery is not that all will die, but that "such brevity—/ makes the world/ so full, so
good."

In spite of her understanding of the oneness of all nature and the coexistence of life
and death, Oliver is not above or beyond fear. In several poems, the trembling of trepidation is palpable. For example, in "Maker of All Things, Even Healings," Oliver
writes of the fox, who "moves through the darkness/ with a mouthful of teeth/ and a
reputation for death." In this poem, Oliver clearly sides with the hunted mice as she
pleads with the Maker of All Things to let her "abide in your shadow."

In what might be the most disturbing poem of the collection, "Sometimes," Oliver describes a cat-headed creature that rises from the water that she immediately associates with death, or perhaps with God: "I don't know what God is./ I don't know what death is./ But I believe they have between them/ some fervent and necessary arrangement." This paradox, this necessary deal between the creator of all and the destroyer of all, is the puzzle Oliver returns to again and again. The poem is divided into seven segments. After the eerie opening, Oliver reports "sometimes/ melancholy leaves me breathless." She is not one to linger in that dark state, however, and soon she finds herself in the middle of a storm, filled with the creative energy of primordial soup, thunder, and lightning. The penultimate segment reads like a prayer: She asks God to strengthen her and to take away her need for answers. Finally, after fear and prayer, she reaches reconciliation, noting that "Death waits for me, I know it, around/ one corner or another." This thought does not trouble her, nor does she find it ironic. It simply is.

Toward the end of the book, Oliver stretches her poetic persona by including a number of poems about love, including the touching poem cycle, "Eleven Versions of the Same Poem." The poems move from the assertion that the poet is lost without the companion she loves, to the contemplation of how the heart heals. Even in healing, however, the heart is not without pain, something made abundantly clear in poems such as "There you were, and it was like spring." The recollection of love causes the poet to cry out, "Why are we made the way we are made, that to love is to want?"

In the final two segments of the cycle, Oliver announces her intention to return to the world or at least to try. In the poem "I Will Try," she calls herself "a woman whose love has vanished,/ who thinks now, too much, of roots/ and the dark places." In spite of this darkness, she nevertheless feels a singing inside her, and she calls upon the totemic red bird, the bringer of passion, song, and life.

While most of the poems in this book are lovely nuggets of life, love, and the mystery of death, some of them turn to larger issues of the world. Oliver takes the United States and its government to task for war and cruelty in poems such as "Of the Empire," and "Iraq," among others, and she warns everyone that humans are rapidly destroying the flora and fauna of the planet in "Showing the Birds." These poems do not seem to work as well as others in the collection. There is no doubt that the thoughts expressed are sincerely held and worthy of serious consideration. Nonetheless, the poetry is less effective than in her other poems, largely because often the language falls into pronouncement and admonishment, as opposed to the subtle and effective intimations of the other works. Contrasted with the delicate and profound poetry of "Ocean," for example, the polemic poems seem heavy handed.

At the end, it might be the Percy poems, written about her dog, that hold the best instructions for reader and poet alike. Oliver places the three poems roughly equidistant one from the other in the book. These wry little gems offer a dog's eye view of the world. In "Percy and Books," readers discover a talking Percy who passes his judgment on literature: "Books? says Percy. I ate one once and it was enough." In the next Percy poem, Oliver describes how the dog acts when he knows that a friend is coming to the door. Again, she opposes the world of language, words, and ideas, the world of literature and Ralph Waldo Emerson, with the world of a dog who runs trustingly into the future without need for thought or explanation. Taken individually, the three poems offer some gentle comic relief and lighthearted fun. Taken as a sequence, however, the three Percy poems are a kind of evolving theology for Oliver. For Percy, life is immediate, lived in the present moment. He does not experience the melancholy of loss or a fear of the future. He tells Oliver to love, run fast, sleep, and trust.

Red Bird closes with a final appearance of the red bird that makes its presence felt throughout the collection. In "Red Bird Explains Himself," Oliver gives voice to the bird that tells readers that its "true task" is "to be the music of the body." The music of *Red Bird* will linger with the reader long after the book is closed.

Diane Andrews Henningfeld

Review Sources

America 198, no. 14 (April 28, 2008): 38-40.
Booklist 104, no. 13 (March 1, 2008): 44.
The Christian Science Monitor, April 15, 2008, p. 13.
Los Angeles Times, January 6, 2008, p. R10.
Weekly Standard 14, no. 9 (November 17, 2008): 43-44.

RETRIBUTION
The Battle for Japan, 1944-45

Author: Max Hastings (1945-   )
First published: Nemesis: The Battle for Japan,
1944-1945, 2007, in Great Britain
Publisher: Alfred A. Knopf (New York). Illustrated. 615
   pp. $35.00
Type of work: History
Time: 1944-1945
Locale: Asia and the Pacific

Japan was losing the war, and Japanese intransigence,
arrogance, and brutality were bringing retribution

RETRIBUTION
The Battle for Japan, 1944-45

MAX HASTINGS

Principal personages:
   CHESTER NIMITZ, commander of U.S. naval
      forces in the Pacific
   DOUGLAS MACARTHUR, commander of the U.S. Army in the Far East
   CURTIS LEMAY, Army Air Force commander who directed the B-29
      raids on Japan
   CHIANG KAI-SHEK, generalissimo of the Chinese armies, recognized
      leader of China
   MAO ZEDONG, leader of the Chinese Communists, isolated in the far
      north of rural Yan'an province, but building a base among the
      peasantry
   WINSTON CHURCHILL, prime minister of Great Britain and author of
      best-selling histories of World War II
   JOSEPH STALIN, leader of the Soviet Union who hurried to grab Japanese
      possessions before the war ended
   HARRY TRUMAN, president of the United States after Franklin
      Roosevelt's death in April, 1945
   HIROHITO, emperor of Japan

The original British title of this much-praised book was *Nemesis.* The subtlety of
the title change is important. *Retribution* emphasizes Allied (essentially American)
revenge; *Nemesis* emphasizes the Japanese responsibility for their own suffering.
Max Hastings demonstrates repeatedly the failures of the Japanese government and
military leaders to plan properly for such a great conflict. It was one thing to occupy
Manchuria and the coasts of China, something else to take on the greatest industrial
power in the world, and yet something else to awaken the American giant by a surprise attack on Pearl Harbor. Those misjudgments head a long list of mistakes made
by the Japanese militarists. They failed to use submarines against American supply
lines, they neglected preparation for the American submarine campaign, and they did
not build sufficient tankers to bring oil to Japan or escort vessels to protect the tankers
that survived. What was in their minds? Most of all, a belief that will was the essential

ingredient to victory and that the racially and
socially superior Japanese people would always prevail over the inferior races facing
them.

    Even today's understanding of the war re-
flects the Germany-first emphasis of Allied
planning, then the dramatic naval battles of
the central Pacific. Pearl Harbor eclipses the
Japanese preoccupation with natural resources
and the fascistic militarism that lay behind Ja-

~
*Max Hastings was educated at Oxford
and was a foreign correspondent for
leading British newspapers. Knighted
in 2002, he is the author of more than
fifteen books, including* Bomber
Command *(1979) and* Overlord: D-Day
and the Battle for Normandy *(1984).*
~

pan's seizure of Manchuria, its invasion of China, and its lust for the French, British,
and Dutch colonial riches. The Japanese advances of 1941-1944 swiftly humiliated
British and American armies and navies—then everything went wrong.

    The Greater East Asia Coprosperity Sphere was not Asia for Asians, but Asia for
the Japanese. Arrogance and lack of planning by the new occupiers made their predecessors look relatively good; to support their armies and supply the home islands, the
Japanese brought not liberation but starvation and fear. Then, as the Allied counterof-
fensive began, desperation set in. Few Japanese would (or dared to) admit it, but by
1944 it was obvious that the war was going badly.

    On the home front, Japanese civilians were short of food, heating oil, raw materi-
als, and even soap. Bombs were falling on new cities each day; most important, firebomb raids were incinerating tens of thousands per raid. Nevertheless, there was no
peace movement and no talk of surrender or even of peace talks.

    Both the American and Japanese military planners made major blunders. Neither
applied the lessons of the U-boat successes until late in the war, when American submarines practically annihilated Japan's merchant marine, and the Japanese wasted
their own vessels in vain attempts to supply isolated island garrisons. While Americans went to great lengths to rescue downed pilots, Japanese let theirs drown. American blunders were distractions, prolonging the war, but Japanese miscalculations
were disastrous. The Japanese economy could not match that of their enemies, while
the Americans could fight simultaneously two wars on opposite sides of the globe and
win.

    The Japanese expected to prevail—if not in set battles, then by exhausting the
Westerners. The Japanese knew that their soldiers and sailors would sacrifice everything for victory, or, if not victory, then for honor, while their opponents would not.
The Westerners would surely conclude that a compromise peace was better than suffering more casualties, and that the compromise peace would leave Japan with most
of its conquests.

    The result was a series of dreary and now-almost-forgotten campaigns: Burma,
New Guinea, and the Philippines. Most of those campaigns were unnecessary, because the Americans could have bypassed the isolated garrisons, but the combination
of pride, the desire for revenge, the need to use the forces available, and ambition
drove the Americans forward. The foremost personality of these destructive but inde-
cisive campaigns was Douglas MacArthur, the most visible public hero of the era and

the general most despised by military historians. In the background was Winston Churchill, whose slim hopes to preserve the British Empire seemed to depend on making some contribution to the war, but whose efforts were largely spurned by the Americans.

When American forces landed on the Philippines, the Japanese began the first of the suicide attacks that became more formidable the next year. First, there were the forlorn efforts of the Japanese fleet to challenge the overwhelming numbers of American naval vessels, and then came the more deadly kamikaze attacks—explosive-laden airplanes diving onto American ships. They might as well, it was reasoned. Japanese aircraft that had been superior at the start of the war became hopelessly outclassed by American fighters, and Japan had lacked the resources to bring out improved models. It was a tactic of desperation, but it worked. There were plenty of pilots ready to die, and they did not even need to be well trained.

Rooting the Japanese out of the Philippine mountains was a foretaste of Okinawa and what could be expected in the home islands. Surrender was a rarity, and soldiers who seemed to want to surrender were likely to throw a grenade at their captors. This discouraged American soldiers from taking risks to bring them in alive. The American commanders were mediocre at best in dealing with the difficult terrain and the challenges of the climate; they hardly knew what to do with an enemy who would not quit when obviously beaten, but even increased the foolish sacrifice of men.

Chester Nimitz had the right strategy—to drive straight toward Japan, cut off the home islands from food and oil, force the imperial navy to come onto the high seas where it would be destroyed, then impose a blockade until Japan surrendered. However, even he agreed to costly assaults on Iwo Jima and Okinawa, and he lacked the personality to dominate the talks on strategy. Instead, MacArthur was allowed to run his own parallel war, one which drew Nimitz's forces to the Philippines instead of moving on Japan. America was rich enough to finance two strategies, so why not? There was not much thought in Washington about the Pacific theaters compared to that given to the European war.

The Americans placed much hope on China. After all, the bulk of the Japanese army was there, and the Chinese had an almost unlimited supply of men. Chiang Kai-shek and Mao Zedong, however, were both quite willing to stand on the defense. They understood that the Americans would defeat their common enemy; meanwhile, they would husband their resources for the civil war that would follow. It was an unbelievably cruel war, fought in obscurity. Few Western reporters were present, and no Japanese newspapers dared print any criticism of the official press releases.

B-29 operations were much more complicated than was publicly revealed. The aircraft were delicate, prone to malfunctions, and more effective at low altitudes than high ones. The Australians, praised at the time for their valor in the Near East and in the early stages of the war, lost enthusiasm for this war as the dangers waned. Australian dockworkers went on strike; the Australian merchant marine worried about the nonexistent Japanese submarine threat. (Australians have not been pleased by this chapter in the book.)

Hastings's style is to use anecdotes, the personal stories that emphasize the tragedy and the suffering. Quoting from memoirs, letters, and interviews, he draws an unremittingly depressing picture of both military and civilian life. There were no meaningful victory parades, few comfortable billets, and few memories of anything but heat, humidity, bugs, disease, and isolation, unless it was rain, mud, and cold. There were heroes, but most soldiers were simply doing their duty, hoping to get the job over with as quickly as possible in order to return home.

Hastings has little patience for those who complain that the United States should not have used the atomic bomb. Those criticisms are offered in a historical vacuum, he feels, with no willingness to look at the options available. The kamikaze attacks and the casualties of the Okinawa campaign made clear what awaited the troops in an invasion of Japan, and Japanese leaders relied on this sacrificial spirit to obtain a favorable peace settlement; moreover, Japanese leaders were aware that fanatics in the officer corps would assassinate anyone who advocated surrender. The massive death tolls from firebomb raids, the collapse of the economy, the potential for starvation—none of these were having the desired effect. The alternative was the starvation of millions, the death of more millions of Chinese and others in Japanese occupation zones, and the end of the last hope of rescuing prisoners of war. The atomic bomb ended the deadlock, while simultaneously warning Joseph Stalin that America had won the war and America would decide the peace terms.

The Soviet invasion of Manchuria did not have the effect that was imagined at Yalta and Potsdam, but it helped demoralize what was left of Japanese militarism. As the Red Army had done in Europe, it raped its way across Manchuria and into Korea, then stripped all machinery and infrastructure for use in Russia. Japanese resistance was inept and ineffective, but heroic in the insane manner that had characterized the army's behavior in the last year of the war.

The emperor finally intervened, broadcasting a message to his people that caused the fanatics to commit suicide and everyone else to breathe a sigh of relief. Contrary to what propaganda had predicted, the Americans did not plan on exterminating the people or reducing them to slavery. MacArthur was a model administrator, making a good end to a war badly fought.

This important book is the culmination of a lifetime of research into aspects of World War II. No reader will put the book down wishing he had been there, yet none should conclude that it did not matter who won.

The war resulted in an Asia for Asians. It was not as the Japanese planned it—an Asia that worked for Japan—but the old colonialism could not be resurrected. It was not just that the Japanese had beaten Europeans and Americans, but in the first year of the war they had beaten them so soundly. Japanese efforts to establish quisling regimes failed miserably; it was obvious that new masters had taken over, masters who believed themselves superior to the colonial peoples in every way. Most important, the Japanese considered honor the essence of life and war the essence of honor. These were not beliefs shared by anyone in their short-lived empire.

There is a strong current throughout the book that the Japanese had begun the war foolishly, had conducted it badly, had misbehaved everywhere (if misbehaved is the right word for countless atrocities and crimes), and at the end refused to believe that the war was lost. The Japanese had earned what they got. It was "retribution."

William L. Urban

Review Sources

Booklist 104, no. 13 (March 1, 2008): 46.
Commentary 126, no. 2 (September, 2008): 74-76.
Kirkus Reviews 76, no. 2 (January 15, 2008): 76.
Library Journal 133, no. 4 (March 1, 2008): 92.
Military History 25, no. 1 (March/April, 2008): 72-73.
The New York Review of Books 55, no. 7 (May 1, 2008): 24-27.
The New York Times Book Review, March 30, 2008, p. 14.
The Wall Street Journal 251, no. 62 (March 15, 2008): W10.

RISING, FALLING, HOVERING

Author: C. D. Wright (1949-   )
Publisher: Copper Canyon Press (Port Townsend,
    Wash.). 96 pp. $22.00
Type of work: Poetry
Time: 2003-2008
Locale: The United States and Mexico

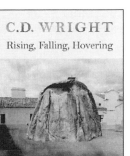

*Wright blends motifs of her private life and details from
a trip to Mexico to create a vehicle through which to express her anguish and rage over the U.S. war in Iraq*

Readers of C. D. Wright's poetry have called the last de-
cade a period of great growth in her work. Beginning with *Just Whistle: A Valentine*
(1993), the work that marked the start of her collaboration with photographer
Deborah Luster, and followed by *Deepstep Come Shining* (1998), a book-length
poem that grew from a road trip she and Luster made through the Deep South, Wright
began to move to longer lines in less narrative poems. Wright moved on to work with
Luster again in *One Big Self: Prisoners of Louisiana* (2003), an extended poem (or
perhaps a number of long and intricately interrelated poems) and photographs of men
and women incarcerated in Louisiana prisons. This poetic growth reduced narration
in Wright's poems and showed her increased interest in extended poems which, although they may still use fragmented narrative, rely heavily on image, language, and
repetition. *Rising, Falling, Hovering* is the next flowering of this growth.

The volume's long title poem is in two parts. Three poems introduce the volume,
followed by the first thirty-three pages of "Rising, Falling, Hovering." Two poems
then form a bridge to the last twenty pages of the title poem. The volume concludes
with an additional nine poems, some of which are completions, or perhaps alternate
versions, of earlier poems. The titles of the shorter poems are almost all introduced
with the word "like," suggesting that they offer metaphors (simile is too limiting a
term for these suggestive works) for the long work they encapsulate.

Scholars have called Wright's early poetry narrative and have suggested that her
interest in language reduced the narrative element in her work. However, the framework of "Rising, Falling, Hovering" describes a trip to Mexico, a friend's health crisis, and the speaker's son's visit to Mexico, and all of this is infused with the speaker's
anger about America's invasion of Iraq, much of which she observes on Mexican television. In addition, the Mexican setting brings to light her painful awareness of the relationship between the inhabitants of a wealthy United States and the Mexicans who
attempt to immigrate to *al otro lado*, the other side of the border. (Appropriately, the
poem is threaded with Spanish words and phrases.) Wright suggests that the U.S.
presence in Iraq, like its presence in Mexico, is based on the power of American economic interests.

Wright's narrative, however, is never focused on anecdote or elements of plot. Instead, fragments of events appear and disappear, elusive as memory. Events that one might expect to be explained or amplified instead remain half-limned, to draw their power from their evocative incompleteness. It is this technique that allows Wright to merge images from disparate settings. Some of the early parts of the poem, for example, suggest Wright's intense early relationship with poet Frank Stanford:

> He would appear central in her book   then go off
> on his own   meanwhile   no one but themselves
> in the kitchen's recessed lighting   in their underpants
>
> Drinking warm beer   not taking calls

Wright's affair with Stanford and its tragic ending with his suicide have often appeared in her work. In this poem, the presence of that lover seems to morph into the figure of the partner who accompanies the speaker to Mexico. On the flight, perhaps, the speaker sees the newspaper report that warns her "the number of their dead to remain unknown," a motif that threads through the poem as the speaker repeatedly compares the unnumbered Iraqi dead with the statistics of dead Americans. The first segment of the poem ends with the ominous statement that "This is no time for poetry."

Before the pair travel into Mexico City, other scenes appear briefly—an old man in a hut or on a burro, a woman (his wife?) who has a special dress she once wore "on the other side," a petal fallen on the arm of a laborer who holds the statue of a saint. In the hotel the "ghoulish glow from a muted TV" shows pictures of the wreckage of Baghdad and its people, "shelled into the memory hole," obliterating a rich past. That past and Mexico's own rich past seem to create an ironic counterpoint. While the headlines cite the number of bombs "blooming in Baghdad," in the city square, the flower market is blooming into a peace demonstration. A short-line passage follows this, offering images that juxtapose growth and life (a pomegranate tree, the courtyard of independence fighter Miguel Hidalgo) with death and decay (a pariah dog, a casket merchant, a desk clerk watching war news on television).

The poem's next segment introduces a boy, perhaps the speaker's son, and a woman whose bones "soften and thin," perhaps the sick friend. The boy uses "chop-logic" on the speaker who returns a "hail of words" that seem to bounce off his eardrums. In a flash forward, the speaker seems to have returned home to discover there none of the destruction that Iraq experiences: "The glorious photographs of their son were not stolen/ from their secondhand frames" nor have any other disasters occurred. Still, "to be ashamed is to be American," she says. "As of Friday 850 of our members/ will be Forever Young." The headlines haunt her, and the ironic "Forever Young" mocks the government's blithe acceptance of the many deaths on both sides.

As the poem opens up, the focus shifts to "her suddenly-grown-tall son" who has long since left behind the child he once was, the one who wanted his mother to read to him. Now a distance seems to have grown between them. "In the event of our death," the poet says, and here she inserts a long space mid-line, "you will have to roll your own poetry." His mother tells the young man he cannot smoke in the house and that he must turn down his stereo's sound, but she is met only with his blank stare. Throughout these

sketchy scenes, some phrases and images reappear—dogs (most of them black), shoes,
and the injunction "Do not think him healed"
(which may apply to the son or to the countless wounded sons of war). Interspersed in this
are passages that seem to describe the sufferings of the *pollos* (chickens), the name for
those undocumented immigrants who struggle to come to this side of the border. "Juan e
Juana Doe" Wright calls them, and they endure the hellish heat, thirst, hunger, and fear

*C. D. Wright has published twelve
collections of poetry and prose,
including collaborations with
photographer Deborah Luster.
Professor of English at Brown
University, she won a MacArthur grant
in 2004. Wright was the poet laureate
of Rhode Island from 1994 to 1999.*

of the *migras* (the immigration officers who patrol the border). "Like they say in Iraq
Now fear up harsh" ends this section.

In the second portion of the poem, the son has been sent to take classes in Mexico
where he is supposed to stay with the friend who seems to be going through chemotherapy. Instead, he opts to rent a room in a private home where he takes up with another student, "call-him-Al," as Wright identifies him. They make a midnight bus trip
to the beach, the son loses his wallet, and they struggle back to town in time for class.
The speaker recalls that she and her husband once had similar adventures in the same
part of Mexico, but these memories do not diminish the fear she feels for the boy's
safety. "If you cannot or do not wish to perform/ this function you shouldn't be in this
century," the narrator remarks wryly. Although the son is now a sophomore in college
and "Walmex" has conquered Mexico, in five portentous one-word lines Wright
warns "Poetry/ Doesn't/ Protect/ You/ Anymore."

The images of the undocumented workers, of the low pay that produces the low
prices at Walmex, and of the U.S. economic interest in Iraq where, with a reference to
T. S. Eliot's *The Waste Land* (1922), Wright says bodies are decomposing in the garden blend in a damning passage where the military "Operation" becomes the key
word:

> Operation hold the line Operation don't drink
> French wine Operation embed the press and
> let them wear the sexy new gear   Operation burn the boots
> with the sand niggers' feet inside   Operation product endorsement

All these operations culminate in a description of the official U.S. government
definition of torture, including references to white phosphorous ("not a chemical
weapon," Wright notes bitterly, quoting the military definition). These join with imagery connected to the undocumented immigrants and to the pain of chemotherapy.
The poem concludes with Wright's indictment of the "current occupants of 1600
Pennsylvania" whose "monosyllabic surnames" she cannot bear to name, and whose
twin daughters will never be sent to invade countries such as Iraq.

Wright's poetic formats for the many sections of this poem vary from short lines to
long, most of them double spaced. Some segments are single spaced in prose.
Throughout, she uses spaces within the line as a sort of punctuation; they often appear

where one might expect commas or dashes and they sometimes seem to set off a particularly ironic or shocking statement.

The volume's other poems make at most oblique reference to the themes of the title poem. In "Re: Happiness, in Pursuit Thereof," the first poem in the volume, the speaker says: "We are running on Aztec time," a time that enjoins the reader to "be ice. Be nails. Be teeth./ Be lightning." The title images of the next two poems suggest ineffable sensations of disorientation: "Like Having a Light at Your Back You Can't See but You Can Still Feel (1)," suggesting an episode explained in the second poem with this title, and "Like Hearing Your Name Called in a Language You Don't Understand," a poem that makes reference to many specifics from the trip to Mexico.

In one of the last poems in the volume, "Or: Animism," Wright weaves in references to the refinery storage tanks that line the highway near her home. They suggest the oil that may be the motive for the war in Iraq, and, like the dead, they are numberless. "Have you ever reeled under the magnitude of petroleum's ruin," the speaker asks. Surveying the age, she concludes: "There must be a reset button for this machine./ Let's be realistic. We are never coming back."

In Nadia Herman Colburn's biographical essay about Wright for *Ploughshares* (Winter, 2002/2003), she quotes Wright as saying, "I am not easy, but I am worth knowing." The same might be said for her poetry. It is not easy, but it is worth knowing. Her voice and vision linger in the reader's thoughts well after the volume is closed.

Ann D. Garbett

Review Sources

Library Journal 133, no. 6 (April 1, 2008): 87.
The New Yorker 84, no. 11 (April 28, 2008): 79.
Publishers Weekly 255, no. 16 (April 21, 2008): 37.

THE ROAD HOME

Author: Rose Tremain (1943-   )
Publisher: Little, Brown (New York). 411 pp. $24.99
Type of work: Novel
Time: Early in the twenty-first century
Locale: A small, unnamed Eastern European country;
London

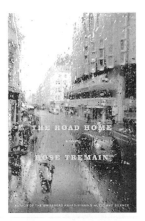

An immigrant tries to adjust to his new surroundings despite his yearning for the home and the family he left behind

Principal characters:
> LEV, a forty-two-year-old widower and an
> immigrant to England from Auror in
> Eastern Europe
> RUDI, his best friend in Auror and the proud owner of a Tchevi
> MAYA, Lev's five-year-old daughter
> INA, Lev's sixty-year-old mother and Maya's caregiver in Auror
> LYDIA, a thirty-nine-year-old translator and another expatriate
> CHRISTY SLANE, an Irish plumber and Lev's landlord
> SOPHIE, a restaurant worker and Lev's lover
> GREGORY (G. K.) ASHE, a thirty-five-year-old restaurant owner and
> Lev's employer
> RUBY CONSTAD, an elderly resident of Ferndale Heights and Lev's
> benefactor

Rose Tremain is known for her sympathetic treatment of ordinary people experiencing isolation, loneliness, and loss. The lutenist in *Music and Silence* (2000) yearns hopelessly for the woman he loves; the courtier in *Restoration* (1989) feels that he cannot survive the loss of his place at court; and the immigrants in *The Colour* (2003) find themselves alone and adrift in their new country. In *The Road Home*, Tremain tells the story of a man who enters a world of strangers in order to provide for those he loves.

The novel begins on a bus from Eastern Europe to London. Lev begins talking to Lydia, a woman from his country who happens to be sitting next to him. Lev's home is in the little village of Auror, he explains, but he had been working at a sawmill in the nearby town of Baryn. When the sawmill closed, he could not find another job. Therefore, he decided to go to London, where he was certain that he could earn enough to support his family, which, since his wife Marina had died recently, now consists only of Ina, his mother, and Maya, his five-year-old daughter. After the bus arrives in London, Lydia and Lev part company, but she has given him her telephone number in case he finds that he needs help. It is not long before Lev realizes that the money he has brought with him will not last long. The one job he finds—delivering leaflets for a friendly Arab—pays so little that he cannot afford to rent a room. Dragging his bag of

～

Among the many awards won by Rose Tremain are the James Tait Black Memorial Prize and the Prix Femina Etranger for Sacred Country *(1992), the Whitbread Prize for* Music and Silence *(1997), and the Orange Broadband Prize for Fiction for* The Road Home.

～

belongings, he sleeps in doorways, hoping that no one will tell him to move on. Cold, filthy, and dizzy from hunger, Lev decides to call Lydia. Though she is staying with friends, she arranges for them to take him in, and from that time on, his life changes for the better.

With Lydia's help, Lev finds a place to live, a room in the apartment of Christy Slane, an Irish plumber. Lev also gets a job as a kitchen porter in an upscale restaurant. His industry so impresses G. K. Ashe, the temperamental chef and owner, that he promotes Lev to vegetable preparation. Lev seizes this opportunity to learn all that he can about cooking and restaurant management. Meanwhile, he embarks on a passionate affair with Sophie, another restaurant worker. Through her, he meets the elderly residents of Ferndale Heights, where Sophie volunteers on Sundays. One of the more difficult residents, Ruby Constad, becomes especially fond of Lev. Unfortunately, as soon as G. K. finds out about Lev's affair with Sophie, he fires Lev, explaining that he does not approve of romantic involvements in the workplace. Lev's next job is as an asparagus picker in Suffolk. It is there that he has an epiphany: He will save his money, return to Baryn, and open up a restaurant. Back in London, he starts working two jobs, cooking both at Ferndale and at a Greek restaurant. A generous gift from Mrs. Constad helps Lev to attain his financial goal, and at the end of the novel, he is back in Baryn as the proprietor of a successful restaurant.

Though almost all these events take place in England, and primarily in London, *The Road Home* gives the impression of having not just one setting but two. In his dreams and in his reveries, Lev re-creates his courtship and his happy life with Marina, and in his nightmares, he watches helplessly as those he loves face some peril from which he cannot save them. In his wanderings around London, he is always looking for something he can buy to send to his daughter Maya, for though it saddens him to hear how much she misses him, he also worries that she will forget him. Even though the money he sends home constitutes his mother's primary means of support, Ina is too negative by nature or perhaps just too defeated by life to appreciate the sacrifices Lev is making or to encourage him in his efforts. Instead, whenever he telephones her, she voices her complaints about whatever gift he has sent her, tells him how miserable Maya is without him, and, evidently incapable of understanding that he went to England in order to support her and his daughter, insists on his coming home.

It is hardly surprising that instead of telephoning his mother, Lev sometimes chooses to call Rudi, his best friend back home. Lev, who has always considered himself a passive person, admires Rudi for his energetic nature. Moreover, unlike Ina, Rudi is an inveterate optimist. Some of the funniest scenes in the novel involve Rudi and the "Tchevi" that he bought, evidently untroubled by the fact that the only vehicle he had ever driven was a heavy hauler at the sawmill. Rudi is confident that he can drive the car home, and indeed he does, though he later admits to Lev that the car is defective because it keeps bumping into things. Whenever he telephones Rudi, Lev is likely to hear the latest development in the Tchevi saga. Rudi fell in love with the Tchevi at first sight, despite such obvious defects as faulty doors and four bald tires. However, he did have in mind a practical use for the vehicle, and with it he actually begins to operate his own taxi service. Unfortunately, the Tchevi develops one serious flaw after another, a broken-down transmission, for example, and finally Rudi has to report to Lev that he is out of business. The demise of his beloved Tchevi, along with the news that Auror is to be flooded when a new dam is built, puts the once-irrepressible Rudi into a state of despair. Ironically, this time it is Lev who rescues Rudi. Back in Baryn, Lev transmits his new confidence to Rudi, with the result that Rudi becomes his old, optimistic self again, as well as an invaluable employee in the new restaurant.

Throughout most of *The Road Home*, the mere mention of Rudi suggests that what follows will be comic in tone. However, other segments of the novel are clearly satirical. Functioning as a naïve foreign observer, Lev finds that the London he had thought of as a promised land is shockingly hostile to immigrants. Instead of bringing him the warm welcome he had anticipated, his foreign accent makes him an object of suspicion. Thus he is stopped and cross-examined by policemen and ordered off the premises when he accidentally ventures into a private park where children are playing. To Lev, the British seem to be a people obsessed with money and status, ready to condemn a stranger for any misstep. When his cell phone rings at a concert of Edward Elgar's music to which Lydia has taken him, the audience reacts so angrily that Lev rushes out and, to Lydia's dismay, does not return. However, while mistreatment by strangers is distressing, what most seems to support Lev's negative impression of the British is his experience with Sophie. At first, she seems truly attached to Lev, but as soon as she has a chance, she deserts him for a celebrity and the glittering, amoral world in which the celebrity lives.

Whenever an author utilizes the device of the fictitious foreign observer, the implication is that the observer's impressions have a considerable degree of validity. Through Lev, Tremain points out some serious defects in her society. In addition, the fact that Lev survives and eventually succeeds is due in large part to the kindness of people who have no connection to him. Admittedly, Lydia is at least from the same country as Lev, though she did not know him until they met on the bus. Early on, she is evidently attracted to Lev, but after he rejects her sexual overtures, she continues to be concerned about his welfare. It is true that when Lev turns to Lydia for the money he needs to finance his restaurant, she turns him down, but by that time her own situation has changed, and her refusal on that one occasion does not diminish her importance in his life. Another chance acquaintance who helps to make Lev feel less alone in London is his Irish landlord, Christy. Christy has his own problems: His wife, who has left him, makes it difficult for him to see their young daughter, whom he adores. Christy's situation makes him uniquely able to sympathize with Lev, who misses Maya so much. Even Ashe, the restaurant owner who fires Lev, plays an important part in Lev's success. Not only does he learn to cook by working for Ashe, but when Lev decides to open his own restaurant, Ashe helps him with the practical details, such as working out lists of the equipment that must be purchased and figuring out how much Lev must save up for his initial investment. Lev's chance contacts with the crotchety residents of Ferndale Heights also turn out to be beneficial. Their enthusiastic response to the meals he plans and cooks helps him develop confidence in his culinary skills as well as in his ability to run a kitchen and even to manage a restaurant. Though he appreciates the residents' praises, Lev does not expect anything more substantial from them than his wages; Mrs. Constad's generous gift to him, which is totally unexpected, is still another proof that despite Lev's first impressions, there are people in England who have open minds and kind hearts.

With its dual settings and its variations in tone, *The Road Home* is a more complex book than it might at first appear to be. However, this reflects the author's intent to explore all the ramifications of the immigrant experience and of the nature of human connections. Tremain's skill in creating believable characters and in developing realistic incidents, along with her intellectual honesty, are again evident in this award-winning novel.

Rosemary M. Canfield Reisman

Review Sources

Booklist 104, no. 21 (July 1, 2008): 37-38.
Kirkus Reviews 76, no. 16 (August 15, 2008): 49.
Library Journal 133, no. 8 (May 1, 2008): 60.
The New York Times Book Review, August 31, 2008, p. 10.
The New Yorker 84, no. 30 (September 29, 2008): 91.
Publishers Weekly 255, no. 16 (April 21, 2008): 30.
The Times Literary Supplement, June 22, 2007, p. 19.

SAVE THE LAST DANCE

Author: Gerald Stern (1925-   )
Publisher: W. W. Norton (New York). 91 pp. $23.95
Type of work: Poetry

Stern's lyrical poems delve into the diffuse worlds of dreams and memory, dwelling especially on feelings of vacancy and loss

Vacancy and loss take central place in the deeply felt, lyrical poems of *Save the Last Dance*. Rarely directly evoked, except in the discursive long poem "The Preacher," which ends the volume, this sense of absence—in Gerald Stern's life and in other lives—takes a variety of forms. The most poignant expressions appear during his meditations upon other, senior poets or in his recollections of his early years. The personal flavor of these lyrics leads the reader to regard the "I" of the poems not as an anonymous speaker, but as Stern himself. In the short poems that make up most of the volume, he infrequently looks on the world immediately outside, for the one within him more pressingly holds his attention. He turns senses inward to rediscover his past—although it seems a past he can only look around and not see directly or hold. In many of the poems, what strikes the reader is that the absences are more powerfully "present" than the people or objects that are, in Stern's elusive lines, supposedly being presented.

A particularly effective poem, "One Poet," speaks of an old poet now in his sixties and expresses Stern's yearning for actions never completed and perhaps never initiated. Stern remembers wanting to tell the "one poet" of reading his book and of treasuring what he found there, "but I couldn't tell him that/ nor did I ever write, since I lost his/ letter." Stern then dwells upon that letter, which he remembers putting into an inside pocket, alongside some pens, and then he imagines how he might have lost it—while looking for something else he has lost: his keys. In dreamlike fashion, his memory then shifts again, and he recalls how the poet, apparently upset at Stern, "barked," ignorant of Stern's strong feelings for the poet's work. In another dreamlike turn, Stern then visualizes a dog that has attacked a park pigeon and has blood on its face.

"One Poet" seems to present a series of individual moments revolving around a real individual in Stern's life, and other poems do make direct, pointed reference to his contemporaries and elders. Nevertheless, the "one poet" remains anonymous—out of discretion, the reader might think. Stern may not have wanted to point out the one who "barked at me not knowing/ how much I loved his work." The poem resists such a reading, however, because of the almost inexplicable first words of the opening lines: "As if one poet then who was in his sixties/ I wanted to tell him that I read his book." The words "As if one poet then" change the reader's understanding of the poem's title. While they might be read as turning the poem back upon the author him-

∼

*Gerald Stern, chancellor of the
Academy of American Poets, is winner
of the National Book, National Jewish
Book, and Wallace Stevens awards and
of the Ruth Lilly Poetry Prize. He has
taught at Columbia University and
Sarah Lawrence, among other
universities and colleges. Until his
retirement in 1995, he taught at the
Iowa Writers' Workshop.*

∼

self, they even more strongly expand the character of the "one poet" to a more generalized being, perhaps a composite of the various respected poets Stern had encountered without making adequate connection. The strong sense of regret—depicted as moments of missed opportunity and embodied in misplaced items of importance—seems greater than a sorrow over a single missed chance. It applies not to one moment but to all such moments, and it applies not just to a lost letter but to the very "keys"—the essential items of a life.

Stern presents other poems about poets or inspired by thoughts and memories of poets—including "Wordsworth" and "Lorca"—that have for their taking-off points literary, not personal, memory. The poem "Rukeyser" is among the most effective in the volume, framing Stern's meditations on absence in terms of a "visit with Muriel in her New York apartment,/ helping her into the kitchen, making her tea." Rukeyser is obviously frail, and their meeting is brief—"we were alone for an hour until her nurse/ came back and scolded her for leaving her bed." The reader senses that Stern's presence in the room is brought about by a sense of devotion—to Rukeyser and to the idea of poetry itself. When he sees her look of "abandonment," however, and then is seized by an image of "when she let/ her poems fall on the floor in Philadelphia," the room becomes someplace he must flee: "but I never finished *my* tea and I escaped/ before the nurse could get to me and I/ turned west, for the record, near Lexington, I think,/ against the sun, for it was March already." In these closing lines Stern brings the reader around to a sense of time passing swiftly, hurrying on to bring the poet not so much the experience of the new as the loss of the old.

All loss in these poems is not entirely on the side of the poet; and all is not debit against achievement or memory. In "Lost Shoe," the title refers not to the loss of the poet's shoe but rather to the finding of one: for the shoe appears like a gift "where there had been/ a feather only a day or two before." "Lost Shoe" is akin to a paean to innocence, to the claiming of the everyday moment in its radiant simplicity.

The poem that gives rise to the book's title, "Save the Last Dance for Me," adroitly combines the senses of recovery and of loss. The poet recalls his "first act of mercy," at age twelve, when the opportunity arises to rescue a Chihuahua that has fallen into a sewer. The act is not heroic, since the poet has descended into that sewer before, but it is a descent into "muck." This reliving of the past is deeply sensory. The Chihuahua has a nearly palpable existence, as do other aspects surrounding the rescue—the lifting of the sewer lid with a hammer, the dog's affection, the offering of the dog's towel for cleaning off the sewer muck—yet the poet finds himself, in retelling the tale, being asked the dog's name, which he does not know, and perhaps never knew. The fullness of memory seems to narrow, and its importance seems to diminish, when this question is raised. At the mention of names, the poet finds himself blurring the picture of his "act of mercy" into the larger picture of his youthful life, and the image of the dog falling into the sewer becomes juxtaposed with "our lives the last/ few years before the war"—a time of limited opportunity when "there were four flavors of ice cream/ and four flavors only." These were the years of the Great Depression. The poet decides on a name for the dog, only to have new questions arise. What was the name of the dog's owner, who had given him the towel to clean himself? Then he must ask himself: "and who was I?/ and what is love doing in/ a sewer, and how is disgrace/ blurred now, or buried?"

Stern is not passively viewing the past. A certain amount of decision comes into this revisiting, and he seems even to acknowledge a certain danger in facing backward, as in the poem "Traveling Backwards." To go backward in time offers him no difficulties, "for here is the brain," Stern says—stating, in essence, with what time machine he accomplishes the feat: "for here is the brain and with it I have relived/ one thing after another but I am wavering/ at *only* reliving though what is hard is being there—." Stern admits hesitation, perhaps even trepidation—"but I am wavering." Some risk attends the act of leaving behind the current moment: for to relive the past is one matter, while to live in the past is another. There is, Stern says, a "rose explaining it"—with the rose being equated with the question of Being versus Not-Being, a bringing together of idea and image that conjures Hamlet's famous indecision at the point of responsibility. The act of looking back seems to nudge the poet, or the reader, back to some "coruscating" time before any such moment of crisis. Reality intrudes, all the same, with the poem's final words: "then came everything." With that conclusion, the normal, forward-flowing course of time seems restored.

The book ends with a longer work, "The Preacher," preceded by a short prose introduction and followed by footnotes. "The Preacher" contains a loose set of reflections, similar to the ones that fill the first two-thirds of the book, and mixed into those reflections are elements of a dialogue taking place between Stern and fellow poet Peter Richards. The speakers dwell upon the theme of absence by speaking of "holes" of all kinds—and also upon the King James Bible's figure of "the Preacher," the speaker in the book of Ecclesiastes. While interesting in its conversational wanderings and insights, "The Preacher" captures little of the lucid brightness of Stern's other works. The heart of the book is contained in those short, lyrical meditations on absence and memory.

Short though most are, the poems of *Save the Last Dance* are not for the impatient. Stern composes his works with the least suggestion of story and with as much floating imagery, reference, and statement as the lines will contain. These disparate thoughts and images are further diffused by being run together into single, long sentences—typically as long as the poem itself. This sometimes gives the poems a breathless quality, as if they were rapid, impulsive statements arising in an utterly natural manner.

Stern's mode of expression is distinctive and appealing, in that it leaves the reader with a feeling of freshness. At the same time, it can become disconcerting and can occasionally even seem artificial, as in parts of "The Preacher." That diffusion of reference and allusion accounts for the poems' lightness and for their dreamlike quality, which Stern draws up to the foreground in poems that seem to be dreams, or hauntings. In "Asphodel," the poet communes with a Korean veteran: "He was dead so he was only a puff/ of smoke at the most . . . " That Stern brings dreams into the foreground makes it seem he, too, may wonder if all this backward-gazing might be much the same as dreaming. In "Rapture Lost" he focuses upon that which cannot be focused upon: "The very thing I was trying not to see was/ so close to my nose that I couldn't see anything/ else . . . " Diffusion itself becomes what he must hold to: "and the smoke crawled to the middle in such a way/ that I had to depend on smoke alone, and fog,/ and clouds and steam and such to light the way."

Stern's indistinct or unmoored sentences and his piquant but elusive expressions on occasion leave the reader at sea. At such times, the sense of vacancy can overcome the lyricism, so that the words seem to be circling around a physical absence, not a poetic one. At such moments the words seem to point more away from meaning than toward it. However, in many, if not most, of his poems, Stern's technique proves itself—as it does to notable effect in "One Poet," "Traveling Backwards," or "Rukeyser." The diverse elements of the poems, however vague and unrelated they may seem at first, assemble themselves in the reader's mind into finished pictures or completed comprehension. In these coalescing moments of understanding, the power of Stern's method and vision shines through with striking clarity.

Mark Rich

Review Sources

Booklist 104, no. 18 (May 15, 2008): 16-17.
Library Journal 133, no. 6 (April 1, 2008): 86-87.
Pittsburgh Post-Gazette, May 11, 2008, p. E7.
Publishers Weekly 255, no. 20 (May 19, 2008): 36.

SAY YOU'RE ONE OF THEM

Author: Uwem Akpan (1970 or 1971-   )
Publisher: Little, Brown (New York). 356 pp. $23.99
Type of work: Short fiction
Time: The 1990's to the early 2000's
Locale: Kenya, Benin, Ethiopia, Nigeria, and Rwanda

Akpan's stunning collection reflects the unspeakable events that have taken place in some modern African nations, as perceived through the eyes of children

Uwem Akpan, a Nigerian who was educated in Africa and in the United States, is a surprisingly powerful writer. *Say You're One of Them* is his first book, in which each of five stories is set in a different African nation. In all cases, a child is either the narrator or the point of view. Akpan, who writes in English, has traveled and lived in several African countries and has done meticulous research on local settings and dialects. His characters speak French, English, and various local languages, and his stories contain only physical details that he has personally observed. When he mentions red earth in his work, it is there.

Akpan's first published story, "An Ex-Mas Feast," initially appeared in the 2005 Debut Fiction issue of *The New Yorker*, offering a glimpse of a family's grim subsistence on the streets of Nairobi, Kenya. The parents, Baba and Mama, their six children, and pregnant dog live in a makeshift shanty of tarpaulin and plastic sheeting at the end of an alley. Although Akpan employs understated humor, his style is mostly naturalistic—from the reek of insecticide fumes inside the shanty, ineffective against the mosquitoes, to the way family members take turns sleeping in the midst of huddled bodies to avoid the cold. Gangs of children also sleep on these streets, where "garbage had spread all over the road: dried fish, stationery, trinkets, wilted green vegetables" and no one can be trusted.

Baba is a pickpocket, Mama drinks, and they all sniff glue to ease their hunger (except the two-month-old baby, asleep in a cardboard box). The oldest daughter, angry twelve-year-old Maisha with her bleached hair and skin, longs to go to school but cannot because, as a prostitute who mostly serves white tourists, she is the true support of the family. Whatever she earns goes toward her younger brother Jigana's school fees and uniform so that he, being a boy, can continue his classes. The underweight and nameless baby is used as a prop to extract sympathy from passers-by whenever Mama or the children go begging.

Every Ex-Mas, Mama follows the tradition of reading the family names inscribed in their battered Bible—a catalog of misfortunes, inasmuch as all are missing or dead. Desperate as they are, the parents still fret over what Christmas gift to give their neighbors—should it be petrol or glue? On this Ex-Mas morning, a disheveled Maisha arrives in a taxi with a feast that she has labored all night to obtain for the fam-

~

*An ordained Jesuit priest, Uwem Akpan
earned an M.F.A. in creative writing
from the University of Michigan in
2006. His story "My Parents'
Bedroom" was a finalist for the Caine
Prize for African Writing in 2007.*

~

ily. Immediately afterward, she moves out to "try full-time" in a brothel, where her income will be less problematic. Naema, ten years old and very pretty, intends to go on the street in her sister's place, even though Maisha disapproves.

A much longer story follows, bearing the cryptic title "Fattening for Gabon" and touching upon several social problems. The ten-year-old narrator Kotchikpa and his obstinate younger sister Yewa, both spirited and smart, speak a patois of English, French, and native Idaatcha. They live with their Fofo (Uncle) Kpee in a poor border village on the coast of Benin, because their parents, dying of AIDS in another village, can no longer care for them. Fofo Kpee survives by smuggling people across the Nigerian border, a delicate task made much easier by the new motorcycle that he has just purchased with money given him by a man known as Big Guy. Even though Big Guy sometimes wears the uniform of an immigration officer, the children are uncertain who he is. In reality, he is only a go-between, being paid by the same secret benefactors whom Fofo identifies as the children's "godparents." These so-called benefactors are human traffickers in prostitution or slavery, to whom Fofo has sold his charges. The adults fully understand this, but the two children do not.

Soon the godparents Papa and Mama, an older man and a beautiful woman, visit Fofo's house, bearing a wonderful array of food. Both children are mesmerized by Mama, who tenderly cuddles the sulking Yewa. Mama renames the children Mary and Pascal, urging them to speak only French. Two other scrawny children are then brought into Fofo's house for a great feast, all to be fattened for their journey to French-speaking Gabon, where they are told they will live with their godparents. The two are soon taken away, but when other children join the group, they will sail together to their fine new home in Gabon.

Fofo teaches his niece and nephew the programmed answers they must have ready for their new life. They must also learn to drink seawater for survival, in case they are put into the sea if their ship is searched. He begins to suffer terrible nightmares, stemming from his decision to betray them into a situation he understands far better than they. When he offers an awkward attempt at sexual instruction, another effort to prepare them, the uneasy youngsters can only suspect he has drunk too much gin. Finally, yielding to conscience, Fofo decides to cancel the arrangement, but several policemen threaten him and he seems to lose heart. Kotchikpa slowly realizes that his uncle's promises are not what they seem.

A brief story, written in second person, provides some relief from all this intensity. "What Language Is That?" is an account of two small Ethiopian girls—one Christian, one Muslim—who live on the same street and are best friends in spite of festering religious and political discord in their little town. While their families are friendly, even attending events together, the sudden riots, burning buildings, and vandalism in the streets force the parents to terminate their daughters' friendship for their safety.

This story is told in short, simple sentences, like the language of a young child. The artistic risk here is that the girls' limited perception downplays the gravity of the situation. All that one sheltered youngster can understand is that her family servants have disappeared and that she will not be allowed to see her friend again, so that a reader may be tempted to dismiss this simply as the story of a broken friendship, a temporary sadness in any child's life. However, the careful reader can see beyond this to the deeper turmoil of a nation.

"Luxurious Hearses," another lengthy story, takes place in the turbulent period after Nigeria's military government has converted to civilian rule. This story is the most ambitious but at the same time least successful, perhaps because the author tries to cover so much ground. At this time, Sharia—Muslim law—is being imposed in northern Nigeria. Sixteen-year-old Jubril, a conservative Muslim, has barely escaped death in religious riots after his childhood friends suddenly turned against him, beat him, and tried to burn him alive. Terrified, he flees the sectarian violence to seek refuge with his father's Christian family in the south. As an infant, he was baptized a Catholic there before his Muslim mother escaped with him to the north. Now he has adopted that Christian identity for his own safety. However, because his right hand has been amputated (a Muslim punishment for theft), he hides his stump in his pocket to avoid recognition and death from the Christians and attempts to mask his northern accent.

At a motor park, Jubril finds a seat on the last of the great southbound buses, called "Luxurious" because one can travel all night on them. While the driver goes to buy black-market petrol, the police insist on bribes and lock Jubril on the bus with many Christian refugees. This Luxurious Bus contains a microcosm of passengers with different, often comic, accents, each representing a particular group, crammed together rather like an African version of the John Ford film *Stagecoach* (1939). Among these is the elderly Chief Ukongo, a "royal father," a proud old man who insists on sitting in Jubril's seat even though he has no ticket; two quarreling young women; a dying man; a contentious passenger; a nursing mother (the source of great discomfort to the Muslim boy); a maddened soldier; and various religious fanatics. The Chief, who favors traditional beliefs, serves also as a vehicle to explain the complex history of the region.

Since the bus is equipped with working television sets, the unruly passengers are temporarily unified by viewing pirated footage from other countries that shows film of the rioting unavailable on the official government station. Jubril watches his own city of Khamfi, two hours from the motor park, become "the corpse capital of the world." The contentious man apparently has a religious fit and is thrown off the bus.

Then Luxurious Buses filled with dead Muslims arrive from the south. Their bodies, originally sent home for burial, have been refused and are being returned to the north. The foreign television monitors the continuing riots in the poverty-stricken south, where the deposed generals permit them. Next comes an announcement that corpses can no longer be ferried from place to place but must remain wherever they died. Jubril realizes that his fellow northerners are trying to escape from the south, where persecution exists as well.

The title of the book comes from the warning given to Monique, a nine-year-old Rwandan girl, in the most brutal but perhaps finest story, "My Parents' Bedroom," during the blood-smeared genocide of 1994 in which an estimated eight hundred thousand people died. As the daughter of a dark-skinned Hutu father and a light-skinned Tutsi mother, Monique is instructed that, no matter who asks for her identity, she must "say you're one of them" to avoid problems. Her parents, both of whom cherish her and her little brother Jean, speak to each other in code so that the children will not fully understand the danger they all face—possible death at the hands of either ethnic group, even from members of their extended family.

Previously, Monique's father had gone with his brother, Tonton André, who also married a Tutsi. Her mother apparently leaves, too, but André returns, tricking the girl into opening the door and allowing in a crowd of Hutus to search the house. When a drunken man attacks Monique, her Hutu great-uncle, the powerful Wizard, rescues her. Next morning, although Monique does not understand what has happened, her little Twa friend crawls to the door, seriously wounded. There is blood on the walls, and someone is hiding in the attic. Monique and her little brother flee.

Critical praise for these stories has been almost unanimous. Four of them deal with the bitter political ramifications of intermarriage and conflict between religious and ethnic groups, and all are affected by poverty. By using children as his protagonists, Akpan is able to reveal events through their innocent eyes even as they struggle to comprehend their world—breathtaking in its madness, heartbreaking in its cruelty, with its darkness lightened by a stubborn glint of humor. Even though these children face a precarious future, what keeps their stories from utter despair is the full humanity of the characters. In a stroke of brilliance, the book jacket displays the photograph of a barefoot African girl running down a dirt road, away from the viewer. By the end of the book, the reader understands why she is running.

Joanne McCarthy

Review Sources

America 199, no. 4 (August 18, 2008): 24-25.
Booklist 104, no. 21 (July 1, 2008): 37.
Chicago Tribune, May 31, 2008, p. 4.
The Christian Century 125, no. 21 (October 21, 2008): 34-37.
Entertainment Weekly, June 13, 2008, p. 72.
Essence 39, no. 2 (June, 2008): 82.
Kirkus Reviews 76, no. 8 (April 15, 2008): 379-380.
The New York Times, June 27, 2008, p. 27.
The New York Times Book Review, July 27, 2008, p. 16.
People 69, no. 23 (June 16, 2008): 47.
Publishers Weekly 255, no. 15 (April 14, 2008): 36-37.
School Library Journal 54, no. 10 (October, 2008): 177.
Time 171, no. 25 (June 23, 2008): 127.
The Washington Post, June 29, 2008, p. T3.

SEA OF POPPIES

Author: Amitav Ghosh (1956-   )
Publisher: Farrar, Straus and Giroux (New York). 528
pp. $26.00
Type of work: Novel
Time: 1838-1839
Locale: Ghazipur and Calcutta, India

*The lives of Deeti, Zachary Reid, Paulette Lambert, and
Raja Neel Rattan Halder become intertwined as their various
paths lead them to the ship* Ibis *bound for Mauritius
with a cargo of indentured laborers*

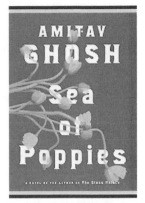

Principal characters:
> DEETI, also known as KABUTRI-KI-MA and
> later as ADITI, wife of Hukam Singh,
> later common-law wife of Kalua
> ZACHARY REID, mulatto freedman from Baltimore, originally ship's
> carpenter on the *Ibis*, but now second mate
> RAJA NEEL RATTAN HALDER, zemindar of Rashkali, whose estates are
> bankrupt
> PAULETTE LAMBERT, also known as PUTTLI and PUGGLI, daughter of an
> unworldly botanist, Pierre Lambert; her mother died in childbirth, and
> she was raised by an Indian woman, mother of Jodu, who became
> Pierre Lambert's mistress
> KALUA, later known as MADHU and MADDOW COLVER, ox-cart driver,
> former prizefighter, and common-law husband of Deeti
> BENJAMIN BURNHAM, owner of an import-export company dealing in
> the shipping of goods, including opium, and legal guardian of Paulette
> Lambert

In Amitav Ghosh's novel *Sea of Poppies*, Deeti lives in a village four hundred miles from the Indian coast. She has never seen the sea or a ship, and she has never left her home district. One day she has a vision of a sailing ship and she knows that it is a sign, although she is not yet certain what it portends. Deeti's life is neither happy nor unhappy; it is a ceaseless round of back-breaking work. She does not love her husband, Hukam, who was injured in battle and now, disabled, works in an opium-processing factory. He has become an opium addict. Their daughter, Kabutri, was in fact fathered by his brother, Chandan, after Deeti was drugged and raped with the family's connivance. Deeti has unexamined feelings for Kalua, a member of the leather workers' caste, whom she rescued, without his apparent knowledge, from a beating. However, when Deeti's husband dies, and she determines to commit sati (throw herself on Hukam's funeral pyre) rather than marry Chandan, it is Kalua who rescues her from the fire and then leaves the village with Deeti, determined to find sanctuary elsewhere. Eventually, they find their way to Calcutta and, aware that Deeti's in-laws are still

Amitav Ghosh was born in Calcutta and grew up in Bangladesh, Sri Lanka, and India. He has studied at the universities of Delhi and Oxford. His first novel, The Circle of Reason, *was published in 1986, and since then he has published five more novels. The* Calcutta Chromosome *(1996) won the Arthur C. Clarke Award, while* Sea of Poppies *was short-listed for the Man Booker Prize.*

searching for her, determine to leave for Mauritius to become indentured laborers.

The ship in Deeti's vision is later identified as the *Ibis*, a former slave ship, in poor condition, that has been sold to Benjamin Burnham and is now being taken to Calcutta for refitting. Zachary Reid, a mulatto freedman from Baltimore, has signed on as ship's carpenter because he cannot find employment in his home town. The voyage to India is little short of disastrous, thanks to the ship's condition. Illness breaks out, and Reid finds himself inadvertently rising to become, at one point, the ship's de facto captain. He is helped by a group of lascar sailors, led by the mysterious Serang Ali, who effectively run the ship and who clearly have plans for the newly minted Zakri Malun. They make over Reid's wardrobe so that he can play the part of a gentleman, and he learns their language and their various ways, coming to appreciate their food as well. What Serang Ali's plans are for Reid remain unclear throughout the novel.

Having brought the ship safely to Calcutta, Reid finds himself among a colorful collection of "old India hands," who represent themselves as understanding the ways of the Indians and the lascars but whose apprehension of local ways is quite different from Reid's. In turn, they look askance at him because he seems able to engage with all segments of the population on apparently equal terms. As a result, they view him with the deepest suspicion. Eventually, the new first mate of the *Ibis*, Mr. Crowle, discovers that when Reid first joined the *Ibis* he had been described on the manifest as "black" and so seeks to blackmail him.

As a presentable member of the crew, and because of his gentlemanly ways, Reid is invited to dine with the Burnhams, and it is here that he encounters Paulette Lambert, whom he previously met when he rescued her foster brother, Jodu, and gave him a place on the ship. Reid and Paulette inhabit a similar place in society, neither native nor gentry. While Reid has been assimilated into the culture of the lascars, Paulette has been brought up by an Indian woman and prefers Indian habits. Her father was a freethinker, and she did not receive a religious education. When she is adopted by the Burnhams, their concern is to rectify this perceived lack rather than to properly understand their new ward. They remain unaware of Paulette's abilities as a scholar, a linguist, and a naturalist, not least because she has the wit to realize that she is best advised to keep quiet. However, Paulette is bored by the enforced lack of occupation that is expected of a white woman. Marriage is the only option, but while Paulette realizes she is attracted to Zachary, she finds to her horror that Judge Kendalbushe, an elderly Englishman, wishes to marry her. Between this and the unwanted attentions of Benjamin Burnham himself, Paulette determines to escape, hidden, on the *Ibis* when it sails. However, her appeals to Zachary for help fall on deaf ears.

Raja Neel Rattan Halder has, by contrast, led a life of almost complete indolence, governed by intricate custom and practice, which is vitally necessary that he maintain in order to preserve his position as zemindar of Rashkali, for his own sake as well as for the sake of the people who look to him for guidance. However, he is well aware that his world will disintegrate because he is in financial difficulties. When he is wrongly found guilt of forgery, Neel finds himself imprisoned and sentenced to be transported to Mauritius on the *Ibis*. Neel shares his imprisonment with an opium addict, Ah Fatt, and almost his first task, having accepted that his life has changed irrevocably, is to nurse Ah Fatt through an enforced withdrawal from the drug. Through this, the two men form an uneasy bond as they await transportation.

Though this disparate group of protagonists provides a microcosm of India in the early nineteenth century, Ghosh presents the reader with an intricate portrait of a multilayered society circumscribed at all levels by convention. It is also a society heavily dependent on one industry for its income; everyone, to a greater or lesser extent, is affected by the opium trade. No one is immune to its effects, economic or otherwise. As the narrative shows, however, this carefully constructed society rests on a fragile foundation. If the opium industry collapses, what will happen to these people?

As the group sails to Mauritius on the *Ibis*, various of its members are beset by danger, most particularly by the fear that they will be revealed to be something other than they have pretended to be. Despite their different backgrounds, the passengers and prisoners gradually form a community, mirroring that of the lascar seamen, and the ship gradually comes to stand for a new India, in which the poor and helpless fight for their rights when they are badly treated by the mostly white officers. Eventually, during a long night of brutality and revelation, the senior officers lose control of the ship, and some are killed. The community is broken asunder, with Serang Ali, Jodu, Neel, Ah Fatt, and Kalua fleeing the ship in a small boat and leaving behind Paulette and Deeti.

At this point, the novel draws to a close, but it is intended to be the first part of a trilogy of novels, the *Ibis* trilogy, in which Ghosh will explore the colonial history of India, principally through the portrayal of the opium industry but also through the transportation of indentured labor to Mauritius and to other British colonies. His approach is necessarily panoramic, with one character representing an entire social group, and yet he manages to portray society as a whole on a personal level. The reader identifies with and cares for the characters, knowing that whatever they have suffered so far is nothing compared to what they are going to experience as they take to the open sea and begin their long voyage into what is, effectively, a new society. Already there are hints that they are, however unintentionally, part of a grander story in which some of them will found dynasties and be remembered. In this novel, Ghosh also explores the ways in which people are perceived in the world, through language and appearance. People are easily persuaded that Zachary is a gentleman by the clothes he wears, although he is acutely aware that he might at any point be found to be not only a mere ship's carpenter but also a mulatto. By the same token, Reid understands far more of the languages used by the lascars than the English officers who command the ship and who attempt to teach him how to speak properly to the seamen. In fact, the English colony prides itself on its ability to communicate with the Indian people, and yet Ghosh deftly shows the ways in which the Englishmen mangle the languages they try to speak because they do not learn them properly. The tragedy of the society that Ghosh portrays is that its disparate parts cannot communicate with one another. The community creating itself on the *Ibis* points the way forward, and it offers hope, although a fragile one.

Maureen Kincaid Speller

Review Sources

Booklist 105, no. 4 (October 15, 2008): 23.
The Economist 387 (May 24, 2008): 108.
Far Eastern Economic Review 171, no. 7 (September, 2008): 71-72.
Kirkus Reviews 76, no. 17 (September 1, 2008): 907.
Library Journal 133, no. 16 (October 1, 2008): 56.
New Statesman 137 (May 5, 2008): 58-59.
The New York Times, November 6, 2008, p. 1.
The New York Times Book Review, November 30, 2008, p. 8.
The New Yorker 84, no. 34 (October 27, 2008): 87.
Publishers Weekly 255, no. 33 (August 18, 2008): 38.
The Times Literary Supplement, June 6, 2008, p. 19.
The Wall Street Journal 252, no. 93 (October 18, 2008): W8.

THE SELECTED ESSAYS OF GORE VIDAL

Author: Gore Vidal (1925-   )
Edited by Jay Parini
Publisher: Doubleday (New York). 458 pp. $27.50
Type of work: Essays
Time: 1953-2004

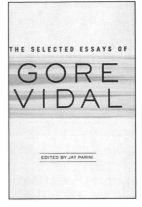

A choice collection of works from the United States' most prolific and provocative writers

Gore Vidal is that rarest of men, one who consistently resists labels in an age of increasing categorization. With the publication of his first novel, *Williwaw* (1946), he immediately established himself as a serious writer by dealing with the then-taboo subject of homosexuality. Had he chosen to do so, he could have continued to produce more groundbreaking novels in the same manner: small works for a select audience that would have eventually found their way into the college classroom. Instead, Vidal went on to excel in every major literary form save poetry. In the 1950's, he had no compunction about writing for the new medium of television, and he even crafted part of the screenplay for one of the most popular films of the period, *Ben-Hur* (1959). On a parallel track to his literary career, Vidal gained a considerable reputation as a political commentator and as a frequent guest on the television talk show circuit in the 1960's and 1970's.

It is as an essayist, however, that Vidal has made his presence felt in the literary world. The essay—at once the most personal and digressive of the traditional forms in the genre of nonfiction—has found in Vidal an impressive and enduring master. It is for this reason that *The Selected Essays of Gore Vidal* is such a welcome addition to any bookshelf. While it is true that an earlier and far more comprehensive volume, *United States: Essays, 1952-1992*, was published in 1993, it was an omnibus collection of 114 pieces. Vidal's reputation is probably better served in this new volume, edited by Jay Parini, which contains essays representing the best of the recurring themes in his work. In addition to Parini's helpful introduction, the book is divided into two sections, consisting of thirteen and eleven essays respectively. In "Part One: Reading the Writers," Parini presents a group of essays dealing with a variety of literary matters spanning the period from the 1950's to the 1990's. Two significant themes emerge in this section: one concerns Vidal's astute analyses of his fellow fiction writers; the other deals with his critiques of other critics. Among the latter, "Novelists and Critics of the 1940's" introduces what has proven to be a common Vidal theme: his lifelong contempt for academic critics. "They tend . . . to be absolutists. They believe that by a close examination of 'the text,' the laws and the crafty 'strategies' of its composition will be made clear and the findings will provide 'touchstones' for a comparative criticism of other works." He then proceeds to point out that this is more effective with metaphysical poetry than with the more open-ended format of the novel.

In addition to many short stories and screenplays, Gore Vidal has published two memoirs, five plays, twenty-four novels, and more than two hundred essays. He won the National Book award in 1993 for United States: Essays, 1952-1992.

For those unfamiliar with the history of Western academic criticism, Vidal's comments require some explanation. What he is describing is what came to be known as New Criticism, a formalist approach to literature that attempted to divorce a work from its historical and cultural context in order to examine it as an isolated artifact. The best-known exponent of this type of critical approach was Cleanth Brooks, whose book *The Well Wrought Urn* (1947) was very influential in the academy. Brooks provided a powerful new tool with which to examine verse; indeed, the book's title derives from John Donne's poem "The Canonization." Vidal's comments on the subject highlight both the strengths and the weaknesses of his writing. On the positive side, Vidal early on recognizes some of the inherent shortcomings in a critical technique that was fast taking root in American universities, and he delivers his verdict with a wit that is as acerbic as it is incisive. As an iconoclast (literally, a destroyer of sacred images), he relishes the opportunity to deflate what he perceives to be the pervasive self-importance of the academy. To be fair, it must be pointed out that, even in its heyday in the 1950's, New Criticism was rarely practiced in its purest form. Good critics then and now employ theory as a tool to be used with caution and not as an intellectual fetish. It should also be noted that New Criticism arose in reaction to the critical strategies of the preceding generation, which centered upon historical and biographical approaches. The severity of Vidal's tone is probably linked to the fact that even then he recognized the gradual demise of such freelance critics as Edmund Wilson, who wrote voluminously about literature from a perspective outside the academy. Nevertheless, Vidal seizes upon what has long been recognized as the primary weakness of academic criticism. While a roving critic such as Vidal espouses what he feels are valuable insights about literature, the academic critic is compelled to do so in order to further his or her own career. It is this "publish or perish" nature of English department criticism that earns Vidal's often scathing remarks.

That his comments are as prescient as they are insightful is witnessed in his later essay, "The Hacks of Academe." When he reviews a volume of essays by lauded academics, it is evident that the nascent and rather modest theories of the New Critics have been further developed by notably less gifted successors. Vidal obviously enjoys picking apart jargon and poorly written articles that often yield little in the way of genuine textual insights. He dispenses with the editor of the book, John Halperin, and proceeds to dispose of the essays themselves.

As entertaining as Vidal's comments often are, the fact remains that he reveals a fundamental weakness in the generation of knowledge in American universities. By adopting questionable theories in an institution that mandates critical production, Vidal claims, academe does a lasting disservice to literature, creating a closed loop in which academics and their students are imprisoned by a self-regulating rhetoric that is ultimately unproductive.

Vidal's comments, however, concern only the generation and practice of literary theory, which represents only a part of the academy and which is mostly confined to the nation's larger Ph.D.-granting institutions. One could argue just as forcibly that in recent decades academic study has successfully enlarged the canon, the body of works that are studied and valued, from a narrow group of male writers to include many works that were neglected in the past. Feminist studies generated by the academy have rescued the once-popular novels of nineteenth century writer Catharine Maria Sedgwick and the groundbreaking early realism of Rebecca Harding Davis. Vidal seems to forget that it was the persistence of a doctoral candidate rummaging through a trunk of old papers that led to the discovery of Herman Melville's last great masterpiece, *Billy Budd* (1924), and the recognition of *Moby Dick* (1851) as one of the greatest works of the American Renaissance. Vidal can be forgiven for being so tough on his fellow critics if only because he himself is so gifted in this field. Surely no one concerned with the serious study of literature would challenge his assertion that a critic's role is to "comment intelligently from his vantage point in time on the way a work appears to him in a contemporary, a comparative, or a historic light."

Vidal's own record as a critic is impressive. As early as 1953, he recognized the genius of writers who later came to be viewed as modern masters: the plays of Tennessee Williams, the stories of Paul Bowles, and the novels of Carson McCullers. That Vidal makes no distinction between high and low art is evidenced by the catholicity of his interests. In the "The Top Ten Best-Sellers According to the Sunday *New York Times* as of January 7, 1973," he gleefully disparages the pervasive influence of the Hollywood dream factory upon popular literature. His analysis of Herman Wouk's novel *The Winds of War* (1971)—one of the most popular books of the 1970's—is an instructive, funny examination of the pitfalls of appropriating the hackneyed themes of film romance by a writer who has little understanding of the milieu he describes at tedious length. The reason Vidal's criticism is so effective, aside from his dazzling intellect, is the impressive range of his literary knowledge. Thus, while many praised the publication of Nobel laureate Aleksandr Solzhenitsyn's *Avgust chetyrnadtsatogo* (1971; *August 1914*, 1972), Vidal is careful to distinguish the honorable life of this Soviet dissident from what he regards as writing that borrows too heavily from Leo Tolstoy. Even if one disagrees with some aspects of his critiques, one has to admit that in his position as an independent critic Vidal is free to make observations that are next to impossible for academics. While writing of the French influence upon American writers of the postwar period, he dismisses James Joyce's *Ulysses* (1922) for what he regards as an unsuccessful use of Greek mythology to structure this lengthy narrative. Given the fact that some academics have devoted entire careers to the study of this novel, such comments within the academy would no doubt constitute professional suicide.

The essays in the second section of the collection, "Reading the World," exhibit the same contrary personality dealing with social and political ideas. Vidal is nothing if not forthright. As an unapologetic, lifelong liberal with a deep attachment to the nation's capital, Vidal was a prominent observer of and participant in the social upheavals of the postwar period. Not surprisingly, he openly questions the establishment's opposition to one of human society's oldest vices, pornography. He engagingly argues that in an overpopulated world, sex can no longer be regarded solely as a means of procreation. If sex is no longer exclusively reserved for this function, then society should be free to accept homosexuality and bisexuality, the latter being a characteristic he attributes to all human beings. Some will no doubt question Vidal's view of pornography as a harmless human activity, but most will applaud his demand for tolerance in sexual preferences.

It is this very call for acceptance, however, that runs counter to evangelism, a topic he explores in "Monotheism and Its Discontents." Whatever one's opinion of Vidal's social views, one cannot help admiring both his courage and the skill with which his impressive intellect tackles such a controversial subject. Rather than simply question the rising power of American evangelism, he challenges the very basis of the world's three monotheistic religions—Judaism, Christianity, and Islam. Asserting that these desert-born religions all worship an intolerant "sky-god," he deems the paternalistic deity of these religions to be an authoritarian who frowns upon liberal ideas. He also contends that American evangelism is a kind of perversion of the Founding Fathers, who he claims "were not enthusiasts of the sky-god. Many, like Jefferson, rejected him altogether and placed man at the center of the world." In reality, the Founders expressed a variety of religious views; most of them felt that religion was necessary on some level for a moral and just society, and Jefferson even crafted his own Bible from selected excerpts from the standard text. Nonetheless, this does not in any way mitigate the substance of Vidal's argument, which is that the rising tide of American evangelism in the 1990's challenged the notions of tolerance upon which the nation was founded. Although many question his provocative ideas, no one doubts Vidal's considerable rhetorical skills. *The Selected Essays of Gore Vidal* will find a ready audience for all who value good writing.

Cliff Prewencki

Review Sources

Library Journal 133, no. 8 (May 1, 2008): 67.
The Nation 287, no. 13 (October 27, 2008): 58-62.
Publishers Weekly 255, no. 14 (April 7, 2008): 50.

SELECTED POEMS

Author: Frank O'Hara (1926-1966)
Edited by Mark Ford
Publisher: Alfred A. Knopf (New York). 265 pp. $30.00
Type of work: Poetry

O'Hara wrote electric poetry expressing the spirit of the mid-twentieth century New York art world, and this new selection of his work showcases his unique gift

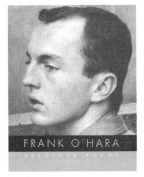

Frank O'Hara was one of the experimental poets of the mid-twentieth century, associated with John Ashbery, Kenneth Koch, and other innovative artists that lived and worked in New York City during the 1950's and 1960's. O'Hara's work is flamboyantly original, capturing the details of the cityscape and the lifeblood that ran beneath it. His energetic and vibrant poems are filled with names and places and events of the time, and even while celebrating life, they hold an elegiac undertone.

This new selection presents the essential O'Hara. The poet's life was tragically short—he was killed at forty in a freak accident. This collection begins with a poem written in 1949 or 1950 (the editor does not know which year) and ends with a poem written in 1966—ironically, an elegy for another poet, Antonio Machado. Thus O'Hara's writing, or at least his publishing, life spanned about sixteen years—long when compared with John Keats's but short if compared with most writers. O'Hara wrote prolifically—editor Mark Ford said of Donald Allen's edition of O'Hara's *Collected Poems* (1971), "I weighed it on my kitchen scales and found it came in at just over three and a half pounds." It seems appropriate to weigh this poetry on a scale, like produce. There is not a lot of change in the poetry—O'Hara's distinctive voice speaks consistently in the same tones, at least most of the time, although the effect is never dulled. The subject matter and style vary, providing different takes on the same life and place.

The selection includes useful material beyond the poems. The verse play *Try, Try* is here, and so are a few prose pieces, including the famous manifesto on Personism, the school of poetics O'Hara founded on a whim, as well as other poetics statements and brief memoirs. Interesting in themselves, the editor's introduction and the concluding chronology help present a poet who has less currency among today's poetry readers, and they consider some of the popular O'Hara myths.

These poems emanate a fiery energy, exploding on the page with a force and a visceral presence, as though the poet were in a small room with you, dancing around with excitement and explaining something crucially important in his life. They flow from line to line without stopping for breath; when they do stop, they are often punctuated with exclamation marks or commas or nothing at all. Nevertheless, the line endings seem appropriate, providing an invisible check to the current of language, reminding the reader that these are poems, that they have a form to guide their flow.

Frank O'Hara helped found the Poet's Theatre and through this work met a variety of postmodern poets. He received an M.A. from the University of Michigan and then moved to New York, where he worked for the Museum of Modern Art. In 1966, he was run over and killed on Fire Island while waiting for the replacement of a disabled beach taxi.

Their topicality ensures these poems are fresh rather than dated. The density of proper nouns in O'Hara's poems is high—many well-known people are addressed directly, or evoked otherwise, always involved in some action that is characteristic. The reader is pulled through a series of rambling speculations that rejoice in the flux and flash of the artistic life, although sometimes glimpsed through the effervescence of the poems is a sadness. This effect is heightened for today's reader because of the names of stars and artists long since faded. Suggestions of transience were always a part of the poems, through their references to news headlines, flowers, and fruit and through their direct descriptions of the persistent awareness of time's passage.

O'Hara's most anthologized poem may be "Poem [Lana Turner Has Collapsed]," in which the intensity of physical, personal presence communicates itself through the imagined connection between the speaker's world and the star's. The speaker is "trotting along" through New York's rainy, snowy weather on his way to meet a friend or lover when he sees a headline, "LANA TURNER HAS COLLAPSED." He thinks about the different weather where she is and comments:

> there is no snow in Hollywood
> there is no rain in California
> I have been to lots of parties
> and acted perfectly disgraceful
> but I never actually collapsed
> oh Lana Turner we love you get up

This poem catches the fast movement of life and its eccentric, electric connections. It appears in many resources, yet it is only one of many similar poems that feature the characteristic O'Hara current that allows the reader to feel invaded by the 1950's and 1960's and carried off. The poems in this collection are all different, despite their shared voice, and they depict a world in which everything is likely to shift at any moment, and this instability is what provides life's savor. Whether O'Hara is doing a riff on Sergei Rachmaninoff ("Onset, Massachusetts. Is it the fig newton/ playing the horn?") or taking delight in the differences among New York men's rooms in "Homosexuality," he projects a sense of nowness—as though complete immersion in the moment would immortalize it. Ideas and images hurtle past. Most of O'Hara's poems are short, a page or less, catching the feel of events flying by. Nev-

ertheless, even the very long "Biotherm" maintains the sense of rush from the beginning:

> The best thing in the world   but I better be quick about it
> better be gone tomorrow
>   better be gone last night and
>   next Thursday better be gone
>   better be
>   always   or what's the use the sky
>   the endless clouds trailing we leading them by the bandanna, red

An atypical poem is "To the Harbormaster," which catches the downside of this
flux. The speaker is on his way in his ship to meet the harbormaster, but the ship "got
caught in some moorings." His intentions were good, he says, but his actions were ineffective. He is not able to achieve the goal of his journey.

>   In storms and
>   at sunset, with the metallic coils of the tide
>   around my fathomless arms, I am unable
>   to understand the forms of my vanity
>   or I am hard alee with my Polish rudder
>   in my hand and the sun sinking. To
>   you I offer my hull and the tattered cordage
>   of my will.

He makes an offering, then, of self, and despite his lack of progress in the right direction, he realizes that he is still sailing, not out of danger. He finally comments that
there may be a reason for his failure to arrive: "Yet/ I trust the sanity of my vessel;
and/ if it sinks it may well be in answer/ to the reasoning of the eternal voices,/ the
waves which have kept me from reaching you."

The humble exploring soul is not seen much in this work, but it is there, and this
apology for not connecting with the harbormaster has a powerful appeal. The tone is
quiet, and the extended metaphor is rare and unusual. This other side to O'Hara gives
his work a metaphysical dimension, even if he denies its presence elsewhere.

Opening the book at almost any point provides a jolt. The poet is open and clear
about everything in his life, including his love affairs with men, but there is nothing
graphic here—the reader gets the desire, the sense of immediacy, the realization that
everything is always subject to change. His delight in the world and his place in it is a
major element in the first poem, "Autobiographic Literaria," which begins with a tale
of a dull and lonely childhood in which the solitary boy had little companionship: ". . .
animals were/ not friendly and birds/ flew away." The expansive conclusion comes in
the style of Walt Whitman: "And here I am, the/ center of all beauty!/ writing these
poems!/ Imagine!" The poems say "Imagine!" in various ways, again and again, in
untoward or in eccentrically happy or unhappy circumstances.

The play *Try, Try* may be included to show that O'Hara, like T. S. Eliot and other
poets, wrote plays, although it is less compelling than anything else in the book, in-

cluding the prose. *Try, Try* seems to make fun of heterosexual love in the deliberately affected interchange among two lovers and her former love who has returned from the war. Like Eliot's plays, it makes for tedious reading, and while it does begin with an Eliot-like situation—infidelity—its concluding acceptance of infidelity as simply how things are is anything but Eliot-like. The play has a curiously flat effect next to the poems—the effervescence missing and the clever, whimsical dialogue lacking persuasiveness.

However, the poetics statements are intriguing, partly because they show where O'Hara placed himself as a poet—a force against the cult of Eliot and against the poetry of denial (of the world, of the self, of pleasure in the moment). "I don't believe in god, so I don't have to make elaborately sounded structures," he said in "Personism: A Manifesto," dismissing the literary theories in Eliot's essay "Tradition and the Individual Talent" and the poetry as well. O'Hara said, "I hate Vachel Lindsay, always have; I don't even like rhythm, assonance, all that stuff. You just go on your nerve." O'Hara believed in expressing the self in moments of heightened consciousness and providing a crackling linkage of network with other selves. This book demands to be read in short snatches, because all that energy all the time is too much for sustained attention.

Editor Ford is a poet who has also written a critical biography, *Raymond Roussel and the Republic of Dreams* (2000). He teaches at University College London and contributes to both *The New York Review of Books* and *The London Review of Books*. Ford's selections are well chosen and will preserve the reputation of this exciting poet for generations of readers. The sensibility of a young poet completely immersed in the New York artistic life provides an insider's look at the movements involved, and the balance of energy and implied elegy remains a powerful force. With the possible exception of the play, everything in this book bears study and rereading, and the whole presents a positive impression of O'Hara as a spokesman for and beyond his time. The *Collected Poems* is a daunting volume that would put off many potential readers; this carefully edited selection is vast enough to satisfy O'Hara's fans and to draw new ones.

Janet McCann

Review Sources

The New Republic 238, no. 9 (May 28, 2008): 47-51.
The New York Review of Books 55, no. 14 (September 25, 2008): 28-34.
The New York Times Book Review, June 29, 2008, p. 1.
Review of Contemporary Fiction 28, no. 2 (Summer, 2008): 172.

SHAKESPEARE'S WIFE

Author: Germaine Greer (1939-   )
Publisher: HarperCollins (New York). 406 pp. $26.95
Type of work: Biography
Time: 1556-1623
Locale: Shottery and Stratford, Warwickshire, England

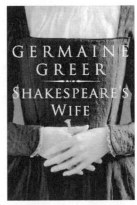

*Greer recounts what is known about the life of Ann
Hathaway, who became Ann Shakespeare, and speculates
on other possibilities that her life might have included*

> Principal personages:
> ANN HATHAWAY SHAKESPEARE, a woman
>   who married England's greatest writer
> WILLIAM SHAKESPEARE, her husband
> SUSANNA SHAKESPEARE, the elder
>   Shakespeare daughter
> JOHN HALL, a medical doctor and Susanna's husband
> HAMNET SHAKESPEARE, son of Ann and William
> JUDITH SHAKESPEARE QUINEY, daughter of Ann and William and twin
>   sister of Hamnet
> RICHARD HATHAWAY, a farmer in Shottery and Ann's father
> MARY HATHAWAY, Ann's stepmother
> JOHN SHAKESPEARE, a glove maker and William's father
> MARY SHAKESPEARE, William's mother

"Anyone steeped in Western literary culture must wonder why any woman of spirit would want to be a wife." Thus Germaine Greer begins *Shakespeare's Wife.* Coming from one of the best known of living feminist writers, the statement is hardly surprising, but it is not what one expects at the beginning of a biography of a sixteenth century woman with only limited control of her destiny. It is not, however, an entirely immaterial point in this book about a woman whose life had never been competently and open-mindedly studied. Ann Hathaway would have been taught that God instituted wifehood as the principal calling of a woman. She spent thirty-four years as William Shakespeare's wife, and she must be recognized as a person who stood closer to him than any future Bardolater and who understood him better than any such latterday expert. Not much is known about her spirit or how much she wanted to be a wife, but Ann is a part of Western literary culture, and her life is a piece of evidence for Greer's hard-nosed assertion.

A Shakespearean scholar, Greer cites the works of many others, often caustically, as for example Stephen Greenblatt's *Will in the World: How Shakespeare Became Shakespeare* (2004). She refers to his comments on the marriage nine times, sometimes approvingly but usually negatively, primarily for his assumption that William Shakespeare tired of his wife after, or as a result of, the confinements related to the births of the couple's three children and that he therefore "contrived" to leave her.

There is no convincing evidence that William did any such contriving, but Greenblatt and others have offered many such uncomplimentary assertions about the woman. To lead Ann into a more favorable light, Greer draws on studies of women and family life, some of them by female scholars such as Alice Clark, author of *The Working Life of Women in the Seventeenth Century* (1982); Lisa Jardine, author of *Still Harping on Daughters: Women and Drama in the Age of Shakespeare* (1983); and Alison Plowden, author of *Tudor Women: Queens and Commoners* (2002).

Being fair to Ann is not an easy task, with so many aspects of her life little or completely unknown and likely to remain so. Any writer of integrity who deals with Ann at any length must use expressions such as "perhaps" and "probably," "would have" and "might have" many times over. Thus they have done, and thus Greer does. She has performed her task more systematically than other scholars, treating the stages of her subject's life in chronological fashion from the standpoint of an observer determined to avoid making easy—and particularly condescending—assumptions about her subject.

Since any biography of a subject such as Shakespeare's wife must speculate, what besides a pitifully small cache of facts does the biographer have at hand? Greer uses available facts pertaining to other young women of that time and place as well as what Shakespeare himself and writers of his time said. No Shakepearean letters are known to exist, and most of what Shakespeare wrote on the facts of life and on modes of thought of his era emanate from the several hundred characters in his plays and poems. This is dangerous territory; most people then, as now, did not think like Lady Macbeth or Iago. What more representative characters in the plays have to say, especially in a more-or-less offhand way, doubtless gives more insight into social norms, and it is interesting to read Greer's compilation of what Shakespeare's characters have to say about the many aspects of common concerns.

One example is the wedding. Although no record has been found, Greer believes that the marriage of William and Ann would have been appropriately solemnized. In her sixth chapter on the events of the big day, she quotes from a song of the period, "The Bride's Goodmorrow," and from Edmund Spenser's account of his own wedding to Elizabeth Boyle in 1594. Then Greer presents a selection of wedding details from *The Merchant of Venice* (pr. c. 1596-1597), *As You Like It* (pr. c. 1599-1600), *The Taming of the Shrew* (pr. c. 1593-1594), and *Twelfth Night* (pr. c. 1600-1602). None of this proves that Shakespeare was recalling the celebration of his wedding in these works, but it reminds the reader that the dramatist took the wedding ceremony and its components seriously.

Everyone has noticed that Shakespeare was only eighteen when he married Ann and that she, almost surely pregnant, was eight years older. Many assumptions can be fashioned from these facts, and most of them remain firmly in the realm of speculation. Was Ann desperate for marriage? Greer notes that many women of Stratford did not marry at all, and some—such as Shakespeare's younger daughter Judith, who married at thirty-one—did not tie the knot when young. Was either Ann or William forced into the marriage? Greer argues that he could have escaped. If Shakespeare's parents had disapproved of Ann thoroughly, they could have stopped the marriage—but they did not. Could Shakespeare have been in love with another woman when he married Ann? A record has been found in the Bishop of Worcester's register of a license for a marriage between "Wm Shaxpere et Annam Whateley," while procedures for William's marriage were underway. There were, however, "lots" of William Shakespeares in Warwickshire in 1582. Greer expresses surprise that no one has speculated that the child who would become Susanna Shakespeare was not his. Even that unlikely possibility could not be established one way or the other.

Shakespeare's "lost years," the later 1580's and early 1590's, may have been spent in Stratford or in London. One of the sonnets attributed to him, 145, has plausibly been suggested as referring to Ann, especially on the basis of its closing couplet, "I hate from hate away she threw,/ And saved my life saying, not you," with language suggesting both her maiden and first names. Some critics refuse to accept this lackluster poem as Shakespeare's, but if it is, it surely must be an early effort, plausibly about his relationship with Ann. If he was spending his time composing such trifles during the couple's early years, Ann might well have sent him off to London, where literary efforts might, for all she knew, be appreciated, especially if he was otherwise idle and unproviding. Greer finds that Shakespeareans have tended to conclude that Ann was illiterate, "that they want her, need her to have had no inkling of the magnitude of her husband's achievement." She could, however, have been able to read and write; her husband might even have taught her.

Considering how little evidence establishes William's presence in Stratford after fathering the twins, Hamnet and Judith, in 1584, was Ann an abandoned woman? Had he deserted her, Greer argues, William would have been a fugitive from the law, unless she did not denounce him. If she did not under those circumstances denounce him, then she was protecting him. Many men spent years away from their wives earning their living, which is what William was doing for most of the time from 1592 until 1610. No Shakespearean scholar, Greer points out, has suggested that William missed his wife and children, but perhaps he did.

That Ann had to support herself during those years seems likely. Greer rejects the notion that she lived with her in-laws and reviews the activities by which women supported themselves: cleaning, washing, tailoring, brewing, malt-making, baking, spinning, weaving, farming, and various other work. There is no evidence of what Ann did, but evidence of what other women did is relevant.

William can be associated with Warwickshire again in his late years, including the well-to-do Combe family, one of whom, in 1614, was seeking to turn much of the open land around Stratford into pasture and thereby endanger the livelihood of farmers who worked that land. Women and children went out, at night, Greer presumes, and, as recorded in a 1602 source, they filled in 275 yards of land that had been ditched as part of the enclosure movement. The law held that if a man had organized an effort of this type, both he and his accomplices could be prosecuted, but if the women had acted spontaneously, the law could not act against them. The temptation was to find a man, guilty or not, to accuse as the instigator, However, in this instance, with women having little legal status, these women were never arraigned, and the Stratford commons were not enclosed. By this time Ann was in her late fifties and both Shakespeare daughters were among the housewives of the area. Whether or not any of these women were involved no one knows, but the event calls attention to the resourcefulness of Tudor females.

William's will introduces another interesting aspect of the relationship between him and his wife. She was not named executor, but Greer refuses to be surprised that he did not name a sixty-year-old woman to this task. Much has been made of the fact that Ann is mentioned only in connection with his "second best bed." It is possible that he left Ann with nothing, but he also might well have given her other property beforehand. Greer doubts that the will represents anything near a full distribution of his possessions.

Does Greer fall into her own unwarrantable and condescending suppositions? Yes, she does, but these suppositions are aimed not at her subject but reflect her judgments of the motives of the Shakespearean scholars who utter their own unflattering surmises anew or repeat old ones indiscreetly. She claims more than once that male scholars have a positive and presumably masculine need to downgrade the woman whom the very young William chose to be his wife.

It is curious and unconventional to write a book about a person not only obscure but also almost completely undocumented. If it had to happen, however, Ann Shakespeare was an excellent choice, for she is a woman often speculated about, either carelessly or, as Greer believes, contemptuously. In a sense, this book is less about Ann and more about the possibilities of obscure women to be more worthy and more enterprising than posterity is inclined to recognize. A book such as this one is not going to convince most Shakespearean scholars that Ann was a force with which to be reckoned, but they may well become more cautious in dismissing her as a nonentity.

Robert P. Ellis

Review Sources

Booklist 104, nos. 9/10 (January 1, 2008): 21.
The Boston Globe, May 28, 2008, p. E8.
Kirkus Reviews 76, no. 3 (February 1, 2008): 130.
Library Journal 133, no. 6 (April 1, 2008): 83.
London Review of Books 29, no. 19 (October 4, 2007): 29-30.
Maclean's 121, no. 14 (April 14, 2008): 80.
The New York Review of Books 55, no. 6 (April 17, 2008): 6-10.
The New York Times Book Review, April 27, 2008, p. 12.
Publishers Weekly 255, no. 5 (February 4, 2008): 46.
The Times Literary Supplement, January 25, 2008, p. 10.
The Wall Street Journal 251, no. 80 (April 5, 2008): W1-W4.

THE SILVER SWAN

Author: Benjamin Black (pseudonym of John Banville, 1945-   )
Publisher: Henry Holt (New York). 308 pp. $25.00
Type of work: Novel
Time: The early 1950's
Locale: Dublin, Ireland

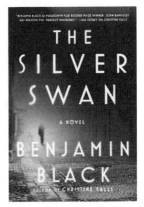

The husband of a drowned woman implores an old schoolmate to ignore protocol and suspend an autopsy on the body, which leads the doctor into a private criminal investigation that produces unexpected results

> *Principal characters:*
> GARRET QUIRKE, a middle-aged Dublin pathologist with an insatiable curiosity
> BILLY HUNT, university classmate of Quirke whom he has not seen in years and only barely remembers
> DEIRDRE HUNT, also known as SILVER SWAN, Billy's much younger wife who has drowned in Dublin Bay
> PHOEBE GRIFFIN, Quirke's estranged daughter
> LESLIE WHITE, Deirdre's business partner and lover
> KATE WHITE, Leslie's disaffected wife
> HAKIM KREUTZ, a spiritual healer and drug dealer

The Silver Swan by Benjamin Black begins in the middle of things with the protagonist, Quirke, puzzling over a note from someone who seems vaguely familiar but whom he does not recall until they meet in a bar. Billy Hunt, a former athletic classmate, informs Quirke, a Dublin pathologist, that his wife has drowned, and Billy pleads that her beautiful body not be disfigured by an autopsy. Quirke reluctantly agrees, only to renege on the promise when he finds a tiny puncture wound on her arm.

At an inquest, Quirke insists that the cause of death was drowning, though he harbors suspicions and spends the rest of the novel learning more than he expected about a host of lives and uncovering the sad truth about Deirdre Hunt's life and death. His investigation uncovers exploitation, blackmail, drug use, and murder, and his primary motivation has less to do with issues of legality or justice than with simple curiosity and protectiveness.

The novel assumes a knowledge of characters and situations that transpired in the first Black mystery, *Christine Falls* (2007), with these events occurring about two years later. Quirke has lost his wife, has remained thoroughly alienated from a daughter he abandoned in childhood, and has betrayed his adoptive father, a judge, who has hidden behind his office. Additionally, although Quirke has given up the drink, he must continually struggle with alcoholic urges that haunt him, just as the novel's events and his shattered life obsess him.

John Banville, who sometimes writes as Benjamin Black, worked as a copy editor for the Irish Press *and then as literary editor at the* Irish Times. *He began his writing career in 1970 with the publication of* Long Lankin, *a series of nine short fictions, and then embarked on his career as a novelist in 1971 with* Nightspawn. The Sea *(2005) won for Banville the Man Booker Prize.*

John Banville, who writes his mystery and detective fiction under the nom de plume Benjamin Black, has had a long and distinguished career, writing challenging fictions dating back to 1970. His fourteen novels have garnered serious critical attention, defining him as one of the most subtle and sophisticated of postmodernists. In addition to having won the James Tait Black Memorial Prize and the Whitbread Prize, he was awarded the prestigious Man Booker Prize for *The Sea* in 2005. In 2007 he surprised many with his next project, *Christine Falls*, a noir murder mystery set in 1950's Dublin that he published, as an open secret, under the pen name of Black. That novel was a finalist for the 2008 Edgar Award and the *Los Angeles Times* Book Prize for Mystery/Thrillers.

Banville has launched a Benjamin Black Web site in which he interviews his alter ego and reveals that to write these latest novels he has rented a small apartment in the Temple Bar area of Dublin, which has encouraged the temporal setting and unique atmosphere of his mysteries. In that interview, Banville admits, "The 1950's fascinates me. It was a remarkable time, here and in America, paranoid, guilt-ridden, beset by fear and loathing, and still shuddering in the after-effects of the war. A perfect period for a novel, if you incline toward a dark view of human beings."

This careful attention to place is a major component of all successful detective fiction, whether it be the village world of Agatha Christie or the mean streets of Los Angeles and San Francisco of Raymond Chandler and Dashiell Hammett. Black knows this genre, and while he seeks to incorporate the atmosphere of hard-boiled writers such as Chandler and James M. Cain, he is not content to strictly imitate them.

Quirke is anything but a tough guy—he is stocky and physically maladroit, far from a ladies' man, and someone who not so much solves a case as he worries it to death, engaging everyone in elliptical conversations. Most detective fictions conclude with the protagonist wrapping up the stray clues, identifying the least-likely suspect, assigning guilt, and solving the case. Quirke puts matters together, to be sure, but he jumps to some erroneous conclusions and essentially argues to let sleeping dogs lie. He is full of suspicions, but in the end he is a thoroughly fallible hero who falls off the wagon and spends a sodden night on a park bench.

Perhaps Quirke's closest association with traditional detective heroes is his individual code of ethics, which places him in conflict with the law and the criminals alike. His fascination with corpses and his overwhelming personal pain make Quirke a complex, distant character. He even regards himself as a divided personality: "For there was another version of him, a personality within a personality, malcontent, vindictive, ever ready to provoke, to which he gave the name 'Carriklea [the orphanage of his youth].' Often he found himself standing back, seemingly helpless to intervene, as this other he made him set about fomenting some new enormity." On the other hand, his sense of justice forces him to turn his adoptive father over to the authorities and public humiliation.

Hard-boiled fictions typically center on a subjective narrator whose deepest feelings and personal ruminations provide as much drama as the plots themselves. Banville is an author who has often emphasized the tortured terrain of his narrators' most intimate thoughts, but Black chooses instead the distance of a third-person narrative consciousness. This narrator, though it favors Quirke, does not focus exclusively on him. Black's narrator is a chameleon, a voice that can often impersonate each of the other characters, and thus whole chapters are often given over to the point of view of different figures. Perhaps the most interesting of these chapters appears at the conclusion, when the reader is allowed purchase into the mind of the killer, someone not as clever as he thinks he is but still eerily perceptive, as for instance when he ruminates on the inevitability of his role as a killer, "Maybe if you looked at anything, any event, closely enough you would see the future packed into it, folded tight, like the tight-folded elastic filling of a golf ball."

The novel develops three separate stories simultaneously—Quirke's, his daughter Phoebe's, and Deirdre's. Each is revealed as a sorrowful figure, burdened by personal guilts and humiliations, and none can rid himself or herself of the embarrassing residue of the past. The three narratives snake uneasily around and through one another, and the principal characters independently become involved with one another.

On the surface, such intricate interconnections may seem contrived and unlikely, but these complicated coincidences are ultimately part of Black's atmospheric purpose. At one point, when Phoebe and the lascivious Leslie White are discussing some of these relationships, Phoebe remarks that in Dublin, "Everyone knows everyone else's business." James Joyce and many other Dubliners have complained that their city, in fundamental ways, is a small town where everyone appears to know one another and their most private secrets. Black seems to insist that a mid-twentieth century Dublin is no different from the place where Joyce escaped because of its narrow and oppressive culture.

The gray, damp fog and omnipresent smoke that surround the action become powerful metaphors for the claustrophobic fog of a society that denies privacy and personal independence. As Banville explains in another interview, "All that fog, all the cigarette smoke, all the Catholic guilt, all those secrets buried deep behind the facade of respectability—[these are] perfect for noir fiction." While all of the characters yearn for escape—through sex, drugs, and tawdry adventures—Quirke chooses the very means that will intrigue yet ultimately depress him. "Do nothing, his better judgment told him; stay on dry land. But he knew he would dive, headfirst, into the depths. Something in him yearned after the darkness down there."

Banville has announced repeatedly in interviews that writing as Black has been a liberating experience. Instead of laboring endlessly over a perfectly wrought sentence, Black writes quickly and spontaneously in a way that brings its author immense joy. Nevertheless, while the style is indeed looser, the novel is laced with many delightful and carefully crafted sentences. For instance, passages devoted to death produce evocative results. When Phoebe ponders the incomprehensibility of suicide, she describes it as the ring of a hammer falling on a dull lump of steel. Perhaps the fascination of it, for her, was merely that she had never known anyone personally, or in the flesh, at least . . . who had vanished so comprehensively, who had become non-flesh, as it were, by one sudden, impulsive dive into darkness.

Quirke also meditates on death in a beautiful passage, nearly reminiscent of Banville:

> Over every scene of violent death Quirke had attended in the course of his career there had hung a particular kind of silence, the kind that falls after the last echoes of a great outcry have faded. There was shock in it, of course, and awe and outrage, the sense of many hands lifted quickly to many mouths, but something else as well, a kind of glee-fulness, a kind of startled, happy, unable-to-believe-its-luckness. Things, Quirke reflected, even inanimate things, it seemed, love a killing.

Banville-Black is a remarkably adroit, perceptive writer. The Dublin he has created in his Quirke novels is thoroughly Irish and an original setting for noir mysteries. The characters in *The Silver Swan* are convincingly believable human types, which the figures in the Banville novels are often not, being cerebral projections of over-wrought consciousness. Like another of his inspirations, Georges Simenon, Black brings a strong sense of existential angst to his creations, even his most vile villains. In keeping with these existential leanings, the crime, while not insoluble, is never neatly resolved, and the cost of the investigation, at least for Quirke, is high, paid in the coin of the soul. The toll, from one novel to the other, is palpable. The Black novels remind readers that of all life's mysteries and secrets, those of the human soul are the most complex and elusive.

David W. Madden

Review Sources

Booklist 104, no. 11 (February 1, 2008): 32.
The Boston Globe, March 10, 2008, p. C6.
The Christian Science Monitor, March 28, 2008, p. 14.
Houston Chronicle, March 20, 2008, p. 1.
Kirkus Reviews 75, no. 24 (December 15, 2007): 1254.
Library Journal 133, no. 2 (February 1, 2008): 51.
Los Angeles Times, March 5, 2008, p. E1.
The New York Times Book Review, April 20, 2008, p. 17.
Publishers Weekly 255, no. 1 (January 7, 2008): 36.
Sunday Times, November 18, 2007, p. 20.
The Times Literary Supplement, November 23, 2007, p. 21.

SITTING BULL

Author: Bill Yenne (1949-)
Publisher: Westholme (Yardley, Pa.). 379 pp. $29.95
Type of work: Biography
Time: The 1840's to 1890
Locale: Mostly the Great Plains of the United States

A narrative account of the life and times of Sitting Bull, probably the best-known Native American leader of all time

Principal personages:
SITTING BULL (1831?-1890), famous
  spiritual, military, and political leader of
  the Lakota nation
WILLIAM "BUFFALO BILL" CODY (1846-
  1917), soldier, bison hunter, and
  showman
JAMES MCLAUGHLIN (1842-1923), Indian agent at the Standing Rock
  Reservation
GEORGE ARMSTRONG CUSTER (1839-1876), lieutenant colonel killed at
  Little Big Horn
CRAZY HORSE (1842?-1877), most famous of the intransigent Lakota
  warriors
RED CLOUD (1822?-1909), Lakota leader who accepted reservation life
  after 1868

In addition to telling the fascinating story of Sitting Bull's life, Bill Yenne's biography, *Sitting Bull*, presents an excellent introduction to the history and culture of Native Americans living on the Great Plains during the nineteenth century. Much of the book necessarily focuses on the violent clashes between two fundamentally different cultures. When Sitting Bull was a young man, he and other indigenous peoples of the region were still living as they had for centuries. They practiced a nomadic way of life without fixed settlements, obtaining their food and other needs by following the great buffalo herds across the plains. Sitting Bull loved everything about this lifestyle, and he grieved to see Euro-Americans (or "wasichu") slaughtering the buffalo and coercing the tribes to settle into reservations. Ironically, the year Sitting Bull was killed, 1890, was the same year in which the census bureau announced that the United States no longer had a definable frontier (or line between settled and unsettled lands) in the American West.

Like any writer on the subject, Yenne sometimes finds it difficult to separate historical facts from legends. He observes that Sitting Bull's "legacy survives in two worlds, with one foot in history, where he remains complex and difficult to understand, and the other foot in popular history." Although dependable knowledge about Sitting Bull's early life is limited, Yenne concludes that Sitting Bull was probably

~

*Bill Yenne is a San Francisco-based
author who has published more than
two dozen nonfiction works, including*
Indian Wars: The Campaign for the
American West *(2005),* The Opening of
the American West *(1993), and* The
Encyclopedia of North American
Indian Tribes *(1986).*

~

born in 1831, close to where the Grand River
enters the Missouri River in present-day South
Dakota. He was initially given the name Jump-
ing Badger, and then he was called Slow because of his careful and deliberate behavior.
At about the age of fourteen, he was allowed
to take his father's former name, Sitting Bull
(or Tatanka Iyotanka), after he first "counted
coup," the dangerous practice of touching a
person from an enemy tribe with a stick. The
Lakota word *tatanka* referred to a buffalo
bull, and the word *iyotanka* implied that the bull was stubborn or intractable. The
name also referred to the first stage in a traditional allegory about the four stages of
life.

Sitting Bull belonged to the Hunkpapa branch of the Lakota tribal group—commonly known as the Western Sioux. The Hunkpapa (which means "head of the
camp") acquired the name from their practice of defending the campsite at large assemblies of Plains Indians. The Lakota people in language and culture are closely related to the Nakota and Dakota (all three names mean "friends" or "allies"). The three
tribal groups did not like to be called Sioux, a name that means "snakes" or "enemies"
in the Ojibwa (or Chippewa) language. The Lakota-Nakota-Dakota were famous for
their skill and organization in warfare, which was the basis for their hegemony over a
large portion of the Great Plains, spanning from the Rocky Mountains to the Mississippi River and from Manitoba to Nebraska.

In contrast to romantic writers who have described Native Americans as living together in peace and harmony, Yenne acknowledges that they frequently engaged in
violent conflict. He writes, for instance, that warfare with the Crow tribe was deeply
embedded in the Lakota culture. Like many indigenous peoples, the Lakota considered the "scalps of women and children, as well as those of defeated warriors, . . .
legitimate trophies long before the wasichu set foot on the plains." Sitting Bull did not
object to the violent methods of U.S. Cavalry, but he was not impressed with their
military skills. He said, "The white soldiers do not know how to fight. They are not
lively enough. They stand still and run straight; it is easy to shoot them." In addition,
he described the wasichu warriors as heartless: "When an Indian gets killed, the other
Indians feel sorry and cry, and sometimes they stop fighting. But when a white soldier
gets killed, nobody cries, nobody cares; they go right on shooting and let him lie
there."

Until the second half of the twentieth century, a large percentage of white Americans looked upon Sitting Bull as a villain opposed to progress and as the person responsible for the death of General George Armstrong Custer. By the late twentieth
century, in contrast, it had become commonplace, especially among intellectuals, to
perceive him as a hero who had defended an oppressed people and who had fought
against imperialism. Yenne writes that "the truth is more complicated than either stereotype." His thesis is that Sitting Bull can be considered a "composite of many reali-

ties." Among his different and complex roles, he was "a warrior, a leader, a shaman, and an 'Indian chief'...a father, and an inspiration to his people."

As a spiritual leader, Sitting Bull was believed to have possessed exceptional and mysterious powers. The Lakota term for such a person was *eikasa Wakan,* commonly translated as "medicine man" by white Americans and as "shaman" by anthropologists. When on a vision quest, Sitting Bull would usually go into a remote location to quietly meditate, but at other times he would participate in a communal Sun Dance, which included singing, fasting, praying, staring at the sun, and pulling skewers through the flesh. According to Lakota spiritual beliefs, revelations came from Wakantanka, or the "Great Spirit," which Yenne defines as the "sacred and mysterious entity" that is "roughly analogous to the Judeo-Christian understanding of an omnipotent God."

For much of his adult life, Sitting Bull had the title of "itancan," which denoted a high position of political and military leadership. The choice of an itancan was not based primarily on heredity; rather, it was achieved from the subjective qualities of character, charisma, and the ability to lead. Much of his prestige, moreover, derived from his outstanding skills as a warrior. By 1869, the year that he finished drawing the story of his life in pictograms, he claimed to have counted coup sixty-three times. Yenne tells about several incidents in which Sitting Bull viciously killed enemies on the battlefield without remorse, although the biographer also describes other times in which Sitting Bull recommended against the killing of prisoners, especially women and children.

Following the signing of the Treaty of Fort Laramie of 1868, the Lakota people were divided into two major factions. The more moderate elements, led by Red Cloud, were willing to move onto reservations and make accommodations with the American government. In contrast, the committed traditionalists were determined to fight to preserve their nomadic existence. In 1869 a large assembly of Lakota traditionalists elected Sitting Bull as their "itancan-in-chief." For a few years, the off-reservation Plains Indians were temporarily allowed to live and hunt in the large region of the Yellowstone River and its tributaries. In 1876, however, President Ulysses S. Grant ordered that all Indians of the region must move to reservations. As the U.S. Cavalry was preparing to enforce the edict, Sitting Bull, after losing consciousness in a sun dance, had his famous vision of soldiers falling like grasshoppers. On June 25-26, when Lieutenant Colonel George Armstrong Custer and his 210-man command were killed at the battle of the Little Big Horn, Sitting Bull did not participate in the fighting, and, contrary to legend, he never came into close proximity of Custer. Yenne suggests that it is symbolic that Sitting Bull was "concerned with and looking after the welfare of the weakest among his people, especially the young children."

After the battle, as the U.S. Cavalry pursued Sitting Bull and other off-reservation Indians, he dictated a note expressing his strong desire to be left alone. "You scare all the buffalo away," he complained. "I want to hunt in this place. I want you to turn back from here. If you don't, I will fight you again . . . I am your friend, Sitting Bull." In October, he agreed to meet with General Nelson "Bear Coat" Miles, but when Miles told him it was inevitable that all Indians would be forced to move onto reservations, he reportedly answered that God had made him an Indian, and that he would rather die than survive as an "agency Indian." Sitting Bull expressed particular abhorrence to the idea of farming and taking food and housing from the wasichu. By this time, however, buffalo herds were quickly disappearing, in large part because of the wasichu's strategy of destroying the food source of the Plains Indians, thereby forcing them to adopt a sedentary way of life.

Escaping to Canada in 1877, Sitting Bull initially had a camp of more than a thousand families. As food became increasingly scarce, however, many of his comrades, including Gall and Spotted Eagle, returned to the United States. By 1881, after Sitting Bull's camp had dwindled to about 125 families, he agreed to surrender at Fort Buford, about fifty miles south of the Canadian border. With sadness, he told the commanding officer that he had yielded "not on my own account, but because my women and children are starving." After spending some time in detention, and then touring with Buffalo Bill's Wild West Show in 1885, he eventually settled into his new life on the Standing Rock reservation, near the place of his birth.

Yenne emphasizes that Sitting Bull did not actively participate in the Ghost Dance movement of the late 1880's. Yenne is highly critical of the stubborn mindset of Indian Agent James McLaughlin, who viewed the aging itancan as a dangerous troublemaker and ordered his arrest in 1890. This unenlightened approach appears to have resulted in the unnecessary deaths of Sitting Bull, his son Crow Foot, and thirteen other Indians. Yenne especially condemns the way in which the Indian police murdered Crow Foot simply because he was Sitting Bull's son. Yenne's account includes a well-written summary of the Wounded Knee massacre of that year, but it does not add anything new about the tragic event.

In concluding his book, Yenne discusses the Standing Rock reservation, Sitting Bull's descendants, and the robbery of his grave. One the most valuable contributions of the book is its report on the status of Sitting Bull's so-called Hieroglyphic Autobiography, which consisted of about sixty-three pictograms that symbolically recorded his memory of major events from 1846 to 1869. Almost all of the drawings depicted battles with warriors of enemy tribes, particularly Crows. Although the original portfolio was destroyed in 1870, Sitting Bull reproduced selective drawings while in captivity, and they are now in different locations: the National Naval Medical Center, the Smithsonian Institution, and a historical museum in Niles, Michigan. Yenne writes that "Sitting Bull's originals may still be out there somewhere."

Like most contemporary historians, Yenne does not try to justify the Indian policies of the U.S. government. Referring to the doctrine of assimilation as "cultural genocide," he condemns the "well-intentioned paternalism" that was based on the idea that Indians "could be saved only by eliminating the essence of their unique language and culture, their 'Indian-ness.'" He especially denounces the practice of taking children away from their parents and punishing them if they spoke their native languages. Yenne, however, appears to recognize that the demise of the nomadic culture was inevitable because of its incompatibility with the modernization of North America, and his account makes it manifestly clear that traditionalists such as Sitting Bull would not have adopted a sedentary culture without coercion.

Yenne's book is the third serious biography to be published about Sitting Bull. The first, Stanley Vestal's *Sitting Bull: Champion of the Sioux* (1932), was a pioneering work that is often quoted by Yenne. Vestal's greatest contribution was to record numerous interviews with survivors who had known Sitting Bull and remembered events from his time. Vestal, however, was primarily interested in writing a literary work, and he did not always utilize critical historical methods. The second major biography, Robert Utley's *The Lance and the Shield: The Life and Times of Sitting Bull* (1993), is a scholarly work that is detailed and richly documented in hundreds of footnotes. Although Yenne does not provide footnotes for documentation, he frequently tells in the text where he has acquired his information. For general readers, Yenne's volume is more concise, better organized, and written in a clearer and livelier style. It is an example of popular history at its best.

Thomas Tandy Lewis

Review Sources

Booklist 104, no. 16 (April 15, 2008): 23.
The New Yorker 84, no. 16 (June 2, 2008): 77.
Wild West 21, no. 4 (December, 2008): 71-72.

SLEEPING IT OFF IN RAPID CITY
Poems, New and Selected

Author: August Kleinzahler (1949-   )
Publisher: Farrar, Straus and Giroux (New York).
 234 pp. $26.00
Type of work: Poetry

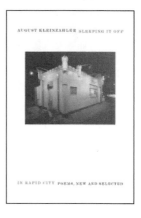

 *A probing and blunt collection from a poet whose rest-
less spirit has taken him to various spots around the world*

Over the years, August Kleinzahler has established
himself as a poet with an almost boundless curiosity for
travel, for seeking greener pastures, for taking leaps into
the unknown. Certain literary critics have noted that he is
itching constantly for the "new," the "different." There certainly is a "restlessness" that pervades his poetry. For the
poet, standing still can be "endured" at best. For decades, Kleinzahler has written concise observations of people and places from the far reaches of the world. He has spent
time on a number of continents, and in each he has written with precision and with
wit.

Kleinzahler is the author of several poetry collections. His first volume, *A Calen-
dar of Airs*, was published in 1978. He is at his best when he is laudatory and critical in
the same breath about a place to which he has traveled. Starting in New Jersey—the
place of his birth—the poet expanded his reach as his dreams grew larger. Poetry has
allowed him to flex his muscles but not in a self-conscious way. He does not, however, blindly circumnavigate the wide landscape or reserve judgment; he allows himself to make harsh—and at times brutal—pronouncements.

Kleinzahler's new volume, *Sleeping It Off in Rapid City*, is divided into five sections. There are new poems and various selected works from previous volumes. These
distinctions are not made clear, so for the uninitiated reader all poems will be new.
Kleinzahler studied with Basil Bunting, an English poet who must be categorized as a
modernist and who had a major influence on his pupil. In later years, Kleinzahler was
influenced by the poet Thom Gunn, from whom he learned the paramount importance
of writing honestly about a subject. Whatever subject matter the poet chooses, it must
be treated with respect and approached directly, without exaggeration and without
flinching.

While the poet has felt driven to travel far and wide, Kleinzahler began in New Jersey. In the poem "Snow in North Jersey," he presents rich details of a region that he
knows well, opening with: "Snow is falling along the Boulevard/ and its little cemeteries hugged by transmission shops/ and on the stone bear in the park/ and the WWI
monument making a crust/ on the soldier with his chin strap and bayonet." As the poet
observes, the snow plays no favorites, not sparing the people and places that are most
vulnerable to the natural elements. The region also gets center stage in the poem "Gray

Light in May," in which it becomes obvious that although the elements can be gloomy, places and people can be transformed between the rains. A richness bursts forth, filling the poem with vivid images, as in: "The soft gray light/ The still moist air/ The azaleas in these yards/ Under the canopies of leaves/ Fiercely abloom in this gray light/ Between rains/ Almost stereoscopic/ The broad green leaves overhead as well/ Painters know it, photographers too." Just as painters and photographers, poets also recognize the beauty. While William Carlos Williams is probably the most famous poet from New Jersey, Kleinzahler appreciates the Garden State, as his home is known, although he has written about it with brutal honesty, too. These poems take him back to his beginnings, so that the reader can see where the poet earned his toughness and built his masculine world from the ground up. Kleinzahler is the fly on the wall, the anonymous observer who just happens to be on the scene. He does not call attention to himself or take himself too seriously. He is a record keeper, the man who is keeping score.

~

August Kleinzahler is the author of several poetry collections, including Storm Over Hackensack *(1985),* Earthquake Weather *(1989),* Live from the Hong Kong Nile Club: Poems, 1975-1990 *(2000), and* The Strange Hours Travelers Keep *(2003), which was awarded the Griffin Poetry Prize. He also is the author of the memoir* Cutty, One Rock: Low Characters and Strange Places, Gently Explained *(2004).*

~

In the role of the poet, Kleinzahler is concerned about being honest in his observations, and he does not pull any punches. There is an urgency in his writing, a burning to be totally accurate. He is less concerned with academic boundaries and popularity and more concerned with precision and toughness of thought in his writing.

Kleinzahler loves details almost to a fault, and in this regard, the poet can be compared to Ezra Pound. This is evident in the title poem "Sleeping It Off in Rapid City." It opens: "On a 700 foot thick shelf of Cretaceous pink sandstone/ *Nel mezzo . . . /* Sixth floor, turn right at the elevator/ "The hotel of the century"/ *Elegant dining, dancing, solarium/* Around the block from the Black Hills School of Beauty." There is a rich tapestry presented for the reader to examine, to decipher with great care. Although Kleinzahler has little respect for stuffy academia, he does not "write down" to an audience. He expects the reader to bring something to the experience, to relish what is presented. Over the years, the poet has held several positions in the academic world, including teaching creative writing at Brown University, at the University of California at Berkeley, and at the Iowa Writers' Workshop at the University of Iowa. In addition, Kleinzahler has taught homeless veterans in San Francisco and has worked as a building manager, a taxi driver, and a locksmith. Each of these endeavors has served him well in his poetry.

Kleinzahler is best described as an amalgam of various influences, including jazz music, Imagism, and Abstract Expressionism. With his ear constantly pressed to the earth and to the wall and pointed toward everyone who passes within shouting distance, Kleinzahler has, with his endless curiosity, created a unique style of poetry. His poetic temperament has compelled him to travel off the beaten path, and in the poem

"Traveler's Tales: Chapter 13," the reader discovers details about another place in time. There are "bicycle paths" that "are busy with peddlers, humorless and good,/ speeding down their privileged corridors,/ kinetic emblems of an enlightened state,/ efficient, compassionate and *on the go*." "*On the go*" is an apt description of the poet, who finds that the world rarely stands still.

In "Poetics," Kleinzahler finds inspiration in the air. He "loved the air outside Shop-Rite Liquor/ on summer evenings/ better than the Marin hills at dusk/ lavender and gold/ stretching miles to the sea." The air at this location is "full of living dust:/ bus exhaust, airborne grains of pizza crust/ wounded crystals/ appearing, disappearing/ among streetlights and unsuccessful neon." Although this atmosphere may not be healthful, it is a part of life and says something about the human condition.

Kleinzahler has stated that he hopes the reader "trusts" him that he would not intentionally lead the reader astray. If a poem at first glance seems difficult, it is not written that way to frustrate the reader but to ask the reader to take a poetic journey that will be enriching. For Kleinzahler, the writing process is invigorating; he has described the writing of a poem as being in a "trance," simultaneously "thrilling" and "very exhausting."

Kleinzahler has voiced strong opinions in his writing and in public forums, becoming "pugilistic" in poetic matters. On occasion, he has become involved in fights at poetry readings. This tough mentality is evident in his poetry. For several years, Kleinzahler has made the Haight-Ashbury section of San Francisco his home, and he has written about this area in such poems as "Sunset in Chinatown." It opens with "The massive cable turns on its spool, pulling/ carloads of tourists to the city's crest// as the sun sits low/ in the hills above Chinatown, exploding// suddenly in the window of Goey Loy Meats, high/ along the top of the glass,// showering light over barbecued ducks."

Kleinzahler adds poignance to the strength of his poetry as he presents his perspective on the world. More than willing to defend his point of view, he considers himself an outsider in the world of poetry. There is little that is genteel about Kleinzahler, and for that reason he has been compared to the rambunctious Los Angeles poet Charles Bukowski. Kleinzahler is also a mischief maker who believes that he is worthy of attention. For some literary critics, Kleinzahler's gritty urban portraits are more "ugly" than "poignant." One of the poems noted for its revolting subject matter is "Meat," in which the poet asks "How much meat moves/ Into the city each night/ The decks of its bridges tremble/ In the liquefaction of sodium light/ And the moon a chemical orange." By the end of the poem, the reader is confronted with the horrors of the "meat" trade: "Hauling tons of dead lamb/ Bone and flesh and offal/ Miles to the ports and channels/ Of the city's shimmering membrane/ A giant breathing cell/ Exhaling its waste/ From the stacks by the river/ And feeding through the night." While Kleinzahler's tendency to almost revel in the seedier aspects of modern society may not earn him many devoted readers, this multifaceted poet is capable of writing in several voices.

A poet of extremes—one part braggart, one part technical expert, one part cultural provocateur, one part sensitive observer—Kleinzahler is revealed in all these aspects in *Sleeping It Off in Rapid City.* It should garner this underappreciated American poet just praise from a far wider audience.

Jeffry Jensen

Review Sources

Library Journal 133, no. 9 (May 15, 2008): 106.
London Review of Books 29, no. 4 (February 22, 2007): 18.
Los Angeles Times, July 28, 2008, p. A1.
The New York Times Book Review, May 25, 2008, p. 15.
The New Yorker 84, no. 11 (April 28, 2008): 79.
Publishers Weekly 255, no. 8 (February 25, 2008): 53.
The Times Literary Supplement, July 11, 2008, pp. 11-12.

THE SOLITARY VICE
Against Reading

Author: Mikita Brottman (1966-   )
Publisher: Counterpoint (Berkeley, Calif.). 233 pp.
    $14.95
Type of work: Literary criticism, memoir

Brottman takes aim at the glorification of reading, suggesting that books (at least some books) are not as good as some people make them out to be

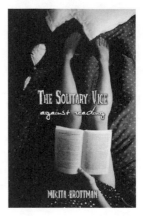

It might seem odd of Mikita Brottman to write a book against reading called *The Solitary Vice*; in truth, she is not against all reading or all books. In fact, she claims to have been a great reader all of her life—too much as an adolescent, when she tried to escape the horrors of family life by immersing herself in gothic horror stories such as Bram Stoker's *Dracula* (1897), Robert Louis Stevenson's *The Strange Case of Dr. Jekyll and Mr. Hyde* (1886), and the short stories of Edgar Allan Poe.

She confesses to have been addicted to reading, and in parts her book reads like an account of a recovering addict warning against the horrors of her particular drug. However, though she begins by seeming to warn against all reading, or at least to mock the campaigns in favor of reading (which say that as long as you read, it makes no difference what you read), it soon becomes apparent that she is actually intent on changing what people read rather than have them stop reading altogether.

Surprisingly, given her youthful addiction to horror stories, those are not the books she warns against. Indeed, she recommends horror stories, though now she is an advocate of true crime stories rather than the fictional tales she devoured as a youth.

What she inveighs against are not gothic novels but the classics, from Sophocles through *Beowulf* (c. sixth century) to Geoffrey Chaucer and Miguel de Cervantes' *Don Quixote* (1605, 1615), all the books she was made to read at university. Forget the classics, she says; if you really must find out about them, watch a film version or read CliffsNotes, a startling point of view from a professor of literature, but her point seems to be to shock or startle and to get readers thinking about what they read and why.

In the end, Brottman says that the point of reading is to learn about other people and oneself, and the best books for that, in her view, are not the classic novels of the past, but nonfiction of various sorts. In addition to true crime stories, which perhaps can instruct about the dark side of life, though mostly they seem as escapist as the gothic fiction of Brottman's youth, Brottman recommends literary memoirs (which in a way is what her book is) and Hollywood gossip, along with psychological case studies, such as the ones Sigmund Freud produced early in his career.

Her interest is in details, because through details one can understand others' lives and measure one's own against them. She is especially interested in the lives of writers, though she delights in puncturing the notion that writers are superior sorts of beings; in fact, she says, they are mostly unpleasant in real life, though she raises the question of what real life is for a writer: Which is the real personality of the writer, she asks, the one revealed in his or her books or the one in the person one meets on the street?

Mikita Brottman is a literature professor at the Maryland Institute College of Art and author of High Theory/Low Culture *(2005). She is also a psychotherapist and the author of* Funny Peculiar: Gershon Legman and the Psychopathology of Humor *(2004), which was nominated for the Gradiva Award of the National Association for the Advancement of Psychoanalysis.*

Brottman is also interested in reading about Hollywood celebrities, and she launches into an analysis of celebrity that seems only tenuously connected to reading. America has become a land of celebrities, she says; celebrity is the true American religion, and celebrities are the true elite, but they are a powerless elite whose worshipers love to read about their setbacks and sufferings.

Brottman says that people like to read about the failings of celebrities because it makes them feel stable and healthy in comparison, and it is interesting that the books she recommends tend to focus on the dark side of life, from true crime to Hollywood gossip to the case studies of sufferers from psychological disorders. She is quick with generalizations and not too concerned about evidence, which may prompt some of her readers to wonder about her accuracy.

Brottman, however, is writing a polemic, perhaps partly with tongue in cheek, and so the fact that some people might want to read more uplifting stories and enjoy others' successes is not mentioned. It is perhaps part of her method to go to such an extreme in order to provoke her readers to think of counter-examples.

On a small scale, for instance, her assertion that everyone agrees that the best way to read is stretched out on a bed seems open to challenge. Her assertion that readers remember not just books in themselves but the situation in which they read them may also warrant challenge. Brottman does seem to believe, or she pretends to believe, that her experience is universal. She mostly draws on her own experiences or on those of people in a very small survey that she conducted.

Brottman also can get almost hysterical at times, for instance, in attacking the reading habits of the popular singer Art Garfunkel and bibliomaniacs, book collectors more interested in books as physical objects than in things to read. Here she seems to be the representative of one cult (the cult of escapist reading) attacking another (the cult of book fetishism).

For all of her digressions and self-absorption, and her brief consideration of Garfunkel and the bibliomaniacs, Brottman does raise serious questions about reading. Why should it be so highly valued, for one thing? On this point, she usefully notes that it was not always so highly valued. In fact, reading was for many years the Internet of its day, a dangerous activity often warned against as distracting people from real relationships in real life. It is amusing to read Brottman's brief account of how the criticisms now made of new media—often by people who recommend reading and who warn of how new media are a threat to books—used to be leveled against books.

Regarding the threat to books today, Brottman notes that there have never been so many books published, and though she characteristically has few statistics to back up this claim, it seems a fair statement. This does raise the question of why some people see such a threat to reading and why various influential figures—from Oprah Winfrey to President George W. Bush's wife Laura—made it a point to campaign for reading.

Perhaps it is an example of moral panic, the sort of thing Brottman talks about in connection with serial killers in the 1980's. Why a moral panic now? Or is it not really such a new thing to worry about the death of reading or books? A more scientific study might be needed to lay out the true history of this issue, but Brottman does not intend to be scientific but to puncture complacent, commonplace views. Video games are more useful than books, she says, and she casts doubt on the claims of the pro-book campaigners that books can cure depression or make you a better person.

Nevertheless, Brottman is a great reader. It seems to be the campaigning and the worshiping to which she objects. It is as if a devotee of crossword puzzles were suddenly to realize that there was a major campaign promoting crossword puzzles as the solution to the world's problems. Brottman wants to read books because she enjoys them, not because they are somehow good for her. She wants her reading to be a guilty pleasure, which is perhaps why she warns away from the uplifting classics and promotes the dark, trashy, sordid forms of literature.

Reading, Brottman says, should be done for pleasure, not because it ought to be done. She warns against reading books one "ought" to read; one should read only what one wants to read, and if a book disappoints, the reader should not feel obligated to finish it. In effect, Brottman is trying to demystify books, to make them more everyday and less sacred, so that a reader feels free to take them or leave them and to abandon them half read.

This may be seen as liberating for readers or as an abandonment of discipline and restraint. It is, in any event, a different point of view from the more common "reading is good for you" approach, and perhaps it is useful to hear that reading is not necessarily good for you, though it is somewhat ironic that this message should come from a book.

Equally ironic is the fact that when Brottman does finally suggest what reading might be good for—to understand the world and other people—the reader is not entirely ready to agree. Remembering Brottman's account of her teenage years, in which reading was a means of escaping from the world and other people, the reader of this book may think that perhaps the best way to understand the world and other people is to go out into the world and mix with other people.

Brottman's title alludes to masturbation, and her introduction explicitly compares reading to masturbation. They are both done alone, in private, often at night, and in bed. Both involve fantasy and imagination, and both can be addictive. Both were once seen as dangerous, and now, if Brottman is to be believed, both are being excessively promoted.

Brottman's view is that both these practices should be performed in moderation.

Sexual knowledge, including self-knowledge, can be useful, she says, just as reading can be if not taken to addictive extremes. It is an ironic lesson to take from a book such as this.

Sheldon Goldfarb

Review Sources

Publishers Weekly 255, no. 44 (November 3, 2008): 24-34.
San Francisco Bay Guardian 42, no. 29 (April 21, 2008).
Shelf Awareness 1, no. 616 (February 20, 2008).

THE SOUL THIEF

Author: Charles Baxter (1947-   )
Publisher: Pantheon Books (New York). 210 pp. $20.00
Type of work: Novel
Time: The 1970's to the present
Locale: Buffalo, New York; Newark, New Jersey; Los
    Angeles

*Divided into four parts, the novel follows the course of a
single character from graduate school until middle age in
an effort to examine the notion that identity theft may be as
much an internal as an external threat*

Principal characters:
> NATHANIEL MASON, the novel's protagonist
> and presumed narrator, good-looking,
> athletic, and emotionally and
> psychologically vulnerable
> JEROME COOLBERG, the title character, an enigmatic figure that seeks to
> fill an essential emptiness in his life by inhabiting other people's
> narratives
> THERESA, a beautiful poseur, Coolberg's temporary accomplice, and
> Nathaniel's occasional erotic playmate
> JAMIE, a lesbian sculptor and the object of Nathaniel's youthful devotion
> CATHERINE, Nathaniel's sister, the victim of verbal aphasia after the
> untimely death of their father
> LAURA, Nathaniel's wife and the mother of his two sons
> JEREMY, Nathaniel's older son, a teenager coveting predictability
> MICHAEL, Nathaniel's younger son, a precocious youth imaginatively
> embracing the plasticity of identity

In the first of four sections of *The Soul Thief*, Charles Baxter opens up a time capsule of student life during the waning years of the Vietnam War when young people were intent on finding new ways to reshape their world. In this time of social and sexual experimentation, protagonist Nathaniel Mason attends, rain-soaked and barefoot, a free-form party abuzz with intellectual discussion and charged with sexual promise. From room to room he wanders, his transit mirroring the trajectory of graduate study as he takes up and discards snippets of overheard conversations on a variety of topics, all the while seeking to reconnect with a young woman, Theresa, whom he met only moments before on his way to the party but about whom he already feels the jolt of "love-lightning." When he does find her, Theresa is part of a rapt audience gathered around the charismatic Jerome Coolberg, physically unprepossessing but compelling because of the strength of his verbal discourse and the intensity of his interest in Nathaniel.

What the reader eventually discovers is that Theresa serves as little more than bait in Coolberg's scheme to possess Nathaniel's soul. Lacking any inner life of his own, this archetypal role player and "virtuoso of cast-off ideas" seeks to mine the core of other people's identities to see if there is anything of value for his use. Coolberg begins his aggressive examination of Nathaniel by intense peeping and probing; he eventually raises the stakes by hiring a junkie to burglarize the protagonist's apartment. Thereafter, Coolberg can be seen around the city, narrating bits of Nathaniel's biography and wearing some of his stolen clothes.

Charles Baxter, a college teacher and an author, began as a poet, but his critical reputation now rests with his fiction, both short stories and novels, including The Feast of Love *(2000), which was a finalist for the National Book Award.*

As subtext to Coolberg's incremental appropriation of Nathaniel's identity are numerable literary and visual references to the nature of selfhood. Early in his affair with Theresa, for example, Nathaniel takes her to visit the Mirrored Room, a 1966 installation by contemporary Greek American artist Lucas Samaras. Visitors to the Albright-Knox Art Gallery in Buffalo can enter this mirrored eight-foot-by-eight-foot cube and sit on a mirrored chair and rest their hands on a mirrored table. Nathaniel and Theresa react differently to the experience. She is turned on, perhaps because her identity itself resides in surfaces and she finds the multiplication of her own physical image intoxicating. Nathaniel, however, regards the space as "monstrous, meant to undermine the soul by wrapping it in reflections."

Even as a graduate student in literary studies, trained in a multiplicity of critical perspectives and therefore comfortable with the concept of the relativity of meaning, Nathaniel still retains the hope of some consistent inner life, some unchanging selfhood. Perhaps this is the essence of his attraction to the seemingly unattainable Jamie, whose basic orientation is not heterosexual; he loves her for her spirit, embodied in the "skeletal flying machines" that she fashions in her studio. His longing is also reflected in the condition of his sister Catherine, with whom he converses by phone each Sunday; in these "conversations," Nathaniel does all the talking because she has lost the power of speech after the premature death of their father. Despite the fact that Catherine does not audibly respond to his weekly, serial narratives, Nathaniel assumes that his sister's essential self, the being that resides within the mute shell, needs to hear his voice.

Most reviewers agree that it is this first part of the novel that packs the most punch because of Baxter's ability to evoke a place and time, a city redolent of the "noble shabbiness of industrial decline" in the early 1970's, and because of the suspense he generates regarding the possible fate of his much too accessible protagonist.

In the second part of the novel, set in New Jersey some thirty years after the events in Buffalo, the reader learns that it is Catherine who restores Nathaniel to himself after he suffers a nervous breakdown caused, in part, by Coolberg's machinations and prompted, in part, by the rape of Jamie, an act that he suspects Coolberg has instigated. Catherine ventures east from a halfway house in Milwaukee to the Manhattan apartment of their mother and stepfather where Nathaniel has been taken after he "fell into the mirror and swam in the glass," a reference to French artist Jean Cocteau's 1946 film *La Belle et la bête* (*Beauty and the Beast*), wherein a mirror serves as a portal between different planes of reality. His sister reads to him from novels until he eventually can "tell the difference between the actual things and the imaginary ones."

Over time Nathaniel feels well enough to tackle a series of mundane jobs, and this "consensual relationship with routine" restores the order of his life and makes it possible for him to reach out to others. In contrast to the romantic passivity of his graduate-school days, Nathaniel now actively cultivates what passes for middle-class normalcy. He marries Laura, an expert in quilts, products of the piecing together of the fragments of material existence, and they raise two boys. The older one appears straightforward and self-directed; the younger is termed a "wily pipsqueak shape shifter," trying on for size a host of different personae. Nathaniel's sons represent the polarities of his personal selfhood, the lure of the predictable and the call of the unexpected.

Nathaniel sums up the before-and-after nature of his biography when he says that in his youth his "soul was mortgaged" but that in his mature years he has "paid it off through regularity, routine, and hard work."

The third part of the novel necessitates a change of scene, from the suburban backdrop of "a time-server in suburban New Jersey" to the Technicolor dreamscape of Southern California, because Coolberg reenters Nathaniel's life with a surprise invitation to revisit his past. No more suitable working environment could be chosen for Coolberg, who continues to inhabit the lives of others, this time by hosting a radio program that gives him license to seduce his guests into sharing the "secret heart" of their personal narratives. Armed with a free plane ticket and the promise of a room at the aptly named Fatal Hotel, Nathaniel prepares to confront his nemesis.

The perceptive reader, however, may wonder if Coolberg really is a villain or just a projection of some aspect of Nathaniel's own personality. Back in their graduate-school days, Coolberg tries to justify his theft of Nathaniel's property, both mental and physical, by arguing that he is doing research for a book in which his fellow student figures prominently. The volume in question is tentatively titled *Shadow*, and the reader may be tempted to see Coolberg as the embodiment of that darker side of the unconscious self defined by modern psychologist Carl Jung. If Coolberg is the shadow, Jamie must surely represent Nathaniel's anima or life force; time and time again, the reader is informed that Nathaniel is attracted to her because of the vitality of her soul. When she is raped and hospitalized, Nathaniel loses his way.

Nathaniel regains his equilibrium only after he assumes a series of roles, not just that of serial employee (postman, insurance adjuster, assistant newspaper editor, bill collector, service representative for the gas and electric company, and grant writer for a local arts agency) but also that of husband and father. "I am in disguise," he admits. In other words, he has constructed a persona, perhaps at odds with elements of his inner self. He rejects his shadow, as represented by Coolberg's fluid approach to personal identity, and he suppresses his anima, as represented by his loss of contact with Jamie and by his subsequent abandonment of poetry and music, two of the mainstays of his student days. During his youth he acknowledged that "if he didn't live in his imagination half the time, he wouldn't be himself." The carefully constructed sanctuary of his middle-class, middle-aged life is made possible only by living not from within but from without.

Nathaniel may indeed offer a case study in the failure to integrate one's inner and outer life. His own story, which Coolberg provides to him in a typed manuscript at the end of the third section of the novel, may offer corroboration of Coolberg's contention that all Americans are "pretenders" and that in constructing a persona from fragments of other people's biographies, real and imagined, any such individual is "just being a good American."

Like the film industry, which dominates the city where he has taken up residence, Coolberg has made a career of making reference, largely without attribution, not only to other people's lives but also to artifacts of high and low culture, from the novels of twentieth century British author E. M. Forster to the scripts of popular films such as Alfred Hitchcock's *Psycho* (1960); he is someone who claims other people's ideas, images, and experiences as his own.

Coolberg's penchant for appropriation underscores the ambiguity of the novel's fourth and final section, which begins with these two sentences: "Nathaniel Mason enters the silent house. I can easily imagine it." The reader is left to ponder whether Nathaniel's homecoming is just another Coolberg script or whether Nathaniel is indeed the author of his own independent narrative.

The Soul Thief joins Baxter's other works of fiction—novels such as *Saul and Patsy* (2003) and collections of short stories such as *Believers* (1998)—that explore how the apparently quiet lives of everyday people can be forever altered by a chance encounter or comment. In these narratives, the main character's resulting shift in direction often occurs because some external happenstance triggers a subversive predilection that had heretofore lain dormant. In essence, any loss of rudder, any drastic recalibration in the individual's previously predictable course in life can be attributed to forces that are both external and internal. The theft of Nathaniel's soul, for example, may be attributed not only to Coolberg but also to Nathaniel himself, just as the burglarizing of his apartment might be part of Coolberg's plan, as Theresa avows, or the result of Nathaniel's own impractical desire to merge his life with Jamie's. In support of the latter contention, Coolberg asserts that Nathaniel emptied his own place to feed the fantasy of his eventual cohabitation with and eventual conversion of his lesbian lover.

"Willful incomprehension" is, according to Coolberg, Nathaniel's greatest survival tactic, and, by extension, such "convenient amnesia" or "strategic forgetting" is symptomatic of the general American experience. In Coolberg's eyes, this country can be seen as a nation built by people unwilling or unable to look within and take responsibility for their own decisions and deeds. As a consequence, Americans rob themselves of their souls.

S. Thomas Mack

Review Sources

Booklist 104, no. 8 (December 15, 2007): 26.
Kirkus Reviews 75, no. 23 (December 1, 2007): 1211.
Library Journal 133, no. 1 (January 1, 2008): 77-78.
The New Yorker 84, no. 6 (March 24, 2008): 83.
Publishers Weekly 254, no. 44 (November 5, 2007): 40.
Review of Contemporary Fiction 28, no. 1 (Spring, 2008): 168-169.

THE SPIES OF WARSAW

Author: Alan Furst (1941-   )
Publisher: Random House (New York). 266 pp. $25.00
Type of work: Novel
Time: 1937-1940
Locale: Poland, France, and Germany

Furst weaves a complicated and rich web of spies, passion, and intrigue in the period immediately preceding World War II

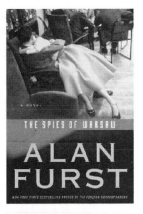

Principal characters:
  COLONEL JEAN-FRANCOIS MERCIER,
    widower, decorated war hero turned
    military attaché
  ARMAND JOURDAIN, political officer and
    Mercier's friend
  ALBERTINE MERCIER, the colonel's cousin
  EDVARD UHL, senior engineer at a munitions plant and reluctant spy
  COUNTESS SCZELENSKA, also known as HANA MUSSER, Uhl's lover
  ANTON VYBORG, Polish military intelligence agent and lover of
    doughnuts
  ANNA SZARBECK, a lawyer for the League of Nations and Mercier's
    sometime companion
  MAREK, Mercier's quiet and complicit driver
  DR. LAPP, Abwehr (Black Front) officer in Warsaw
  MALKA and VIKTOR ROZEN, Russian secret service agents
  AUGUST VOSS, major in the Nazi SS counterintelligence office

As the nations of Europe posture and prepare for war in the autumn of 1937, an intricate subculture of spies and sumptuous living thrives. Initially Alan Furst's *The Spies of Warsaw* appears to be a rather mundane tale of the daily life of mediocre agents: clandestine meetings, bits and pieces of boring information exchanged in protracted secret. Colonel Jean-Francois Mercier has retired from distinguished military service during the war to end all wars (World War I) and has settled into a bureaucratic job. Although it is not his beloved France, there are some gastronomic and other perks seasoned with a dash of minor espionage to be found in Warsaw. Mercier meets periodically with Edvard Uhl, an engineer at an ironworks that produces tanks for the Germans. Uhl proves to be a skittish spy, who only reluctantly provides seemingly innocuous information about tank production.

"Hotel Europejski" starts slowly. The author paints the scenes with care and exquisite detail. Situated in the heart of prewar Warsaw, the hotel is the site of periodic trysts between Uhl and his mysterious mistress, Countess Sczelenska. She captures Uhl's heart but also manages to snuggle comfortably into his pocketbook. She explains to him that, unless he helps to subsidize her living arrangements, her desperate

Alan Furst is considered a master of the historical spy novel. His work, which includes Night Soldiers *(1988),* Dark Star *(1991), and* The Polish Officer *(1995), has been translated into seventeen languages. A New Yorker by birth, Furst divides his time between Paris and Long Island.*

financial situation will force her to move in with her aunt, who resides in Chicago. He does not want to lose her or at least the comfort of her loving. He agrees to a proposal that the countess suggests: her cousin knows a man who hires "industrial experts." Poor Uhl is hooked. The new but profitable liaison introduces him into a game of espionage and fear. The countess's identity is somewhat in doubt: Is she really of aristocratic blood, or is she a part of the shadowy network of spies and intrigue that weaves itself in and out of the novel's pages?

Uhl's life becomes more complicated. His anxiety over what he is doing causes him to appear nervous as he rides the train across the Polish border back home to Breslau. Although he successfully avoids a compromising encounter with Nazi SS officers, a dutiful citizen, Frau Schimmel, reports his suspicious behavior to the authorities. The tentacles of German intelligence, controlled by August Voss, reach out to encircle poor Uhl. Will the contact with Mercier bring him disaster or salvation? At the very least it will become clear that his spying and philandering days are behind him, as is his life as a family man and ordinary engineer of Breslau.

The pace of the book heats up as Mercier moves in "On Raven Hill." Determined to discover the specifics of Adolf Hitler's plans for the invasion of Europe, Mercier travels in his trusty Buick with his faithful and resourceful driver, Marek, to the Polish-German border. The colonel's goal is to ascertain the most likely point of German invasion, which he assumes will be launched with tanks. He ventures into the forest through which he speculates Germany will invade. However, tanks do not go into forests, at least that is the firm opinion of Mercier's superiors. Quick page turning promises to resolve for the reader the questions of whether Mercier's forays into enemy territory will be discovered, whether he will be caught, and whether his assessment of the location of the looming threat is accurate.

The action of the book heats up as additional persons of interest come on stage. Viktor and Malka Rozen, known to be Russian spies, are among the guests at the lavish cocktail party hosted by the Polish Foreign Ministry. Such parties provide ample opportunity for tidbits of rich food as well as of random bits of intelligence, as the guests intermingle in the rich tapestry of spydom. One never knows whom one will meet or whether a morsel of cocktail chitchat is a clue to some important information. The seemingly casual encounter between Mercier and the Rozens illustrates such an exchange. It opens the way to more danger, more clandestine information, and a broadening of Mercier's scope of work into much more dangerous areas than the insignificant bar where money and blueprints are swapped between him and the ill-fated Uhl.

Eventually Mercier is placed in contact with the Black Front, a subversive group of German patriots who are dissatisfied with the leadership and goals of Hitler. Mercier's toe in the door is a mysterious Dr. Lapp, who introduces himself to Mercier at yet another dinner party. This encounter opens a treasure trove of interesting information about the war plans of Hitler's regime and introduces him to people who will put Mercier's life and theirs in greater danger. He moves in and out of territory under the control of the Germans, often right under their noses or their probing spotlights. He risks his own life and safety, as he helps to bring his contacts to freedom and security.

The final pages of the novel are increasingly under the "Shadow of War." By spring of 1938, the Allies more and more expect the Germans to move against them. Mercier himself is shadowed by the tenacious Voss. Because of the affair with Uhl, Mercier has made himself a virulent enemy. During a visit to an outlying factory, Mercier is brutally attacked by a group of thugs. This assault is a function of Voss's private vendetta rather than a discovery of Mercier's work. Although Mercier narrowly escapes, due to the quick action of his faithful chauffeur, Malek, this is not the end of his troubles. A foray into Berlin, to make contact with members of the Black Front, will ratchet up the danger for Mercier as well as the anxiety of the reader. Plots involving gathering information about the invasion, attempts to engineer the escapes from Germany of two men who agree to supply information to Mercier, and close encounters with the bad guys are all well played out.

Exquisite description drips from every page of the book. The lavishness of the scenery, with details on everything from the soft texture of the earth that hides tank traps in a border forest to the entertainment at a lavish party (a magician as well as a songstress), presents a vivid canvas into which the reader can almost step. One can smell the fragrance of the ponczkis, the irresistible jelly doughnuts that inevitably insert themselves between Mercier and Polish intelligence officer Anton Vyborg whenever they meet. One can almost taste the select wine, the perfectly cooked sole, the Polish chicken soup with heavy twisted noodles, the pork and sauerkraut. The reader is left drooling for more, even as the characters in the book are sated and push away their plates. Even Mercier's lady's lacy underwear—another "black front"—is carefully described, leaving little to the imagination.

The author uses an occasional interlude into Mercier's family life perhaps to allow the reader to rest from the novel's constant sense of danger and foreboding. He tells of Mercier's boyhood introduction to sex by his cousin, the assertive Albertine. He details the loneliness and longing of the widowed colonel, which is eventually abated by the beautiful Anna Szarbek in a passionate affair. Furst opens a window to the family holiday celebrations as well as to the aristocratic history of the Mercier family. With the introduction of Mercier's two daughters, now living in other countries, some insight into the foreshadowing of war is seen from the perspective of countries less prominent in the lead-up to the war. Detailed is the selling of Jewish assets, the general fallout of Hitler's corrosive projects.

The Spies of Warsaw is not just a compelling story of intrigue and sometimes caricatured behavior. It is a lavish picture of a certain slice of international life in the late 1930's, which draws the reader into the intimacy of the private life of its main character and the vast reach of the world scene of the time. The wine, the six-course dinners, the sets at the tennis club, the clandestine sexual encounters—all provide the reader with a savory picture. It is no wonder Furst is known as the master of the spy novel.

His marvelous descriptions of great food and drink show why he is featured in the Absolut vodka commercial. His work is absolutely satisfying.

Occasionally the author comes close to sinking into clichés that might have been stolen from hackneyed spy films. There are the required false-bottom suitcases, the exchange of secret messages, the stereotypical SS men, the message left on a certain page in a specified phone book. Even so, the author holds himself to an effective discipline of structure.

A minor annoyance is the surfeit of characters, which forces the less diligent reader to page back in order to remember. The author would have done well to use the technique of reestablishing the identity of those who come and go in the many pages. Perhaps that is part of the intrigue of the spy novel, however. One never quite knows who is who and who will turn out to be someone—or something—else than they appear. The many layers of the book—family and personal stories, the extravagant description, and the shivers of danger under the cold shadow of impending war—hold the attention of the reader throughout. Likely, with some conflation of several characters, the novel will find its way to a successful film. One is eager to see Vyborg's ponczkis and Anna's black lace underwear on the big screen.

Dolores L. Christie

Review Sources

Booklist 104, no. 14 (March 15, 2008): 6.
Forbes 182, no. 7 (October 13, 2008): 20.
Kirkus Reviews 76, no. 8 (April 15, 2008): 383.
Library Journal 133, no. 6 (April 1, 2008): 75.
The New York Times, June 14, 2008, p. 7.
The New York Times Book Review, June 29, 2008, p. 9.
Publishers Weekly 255, no. 15 (April 14, 2008): 35.
The Times Literary Supplement, July 25, 2008, p. 20.

A STEP FROM DEATH

Author: Larry Woiwode (1941-   )
Publisher: Counterpoint (Berkeley, Calif.). 272 pp.
    $24.00
Type of work: Memoir
Time: The present and the 1970's
Locale: North Dakota

*Woiwode's memoir juxtaposes a series of traumatic ac-
cidents against the composition of his most important novel,*
Beyond the Bedroom Wall

> *Principal personages:*
> LARRY WOIWODE, an author, farmer, and
>   part-time professor
> CARE WOIWODE, his wife
> JOSEPH WOIWODE, his son
> EVERETT WOIWODE, his father
> WILLIAM MAXWELL, his friend, an editor at *The New Yorker* magazine

Larry Woiwode's memoir *A Step from Death* is more a successor than a sequel to
his first memoir, *What I Think I Did: A Season of Survival in Two Acts* (2000). Much
like its predecessor, *A Step from Death* is a loosely structured and meandering memoir focused on ideas more than a simple recounting of a straightforward, linear narrative rendering a particular time in an author's life. As such, the book's shifting structure is anchored by two conceits. First, the book is presented as a letter to the author's
son, Joseph, in the tradition of the *Autobiography of Benjamin Franklin* (1791). The
book begins, "So, dear son, where to begin?" As reviewers have noted, this conceit
becomes slightly tenuous at times because Woiwode, in telling stories from his past,
must recount and elaborate upon events and circumstances that his son Joseph presumably would already know about in some detail. Nevertheless, Woiwode explains
both his aim and his method when he addresses his son and readers, stating,

> Every detail I stumble over or move away to clear a path to the exit is a fragment of
> memory, and memory is a contract between the past and our instinct to shape it into a
> story that will cohere far into the future. A memoir should recognize that contract and
> dissolve the distance between us, and by that I mean not only the attentive reader, my
> soul's semblance, my mirror, my brother or sister, but mostly you, Joseph, my only son.

The other tactic used in *A Step from Death* to build a thematic and idea-focused
memoir (as opposed to a conventional chronologically organized narrative) is the
story's springing back and forth between an alarming number of traumatic accidents.
Woiwode tells of a recent tractor accident in which he is almost killed that requires
him to endure painful rehabilitation for months; another time, he is involved in an al-
most-fatal car wreck. His son Joseph is a victim of so many accidents that he seems to

Larry Woiwode has won the William Faulkner Foundation Award for What I'm Going to Do, I Think *(1969), a Guggenheim Fellowship (1971-1972), the John Dos Passos Prize in 1991, and the* Southern Review *Award for Short Fiction. His book* Beyond the Bedroom Wall *(1975) was nominated for the National Book Award and the National Book Critics Circle Award. He was designated the North Dakota Poet Laureate in 1995.*

be prone to them: He is seriously injured by a horse, suffering brain damage and lying in a coma for a time; he is shot in the leg by a loaded gun that falls to the floor and discharges; he burns down the barn with his brother; and he almost loses part of his hand in a lawn-mower accident.

Despite the use of the two conceits as thematic guideposts, the book's structure is wandering and scattered, operating scene by scene and vignette by vignette in an almost stream-of-consciousness way, although Woiwode's sentence-to-sentence prose style is as clear and as carefully crafted as ever. However diverse and random the varied narratives telling the back and forth of Woiwode's life, on a thematic level the stories build upon each other and slowly help the reader to grasp the author's subtle but evident aims. Even as the memoir depicts Woiwode's tractor accident (when a power takeoff shaft on a baler pulled his loose jacket down into the device, slamming him against the implement, binding him brutally, breaking a number of ribs, and savagely wrenching his arms) and then his subsequent difficulties with recovery, the narrative springs back to his early days as a newly successful writer, having completed *What I'm Going to Do, I Think* (1969) and moving on into the series of vignettes that would eventually cohere into *Beyond the Bedroom Wall* (1975). In many ways, the memoir is about this tractor accident (just as it is about fathers and sons and the ever-present reality of death and writing): It is about the things that wrench, bind, and hurt individuals—and how they can free themselves from such bonds.

As Woiwode recounts the early days and his work on his novel, he emerges as a man obsessed with his work and driven to write and rewrite his book over many years. He describes (in perhaps too little detail) how his singular focus on completing his book almost destroyed his marriage and how he eventually learned to place the things in his life in their proper priority.

Even as the book bounces between Larry and Joseph Woiwode's various accidents and a fragmented portrait of the artist as a young man, father, and husband emerges, the setting of the old farm purchased by Woiwode and his wife remains central to the story. Woiwode and his wife strove to maintain the place as a working farm, raising "organic" produce even before that label became popularized. His various academic positions seem to fall short in his estimation when compared to working the farm, and, as he puts it, the farm and working on the land represent an Edenic escape.

One never knows how much weight to place on metaphors in a work of nonfiction, but in this case the figurative link is undeniable: Even as a farmer must nourish and nurture his land to make it fruitful and profitable, Woiwode, as both artist and man, had to maintain a grip on the things in life that truly nourished him, such as his wife and children, his North Dakota farm, and his connection to the land. Only through keeping matters in perspective could he truly grow and prosper.

As much as the book is a memoir, it is also—as indicated by how it is addressed to Woiwode's son, Joseph—a book about fathers and sons. Chapters are titled "Sonship," "Child as Father," and "Father as Child." Woiwode's thoughts about Joseph (and Joseph's near brushes with death) lead him to think about his own father and his conflicted feelings, equal parts reverence and resentment. As he states, "I was not a dependable son, no stalwart behind my father. It was too easy for me to find flaws in him, and this blurred my ability, I believe, to be transparent with you, Joseph, as the best fathers are." Not only does Woiwode think about his father (a man twice widowed—Woiwode's mother died when he was a young man, similar to how the Neumiller children lose their mother in *Beyond the Bedroom Wall*), but also he spends a good deal of time describing famous *New Yorker* magazine editor and novelist William Maxwell, a surrogate father figure and a father to the artistic side of Woiwode's life.

The focus upon fathers and sons, when considered alongside the various times that Woiwode and Joseph are "a step from death," perhaps shows how the scattered and varied pieces of the puzzle of *A Step from Death* can be placed into a coherent and cohesive whole.

As his career grew, Woiwode became known as a spiritual writer, and at heart *A Step from Death* is a spiritual book. Woiwode describes how, after having pushed his wife as far as he could in his need to finish the sprawling *Beyond the Bedroom Wall*, she finally confronted him, saying, "I've stood by you all these years. . . and this last year was the worst. I need a spiritual connection!" When Woiwode asks her, "What do you mean, 'a spiritual connection'?" she tells him, "*God*, you ass!" At some level, the focus throughout the book on fathers and sons—including Woiwode's almost adulatory stance toward his son (a helicopter pilot serving in Iraq at the time of the book's writing), his relationship as a son to both his biological father and his artistic one, William Maxwell—perhaps relates to his spiritual growth and relationship with God, his heavenly father. If, as the memoir suggests, life is fleeting and short, and death can take anyone at any time and in any way (a horse can fall on a boy, a farmer's jacket can catch in a spinning shaft, a driver can lose control of a car on an icy road, a loaded gun can fall and discharge a bullet into its owner), then life is that much more precious. Lives must be worth living, and they must stand for something when they are over. In some ways, the author clearly has regrets, and he lists more moments of embarrassing failure and immature actions on his part than he does his successes. He gets drunk and makes an abortive attempt at seducing his agent, he is unkind to his father, and he even drives away his young wife. His son Joseph, on the other hand, is liked by all, an eternal optimist, a hard worker, and intent on dedicating himself to helping others.

Ultimately, the author's decision to springboard between vignettes and proselytizing commentaries anchored by thematic unities (brushes with death, ruminations upon fatherhood, the importance of farm life, the problems with academics) is both a strength and a weakness. A certain tension builds as the writer rotates back to his crisis when bound against the hay baler or to his son's comatose state and slow recovery after his accident with a horse, and the sporadic shifts help highlight the thematic connections among the various scenes. On the other hand, there are too many instances in which the memoir fails to adequately follow through on a topic, not fulfilling a reader's reasonable expectations. For example, the memoirist's reconciliation with his wife in the waning days of his work on *Beyond the Bedroom Door* is given short shrift, although presumably this time would have been the beginning of a period of spiritual awakening for him.

In the end, *A Step from Death* is the kind of book a reader would expect from a writer who had previously published books about men driven to the edge by their obsessions (as in *What I'm Going to Do, I Think*), a book composed of a series of thematically related sequences and scenes (as in *Beyond the Bedroom Wall*) and a book on modern Christianity (*Acts*, published in 1993). Despite its structural complexity, it serves as a memoir not so much of a particular time in a writer's life so much as an explanation of how he became who he is today—in heart and in soul.

Scott Yarbrough

Review Sources

America 199, no. 4 (August 18, 2008): 26.
Booklist 104, nos. 9/10 (January 1, 2008): 21.
The Christian Century 125, no. 13 (July 1, 2008): 41.
Christianity Today 52, no. 8 (August, 2008): 58.
Entertainment Weekly, March 21, 2008, p. 63.
Kirkus Reviews 76, no. 1 (January 1, 2008): 34.
Library Journal 133, no. 4 (March 1, 2008): 83.
The New York Times Book Review, March 30, 2008, p. 17.
Publishers Weekly 255, no. 2 (January 14, 2008): 52.
The Wall Street Journal 251, no. 56 (March 8, 2008): W8.

THE STORY OF A MARRIAGE

Author: Andrew Sean Greer (1970-   )
Publisher: Farrar, Straus and Giroux (New York).
   195 pp. $22.00
Type of work: Novel
Time: World War II to the late twentieth century
Locale: San Francisco

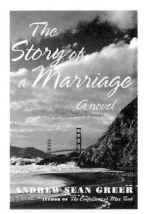

An unusual triangle is at the center of this novel about love and war, told from the point of view of a black woman transplanted from a Midwestern farming community to the city

Principal characters:
> PEARLIE COOK, the narrator of the novel
> HOLLAND COOK, her teenage sweetheart
>   and later husband
> CHARLES ("BUZZ") DRUMER, a white man who befriends Holland in the war
> SONNY ("WALTER") COOK, Pearlie and Holland's only child
> ALICE and BEATRICE, Holland's elderly cousins, considered his "aunts"

The year is 1953, and when Pearlie Cook, the narrator of Andrew Sean Greer's quietly affecting novel, *The Story of a Marriage*, sits down each morning, she dutifully clips the bad news from the paper to prevent her husband, Holland, from reading anything that would upset his supposedly delicate health. There is, at this time in America, much that she needs to censor: the Korean War and the Cold War spread of nuclear weapons; the House subcommittee hearings on Communist sympathizers and the entrapment of sexual deviants who might prove a special threat to national security; the execution of Julius and Ethel Rosenberg on charges of spying for Russia, and Eisenhower's refusal to commute that sentence; the regulations against burying Negro soldiers in certain cemeteries, Ku Klux Klan cross burnings, and racial discrimination in housing. The last items are of interest because Pearlie and Holland are black. Greer masterfully limns this background against which the story of the Cooks' marriage plays itself out, reminding readers that the early 1950's, with their fear and paranoia, were not nearly as placid as they often have been portrayed.

Pearlie and Holland met each other when they were growing up in rural Kentucky during World War II. A bright girl who memorized poetry but accounted herself as less than attractive, Pearlie was smitten by something as simple as Holland holding her hand. When Holland's mother—for this is partly a story about how women try to keep their men from having to go off to war—hid him from the draft until an illness necessitated calling in a doctor, Pearlie visited and read to him. After he was drafted, a government official persuaded her to go to California and work in an airplane factory, where she could gather evidence of any unpatriotic behavior. After Holland returns

Andrew Sean Greer, who lives in San Francisco, has published a collection of short stories, How It Was for Me *(2000), and two earlier novels, including the acclaimed best seller* The Confessions of Max Tivoli *(2005). He has been awarded the New York Public Library Young Lions Fiction Award.*

shell-shocked from a naval attack in the Pacific, they meet again by accident in San Francisco, where Pearlie immediately feels an urge to care for the ashen-faced, despairing ex-soldier, who still exudes "masculine grace" and seductive beauty. Holland, like many soldiers craving the normalcy of civilian life, has a desperate need that she marry him. So they do marry and settle down in the barely integrated community of Ocean Beach. His maiden "aunts," Alice and Beatrice, who fabricate a Hawaiian rather than an African American ancestry and prefer to live in a segregated area, hint at Holland's "bad blood" and "crooked heart" that must be protected. By 1953, after having fathered Sonny, who contracts polio, Holland is sleeping in a separate bedroom.

It is not until a mysterious white stranger, Charles "Buzz" Drumer, appears on their doorstep bearing a gift of silver top-hat cufflinks for Holland's birthday and confesses to having been "together" with Holland as lovers during the war that Pearlie finally understands what has been eating at her husband's heart that the two cousins refused to name. It is recalling the shock of this newfound awareness that propels Pearlie's retrospective meditation—by the time she tells the tale, Holland is long dead from kidney failure and Sonny is fifty years old—on how lovers, at base, remain always strangers to one another. Greer has Pearlie assert this insight at the novel's beginning and reiterate it several times throughout. As the story opens, Pearlie remarks about being able to love only "the poor translation" she has made of the other, without being able to "get past it to the original." Later she comments on the loneliness and heartbreak that come from the "silence and lies" between even husband and wife that make their life at best "a fiction." Still later she muses about how, in the face of the heart remaining hidden, the lover re-creates the loved one according to how she wishes him to be.

Pearlie, in fact, comes to know Buzz Drumer better than she ever knew her husband, though perhaps she just fails—or consciously chooses not—to report more of what goes on behind the closed doors of their marriage. If Holland fought in the war only because he was dragged off to it, Buzz, who now owns a profitable business that makes women's foundation garments but lives sparely in a rooming house, was a conscientious objector. Sent to a Quaker-run work camp rife with bigotry and prejudice that was as much a prison as a site for enforced labor clearing tree stumps, he apparently found there gay companions before he was chosen to participate in a medical experiment designed to see how little food war refugees needed to survive. Starved and emaciated, so that no one could possibly love him, he eventually plunged into a kind of madness, finally eating off his little finger. It is thus that he comes to share a room in a veterans' hospital with Holland and their affair begins. Now he reappears in Holland's life and tries to wrest him away from Pearlie.

Instead of demanding that Holland reject the interloper and throw him out, Pearlie somewhat surprisingly insists he make a choice between her and his former lover. Knowing that Holland, whom she describes as physically "beaten out of gold," has always been an object of admiration and alluring to the eyes of both sexes, she wants him to name his desire rightly. The "aunts," who have always known more of the truth than they let on, caution her against jealousy and counsel her to avert her eyes from the unpleasant facts. Pearlie, who feels that she has at times tried to pass for white, even surreptitiously visits a gay bar in North Beach to see what she calls "the change-ling boys," transvestite dancers forced to wear badges announcing their true gender to ward off being arrested. Ready to be won over by Buzz's need, she entertains his offer of financial security for her and Sonny, which makes her feel little better than her "husband's procuress." She and Buzz even concoct a plan to turn Holland's attentions away from a white woman, Annabel, to whom, in his sexual uncertainties, he seems to be attracted. They report her fiancé Walter, who has been excused from the draft because of a clerical error that lists his brother as already serving overseas, to the authorities, only to suffer guilt when he is seriously injured in boot camp and returns home permanently disabled. Given the chance, however, to be free of his marriage, at the last minute Holland, after a physical altercation, decides to stay with her and Sonny.

If Holland remains unknowable to her, so, too, was Pearlie a "greater mystery" to him: Believing she wanted what only Buzz could give her, he "got [her] wrong." When thinking back on how she defined her role, Pearlie calls upon the example of two of "history's wives" who also did not speak out against their husbands: Eslanda Goode Robeson, who took the Fifth Amendment rather than incriminate her actor husband Paul, and, especially, Ethel Rosenberg, who was forced to bear with her husband the shame of the whole affair and to see her silence blamed for war, communism, death, and possible annihilation. Pearlie, who shed tears that it took two shocks to kill Ethel (after she had bloodied her hands on the mesh screen that kept her apart from Julius), wonders why she did not confess to save her life, concluding that Ethel remained steadfast to the principle of "the smallest atom of a wife that cannot be split apart."

More than forty years later, Buzz unexpectedly reenters Pearlie's life, through a chance meeting of Sonny, long after Sonny had been called upon to make his own difficult choices during the tumultuous period of the Vietnam War, whose peace demonstrations and draft card burnings are tellingly sketched in by Greer. Pearlie punctuates her narrative by remarking that although it began as a story of love and marriage, "the war has stuck to it everywhere like shattered glass," providing a perspective on three different conflicts: World War II, Korea, and Vietnam. Holland's mother tried to keep him safe from a war that was not "our war," referring to the fact that blacks were even segregated in the armed forces. Pearlie, on the other hand, in a misguided moment, effectually sent Walter off to fight in Korea. When it comes time for Sonny to be drafted, however, she supports his decision to flee to Canada, where he has a child by a Chinese woman. Men either go to war or do not go to war: During World War II, men felt both fear of and shame over not serving, and threats to their manliness on both counts; during the Vietnam War, personal integrity might require a quite different response. Women either send their men to war or, in Greer's hands, do everything in their power to protect them from it. In this case, Pearlie decides to shelter Sonny from something else as well. Now an executive with a nonprofit agency in the East, married to a white woman, and father of a son, he comes to San Francisco on business, inviting his mother to breakfast and to renew her acquaintance with Buzz. Questioned by Sonny about the nature of her relationship with this other man, she is unwilling to admit the truth and does nothing to disabuse her son of the notion that she and Buzz must once have been lovers. And so the true nature of Holland's sexuality remains hidden, even to his son. She cannot confront Buzz again after all these years, unwilling to tell him that Holland "loved [her] more."

Of the three central players in Greer's triangle, Holland is the most elusive, with the reader never really let into his life—even though it is told by the one he chose to stay with and who remained with him until his death. This, however, may well be a deliberate strategy on the author's part. Not only does it reemphasize the unknowability of the loved one to the lover, but it foregrounds the closeted nature of Holland's existence in mid-twentieth century America. He was black, and being homosexual as well made him doubly the outsider. So the nature of Holland's love puts him at war with himself. Forced into a heterosexual marriage that accorded with society's norms, he could never truly be himself or articulate an identity in keeping with his nature. As Greer writes in a haunting line that introduces the final section of this understated short novel with its masterful control of first-person viewpoint, "America, you give a lovely death."

Thomas P. Adler

Review Sources

Booklist 104, no. 17 (May 1, 2008): 73.
Entertainment Weekly, May 9, 2008, p. 67.
Kirkus Reviews 76, no. 5 (March 1, 2008): 210.
The New York Times Book Review, May 11, 2008, p. 35.
The New Yorker 84, no. 12 (May 5, 2008): 78-79.
Publishers Weekly 255, no. 4 (January 28, 2008): 38.
The Times Literary Supplement, June 27, 2008, p. 20.

THE STORY OF EDGAR SAWTELLE

Author: David Wroblewski (1959-   )
Publisher: Ecco Press (New York). 566 pp. $25.95
Type of work: Novel
Time: 1919 to 1970
Locale: Wisconsin and South Korea

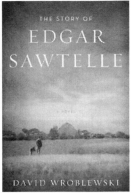

*The mute Sawtelle grows up in rural Wisconsin, helping
his parents raise and train highly intelligent dogs*

Principal characters:
EDGAR SAWTELLE, a mute boy
GAR SAWTELLE, his father, a dog breeder
TRUDY SAWTELLE, his mother, a dog
trainer
JOHN SAWTELLE, his grandfather, a dog
breeder
MARY SAWTELLE, his grandmother
CLAUDE SAWTELLE, Gar's mysterious brother
DOCTOR PAGE PAPINEAU, a veterinarian
GLEN PAPINEAU, his son, a sheriff
HENRY LAMB, Edgar's friend
DOCTOR FROST, a physician
ALMONDINE, a dog who becomes a second mother to Edgar

Few first novels receive the kind of attention afforded David Wroblewski's *The Story of Edgar Sawtelle*. The forty-nine-year-old writer's initial effort won glowing reviews, reached the top of *The New York Times* best-seller list, and was chosen by Oprah's Book Club, a guarantee of good word of mouth and brisk sales. A coming-of-age story, a dog tale, and a nostalgic look at America's recent past, the book is also highly literary.

After opening with a prologue set in South Korea during 1952, an episode that seems to have little relation to the rest of the novel until midway through, *The Story of Edgar Sawtelle* traces the evolution of the Sawtelle family's dog-breeding enterprise. After John Sawtelle fails as a dairy farmer near Mellen, Wisconsin, in the 1920's, he discovers he likes having the seven puppies of his dog, Violet, around, and he has a vision of breeding perfect dogs by following the theories of geneticist Gregor Mendel: "dogs so unlike the shepherds and hounds and retrievers and sled dogs he used as foundation stock they became known simply as Sawtelle dogs."

Much of *The Story of Edgar Sawtelle* examines the disappointments of family life experienced by John's son Gar, his wife Trudy, and their mute son Edgar during the early 1970's. A foster child, Trudy has a strong need for family ties, and she is crushed by a miscarriage before Edgar is born in 1958. His muteness is a small price to pay for his survival. Then there is Gar's estranged brother, Claude, who returns after an absence of many years to help with the dogs, despite fluctuating tensions between the

~

David Wroblewski grew up in a dairy region near the Chequamegon National Forest, where The Story of Edgar Sawtelle *is set. After studying acting at the University of Wisconsin, he switched to computer science and worked in software development for twenty-five years. He has a degree from the Warren Wilson M.F.A. Program for Writers in North Carolina and lives in Colorado with writer Kimberly McClintock.*

~

brothers: "Edgar got the idea that Claude and his father had slipped without their knowing it into some irresistible rhythm of taunt and reply whose references were too subtle or too private to decipher." Wroblewski explains the troubles between the brothers a bit at a time, and when matters seem resolved, the unexpected arrives. The narrative seems to flow smoothly for long periods only to backtrack upon itself with each new surprise.

Wroblewski describes the daily activities with the dogs in detail: feeding, training, exercising, playing, observing, cleaning their quarters in the barn. No time off is possible from "the work that never ended." Because of the immaculate records they keep, Gar and Trudy have photographs of every dog they have raised but none of themselves. These records form a strong bond between Edgar and the past, which he explores in an effort to understand the present.

When Edgar is finally old enough to be given a litter to look after, he takes delight in naming them, consulting *The New Webster Encyclopedic Dictionary of the English Language* to find fitting names: Baboo, Essay, Finch, Opal, Pout, Tinder, and Umbra. The boy counters his muteness with pleasure in the meanings and sounds of words. Language is a means of exerting some control over his life, and not being able to hear or read words when circumstances force him to run away with three dogs makes him feel even more isolated. As he ages and takes on more responsibilities, Edgar realizes how much he is like his father, "so certain he was right," and comes to see the possibly malevolent Claude with Gar's suspicious eyes, realizing there is "not one Claude but many." Trudy's acceptance of Claude's presence leads to further tensions.

Because of Edgar's muteness, the dogs must learn a modified version of the signs he uses to communicate with his parents, signs he first tests on Almondine, the family's only pet. These signs become especially important when Edgar runs away. Much like Charles Frazier did in *Cold Mountain* (1997), whose style and pace *The Story of Edgar Sawtelle* resembles, Wroblewski shifts his narrative focus several times. Edgar's adventure in the Wisconsin woods, similar to the homeward journey of Frazier's hero, is the most tightly constructed and gripping part of the novel, as Edgar steals food from vacation cabins, hides from the police, and is injured in a freak accident. Again like Frazier, Wroblewski is an outstanding storyteller, embellishing his narrative with literary archetypes, such as the symbolic uses of fire and water, which can both purify or destroy.

Several of the dogs are almost as fully developed as the humans. Almondine assumes responsibility for the infant Edgar, instinctively realizing his silence means he needs extra care. His earliest memory is of her beside his crib. During the following years, she is always there to love, to help, even to scold, becoming like a second mother. Edgar exults in having different relationships with Trudy, Gar, and the dog:

"If he managed to share one secret with his father and a different one with his mother and yet another with Almondine the world felt that much larger."A mysterious stray dog spotted several times in the woods seems to be the reincarnation of an earlier Sawtelle dog and also has parallels with Claude.

Wroblewski's style often echoes the short, simple declarative sentences of another Midwestern writer, Ernest Hemingway: "They walked into the dark kitchen together. The kitchen clock read 2:25. Almondine lay near the porch door." Wroblewski's evocation of nature, specifically the glories of the American Middle West, recall the descriptive writing of Hemingway in such stories as "The Big Two-Hearted River" (1925). In addition to conveying the sights, sounds, and smells of the land, Wroblewski presents rural Wisconsin as a calming, peaceful place until humans interfere. Edgar considers his home a self-contained world where everything has a degree of logic. When this is no longer true and he leaves, his universe expands in surprising ways. As in Hemingway's story, nature offers the possibilities of escape and of healing. However, like Hemingway's hero, Edgar must return to a more threatening reality.

Edgar identifies with Mowgli in Rudyard Kipling's *The Jungle Book* (1894), but the major literary influence does not become clear until Gar's death, with similarities to William Shakespeare's *Hamlet* (pr. c. 1600-1601). Shakespeare's play and *The Story of Edgar Sawtelle* share treatments of discord and suspicions within families, revenge, and the psychological turmoil of their protagonists. Edgar is Hamlet; Gar, or Edgar, Sr., is the ghost of Hamlet's father, also named Hamlet; Trudy is Gertrude; Claude is Claudius; Page Papineau, the family veterinarian and business investor, is Polonius; his son, Glen, the sheriff, is Laertes; and Almondine, in an unusual twist, resembles Ophelia.

Wroblewski does not allow his homage to become predictably mechanical, with some character similarities and plot developments much stronger than others. For example, Edgar's biggest dilemma, like Hamlet's indecision, is "To wait and watch or to run away." The *Hamlet* subplot, although significant, is also only a portion of a larger canvas on which Wroblewski paints his characters and their way of life. Familiarity with Shakespeare's masterpiece is not essential to appreciating *The Story of Edgar Sawtelle*, though the novel's conclusion will make more sense to those who know Hamlet's story.

Wroblewksi's prose is often poetic, as with this prophetic description of Gar: "As he passed through a stand of aspen saplings he seemed to shimmer into place between their trunks like a ghost." A disused car gives "the impression of an animal that had crawled to within inches of its lair before expiring." When John buys the farm where he will breed his dogs, he receives a telegram from his lawyer: "OFFER ACCEPTED SEE ADAMSKI RE PAPERS." Edgar periodically looks at this document, and every time he takes out this telegram, a word falls off until only ACCEPTED is left. Wroblewski pays close attention to such details throughout the novel, making such minutiae reflect the larger picture.

Compared with such popular nonfiction dog books as John Grogan's *Marley and Me: Life and Love with the World's Worst Dog* (2005), *The Story of Edgar Sawtelle* is full of touching moments but is generally restrained, more in keeping with the tone of Jon Katz's *A Dog Year: Twelve Months, Four Dogs, and Me* (2002). In addition to Almondine's touching devotion to Edgar and her ability to experience an even deeper grief than the humans, owners bring their Sawtelle dogs to Gar's funeral, both in tribute and in showing an awareness that these dogs have an active emotional life. Wroblewski makes the almost human qualities exhibited by the dogs, with their distinct personalities, credible by constantly reinforcing how they differ from ordinary dogs: "From the moment they opened their eyes the dogs were taught to watch and listen and trust. To think and choose. This was the lesson behind every minute of training. They were taught something beyond simple obedience: that through the training all things could be spoken." In a pivotal scene late in the novel, some dogs are faced with making an important decision and, after seemingly weighing their options, make the right choice. Edgar both teaches the dogs and learns from them, becoming an unusually keen observer, a characteristic central to his quest to distinguish between possible versions of the truth. This quest leads him to using the dogs to stage a canine variation of "The Mousetrap" scene from *Hamlet*.

Wroblewski creates vivid characters with seeming ease. In addition to Edgar and Trudy, the most sympathetic characters, there is Henry Lamb, a lonely man Edgar meets well into his journey away from home. The guileless, trusting Henry serves as counterpoint to the moral confusion Edgar is fleeing. The way the dogs take to him proves he is a good man. Henry is, however, far from a sentimental creation: He is a forlorn defeatist who retreats from life after his fiancé rejects him for being too ordinary. He and Edgar help each other become wiser and more alive. The sequence in which Edgar cleans out Henry's crammed, untidy shed only for his friend to decide to put everything back is a miniaturization of the novel's treatment of the importance of work and the need to impose order on chaos.

Trudy tells Edgar about a theory of Doctor Frost, their family physician, that all people have flaws in their veins and arteries that can be fatal, though no one knows why only some are affected. These flaws are metaphors for the lives of Wroblewski's damaged, imperfect characters, each of whom responds differently to the crises in their lives. *The Story of Edgar Sawtelle* celebrates the commonplace while gazing at the mysteries lurking within the ordinary. Wroblewski summarizes his theme after a series of important decisions have been made: "Life was a swarm of accidents waiting in the treetops, descending upon any living thing that passed, ready to eat them alive. You swam in a river of chance and coincidence. You clung to the happiest accidents—the rest you let float by. . . . You looked around and discovered the most unusual thing in the world sitting there looking at you."

The Story of Edgar Sawtelle is about the value of work, about balancing independence with the need for companionship, and it never pushes its themes too hard. Equally compelling as a family drama, an adventure story, and a murder mystery, the novel deserves its lavish praise.

Michael Adams

Review Sources

Booklist 104, nos. 19/20 (June 1, 2008): 45.
Entertainment Weekly, June 13, 2008, p. 75.
Kirkus Reviews 76, no. 7 (April 1, 2008): 329.
Library Journal 133, no. 5 (March 15, 2008): 65.
New Statesman 137, no. 4907 (July 28, 2008): 51.
The New York Times, June 13, 2008, p. 23.
The New York Times Book Review, August 3, 2008, p. 6.
Publishers Weekly 255, no. 7 (February 18, 2008): 132.
USA Today, June 19, 2008, p. D4.

A SUMMER OF HUMMINGBIRDS
Love, Art, and Scandal in the Intersecting Worlds of Emily Dickinson, Mark Twain, Harriet Beecher Stowe, and Martin Johnson Heade

Author: Christopher Benfey (1954-   )
Publisher: Penguin (New York). Illustrated. 288 pp.
   $25.95
Type of work: Literary biography, literary history
Time: 1860-1900
Locale: Amherst, Massachusetts; Jacksonville and St.
   Augustine, Florida; New York City; various capitals of
   Europe

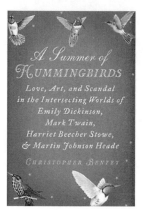

Benfey describes the intersecting lives of some of the most famous American writers and artists of the Gilded Age, and he examines their artistic responses to the changing post-Civil War world

Principal personages:
> GEORGE GORDON, LORD BYRON (1788-1824), the British Romantic poet whose life and writings captivated Americans in the nineteenth century
> HARRIET BEECHER STOWE (1811-1896), the author of *Uncle Tom's Cabin* (1851)
> HENRY WARD BEECHER (1813-1887), her brother, the most popular preacher in America
> MARTIN JOHNSON HEADE (1819-1904), an American landscape painter
> EMILY DICKINSON (1830-1886), the reclusive Amherst poet
> THOMAS WENTWORTH HIGGINSON (1823-1911), the writer to whom Dickinson first sent her poems
> MARK TWAIN (1835-1910), the comic writer and member of several New England social and literary circles
> HENRY JAMES (1843-1916), American novelist, who lived most of his career in Europe
> MABEL LOOMIS TODD (1856-1932), a painter, a writer, the lover of Emily Dickinson's married brother Austin, and the editor of the poet's work after her death
> JOSEPH CORNELL (1903-1972), an American artist known for his surrealist boxes

The Civil War was a watershed in American history. Before the war, American life was built upon a series of religious and social truths few people questioned. After the war, America began its transformation into the modern world, and the pre-war certainties gave way to doubt and instability. The exploding growth of the Gilded Age following the Civil War was accompanied by intellectual tremors set off by Charles Darwin, Karl Marx, and other skeptics of inherited Calvinist ideas. Historians have charted this transformation in the second half of the nineteenth century in a number of different ways, but in *A Summer of Hummingbirds*, Christopher Benfey has found a unique expression of the change.

He follows a group of American artists and writers linked by family and friendship, tracing their responses to the changing postbellum world through their poetry and art, their motifs and metaphors, and in particular the striking image of the hummingbird. "In science and in art, in religion and in love, they came to see a new dynamism and movement in their lives, a brave new world of instability and evanescence. This dynamism, in all aspects of life, found perfect expression in the hummingbird."

~

Christopher Benfey has written Emily Dickinson: Lives of a Poet *(1986),* The Double Life of Stephen Crane *(1992),* Degas in New Orleans *(1997), and* The Great Wave: Gilded Age Misfits, Japanese Eccentrics, and the Opening of Old Japan *(2003). He writes for* The New York Times Book Review, *The* New Republic, *and* The New York Review of Books. *Benfey is Mellon Professor of English at Mount Holyoke College.*

~

Benfey divides his study into three parts: from conflict (images of the Civil War), through confinement (images of prison), to release (images of flight or of escape). Part One is called "An Oblique War," from a phrase Emily Dickinson used in a letter to Thomas Wentworth Higginson in 1863, and focuses on the effects of the Civil War on this group of writers and artists. Harriet Beecher Stowe, who wrote the antislavery novel *Uncle Tom's Cabin* that President Abraham Lincoln claimed had started the Civil War, had a son, Captain Fredric Stowe, permanently wounded in the war in 1863. Stowe was drawn to the image of the fragile hummingbird, and in fact she painted one in 1864, a figure, Benfey suggests, that may have reminded the writer of her vulnerable son. The war was actually a stimulant to Dickinson, for she produced many of her greatest poems in a burst of creative energy during the war, although most would not be published until after her death. Her famous line "I taste a liquor never brewed," for example, was written in 1861; the hummingbird narrator of the poem was for Dickinson a figure of "ecstasy," Benfey writes; the same figure for Stowe was one of "vulnerability." Henry Ward Beecher, the most famous minister in America, and the brother of Harriet, collected stuffed hummingbirds, while the artist Martin Johnson Heade in 1863 headed to Brazil—where the greatest number of species of hummingbirds lived—to try to become the John Jay Audubon of the bird.

Part Two, "At the Hotel Byron," opens with Stowe on Lake Geneva in Switzerland, the setting for Lord Byron's popular 1816 poem "The Prisoner of Chillon," which tells the story of the sixteenth century hero of Swiss independence, François Bonnivard, who was imprisoned for six years in the Castle of Chillon, and, when released, hesitated to leave his familiar dungeon. The romantic Byron was a favorite with American readers. "He represented, with his passions and his flair, an escape from the prison of Puritan repression," Benfey suggests. Lyman Beecher (Harriet and Henry's father) preached a funeral sermon when the poet died in 1824, while Harriet called his popularity in America "Byronic fever," modeled the heroic Augustine St.

Clare in *Uncle Tom's Cabin* on the poet, and later published a book-length defense of the wife abandoned by the poet, titled *Lady Byron Vindicated* (1870). Henry James used Chillon as a crucial setting in his novella *Daisy Miller* (1879), when the title character visits the castle with a potential suitor. Finally, Mark Twain made fun of the castle and its famous prisoner in his narrative of travel through Europe, *A Tramp Abroad* (1880), claiming Bonnivard should have amused himself with the swarms of tourists Twain encountered on his visit there three centuries later. Benfey finds a deeper significance in the image of the prison that its frequent use by artists and writers only hints at. Dickinson, for example, who spent the two decades after the war as a virtual self-prisoner in her house in Amherst, was also drawn to the poetry of Byron: "What Byron's poetry promised—for Stowe, Dickinson, and Henry James—was escape from the wintry prison-house of custom and Calvinism, and access instead to nature and feeling." The literature produced in the United States after the Civil War, and in particular the realism of James and Twain and other writers who would come to dominate fiction, demonstrated that escape from literary and social custom and convention in numerous ways.

Part Three, "Transits of Venus," completes the study's triptych with its theme of release, flight, and escape, all three as much physical as artistic. Martin Johnson Heade created his most accomplished paintings, including those of hummingbirds, after the war. Heade was in love with Mabel Loomis Todd, the wife of astronomer David Todd, a member of the commission charting the rare passage of Venus between the earth and the sun in 1882. Heade pursued her, unsuccessfully, to Amherst during the summer that Mabel became the lover of Dickinson's married brother Austin. Apart from her extramarital affairs, Mabel recognized the importance of Dickinson's poems and edited the first selection of them, with Higginson's help, after the poet's death in 1886. The links are even closer, Benfey reveals: Mabel's recognition of Dickinson's talent "was shaped and nurtured by her apprenticeship with Martin Johnson Heade. It was in Heade's studio in Washington that Mabel saw what could be done with a few hypnotic images—flowers, mysterious lights on meadows, hummingbirds." As critics have noted, Dickinson's poetry often has a painterly perspective, including the effect of light on landscape that artists such as Heade were trying to achieve at the time. The changing light is only one of the ways the new "dynamism" of the Gilded Age was illuminating and transforming American life. Henry Ward Beecher, who collected stuffed hummingbirds and knew Heade and bought at least one of his paintings, was the subject of one of the most sensational trials in America in the 1870's, resulting from his affair with his parishioner Elizabeth Tilton.

Benfey's last chapter, "Florida," includes an account of the construction of the lavish Hotel Ponce de Leon that industrialist Henry Morrison Flagler built in St. Augustine and where he installed Heade as one of the resident artists. James later stayed there, writing that the hotel "comes as near producing, all by itself, the illusion of romance as highly modern, a most cleverly-constructed and smoothly-administered great modern caravansary can come." Passion and romance were spilling out all over America by the end of the nineteenth century, giving way, at times, to extravagance and ostentation. The Gilded Age was becoming the Age of Excess.

In his "Epilogue," Benfey turns to another American artist, the twentieth century collagist Joseph Cornell, and studies his affinity for the writers and artists of the previous century. "In Cornell's work, the familiar romantic objects of Beecher and Stowe and Dickinson—birds and flowers and jewels and planets—reappear with a ghostly majesty and strangeness." Benfey calls "Toward the Blue Peninsula (For Emily Dickinson)" (c. 1953), a collage of wire and cage, "the single most trenchant interpretive response, in all of American art, to the meaning of her life and work."

Benfey's thesis is not new, but his exploration of it certainly is. "This book is about a cluster of American artists and writers adrift during the seismic upheaval of the Civil War and its wrenching aftermath," artists and writers who "found meaning in the shifting light on a river at dawn, or the evanescent flash of a hummingbird's flight."

At times, however, Benfey's focus gets lost in his complex story. *A Summer of Hummingbirds* recounts numerous episodes from the lives of Twain, Dickinson, Beecher, Stowe, and a dozen other artists and writers, and it is easy to lose sight of Benfey's focus—that these creative people found themselves caught between the Calvinist prewar world of convention, custom, and restraint, and a more romantic postwar world in which nature and passion prevailed. Fortunately, Benfey starts this study with a three-page "Dramatis Personae" that gives brief biographies of the fifteen major characters in the book, which helps readers to keep them straight. His focus on tropes and motifs, however, and particularly the figure of the hummingbird—an image "of freedom in a world of captivity," as he writes—sometimes seems too fragile to carry all the weight that Benfey wants it to hold. There are a number of ways of dramatizing this shift in nineteenth century America. Benfey begins his study with a glance at Twain's *Life on the Mississippi* (1882), which represents a stronger metaphor, as Twain contrasts life on the great river before the war, when he was a cub riverboat pilot, and after it, when he returned to discover the Mississippi swamped by commercial traffic as the United States opened westward. Many studies such as Benfey's are overweighted by theory, and his tends to err on the side of narrative detail and metaphor.

Benfey does evoke powerfully the mid-nineteenth century literary and artistic world—particularly the cloistered life of Dickinson, and the nomadic journeys of Heade—and shows how intertwined that world became. The book also contains a number of photographs and reproductions of the artworks Benfey studies by Heade, Stowe, and Cornell. Benfey helps to unlock the complex artistic and intellectual links among this talented and passionate group of Americans, and he uses their art and literature to show the transformation the United States was undergoing through the end of the nineteenth century.

David Peck

Review Sources

ARTnews 107, no. 9 (October, 2008): 50.
The Atlantic Monthly 302, no. 1 (July/August, 2008): 141.
Booklist 104, no. 16 (April 15, 2008): 18-19.
Library Journal 133, no. 6 (April 1, 2008): 83.
The New York Times Book Review, May 4, 2008, p. 20.
Publishers Weekly 255, no. 7 (February 18, 2008): 144.
The Times Literary Supplement, January 2, 2009, pp. 7-8.

TAKING ON THE TRUST
The Epic Battle of Ida Tarbell and John D. Rockefeller

Author: Steve Weinberg (1948-   )
Publisher: W. W. Norton (New York). 256 pp. $25.95
Type of work: Biography
Time: 1839-1944
Locale: Titusville, Pennsylvania; Cleveland, Ohio; New York City

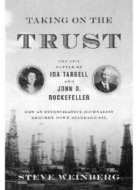

This dual biography traces the trajectories of two great American lives and their collision over the proper role of business in the nation's economy, politics, and morality

Principal personages:
>JOHN D. ROCKEFELLER, the founder of the Standard Oil Trust
>WILLIAM AVERY ROCKEFELLER, his con-man father
>ELIZA DAVISON ROCKEFELLER, his pious mother
>HENRY FLAGLER, his Florida business partner
>IDA TARBELL, one of the United States' first investigative journalists
>FRANK TARBELL, her father, an oil refiner, and the inventor of oil storage tanks
>ESTHER TARBELL, her supportive mother
>S. S. McCLURE, the founder of *McClure's Magazine*, the venue for many of Tarbell's articles
>THEODORE ROOSEVELT, the first president to attack trusts such as Standard Oil

The History of the Standard Oil Company (1904) remains Ida Tarbell's lasting contribution to the development of American journalism. An indefatigable researcher and fearless reporter, Tarbell assembled a painstaking and unassailable case against the Standard Oil Trust, accusing it of ruthlessly ruining its competition, fixing railroad shipment rates, and engaging in other anticompetitive practices that made it impossible for independent oil producers and refiners to make a profit. Prone to biographical interpretations of history, Tarbell viewed the Standard Oil Trust as the embodiment of John D. Rockefeller's rapacious personality. After publishing her landmark book, she followed up with a profile of Rockefeller in *McClure's Magazine*, suggesting that his various charities were merely a public relations front to rescue the reputation of a man who engaged in restraint of trade and other unethical practices that contributed to his company's monopolistic control of the refining of oil in the United States and abroad.

In *Taking on the Trust*, Steve Weinberg emulates Tarbell's biographical approach insofar as he regards the clash between Tarbell and Rockefeller as deeply rooted in their family backgrounds, the former deeply influenced by her entrepreneurial father

⁓
Steve Weinberg has written seven
books and dozens of investigative
reports for magazines and newspapers.
He teaches at the top-ranked University
of Missouri Journalism School and
lives in Columbia, Missouri.
⁓

and strong mother, the latter influenced by his mother's religious convictions and his father's deceitful business practices.

Both were innovators. Early on in her education at Allegheny College, Tarbell learned the value of consulting primary sources—the documents that could establish the truth behind the stories people told her. Before taking on the enormous task of investigating Rockefeller and Standard Oil, Tarbell researched the lives of European and American historical figures, notably the biography of Abraham Lincoln. She searched courthouses and other public institutions for records of Lincoln's life and found much new evidence overlooked by the president's authorized biographers. Indeed, Tarbell can rightly be considered one of the inventors of American unauthorized biography, since she began with no one's sanction or approval but rather with a series of questions and issues that she pursued with relentless determination and ingenuity. Heretofore, biography had been a rather staid genre—distinguished, to be sure, by a few biographers such as James Parton—but lacking in the kind of undaunted and resourceful independence that Tarbell patented.

Weinberg shows that Tarbell's initiative derived from close observation of her father's experiences in the oil business. Frank Tarbell knew at first hand about Rockefeller's efforts to intimidate his competition. Tarbell's mother, Esther, early on recognized that her daughter would not fit the conventional mold of the conforming, sedate, and conventional nineteenth century woman. In sum, Tarbell had the staunch support of her family that enabled her to pursue her radical search for truth.

At nearly the same time, Rockefeller arose from a family marked by a curious blend of the raffish and the religious. His father was often away from home on business trips, indulging in sexual affairs, and bent on bilking others in get-rich-quick schemes. Rockefeller never acknowledged his father's unethical and illegal behavior or that he may have learned a trick or two from dad. On the contrary, Rockefeller overly identified with his mother's piety. A devout Christian, Rockefeller apparently believed that his business dealings were honorable.

Like Tarbell, Rockefeller showed remarkable initiative. He pioneered better ways to refine oil, and he was constantly making other improvements in the exploration and distribution of fuel at a time when other refiners relied on shoddy equipment that often led to fires and other industrial accidents. A keen appraiser of talent, Rockefeller employed the best executives, often drawn from the companies Standard Oil took over.

Drawing on the later scholarship of writers such as Allan Nevins and Ron Chernow, Weinberg shows that Tarbell had an excessively narrow view of Rockefeller's personality. It seems unlikely—as Tarbell supposed—that Rockefeller established his charitable foundations out of guilt or in an effort simply to restore the reputation Tarbell had denigrated. Rockefeller often provided funding for worthy projects without expecting publicity or any sort of public acknowledgment.

Tarbell did not merely attack Rockefeller. She acknowledged that he had done much to improve the oil business. She was not against big business per se but rather against the abuses of the capitalist system. Indeed, her reporting led to court cases and legislation that made illegal what was, in Rockefeller's early years, only unethical.

How Rockefeller viewed himself is difficult to say since his autobiography is reticent and he left behind no documents that decisively reveal his inner life. He rarely answered his critics directly and took care—as Weinberg demonstrates—to make sure his name appeared on very few internal company documents. He rarely mentioned Tarbell by name, but on those few occasions when he did defend himself (he hired an interviewer for precisely this purpose), it is clear he had Tarbell in mind. At one point, he did refer to her directly, suggesting she was misguided, although he acknowledged that in some respects her book presented a favorable view of Standard Oil.

Like Rockefeller, Tarbell produced an autobiography, and yet she revealed little about her inner or private life. Why did she not marry? Did she have lovers? Neither Weinberg nor previous biographers can tell. Consequently, Tarbell, like Rockefeller, remains something of a mystery. Weinberg, a superb journalist, does not attempt to psychoanalyze his subjects or to speculate unduly about their motivations.

Weinberg began his work intending a full biography of Tarbell, but given the paucity of material about her inner life, it is understandable why he turned to this dual biography. It provides him with the opportunity to do full justice to his main story and to the events that led to the clash between Rockefeller and Tarbell.

While these two figures never met, they remained to the end of their days aware of each other. After all, Tarbell's work influenced Theodore Roosevelt and others to condemn the monopolistic practices of Standard Oil and other trusts. In addition, Tarbell was certainly one of the principal reasons why in 1912 the Supreme Court rendered a decision that effectively broke up the Standard Oil Trust.

The irony, however, is that the breakup made Rockefeller richer—the richest man in the United States, in fact—because he had stock in all the companies carved out of the Standard Oil leviathan. Tarbell's career flourished and Rockefeller remained the chief symbol of ravenous big business. He was never able to rectify the damage Tarbell had done to his reputation.

Weinberg shows that Tarbell's legacy consists of much more than her classic work on Standard Oil. She not only pioneered the craft of investigative journalism but also insisted on the meticulous analysis of documents, becoming at the same time the first woman and perhaps the first journalist to join the staff of a major magazine (*McClure's*) to concentrate exclusively on in-depth and well-researched articles.

For Tarbell, there was no such thing as received wisdom. She argued that reporters should begin afresh, jettisoning opinions and looking for new material. When Lincoln's son denied her access to his father's papers, and one of Lincoln's secretaries, John Nicolay, rebuffed her, Tarbell pursued her own quest for documents and scoured newspapers for leads. Impressed with her efforts, the son, Robert Todd Lincoln, eventually provided some assistance, persuading sources to speak with her. In this way, Tarbell built up a network of contacts that led her to collectors of Lincoln material that had not been shared with other biographers.

Weinberg uses a phrase (the "era of heroic biography was fading") that demarcates the changes Tarbell promulgated in American biography and journalism. He notes that she "glossed over Lincoln's faults" but with Rockefeller she "went to great lengths to pull back the curtain." In other words, she was on her way to making biography itself a more critical genre a full generation before iconoclasts such as Lytton Strachey would do so in *Eminent Victorians* (1918).

It is no longer standard practice for biographers to quote large portions of their subject's prose. The contemporary fashion is to write swiftly moving narratives peppered with brief sound-bite quotations. Weinberg does quote a few extended passages from Tarbell, however, that reveal what a marvelous writer she remains. However much her biographies have been superseded by later research, her prose repays study. Here is just one pithy example from her *McClure's* profile of Rockefeller: "Mr. Rockefeller may have made himself the richest man in the world, but he has paid. Nothing but paying ever ploughs such lines in a man's face, ever sets his lips to such a melancholy angle." This is a devastating portrait, combining moral judgment and observation, sound, sense, and imagery in just two sentences. The pacing of such prose never ages.

Although Tarbell could claim many "firsts" as a woman working in what was still mainly a man's occupation, she rarely adopted a feminist viewpoint. To be sure, she wrote about women's issues, but she was not keen, for example, on votes for women. In this respect, she took a rather staid, nineteenth century old-fashioned view of women who should shy away from the rough-and-tumble of the political world. Somehow a woman's authority as above or beyond the fray appealed to her, although she herself hardly provided a good example. Nevertheless, she did not think women's involvement in politics would change the world all that much.

In another sense, like Rockefeller, Tarbell remained a conventional American tied to her family. She took an active interest in her relatives and often supported them even when her income (derived solely from writing) diminished. Similarly, Rockefeller devoted himself to family, sometimes even taking part of a day off to return home and play with his children. Even though both resided in New York City for long periods, Rockefeller saw himself as rooted in the Cleveland of his youth just as Tarbell remained at heart a citizen of Titusville. Given their antagonism, it was impossible for one to see the other's full humanity. This, however, is the work of biography, and one that Weinberg accomplishes with admirable dexterity, compassion, and perception.

Carl Rollyson

Review Sources

The Boston Globe, April 3, 2008, p. C7.
The Christian Science Monitor, April 22, 2008, p. 17.
Columbia Journalism Review, March/April, 2008, p. 58.
Journalism History 34, no. 3 (Fall, 2008): 180.
Kirkus Reviews 75, no. 24 (December 15, 2007): 1288.
Library Journal 133, no. 2 (February 1, 2008): 84-85.
Publishers Weekly 254, no. 50 (December 17, 2007): 42.
St. Petersburg Times, March 7, 2008, p. 1E.
The Wall Street Journal 251, no. 73 (March 28, 2008): W5.
The Washington Post Book World, April 27, 2008, p. 8.

THE TEN-CENT PLAGUE
The Great Comic-Book Scare and How It Changed America

Author: David Hajdu (1955-   )
Publisher: Farrar, Straus and Giroux (New York).
  434 pp. $26.00
Type of work: History
Time: 1890 to the 1960's
Locale: The United States

Hajdu describes the suppression of comic books in the immediate aftermath of World War II

At the end of World War II, the enemy defeated and the peace secured, the United States was poised to enjoy a period of security and prosperity. While the country did experience a sustained economic growth into the 1960's, growth unparalleled in modern times, a sense of security seemed to elude the postwar generation, according to *The Ten-Cent Plague* by David Hajdu. The American nuclear monopoly, which ended the war with the bombing of Hiroshima and Nagasaki, was shattered by the Soviet Union's development of its atomic bomb and nuclear arsenal. Internal security was challenged by Senator Joseph McCarthy's crusade against what he claimed was widespread domestic subversion by Communists in the federal government, the entertainment industry, and the Army. Estes Kefauver, a senator from Tennessee, chaired governmental investigative committees that examined the growing concern with domestic crime and juvenile delinquency. Paranoia appeared to reign throughout the land.

On April 22, 1954, postwar paranoia coalesced in two U.S. Senate hearings. As Hajdu points out, both were decisive but in contrary ways. In Washington, Senator McCarthy's probe into Communist infiltration of the Army marked the end of a movement in decline and destroyed the credibility and reputation of the junior senator from Wisconsin. The other Senate hearing was conducted in New York by Robert C. Hendrickson, a first-term Republican from New Jersey, into the link between juvenile delinquency and comic books that boosted a crusade on the rise that would prove devastating to the comic-book industry.

Comic books that would raise such outrage and concern in the late 1940's and into the mid-1950's began innocently enough as the brainchild of Joseph Pulitzer in order to increase the circulation of his *New York World* by creating a largely visual feature that would appeal to the paper's non-English reading public. "The Yellow Kid" was set in the streets of Manhattan's Lower East Side where the multiple boxes of drawings depicted the adventures of a gang of slum kids. Created by Richard Felton Outcault, the Kid became a caricature of the immigrant poor. He and his pals were vulgar stereotypes, inarticulate, violent, violators of the social order, in short, as Hajdu points out, juvenile delinquents. The popularity of the Yellow Kid, who also

incidentally gave his name to "yellow" journalism, was enormous, and it gave birth to
dozens of newspaper cartoons, some based on
the Kid himself. In their earthiness, freedom,
and challenge to authority, these early newspaper comics spoke directly to the burgeoning immigrant population swelling the major
American cities, and because of their subversiveness they attracted the attention of civic
groups and local do-good societies. Similar to
the criticisms directed at the dime novels of
the nineteenth century, comics were found in-
fantile, brutal, unsophisticated, subliterate, all
of the things that offended the cultural arbitra-
tors of the time. The syndication of the popular strips plus the creation of new ones in local
newspapers across the country spread the new visual form.

∼

*David Hajdu teaches at the Journalism
School at Columbia University. He
writes a column on music and popular
culture for* The New Republic *and
contributes to* The New Yorker, Vanity
Fair, *and* The New York Times. *His
books* Lush Life: A Biography of Billy
Strayhorn *(1996) and* Positively Fourth
Street: The Lives and Times of Joan
Baez, Bob Dylan, Mimi Baez Farina,
and Richard Farina *(2001) were*
National Book Critics Circle Award
finalists.

∼

Soon tear-outs were being printed to be sold with the newspaper or as separate
newspaper promotions. Comic strips were collected and printed as separate publications. As their popularity grew, so did the characters and the formats diversify. Historically, the first comic book has been identified as *Funnies on Parade*, from 1933,
and it was not for sale but rather was a free premium for Procter & Gamble. In February
of 1935, Malcolm Wheeler-Nicholson published a thirty-six-page, black-and-white,
tabloid-sized collection of never-before-published comic strips. He thus created the
first published for-sale, stand-alone comic book that was designed for syndication
and future sales. The comic book was born.

By the late 1930's, Wheeler-Nicholson's idea had given rise to several comic-
book studios, most of them located in New York City, which allowed them to take advantage of the city's concentration of artistic talent, much of it unemployed or under-
employed because of the Depression. For a low cost, comic-book entrepreneurs could
turn out dozens of comic books a month. The contents of these books varied, and as
the market expanded so did the stories, eventually to include everything from romance to science fiction to adventure and crime, Westerns, kiddie cartoons, and war.
In June of 1938, in *Action Comics*, there appeared a caped crusader with superhuman
powers dedicated to right and the American way. Superman was to be followed by
dozens more superheroes (and superheroines) that are still present today, both in print
and on the large screen. The physical strength, gallantry, and moral righteousness of
the superhero moved the comic book beyond the tawdriness of the early newspaper
days. As Hajdu puts it, if the Yellow Kid appealed to the newly arrived immigrant at
the turn of the century, Superman celebrated the virtues and goodness of American
life of the 1930's.

The newfound success of the comic-book superheroes provided a financial stability that allowed expansion of the industry. As the business grew, and more and more
children spent their nickels and dimes on the millions of comics churned out each

year, the cultural establishment maintained its vigilance and the sniping at comics continued unabated. Articles with titles such as Stirling North's "A National Disgrace" appeared regularly in up-culture journals. His "The Antidote to Comics" was published in the magazine of the National Parent-Teacher Association, claiming comics promoted a pre-fascist pattern for American youth. What bothered many of the prewar critics was the turn comics had taken toward the depiction of crime and criminal behavior. As would happen when comics turned to horror in the early 1950's, this new venture would provoke a substantial backlash.

The comic-book "problem" was exacerbated by their appeal not only to the young but also to adults. This appeal became especially evident during World War II when soldiers bought huge numbers of comic books, apparently preferring them to other more elevating reading matter with which they were provided. All of this must also be placed in the context of the ongoing modernist conflict involving the confluence of popular and high art, a movement that obscured the differences between the two and called into question traditional hierarchies of aesthetic taste and conventions of aesthetic evaluations. If comic books could be considered art, what did that say about other forms of popular expression? Elevating the popular arts was the thin edge of the wedge and complemented various other forms of paranoia that flourished in the aftermath of World War II.

The postwar years brought rapid and often socially upsetting cultural change. The expansion of the opportunities of the war years for African Americans and women laid the foundation for both the women's and Civil Rights movements of the 1950's. The emergence of a teen culture in the war's aftermath also was unsettling for many, and much of the individuality in dress, music, and language that teenagers exhibited was attributed to the reading of comic books, especially those featuring crime and horror. This perception made it easy to tie together the rise of juvenile delinquency and comic-book reading and set the stage for the crackdown on comic books and their publishers, writers, and illustrators.

From the late 1930's through the war years and into the early 1950's, there was a persistent movement to suppress comics. There were local and even national drives to have kids collect their comic books to be publicly burned. The similarities with the Nazi book burnings were not lost on critics of the practice; nor was the more than a whiff of anti-Semitism in the crackdown since so many of those involved in the making and distributing of comics were Jewish. Nevertheless, municipalities passed laws to forbid the sales of certain comic books or certain categories of comics. Local bodies, including churches and service organizations, were especially involved, often making up a list of offensive titles to aid in the control of those comics thought offensive. The graphic detail of the drawings illustrating many of the crime and horror stories contributed to the fear that comics were creating a depraved generation of readers.

Senator Hendrickson's 1954 hearings delivered a devastating blow to the comic-book business. The excessively gruesome covers and stories of the horror comics, the continued appearance of crime in the ten-cent magazines, and the increasing public fear of crime, communism, and the bomb finally resulted in a more concerted effort to clean up the industries' product. Civic committees across the country drafted lists of unacceptable titles, which were then distributed to newsstands and cigar stores that sold comic books. Youths were exhorted to seek more wholesome reading matter; the comic book had reached the end of an era.

In order to stem the tide of criticism, the comic-book publishers formed the Comics Magazine Association of America, which issued a code of standards for comic-book contents. The group agreed to an independent overseer, and the position was offered to Fredric Wertham, author of the *Seduction of the Innocent* (1954), his "study" of the effects of comic books on the psyches of American youth, a book much influential at the time but now largely discredited. The subversiveness and edginess of comics that had appealed to kids was sapped from the publications. There were spinoffs in other formats, such as Harvey Kurtzman's *Mad* magazine, and comic books did continue, but it would be years before some of the old moxie returned. Now there flourishes a healthy business in comics, fantasy books, and graphic novels. Even the original artwork from the postwar years fetches healthy prices in the art-auction market. The content and graphic display in many of today's illustrated publications, as well as video games, would make Hendrickson and Wertham spin in their graves.

In *The Ten-Cent Plague*, Hajdu has written a fascinating study of a little-remembered episode in American history. Certainly the postwar years and the paranoia that produced the Communist hysteria of the House Un-American Activities Committee and McCarthy have been widely researched and written about, but the comic-book slice of that history has not been. Examining the depth and breadth of the controversy extends knowledge of this truly strange period in American history.

Hajdu has also performed a wonderful service by interviewing many of those artists and editors who worked in the field, some of them from the 1930's and the beginnings of the boom period, before their stories were lost through failing memory or health. The stories they tell are at the same time informative, funny, and outrageous. It would have been a shame to have lost this oral history.

For those readers who remember the period and the subversive fun of saving up dimes and buying the comics their folks did not want them to read as well as those readers who may be shocked to learn how widespread was the postwar fear and paranoia, *The Ten-Cent Plague* is an enjoyable read as well as an instructive one.

Charles L. P. Silet

Review Sources

Booklist 104, no. 12 (February 15, 2008): 18.
Entertainment Weekly, March 21, 2008, p. 62.
The Humanist 68, no. 4 (July/August, 2008): 40-41.
Kirkus Reviews 75, no. 23 (December 1, 2007): 1230.
Library Journal 133, no. 9 (May 15, 2008): 86.
Mother Jones 33, no. 2 (March/April, 2008): 93.

The New Yorker 84, no. 7 (March 31, 2008): 124-128.
Publishers Weekly 254, no. 49 (December 10, 2007): 44.
The Wall Street Journal 251, no. 61 (March 14, 2008): W2.
Washington Monthly 40, no. 4 (April, 2008): 54-56.

TERROR AND CONSENT
The Wars for the Twenty-first Century

Author: Philip Bobbitt (1948-   )
Publisher: Alfred A. Knopf (New York). 672 pp. $35.00
Type of work: Current affairs, history, law

Bobbitt argues that the nature of terrorism is largely misunderstood because it is adapting to globalization and to the market orientation of the terrorists' primary target, secular democracies

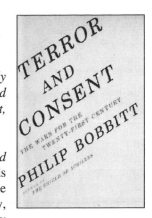

The most stirring part of Philip Bobbitt's *Terror and Consent* is its discussion of the latter. Bobbitt reminds readers that government legitimized by the consent of the governed—all of them, not just those of a particular party, creed, gender, or race—is relatively new in human history and precious. It can exist only in nations that have constitutionally guaranteed human rights and the rule of law. However, in the twenty-first century, despite the triumph of democratic governments over fascism and communism in the wars of the previous century, consent is imperiled. Variously political analysis, historiography, outline for reform, and plea, this intriguing, provocative tome identifies the peril: a new form of terrorism that is global in its reach, technologically sophisticated, decentralized, indiscriminate, and capable of havoc.

However, it is not just terrorist organizations that Bobbitt addresses. Terror itself is his worry. Accordingly, Bobbitt defines terrorism functionally: "use of violence in order to advance a political agenda by preventing persons from doing what they would otherwise lawfully do." Terror is a threat from those to whom the free consent of a nation's people is unimportant, or even anathema, because the terrorists derive their authority from some other source: for instance, god, ideology, or ethnicity. There is simultaneously the worrisome possibility that free, democratic societies, out of the need to protect themselves from the likes of al-Qaeda, might resort to terror. For this reason, Bobbitt says the great conflict of this age is not a war on terrorism, as the administration of George W. Bush termed it, but "Wars on Terror," which he might just as well have called "Defense of Consent."

In this way of looking at it, terror includes more than violence or the threat of violence. It includes the disenfranchising of a group (such as women or atheists), restriction of rights (such as freedom of assembly), reduction of opportunity (by, for example, limiting education or access to the Internet), isolationism, and abnegation of legal due process. Terror is so deadly, Bobbitt argues, because it preys upon countries such as the United States and federations such as the European Union at a time when the internal and external nature of the state is changing. The developed nations of the twentieth century were "nation-states," whose primary duty was to foster a national identity and the welfare of citizens as a whole; the nation-state was protectionist and

～

Philip Bobbitt taught at Oxford
University and King's College, was a
counselor to the president of the United
States and Senate, and advised on
strategic planning at the National
Security Council. He is the Herbert
Wechsler Professor of Federal
Jurisprudence and director of the
Center for National Security at
Columbia University.

～

maintained entitlement programs for its citizens, such as welfare, to promote equality. Now the nation-state is evolving into the "market state" because of the telecommunications revolution and the globalization of markets. Shifting away from the old entitlements and internal market protections, such as tariffs, the market state behaves more like a multinational corporation, relying less on regulations and laws and more on incentives in order to provide its citizens with the means for self-improvement (economically, intellectually, or socially, for instance). It seems as if the famous appeal of President John F. Kennedy is to be reversed: Citizens should now ask what their country can do for them.

The greater ease of travel and trade, the vastly increased access to information through the Internet and communications through such inventions as the cell phone, the diasporas of ethnic groups, and the decentralization of power that underpin the market state—in a term, globalization—also create vulnerabilities. Attack any of these, and the market state cannot ensure opportunities to its citizenry; attack or threaten to attack the citizens and they cannot avail themselves of the opportunities. Such is the strategy of al-Qaeda: to destroy the means and ends of consent. As al-Qaeda leader Osama bin Laden asserted in the mid-1990's, any member of a nation of consent is responsible for the actions of the government and so is a legitimate target. The duty of the government is to foil this strategy and prevent attacks.

Bobbitt recognizes, however, that it is not only terrorists that threaten the free exercise of consent and pursuit of opportunities. In one of his book's most telling arguments, he points out that natural disasters—deadly hurricanes or earthquakes, for example, or a pandemic—have the same effect. The government of a market state must therefore equally prepare for such disasters and handle them with greater efficiency than was the case for Hurricane Katrina in 2005. (Bobbitt's review of that debacle is scathing.) In both cases—preventing or responding to terrorism and preparing for natural disasters or restoring order after them—a government must not employ such draconian, exceptional emergency measures that it itself prevents its citizens from enjoying their human rights, in effect creating terror. This restraint is particularly difficult because terrorists may soon get their hands on weapons of mass destruction (WMDs)—nuclear, chemical, or biological. It is only a matter of time, Bobbitt darkly warns. Either a nuclear-armed state that aids terrorists, as Iran may become, or the black market will make WMDs available. Neither Bobbitt nor the many experts whom he cites doubt that, once acquired by terrorists, WMDs will be used against ordinary people.

Compounding the problem is the new character of terrorism. Al-Qaeda has adopted many of the structural properties of multinational corporations. It is decentralized, franchising its violent operations to local affiliates; it exploits the networking capacities of the Internet and telecommunications; and regional commanders, although adhering to a master strategy to establish a Muslim hegemony, have wide leeway in deploying forces to attack states of consent. It is elusive and flexible, and although by its very nature al-Qaeda has no fixed territory, Bobbitt considers it to be a "virtual state," an evil shadow of the market states that it seeks to intimidate. Accordingly, to fight it, new tactics are needed. Bobbitt spends the first section of *Terror and Consent* considering needed basic innovations. For instance, military forces must not only defeat their enemy on the battlefield but protect the population from guerrilla reprisals, kidnapping, and suicide attacks. The Iraq War is his example of failed tactics: After a brilliant campaign to oust Saddam Hussein, the Bush administration bungled the occupation by committing too few troops to keep the peace, allowing nationalists to create an insurgency and an al-Qaeda affiliate to infiltrate. Iraq became a proving ground for terrorism, which threatens to stymie the creation of a government of consent. Bobbitt insists that military and police duties will have to overlap for free governments to protect their citizens, and the conception of "victory" will change. There will be no decisive event followed by peace. In fighting terrorism, victory is a process: the process of never losing. It will be a long process, too. Bobbitt believes that al-Qaeda is but a forerunner of more deadly and sophisticated terrorist networks.

After his reelection in 1864, President Abraham Lincoln remarked, "It has long been a grave question whether any government, not *too* strong for the liberties of its people, can be strong *enough* to maintain its own existence, in great emergencies." In Bobbitt's analysis the answer yet hangs in the balance, and it is up to states of consent to decide it. That is his major theme, and the fundamental tool that protects a democracy is the rule of law. A widely experienced legal expert himself, he has great faith in the law and decries governments that slight, ignore, or twist either constitutional provisions or statutes. That does not mean, however, that Bobbitt wants to restrict governments' activities by emphasizing civil liberties. On the contrary, he calls for the strengthening of security powers through well-made laws. Above all, he wants nations to wed law to strategy in combating terrorism. That means reforming constitutions to accord with security measures, clarifying intelligence-gathering powers, finding leaders who understand the full import of their obligation to protect citizens, and allocating power to branches of government. In addition, it requires engaging in alliances based on a set of international standards, something the United States has been reluctant to do.

Bobbitt offers suggestions for reform. As he acknowledges, among them there is something for everyone to dislike, but as such they are starting points for debate. At the level of abstract policy he insists that extreme public danger excuses extreme methods—in other words, that ends can justify the means, including preemptive wars such as the 2003 invasion of Iraq. More particularly, he endorses the proposal that the United States ought to have an emergency constitution that, invoked for limited periods during national disasters, clarifies and expands the powers of the executive branch. Additionally, he recommends a broader isolation and quarantine statute, the use of a national identity card, the repeal of the Posse Comitatus Act that restricts use of military forces within the United States, the presidential authority to declare a national emergency, data mining (after judicial authorization), the preventive detention of suspected terrorists, a constitutional amendment to hasten the replacement of dead or disabled members of the House of Representatives, the revision of the Presidential Succession Act of 1947 to remove the Speaker of the House and president pro tempore of the Senate from the line of succession (they are currently second and third in line after the vice president), provisions for emergency succession for the Supreme Court, the restriction of information about dangerous diseases, a special federal court to try terrorist cases, and statutes protecting the assets of private companies that share information with the government about their customers. Moreover, Bobbitt calls on the United States to draw more on such nongovernmental sources of information, engage with other countries to reform the laws of war, and reconsider the nature of sovereignty.

Terror and Consent is challenging to read. Bobbitt strives to lay out his ideas with precision, especially in legal matters, because, as he notes, how a problem is solved depends upon how it is framed. This effort entails use of legal and political-science terminology in extended definitions and distinctions that may try the patience of readers. Given the book's basically earnest, practical-minded tone, Bobbitt's occasional attempts at historiography (for instance, in adapting Georg Wilhelm Friedrich Hegel's theory of "antimonies") seem to burden rather than clarify the discussion. His occasional bursts of sarcasm and outrage betray his deep worry about the state of the world.

If challenging, *Terror and Consent* is yet rewarding for readers interested in grasping the terms of change in contemporary politics and war. It would be a mistake to read it as a prospectus for the twenty-first century. Certainly, beyond its purview lie important concerns that are sure to shape nations of consent and their response to war and terrorism, notably dwindling resources for an expanding human population and whether consumerism and market dynamics should be the foundation of global culture. Bobbitt makes only passing reference to such matters, but then he should not be expected to address everything. The book is long enough as it is. Rather, its value lies in stimulating rational debate and instilling both a sense of urgency and of opportunity.

Roger Smith

Review Sources

Booklist 104, no. 16 (April 15, 2008): 11.
The Economist 387 (April 5, 2008): 87.
Kirkus Reviews 76, no. 5 (March 1, 2008): 225-226.
National Review 60, no. 9 (May 19, 2008): 50-52.
New Statesman 137, no. 4902 (June 23, 2008): 54-56.
The New York Review of Books 55, no. 19 (December 4, 2008): 15-18.
The New York Times Book Review, April 13, 2008, p. 1.
Publishers Weekly 255, no. 8 (February 25, 2008): 67-68.
The Spectator 307 (May 24, 2008): 33-34.
Sunday Times, June 1, 2008, p. 4.
The Times Literary Supplement, July 25, 2008, pp. 8-9.

THAT LITTLE SOMETHING

Author: Charles Simic (1938-   )
Publisher: Harcourt (Orlando, Fla.). 73 pp. $23.00
Type of work: Poetry

*An accomplished poet of the vaguely ominous moves
closer to the dark heart of history and human behavior*

Whimsy, usually defined as "curious, quaint, or fanciful humor," has a contract with oddity, and the "odd" has a way of flirting with the darker side of experience. One does not think of Lewis Carroll's *Alice in Wonderland* (1865) or Charles Lamb's *Essays of Elia* (1823) as dark works, and this is because their whimsy falls just short of embracing oddity too warmly. Alice is constantly stepping back from the darker aspects of the oddity forced on her at every turn. She walks out on the Hatter's "Mad Tea-Party" at just the point where highjinks turn into mayhem:

> —the last time she saw them, they were putting the Dormouse into the teapot.
> "At any rate I'll never go there again!" said Alice, as she picked her way through the wood. "It's the stupidest tea-party I ever was in all my life!"

Charles Simic rarely gives his readers the choice to escape the darkness of his whimsy in his collection *That Little Something*. Rather than implicit, the darkness is explicit and no more avoidable than the owlish laughter that resonates long after his poems are read. That laughter is often silent, largely because his poetry does not invite a voiced reading. Without rhyme and often flat in diction, the metrical precision of his verse bites into the mind and holds the reader's thinking on a tight leash. After leapfrogging from quaintness to terror, his poems usually leave readers thinking thoughts that they cannot always easily connect or explain to their deepest selves. In this collection, one of several eight-line poems describes this effect perfectly:

> Thoughts frightened of the light,
> Frightened of each other.
> They listen to a clock ticking.
> Like flock of sheep led to slaughter,
> The seconds keep a good pace,
> Stick together, don't look back,
> All worried, as they go,
> What their shepherd may be thinking.

What are these "thoughts" that Simic forces on the reader? The first poem of this new collection, "Walking," invites readers to take a prosaic stroll through the proverbial old neighborhood, a place that everyone knows intimately but where the speaker can "find nothing remotely familiar." The "trees . . . the bus that passed this way . . .

~

*Charles Simic, born in Belgrade, was
sixteen years old when his family
emigrated to the United States in 1954.
He has published nineteen books of
poetry, won the Pulitzer Prize, and
received a MacArthur Foundation
grant. Simic was appointed the fifteenth
poet laureate of the United States in
2007.*

~

the greengrocers and hairdressers," all the ordinary things and places he remembers cannot be found. Things become desperate when,
despite his inability to find any of the things
his memory tells him should be there, he realizes that he has "no return ticket/ To wherever
it is I came from earlier this evening." The
whimsical absurdity produced by the mis-
alignment of memory and experience gives
way to the terrifying discovery that memory
deceived can actually cut one off from the experience of the present. One relies on the past
to flesh out the moment at hand. Robbed of
that past, one has nowhere to go—or to be.

This is the kind of primal anxiety Simic's
poetry brings into comic relief again and
again. He makes readers grin, almost fever-
ishly, at their helplessness. Often the sensa-
tion is dreamlike, a nightmare brought under
control with wit and humor. Phantasmagorical
images abound. In "The Elevator Is Out of Order," a "monkey dressed in baby
clothes" and an "old man, with a face powdered white" frighten a protagonist "fraz-
zled and descending in a hurry" down the staircase of what seems to be the proverbial
house of life. When the elevator is not working, one has to keep one's eyes open in the
stairwell, and suppressed memories rise up from nowhere.

If the past is both elusive and overpowering, the future is no less maddening. The
future is not dependent on memory, but it teases one into thinking that it is moored in
the past. In the poem "Clouds," which sails by in three perfectly balanced stanzas—
very much like a series of clouds in a quiet sky—the future seems at first to be riding
the crest of Nature's being: "To those worried about the future,/ You bring tidings,/
Shapes that may recall things/ Without ever shedding/ Their troubling ambiguity."
Even Nature seems to be playing games: "Like a troupe of illusionists/ Traveling in
circus wagons/ You play hide-and-seek with the light/ In country fairgrounds/ Until
overtaken by the night."

Although above and beyond the self, the clouds fall into the same darkness that
Simic's whimsy cannot avoid. They do not belong to themselves. Nature's voice is no
more independent than the bemused speech of the bracketed poet: "Taking a break
from prophecy/ Over small prairie towns/ In company of dark trees,/ Courthouse statues, crickets,/ And other amateur ventriloquists." The odd marriage between past and
future can propel one into illusions about the present. Here is the first stanza of
"Crickets": "Blessed are those for whom/ Time doesn't run/ Into dark of night,/ But
drags its feet . . . " Those who allow themselves a prolonged stasis, who give in to the
moment, who embrace the stationary, and who give up "walking," "staircases," and
fleeting "clouds" in the sky are "blessed"—for the moment. They think they can es-

cape the "dark of night" and have wrestled "Time" to a halt. Simic puns on the illusory self-deception of the mind when it believes in the possibility of diverting "Time" from its relentless progression: "Time . . . drags its feet." The metrical feet, indeed, drag their accents in the second stanza: "A moment's captive,/ Like a lone sail/ At sunset/ Suspended on the bay . . . "

Simic's imagery has been compared to Edward Hopper's bleak and lonely depictions of American rooms and offices. This stanza's seascape recalls Hopper's early paintings of sailboats etched against linear shores and monochromatic blue skies. Note that the "moment" is not captured (by poet, painter, or reader) but rather the moment has captured the viewer into believing in a form of liberation from Time's progress, which is a kind of imprisonment, a loneliness and isolation approaching extinction ("lone sail . . . sunset . . . suspended"). The last stanza ends in muted, sardonic laughter: "A few gulls in the sky/ Keeping it company,/ And closer to home,/ Crickets, crickets, crickets." The gulls keep the illusion of fleeting "company," but the relentless and monotonous chirping of the crickets is the dominating music for those who have chosen the false blessing of detachment.

There is no way out from under the "darkness" that closes in on every human experience. The endless dialectic between imagination and reality, however, precludes the "darkness" from having the last word. Simic's boyhood in postwar Yugoslavia was not a carefree experience, to say the least. It toughened him to the point that he acquired what can be called a muscular anxiety, a tolerance for contradiction and alienation, an acceptance of history's bad faith.

In the poem "House of Cards," Simic recalls the unsettling everyday reality of his family's life in a police state. The title is ironic. It underscores the fragility and vulnerability of the family's home, while at the same time it invokes the solace provided by a family game of cards. He remembers the "shut lips of my mother" and the "held breaths" of the family "as we sat at a dining room table." The mother deals out the cards, and as they wait "for them to fall . . . the sound of boots in the street" makes them all "still for a moment." The last stanza emphasizes the terror and hopelessness of the moment. Even Nature seems to have turned her back: "There's no more to tell./ The door is locked,/ And in one red-tinted window,/ A single tree in the yard,/ Leafless and misshapen." What is astonishing about this poem is its first two lines: "I miss you winter evenings/ With your dim lights . . . " One takes Simic at his word. He does "miss" the closeness of that family scene despite the terror that provides its context in time and memory. Memory makes that moment precious. It may be whimsical to think of it as a moment one would want to live again, but to imagine a life without a moment like it is to give up the reality of life itself.

Simic has enlarged his whimsical worldview into a wide lens that collapses history, European and American sensibilities, humor and tragedy, into a panorama on a kitchen table. He can bring together different worlds without a shattering collision; often he seems to suggest a consanguinity of emotions and feelings where most would turn away in confusion, distrust, fear, or boredom. He does it by insisting on the relevance of the ordinary. Indeed, one could argue that he establishes the metaphysical authority of the ordinary. Without the ordinary, the extraordinary could not exist.

"The Late Game" records what happens when the tension of a prolonged baseball game dissolves into the physical demands of fatigue, hunger, lust, and urination. Ironically, it is not the players who succumb to these ordinary reminders of the body's needs. Instead, the fans, mere observers of the sport, are the impeded agents. A waiter carrying "burgers and fries" is described as "sleepwalking" as he takes the food out of the restaurant and brings it to the "small field across the road" where "the baseball game . . . has gone past midnight . . . because the score is tied/ And now someone's hungry." In the poem's last stanza, the speaker imagines what must be happening "In the near-empty bleachers,/ Or out in the back/ Where couples make out in the bushes/ Young boys smoke reefers,/ And take long pees side by side." The ordinary game of life overwhelms the unusually prolonged game of baseball. The poem's title, "The Late Game," resonates strangely once the poem is read to the last line.

However ominous the tone and imagery in Simic's poems, they are firmly rooted in aesthetic values. There is a trade-off between the overpowering anxieties of life and the equally demanding but sustaining laws of poetic order. The metrical control is matched by subtlety in the shading of light and colors. Images, often prosaic or banal, are carefully arranged and distributed as if they were parts of a painterly composition. Yes, most of Simic's "paintings" recall the detached realism of Hopper, but Simic is also capable of reaching toward brighter and more vivid effects for purposes of ironic contrast.

A good example is "Waiting for the Sun to Set." The title itself plays with an image—sunset—that has strong associations with beauty in Nature and is therefore poised and ready to fulfill an aesthetic function in the poem. Note that the speaker is "waiting." The distance between the beauty of the moment and the speaker's mindset is the measure of Simic's thematic distance from the very aesthetic statement that he is intent on making. In the first stanza "palm trees . . . white villas . . . white hotels fronting the beach and the sea" all seem out of tune with the speaker's mood and mental state. The entire scene seems "most improbable" to him.

All the luxuries of the scene—the laziness of the afternoon, the "cane rocking chair" in which he is comfortably ensconced on a "small secluded veranda" that is overrun "with exotic flowers"—are foreign to his nature, sensibility, memory, and experience.

The mariner of troubled seas (a skeptical soul with a traumatic childhood), Simic is tossed up on the beach of the Lotus Eaters. It is not his scene. He does not even "know the names" of the flowers: "Raised as I was by parents/ Who kept the curtains drawn,/ The lights low, the stove unlit." However, just when the darkness seems to have taken over and Simic's ironic deflation is about to eclipse the beauty of the sunset with the dark memories of his youth, the "waiting" of the poem's title is redeemed. The speaker cannot remove himself from the scene; he cannot stop the sun from setting. He cannot deny the splendor about him any more than he can erase the memories of the past. So he is left with a guarded perception, a vision that remains true to his nature but permits itself the sublimation of art. In this case, the art seems to derive from images associated with Matisse. After the drawn curtains and lowered lights of his parents' home, Simic's speaker is left "wary as they'd be/ At first seeing oranges in a tree,/ Women running bare breasted/ Over pink sands in a blue dusk."

Peter Brier

Review Sources

Booklist 104, no. 13 (March 1, 2008): 44.
Library Journal 133, no. 3 (February 15, 2008): 108.
The New York Times Book Review, May 18, 2008, p. 22.
Publishers Weekly 255, no. 11 (March 17, 2008): 51.
World Literature Today 82, no. 6 (November/December, 2008): 73.

THEODOR W. ADORNO
One Last Genius

Author: Detlev Claussen (1948-   )
First published: Theodor W. Adorno: Ein leztes Genie,
   2003, in Germany
Translated from the German by Rodney Livingstone
Publisher: The Belknap Press of Harvard University
   Press (Cambridge, Mass.). Illustrated. 440 pp. $35.00
Type of work: Biography, philosophy
Time: 1903-1969
Locale: Frankfurt, Germany; Oxford, England; New
   York City; Los Angeles

A student of Adorno at the Frankfurt Institute for Social
Research in the 1960's, Claussen has written a sweeping
survey of Adorno's career and valuable accounts of many
of Adorno's associates

Principal personages:
   THEODOR ADORNO, a sociologist and music theorist prominent in the
      Frankfurt School
   WALTER BENJAMIN, a critic who died trying to escape from Nazi
      Germany
   MAX HORKHEIMER, a sociologist who in 1930 became the director of the
      Institute for Social Research
   SIEGFRIED KRACAUER, an early mentor of Adorno with whom he read
      Immanuel Kant
   GYÖRGY LUKÁCS, the author of influential Marxist studies
   JÜRGEN HABERMAS, a student of Adorno at the Frankfurt School in the
      1960's
   ERNST BLOCH, an early associate who clung to Soviet communism

Detlev Claussen has designed the biography *Theodor W. Adorno* so that each
chapter stands on its own, and he views Theodor Adorno's work as a "palimpsest" of
overlapping ideas. He begins his account of Adorno's life and work by immediately
introducing the name of Johann Wolfgang von Goethe, an "exemplary genius" to
whom he compares Adorno, the *One Last Genius* of the subtitle. The precocious
Adorno was born on September 11, 1903, in Frankfurt am Main, Germany. His father,
Oscar Alexander Wiesengrund, was a prosperous wine merchant, and his mother,
Maria Barbara, born Calvelli-Adorno, was a talented musician. His father was an assimilated Jew, and his mother was a Catholic. In 1933 Adorno was expelled by the
Nazis.

Adorno's comfortable bourgeois childhood was spent on the Frankfurt street
known as Schöne Aussicht (beautiful prospect). In his teens, Adorno became close to

Siegfried Kracauer, fourteen years his senior and from a lower-middle-class background that, Claussen surmises, must have "disconcerted" the "adored prodigy" Adorno. Claussen stresses the importance for Adorno's early years of the poet Heinrich Heine, who as a successful Jew represented a "social metaphor" for the aspiring Jewish middle classes but whose memory was desecrated by the Nazis.

Detlev Claussen teaches social theory, culture, and sociology at the University of Hanover in Germany. Rodney Livingstone has translated books by Walter Benjamin, Theodor Adorno, and Max Weber, among others.

The main themes of *Dialektik der Aufklärung* (1944; *Dialectic of Enlightenment*, 1972), Adorno's major work, written with Max Horkheimer, are foreshadowed in Heine, Claussen says, referring to "the idea of the inexorable advance of a modern, enlightened culture that liberates self-destructive forces."

Felix Weil, born in 1898, was to play an important role in the lives of both Adorno and Horkheimer. He was heir to millions from his family's huge trade in grain, and in 1918 he joined the short-lived Workers and Soldiers Council in Frankfurt. This experience eventually led him to financing in 1923 the Institute for Social Research, "the product of the spirit of practical socialism" and the professional home for many years of Adorno and the other Critical Theorists, especially Horkheimer, who became its director in 1930. The ideology of the Institute for Social Research soon became clear with the declaration of the First Marxist Work Week, an event that brought the Hungarian aristocrat György Lukács into prominence. Adorno and Kracauer had already read Lukács's early *Die Théorie des Romans* (1920; *The Theory of the Novel*, 1971), an indictment of science for its influence on thought that was followed in 1923 by *Geschichte und Klassenbewusstsein* (*History and Class Consciousness*, 1971), an idealizing version of communism.

Adorno earned a doctorate from Frankfurt University in 1924, and in 1925 he went to Vienna to study musical composition with Alban Berg, an admirer of the brilliant composer Arnold Schoenberg. The brief sojourn in Vienna did not work out well for the immature Adorno, but it proved a turning point in his life, and it was at this time that he met Lukács.

Lukács's influence can be seen in Adorno's Habilitationsschrift (dissertation) in 1931 on Søren Kierkegaard, in which he rejects idealism as the prime bourgeois ideology, a theme that was to appear repeatedly in *Negative Dialektik* (1966; *Negative Dialectics*, 1973) and other works. The failure of the bourgeois class to change the world made social critics of Adorno, Kracauer, and Lukács, as well as of Adorno's new friend Walter Benjamin, and for them "Marxism" meant the exhaustion of bourgeois society. It was a nervous Marxism, however, for, as Claussen notes of Benjamin, he closer he came to orthodox communism, the more he felt repelled by what it meant in practice.

After three years in New York, Adorno became Thomas Mann's neighbor in Los Angeles, and Claussen devotes a whole chapter to Adorno's contribution to the composition of Mann's novel *Doktor Faustus* (1947; *Doctor Faustus*, 1948), the story of a composer, Adrian Leverkün, whose musical inventions "in reality" belong to Schoenberg. The relationship, however, was not without some clash of egos, with Mann's daughter, Erika Mann, faulting Adorno for his account in 1962 of their working routines. Mann and Adorno both knew that *Doctor Faustus* would be "the last bourgeois novel in the German tradition," as Claussen calls it. Adorno thus speaks of his being "non-identical," a younger man than Mann and a different one. He was different in a further sense, for in 1942 he had dropped the surname Wiesengrund and become simply Theodor Adorno.

Claussen tells the stories of two of Adorno's friends in his chapter on "Transitions." Hanns Eisler and Adorno collaborated in 1944 on *Komposition für den Film* (*Composing for the Films*, 1947), but the original edition caused a great stir when it was published a year after Adorno's death in 1969. It had been published in 1947 under Eisler's name alone, a subterfuge necessitated by the radical political activities of Eisler's brother, Gerhart, and Adorno's desire to avoid being smeared by the notoriety. Adorno and Eisler were friends of long standing, but the Cold War split them, with Eisler living in the German Democratic Republic and Adorno returning to the Federal Republic. Eisler, like the dramatist Bertolt Brecht and the Marxist critic Ernst Bloch, had been careful, however, to spend the Stalinist period in the United States. Another close California associate of Adorno was film director Fritz Lang, whom he met in Hollywood and who remained a good friend until Adorno's death. Lang helped Brecht immensely, not least by financing his escape from Vladivostok to California in 1941, but Lang ran into financial problems and returned to West Germany. Later, in the 1960's, European cinema theorists took up his work in publications such as *Cahiers du cinema* and the Frankfurt *Filmstudio*.

When Horkheimer left New York to live in California, the Institute for Social Research, now housed at Columbia University, was taken over by Paul F. Lazarsfeld, an ambitious Viennese who had established himself as director of the Princeton Radio Research Project. In that capacity, he hired Adorno as music director, a job unsuited to a theorist with no background in empirical research. One of Adorno's later conclusions about music insisted that the distinction between serious music and light was the result of America's capitalist division of labor, an observation that reveals something about the depth of Adorno's grasp of American music culture. After his return to Frankfurt, in 1953 Adorno published "Perennial Fashion—Jazz," an account of jazz as obsolete. In the chapter on the culture industry in *Dialectic of Enlightenment*, jazz is treated as one of the running sores of advanced capitalism. Claussen observes, "Again and again Adorno's critique of jazz establishes a far from convincing linkage of jazz and sadomasochism, utility music and castration."

Adorno stayed in the United States, mostly in California, from 1938 till 1949, but even after returning to Frankfurt he made periodic trips to Los Angeles, partly to keep his American passport. He never again returned to the United States after 1953. The volume of wide-ranging essays titled *Prismen* (*Prisms*, 1967), published in 1955 soon after his return to Frankfurt, marked the beginnings of Critical Theory. Previously restrained in his political commentary except when excoriating Soviet cultural policies, Adorno speaks out bluntly in his essays in *Prisms*. He attacks directly the "politicization of intellectuals" encouraged by Karl Mannheim in his advancement of a sociology of knowledge, a direct descendant of the bourgeois sociology of such thinkers as Max Weber. He saw in Germany the revival—the reification—of a culture presenting itself as timeless, and he soon settled into a role as "the critic of a schizoid restoration of culture."

Adorno's relationship with Horkheimer was long and fruitful for both men, with Adorno following Horkheimer to New York in 1938. The great achievement of their California period was *Dialectic of Enlightenment*. Back in Frankfurt in 1956, they contemplated a new version of Karl Marx and Friedrich Engels's *Manifestder Kommunistischen Partei* (1848; *The Communist Manifesto*, 1850) that would address the issues of their times. Horkheimer was disturbed by the collectivization of agriculture just undertaken in China, fearing a repeat of the Soviet collectivization of the 1930's. He was especially shocked by the reports of twenty million victims of Chinese industrialization, and his political awareness exceeded Adorno's. Horkheimer had been alert to the viciousness of Stalinism from early on. He told Benjamin in 1942 that the degradation of traditional Marxism into the commodity fetishism of the Stalin era was an aspect of authoritarian states like fascism and communism. During the 1950's Adorno stayed in Frankfurt, minding the Institute for Social Research and becoming a public figure, while Horkheimer commuted occasionally to teach at the University of Chicago. Indeed, he broke mildly with Adorno on the latter's indictment of the Culture Industry, opining that it would be best to retain America's achievements. When Adorno sneered at television programs, Horkheimer responded that it was the most progressive workers who were buying television sets. In their relationship, Horkheimer continued to favor the nontheoretical side of radical theory as opposed to Adorno's determined updating of theory.

After the war, back in Frankfurt, Adorno revived several old relationships, especially with Bloch and Kracauer. Bloch had alienated Adorno with his defense of the Moscow trials, but he was cautious enough to escape to the United States through Prague. Bloch remained, along with Brecht and Eisler, an unrepentant champion of Soviet communism. Adorno could not accept Bloch's optimism. He sharply criticized Bloch's *Erbschaft dieser Zeit* (1935; *Heritage of Our Times*, 1991) on its publication, and the controversy over it was resumed in the 1960's, although Adorno continued to praise Bloch's first book, *Geist der Utopie* (1918; *Spirit of Utopia*, 1970).

Adorno's relationship with Kracauer was a different story. Adorno hoped to arrange Kracauer's assimilation back into German intellectual currents by convincing Suhrcamp to publish his volume of essays *Das Ornament der Masse* (*The Mass Ornament*, 1991) in 1963. Adorno's 1964 essay on Kracauer, "The Curious Realist," in which Claussen says he "drip-fed the memory of inextinguishable mass atrocities," resonated with the many discussions held by the exiled intellectuals of the prewar period. In addition, Kracauer's perceptive 1930 study of white-collar workers, *Die Angestellten* (*The Salaried Masses*, 1998) was reissued in 1959. Nevertheless, despite the collaboration involved in these publishing successes, Kracauer and Adorno grew apart in their thinking before Kracauer's death in 1966.

Adorno's early years of teaching at the Institute for Social Research in Frankfurt must have been satisfying, because he enjoyed the respect of his students and a growing public reputation. In 1957 his assistant, Jürgen Habermas, debuted as a political theorist with a "brilliant" essay on "The Philosophical Discussion Around Marx and Marxism," but he was soon forced out of the Institute for Social Research by Horkheimer. Horkheimer's wife, however, once remarked that "Teddie (Adorno) is the most monstrous narcissist to be found in either the Old World or the New," and Claussen observes that in 1996 "Adorno was widely regarded as an academically obsolete elitist aesthete from an indeterminate epoch lying in the remote bourgeois past." For the last two years of his life, Adorno struggled to establish good relations with Herbert Marcuse, whose student followers preached hope for the future. The protest movement in Frankfurt peaked in the spring of 1969, and when the students occupied Frankfurt University Adorno and his colleagues could only call on the police for support. Horkheimer denied that these conflicts hastened Adorno's death, but in 1969, he escaped to the Hotel Bristol in Zermatt, Switzerland, and there he died on August 6.

Frank Day

Review Sources

Library Journal 133, no. 4 (March 1, 2008): 84-85.
London Review of Books 30, no. 12 (June 19, 2008): 9-10.
Publishers Weekly 255, no. 6 (February 11, 2008): 64.
The Wall Street Journal 251, no. 91 (April 18, 2008): W5.

THERE A PETAL SILENTLY FALLS
Three Stories

Author: Ch'oe Yun (1953-   )
First published: Chogi sori opsi hanjom kkonnip i chigo,
   1992, in South Korea
Translated from the Korean by Bruce and Ju-Chan Fulton
Publisher: Columbia University Press (New York). 192
   pp. $24.50
Type of work: Short fiction
Time: 1980 to the present
Locale: South Korea

*Three lyrical stories by one of South Korea's most re-
spected writers*

Ch'oe Yun is a professor of French literature at Sogang
University in Seoul, South Korea, where she was born and
where she studied Korean language and literature. After graduation, she studied in
France where she received a doctorate. Her first publications were critical essays on
literature, but in 1988, her first fiction, a novella entitled *There a Petal Silently Falls*,
appeared. Since then, she has won a number of awards.

Although her first story in this collection of three depicts the aftereffects of the
1980 Kwangju massacre, she denies that she is an ideological writer, arguing that all
literary works, no matter how neutral, have a message. She also denies that her work
is experimental, as often suggested by critics. She says that to depict a constantly
changing reality one must use a unique language and form because you cannot change
the world with conventional methods and language. Because writing is a struggle to
transcend time, she cherishes her novella *There a Petal Silently Falls* more than any
of her other works for its timelessness and universality.

The story focuses on a fifteen-year-old girl whose brother, a victim of the repressive military government, has disappeared and whose mother has been killed in the
1980 Kwangju massacre. The riots took place a few months after a military coup,
when students and labor activists engaged in a series of nationwide demonstrations,
insisting on democratic elections and an end to martial law. Paratrooper units of Korea's Special Forces Command were ordered into the city of Kwangju, killing a number of people; the government says less than two hundred; the survivors say nearly
two thousand, claiming that the military burned many bodies and dumped the rest into
the sea.

Influenced by her study of the critic Mikhail Bakhtin, Ch'oe Yun creates a story of
several voices in polyphonic counterpoint told from three viewpoints: the young girl
who has been driven half mad by her losses; a man who takes her in and abuses her;
and a small group of her brother's friends who search for her.

The story begins with a cautionary warning about a young girl haunting the

*Ch'oe Yun is professor of French
literature at Sogang University in
Seoul, South Korea. She received the
1992 Tongin Literature Prize and the
1994 Yi San Literature Prize. Her
works have also been translated into
French and Spanish.*

gravesites in the city who may follow you (especially if you are a young man in your twenties), crying, "Brother." The story then moves to a man who is followed by the girl. Unable to get rid of her, he takes her in and has sex with her, although she remains silent. The story shifts to the voice of the girl, as she recalls her mother lying in the street, shot, and a black curtain falling over her mind. The voice of the girl reflects her loss of contact with reality and her increasing hallucinations. She recalls the previous year, when two men came to her house and told her mother something about her brother that made her mother scream and cry.

The story shifts to the point of view of some of her brother's friends who are searching for her, describing how she turns up in Okp'o and is made an errand girl. When the perspective shifts back to the girl again, she is not sure whether she is experiencing reality or a dream, as she finds refuge in a cave where she has to fight off a horde of beetles as big as toads. She walks for days in the mountains until she is taken in by a mute who feeds her, washes her clothes, and has sex with her, which she describes as a bluebird entering between her legs. However, once again, she cannot be sure if this happened or it if was an illusion.

In one crucial scene, she describes being on a train and seeing the face of a woman in the window, which she eventually recognizes as her own. The face in the glass becomes that of a monster that says it is going to open up her skull and remove the black curtain, until she shatters the window with her head. She now accepts the fact that she has created the black curtain to cover up everything that happened on the day her mother was killed.

In the penultimate section of the story, the girl has a hallucinatory conversation with her brother, telling him what happened on the day of her mother's death. She confesses her mother did not want her to come with her, but that she insisted and ran after her. She feels guilty that when her mother is shot, the girl must step on her mother's arm to free her hand, feeling the slippery blood under her feet. She laments that she can never return to that day when she committed the terrible crime of stamping on her mother's arm so she could get away and live, feeling she has no place to go now but to the grave with her brother.

The story ends with the point of view of the young men who continue their search for the girl. A year after the death of the brother, they see a photo of the girl that a man has put in the paper, and they go to talk to him, recognizing a similarity to the girl's brother. They are not sure why they have engaged in this search—to comfort their lost friend that they had found her, to pacify the soul of her departed mother, or to fulfill their sense of obligation. Maybe, they think, they were only indulging in cheap humanitarianism.

The second story in the collection, "Whisper Yet," is also a polyphonic piece, this time alternating back and forth in time as a mother talks with her young daughter and remembers her childhood, especially her relationship with a farmhand, Ajaebi, a former prisoner of war and a fugitive from the South Korean government, who lived with her family. When her father, who left North Korea because he hated communism, becomes ill, Ajaebi nurses him. The two men become like brothers, practically inseparable, often whispering together. When the young woman goes home from school for the summer, Ajaebi gives her a folded slip of paper, asking that she deliver it to a house. Before depositing the message she reads its one line—"No time for the moon to rise on the water of the stream."

In her internal monologue to her child, the woman warns her it is a war out there and says she wants her to become a poet who turns ugly words into beautiful ones. She recalls the notebooks that Ajaebi left after his death, filled with lines of poetry. In a ten-year period, she delivered one-line poems to five different houses for Ajaebi, learning that the recipients were his wife and his young son, from whom he has been separated because he faces a death sentence from the Korean government. The story ends with the mother's brief internal monologue to her daughter, saying she has much to whisper to her, asking what kind of story she should tell, a story of tears, of laughter, of days gone by, of days yet to come—a story like she told her unborn child when the two were one body.

The third story, "The Thirteen-Scent Flower," has a different tone. Although it retains some lyrical beauty, it changes at the end into a satire on bureaucrats and academics who try to commercially appropriate beauty. The story begins with a young man, aged twenty, who comes to Seoul to work as a truck driver. However, his dream is to live in the Arctic. Each evening he lies in bed and looks at a map on his wall and dreams of walking the Arctic wastes by himself. He names himself Bye, which he says means "a man who walks the Arctic flats." A young girl, aged sixteen, is introduced hiding by the side of the road. She is from a remote mountain village; her parents are dead, she has no siblings, and she was raised by her grandmother, who named her Green Hands because she did such good work producing crops in stony ground. Death seems to her to be a nymph hovering to solve her problems. When she sees a truck with only one headlight coming toward her, she starts to run out in front of it when it sputters to a stop. In typical fairy-tale inevitability, the driver is Bye, and the young girl rides away with him.

The two fall in love and decide to seek out a desert island where they can live. After driving for several months, they arrive at Green Hand's ancestral home. In fairy-tale fashion when they arrive, the grandmother, who has waited for the girl's return so she could die, asks that they plant some seeds on her grave. In the coldest part of the winter, a flower grows from the seeds. After discovering that the flower, which they name wind chrysanthemum, prefers dark, cold earth, they devise a propeller that simulates an Arctic wind, making the flower give off powerfully strong scents. Unable to sell the flowers, they decide to leave one with each family in the village. As a result of the flower's magical scent, several people move to Land's End, where the young couple lives.

The story continues in the fairy-tale mode, as people come from far and wide to smell the scent of the wind chrysanthemums. A forty-two-year-old man named Ko comes to study the plant, saying he suffers from low-altitude sickness and that, like the wind chrysanthemums, he needs cold air and strong mountain winds to stay alive. With the arrival of Ko, who seems to be the only person in the world who has low-altitude sickness, the story shifts to the comic and the satiric. The wind chrysanthemum becomes a craze; a man writes a poem about it, which is then made into a song that everyone sings. Reporters and photographers come to Land's End. Horticultural specialists offer Bye and Green Hands money for rights to cultivate the wind chrysanthemums. People come to buy the essence of the flower's scent for perfume. Ko decides to write a history of Bye and Green Hands's cultivation of the flower, titled *Everything You Wanted to Know About the Wind Chrysanthemum.*

Pharmaceutical experts come to procure the flower's scents, which they say have healing properties, for alimentary and urinary ailments. Plans are even made for a theme park near Land's End. Horticulturalists battle over rights to give the flower a Latin name. Inevitably, a reaction sets in and articles appear in magazines warning that if you smell the flowers your hair will fall out. As if they know that the wind chrysanthemums only exist in the realm of fairy tale, Bye and Green Hands drive to the seashore and walk into the waves.

Ch'oe Yun is a major new Asian fiction writer whose stories have the formal delicacy of fairy tale and legend, carefully controlled, perhaps as a result of her academic training. Her fabulistic formality is beautifully sustained by her translators.

Charles E. May

Review Sources

Booklist 104, no. 18 (May 15, 2008): 22.
Publishers Weekly 225, no. 13 (March 31, 2008): 38.

THIS REPUBLIC OF SUFFERING
Death and the American Civil War

Author: Drew Gilpin Faust (1947-   )
Publisher: Alfred A. Knopf (New York). 346 pp. $27.95
Type of work: History
Time: 1861-1865
Locale: The United States

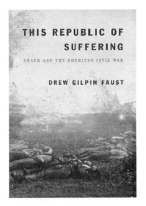

An examination of how the unprecedented carnage
caused by the Civil War changed the American perceptions
of death and dying

Principal personages:
>WALT WHITMAN, an American poet who
dedicated himself to visiting the
wounded and dying in Civil War
hospitals
>AMBROSE BIERCE, an American writer who served in the Civil War and
wrote about his experience
>CLARA BARTON, an American nursing pioneer who devoted herself to
identifying the Civil War dead
>EDMUND B. WHITMAN, assigned to locate and identify Union dead after
the war
>ELIZABETH STUART PHELPS, the author of *The Gates Ajar*, a best-selling
nineteenth century novel

In *This Republic of Suffering*, Drew Gilpin Faust demonstrates how the unprecedented carnage, both military and civilian, caused by the Civil War forever changed
American assumptions about death and dying, and how the nation and its people
struggled to come to terms with death on an unimaginable scale. As Faust explains,
"Death transformed the American nation as well as the hundreds of thousands of individuals directly affected by loss." The war created a veritable "republic of suffering,"
in the words that Frederick Law Olmsted chose to describe the wounded and dying arriving at Union hospital ships on the Virginia Peninsula. Her chapter titles—"Dying,"
"Killing," "Burying," "Naming," "Realizing," "Believing and Doubting," "Accounting," "Numbering," and "Surviving"—succinctly yet vividly portray the United
States' ordeal and transformation during and after the war as the country struggled to
invent new ways of dealing with the onslaught of death.

The scope of death caused by the Civil War is almost incomprehensible today. Between 1861 and 1865, an estimated 620,000 soldiers died, a number approximately
equal to the total American fatalities in the Revolutionary War, War of 1812, Mexican War, Spanish-American War, World War I, World War II, and the Korean War
combined. The rate of death was six times that of World War II, about 2 percent of the
population, which would total six million dead in a war today. Confederates died at a
rate three times that of Union soldiers; in fact, one in five Southern men of military

∿

Drew Gilpin Faust earned an M.A. and Ph.D. in American civilization at the University of Pennsylvania. In 2001, she became the founding dean of the Radcliffe Institute for Advanced Study. Faust was appointed president of Harvard in 2007 following controversy regarding then-President Lawrence H. Summers. She is an eminent scholar of the Civil War and the antebellum South.

∿

age died in the war and more than fifty thousand civilians also perished.

This unprecedented loss of life was neither expected nor prepared for as the war began. The Union army assumed it would make short work of the rebels, and it made no provisions to deal with the carnage that was to ensue. Until 1864 the Union army did not even have an ambulance service. More than two weeks after the battle at Antietam, a horrifying number of corpses remained unburied on the battlefield, stacked in rows a thousand long. Following the battle at Gettysburg, more than six million tons of animal and human bodies were left for disposal. There was no provision for burying the dead, a job which usually fell to the victorious army, which often had neither the will nor time to take care of its own dead, let alone those of the enemy.

The Union and Confederate armies did not have a process in place for burying their dead, and they had no procedure for identifying the bodies or informing the families of deceased soldiers. There were no dog tags or any other official means of identification, no procedure for counting the dead, and no national cemeteries in which to bury them. Only officers had access to coffins; at best, enlisted men might be wrapped in a blanket before being buried in a mass grave, and others were left where they fell. Chaotic record keeping led to reports of deaths of soldiers who were still alive. Nurses and hospital volunteers did their best to contact family whenever possible, but often family members traveled to battlefields in search of news of their loved ones. The poet Walt Whitman regularly visited hospitals to write letters for wounded soldiers to their families, and he made every effort to inform them when their son, husband, father, or brother had died. Nursing pioneer Clara Barton devoted her time after the war to identifying the war dead as well.

In the mid-nineteenth century, people generally died at home, surrounded by family members and comforting rituals. It was thought that the way one met death indicated one's state of readiness to meet God and was crucial to one's successful passage into Heaven. In this so-called good death, the dying person was expected not only to express an awareness of his impending fate and acceptance of it but also to state his belief in God and salvation. These last words were considered critical to achieving the good death. The war, however, forced Americans to redefine a good death, since their fathers, sons, husbands, and brothers were dying in unimaginably horrible ways, alone and far from home. In order to reassure their family that they met a good death, many soldiers wrote letters that they carried with them, assuring their families that they were at one with God and prepared to meet their fate should the occasion arise. The letters written to families by nurses, volunteers, and fellow soldiers describing the deceased's last moments have an eerie similarity, as if they were completing a mental checklist of the good-death requirements.

With pressure from grieving mothers, wives, and sisters, who could not bear not knowing how their loved ones faced death, the government ultimately took up the task of identifying and caring for the remains of its war dead. After the war the federal government gathered the Union dead from Southern battlefields and buried the bodies in new federally funded national cemeteries. It took six years to complete this job, and, at its conclusion in 1871, 303,536 Union soldiers, nearly half of whom were never identified, had been buried at a cost of four million dollars. This massive effort of identifying and burying the war dead created a federal bureaucracy that forever changed the relationship between the individual citizen and the government, and, contends Faust, it helped to create our modern American state.

This federal program, however, covered only Union soldiers, not the Confederate dead, and while Union soldiers were returned from Southern battlefields and buried in the national cemeteries, the Confederate bodies were left where they fell, often still unburied. Southern women took up the cause of taking care of their deceased soldiers, raising funds to gather up and bury their dead in private cemeteries. The resentment caused by the government's treatment of Southern casualties helped to foster the strong feelings of separatism that linger in the South to this day and to promote the cult of the Lost Cause.

The war's overwhelming death counts also caused a crisis of faith in this country. In a world that allowed such terrible, often anonymous deaths, God's benevolence was questioned, and a search for meaning ensued, including new ideas of heaven and earth. Profound spiritual and intellectual questions were raised, some of which previewed modernist disillusionment. Some writers, such as Ambrose Bierce, a soldier himself, wrote of his war experiences in an unromanticized manner, rejecting an idealistic view of the war. At the opposite extreme, Elizabeth Stuart Phelps, in *The Gate Ajar* (1868), the second-best-selling book of the nineteenth century after Harriet Beecher Stowe's *Uncle Tom's Cabin* (1852), reimagined heaven not as a kingdom of winged angels playing harps but rather as a place similar to home, where families were brought together again, husband and wives were reunited, and Abraham Lincoln blessed fallen soldiers, bringing comfort to those who had lost loved ones in the war.

As Faust notes, "Men and women approach death in ways shaped by history, by culture, by conditions that vary over time and across space. Even though 'we all have our dead,' and even though we all die, we do so differently from generation to generation and from place to place." Before the war, death was an accepted part of life, accompanied by familiar rites and traditions, but with death now happening to young, healthy men, it took on a whole new meaning. Although Americans of the era may have been culturally prepared to die, they were not prepared to kill. They were not morally ready to take the lives of their fellow Americans, and many found killing more difficult than dying. Snipers, who caused the majority of deaths during the war, were considered immoral by their fellow soldiers because they did not face their victims. Only by being absolutely certain of the rightness of their cause could the young men bring themselves to take a human life.

This Republic of Suffering is a masterful study of American history and culture, revealing not only fascinating historical details on nearly every page but also new insights into the American psyche. As absorbing as an engrossing novel, *This Republic of Suffering* captivates and excites the reader at every turn. Examining the Civil War through the lens of death provides a unique and revealing perspective on American culture. As Faust explains:

> Americans had to identify—find, invent, create—the means and mechanisms to manage more than half a million dead: their deaths, their bodies, and their loss. How they accomplished this task reshaped their individual lives—and deaths—at the same time that it redefined their nation and their culture. The work of death was Civil War America's most fundamental and most demanding undertaking.

Mary Virginia Davis

Review Sources

America 198, no. 16 (May 12, 2008): 32-34.
American Historical Review 113, no. 4 (October, 2008): 1108-1110.
American History 43, no. 2 (June, 2008): 67.
American Scholar 77, no. 1 (Winter, 2008): 120-123.
The Christian Century 125, no. 13 (July 1, 2008): 40-41.
Journal of American History 95, no. 3 (December, 2008): 808-809.
Kirkus Reviews 75, no. 20 (October 15, 2007): 1083.
Publishers Weekly 254, no. 40 (October 8, 2007): 45-46.
The Times Literary Supplement, July 25, 2008, p. 7.
The Wilson Quarterly 32, no. 1 (Winter, 2008): 98-99.

TRAFFIC
Why We Drive the Way We Do (and What It Says About Us)

Author: Tom Vanderbilt (1968-)
Publisher: Alfred A. Knopf (New York). 402 pp. $24.95
Type of work: History, sociology, technology, psychology

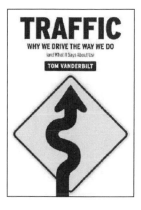

Vanderbilt draws upon wide-ranging research to describe the complexity of traffic, the technology and infrastructure making it possible, and the often ill-advised behavior of drivers

It just may be as most drivers, at some point or other, come to suspect: Motor vehicle traffic is part miracle, part mass psychosis, and, if a person is to survive, a matter of oblivion to statistics. While Tom Vanderbilt's marvelous exposé, *Traffic: Why We Drive the Way We Do (and What It Says About Us)*, does not exactly confirm that dark surmise, it does consider why perfectly agreeable, well-socialized, intelligent people undergo a transformation behind the steering wheel and behave in ways contrary to their own interests and safety. Partly that arises from advances in technology and infrastructure supporting ground transportation. As Vanderbilt shows, however, traffic is above all things a social act, but one in which participants are inhibited from divining the intentions of each other through the means that normally smooth social intercourse. Added to this problem is the paradoxical nature of traffic.

The focus of *Traffic* is largely on modern cars (although Vanderbilt discusses transportation history) and their drivers. "In traffic," he writes, "we struggle to stay human." Why this should be so is the most fascinating theme in the book. Essentially, isolation, inattention, frustration, and conceit cause the trouble. For one thing, drivers can see what others do but cannot convey what they think about it. For another, the eye contact that usually mediates social interaction is seldom possible in traffic. Each driver, alone in a car, becomes identified with the car. Unable to converse directly with others on the road, drivers make up independent narratives about their behavior and that of others based wholly on what they see cars do. The narrative easily segues into moral drama when the behavior of one driver makes another feel victimized. Worse, the anonymity of drivers, cocooned in their vehicles, increases aggressiveness in traffic, often expressed in an unfocused need to dominate. On top of such impulses, drivers have many distractions: talking to passengers, making cell phone calls, eating, drinking, smoking, fiddling with the radio, gaping at the scenery, even reading. All the while each driver typically believes that he or she is more law-abiding and skillful than those nearby. (The well-established "Baker's law," formulated by crash expert J. Stannard Baker, contends that drivers want to explain away their traffic mishaps by reporting circumstances of "lowest culpability compatible with credulity.")

~

Based in New York City, Tom
Vanderbilt writes and lectures on
architecture, design, technology, and
science. He is a contributing editor to
the design magazines I.D. *and* Print
and contributes to numerous
publications, such as Wired, The New
York Times, The Wilson Quarterly,
and Rolling Stone.

~

The impulse to drive assertively, the inattention, and the susceptibility to taking umbrage, as if other drivers are intentionally set upon harming each other, lead to anger, and anger impairs judgment. Every driver has had enough upsetting encounters to recognize that the following hypothetical incident on a four-lane highway, however absurd, is yet possible. Driver A, while talking on a cell phone, glances into the rear-view mirror, glimpses an opening into the faster traffic of the lane to the left, and swerves into it, flicking on the turn signal in the process. Satisfied the maneuver was legal and safe (because successful), Driver A moves on. At the beginning of the maneuver, however, Driver B, in the fast lane, is singing along to a rock-and-roll classic so that when Driver A swerves in front, Driver B is startled and reflexively taps on the brake. Driver C, meanwhile, impatient with Driver B for poking along in the passing lane, has edged close to Driver B's rear bumper (and is annoyed to read there a bumper sticker with a disagreeable political slogan). Interpreting Driver B's brake light as a message to back off (passive-aggressive braking), Driver C is irked. Accordingly, Driver C accelerates into the space vacated by Driver A, pulls even with Driver B, and makes an uncomplimentary hand gesture. Astonished and offended, Driver B replies in kind, unconsciously pressing down on the accelerator. The ensuing minor rear-end collision between Driver B and Driver D results in a rush-hour traffic jam that slows the progress of hundreds. Driver A, blithely unaware of what lies behind, is not among them.

Even relatively minor collisions can prove deadly, given high speeds and dense traffic. In 1999, for example, some forty-one thousand people died in crashes. Although that number represents a decline in fatalities since the 1950's, it still leaves traffic as a leading killer of healthy Americans. (In countries such as China and India, which have had a sudden influx of new drivers and inadequate infrastructure and driving customs, the numbers of fatalities and injuries are shocking.) Given the vast improvement in car technology, especially safety features, and the expansion of roadways, it is still surprising that so many crashes occur. Naturally, much of the responsibility lies with drivers. Lulled by the illusion of firm control behind the wheel, some, believing that they drive better than they do, drive carelessly, drive in a state of "selective awareness," and, essentially, do any number of things that make crashes unpreventable. "[T]he safer cars get," writes Vanderbilt, "the more risks drivers choose to take."

Still, a share of the problem lies in the sometimes paradoxical nature of traffic itself, a fact complicating the task of engineers to increase safety. Vanderbilt opens his book with a brilliant example: when to merge because of a lane closure. The majority of drivers merge as soon as they see the warning sign of a closure ahead, feeling that they have done the socially correct thing, and then seethe as a few mavericks forge on past them and cut in right before the choke point, slowing everyone behind. Is merging early really the right thing to do, though? As Vanderbilt points out, if everyone merges early, one entire lane is left unused. It would be more efficient for both lanes to be filled right up to the choke point and then have cars move into the unobstructed lane with a "zipper merge." So in the case of merging, the socially considerate action (merging early) decreases, rather than increases, efficiency. There are many other examples: More roads mean more traffic, not less, because they encourage use by those who would otherwise have stayed home to avoid traffic. Narrow roads are safer than wide roads, because they force drivers to slow down. Traffic circles are less dangerous than intersections for much the same reason. In altercations between truckers and car drivers, the latter are in the wrong the overwhelming majority of the time. Large, high cars, such as SUVs, are less safe than small cars because it is more difficult to judge speed and the distance to the next car; accordingly, drivers regularly exceed safe speeds for their vehicles' design. Women are more likely to crash than men but are less likely to be in fatal crashes. In heavy traffic, slower speed can get drivers to their destinations faster, because there is less braking, and braking has a cascading effect, slowing traffic in general until it lapses into "stop-and-go" behavior.

Perhaps it is a testament to human adaptability that traffic proceeds as smoothly as it does. At all events, *Traffic* argues, remedies exist for many current deficiencies. Primary is to slow down and to pay attention. Beyond that, engineers are becoming aware that designing highways only for speed can be counterproductive. Some propose controversial measures, such as narrowing lanes and shoulders, especially in congested areas, or reducing signage, or making pedestrian crossing easier. Another proposal is congestion pricing on toll roads—that is, charging higher tolls during high-use periods to discourage driving. Vanderbilt also mentions, although is skeptical of, new technology, such as navigation devices that detect highway congestion ahead and propose alternative routes.

Vanderbilt is engaging and writes plainly. When he must quote the jargon of engineers or psychologists, he frequently accompanies the quotation with a punchy translation. He avoids euphemisms, for instance, using "crash" instead of the mushy, often disingenuous "traffic accident." He is sententious ("affluence breeds traffic"), witty, and provocative. Consider just two chapter titles: "Why Ants Don't Get into Traffic Jams (and Humans Do): On Cooperation as a Cure for Congestion" and "Why You Shouldn't Drive with a Beer-Drinking Divorced Doctor Named Fred on Super Bowl Sunday in a Pickup Truck in Rural Montana: What's Risky on the Road and Why." He ranges widely in coverage, discussing traffic behavior in China, India, Europe, and Latin America as well as in the United States. Still, *Traffic* has limitations. Vanderbilt admits that the environmental effects of traffic are an important topic but, unfortunately, declines to address it. The focus of the book is trained largely on car drivers (they do, after all, constitute the largest share of traffic), yet after learning that tractor-trailer drivers are usually the victims of mishaps rather than the cause, readers may well want to learn more about them, if only to understand how to behave near them. About one matter readers must particularly prepare themselves: statistics. *Traffic* draws heavily on psychology, economics, and sociology. All three disciplines rely on statistical analyses of data, and so does Vanderbilt. Even though the statistics in his book are not stultifyingly dense, they sometimes seem incongruent and so can create a cognitive traffic jam of their own, with a 31.4 percent chance of sudden comprehension failure for readers unwilling to slow down and proceed through them cautiously.

Intriguingly, Vanderbilt shows how traffic both reflects and amplifies larger cultural trends. Greater mobility expands the distances that people are willing to travel for simple chores. Accordingly, shopping malls, huge discount stores such as Wal-Mart and Costco, and supermarkets, all with acres of parking, were built to accommodate them. Between 1983 and 2001, trips to malls alone increased twofold. School districts save money by building fewer, larger schools because children can come from farther away. Fast food restaurants featuring drive-through lanes attract diners who do not want to get out of their cars for meals. These shifts in behavior not only meant the end of the corner grocery store, a great reduction in children walking to school, and the decline in home cooking but also increased and redistributed traffic: heavier traffic in the morning as school buses and parents transporting students join in the rush hour and more traffic spread through the day as shoppers fan out. In a phenomenon called "trip-chaining," drivers now regularly stop en route to a traditional daily destination, such as a job site, to drop off children at day care, take clothes to the cleaners, pick up breakfast, and the like. The related "Starbucks' effect" involves stops simply so that people (increasingly men) can have some time to themselves away from job and family—by, for example, sipping a latte.

Traffic astonishes, sometimes amuses, and frequently corrects misconceptions, but its real contribution lies in demonstrating—in concrete, familiar detail—the plasticity of modern society. People adapt to cars as cars are adapted to them, and traffic, remarkably, flows. Moreover, the book has some crossover value as cultural analysis. For instance, it is nearly impossible, while reading *Traffic*, not to be reminded of the financial market, another human activity that inspires reckless self-interest yet seems to move with miraculous facility—until, that is, there is a crash.

Roger Smith

Review Sources

Booklist 104, nos. 19/20 (June 1, 2008): 4-5.
Discover 29, no. 8 (August, 2008): 74.
Entertainment Weekly, September 19, 2008, p. 79.
Kirkus Reviews 76, no. 11 (June 1, 2008): 75.
Library Journal 133, no. 11 (June 15, 2008): 83-84.
The New Republic 239, no. 2 (August 13, 2008): 36-39.
The New York Times Book Review, August 10, 2008, p. 1.
The New Yorker 84, no. 25 (August 25, 2008): 81.
Newsweek 152, no. 6 (August 11, 2008): 10.
Publishers Weekly 255, no. 20 (May 19, 2008): 43.
Time 172, no. 5 (August 4, 2008): 23.

THE TREE OF MEANING
Language, Mind, and Ecology

Author: Robert Bringhurst (1946-   )
First published: The Tree of Meaning: Thirteen Talks, 2006, in Canada
Publisher: Counterpoint (Berkeley, Calif.). 336 pp. $28.00
Type of work: Literary criticism

Thirteen lectures delivered by Canadian poet, translator, and linguist Bringhurst at universities and academic institutions cover the relationship of Native American oral literature to other world literatures, emphasizing their unappreciated similarities, their narrative methods, their prosody and literary form, and their connections to the natural world

Principal personages:

ROBERT BRINGHURST, the author, whose personal experiences with Native American oral poets are recounted throughout the lectures

EMILE PETITOT, a French missionary who first wrote down the songs and stories of Lizette K'atchodi, Big Rabbit Woman, the first Native Canadian woman recorded in her own language

FRANZ BOAS, the father of modern anthropology, trained in physics and geography but bringing scientific analysis to Native American oral poetry, especially by transcribing the rapidly disappearing oral poems largely ignored by experts in Indian languages

Q'ELTI´, ranked by Bringhurst with Emily Dickinson and Wallace Stevens, whose oral performances were first recorded by Boas in the 1890's

SKAAY, of the Qquuna Qiighawaay lineage, and GHANDL, of the Qayahl Llaanas line, Haida oral poets Bringhurst ranks as among the best in any language, possibly equal to Homer

JOHN SWANTON, Boas's student who transcribed Skaay's poems

EDWARD SAPIR, another student of Boas who went on to do groundbreaking work in Native American languages and who is considered by Bringhurst a true humanist, in comparison to more technically oriented modern linguists

BILL REID, a Haida sculptor and artist of worldwide renown who is the subject of one of the memorial lectures

The thirteen lectures in *The Tree of Meaning* were delivered by Robert Bringhurst at eminent Canadian, U.S., and European universities and academic venues, including the University of British Columbia, Vancouver; the University of Victoria, British Columbia; the College of France, Paris; and the Universidad de la Laguna, Tenerife (delivered in Spanish). At least five were named memorial lectures. While all are

~

Robert Bringhurst is one of Canada's most published poets, a translator of Haida and other Native American oral works, a frequent lecturer on literature and humanistic issues, an environmental advocate, and an expert in typography. He lives on Quadra Island, off the east coast of Vancouver Island.

~

serious academic performances, the tone and style vary, ranging from fairly casual and relaxed student-centered talks about vocation to a sensitive and nostalgic memorial to a deceased Haida artist friend to uncompromisingly scholarly anatomies of Native American prosody and literary technique, rife with extensive quotations from any number of languages, including Native tongues. (Translations follow all quotations.) All are unified by Bringhurst's charm, articulate speech, and engaging ideas, but even more so by continuing threads and themes returned to with fresh perspectives in each talk. There is no repetition or recycling; even when Bringhurst refers to earlier work, the new context changes our understanding artfully. The goal is to provide what amounts to a unified field theory, not of physics (the term was coined by Albert Einstein), but of language and literature, and especially of North American Native languages and literatures. A Theory of Everything, as field theories are sometimes called jokingly, attempts to explain how disparate phenomena and systems work as a meaningful whole, a particularly relevant exercise given the scores of indigenous American languages, their fearsome appearance when transcribed phonetically, and the seemingly bizarre myths and creation stories they tell. How do these apparently alien works couched in inaccessible languages fit in to world literature? The traditional response has been to say they do not, relegating the thousands-of-years traditions of the first American literature to quaint folklore or puzzling religious myth.

Bringhurst credits Franz Boas (1848-1942), the progenitor of modern anthropology, with taking the first step toward understanding in the late nineteenth century. Boas was a physicist and later a geographer; he pushed his students, occasionally against their will, to record phonetic versions of disappearing oral narratives. Bringhurst is a kind of modern version of Boas, born to a widely traveled family and beginning as a physics student at the Massachusetts Institute of Technology (1963-1964) and finishing at the University of Utah, Salt Lake City (1964-1965). Bringhurst studied Arabic at the Defense Language Institute, Monterey, California (1966-1967) and served in the U.S. Army in California, Israel, and the Panama Canal Zone (1967-1969). He worked as a journalist in Beirut, Lebanon (1965-1966), before beginning a long residence in Canada, mostly in British Columbia, where he taught at a number of universities and practiced his main profession, poetry. Now a Canadian citizen, Bringhurst is widely admired as among the best practicing Canadian poets, with nearly thirty books to his credit, including *A Story as Sharp as a Knife: The Classical Haida Mythtellers and Their World* (1999). He is the author of *The Elements of Typographic Style* (2004), a respected work on print graphics now in its third edition.

Though an expert in oral literature, Bringhurst wrote an important book about print, seemingly contradicting the emphasis of his primary interest, orally delivered poetry. In like manner, his linguistic accomplishments defy easy categorization. Like

Boas and Sapir, European-trained experts who became consumed with the study of North American languages, Bringhurst brings to his New World languages and literatures insights from the Old. He has translated the ancient Greek writer Parmenides, reads Arabic, delivered one of the lectures from his book in Spanish, and seems familiar with Chinese and Japanese. In every case, unlike many modern linguists he criticizes, he has mastered these languages for the insights their poetry and literatures provide, not simply as a technical exercise in phonetics and syntax. Bringhurst rightly sees much linguistic research limited by its refusal to consider issues that extend beyond the sentence; language students often observe that the focus on what happens between the capital letter that initiates the sentence and the period that ends it has produced wondrous insights into grammar but has left the relationship between sentences—the "grammar" of paragraphs, for example, and the semantics of metaphor—relatively unexplored. Bringhurst is highly persuasive in arguing, especially in "Prosodies of Meaning: Literary Form in Native America," the tenth lecture, that understanding how oral poets hold the attention of their listeners requires attention to larger units of form than end rhyme, assonance, and the sometimes decorative discrete metaphors of Western poetry. The Native genius is not with artful figures of speech and conceits, as with seventeenth century metaphysical poet John Donne, for example, but rather with structural repetitions in threes, fours, or fives, repetitions that ironically were sometimes deleted by early translators as ritualized beginnings and endings. While Westerners search for the jewels in the crown and find them missing, they fail to examine the crown itself and misunderstand its purpose. The units of discourse, according to Bringhurst, are larger than those of much poetry in the Christian and Islamic traditions.

It should be evident why someone with polymath interests and a spectacularly diverse resumé should aspire to a unified field theory that connects his enthusiasms. Bringhurst's other great passion is the environment, and he is eloquent about how colonialism despoiled an edenic North America, killing its animals (the buffalo), parceling up the land (a process ongoing even on the small island where he lives), turning the natural into the profit-making and uniform (old growth becoming factory tree farms), and eradicating the ancient cultures and languages that had longer histories than the modern European countries that destroyed them. He is particularly hard on the missionaries who translated Native languages but only to proselytize, not to listen and learn. Bringhurst argues that language and poetry have an existence beyond the humans who speak it, evolving and changing; the language speaks through humans rather than the other way around and is in fact possibly prehuman. Language and poetry are life forces reflected in plant and animal biology and are not simply a cultural product, the sum total of speakers; humankind is not the measure of all things, says Bringhurst, refuting the statement of philosopher Protagoras as ethnocentric and self-serving. "Elemental biological mechanisms really are linguistic," and human language is simply one expression of this force.

This Platonism goes well beyond the suggestions of Noam Chomsky, the preeminent linguist of our time, that human language may have some biological basis, a readiness in infants to accept the input of a given culture, the vocabulary of Japanese or the syntax of German. Bringhurst looks at the natural world as a whole, with humans one small part of it, a part out of control, like a cancerous growth, he would argue. Language, poetry, art—all are manifestations of deep biological-natural instincts (or Forms? Ideas?) which cannot be parsed away or nailed down to a firm definition. "Stories" seem to be able to exist outside language: Trees have their own stories, for example, as do landscapes. Bringhurst uses the word "language" in a variety of ways, speaking of the language of music, of mathematics, and so on. While such usage is common as metaphor, the theory of language here is far broader, in direct opposition to the more conventional view of language as a cultural artifact.

Bringhurst's ideas about language and poetry might be thought to be attuned to Native American philosophy, although he does not make this claim and is in fact far too sophisticated to practice such reductionism: There are many Native cultures and competing philosophies. He is excellent at explaining how individual storytellers leave the imprint of their own lives and personalities on their cultural productions, introducing the personal into the seemingly monolithic. What is evident is that *The Tree of Meaning* attempts to show the reader through a charming, witty, and engaging series of views of its varied subjects how to think about poetry and language anew, as having deep roots in all cultures at their most elemental, biological levels, expressing the essence of what it means to be living and human. Bringhurst certainly learned from his oral storytellers how to hold an audience, but his ideas, beyond giving due respect to nature and advocating reduction of the huge colonial-capitalistic footprint, seem to be mostly his own.

Some critics of unified field theories such as Bringhurst's point out that such attempts to explain everything usually fail and more important can be dismissed with the phrase, "Who cares?" His proposals can be frustrating: Many students of far more accessible languages than Haida, Navajo, or Cree will blanch at Bringhurst's suggestion that the curriculum include readings in the original Native languages, a formidable task for most. Bringhurst might answer that attempts to understand are always admirable (the colonizers and proselytizers made little or no attempt to understand the Native culture or languages) and that in a period of overpopulation and scarcity people must care, learning to respect nature rather than taming it. While *The Tree of Meaning* reflects Bringhurst's poetic identity much more than his other identities as an expert on print and a master of the mechanics of language, he provides an intellectual challenge that is difficult to dismiss. Yes, the theory of language and poetry is heavily metaphorical, but as he points out in his last lecture, the interplay between the two parts of all metaphors, the similarities and disparities between tenor and vehicle, forces people to reexamine the world and revise their thinking. Returning to his first field of study, he notes that cutting-edge physics hypothesizes about unseen subatomic worlds and alternate universes that make Native American creation myths look tame. Metaphors all, the hardest science shares much with Bringhurst's poetic view.

The Tree of Meaning also reflects Bringhurst's enthusiasm for fine printed copy: The book is a lovely artifact, printed on soft, creamy paper with fine print faces that create a very readable text. The books sits happily in the hand, has markers front and back, and each graphic is perfectly placed after its first reference in the text, allowing the reader to look forward to view the example. The advocate of oral communication also thought through this print version of his lectures.

Andrew Macdonald

Review Sources

Canadian Literature, no. 196 (Spring, 2008): 127-128.
Poetry 191, no. 5 (February, 2008): 438-440.
University of Toronto Quarterly 77 (Winter, 2008): 451-453.

2666

Author: Roberto Bolaño (1953-2003)
First published: 2004, in Spain
Translated from the Spanish by Natasha Wimmer
Publisher: Farrar, Straus and Giroux (New York). 898
  pp. $30.00
Type of work: Novel
Time: 1920 to 2001
Locale: Europe, the United States, and northern Mexico

Bolaño's five-part saga centers on the vicious murders
of young women in a northern Mexican city and the life of a
mysterious German writer, Benno von Archimboldi

Principal characters:
  BENNO VON ARCHIMBOLDI, the nom de
    plume of German novelist Hans Reiter
  JEAN-CLAUDE PELLETIER,
  MANUEL ESPINOZA,
  PIERO MORINI, and
  LIZ NORTON, literary critics and Archimboldi scholars
  OSCAR AMALFITANO, a professor of literature at the University of Santa
    Teresa, Mexico
  QUINCY WILLIAMS, also known as OSCAR FATE, an African American
    journalist
  JUAN DE DIOS MARTÍNEZ, a detective for the Santa Teresa police
  SERGIO GONZALEZ, a newspaper reporter
  KLAUS HAAS, a German-born American businessman and murder
    suspect
  AZUCENA ESQUIVEL PLATA, a Mexican congresswoman
  LOTTE REITER, Archimboldi's sister

Nearly nine hundred pages long in Natasha Wimmer's superb translation, Roberto
Bolaño's novel *2666* pieces together diverse types of fiction—among them murder
mystery, war story, love story, portrait of an artist, and police thriller—into a story as
garish, moving, and perplexing as a ralli quilt. Above all, it concerns families and
friendship. In each of its five parts the narrative resolution involves some decisive action intended by one person to save a loved one, often from one of the most hellish
places ever conceived in modern literature.

That place is Santa Teresa, a Mexican border city in the Sonora Desert. Fictional,
Santa Teresa is nevertheless closely modeled on Ciudad Juaréz, which lies across the
border from El Paso, Texas. Like Juaréz, Santa Teresa is a city rapidly expanding with
workers attracted to its maquiladoras (assembly factories for foreign companies); like
Juaréz, it is a violent, corrupt place, overrun by drug gangs. Most of all, from the early
1990's onward, Santa Teresa witnesses the unsolved rape-murders of hundreds of

girls and young women, whose bodies, often mutilated, are discovered unburied in the desert. The major characters in *2666* come here, for one reason or another, and its atmosphere of motiveless menace alters them all.

If there is a mysterious city at the heart of the novel, there is also a mystery man, a novelist, who is its antipode. As in *Los detectives salvajes* (1998; *The Savage Detectives*, 2007), Bolaño makes this literary figure, legendary and elusive, the object of a quest. "The Part About the Critics" introduces him in the first sentence: "The first time that Jean-Claude Pelletier read Benno von Archimboldi was Christmas 1980, in Paris, when he was nineteen years old and studying German literature." Pelletier is soon joined in his interest by three other literature professors—Manuel Espinoza in Spain, Liz Norton in England, and the wheelchair-bound Piero Morini in Italy. Together they bring Archimboldi's nov-

Before his death in 2003 in Barcelona, Spain, Roberto Bolaño gained a reputation as the greatest Latin American novelist of the late twentieth century. Born in Santiago, Chile, and raised in Mexico City, Bolaño wrote short stories, poetry, and essays as well as novels.

els to international academic prominence, to the point that he is listed for the Nobel Prize. At the same time, the four critics form a tight-knit group, a family of sorts. Pelletier, Espinoza, and Norton carry on a ménage à trois, and all four are constantly in close contact. Meanwhile, Archimboldi remains a shadowy figure to them, eluding all of their attempts to track him down until a chance remark suggests that he has gone to Santa Teresa, Mexico. Espinoza, Pelletier, and Norton set off in pursuit. After scouring the city for weeks, they despair of finding him. At the same time, the horrendous city depresses them, as does their erratic sex life. They leave—Norton to move in permanently with Morini in Italy, Pelletier to brood, and Espinoza to consider marrying a Santa Teresa teenager. Their quixotic pursuit of the novelist illustrates how art eludes criticism, and, more, it reveals a group of people who form a family that at least succeeds in freeing them from a literary obsession.

The critics' host at the University of Santa Teresa is Oscar Amalfitano, a professor of literature, and he becomes the protagonist in "The Part About Amalfitano," the shortest of the five sections. Born in Chile and educated in Spain, he has come with his college-age daughter, Rosa, to Santa Teresa from Barcelona to escape his insane wife and crumbling career. He finds only growing despair for himself, symbolized in what at first is a impulsive joke: hanging a copy of a geometry book on the clothesline, as if logic itself is left to dry and fade in Santa Teresa. For Rosa, he fears the near certainty of kidnap and murder. Her rescuer arrives in the next section, "The Part About Fate," in the person of African American journalist Quincy Williams, also known as Oscar Fate. His magazine has sent him to Santa Teresa as a last-minute replacement for a sports reporter to cover a boxing match. He falls in with a group of

Mexican journalists, learns of the murder epidemic, grows interested, and through them works his way deep into the chillingly sleazy underworld of the city, which, he concludes, exists as if "outside of society." At the boxing match, Williams meets Rosa Amalfitano and falls in love with her. Not long afterward, he comes across her in a drug house and, when it appears she is on the verge of becoming another victim, leads her away and, with her father's approval, spirits her across the border into the United States.

"The Part About the Crimes" is the longest and most excruciating section of the novel to read. Several subplots run through it, but its overriding power comes from the short subsections describing the discovery of individual victims—dozens of them, presented for the most part one by one. They read like police case reports, detached in tone and gruesomely detailed. Coming sometimes ten in a row, these case reports have the effect of saturating the reader's compassion and overcoming all emotional responses except revulsion. It is a devastating technique, relentlessly used. Further-more, behind the reports, readers perceive the hundreds of families bereft of daugh-ters, the police connivance, shadowy organized crime, and a thoroughgoing indiffer-ence among Santa Teresans (except worried mothers of young daughters and a handful of protesters). As a reporter comments, "No one pays attention to these kill-ings, but the secret of the world is hidden in them."

Among the subplots, three particularly highlight the twisted mentality of the city. One follows the outbreak of another crime spree: the desecrations of Catholic churches in the city. The vandalism is investigated by a Mexico City reporter, Sergio Gonzalez, and Santa Teresa detective Juan de Dios Martínez. A second subplot fol-lows a loveless affair between Martínez and a much older psychiatrist. He is looking for love, but the psychiatrist wants only to be desired by a younger man as a way to hold on to her vanity and vitality. A third involves the leading suspect in the murders, a German-born American named Klaus Haas. As he fights to keep alive in a brutal Mexican jail, his lawyer falls in love with him, he holds press conferences, his trial is repeatedly delayed, and the murders continue without him.

The section comes to an end with a twist that is strange even by this novel's tangled standards. Azucena Esquivel Plata, a member of the national congress, recruits Gon-zalez to help her investigate the Santa Teresa murders. She has become interested be-cause of the disappearance of a childhood friend. Esquivel is estranged from her wealthy family, and the friend, practically the only acquaintance from her coddled youth in the Mexican aristocracy, is the person to whom she feels most obligated. The ensuing private investigation turns up a horrific surprise. The friend has been running a prostitute ring serving orgies for drug lords, and she may have gone even further by helping kidnap girls in Santa Teresa. Although she is beyond redemption, Esquivel tries to find her. Together these and other narrative strands form a bewildering portrait of a hellhole. Even the scenery conspires to terrorize: "The sky, at sunset, looked like a carnivorous flower."

The last section, "The Part About Archimboldi," begins almost as if it is a fairy tale. Hans Reiter, born in 1920 to a one-legged war veteran and a one-eyed woman, grows up in a small northern German village with his adoring younger sister, Lotte.

His mother works as a servant to the local baron. Accompanying her one day, he meets the baron's nephew, an artist, who starts young Reiter reading. Dropping out of school, the boy educates himself, after a fashion, and runs away to improve his life. He ends up in Berlin, working as a factory night watchman until he joins the German army. Fighting in Poland, France, and then Russia, he is decorated for bravery and wounded; he witnesses horrific brutality, including the murderous campaign against Jews by Germany's death squads, known as Einsatzgruppen. At war's end, he is in an American prisoner-of-war camp. Hidden among the soldiers are Nazi war criminals. Reiter murders one of them before escaping and working as a bouncer at a bar in Cologne. He rents a typewriter and begins writing novels in his spare time under the name Benno von Archimboldi. One after another he publishes them, at first to little success but eventually attracting a cult following. By the time that the critics in the first section of *2666* discover him, Archimboldi has left Germany and roams the Mediterranean, haunted by his past and living for little other than his writing.

Meanwhile, Lotte, whom Archimboldi has not seen since she was ten years old, grows up among hardship and loss, marries a mechanic, and works her way into the German middle class, a solid postwar success story. Her son, however, is a scapegrace. After getting in trouble with the police, he leaves Germany for the United States and changes his name and citizenship. Then he disappears. Late in life, Lotte tries to track him down, and in 1995 she locates him in the Santa Teresa jail. He is Klaus Haas, accused of the Santa Teresa murders. Over the next six years, Lotte bends all of her efforts to freeing her son. While on a plane trip, she happens to read a novel that exactly describes her childhood. She contacts the publisher and learns that the author, Archimboldi, is Hans Reiter, her brother. After nearly fifty years, they reestablish contact. In the novel's last line, Archimboldi sets off for Santa Teresa in an attempt to help his nephew, a gesture of hope that brings him back into his family and a gesture of commitment by the writer to confront evil directly.

"All eloquence springs from pain," one of Bolaño's characters insists. The pain of history, both social and personal, and the obligations of love are the thematic counterpoints of *2666*. Before he died in 2003, Bolaño left instructions to issue each major part as a separate novel. His publisher decided to bundle them together (a decision defended in an epilogue, along with speculation about the novel's enigmatic title). Readers may well regret that decision. The long, repetitious, often surreal, crushingly cruel "Part About the Crimes" so dominates *2666* that reading all five parts straight through may leave the reader with the impression that to Bolaño humanity as a whole is irredeemably self-destructive. Read individually, however, each of the five parts manifests Bolaño's confident faith in the power of literature to refresh awareness of the deepest human bonds.

Roger Smith

Review Sources

Esquire 150, no. 5 (November, 2008): 28.
Kirkus Reviews 76, no. 18 (September 15, 2008): 967-968.
The Nation 287, no. 19 (December 8, 2008): 13-22.
The New York Times, November 13, 2008, p. 1.
The New York Times Book Review, November 9, 2008, p. 1.
The New Yorker 84, no. 37 (November 17, 2008): 105.
Newsweek 152, no. 21 (November 24, 2008): 60.
Publishers Weekly 255, no. 30 (July 28, 2008): 52.
Time 172, no. 21 (November 24, 2008): 60.
The Times Literary Supplement, September 9, 2005, p. 23.

UNACCUSTOMED EARTH

Author: Jhumpa Lahiri (1967-   )
Publisher: Alfred A. Knopf (New York). 333 pp. $25.00
Type of work: Short fiction
Time: The present
Locale: Massachusetts, Pennsylvania, Washington State, London, Rome, and Thailand

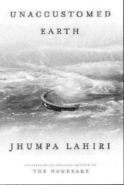

An exquisite collection of eight stories focusing on the Indian diaspora in generation 1.5, those who were either born in the United States or immigrated as young children

Principal characters:
> RUMA, a lawyer who has abandoned her profession to tend to her husband, Adam, and son, Akash, in Seattle
> RUMA'S FATHER, a widowed, retired biochemist living in Pennsylvania
> PRANAB CHAKRABORTY, an engineering student at the Massachusetts Institute of Technology
> APARNA, a married woman who befriends Pranab and falls in love with him
> AMIT SARKAR, a medical editor who had been left behind at the Langford Academy when his parents moved back to Delhi
> MEGAN, Amit's physician wife
> RAHUL MUKHERJEE, a college dropout who continually disappoints his family
> PAUL, a Harvard graduate student who takes an obsessive interest in the romantic tribulations of his Indian housemate
> KAUSHIK CHOUDHURI, a photojournalist who wanders the globe on assignment
> HEMA, a classics professor who knew Kaushik as a child in Massachusetts and encounters him again in Rome

"Indians are everywhere these days," observes a native of Calcutta after returning home to Pennsylvania from a tour through Italy. South Asian Americans and their children populate and animate Jhumpa Lahiri's second collection of short fiction, a gathering of eight exquisite stories. If her Indians are everywhere, they are at home nowhere. "He was furious that we left," says a father who moves his son from Massachusetts to Bombay and back to Massachusetts, "and now he's furious that we're here again." *Unaccustomed Earth* is a wistful record of people who, even while retaining traces of their ancestral customs, have lost their roots.

In addition to one billion in south Asia, Indians have a diaspora numbering some twenty-five million worldwide, three million in the United States. Authors of Indian background—including Salman Rushdie, Bharati Mukherjee, Vikram Seth, Rohinton Mistry, Arundhati Roy, and Anita and Kiran Desai—are prominent and proliferating.

~

Nilanjana Sudeshna Lahiri was born in London and at age three moved with her family to Rhode Island, where a kindergarten teacher found it easier to call her by her pet name, Jhumpa. Lahiri graduated from Barnard with a degree in English literature and earned three master's degrees, in English, creative writing, and comparative literature, and a Ph.D. in Renaissance studies from Boston University.

~

With her first book, *Interpreter of Maladies* (1999), a story collection that won the 2000 Pulitzer Prize, Lahiri emerged as the Bernard Malamud, Aleksandar Hemon, and Junot Diaz of Indian emigrant experience. *The Namesake*, a 2003 novel that was adapted into film by Mira Nair, consolidated Lahiri's reputation. *Unaccustomed Earth* arrived next as that rare phenomenon, a triumph both commercially and artistically. It debuted as number one on *The New York Times* best-seller list, and critics have been virtually unanimous in its praise. Lahiri's third book has earned the admiration it inspired.

Unaccustomed Earth takes its title—and epigraph—from the essay that serves as preface to Nathaniel Hawthorne's *The Scarlet Letter* (1850). In "The Custom-House," as the preface is titled, human nature is compared to potatoes, which cannot flourish if planted and replanted "in the same worn-out soil." Hawthorne's narrator declares: "My children have had other birthplaces, and, so far as their fortunes may be within my control, shall strike their roots into unaccustomed earth." Lahiri's characters strike their roots in Massachusetts, Pennsylvania, and Washington State, corners of the earth unaccustomed to Bengalis. However, the transplantation does not produce the vigor Hawthorne expects in relocated tubers. Most of the characters in these pensive stories are transplants who never find a soil in which to thrive.

Lahiri was born in London, to Bengali parents, but she has lived in the United States since age three. Her characters belong to generation 1.5; children of immigrants, they were either born in the United States or arrived too young to have formed an Indian identity. They tend to be affluent professionals—doctors, lawyers, engineers, professors—educated at prestigious American colleges such as Harvard, Swarthmore, Columbia, and Princeton. Though dragged along on family visits to Calcutta, they lack an appetite for Indian foods, languages, and spouses. In "Hell-Heaven," when Pranab Chakraborty, an engineering student at the Massachusetts Institute of Technology, announces his engagement to an American named Deborah, it so upsets his parents back in Calcutta that they disown him. In "A Choice of Accommodations," Amit Sarkar is deposited in a New England prep school when his ophthalmologist father decamps for a position in a Delhi hospital. The only Indian at Langford Academy, Amit falls in love with the headmaster's daughter, Pam, and later with a medical student named Megan. In the title story, "Unaccustomed Earth," Ruma, a lawyer who cannot read Bengali and has lost the Asian habit of eating with her hands, marries a hedge-fund manager named Adam. Though Adam adores the Bengali dessert called mishti, Ruma's mother, who met her father through an arranged marriage, regards her daughter's conjugal choice as treason: "You are ashamed of yourself, of being Indian, that is the bottom line." In "Hema and Kaushik," the sequence of three connected stories that concludes the entire volume,

Kaushik, who spends his childhood shuttling between Massachusetts and Bombay, becomes a professional nowhere man, a freelance photojournalist who wanders the world recording others' misfortunes and expunging any evidence of his own existence. The final pages of the book take Lahiri's chararacters beyond the United States and India, to Rome and Thailand, where a catastrophic historical event links them at last, tenuously, to other victims.

For Lahiri's characters, the tension between Old World and New World identities is often embodied in the generation gap between parents who look back to India for models of behavior and of thought and of children who strive, however futilely, to pass for unhyphenated Americans. "Unaccustomed Earth," the story that leads the volume, turns on Ruma's unsuccessful effort to persuade her widowed father, a retired biochemist who clings to the customs of the country he was born in, to move in with her family in Seattle. The discovery of her father's secret romance, with a Long Island Bengali named Mrs. Bagchi, reinforces the realization that, despite the rapport he establishes with his young grandson, father and daughter inhabit separate solitudes. The narrator of "Heaven-Hell" lacks sympathy for her mother, trapped in a loveless marriage in the suburbs and missing India, as well as the Indian student, Pranab, who had not reciprocated her affections: "I began to take my cues from my father in dealing with her, isolating her doubly. When she screamed at me for talking too long on the telephone, or for staying too long in my room, I learned to scream back, telling her that she was pathetic, that she knew nothing about me, and it was clear to us both that I had stopped needing her, definitively and abruptly, just as Pranab Kaku had." In the volume's final fictional sequence, after Kaushik's widowed father imports a second wife and her two daughters to the United States, Kaushik maintains a glacial distance from them all.

Nevertheless, even if they savor salads instead of chorchoris or refuse to embrace a match made in Asia, Lahiri's Indians in America are expected to make their parents and siblings proud of their achievements. However, in "Nobody's Business," not only does Sangeeta, a graduate-school dropout who works part time at a Harvard Square bookstore, rebuff all calls from eligible Indian suitors but also she loses her heart to a callous Egyptian philanderer. In "Only Goodness," Lahiri offers an even more acidic portrait of an Indian American ne'er-do-well. After dropping out of Cornell and moving back home, where he works in a Laundromat, Rahul disgraces himself through public drunkenness: "And so, he became what all parents feared, a blot, a failure, someone who was not contributing to the grand circle of accomplishments Bengali children were making across the country, as surgeons or attorneys or scientists, or writing articles for the front page of *The New York Times*." My son the slacker is not a boast that Lahiri's Old World mothers are eager to make about their American children.

Nevertheless, even those children who manage to attain worldly success are haunted by a sense of loss. In "Hell-Heaven," though Pranab sacrifices his family ties to make Deborah his wife, the marriage ends in divorce. After the breakup, Deborah confesses that she envied a Bengali friend "for knowing him, understanding him in a way I never could," as if Americans and Indians who long for concord are doomed to failure at achieving it. In "A Choice of Accommodations," Amit Sarkar, attending a wedding, reveals to a stranger the hollowness of his own marriage to Megan. Though Hema, in "Hema and Kaushik," grows up to become an accomplished scholar, resourceful and independent, she accedes to a traditional arranged marriage to a Punjabi, one that she realizes will not bring genuine fulfillment. However, the problem for Lahiri's characters is only in part an unbridgeable chasm between cultures. She depicts a world in which to be human is to fail.

In an interview with *Bookforum*, Lahiri explained that "bits and pieces" of the stories in *Unaccustomed Earth* are drawn from her own family and acquaintances. However, though she is fated to be categorized as an author of the Indian diaspora in the United States, she also insisted that the characters and experiences she depicts are universal:

> The thing I took for granted when I was growing up is that I was living in a world within a world. It was a tight world, but I knew a lot of people and was privy to the whole spectrum of types and personalities and characters. To me, they don't represent immigrants or anyone specific. They just represent the human condition.

Built upon the patient accumulation of detail and spare, incisive sentences, Lahiri's stories lack the spectacular effects found in Rushdie or Roy. Her style approaches tragical—not magical—realism, a clinical but gracefully poised account of lives unmoored and thwarted. The devastating epiphany that concludes "Only Goodness" is downright Chekhovian in Lahiri's ability to expose a universal anguish not unique to Indian Americans. At the conclusion of the story, when the full extent of Rahul's failure—as a son, brother, and responsible adult—is exposed, the reader is suddenly left with: "the fledgling family that had cracked open that morning, as typical and as terrifying as any other."

Steven G. Kellman

Review Sources

Booklist 104, no. 11 (February 1, 2008): 5.
The Boston Globe, April 6, 2008, p. C6.
The Christian Science Monitor 100, no. 88 (April 1, 2008): 17.
Entertainment Weekly, April 4, 2008, p. 64.
Library Journal 133, no. 2 (February 1, 2008): 65.
Los Angeles Times, March 30, 2008, p. R1.
The New York Review of Books 55, no. 8 (May 15, 2008): 28-29.
The New York Times Book Review, April 6, 2008, p. 1.
Newsday, April 20, 2008, p. C24.
People 69, no. 13 (April 7, 2008): 49.
Publishers Weekly 255, no. 4 (January 28, 2008): 39.
USA Today, April 3, 2008, p. 5D.
The Washington Post Book World, April 6, 2008, p. BW06.

THE WAITRESS WAS NEW

Author: Dominique Fabre (1960-   )
First published: La Serveuse était novelle, 2005, in
France
Translated from the French by Jordan Stump
Publisher: Archipelago Books (New York). 117 pp.
$15.00
Type of work: Novel
Time: Contemporary to 2005
Locale: Asnières suburb of Paris

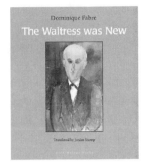

*In Fabre's novel, Pierre, the barman at Le Cercle, re-
counts the events of his final three days at the café, during
which his entire lifestyle slips away from him*

Principal characters:
> PIERRE, a fifty-six-year-old barman at Le Cercle café
> HENRI, his boss, café owner
> ISABELLE, Henri's wife
> SABRINA, the waitress at Le Cercle
> MADELEINE, the new waitress at Le Cercle
> AMADÉE, the Senegalese cook at Le Cercle
> ROGER, Pierre's friend who also works as a barman

In Dominique Fabre's *The Waitress Was New*, the main character Pierre, a barman
at Le Cercle, gives the reader a first-person account of the events that lead to the closing of the café. Pierre is fifty-six years old, he lives alone, and he has worked as a barman the greater part of his life. He has one good friend, Roger, also a barman. Although Pierre is an ordinary man who works at an ordinary job, Fabre captures
readers' interest by creating the special world in which Pierre lives. Pierre performs
routine tasks every day; however, his life has significance as he interacts with his
boss, his boss's wife, the other employees, and the customers.

Pierre knows his clientele: He is not only a good listener but also, as every barman
must be, a keen observer. Pierre provides the reader with detailed descriptions of the
various regular customers and the ones who stop occasionally or only once. There is
the young man always dressed in black, who reads Primo Levi. There is the regular
Mr. Dilman, who has not paid his bill for some time. It is Pierre who takes care of the
matter and remains on good terms with the customer while collecting the bill. There is
the beautiful young woman whom Pierre notices walking outside the café. Pierre
rarely looks outside, as he says what interests him is in the café, seated at the bar.
Somehow, he had a need to look outside as she passed. She has a coffee at the café,
and Pierre is very intrigued by her. He almost creates a fantasy about her, but, calling
himself "Pierrot, my friend," he tells himself that she is too young and too beautiful
for him.

Dominique Fabre published his first novel, Moi aussi, un jour j'irai loin, *in 1995. He received the Marcel Pagnol Prize for his novel* Fantômes *in 2001.* The Waitress Was New, *published in France in 2005, is his first work to appear in English. He has written nine novels.*

∾

The plot of the novel is simple, almost thin. Sabrina, the regular waitress, is off work, supposedly ill. The temporary waitress, Madeleine, arrives and meets Pierre and Amadée the cook. The boss leaves the café that morning and does not come back. No one knows where he has gone. He is apparently having some sort of midlife crisis, and his wife Isabelle is disconsolate, fearing he has left her for another woman. How will the café run without the boss? Where is the boss?

Pierre is the cog that keeps everything running at the café. When Madeleine arrives, Pierre immediately looks her over, worried that things may not run smoothly with a new waitress. He is relieved when she appears to get along well with the Senegalese cook Amadée. As the day wears on, Pierre's life becomes more and more complicated. Isabelle is so preoccupied with where her husband has gone that she is little help, leaving only Pierre, Madeleine, and Amadée to keep the café functioning. Pierre knows that without the boss, the café will have to close.

Pierre desperately needs the café; it is his life. He may just be a barman, but he is a barman with routine duties, with an organized existence that occupies his mind and protects him from life. Each night the café closes, but Pierre's existence does not stop. It is at these moments that Fabre poignantly portrays Pierre assailed by his fears of aging, by loneliness, by helplessness, by the agonizing human condition.

Pierre must somehow get the boss back to the café. Pierre comes up first with the solution that Henri is with Sabrina. Isabelle has also thought of this possibility but refused to pursue it. Pierre goes to Sabrina's apartment, where he finds she really is ill and the boss is not there. She admits to having an affair with Henri, but she has no idea where he is. Pierre then finds another solution: Henri has gone to visit his daughter in England. Isabelle, however, has talked to the daughter, and Henri is not there. Then, Isabelle tells Pierre that she is closing the café for a week. She asks him to accept the deliveries on Tuesday; he agrees, but he has a week to get through without a job. He checks his eligibility for his pension and finds he has thirteen more trimesters to work. Pierre goes to the café each day, wiping down the bar, checking on everything. Then, at the end of the week, Pierre is alone in the closed café when the telephone rings and he recognizes his boss's voice. The café has been sold. Pierre feels betrayed and refuses to tell Amadée. After the phone call, alone in the café, he lets out a yowl. His life as a barman there is over.

In a self-indulgent response to this devastating blow, he opens the café for business. Soon the regulars, including the young man who reads Levi, begin to come into the café. Amadée arrives and Pierre serves free drinks to everyone. They close at nine-thirty, and Pierre is alone with the café. He wipes down his bar, cleans the glasses, takes out the trash, and when everything is in excellent order, he locks the café door, taking the key with him. Pierre has had one last time as a barman, one last existence. After that, he avoids going home as long as possible. Once home, unable to read and unable to think of anything else to do, he goes to bed.

Fabre's use of description, of monologue, and of Pierre's relationship with objects fleshes out the novel, making it more than a "slice-of-life" work. Through his descriptions of the lights of the café, the street lights, the dead leaves on Isabelle's Audi, and the poorly pruned sycamore trees, he creates strong visual impressions that give the novel qualities of a painting. Pierre's monologues, recounting his thoughts during the three days that drastically change his life, give the novel a philosophical depth. Pierre is really trying to figure out what life is about, why things happen as they do. It is in Pierre's thoughts, as he attempts to deal with his life, that Fabre emphasizes the helplessness of the human condition. Here, also, he examines the problem of loneliness and the difficulty of lasting commitment to other human beings. Pierre was married but soon divorced. All of his love affairs have been of short duration. This does not mean that Pierre is lacking in compassion for other people. He tries to help the distraught Isabelle by taking her to dinner and listening to her talk about her life with her husband; he is concerned for Sabrina, a single mother with children. He likes Amadée and his regular customers. However, Pierre refers to the regulars at his bar as people he listens to but does not know. He remains always separated from them. His only enduring friendship has been with Roger, a fellow barman who is possibly a reflection of Pierre.

Pierre's strongest relationships are not with people: His apartment, his possessions within it, and his housekeeping tasks occupy a good part of his time when he is not at Le Cercle. He wants things a certain way; the condition of his surroundings is always important to him. The café Le Cercle is as much a character in the book as Amadée or Sabrina. For Pierre, wiping down his bar is an essential part of his existence. He is a barman and a barman takes care of his bar.

Pierre's dream adds to the texture of the novel. His dream life is almost always frightening to him. He would like to dream about the beautiful young woman he noticed outside of the café, but instead he dreams about Le Cercle locked with its tile floor covered with dead leaves. Inside he glimpses Sabrina and her children, who flee when they see him at the door. He does not like the dream and fears its return.

However, the novel is neither morbid nor pessimistic—it simply portrays life as it is for an ordinary man such as Pierre. Fabre adds a tone of levity to his novel in the many comments Pierre makes as he accepts how things are and his inability to change them.

The overlapping or folding structure of the work makes it seem longer than its 117 pages. Events and observations constantly trigger memories in Pierre's mind, and he takes the reader to earlier moments in his life and to past experiences in such a way that there is almost another story within the novel. Pierre's life unfolds along with the story of the search for the boss.

The novel is the first of Fabre's works to be published in an English translation. It has been successful among American readers and critics, elciting hopes that more of his novels will be translated into English.

Shawncey Webb

Review Sources

Booklist 104, no. 8 (December 15, 2007): 27.
Kirkus Reviews 75, no. 24 (December 15, 2007): 1258.
Publishers Weekly 254, no. 42 (October 22, 2007): 33.
The Village Voice 53, no. 9 (February 27, 2008): 49.

WALLACE STEGNER AND THE AMERICAN WEST

Author: Philip L. Fradkin (1935-   )
Publisher: Alfred A. Knopf (New York). 370 pp. $27.50
Type of work: Literary biography
Time: 1909-1993
Locale: Various locations in the West, especially Palo
    Alto, California; Greensboro, Vermont

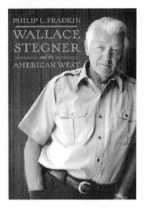

*Fradkin's detailed study of Stegner includes valuable
discussions of the American West, conservation, Western
writers, and the relationship between region and literature*

> *Principal personages:*
> WALLACE STEGNER, a writer, teacher, and
>   conservationist
> MARY STEGNER, his wife for almost sixty
>   years
> PAGE STEGNER, their only child, a writer and teacher
> BERNARD DEVOTO, the American literary critic and conservationist who
>   was one of Stegner's early mentors
> STEWART L. UDALL, the Secretary of the Interior in the administration of
>   President John F. Kennedy in the early 1960's
> DAVID BROWER, the controversial president of the Sierra Club when
>   Stegner worked with the organization in the 1960's

Wallace Stegner was the first writer in the twentieth century to turn "Western" into a positive adjective in front of "writer" or "literature." He founded the creative writing program at Stanford University in 1945, and for twenty-five years he shepherded through it students who would become some of the finest writers in America: Wendell Berry, Terry Tempest Williams, Ernest J. Gaines, Robert Stone, and dozens of others. His books opened up Western landscapes for both fiction and nonfiction, debunking the romantic myths about the West and revealing the truth about its vast plains and deserts. Finally, his work with the Department of the Interior, the Sierra Club, and other conservation groups helped to preserve those Western locales that had given him such a sense of place, and the personality out of which he would teach and write for more than half a century. Philip Fradkin's biography is significant not only for uncovering Stegner the man and a writer who has grown in reputation since his death in 1993 but also for providing the larger canvas: Stegner's pivotal role in establishing the literary and ecological West in the American imagination, the literary shift of power between the West and the East Coasts in the second half of the twentieth century, and the sense of place that so grounded Stegner on both coasts. In writing an authoritative biography of a great Western writer, Fradkin has redefined the terms of the debate about region and literature in American letters.

Stegner's roots were nourished in shifting soil. His father was a gambler and

~

Philip L. Fradkin has been a reporter with the Los Angeles Times, *where he shared a Pulitzer Prize, and he was Western editor of* Audubon *magazine. He has written more than ten books, including* A River No More: The Colorado River and the West *(1996).*

~

drinker who moved the family all over the West. Stegner was born in Iowa, but he spent time in Great Falls, Montana, in an orphanage in Seattle, and on a homestead in Saskatchewan, before settling with his family in Salt Lake City, still not a teenager. He attended the University of Utah and launched himself from there: to the University of Iowa for an M.A. and a Ph.D. in English, and then through a series of teaching jobs at the University of Wisconsin, Harvard University, and back to the University of Utah. He also began to produce short stories and novels (*The Big Rock Candy Mountain* in 1943 was his first substantial work), to attend the Bread Loaf Writers' Conference near Middlebury, Vermont (he went eight times over fifteen years after 1938), and in 1945 he was brought to Stanford to found the academic unit that would become one of the most famous and successful creative writing programs in the country. Until 1971, when he retired to devote more time to his own writing, Stegner helped dozens of writers, from Edward Abbey, Ivan Doig, Barry Lopez, and Harriet Doerr, to William Kittredge, Ken Kesey, and Larry McMurtry—many of them Western writers and most with a natural taste for Western topics—to establish themselves in American literature.

As Fradkin shows in detail, Stegner had another career as a conservationist, through both his writing and his personal efforts. His early biography of one of the most important explorers of the West, *Beyond the Hundredth Meridian: John Wesley Powell and the Second Opening of the West* (1954), has become a classic in Western history, for it identified the land and the water issues that continue to be so crucial in the West. Later his famous "Wilderness Letter" helped to define the terms on which environmental battles would be fought for the next half century. "We simply need that wild country available to us," he wrote about wilderness in that piece in 1961, "even if we never do more than drive to its edge and look in. For it can be a means of reassuring ourselves of our sanity as creatures, a part of the geography of hope." He worked under Secretary Stewart Udall at the Department of the Interior, where he helped to shape New Frontier environmental policy such as the Wilderness Act of 1964, as well as federal cultural policy that would lead to the National Endowments for the Arts and the Humanities. He worked with organizations such as the Sierra Club and the National Parks Advisory Board for years. Besides lobbying on national issues, Stegner fought locally to halt the spread of Silicon Valley developers into the Los Altos Hills above Palo Alto where he and his wife Mary had built their first house and raised their son Page. The changes to that locale finally drove him away; he died in Santa Fe, New Mexico, in 1993, and his ashes were scattered near his summer home in Greensboro, Vermont.

All of his writing reveals his crucial relationship to the land and his recognizable sense of place. *Angle of Repose* (1971), the novel for which he is probably best known, won the Pulitzer Prize for fiction and helped to establish the West as a fitting subject for modern fiction. *The Spectator Bird* (1976) moved between California and

Denmark and won the National Book Award for fiction, and *Crossing to Safety* (1987) bridged the continent in subject between his two coastal residences, in California and in Vermont. Stegner won three O. Henry prizes for his short stories over his career, and his *Collected Stories* were published in 1990. In 1980 he received the Robert Kirsch Award from the *Los Angeles Times* for his lifetime literary achievements.

The conflict between East and West is one of the threads running through Fradkin's story. For much of the twentieth century, the East Coast literary establishment (epitomized by *The New York Times Book Review*) treated California and the West as a kind of literary frontier, denigrating or ignoring literary efforts on the West Coast by referring to West Coast writers as "regional." (If California writers were regional, then why did not the same label apply to East Coast writers such as Philip Roth, John Updike, and Kurt Vonnegut, Jr.? *The New York Times* never recognized this double standard.) Stegner helped to break that stigma. His fiction revealed the rich literary resources of the West, as in *Angle of Repose*, for which he used historical documents—the memoirs and letters of California writer Mary Hallock Foote—as the basis for a moving fictional re-creation of the life of a mining engineer and his young family in California and other Western states in the second half of the nineteenth century. His nonfiction—his book about growing up on the isolated Saskatchewan prairie, *Wolf Willow: A History, a Story, and a Memory of the Last Plains Frontier* (1962)—like his study of Powell helped to establish the standards for American nature writing. It is significant that so many of the writers who came through Stanford's creative writing program—including Abbey, Williams, and McMurtry—would continue this tradition of exploring the West's possibilities in both fiction and nonfiction. In the process of establishing the West as a rich resource for writers, Stegner also demystified it, debunking the cowboys and Indians romance of the West in order to establish the truth of its history and its culture: the limits of its land, its lack of water, its differences from and similarities to the East Coast. In his introduction to *Beyond the Hundredth Meridian*, Stegner's friend Bernard DeVoto writes at length about the romantic misconceptions historians hold about the West that Stegner so tellingly put to rest in the biography. Although Stegner destroyed many of the myths about the West, he elevated the region as a literary resource.

If Fradkin has a thesis, it is this influence of place on his subject, "the effect of landscape—meaning nature—on human destiny, history, culture, and character." He spends the first seventy-five pages of this biography placing the young Stegner in the various locales that would be so influential, especially the patch of the Saskatchewan plains where his family tried to homestead for four years before 1920 and a little later Salt Lake City and southern Utah, which "remained central to who he was and what he thought about the West" throughout his career. In both his "Prologue" and his "Epilogue," Fradkin describes visiting the various locations where Stegner settled, from Palo Alto to Greensboro, places where Stegner found "a convergence of nature and human history." The biography of the writer thus becomes a meditation on the complex relations between American regions and American literature.

The only place Fradkin goes off track in this admirable study is in detailing the controversy following the publication of *Angle of Repose*. Stegner used historical documents—including the reminiscences of Foote and her letters purchased by Stanford University in 1955—receiving only vague permission from heirs. However, his transformation of these materials into fiction was both less and more than what he had asked for or what he acknowledged in the brief prefatory note to the novel. A critical scuffle broke out soon after the novel appeared that has continued, at least in scholarly journals, for more than thirty years. Fradkin is clearly proud to be relating the "full story—told here for the first time" in the longest chapter in the book (forty-five pages). Because the controversy is less important than Fradkin thinks it is, that chapter tends to outweigh its subject. The lines between fiction and nonfiction have been deeply eroded in the twenty-first century—Stegner's work may have helped to erase them—when novelists routinely drop historical figures into their fiction, and nonfiction writers take fictional license in their work by creating characters and imagining conversations between them. Therefore, Fradkin's editorial judgment in spending such an inordinate amount of time on the matter must be questioned. In spite of this imbalance, Fradkin's study stands as a major accomplishment, not only in bringing Stegner's life and career into focus but also in showing how that life and career represented larger themes that continue to be important in American culture and literature.

David Peck

Review Sources

Audubon 110, no. 4 (July/August, 2008): 86-88.
Booklist 104, no. 12 (February 15, 2008): 31.
The Boston Globe, March 30, 2008, p. C7.
The Chronicle of Higher Education 54, no. 28 (March 21, 2008): B19.
International Herald-Tribune, May 22, 2008, p. 10.
Los Angeles Times Book Review, February 10, 2008, p. 2.
The New York Times Book Review, May 18, 2008, p. 18.
The New Yorker 84, no. 4 (March 10, 2008): 123.
Outside 33, no. 3 (March, 2008): 30.
The Wilson Quarterly 32, no. 3 (Summer, 2008): 102-103.

WELLSPRINGS

Author: Mario Vargas Llosa (1936-   )
Publisher: Harvard University Press (Cambridge, Mass.).
   202 pp. $17.95
Type of work: Essays, literary criticism

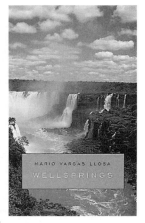

In seven essays, Peruvian novelist and essayist Vargas Llosa critically examines the literary, cultural, and political "wellsprings" of his work

Since the publication of his first novel, *La ciudad y los perros* (1962; *The Time of the Hero*, 1966), more than forty years ago, Peruvian novelist Mario Vargas Llosa has become one of the modern world's most important writers. Not only has he written sixteen diverse novels, from political thrillers such as *Fiesta del Chivo* (2000; *The Feast of the Goat*, 2001) to a contemporary retelling of Gustave Flaubert's *Madame Bovary* (1857) titled *Travesuras de la niña mala* (2006; *The Bad Girl*, 2007), but he has also written critical essays on topics ranging from fellow Latin American novelist Gabriel García Márquez to Flaubert in *La orgía perpetua* (1975; *The Perpetual Orgy*, 1986) and the craft of writing in *Cartas a un joven novelista* (1997; *Letters to a Young Novelist*, 2002) and *A Writer's Reality* (1991).

Like many Latin American novelists, Vargas Llosa has been politically active, running for president of Peru in 1990, and many of his novels and essays focus on the intricate ways that politics often intertwine with everyday life. The essays in *Wellsprings* range over writers as diverse as Miguel de Cervantes and Jorge Luis Borges, Isaiah Berlin and José Ortega y Gasset, exploring topics as wide-ranging as the dangers of nationalism and the challenges of liberalism. At least two of the essays explore the dangers of totalitarian approaches to political or religious thinking and the challenges to freedom of such approaches. In all of his writings, Vargas Llosa has experimented with different styles, from literary modernism to postmodernism. His novels and essays demonstrate that he is one of the most playful, inventive, and thoughtful contemporary Latin American writers.

At first glance, the essays in *Wellsprings* seem to be disparate meditations on a variety of unrelated topics. Nevertheless, while each essay can indeed be read as a discrete reflection on a particular topic, the essays do exhibit a thematic unity. Much like Milan Kundera's essays in *Le Rideau* (2005; *The Curtain*, 2007) and *L'Art du roman* (1986; *The Art of the Novel*, 1988), Vargas Llosa's essays in *Wellsprings* attempt to explain the development of the novel against the backdrop of politics, history, and culture. In the first two essays in the collection, Vargas Llosa cites the two writers, Cervantes and Borges, who have influenced not only his own writing but also Spanish literature, in particular, and world literature, in general. He calls Borges a liberating force for Latin American fiction, and he declares that Borges's fiction is the most ex-

~

Peruvian essayist, politician, and journalist Mario Vargas Llosa's novels include La tía Julia y el escribidor *(1977;* Aunt Julia and the Scriptwriter, *1982),* El hablador *(1987;* The Storyteller, *1989), and* Travesuras de la niña mala *(2006;* The Bad Girl, *2007). His collections of critical essays include* La orgía perpetua *(1975;* The Perpetual Orgy, *1986) and* La tentación de lo imposible *(2004;* The Temptation of the Impossible, *2007).*

~

citing and important event for imaginative writing in the Spanish language in modern times. In canny fashion, Vargas Llosa shifts his gaze from fiction to politics in essays on nationalism, Ortega y Gassett, Berlin, and Karl Popper. The novel, according to Vargas Llosa, acts as an arbitrary organization of human reality that protects individuals against the anxiety unleashed by the political or social disorder that is part of their everyday lives. The greatest novelists—Marcel Proust, Henry James, Leo Tolstoy, William Faulkner—ingeniously construct orderly fictitious worlds where life flows with order and coherence and which encourage confidence in individuals that they can know themselves, their world, and their hopes.

Wellsprings opens with Vargas Llosa's reflections on Cervantes's *Don Quixote* (1605, 1615), "Four Centuries of Don Quixote." In the manner of Dante and William Shakespeare, Cervantes uses his writing to explore the nature of humanity, questioning the extent to which illusion intrudes on reality. *Don Quixote* is a perfect example of Vargas Llosa's notion that fiction provides an order that the real world cannot provide. Such an order is not always perfect, though, since Quixote and his sidekick, Sancho Panza, not only humorously tilt at imaginary windmills but also destroy villages and injure people in their adventures. At best, *Don Quixote* enriches the reader by showing that individuals, through artistic creation, can overcome the limitations of their existence and achieve a nobility and an immortality. Thus, just as Hamlet remains forever a model of indecision, Quixote will live eternally as a model of the good-hearted but inept hero, dreaming of a better world. At the same time, however, Cervantes makes writers feel small with his glorious creative accounts of Quixote and Panza. Vargas Llosa praises Cervantes for taking the Spanish language to new heights as well as creating a challenge for those who write in Spanish.

The powerful model of *Don Quixote* demonstrates for Vargas Llosa the nature of fiction. While fiction is entertaining and magical, it is also an escape from the prison of everyday life. The novel, like many others, provides individuals with an opportunity to step out of their worlds and into another world where they can play roles that are richer or more sordid than the lives they are destined to live. Using *Don Quixote* as his starting point, Vargas Llosa proclaims that fiction is at once a witness to and a foundation of our nonconformity. After four centuries, the most enduring image of Cervantes's novel is that odd couple, Quixote and Panza, riding through the novel's pages and their adventures, revealing the remarkably rich power of the human imagination in re-creating individual's lives.

Vargas Llosa continues to explore the nature of fiction and the writers who have influenced him in his second essay, "The Fictions of Borges." Much like Cervantes, the twentieth century Argentine writer elevated the artistic bar for Latin American writers. According to Vargas Llosa, Borges brought to an end the timidity of Latin American writers who felt that their fiction could deal only with provincial subjects. Before Borges, Latin American writers shrank from writing novels or stories that might deal with universal themes. Embraced by European and North American writers, Borges's fiction opened the doors for Latin American writers to enter into a larger cultural conversation without feeling foolish or deluded about their writing. Borges's prose is revolutionary because it contains almost as many ideas as words, and he is precise and concise in the execution of stories such as "The Circular Ruins," "The Theologians," and "The Aleph." Borges's manifesto for fiction—that the habit of writing long books to state an idea that can be expressed in a few minutes is a laborious and exhausting enterprise—reveals his theory of fiction. As much as Vargas Llosa disagrees with Borges—if Vargas Llosa had emulated Borges's theory, Vargas Llosa's novels would have been the length of short stories—he does find it useful as a way of thinking about the central issues of Borges's fiction (conjecture, speculation, theory, doctrine) and its broad appeal to novelists of ideas. Without Cervantes and Borges, Latin American literature, in particular, and world literature, in general, would have been impoverished, for, as Vargas Llosa so elegantly illustrates, each writer opens the windows on imagination and freedom.

In a final essay devoted to the nature of fiction, "Fiction and Reality in Latin America," Vargas Llosa explores the relationship between fiction and history while at the same time praising one of his mentors, Raúl Porras Barrenechea, a historian who was working on a history of the conquest of Peru by the Spaniards at the time of his death. According to Vargas Llosa, Barrenechea masterfully turned history into story, anecdote, and adventure. Barrenechea, in Vargas Llosa's telling, is something of a comic character—a potbellied little man with a large forehead—who resembles the character Casaubon in George Eliot's *Middlemarch* (1874). Like Casaubon, Barrenechea spent his career so intently collecting documents related to the conquest of Peru that he never got around to writing his book on the subject. Vargas Llosa served as his assistant one semester and spent his time looking over chronicles of conquest and discovery; in those documents he discovered the source of much of the magical fiction that eventually grew out of Latin America. Without these chronicles, books such as García Márquez's *Cien años de soledad* (1967; *One Hundred Years of Solitude*, 1970) and Julio Cortázar's short stories would not have been possible. These chronicles, which purport to be historical accounts of certain events, are in fact a type of writing that weaves together literature and history, fiction and reality, truth and falsehood, in ways that create new ways of looking at the world. More important, though, for Vargas Llosa are the lessons that these chronicles teach. The chronicles reveal the stories that Peruvians made up to vilify the conquistadors and persuade the Peruvians that their problems had been imposed from abroad. As fiction, the chronicles mask the historical fact that, as Vargas Llosa points out, the Peruvians defeated themselves. Once again, Vargas Llosa demonstrates the power of fiction to change the world.

The remainder of the essays in *Wellsprings* are less compelling than those on fiction, exploring mostly political topics, and range from portraits of the Spanish philosopher Ortega y Gasset ("Ortega y Gasset and the Revival of a Liberal"), Berlin ("Isaiah Berlin, a Hero of Our Time), and Popper ("Updating Karl Popper") to an examination of the dangers of an unbridled nationalism ("The Challenges of Nationalism"). In "The Challenges of Nationalism," Vargas Llosa uses the examples of the suppression of the Catalans and the Basques in modern Spain to challenge stridently the elevation of a national identity that suppresses the freedoms of the various groups that make up the nation. Returning to the creative spirit, he declares that the only legitimate role of any government is to create the conditions in which cultural life can flourish. Governments ought not to interfere with such cultural life, and they should guarantee freedom of expression and the free flow of ideas as well as foster the arts and provide access to education. Any government that suppresses the creative spirit in the jingoistic spirit of nationalism invites its own demise, leading often to the silencing of the very voices that might provide the most ingenious solutions to political issues.

Vargas Llosa's most powerful essays in *Wellsprings* focus on the power of literature and the relationship between imagination and reality. These essays reveal Vargas Llosa's tenacious commitment to the power of storytelling and to the ability that writing and art have to transform individuals. His compelling essays on Cervantes and Borges encourage individuals to savor those writers and their fiction, by rereading them or by picking them up to read for the first time. Vargas Llosa asks readers to consider the task of good fiction. Does it succeed in offering an alternative to the disorder of the worlds and offer an orderly and coherent world into which a reader can escape to lead a richer life? Does the fiction of Borges offer a sufficiently coherent world into which readers may retreat to find themselves and reorder their lives? What can philosophical fiction or the novel of ideas offer readers? Vargas Llosa's political essays, while not as powerful as his literary ones, nevertheless form a unity with his literary essays. It is the power of fiction and literature, for Vargas Llosa, that can indeed challenge the sometimes misguided doctrines and policies of governments. Vargas Llosa's *Wellsprings* will persuade readers that the freedom of expression keeps political regimes from calcifying, and the imaginative spirits of novelists and artists are a necessary feature of all cultures that value their futures.

Henry L. Carrigan, Jr.

Review Sources

Hispanic 21, no. 11 (November, 2008): 72.
Publishers Weekly 255, no. 8 (February 25, 2008): 60-61.
The Times Literary Supplement, November 7, 2008, p. 29.

WHAT I TALK ABOUT WHEN I TALK ABOUT RUNNING
A Memoir

Author: Haruki Murakami (1949-   )
*First published: Hashiru koto ni tsuite kataru toki ni boku
    no kataru koto*, 2007, in Japan
Translated from the Japanese by Philip Gabriel
Publisher: Alfred A. Knopf (New York). 180 pp. $21.00
Type of work: Memoir
Time: 1978-2007
Locale: Tokyo, Hokkaido, and Murakami City, Japan;
    Kauai, Hawaii; Cambridge, Massachusetts; New York
    City; Athens and Marathon, Greece

*A famous Japanese novelist describes how his lives as a
distance runner and a writer overlap*

Haruki Murakami is arguably the most popular Asian writer in the world because of such novels as *Nejimaki-dori kuronikuru* (1995; *The Wind-Up Bird Chronicle*, 1997) and *Umibe no Kafuka* (2002; *Kafka on the Shore*, 2005). His often whimsical accounts of the struggles of ordinary, usually young people to understand the vicissitudes of daily life have moved international readers. *What I Talk About When I Talk About Running* is ostensibly an account of his twenty-five years as a serious distance runner, yet it reveals much more. The leisurely, free-association book is as much about Murakami the artist and, in his words, the difficult individual as about his athletic exploits. While runners may find something of interest here, the book is primarily for Murakami's fans seeking more insight into his character and creative process.

Murakami got the idea for the book from an *International Herald Tribune* article about what marathoners said they thought about while running. It took him ten years to decide upon a suitable approach. Writing the book during 2005-2006, he quickly discovered that writing about running was the same as writing about himself, so the project took the form of a memoir, alternating accounts of running with what he calls "life lessons," what he has "learned through actually putting my own body in motion, and thereby discovering that suffering is optional." Running is essential for his mental well-being, clearing his mind of the pressures of creating. He claims not to think of anything while running.

Murakami describes how he had an epiphany during a 1978 baseball game between the Yakult Swallows and the Hiroshima Carp and decided he could be a novelist. Ironically, the idea came to him when an American player, Dave Hilton, got a hit. It is perhaps understandable that Murakami has been criticized in Japan for letting American culture have too great an influence on his writing. After publishing his first two novels, *Kaze no Uta o Kike* (1979; *Hear the Wind Sing*, 1987) and *1973-nen no Pinboru* (1980; *Pinball 1973*, 1985), Murakami decided to close the jazz club he and his wife had been operating and write full time. Realizing good health would be es-

~

Haruki Murakami has published novels, short fiction, and nonfiction. His many awards include the Yomiuri Literary Award for The Wind-Up Bird Chronicle. *He has taught at Princeton and Tufts universities.*

~

sential to a long career as a novelist, he quit his sixty-cigarettes-a-day habit and took up running.

He began running seriously in 1982, running almost every day and competing in at least one marathon a year with occasional other long-distance races. Although he played baseball and soccer as a young man, he never felt comfortable with team sports or with the competitive nature of one-on-one sports such as squash, but he found peace with the solitude of running. He competed in his first road race, a five-kilometer event, in 1983 and gradually built up his endurance to try marathons. Training for long-distance events resembles his approach to writing, which involves driving himself physically and devoting considerable time and effort. When "a mental gap" began to develop between him and running, he accepted the challenge of the triathlon, adding swimming and cycling to his routine. Contemplating this challenge made him think that his entire life up this point had been "a total waste."

Murakami's normal routine is to run an hour a day, six days a week, while listening to rock by such performers as the Beach Boys, Beck, Credence Clearwater Revival, Gorillaz, the Lovin' Spoonful, and Red Hot Chili Peppers and occasionally to jazz. Of running to the songs from Eric Clapton's album *Reptile* (2001), he writes, "It's not too brash or contrived. It has this steady rhythm and entirely natural melody. My mind gets quietly swept into the music, and my feet run in time to the beat."

Music figures prominently in Murakami's fiction, with his characters constantly listening to and discussing jazz, rock, and classical music, and several of his titles are drawn from pop music, as with *Dansu dansu dansu* (1988; *Dance Dance Dance*, 1994) and *Noruwei no mori* (1987; *Norwegian Wood*, 2000). Hearing popular music from the 1960's brings back memories of his youth, though he admits there is nothing special about them. Throughout *What I Talk About When I Talk About Running*, Murakami is modest and self-deprecating: "Those kinds of memories—unpretentious, commonplace. But for me, they're all meaningful and valuable . . . the accumulation of these memories has led to one result: me."

Strenuous exercise is necessary for Murakami because he sees writing as an unhealthy enterprise, releasing "a kind of toxin that lies deep down in all humanity." As a result writers and other artists are often antisocial or decadent. Despite attempts at grumpiness, Murakami often makes fun of himself, as when a seventy-year-old woman passes him during a sixty-two-mile ultramarathon in Japan and shouts, "Hang in there!"

What I Talk About When I Talk About Running deals with the similarities between running and writing. When training for a marathon, he increases his pace each day while shortening the amount of time "to let the exhilaration I feel at the end of each run carry over to the next day." While writing a novel, "I stop every day right at the point where I feel I can write more." The worlds of Murakami the athlete and Murakami the writer collide when a woman spots him running by in Tokyo and shouts that she has been a fan for twenty years.

Much of *What I Talk About When I Talk About Running* is concerned with Murakami's life as a writer. He tries to explain what enables him to be a writer: "It's precisely my ability to detect some aspects of a scene that other people can't, to feel differently than others and choose words that differ from theirs, that's allowed me to write stories that are mine alone." Being an essentially lonely person helps him deal with the solitude of both writing and running. The qualities making him a writer, he claims, also make him a difficult person to deal with: "I just can't picture someone liking me on a personal level. Being disliked by someone, hated and despised, somehow seems more natural." Murakami considers his highest priority to be his writing, not dealing with other people, though he calls his most "indispensable relationship" to be with his readers. Because readers have responded to his books, he gained the freedom to write "the kind of things I wanted to write, exactly the way I wanted to write them."

Though Murakami writes in his usual style, occasionally there are echoes of other writers, at least in Philip Gabriel's sometimes colloquial translation. A paragraph about running is full of short sentences and compound sentences with short independent clauses, as if trying to approximate the rhythm of running. It begins, "It rained for a short time while I was running, but it was a cooling rain that felt good." Just as Ernest Hemingway's characters merge with their landscapes, Murakami feels at one with the weather, the terrain, and whatever he sees while running. His seemingly simple style also recalls that of Hemingway's friend, F. Scott Fitzgerald. While translating Fitzgerald's *The Great Gatsby* (1925), Murakami marvels at how the novel nourishes him, how he discovers something new each time he reads it, and how mysterious the creative process is. He still cannot understand how Fitzgerald accomplishes what he does.

Murakami contrasts the physical peak reached by athletes when young with the productivity of Fyodor Dostoevski and Domenico Scarlatti in their fifties. Murakami repeatedly addresses the question of aging: "Mick Jagger once boasted that 'I'd rather be dead than still singing "Satisfaction" when I'm forty-five.' But now he's over sixty and still singing 'Satisfaction.' Some people might find this funny, but not me." Most of Murakami's characters are young people, and he clearly continues to identify with them, seeing himself as a slightly wiser version of the man he used to be. While running is a means of staving off some of the consequences of aging, he is reconciled to the inevitability of change and that it is not a laughing matter.

While *What I Talk About When I Talk About Running* consists mostly of Murakami's seemingly random thoughts, there are many wonderful passages illustrating why he has such a lofty reputation. One describes his 1983 trip to Greece and a lonely run from Athens to Marathon to experience what the ancient Greek messenger did on his journey that gives the sport its name, though Murakami chose to run in a direction opposite that of the original. He deals with speeding traffic, encounters dead cats and dogs, and develops an intense thirst for a beer, becoming angry at the placid calm of the grazing sheep he passes. When he finishes this, his first marathon, and goes to a café for the longed-for beer, it does not taste as good as the one he had been imagining. The descriptive passages in this section are matched by his account of the change from brisk autumn to much bleaker weather in Cambridge, Massachusetts, where he trained for the New York City Marathon in 2005. He creates a vivid image of a homeless man pushing a shopping cart and singing "America the Beautiful."

Throughout his writing Murakami uses sports metaphors. In *What I Talk About When I Talk About Running* he compares the modifications necessitated by aging that every writer goes through to a baseball pitcher who relies upon fastballs learning to be more clever and learning a changeup. As in his fiction, Murakami's major points of reference are the arts. During the ultramarathon he spots clouds "like something out of a nineteenth century British landscape painting." Occasionally, historical references are called for, as when his body rebels during this grueling race: "Like Danton or Robespierre eloquently attempting to persuade the dissatisfied and rebellious Revolutionary Tribunal, I tried to talk each body part into showing a little cooperation."

In his afterword, Murakami says that he thinks of *What I Talk About When I Talk About Running* "as a kind of memoir," allowing him "to sort out what kind of life I've led, both as a novelist and as an ordinary person, over these past twenty-five years." He wrote the book to discover something about himself, and, when he had finished, he felt a weight had been lifted. Murakami takes his title from Raymond Carver's short-story collection *What We Talk About When We Talk About Love* (1981), which he has translated into Japanese. While Carver's stories focus on the often insurmountable burdens life places upon his characters, Murakami's book celebrates an individual's struggle to make sense of his life and his art by exerting control over every facet of his daily existence.

Michael Adams

Review Sources

Booklist 104, no. 16 (April 15, 2008): 5.
Christianity Today 52, no. 10 (October, 2008): 104.
The Economist 388 (July 26, 2008): 95-96.
Entertainment Weekly, August 8, 2008, p. 73.
Library Journal 133, no. 11 (June 15, 2008): 69.
Los Angeles Times Book Review, July 27, 2008, p. 2.
Nature 454 (July 31, 2008): 583-584.
The New York Times Book Review, August 10, 2008, p. 16.
Publishers Weekly 255, no. 19 (May 12, 2008): 43.
Sports Illustrated 109, no. 4 (August 4, 2008): 26.
The Times Literary Supplement, September 12, 2008, p. 5.

WHEN YOU ARE ENGULFED IN FLAMES

Author: David Sedaris (1956-   )
Publisher: Little, Brown (New York). 336 pp. $25.99
Type of work: Essays, memoir

*A collection of autobiographical essays that reveal ab-
surdity in the mundane*

As a writer, David Sedaris relates personal experiences
that he exaggerates for comic effect and from which he
draws insights about the human condition. A witty and wry
observer of everything from natural childbirth to forensic
pathology, Sedaris has earned a loyal following, periodic
speaking tours, and various awards. Using the first-person
voice, Sedaris unabashedly describes himself self-criti-
cally, not just admitting but perhaps magnifying his shortcomings. This sometimes
comes across simply as self-deprecating humor, but cumulatively Sedaris's essays
create a picture of a man who is manipulative, wheedling, lazy, greedy, petty, dishonest, arrogant, and hypercompetitive. Even in stories intended to be funny, these revelations can at times make it hard for the reader to feel sympathy for Sedaris.

Sedaris's writing is defined by a deadpan delivery, exquisite word choice, and colorful imagery. The first of these—a narrative voice that is composed and straight-
faced—becomes itself a source of humor as his stories become increasingly absurd,
as when he describes in some detail an "external catheter" that is marketed to people
who desire to sit through an entire football game without having to get up to go to the
bathroom. His writing is also defined by a precise vocabulary and a good feel for vernacular that allows him to convey experiences and feelings with precise shading that
comes alive for the reader. He describes a flight during which he sat next to a richly
dressed senior couple whose conversation was filled with foul-mouthed complaints
about the airline: "It was as if they'd kidnapped the grandparents from a Ralph Lauren
ad and forced them into a David Mamet play." Sedaris's imagery is always evocative:
a hotel room for smokers that "smells like a burning mummy"; a woman with hair
"the color of a new penny"; the difference between a regular and a "mild" cigarette is
"the difference between being kicked by a donkey and being kicked by a donkey that
has socks on."

The essays in *When You Are Engulfed in Flames* can at times be slightly weightier
than those in Sedaris's previous collections. Still, the style and attitude that built his
reputation in previous volumes remain largely the same. In this sixth of his published
collections of essays, Sedaris focuses primarily on three areas: his childhood and
coming-of-age experiences; his life (mainly living in France) with his longtime partner, Hugh; and his efforts to quit smoking.

In his previous volumes, Sedaris's most poignant humor is drawn from his childhood. The son of a Greek Orthodox father and a Protestant mother, Sedaris and his

~

David Sedaris became well known in 1992 after reading his essay about working as a Christmas elf at Macy's on National Public Radio. Since then, his essays have been collected into books appearing on The New York Times *best-seller lists and collectively selling more than seven million copies. In 2001, he received the Thurber Prize for American Humor and was named* Time *magazine's "Humorist of the Year."*

~

five siblings grew up in the 1960's in Raleigh, North Carolina. His past experiences have provided rich material for Sedaris to train his wit on suburban life, family relations, alcohol and drug abuse, sex, school, and myriad other topics. In the current volume, however, Sedaris offers only one story exclusively about his childhood—an especially rich and entertaining topic in many of the essays in earlier collections. In the single childhood essay in the current volume—"The Understudy"—Sedaris describes the time his parents went away for a week and left the eleven-year-old David and his sisters with a lazy and tyrannical "sixty-year-old woman who was not just heavy but fat, and moved as if each step might be her last." It's difficult to know which details in the story are genuine. Was this woman really dropped off at Sedaris's house in a jalopy driven by a shirtless teenager? Did she really cook nothing but Sloppy Joes for them the entire week? Did she really tell them "First rule is that nobody touches nothing, not nobody and not for no reason"? However, separating factual details from fictional ones and slight exaggerations from outright fabrications misses the point of Sedaris's work. Each story illuminates some aspect of humanity—especially the shortcomings and failings in interactions with one another. The story of the tyrannical sitter is not important in its particulars, but rather in what it says about how children view an adult from the other side of the tracks.

Among the several coming-of-age stories in this volume, one stands out for its authenticity and sensitivity. "Road Trips" describes the author's coming out as a gay man. There are many ways such a story could go wrong, either falling into smug self-congratulation or proselytizing about social and moral issues. Instead, Sedaris manages to share his inner conflict and discomfort without making a cloying play for the reader's sympathy and without delivering a polemic about society's treatment of homosexuals. He simply offers his story with honesty and weary bemusement, in a way that readers of any sexual orientation could identify with.

Another contribution in the coming-of-age vein is "This Old House," in which Sedaris describes how he became infatuated with a romanticized ideal of the past and contrived for himself a wardrobe and lifestyle from the early twentieth century. His outfits supposedly included knickers, suspenders, and a top hat, and he moved into a boarding house run by a woman with a similar desire to live in the past. Even allowing for the author's tendency to exercise exaggerated self-deprecation, one gets the sense that Sedaris was losing his connection with present reality.

The only essay in this volume that clearly misses its mark is "What I Learned," which Sedaris delivered as a commencement address at Princeton in 2006. The story completely overreaches, which is an unusual departure from his typically well-paced and balanced storytelling. The essay amounts to a fake reminiscence about attending

Princeton so long ago that Jesus Christ had not yet been born and students worshiped a god named Sashatiba during the daily compulsory prayer. (Sedaris never in fact attended Princeton.) It describes in a singularly humorless fashion how students were burned alive if they failed a class; how the school mascot was a sabertooth; and how Sedaris himself majored in literally killing his parents. If Sedaris is trying to satirize certain aspects of Princeton or of higher education in general, it is not at all clear what these might be. The story lacks any evident kernel of truth that would allow it to make a larger point.

A large portion of the essays in this volume are drawn from Sedaris's life with his partner, Hugh Hamrick. The two have been together since 1990, and much of their time has been spent in Paris. Unlike most of Sedaris's family members and acquaintances, Hamrick is treated kindly in these essays. He comes across as a calm, sensible, and capable individual, and as such he does not figure into much of the humor in this volume. Instead, it seems his main purpose in these essays is to serve as a straight man to Sedaris's neurotic, hyperactive self.

Many of these stories focus on Sedaris's life in France, suggesting a fish-out-of-water theme. "In the Waiting Room," for example, recounts confusion and mishaps caused by Sedaris's limited French vocabulary. "Keeping Up" starts out by describing American tourist couples that Sedaris observes from his office window, then segues into a (supposedly grudging) tribute to Hamrick. A fuller and more unabashedly loving tribute to Hamrick is offered in "Old Faithful," in which Sedaris describes how the two of them met and became what Sedaris describes as a fairly conventional, monogamous couple. Sedaris certainly makes no effort to hide or downplay his homosexuality, but it is incidental to this relationship between two loving individuals.

Especially poignant is "That's Amore," an essay about an elderly, foul-mouthed, and combative woman who lived in the same apartment building as Sedaris and Hamrick in the 1990's. (The story actually takes place in New York rather than Paris.) Despite various ups and downs, Sedaris and the woman became friends of sorts, and by the end of the story it becomes evident that Sedaris truly cared for her.

The final essay, "The Smoking Section," is the longest and the one from which the book's title is drawn. It is written in three parts. "Before," "(Japan)," and "After." The first section describes the author's life as a smoker, from when he smoked his first cigarette at age twenty until his mid-forties, when he found smoking to be increasingly intolerable. The trouble was not so much the health effects or cost, but rather society's mounting restrictions on where smoking remained permissible. Thus, it was not watching his mother dying of smoke-induced cancer that drove him from cigarettes, but rather it was being excluded from decent hotels, which one by one converted to smoke-free environments. Sedaris's frank description of his smoking addiction is as entertaining and as illuminating as it is painful and revolting. It is a singularly honest, firsthand description of powerful addiction.

The second section of the essay takes place in Japan, where Sedaris lived for three months as a way to reinforce his decision to give up smoking. He had read that a change of scene would make it easier to stick with his decision to give up his smoking habit. This section is written as a diary, with entries from throughout his three-month stay. While entertaining, this section offers relatively little insight into Sedaris's struggle to give up smoking, instead focusing to a large extent on his efforts to learn the Japanese language and immerse himself in the Japanese culture. The entry for January 31, for example, opens with "Four weeks without a cigarette," and then goes on for three paragraphs about English translations in Japanese marketing.

The concluding, short section feels as though it should sum up some larger truths about smoking, addiction, or kicking the habit, but instead it mainly focuses on Sedaris's feelings about litter. He offers that his only real regret about having smoked for so many years is that he'd generated so much litter in the form of cigarette butts, and he goes on to describe how he was once arrested for littering. It's not much of a conclusion for such a long essay, but it's in character for this writer who specializes in the mundane.

Steve D. Boilard

Review Sources

Booklist 104, no. 16 (April 15, 2008): 5.
Entertainment Weekly, June 6, 2008, pp. 66-68.
Kirkus Reviews 76, no. 8 (April 15, 2008): 412.
Lambda Book Report 16, nos. 1/2 (Spring/Summer, 2008): 13.
Library Journal 133, no. 14 (September 1, 2008): 179.
New Statesman 137 (July 28, 2008): 49.
The New York Times, June 10, 2008, p. 7.
The New York Times Book Review, June 15, 2008, p. 5.
People 69, no. 22 (June 9, 2008): 55.
Publishers Weekly 255, no. 17 (April 28, 2008): 128.

WHERE HAVE ALL THE SOLDIERS GONE?
The Transformation of Modern Europe

Author: James J. Sheehan (1937-   )
Publisher: Houghton Mifflin (Boston). 284 pp. $26.00
Type of work: History, current affairs
Time: 1900-2007
Locale: Europe

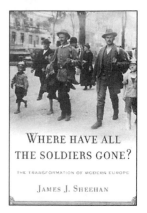

Sheehan examines the radical shift of Western Europe after World War II from a collection of competitive, warring states to an interconnective, peaceful society

The pendulum between peace and war among the major European states has swung slowly during the last four centuries. The two centuries of almost consistent warfare among these nations—from the outbreak of the Thirty Years' War in 1618 until the fall of Napoleon in 1815—was replaced by a relatively peaceful century, stretching until the outbreak of World War I in 1914. Most striking, from 1871 to 1914, there was peace among all the great powers, the longest stretch without fighting among the larger European countries in three hundred years. That tranquillity was replaced by the bloodbath of World War I, which drew in every major and most minor European nations. Then came two decades of uneasy international peace, a period Sheehan calls the "Twenty-Year Truce," marked by internal social and political revolutions. The truce was broken in 1939, and the resulting conflict almost destroyed Europe. The peace established in 1945, however, has held, resulting in the longest recorded period of noncombat among the major European powers.

This study, by a senior scholar of German history, provides the historical background, context, and explanation for these two generations of peaceful coexistence. Sheehan also looks at the challenges that Europe must overcome if the transformation that occurred after World War II will continue into the twenty-first century. This is not an interpretation based on the uncovering of new documentary evidence. Instead, Sheehan has reexamined, synthesized, and reinterpreted previous research. The result is a fresh and insightful examination of the history of modern Europe.

Europe at the turn of the twentieth century was a world, as Sheehan puts it, "living in peace, preparing for war." It was a time of relative civil and international tranquillity, but it was also a time of widespread militarism. According to Sheehan, nations at the turn of the twentieth century believed their essential responsibility was national defense. The major powers of Europe were what he called war states, with large citizen armies. The public face of the nation—whether it was Germany, Austria-Hungary, or even France—was the soldier. Because of the great expense of maintaining large armies in time of peace, an expense that included both the direct costs of equipping and otherwise paying for the armies and the indirect expense of the drain a large standing army made on the manpower available for the civilian economy, the nations

~

The Dickason Professor in Humanities at Stanford University since 1986, James J. Sheehan is the author, editor, or coeditor of eight other books focusing on German history in the nineteenth and twentieth centuries. He was president of the American Historical Association in 2005.

~

utilized a system of mass reserves. (The exception to this rule was the United Kingdom.) Conscripts were initially brought into the military system for a relatively short period of time for training, and then they returned to the civilian workforce, ready to be called back to military service should the need arise. Communications and transportation technology and elaborate and sophisticated planning were additional essential elements in the evolution of the large citizen armies. Large reserve forces needed to be recalled from civilian life, equipped, and deployed swiftly. The result was a similar political and social system throughout Europe. Sheehan emphasizes that this was a period that actually encouraged a sense of optimism in the future. War was accepted as a possibility that hung over everyone's head, but internal violence was limited, and standards of living for many Europeans rose during the century.

At the same time that Europe was involved in a massive military buildup and in perfecting a system of deploying mass armies, nations and individuals were also trying to develop ways of restraining the destruction of war. Ironically, alongside the growing militarism of the late nineteenth and early twentieth centuries was a growing and strong pacifist strain. Writers such as the Polish industrial warfare expert Ivan Bloch and the British journalist Normal Angell warned of the destructive nature of modern warfare. Their argument for turning away from war was not, unlike the Quakers, for example, based on any moral objection to war. Instead, they argued that modern war was so horrible that it would destroy social and economic stability. There were also some stirrings among governments. In 1899 and again in 1907, international peace conferences were held in The Hague, in the Netherlands. Sheehan, however, interprets these conferences, especially the later one, as little more than window dressing. Pacifism and militarism struggled for the soul of European governments during the first decade of the twentieth century, but militarism won. Although governments did not want to appear publicly opposed to efforts to find lasting peace, they did not want to have their ability to wage war restricted. This led to a certain amount of hypocrisy. For example, the Germans signed the convention in 1907 guaranteeing neutral territory, despite the fact that German war plans already included an invasion of neutral Belgium in order to defeat France.

Sheehan emphasizes that he is only speaking of what might be considered the central core of Europe when he writes of relative domestic and international peace. The rest of the world continued to be a violent and dangerous place. Throughout the peaceful century in Europe after the Napoleonic Wars, there was fighting in Africa and Asia as European nations expanded their colonial holdings or defended economic rights. Violence was also more likely to be the norm in life in the periphery of Europe. In Ireland, Spain, southern Italy, and the Balkans, for example, there was continuing conflict between nations or between the national government and elements of the population. Sheehan points out that conditions in the periphery of Europe resembled those of the colonial world: underdeveloped economies, inhospitable terrain, weak state institutions, communal or kinship loyalties, and feeble identification with the nation. In such circumstances, violence was a way of life.

One of the perennial questions confronting historians of twentieth century Europe is why did the assassination of the heir to the Hapsburg throne, the Austrian archduke Franz Ferdinand, lead to World War I? Having described an environment of violence (in the periphery of Europe) and militarism (among the great powers), Sheehan responds to the question by asking whether war in 1914 was inevitable. He concludes that given the atmosphere and the stresses being placed on the European powers during the second decade of the century, some sort of conflict between the major European states was probably unavoidable. However, diplomacy might have avoided war during the summer of 1914. More important, the conflict needed not, as it did, engulf every major European country.

The war that came left behind two different views of the place of war in European culture. For many Europeans, perhaps the majority, World War I proved the truth of the prophecies of Angell and Bloch. War was far more destructive than many had anticipated, and the lesson learned was the need to develop means to prevent a future large-scale European conflict. For other Europeans, probably fewer in number than the first group, but perhaps more energetic in seeking their objectives, and possessing political philosophies that required violence to succeed, such as the Communists and the Fascists, there was a belief in the "regenerative value of violence." War was a positive good.

In the end, the advocates of violence won, and the world was plunged into a second world war, this one of unparalleled destruction, especially in the east of Europe, where the total war between the tyrannical governments of Germany and the Soviet Union was characterized by a complete disregard for human life. When the conflict finally ended, it left the surviving population of Europe hungry, displaced, and disoriented. In Western Europe at least, there was a demand for a new approach to political and social life. The views of Angell and Bloch were firmly in ascendance.

That new approach is what Sheehan calls the "Rise of the Civilian State." In a sharp contrast to their pre-World War I counterparts, national defense was no longer the most important obligation of the post-World War II European states. Instead, public welfare was the highest priority on the minds of most European citizens. According to Sheehan, in the postwar period "the legitimacy of every Western European government depended upon its capacity to sustain growth and prosperity." Thanks to the economic cooperation among the European nations and the time of peace, the quality of life improved manifold. Consumer goods and automobiles, foreign travel, and secure retirement became commonplace. For those unable to take advantage of the economic boom, there is an expectation of government-provided social services, such as education, pensions, health care, and subsidized housing.

A number of factors allowed Europe to move in this direction. The most significant was the continuing presence on the European continent of the military might of the United States. The United States took on a significant portion of the defense burden of Western Europe in the confrontation with the Soviet Union. Another was the rapid decolonization that took place during the fifteen years after the end of World War II. Attempts to reestablish or maintain colonial empires were met with violent opposition by the indigenous peoples. The important point, according to Sheehan, was not that the Europeans suffered military reversals. That had happened before. However, instead of returning to the fray with renewed determination, the Europeans eventually admitted defeat. By letting go of their colonies, they were able to turn inward and focus on the welfare of Europe.

In many respects, the postwar history of Europe is a great success story. At the time Sheehan wrote, the European Union was the largest economic bloc in the world. Life was never so good for so many in a material sense, and this was accompanied by a historically low level of political violence.

There remains, however, one significant problem: external security in a dangerous world. When Europe had to confront a military issue on its own, such as the ethnic conflict in Bosnia in the early 1990's, it failed miserably. Only when NATO, with leadership from the United States, intervened by bombing the Bosnian Serbs was the fighting ended. For Europe to truly take its place as a major power in the world, it needs an independent security system. Sheehan, however, believes that this is unlikely to happen because of cost and other factors. The transformation of Europe from militant to peaceful may continue to be dependent in the future, as it has in the past, upon the protective umbrella of the United States.

Marc Rothenberg

Review Sources

Booklist 104, no. 2 (September 15, 2007): 22.
Commonweal 135, no. 6 (March 28, 2008): 22-23.
Foreign Affairs 87, no. 3 (May/June, 2008): 147-148.
Kirkus Reviews 75, no. 20 (October 15, 2007): 1092-1093.
Military History 25, no. 4 (September/October, 2008): 68-69.
The New York Times Book Review, February 10, 2008, p. 26.
The New Yorker 83, no. 45 (January 28, 2998): 83.
Publishers Weekly 254, no. 38 (September 24, 2007): 56.
The Virginia Quarterly Review 84, no. 1 (Winter, 2008): 258.
The Wall Street Journal 251, no. 14 (January 17, 2008): D7.

WHITE HEAT
The Friendship of Emily Dickinson and Thomas Wentworth Higginson

Author: Brenda Wineapple (1949-   )
Publisher: Alfred A. Knopf (New York). 416 pp. $27.95
Type of work: Literary biography, literary history
Time: The nineteenth century
Locale: New England, especially Amherst, Massachusetts

Wineapple traces the friendship between Emily Dickinson, the reclusive poet of Amherst, Massachusetts, and her more worldly friend, the older, former pastor, soldier, essayist, and abolitionist Thomas Wentworth Higginson

Principal personages:
> EMILY DICKINSON, a nineteenth century American poet
> EDWARD DICKINSON, her father
> LIVINIA DICKINSON, her sister
> WILLIAM AUSTEN DICKINSON, her brother
> SUSAN DICKINSON, her sister-in-law
> THOMAS WENTWORTH HIGGINSON, a nineteenth century man of letters, soldier, editor, abolitionist, and early editor of Emily Dickinson
> MABEL LOOMIS TODD, a poet and friend of Emily and her early editor

On April 17, 1862, Thomas Wentworth Higginson, minister, soldier, and man of letters, received a curious letter from a retiring spinster of Amherst, Massachusetts, Emily Elizabeth Dickinson. The letter asked his advice about the writer's poetry and enclosed were three of her poems. Wentworth was used to receiving such letters, especially after the publication of his essay "Letter to a Young Contributor," in which he gave advice to would-be authors. Nevertheless, he was not prepared for this particular letter, with its query about whether or not her poetry was "Alive," or for the strange poems enclosed. Thus began one of the most unusual literary correspondences of the nineteenth century, or of any century, and it forms the basis for this scrupulously researched and documented, fascinating, and wonderfully written study of nineteenth century American literary culture.

Thomas Wentworth Storrow Higginson (he was called Wentworth) was born in 1823, descended from seven generations of a New England family, beginning with the Reverend Francis Higginson, who arrived in the New World from England in 1629. He settled in Naumkeag, which he renamed Salem, and established the village's first church. Cotton Mather would describe him as the Noah of New England. Wentworth's ancestors were involved in the banishing of Quakers from Massachusetts, in the witch trials in Salem, but also in promoting freedom of the press, the antislavery movement, and education reform. Wentworth's father helped to found the Harvard Divinity

∼

Brenda Wineapple wrote the award-winning Hawthorne: A Life *(2003),* Genêt: A Biography of Janet Flanner *(1989), and* Sister Brother: Gertrude and Leo Stein *(1996). Her essays and reviews appear in* The New York Times Book Review *and* The Nation. *Wineapple has received grants from the National Endowment for the Humanities and the Guggenheim Foundation and teaches creative writing at Columbia University and the New School.*

∼

School, but he later lost his post when state funds were withdrawn, partly because of the rise of Unitarianism at the school. Nevertheless, Wentworth grew up in Cambridge surrounded by the atmosphere of Harvard. Later, as a Harvard student, he studied under a stellar group of academics and made contacts among the next generation of intellectual leaders. In 1844, he enrolled in Harvard Divinity School but left to pursue a life of poetry and social action, especially in the burgeoning abolitionist and women's rights movements. His subsequent life would be torn between direct social action on behalf of both women and slaves, and his desire to live the more private and secluded life of a man of letters.

Emily Elizabeth Dickinson was born December 10, 1830, some two hundred years after the first Dickinson had arrived in Massachusetts Bay Colony. Her antecedents in the New World had been in Massachusetts as long as Wentworth's, even if they were not as prominent. Emily's grandfather settled in Amherst, Massachusetts, and became one of the town's leading citizens. Her father, Edward, helped to found Amherst College as a bulwark against the religious liberalism of Harvard Divinity School, and when the state legislature pulled its financial support for Harvard, Wentworth's father lost his job with the Divinity School. As Wineapple notes, it was one of the connections, albeit an odd one, between the two correspondents. Emily received some education in the local schools and then passed a year at Mount Holyoke Seminary in nearby South Hadley. Then she returned to Amherst, her father's house, and the domestic retreat of her family, which for the most part she left only infrequently as a young woman and less frequently as she grew older, ultimately becoming a virtual recluse.

They met only twice, and Wentworth visited Amherst only three times in all the years of their correspondence, twice to see Emily and once to attend her funeral in 1886. He confessed that the two visits left him drained, for in the face-to-face contact her intensity simply sapped the energy from him, an experience that he wrote about later. Apparently, it quite frightened him. Emily appears to have been somewhat passive-aggressive, distant and reclusive but needy and obsessive, in her relationships with men. Throughout their long correspondence, she would send him poems asking for his help and then ignore his suggestions. An incredibly busy man, with his writing and with the various social causes he supported, Wentworth at times seems to have been perplexed as to how to respond to her queries. For her, the letters were a way to relate to the outside world, reaching beyond her family's garden.

As they lived their separate lives through the history of their times, they shared periodically their thoughts on verse, on their families, on the Civil War, and more: he directly; she obliquely. She would send often-obscure poems that mirrored or commented on something he had stated previously or had published. He wrote of the times, of history, of events of the wide world. She wrote of her garden, of her family, of the diurnal world of Amherst. She chided him for not coming to visit her, and he put off the visits for various reasons, one of which Wineapple speculates was a growing affection Wentworth was developing toward his correspondent. He apparently had had several relationships of varying depths with female acquaintances that annoyed his bed-bound wife. Emily, too, seems to have invested the epistolary friendship with an intensity that became apparent during Wentworth's two visits. After his second marriage, things cooled between them, and Emily developed another passion, this time with a local widowed judge, Otis Lord. Her friendship or relationship, however described, with Wentworth does appear to have been her longest one with a male not of her family.

One of the main purposes of this study is to recast the relationship between the two correspondents. The major biography of Emily is by Richard Sewall, who paints a rather unflattering portrait of Higginson that Wineapple is at some pains to revise. Much of the current literary opinion of Wentworth comes from his relationship with Emily, as his own voluminous writings are nearly forgotten. In addition, the negative opinion of him in some measure originates with the three-volume edition of the poet's work in part edited by him. After Emily's death, Mabel Loomis Todd and Wentworth gathered her poems that for the most part she had steadfastly refused to publish. Emily did publish a few under her name and, during the Civil War, several more anonymously. However, she published only one after the war. Ralph Waldo Emerson described such writers as "portfolio poets," those who wrote only for themselves and not to be published, presumably keeping their poems in a portfolio for their eyes only. Wentworth helped with the initial volume, wrote an introduction, and quarreled with Todd, who insisted on editing the poems by adding punctuation marks, rearranging the lines, and in some cases rewriting the texts. Wentworth opposed this practice, a fairly common one during the nineteenth century, but he appears in his later years to have lost much of his earlier spunk and, perhaps faced with Todd's insistence, seems to have caved in to her meddling. He had little or nothing to do with the next two volumes of poetry. When Emily's work was rediscovered in the early twentieth century, those early volumes of the poems were widely criticized, and rightly so, for the liberties taken with the poems.

According to the details provided in *White Heat*, Wentworth appears to have been unfairly criticized all these years for not understanding the genius of his correspondent or not providing her with sufficient support during her lifetime. Wineapple supplies ample evidence that Wentworth offered what encouragement he could, given Emily's eccentric behavior and her unique poetic style. Nothing in the nineteenth century literary culture could have prepared him for the eccentricity and advanced style of her prosody. He seems to have done the best he could under the circumstances, and apparently he did genuinely appreciate her poetic gifts, however strange they may have appeared. He encouraged her to publish, but when she was reluctant, he respected her wishes. The calumny heaped on him later by literary critics seems unnecessarily harsh.

White Heat is a carefully documented, well-written book that presents a compelling history of the strange friendship between the worldly activist, soldier, and writer Wentworth and the reclusive poet Emily, a relationship carried on primarily through letters. The fascinating frisson between the correspondents makes for an interesting collision of sensibilities. Wentworth brought to the self-isolated Belle of Amherst news of the outside world, through his letters and through the vast literary journalism he produced throughout his career. Emily saw the world close and, as she put it, "slant," and that perspective, delivered in the prose of her letters and in the poems she sent him, somewhat expanded his literary world. She exposed him to a poetry so unlike any he had experienced that it broadened, even if only privately, his literary horizons.

Wineapple has created in her study a marvelous dance of sorts between the enclosed world of Emily's household, with her extraordinarily inventive poetic style that would not be fully appreciated until deep into the twentieth century, and the active and open world of Wentworth, with his full participation in the central events of his time: the antislavery movement, the fight for women's rights, the expanded freedom of expression in the arts, the reform of education. The interaction between these two worldviews makes for a compelling narrative, and it also allows Wineapple to provide a survey of nineteenth century culture—religious, political, social, and literary—that enlarges the book from its simple discussion of the correspondence of two literary figures. The reader glimpses a broad sweep of nineteenth century American history, with its religious denominational conflicts, its various literary tensions, and its political tensions, especially following the emancipation and during the Reconstruction. In addition, there is the Civil War itself, in which Wentworth made history and which interacts with Emily's letters and life, providing a heart-rending close-up of the sufferings of the home front, albeit at a slant. *White Heat* offers an eminently readable study of two literary figures at the opposite ends of the genteel tradition in American letters. Wineapple has written a fascinating book, one that will educate as well as entertain.

Charles L. P. Silet

Review Sources

Booklist 104, no. 21 (July 1, 2008): 28.
The Economist 388 (July 26, 2008): 96-97.
Kirkus Reviews 76, no. 12 (June 15, 2008): 64.
New Criterion 27, no. 5 (January, 2009): 76-78.
The New Yorker 84, no. 23 (August 4, 2008): 68-72.
Publishers Weekly 255, no. 25 (June 23, 2008): 48-49.
The Wall Street Journal 252, no. 40 (August 16, 2008): W6.
The Wilson Quarterly 32, no. 4 (Autumn, 2008): 100-101.

THE WHITE TIGER

Author: Aravind Adiga (1974-   )
Publisher: Free Press (New York). 276 pp. $24.00;
    paperback $14.00
Type of work: Novel
Time: The early twenty-first century
Locale: Delhi and Bangalore, India

Adiga's compelling story of the coming of age of a young man caught in the tension between wealth and poverty in a newly globalized India examines deeply questions about human nature and its struggles with good and evil, justice and injustice, equality and inequality

> Principal characters:
> BALRAM HALWAI, also known as the White
>   Tiger, the young narrator raised in poverty who becomes the
>   chauffeur for a wealthy landlord
> ASHOK, the wealthy landlord and the White Tiger's employer
> PINKY MADAM, Ashok's wife
> MONGOOSE, Ashok's brother

In October, 2008, Aravind Adiga became the second youngest writer to win the prestigious Man Booker Award. He beat out fellow Indian writer Amitav Ghosh for *A Sea of Poppies* as well as the Irish writer Sebastian Barry for *The Secret Sculpture*, among others. Winning thrust Adiga, a former *Time* correspondent and freelance journalist, into the limelight for his acerbic and satiric look at contemporary India, especially the great divide between castes and classes that the drive toward globalization and wealth in the South Asian country has exacerbated. Reminiscent of Charles Dickens's *Great Expectations* (1861) and Salman Rushdie's *Midnight's Children* (1981) and *The Satanic Verses* (1988), Adiga's novel teems with the assorted misfits, ragamuffins, and other denizens of the slums, back alleys, and gleaming corporate towers of the new India of the twenty-first century.

When Balram Halwai learns that Wen Jiaboo, the premier of China, plans a visit to India to learn more about the country's success with capitalism, Halwai sets out to offer the premier his own insights into the nature of the modern India. Over the course of seven days and nights, Halwai writes letters to Jiaboo, providing details into his life of entrepreneurship and chronicling the way that he was able to move from poverty to wealth. These letters paint a picture of an India divided by wealth, a class of workers enraged by their treatment and striving to overcome their lowly position for a piece of the wealth, and a political system that is so corrupt that murder can go unpunished if enough money can be paid to the police. Although a statue of Gandhi stands in the center of Bangalore, where Halwai lives, Gandhi's memory is more mocked than venerated. To succeed in the new India requires cunning, desire, and the will to power.

~

*Aravind Adiga studied at Columbia
University—where he was salutatorian
in 1997—and Oxford University.
Before becoming a novelist, he served
as a South Asia correspondent for*
Time. *His articles have appeared in*
The Wall Street Journal *and* Financial
Times. *The White Tiger,* Adiga's first
novel, *won the Man Booker Prize. He
lives in Mumbai, India.*

~

Without these, life, according to the narrator, is a joke.

Halwai is no stranger to poverty. Born in the village of Laxmangarh to a rickshaw driver, he does not even have a name until he begins school. On the first day of school, when the teacher asks the pupils their names, Halwai replies that his name is "boy." When the teacher further questions Halwai, the narrator says that everyone in his family called him that and that they had no time to give him another name. The teacher then names the boy Balram, which means "sidekick to Krishna," one of the many gods of Hinduism. Even though the narrator possesses a religious name, he hardly feels religious. His family's poverty is so pressing that all he feels is the darkness of the India in which he lives. This poverty becomes even more crushing when Balram's father dies of tuberculosis, and he soon finds himself working in a tea shop to help his family make ends meet. He gets his last name, Halwai, or "sweet-maker," from his new job at the tea shop. Although his destiny seems settled, he eventually is hired as a chauffeur for one of the wealthiest men in the village, and his education about the nature of humanity and the deep political and social fissures in India soon begins.

Mr. Ashok, Balram's new employer, represents the new wealth in India. Although the sources of his wealth are mysterious, he has enough money to hire servants and to keep ostentatious living quarters in the wealthy section of Delhi. He is also able to use his money to help, or try to help, influence political elections and to hire Western prostitutes. A fat man whose wealth has not made him especially happy, Ashok is married to a demanding Westerner named Pinky Madam, who makes life hell for her husband and his servants. Although Ashok's family did not approve of his marriage to Pinky Madam, Ashok went ahead with the marriage. When Balram becomes Ashok's driver, he soon begins to learn what life is like in the part of India that lives in the Light, away from the darkness of poverty and the superstition bred from centuries of religious observance. When Ashok's brother, Mongoose (his real name is never revealed; this is the name that Balram gives the brother in order to represent the brother's personality), meets Balram, he tells this new driver that the road is a jungle and that he will soon learn that he will have to roar to get ahead on it.

When Balram moves with Ashok and Pinky Madam to their home in Delhi, he sees the great gap between the two Indias—the Light (rich) and the Dark (poor)—and he plots a way to make his move from the darkness to the light. Ashok attempts to be an enlightened master to his hired help, and he treats Balram the way he thinks Balram wants to be treated, as a member of his family. Pinky Madam and others around Ashok recognize Balram for the servant he is, and they encourage Ashok to treat this young chauffeur accordingly. Ashok refuses, but Balram does not think of Ashok's treatment as kind; he feels as if his employer is patronizing him and becomes angry.

Balram's anger is exacerbated as he watches his employer engage in political corruption as he tries to influence an election and as he tries to frame Balram for a hit-and-run accident for which Pinky Madam is responsible. Late one night on the way home from the mall, a drunken Pinky Madam demands to drive the car, and Ashok allows her to do so. Racing down a dark street, she hits and kills a young child. The next day, Ashok's brother makes Balram sign a statement admitting that Balram was the driver when the accident occurred. After this incident, Balram begins to look for ways to betray and finally to escape Ashok.

Balram recognizes that having a great deal of money is the only way to survive in the jungle that is the new India. In order to escape his servitude, he begins to steal in devious ways small amounts of money from Ashok, whom he has now come to hate. When his employer withdraws a large amount of money from the bank, Balram decides to murder him and steal the money. One night on a deserted road, Balram succeeds in his plan, and he escapes undetected to southern India. He sets himself up as an example of entrepreneurship to Jiaboo because he took this first step to wealth. Once he gets to his new home, he hatches a plan to provide taxi service to employees leaving early in the morning from their jobs in new industries such as telemarketing. When he discovers that such car services already exist, he buys off the local police—who talk to him about this plan even though he is standing next to a wanted poster of himself in the police station—and they arrest the drivers in the taxi companies for having expired licenses. Balram's company begins to thrive, and he survives in the jungle like a white tiger, that unique animal that is born only once every several years, whose roar is loud, and whose desire for conquest is unquenchable. Like Pip in *Great Expectations*, Balram has succeeded in far greater ways than he ever imagined; in his success he now resembles his now-dead ex-employer and can live in the Light and never again in the Dark.

Much like Salman Rushdie's *The Satanic Verses*, *The White Tiger* explores the tremendous disparities between rich and poor, Muslim and Hindu, that exist in post-1947 India, when the newly independent country is struggling to define itself and to establish its power. As Balram asserts in *The White Tiger*, the old India was like a well-kept and orderly zoo where every animal knew its place. In those days cowherds tended to cows and women wore veils and kept their eyes averted from strangers' faces. When the British pulled out in 1947, the doors to the cages were suddenly opened and the animals began to destroy one another. The law of the jungle replaced the law of the zoo, and the most ferocious animals ate the others and grew big bellies. In Balram's experience, there are now only two castes: men with big bellies and men with small bellies. Destiny in the new India is to eat or to be eaten. Thus, as in Rushdie's novel, where in a famous scene the Indian immigrants to England become animals such as snakes and water buffaloes, Balram sees everyone around him in terms of their animal nature and gives them animal names. He is the white tiger because of his cunning; when he sees a white tiger at the zoo, he faints because he realizes he can no longer live in the cage of his existence. His employer's brother is the Mongoose because of his fearlessness and his deceitful ways; his employee's father is the Stork because of the length of his legs. In addition, Balram tells his grandmother that men and women in Bangalore live like animals in a jungle. Balram likens Bangalore to a chicken coop in which the animals' movement is limited. Ironically, in order to break out of the chicken coop, he must embrace his animal nature—which he has tried to rise above in believing that obedience and humility were virtues—and eat rather than be eaten.

Balram's new India is one of deep contradictions. On the one hand, there is the wealth of the new middle classes brought about by globalization and the creation of middle management positions in jobs outsourced from Western countries at businesses such as call centers. On the other hand, the suffocating poverty of rural villages and of slums in the cities exists in the shadows of these new jobs. Class warfare continues to define India in a way that even Ashok is unable to see or admit. His patronizing treatment of one of his own countrymen resembles the way that a British colonial governor would treat one of his Indian servants. Balram's murder of Ashok is both an act of class warfare and an act of individual entrepreneurship that enables Balram to get ahead. Thus, the greed that drives the new middle class in India touches the lower classes, making greed the consuming trait of the new India. In a world where life is a joke, as Balram tells Jiaboo early in the novel, even the act of murder can be seen as a self-congratulatory act of getting ahead in life.

As many of the reviews of the novel pointed out, Adiga's novel is often simplistic and the characters are not fully developed. Neither of the two main characters— Balram or Ashok—is complex or thoughtful; they are instead symbols of the poor and the rich. Each is driven by an almost physical desire to consume and conquer and thus is reduced to his animal nature. The contest between these two animals is exactly the point of Adiga's novel, and he succeeds by using parody and satire to draw readers into the arena to watch this battle.

Henry L. Carrigan, Jr.

Review Sources

The Economist 388 (September 13, 2008): 94.
Kirkus Reviews 76, no. 4 (February 15, 2008): 159.
Library Journal 133, no. 3 (February 15, 2008): 89.
New Statesman 137 (March 31, 2008): 59.
The New York Times Book Review, November 9, 2008, p. 13.
The New Yorker 84, no. 9 (April 14, 2008): 75.
Publishers Weekly 255, no. 2 (January 14, 2008): 37.
The Times Literary Supplement, April 11, 2008, p. 21.

THE WIDOWS OF EASTWICK

Author: John Updike (1932-2009)
Publisher: Alfred A. Knopf (New York). 308 pp. $24.95
Type of work: Novel
Time: 2006-2007
Locale: Canada, China, Egypt, and Rhode Island

In his final novel, Updike continues the story of the women first introduced to readers in The Witches of Eastwick, *tracing their lives as they return to Eastwick and attempt to atone in some ways for their past transgressions*

Principal characters:
ALEXANDRA FARLANDER, a widow living in New Mexico
SUZANNE (SUKIE) MITCHELL, a widow living in Connecticut
JANE TINKER, a widowed Boston socialite
CHRISTOPHER GABRIEL, an Eastwick resident
GRETA NEFF, a longtime resident of Eastwick

A sequel by its nature invites comparison with its predecessor, and John Updike's *The Widows of Eastwick* is no exception. The novel picks up the stories of the three principal characters Updike first created in his 1984 best seller *The Witches of Eastwick*, a mixture of graphic realism and magical fantasy set during the early 1970's in a socially conservative Rhode Island seaside community. In that novel Alexandra Spofford, Jane Smart, and Sukie Rougemont, all in their thirties, seem to possess the ability to perform black magic. When they come under the spell of the mysterious Darryl Van Horne, a stranger recently relocated to Eastwick, they begin engaging in a series of sexual orgies and rites of black magic that wreak havoc on people who cross their paths. This tale of powerful women, published when discussions of feminism and women's roles in society were still center stage in the American consciousness, was widely popular at the time of its publication—although it was heavily criticized by many ardent feminists for treating serious women's issues with a certain sense of patronizing smugness. Additionally, millions who never read the book became familiar with the story through the 1987 film adaptation starring a trio of screen celebrities—Cher, Susan Sarandon, and Michelle Pfeiffer—as the witches, and legendary film star Jack Nicholson as Van Horne.

Some of the same attractions—and faults—of the earlier novel are present in *The Widows of Eastwick*, which picks up the stories of Alexandra, Jane, and Sukie as they find themselves alone, widowed after years of marriage to men whom they met after fleeing Eastwick some three decades earlier. It is possible to read this novel without knowing anything about Updike's earlier story featuring these characters. Enough hints are provided in *The Widows of Eastwick* to let readers know what had happened thirty years before to explain why the return of these women to Eastwick would be

John Updike had a highly successful career as a novelist, poet, and essayist. The author of more than fifty books, he received numerous honors, including the Pulitzer Prize, the National Book Award, the National Book Critics Circle Award, the Howells Medal, and the 2007 Gold Medal for Fiction from the American Academy of Arts and Sciences. Updike died of lung cancer shortly after the publication of The Widows of Eastwick.

cause for concern, not only to the townspeople but to Alexandra, Jane, and Sukie as well.

To resurrect these characters who were once examples of female power involves quite a gamble, but Updike manages to use these women to elucidate new themes about the problems of growing old in American society. At the same time, readers familiar with Updike's earlier novel will find his portrait of the aging witches particularly poignant. These once-strong women are now merely aging grandmothers whose everyday struggles with failing health add to their deep awareness of their inconsequential presence in a society that values youth and physical fitness.

The first third of the book focuses on attempts by all three women to fill the void in their lives created by the deaths of their husbands. The opening scenes trace the journey of Alexandra, widow of New Mexico potter Jim Farlander, through the Canadian Rockies, where she tries with mixed success to enjoy the scenery and the company of fellow travelers, one of whom seems to take a romantic interest in her. Not ready for new commitments, she returns home to New Mexico and shortly thereafter reestablishes contact with former friend (and fellow witch) Jane Tinker, who has recently lost her husband, a rich Bostonian. The two arrange for a trip to Egypt, during which they reminisce about their days in Eastwick, Rhode Island. Although the excursion is not as pleasant as Alexandra had hoped it would be, within a short time the two find themselves traveling together again, this time in the company of their Eastwick friend Sukie Mitchell, also a recent widow, who prompts them to join her for a tour of China.

These journeys allow readers to see how the women have changed in thirty years. They are also intended as prelude for a more important trip that takes the three back to Eastwick, where they had originally met and where, under the influence of the diabolical Van Horne, they had virtually abandoned their families (and eventually divorced their first husbands) to engage in a series of sexual orgies that had allowed them to demonstrate to themselves and the community their newfound freedom and power as independent women. Unfortunately, they are painfully aware that their earlier experience had ended in disaster: Several people lost their lives, and the three women were convinced that their magic had led to these deaths. As a result, in the sequel, the three agree to return to Eastwick, where they hope to make amends for the calamities they had helped bring about. They manage to rent space in the same mansion Van Horne had owned—now refurbished into apartments—where they intend to reconstitute their witches' coven to see if they can reverse some of the damage they had caused.

The plan has problems from the outset, as the townspeople in Eastwick prove to have long memories, and the women are not welcomed back into the community. Among those most outraged by their return are Greta Neff, whose husband had been seduced by one of the witches, and Chris Gabriel, who believes that his teenage sister Jenny died as a result of a spell cast on her by the three. Greta and Chris are still living in Eastwick, and when the witches return the two decide to exact revenge. Chris takes an active role in stalking the witches and even issues some veiled threats against them. Only when Sukie manages (somewhat improbably) to thwart Chris's scheme by seducing him do the three women feel they are out of danger and can attempt to re-create the magical rite, hoping they might conjure some permanent good. Instead, at the height of the ceremony, Jane suffers an aneurysm and dies. Their coven fractured, the two remaining witches leave Eastwick, making what they both sense are empty vows to meet again for future travels. It is a sobering farewell to these once-powerful figures whose earthy seductiveness has been replaced by a sentient awareness of their own frail mortality.

As complicated as the foregoing plot summary may appear, it does not do full justice to the complexity of this novel. *The Widows of Eastwick* is filled with humor, irony, and pathos. Updike deals directly with the problems of aging in American society and seems to call out, as Linda Loman does over the body of her dead husband Willy in Arthur Miller's play *Death of a Salesman* (pr. 1949), that "attention must be paid" to these women who might otherwise be shunted aside by a culture that no longer values what they can contribute—or even wishes to acknowledge their existence.

While it is clear that Updike intended to deal seriously with an important problem in American society, his use of the language of sophisticated comedy to express a serious and sensitive topic and his insight into his principal characters were almost immediately challenged by the first reviewers of this novel. Quite a few criticized it as a serious falling-off from Updike's earlier achievements such as the Rabbit Angstrom novels or even *The Witches of Eastwick* (which also received mixed reviews when it first appeared in 1984). Three principal criticisms emerge from these early critiques. First, some attacked the novel as being formless, dismissing the first third of the book as a well written but irrelevant travelogue. This observation seems to miss the point Updike is making in the early sections of the book. The descriptions of the Western Rockies, the Egyptian pyramids, and the Chinese antiquities are rendered in such detail as to make them almost tiresome at times, but that seemed to be Updike's intention, since he has the women themselves complain about the tedium of their journeys. It seems clear that these excursions serve an important function in the novel, demonstrating the desperation that the widows experience as they try to replace the husbands whom they have recently lost.

A second charge reflects a larger problem that Updike had faced at least since the publication of *Couples* (1968), a novel that deals frankly and playfully with American sexual mores. While a few more straitlaced critics have complained about his gratuitous descriptions of sexual activities (almost totally absent in *The Widows of Eastwick*), what has bothered many is Updike's rather glib handling of women's issues and what some have described as his inadequate understanding of the psychological makeup of his female characters. Similar complaints were almost immediately launched against *The Widows of Eastwick*; one reviewer was particularly put off by Updike's inability to depict the emotional dimensions and even the social interests of older American women.

A third charge is that the exceptional vitality which characterized *The Witches of Eastwick* is missing from the sequel. Perhaps, however, such criticisms are driven by the expectations of the reviewer as much as by anything Updike has done or failed to do. *The Widows of Eastwick* lacks vitality precisely because it reflects the sad state in which the three witches find themselves. Where once these women could (literally) work magic, they are now unable to influence their own lives, or those of others, through their special abilities. What is clear is that in this novel Updike is attempting to present characters who suffer immensely not only from guilt for past transgressions but also from the feeling of powerlessness that accompanies advancing age.

Although it may be possible to answer the charges of early reviewers regarding the novel's organization, treatment of women, and lack of vitality, one significant problem remains for those trying to comprehend Updike's intentions in this novel. The same problem exists for those trying to make sense of *The Witches of Eastwick* as well. It evolves from what might be called a confusion of genres, rooted in Updike's decision to move fluidly between the worlds of realism and fantasy, particularly in his willingness to treat witchcraft as a part of the real world. His three protagonists believe they can affect others' lives (and their own) through conjuration, and events do seem to happen as a direct result of their casting of spells. In the 1984 novel, badminton shuttlecocks are turned into bats, and people are made to spit out feathers and other debris when they cough. More seriously, two deaths in that book are brought about as a result of the witches' malevolent activities. In the sequel, even though the witches fail in their major attempt to reverse some of their earlier malevolent work, their good offices do seem to cure a young woman of infertility. Is this really magic, or is there another explanation? Additionally, one is never certain how to understand the notion, expressed more than once in the book, that the three women conjured up their new husbands when they all fled from Eastwick. If they did, could they not have used their powers to prevent those husbands from dying? Is this conjuring simply a metaphor, suggesting that conventional feminine wiles are somehow akin to magic? If it is, then should other events of witchcraft be interpreted metaphorically as well? Unfortunately, these questions remain unanswered, perhaps intentionally. For witchcraft is a mystery that remains unfathomable, one among many that Updike deals with in this and other novels: sex, religion, and, most notably in *The Widows of Eastwick*, death. (Updike himself died of lung cancer three months after the novel's publication.) As the witches-turned-widows of Eastwick come to realize, they cannot hold back the forces of time, and their attempts to come to grips with their own mortality give readers some insight into the greatest of all of life's mysteries, one for which Updike—despite his exceptional ability to offer insight into the human condition—is unable to provide answers.

Laurence W. Mazzeno

Review Sources

Booklist 104, no. 22 (August 1, 2008): 8.
Commonweal 135, no. 22 (December 19, 2008): 20-21.
Kirkus Reviews 76, no. 16 (August 15, 2008): 15.
Library Journal 133, no. 14 (September 1, 2008): 123.
The New York Times Book Review, October 26, 2008, p. 1.
Publishers Weekly 255, no. 30 (July 28, 2008): 48.
The Spectator 308 (November 1, 2008): 46-47.
The Times Literary Supplement, October 31, 2008, p. 19.
The Washington Post Book World, October 26-November 1, 2008, p. 7.

WILLIE NELSON
An Epic Life

Author: Joe Nick Patoski (1951-   )
Publisher: Little, Brown (New York). 567 pp. $27.99
Type of work: Biography

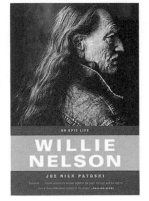

*A country-western music journalist with thirty-five years
of experience writing about Willie Nelson tells the singer's
epic story*

Principal personages:
> WILLIE NELSON, the legendary maverick of
> country-western music
> BOBBIE LEE NELSON, Nelson's older sister,
> who is also his pianist and his close
> friend
> ALFRED NELSON, grandfather of Willie and
> Bobbie, who raised them with his wife, taught them faith, and gave
> them a love of music
> NANCY NELSON, Alfred's wife, grandmother of Willie and Bobbie
> PAUL ENGLISH, Nelson's lifelong friend, bodyguard, and drummer
> WAYLON JENNINGS, the famous country-western singer, cofounder with
> Nelson of "Outlaw Country"

With *Willie Nelson: An Epic Life*, Joe Nick Patoski has fulfilled a lifelong quest for knowledge, not only about a legendary singer but also more broadly about the Texas milieu they share. The biographer's family moved to Texas when he was two years old, and he has been "trying to figure out Texas and Texans ever since . . . . I realized the answer had been right in front of me for most of my life," meaning in the person of Willie Nelson. Most people would probably agree with Patoski that Nelson is the quintessential Texan.

Patoski also has the professional background to write this story. He has written two other book-length biographies, numerous magazine and newspaper articles as a staffer or freelancer, and liner notes for nearly a dozen country-western albums; he has served as a radio commentator on the country-western scene, manager of two country bands, and Grammy Awards judge for the National Academy of Recording Arts and Sciences.

These qualifications, personal and professional, should satisfy those wondering why a new book about Nelson joins some seventeen others already published, including Nelson's autobiography. Patoski offers something extra for those who share his thirst for knowledge: a wealth of details on the history of American music, whose particulars must be recounted if the reader is to understand Nelson's place in it. For educational value, Partoski's chapters on Nashville and Austin are outstanding.

The biographer presents Nelson's life in chronological order, titling each chapter with a place name and a year, such as "Abbott [Texas], 1933" (the year of Nelson's birth) or "Nashville, 1960." At key points, however, the author interrupts this sequence to provide background on the Nelson family, the development of American folk music, or the intricacies of the music business. Thus, in a chapter titled "East of Western Grove on Pindall Ridge, 1925," Patoski reveals that "[m]usic was in the Nelson blood long before Texas, back in the rugged hills of north central Arkansas." Another chapter, on Fort Worth, describes Western swing as

> an amalgam of popular American music—country, of course, swing, jazz, pop, Dixieland, and country blues—tailored for dancing, with a strong Texas flavor. Swing in Fort Worth wasn't just a western thing, either. It was the hometown of big-band orchestra leader Paul Whiteman and numerous other swinging big-band musicians.

As for Nelson's life, the broad outlines will be familiar to most fans; they include an impoverished but contented childhood, an early stint in a Western swing band, service in the Air Force, work as a disc jockey, and writing wildly successful songs in Nashville, Tennessee. However Nelson's efforts to record his own work, on his own terms, were disappointing. Nashville was "the promised land" to Nelson and hundreds of other country musicians. "The home of the Grand Ole Opry and Music Row was where country music's stars shined brightest and where the hits were made," but Nashville was "much more than that," as Patoski shows in generous detail. He relates that it was the city's African American community that first established its position as a music center. Patoski describes the Nashville recording industry, the participating artists, and even the studios where they played. The radio program that was to become Grand Ole Opry, he says, was launched in November, 1925, as *WSM Barn Dance*.

As Nelson found it in 1960, the Grand Ole Opry was "a friendly, folksy, and family-oriented showcase of all styles of southern, western, and mountain music, in a tightly regimented format." Nevertheless, he would have to work hard to break into the Grand Ole Opry and the Nashville recording scene. Nelson's first job in the city was selling encyclopedias door to door. In time, the popular Faron Young asked to record Nelson's song "Hello Walls," which rose to the top of the country singles chart in 1961 and soon yielded Nelson an initial royalty check of $14,000.

Nelson was on his way as a songwriter. After "Hello Walls," Nelson penned, in short order, "Crazy," "Night Life," and "Funny How Time Slips Away," all of which made their way into the iconic book *Heartaches by the Number* (2003), listing the five hundred best country songs. Still, it was other singers who made these songs famous. Nelson wanted desperately to present his music according to his own vision. He formed his own band and toured the country. In 1964, he enjoyed the prestige of Grand Ole Opry membership, but

Joe Nick Patoski began writing about Willie Nelson in 1973. He has also authored the biographies Stevie Ray Vaughan: Caught in the Crossfire *(1993) and* Selena: Como la Flor *(1996). He has written for* Country Music, Rolling Stone, Spin, *and* The New York Times, *among other publications. Patoski has served as a Grammy Awards judge for the National Academy of Recording Arts and Sciences.*

he left abruptly when he realized he could not fulfill his contractual obligation to perform twenty-six Grand Ole Opry dates a year and still maintain his road-tour schedule—his larger source of income by far. Moreover, although the Grand Ole Opry was hospitable to all country genres, on Nashville's Music Row these genres had to be kept strictly separate.

As Patoski notes, many Texan performers tend to switch or blend musical genres; Nelson found a model from earlier years in Bob Wills. Stylistic diversity, however, was not acceptable to Music Row's record producers, who favored the commercially safer single-genre formula. That made conflict between Nelson and them virtually inevitable. As if this were not enough, Nelson's voice and appearance also counted against him with the Nashville music companies. Finally, in exasperation, Nelson returned to Texas in 1965. Many thought this move would destroy his career, but he persisted and defied the odds. For years, Texas fans, especially in Austin, provided support and revenue even when Nelson's record sales elsewhere were slow.

Paradoxically, the song that turned around his performing career a few years later was not one of Nelson's compositions. It was "Blue Eyes Crying in the Rain," written by Fred Rose in 1945 and recorded previously by Hank Williams, Gene Autry, and Elvis Presley. Nelson's cover was part of his 1975 Columbia Records debut, *Red Headed Stranger*. The first recording produced by Nelson, this stripped-down concept album was initially greeted with skepticism in the music industry, but it became a popular triumph, bringing Nelson some measure of financial security and a new credibility that freed him to create the kind of music he had long envisioned. As a single, "Blue Eyes Crying in the Rain" reached the top of the country-western charts before moving onto the pop charts, where it shortly reached number 21.

With this fresh start, Nelson pioneered "Outlaw Country" with his close friend Waylon Jennings, not only loosening the hold of Nashville but also winning over large numbers of new country-western fans, especially among rock enthusiasts. Nelson had seen possibilities in Austin's rapidly developing "hippie" music scene, dominated in the 1970's by the city's Armadillo World Headquarters music hall. Soon Nelson built his own Pedernales Studio near Lake Travis in Austin. He realized his dream of playing and recording his own brand of country music, strongly influenced by rock and roll, jazz, Western swing, and folk.

The "crossover" phenomenon at the heart of Patoski's tale is one reason for the subtitle "An Epic Life." Indeed, like the hero of Homer's *Odyssey* (725 B.C.E.), Nelson has lived by his wits and taken things as they came. Epic heroes also tend to have flaws, however, and, notwithstanding his clear admiration of his subject, Patoski duly details those of his epic hero. One such flaw was Nelson's tolerance of gun-toting by some members of his staff, leading to tension in the "hippie-oriented" venues where he performed, including the Armadillo. Conversely, the biographer also notes how Nelson's forbearance of "scalawags" can make the way thorny for the honest members of his circle. Patoski also examines Nelson's marital infidelities and his periodic financial and emotional neglect of his family. He reports that Nelson's eldest son, Billy, committed suicide in 1991.

Much of the hardship in Nelson's life, however, had other origins than his personal shortcomings. In the early 1990's, a failed tax-shelter investment—one his accountants had told him was perfectly sound and legal—led to his arrest by Internal Revenue Service (IRS) agents who seized all of his property for back taxes. He acknowledged the debt and paid it all, auctioning much of his land and selling his 1992 album *The IRS Tapes: Who'll Buy My Memories?* via late-night television commercials. His friends and admirers did what they could to minimize Nelson's humiliation, for example by bidding up land prices at the auctions. Many of his supporters wanted to repay the kindness he had shown with his famous Farm Aid concerts. To Kinky Friedman, a longtime associate, the important thing about Nelson's payment of the tax debt was that "[h]e didn't do it the easy way and plead bankruptcy. He did it the cowboy way."

Patoski does an excellent job of showing how, despite setbacks, Nelson exhibits a quiet resolve and an untiring focus on the goal, which has helped him to artistic success. The writer also traces clearly Nelson's gradual but steady evolution into the gentle, laid-back secular saint he has become.

Patoski is plainly elated at having produced such an authoritative biography, based on more than one hundred interviews and scrupulous research. Nelson's loyal fans will appreciate the wealth of detail Patoski shares about all aspects of the singer's life. However, at times too much detail is crowded into the narrative, as in the meticulous descriptions of the singer's real estate transactions during the 1970's. In addition, the accumulation of detail sometimes can make for awkward syntax, as in this passage from the chapter "Fort Worth Again, 1958," about a publishing deal with disc jockey Jack Rhodes:

> [Rhodes] had cowriting credits with Red Hayes on "A Satisfied Mind," which Porter Wagoner, Jean Shepard, and Red and Betty Foley had just recorded, and would share credits on "'Silver Threads and Golden Needles," and "Woman Love," which were covered by the likes of Hank Snow, Sonny James, Ferlin Husky, Jim Reeves, Porter Wagoner, and Gene Vincent. Before that, Rhodes led the Western swing band Jack Rhodes and His Lone Star Buddies ("Mama Loves Papa and Papa Loves the Women"), formerly Jack Rhodes and His Rhythm Boys, which featured Rhodes's stepbrother Leon Payne, whose loose style influenced Willie.

Even so, in a book the size of Patoski's—especially one purporting to relate a true-life epic—something had to be left out. The author has concentrated on the history of Nelson's music and its antecedents but has not truly plumbed the depths of Nelson's artistry and creative process. After all, it was Nelson's music that made possible one of his most epic accomplishments—bringing together disparate, potentially clashing audiences with his blend of musical genres and compassionate portrayals of human life. Nelson bared his heart concerning his musical endeavors in 1988 with *Willie: An Autobiography*, and, given the consummate success of that autobiography, Patoksi's omissions may have been for the best. Arguably, a reader needs both books to understand the full significance of Nelson's life and work.

Patoski most certainly has accomplished what he explicitly set out to do: understand Texans and Texas, the strange land to which he was transplanted so young. In an

"Author's Note" at the end, he describes how writing the biography of Nelson helped him understand that "Texans by nature are independent, free-thinkers, open, outgoing, and friendly. Iconoclasts, they respect tradition but are not beholden to it. Whether it's God or sin, they tend to embrace excess. The good ones have a whole lot of heart." He adds, "I can now safely say that no single public person living in the twentieth or twenty-first century defines Texas or Texans better than Willie Hugh Nelson."

As portrayed by Patoski, Nelson in the twenty-first century is

> pretty much the same old guy that Waylon had described years ago: "He'll give you everything, say yes to anybody and trust events will turn out fine." For all the hurt, emotional scars and financial challenges he had endured, he hadn't changed that much. More often than not, his instincts had proved right. What Willie started almost thirty years earlier [the merging of musical genres, with peace between their respective fans] . . . was still in play.

Thomas Rankin

Review Sources

Booklist 104, no. 14 (March 15, 2008): 4.
Kirkus Reviews 76, no. 5 (March 1, 2008): 235-236.
Rolling Stone, May 1, 2008, p. 22.
Texas Monthly 36, no. 4 (April, 2008): 64.
The Village Voice 53, no. 16 (April 16, 2008): 77.

THE WINTER WAR
Russia's Invasion of Finland, 1939-40

Author: Robert Edwards (1955-   )
Publisher: Pegasus Books (New York). Illustrated. Maps.
   319 pp. $26.95
Type of work: History
Time: 1915-1945
Locale: Finland, Sweden, and northwestern Russia, especially Leningrad

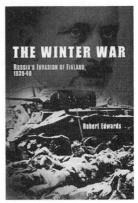

Edwards explores in daunting detail the events, political and social, that led up to Russia's invasion of Finland in 1939 and the ensuing war that lasted from late November, 1939, until March 12, 1940

Principal personages:
BARON CARL GUSTAV EMIL VON
   MANNERHEIM (1867-1951), a Finnish military leader and statesman
KURT WALLENIUS (1893-1984), a Finnish major general, a superb
   military leader
KLIMENT VOROSHILOV (1881-1967), an overconfident Soviet commissar
   for defense
WIPERT VON BLÜCHER (1883-1963), German minister to Finland in the
   1930's
ADOLF HITLER (1889-1945), Nazi dictator
JOSEPH STALIN (1897-1953), Soviet dictator
NEVILLE CHAMBERLAIN (1869-1940), British prime minister, 1937-1940
WINSTON CHURCHILL (1874-1965), British prime minister, 1940-1945
   and 1951-1955
FRANKLIN DELANO ROOSEVELT (1882-1945), president of the United
   States, 1933-1945

The winter war that the Soviet Union launched against Finland in 1939 grew out of territorial disputes that had existed between the two nations for more than two hundred years. Their common border extended for eight hundred miles from an area west of Leningrad to Lake Ladoga, the largest lake in Europe, and northward to the Arctic Ocean and seaport city of Murmansk on the Soviet side of the boundary.

Russian-Finnish political involvements date back to before the time of Peter the Great, the Russian czar from 1682 until his death in 1725. The eight-hundred-mile border that the two countries share has always been a bone of contention.

In the early eighteenth century, Czar Peter, in an alarming statement whose subtext suggested that sex-starved Finnish barbarians were on the verge of invading St. Petersburg and raping its women, warned that "[t]he ladies of St. Petersburg could not sleep peacefully as long as the Finnish frontier ran so close to our capital." He used this fear, ungrounded and irrational, as a means of justifying his invasion and con-

∽

Robert Edwards, in his own words,
"resides in a damp, collapsing
farmhouse in Somerset, England." The
Winter War *is his first book on military*
history. An occasional contributor to
the Daily Telegraph *and to* Motor
Sport, *Edwards holds a degree in*
international politics from the
University of Wales and spent two
decades as a financial analyst and a
trader in London and on Wall Street.

∽

quest of Viipuri and Karelia. The tensions between the Russians and the Finns were ever palpable during the two hundred fifty years separating Czar Peter's warning from the 1939 invasion of Finland by the Soviets.

Just as Peter feared for the safety of St. Petersburg, Joseph Stalin, two hundred years later, had similar fears for the city, under the Soviets renamed Leningrad. Twenty years before the winter war, Stalin produced a document that called for six provisions that would presumably assure the safety of Leningrad. His document called upon Finland to lease the entire Hanko peninsula to the Soviets for thirty years so that they could establish a Soviet naval base there. Fortified by artillery, this base would, in essence, seal off the Gulf of Finland and all the entrances to Leningrad by sea.

Stalin called upon the Finns to permit the Baltic fleet to use the Lapvik Bay as an anchorage and to cede the Gulf islands, as well as Björk, to the Soviet Union. Stalin demanded that the Soviet-Finnish border on the Karelian Isthmus be altered in such a way as to place it further from Leningrad than originally sited. He also called for the dismantling of the Finns' fortifications on the isthmus and for Finland to cede the western reaches of the Fisherman's peninsula to the Soviets.

Stalin's confiscatory proposals incensed the Finns, who were building their nation into an economic utopia during the globally bleak years of the Great Depression. Finland was the only European country that prospered during the 1930's: With the country's brisk foreign trade, Finland had paid off most of its World War I debt, the only European country to do so, and it had a manageable unemployment rate of slightly more than 2 percent. It spent as much on education as it did on defense, achieving a literacy rate approaching 100 percent.

As war clouds gathered over Europe in the late 1930's, Finland was poised between the Nazis, who were clearly aligned with the political right and fascism, and the Soviets, their untrustworthy neighbors, who were aligned with the political left and socialism. Adolf Hitler and Stalin clearly distrusted each other. Finland, whose populace included substantial numbers of supporters on both sides of the political spectrum, attempted to observe the Nordic neutrality that had served the country well during the early 1930's.

With Germany's invasion of Poland in September, 1939, a glaring violation of the nonaggression pact that Great Britain's prime minister, Neville Chamberlain, signed with Hitler just months before, it became clear that Hitler could not be trusted. Chamberlain, soon to be replaced as prime minister by Winston Churchill, had lost credibility by attempting to deal diplomatically with Hitler's fascist tactics.

Meanwhile, the Finns were enduring pressure from the Soviets, a development closely monitored by the German minister to Finland, Wipert von Blücher, who kept the Germans informed of Finland's looming threat from the Soviet Union. As Soviet pressure on the Finns increased, they were faced with a Hobson's choice in which no alliance would be to their advantage. Their preferred course of neutrality was no longer viable. Tension between the Soviets and the Finns quickly reached a boiling point, and in November, 1939, the winter war between the Soviets and the Finns began as more than a million Soviet troops were deployed to Finland.

The Soviet aggressors outnumbered their Finnish opponents by ten to one. In view of being so incredibly outnumbered, the resistance of the Finnish army under the outstanding leadership of Baron Carl Gustav Mannerheim and General Kurt Wallenius was remarkable. The Finns stood their ground against the Soviet troops for 105 days in mid-winter, a truly extraordinary feat.

Even though the Finnish commander, Wallenius, was a heavy drinker, he was an accomplished military strategist. Often forced to make crucial decisions when he was intoxicated, he somehow managed to keep a clear head when he was called upon to make strategic judgments.

The Soviet forces were led by Klimert Voroshilov, the Russian commissar of defense, who had an overblown vision of the strength of his forces and of his ability to lead them. Robert Edwards describes him in striking detail: "It is hard to identify a more overrated figure in military history than Kliment Yefremovich Voroshilov. A year older than [Chief of the General Staff Boris] Shaposhnikov, he had, in a long and undistinguished career, progressed from semiliterate roustabout to marshal of the Soviet Union without delivering a single example of leadership or military vision, instead taking the easier route of becoming a symbol of rugged Bolsevik 'soundness.'"

In this description, Edwards skillfully highlights the internal problems that had long afflicted the Soviets. Theirs had become essentially a government of personalities rather than one based on demonstrated performance. Voroshilov was a striking example of this weakness that, in the long run, proved devastating in many Soviet military and political undertakings. The Soviet Union's terrible losses in the winter war forced Stalin to purge the high command of the Soviet army.

Voroshilov had substantially underestimated the difficulties involved in invading Finland during the winter, particularly in view of the fact that his Finnish opponents were well accustomed to functioning in the brutally cold weather and pervasive darkness that typify Finnish winters. Given the climatic conditions, the Soviets could not have chosen a less favorable time of year to begin their assault on Finland.

The Finns traversed their country's difficult terrain effectively, often moving about on skis, transporting with them automatic weapons and the devastating mortars they fired with great precision against the enemy. Edwards relates how they completely disabled most of the Soviet's sixty field kitchens by hurling mortars at them and making direct hits, rendering them useless and unable to prepare meals to feed Soviet troops that were starving and suffering from sleep deprivation because of Finnish attacks in the dark of night when, with temperatures approaching minus thirty degrees Celsius, trees exploded loudly around them as their sap froze.

Soviet troops resorted to building log fires to warm themselves and to cook their food. This, however, was a hazardous thing to do because Finnish troops, perched in nearby trees, used their automatic weapons to shoot the soldiers clustered around these fires.

There was no shortage of vodka among the Soviet troops, and most of them partook generously of it. Edwards remarks on this, writing "a high alcohol consumption in cold weather merely produces the illusion of warmth and comfort; in reality, it has the effect of opening the pores of the skin and the consequent loss of body heat, with no reliable sources of external warmth save the suicidal log fires, can be terminal, even over as short a period as that endured by the 44th Division."

Edwards is at his best in describing vividly and in detail the field conditions and the terrain in which the winter war was waged. He is fully in command of the details of how the Finns fought the enemy. His extensive command of the political convolutions that led to the war is comprehensive and reveals much information that was not available to earlier students of the winter war.

Väinö Tanner's landmark study *Olin ulkoministerinä talvisoldan alkana* (*The Winter War: Finland Against Russia, 1939-1940,* 1957) was published in 1951, and Eloise Engle and Lauri Paananen's useful study *The Winter War: The Russo-Finnish Conflict, 1939-40* was published in 1972 and reissued in 1992 as *The Winter War: The Soviet Attack on Finland, 1939-1940.* Since then, Russia has opened archives to which these earlier scholars were denied access.

After Germany invaded Poland, the Soviets wanted tangible proof that Finland, then a neutral, democratic country, would work to protect Leningrad from attacks, presumably from Great Britain and France, but in actuality from Hitler's Germany. When Finland refused to permit the Soviets to establish military and naval bases in its sovereign territory, the Soviet response was a preemptive invasion of Finland.

The Soviets anticipated that they would defeat the small Finnish forces quickly and easily, thereby proving to Hitler that the Soviet forces were formidable. Because of the utter ineptitude of the leadership of the invading Soviet forces, the message Hitler received was completely the opposite of what was intended.

When, on March 12, 1940, the Finns were finally forced to sign a peace treaty with the Soviet Union after repeated bombings of their country by the Soviet air force and a frontal attack by the Soviets on the Karelian Isthmus, they had no recourse except to cede part of the isthmus to the Soviet Union as well as Vyborg (Viipuri) and some border territory.

The world at large, particularly the United States and its president, Franklin Delano Roosevelt, and Great Britain and its prime minister, Winston Churchill, had great sympathy for the Finns, but neither country came forward with tangible help. The League of Nations, by this time a virtually toothless organization, made no attempt to enter into the fray.

The winter war was strategically important to Hitler because it revealed weaknesses in the Soviet Union's armed forces. As a result of this abbreviated war, Hitler concluded that his plan for the German invasion of the Soviet Union, called Operation Barbarossa, was tenable. The long-term result was the siege of Leningrad, an encounter that lasted for a thousand days during which most of the city's population perished along with hundreds of thousands of the German aggressors.

In June, 1941, warfare resumed between the Finns and their Russian neighbors, but this conflict became a part of World War II. In this war, the Finns again demonstrated their strength and determination.

Edwards's research for this book was exhaustive. Although at times one might wish the author had presented his account with less information, the accumulated details provide evidence of Edwards's comprehensive command of his subject. His writing style, aside from frequent parenthetical intrusions that can prove distracting, is appealing and happily leavened by his unfailing wit.

R. Baird Shuman

Review Sources

Booklist 104, no. 13 (March 1, 2008): 46.
Kirkus Reviews 105, no. 6 (March 15, 2008): 283.
Publishers Weekly 255, no. 16 (April 21, 2008): 47.

WITHOUT SAYING
New Poems

Author: Richard Howard (1929-   )
Publisher: Alfred A. Knopf (New York). 265 pp. $30.00
Type of work: Poetry

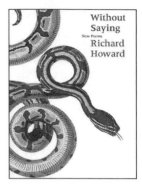

*In his fourteenth collection of poetry, Howard provides
more of his famous dramatic monologues, supplemented
by a number of other poems filled with wit and wordplay*

> *Principal personages:*
> HENRY JAMES, a major American-British
>   novelist
> L. FRANK BAUM, the author of *The
>   Wonderful Wizard of Oz* (1900)
> EDITH WHARTON, another major expatriate
>   novelist, an American who lived in France
> HUGH WALPOLE, a British novelist and key member of a London literary
>   clique

Richard Howard is known as a poet and a translator with an uncanny agility with language; as a young man he worked briefly as a lexicographer. He is best known for dramatic monologues that not only capture the spirit of a time period but also explore subtleties of character of historical literary figures, often Victorian, whose complex works have made them part of the canon. In his thirteen previous collections, these sparkling monologues have been most frequently commented on, anthologized, and honored. They carry with them the richness of the era as well as insights into how the most profound thinkers and artists confronted the problems in their lives.

Beginning with his first book of poems, *Quantities* (1962), Howard has been compelled by the dramatic monologue. The monologues are perhaps most concentrated in his 1969 book, *Untitled Subjects*, which gives the voices of Oscar Wilde, Alfred, Lord Tennyson, and others. For *Untitled Subjects*, Howard used Victorian photographs as the spur for a series of poems involving imagined speeches and letters by people photographed by Nadar, whose real name was Gaspard-Felix Tournachon. Nadar was a nineteenth century photographer who believed in reading the sitter's character into the photograph; he noted that "[i]n teaching photography it's this immediate contact which can put you in sympathy with the sitter, helps you to sum them up, follow their normal attitudes, their ideas, according to their personality, and enables you to make not just a chancy, dreary cardboard copy typical of the merest hack in the darkroom, but a likeness of the most intimate and happy kind." Howard grafted his own understanding of his subjects onto Nadar's likenesses, and his book, which included some of the Nadar likenesses, won the 1970 Pulitzer Prize.

Howard's poetry often seems preoccupied with the question of how events turn into history—with the sense of disjuncture between experience and record. His po-

ems trace constructions and reconstructions
of historical truth, playing with story and life.
The minute detail with which he creates people and events makes the reader both feel a
part of his scenes and a secret listener in the
shadows. Many of his works either mention
or identify themselves as physical records—
letters, books, tapes, pages. One has a strange
sense of walking into a picture through its
frame and yet knowing that it is a framed picture, not life, one is walking into. The sepia
background remains sepia. The museum feel
is deliberately maintained.

*Richard Howard studied at the
Sorbonne and worked briefly as a
lexicographer. A graduate of Columbia
University, he has taught at his alma
mater. His awards include the Pulitzer
Prize for* Untitled Subjects *(1969), a
PEN translation award, and an
American Book Award for translating
Charles Baudelaire's works. He has
been poetry editor of* The Paris Review
and Western Humanities Review *and
chancellor of the Academy of American
Poets.*

Howard's monologues are very different
from those of other current practitioners of
the popular medium, as they are all one voice
and at the same time separate voices. The penetrating intelligence they share and the
mixture of wisdom and cynicism appear in poem after poem, yet the personal idiosyncrasies, the quirks, of each character come through. The poems are also visually intriguing as he uses a flexible blank verse in some, experimental designs in others, and
occasionally rhyme. The appearance of the poems on the pages reinforces the sense
that different individuals are being portrayed who speak in different tones although
their language may be similar.

Without Saying: New Poems contains more historical monologues as well as other
voices, of myth figures and of Howard's other selves. The title is teasing, evoking the
cliché "It goes without saying"—which is always followed by full disclosure. There
are all sorts of ways silence speaks in these poems, too—one hears things that would
not or could not be said and witnesses failed communications and missed connections, whether these involve an aborted meeting between two writers, telephone messages to an absent recipient, a teacher who gets across unintended lessons, or a Nobel
Prize that is not awarded to the desired recipient.

A major figure in this collection is Henry James, who features in the opening and
closing sequences. The first sequence, "Only Different," is set in 1904, and James is
threatened, for the edification of all involved, with a meeting with L. Frank Baum, author of *The Wonderful Wizard of Oz.* Since both writers were staying at the Hotel del
Coronado, near San Diego, California, young relatives of James—his niece Peg and
her fiancé, Stanford professor Bruce Porter—thought it would be a favor to the two
writers if they would meet at a luncheon party. Each writer was invited to read the
other's works, after which each rejected with horror the prospect of meeting the other,
leaving their would-be introducers with egg on their faces. The imagined reception of
the work of the popular children's writer by the hypercerebral James is particularly
funny.

The last poem is a long discussion supposedly from the journal of a young Hugh
Walpole. Edith Wharton has led a major effort to have the Nobel Prize awarded to

James, but it has been given instead to "a writer known (in Belgium) as/ the Belgian Shakespeare, Maurice Maeterlinck." The lengthy poem, "Notes of an Industrious Apprentice, or What the Master Knew," contains twenty-four pages of eight-line stanzas exploring the attempt to garner the prize, the behavior of Wharton in giving the bad news to her friends, and Walpole's attitudes toward James. The poem is a subtle study of literary sonship and the nature of the relationship between Walpole and James. James had intuited and understood a great deal about Walpole's personal life, which he used in his criticism of Walpole's works. James had in fact interacted with Maeterlinck and had a certain appreciation for him; this he shared with Walpole. Moreover, James had referred to Maeterlinck in *The Wings of the Dove* (1902). Walpole, who finds Wharton too crude and unsubtle in her adulation of James, is baffled, awed, and overwhelmed by James, but can give him only the silent reverence of reading and understanding his work.

Another poem filled with delights is "School Days," probably based on Howard's early education in an experimental school that seemed to mix permissiveness, neglect, and quirkiness. The speaker is addressing the teacher, Mrs. Masters, on the subject of field trips and other learning experiences. The students are far more vivid than the teacher, whose progressive attitudes and practices seem without understanding of the child mind and the unexpected uses to which lessons may be put. The final segment has the students propose a sex-free world as a project. It is entertaining to see how the typical worldly wise Howard speaker is slightly adjusted to produce cynical, worldly wise children. When Howard presents what are apparently his own childhood memories, too, the child seems to know too much, too soon.

Other poems include "Ediya, an Interview," recording an interview with Medea's mum on the subject of her daughter's untoward behavior, and "Exposures," revealing monologues presented as messages on an answering machine. All Howard's devices objectify and distance the major human issues the poems narrate, and it is appropriate to find recordings as messages—the medium of the tape suggests that the message is passed somehow anonymously, without interaction or connection. The message is given and received but without true communication. There is little of the face-to-face in Howard's constructed world. "Ediya, an Interview" gives the responses of Medea's crone mother, a self-indulgent, rather silly old socialite with a lapdog, to the questions a reporter poses, presenting a superficial analysis of how her daughter came to be the person she is. More sustainedly comic are "Exposures," three complex narratives left by callers on the answering machine of "Richard," all of which involve stripping or unclothing in some way. The funniest is the third, which tells of a woman speaker's adventures with the "Backscatter Body Scanner" at the airport. The recorded confessional outburst catches the play with disclosure, exposure, concealment, and revelation that is echoed throughout the collection. The speaker wants the recipient of the message to keep it for her.

And isn't recognizing
           sacrilege (by which I mean

               my feeling of outrage caused
       by that Backscatter Body Scanner)
           somehow recovering the meaning
   of the Sacred? Richard, didn't I tell you it was
           a religious experience? Would you please
   save this message for me: I'd like to read it
               over and avoid making
               a fool of myself next time

So much of Howard's poetry involves the passion for keeping things—often small, unimportant things, but also items and words that were part of the world's furnishings, for a given person, in a certain time. His characters are frantic to keep mementos of their lives, as if saving an object, a letter, or a record could prevent the passage of time. The irony of their desire to save themselves by saving these aspects of their worlds enhances the museumlike atmosphere often present in the poems. The poet is also a collector of things from the past.

This book is filled with glittering wit and acute psychological insight, and some passages actually provoke laughter, with humor ranging from the intriguing double meanings of the titles to something close to farce. These poems will be savored and reread; they give the reader the sense of overhearing turn-of-the-century literary gossip. They show a version of the early twentieth century elite literary society that is entertaining and persuasive; the characters are often petty, insufferable, and grandiloquent. The reader is glad to experience them at some remove. These poems do not have the banked passions of some of the earlier Howard Victorian monologues, such as "A Pre-Raphaelite Ending"—a poem from *Untitled Subjects* that makes a reader awaken at midnight and hunt for the book, having suddenly recognized one more allusion. The narratives in this collection, however, are appealing for the tales they tell. Their dexterity, their capsule characterizations, and their glimpses into an era make them poems to which a reader desires to return.

Janet McCann

Review Sources

Antioch Review 67, no. 1 (Winter, 2009): 191.
Booklist 105, no. 1 (September 1, 2008): 26.
Publishers Weekly 255, no. 29 (July 21, 2008): 142.

WOMAN'S WORLD

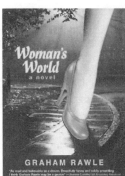

Author: Graham Rawle (1955-　　)
First published: 2005, in Great Britain
Publisher: Counterpoint (Berkeley, Calif.). 440 pp.
　$25.00
Type of work: Novel
Time: The 1960's
Locale: Great Britain

　A cutup novel of a 1960's British woman with a terrible secret

Principal characters:
　　ROY LITTLE, a young man in love with Eve
　　NORMA LITTLE, who calls herself Norma
　　　Fontaine and is actually Roy's alter ego
　　MARY, who may be Roy and Norma's mother or their housekeeper
　　EVE, Roy's fiancé
　　MR. HANDS, a photographer who tries to seduce Norma

In *Woman's World*, Graham Rawle presents an authoritative example of the cutup technique initially made popular by William Burroughs with the Nova trilogy, consisting of *The Soft Machine* (1961), *The Ticket That Exploded* (1962), and *Nova Express* (1964). Rawle's novel, published in Great Britain in 2005 and in the United States in 2008, is the culmination of years spent cutting up women's magazines from the 1960's and painstakingly assembling a 437-page tale from bits of text. The result is visually striking as typography and psychologically compelling as narrative.

Whereas Burroughs conformed the content of his cutup novels to the pieces he cut out of magazines, Rawle in *Woman's World* shaped the tale while the cutup text determined the actual phrasing. Rawle drafted *Woman's World* in a word processor, while also collecting text from magazines and organizing it by topic. Then he entered the magazine text into a computer database, enabling him to substitute this magazine text for phrases in his original draft. Using the result as a guide, he physically pasted the magazine cutouts into the draft he ultimately submitted to publishers. The entire project required five years.

The story's protagonist, Norma Fontaine, is a recluse who believes that "as a woman, you must never look less than your loveliest." Her chief pastime at home is to read up on "the latest fashions, beauty tips, and handy hints for the home" in women's magazines. She reflects,

　　I really must think about starting a scrapbook. My dressing room is piled high with all the women's magazines I have saved over the years. Wouldn't it be wonderful to collect together my favourite fashion features, all the hints and tips on glamour and etiquette that I have found especially useful, and keep them together in one big book?

Her loving brother, Roy, has learned as much from the magazines as has Norma; he is continually bringing the housebound woman exquisite dresses, scarves, and cosmetics.

∾

Graham Rawle is a British writer and artist who has contributed series of stories, word games, and visual puzzles to newspapers The Guardian, The Observer, *and* The Sunday Telegraph Magazine, *some of which have been collected in book form. He has exhibited his artwork in Great Britain and around the world.* Woman's World *is his first novel.*

∾

With text scissored from old magazines and creatively spliced into narrative, Rawle can make Norma's choice of words read like advertising copy, often with amusing effect: Raindrops fall like "chocolate-covered Payne's Poppets thrown from the branches above them by playful confectioners." Sometimes her dialogue, though awkward, is more inventive than commonplace expressions: She describes someone as tiptoeing "with the stealth of a cartoon mouse." She recalls that when her brother, Roy, failed to meet up with a woman who has strongly attracted him, "his heart had slipped deep into the lining of his overcoat."

Despite this hilarity, an ominous undertone soon becomes apparent in the story, and the book's title begins to seem ironic. The perfect "woman's world" of Norma's magazine-fueled imagination clashes with the realities outside her home. She shows up to interview for a delivery job for which her brother is applying. "'Good morning,' I began, my voice a light and airy soufflé, straight from the oven. 'I've come about the vacancy.'" Told she is not qualified, she complains to the boss, "You recognize me as the perfect woman, yet you are unable to see me as the perfect man for the job." Though she nearly spoils Roy's chance of getting hired, he does land the job, however, and in the process meets Eve, his future wife.

Meanwhile, Norma meets a photographer named Mr. Hands, who proves to be the villain of the story. (Rawle, the cutup artist, has said, "I decided on Mr. Hands for my antagonist because the word hands is easy to come by in adverts for nail polish, soap powders, and the like. The name also describes his licentious, groping nature.") In a familiar ploy, Mr. Hands lures Norma to his apartment by offering to take glamorous photographs of her. Finding the name "Syms" on his apartment-house entrance, Norma wonders if she will be greeted by "Sylvia Syms, star of stage and screen who keeps her skin so young-looking." Instead, the door is opened by a woman "whose resemblance to Sylvia Syms could be measured in nautical miles . . . . At her feet, a small, highly strung poodle wriggled and worried itself into a rich, creamy lather." The woman directs Norma to Mr. Hands's apartment, whose squalid condition alarms her. Her thoughts immediately stray off into magazine home care tips, one of which she recites inwardly as she stares at a filthy lamp shade: "If your shade is only slightly soiled, rub it over with cotton wool dipped in fine oatmeal." Then, flattered by the photographer's attention, Norma displays a streak of narcissism, again expressed in the journalistic prose of the day: "My gaze ate into the mirror, fixated as I was by the image of my leg-flatteringly lovely pose." However, Mr. Hands assaults her brutally, and, realizing that he has "underestimated the inner strength of the modern woman," she fights him off and hits him in the head with her Cinderella slipper. Believing she has killed him, she flees.

Fearing arrest for murder, Norma laments that the magazines offer no guidance for her dilemma. "In all the romantic stories I have ever read in my magazines, not one of the men, and certainly none of the women, has ever killed anyone." She slips out of Hands's apartment and makes her way home, to be confronted by Mary, who is either her mother or her housekeeper. Mary reproaches her for "dressing," and suddenly it is revealed and Roy that Norma are the same person.

The relationship between the personae of Roy and Norma is difficult to understand, rooted as it is in multiple forces. The beginning of the book contains a hint that there was a real Norma who in childhood was killed by an automobile, her older brother being at fault for not protecting her from traffic. In that case, in addition to the fascination with cross-dressing noted by some reviewers, Roy may be obsessed with living the life of a lost sibling in parallel with his own. Perhaps Roy has been channeling the spirit of the disembodied Norma. Finally, there is the question whether Norma ever existed or was simply a figment of Roy's imagination.

In any case, Roy and Mary frantically try to get rid of evidence that Norma is connected to Hands's presumed death, and this comes to mean destroying every indication that Norma has existed at all. When, several days later, Roy spots Hands in a theater and realizes the photographer has survived the blow to his head, Roy decides to burn Norma's clothing just as, twenty years earlier, he had burned pictures of her along with her childhood drawings and stories. Though greatly relieved that Hands is alive, Roy is now obsessed with the possibility that Hands recognized his "family resemblance" to Norma. Roy has the additional goal of clearing the way for a male-female relationship with Eve. Still, his life as Norma, bolstered by the women's magazines, has made him extremely knowledgeable about women's fashions—much to Eve's delight, though she is unaware of the source of his education.

Then Hands traces Roy to his home. Aware that Roy and Norma are identical, he demands compensation for the injury, even though he had been the aggressor against Norma. Roy and Mary drive Hands away, countering his bluster and threats with bigger threats. However, because of the attendant stress, Norma makes a brief reappearance, her hysteria rising. Further uncertainties arise, however, when at the end of the book Norma, willing to sacrifice herself for the sake of Roy's marriage to Eve, steps in front of a moving vehicle—a re-creation of her childhood accident. This puts an end to Roy as well as Norma. As the dying Roy imagines Eve forgiving his subterfuge, he and Norma both relinquish their claims to a single body. "In that moment of mutual surrender, bliss touched them with a sweet and gentle hand as they learned from one another the unselfishness of true love."

With this ending, the novel poses deep questions about the nature of gender. Some readers and some reviewers may consider Roy to be just a transvestite eager to learn how to apply lipstick or look demure—giving his alter ego Norma reason enough to peruse the women's magazines. Another view is that, because Norma's self-expression is limited to the bland sentiments of the women's magazines, she has been bound all along to lose out in the real world. Nevertheless, from some source the troubled young man has learned much more than superficial femininity, for in the end he manifests what are commonly regarded as cardinal female virtues, namely, compassion, forgiveness, and self-sacrifice. This is one of this story's paradoxes: that the quest to become an ideal woman, as defined in contemporary magazines, is realized by a man at the moment of his death. Did he have some innate understanding not garnered from the women's magazines? Or are the virtues generally assigned as female really limited to that sex?

The fact is that, despite their use of language culled from ephemeral publications of long ago, Roy and Norma truly are original characters. They cannot be depended upon to remain within the single frame of reference apparently set out for the story.

It is true that the borrowed text, with its often decorative type fonts in varying sizes, provides a constant reminder that the characters' ideas and the language in which they express them are derived from sources outside themselves. In a sense, as an example of cutup fiction, *Woman's World* explicitly bears out the assertion of philosopher Roland Barthes that every piece of literature is derivative, "a tissue of citations, resulting from the thousand sources of culture." Barthes made this claim, however, in his essay "The Death of the Author" (1967), to minimize the role of authors as "owners" of their work, with the right to confer fixed meaning upon that work. *Woman's World*, in fact, shows an authorial intelligence juxtaposing the novel's text bits in such a way that the whole conveys different, and even deeper, meanings from those originally intended.

In recombining the clichés of 1960's women's magazines, Rawle brings forth highly inventive expressions, many of them hilarious and some of them subversive of their original spirit. In the end, through the same technique, he also reveals something noble and affecting in his characters which they could never have absorbed solely from popular magazines.

Thomas Rankin

Review Sources

Bitch Magazine: Feminist Response to Pop Culture, no. 39 (Spring, 2008): 70.
Gay Times, no. 325 (October, 2005): 91.
New York 41, no. 11 (March 31, 2008): 63.
Publishers Weekly 254, no. 45 (November 12, 2007): 33.
The Spectator 299 (November 26, 2005): 44.

THE WORD OF THE LORD IS UPON ME
The Righteous Performance of Martin Luther King, Jr.

Author: Jonathan Rieder (1948-   )
Publisher: The Belknap Press of Harvard University
Press (Cambridge, Mass.). 394 pp. $29.95
Type of work: Sociology, biography
Time: 1950-1968
Locale: The United States, primarily the South

*An exploration of the various modes of speaking that
King employed in communicating in particular situations,
with a special emphasis upon distinctions between public
and private, black and white audiences*

National heroes, once they become enshrined as such,
tend to flatten out into one-dimensional paragons of virtue.
Now that almost every major city in the United States has named a street for Martin
Luther King, Jr., and the country celebrates his birthday as a national holiday, King
has clearly entered the pantheon of great Americans, and in the process he has lost
some of his sharper edges. In the short span of forty years since his death, King's image has shifted from that of a controversial civil rights leader (mainly associated with
African Americans) to a universal representative of freedom and good will.

Jonathan Rieder's *The Word of the Lord Is upon Me* aims to recapture the complexity of King. He argues correctly that "the idolatry of King has come at a cost; it
has sifted out the unsettlement that King inflicted, and meant to inflict, on a noncha-
lant, often clueless nation." King's "I Have a Dream" speech in 1963 aimed at highlighting harsh racial injustice, pointing out the faults in the United States. Now the
endless replays of that speech, especially on the holiday of his birth, subtly imply that
King's dream has been mostly fulfilled and that his words describe what is rather than
what one day might be. Rieder's book shows that there is much more depth to King
than one would glean from the famous lines spoken in front of the Lincoln Memorial.
Through an analysis of King's rhetoric, Rieder points to how difficult it is to describe
King in sound bites.

Rieder focuses upon four different arenas in which King communicated: the company of fellow African American leaders, the black church pulpit, the mass meetings
of the Civil Rights movement, and the broader, general public that included white
Americans. Depending on the audience, King crafted his speech in startlingly different forms. Among his close circle of friends, almost all of whom were also black
preachers, King could sound earthy and even vulgar. In his public addresses and published essays, he achieved a high degree of refinement and erudition. When he took
the pulpit of a black Baptist church, King's language would fall within the black idiom, in content and style. When whites were part of the audience, he leaned toward
universal language and universal humanity.

Some might call this pandering, but Rieder is careful to demonstrate that such a charge would be wrong. During his lifetime King sometimes received criticism from those who thought he sold out by making overtures to white audiences. (Here is the most obvious difference between King and Malcolm X, who almost always remained confrontational.) Less sharply, other critics have said that King's tailoring of his message to white audiences was essentially window dressing. This type of critique separates King's authentic self as a "race man" from his masked self as someone who appealed to white audiences for pragmatic purposes. Rieder's book convincingly demonstrates that any attempt to separate the authentic King from the inauthentic, based on how he delivered his message, overlooks the complexity of the man. His capacious mind and his deep commitment to both black Americans and humanity in general precludes any facile compartmentalization of King into a stereotype.

Jonathan Rieder is a professor of sociology at Barnard College. His research centers on the sociology of race, culture, and ethnicity. He is the author of Canarsie: The Jews and Italians of Brooklyn Against Liberalism *(1985) and coeditor of* The Fractious Nation? Unity and Division in Contemporary American Life *(2003).*

Although he recognizes that King had a chameleonlike ability to appeal to a myriad of audiences, Rieder emphasizes that King's message had a consistent center. As he states, "the core of the man was the power of his faith, his love of humanity, and an irrepressible resolve to free black people, and other people, too." Rieder contributes to King scholarship by demonstrating both the coherency of King's message and the contingent manner in which King clothed his message, depending upon his audience. In every speaking situation, King's context gave meaning to the content. The fullness of King's meaning derives from the larger rhetorical situation. In order to do justice to the depth of King's speeches, therefore, Rieder consistently frames King's language within the conventions in which they were spoken.

The most intriguing sections of the book are those in which Rieder engages in a close rhetorical analysis. One prime example that illustrates the modulations in King's rhetoric is the famous "kitchen experience" as told in written and sermonic form. During the Montgomery bus boycott in 1956, a man telephoned King and threatened him. This phone call broke King's spirit temporarily as he groped for a way to withstand enormous persecution and pressure. In his written narration for his book *Stride Toward Freedom* (1958), King describes his emotional process movingly but with detachment: "At that moment I experienced the presence of the Divine as I had never experienced Him before. It seemed as though I could hear the quiet assurance of an inner voice saying, 'Stand up for righteousness, stand up for truth; and God will be at your side forever.'" Rieder contrasts this account with the way King described the same experience in a sermon entitled "Why Jesus Called a Man a Fool." In the oral performance, King lengthens the story considerably, adding particulars such as the details of the threat ("we're going to blow your brains out"), King's concern for his infant daughter, and the failure of academic theology to assuage his fears. The climax of the sermon sounds remarkably different from the written word. He said that he heard the voice of Jesus (not "the Divine") call him by name and that voice promised to fill him with the spirit. Then, in a poetic elaboration that Rieder shrewdly writes as poetry, "And I'll tell you,/ I've seen the lightning flash./ I've heard the thunder roll./ I felt sin-breakers dashing,/ trying to conquer my soul./ But I heard the voice of Jesus/ saying still to fight on."

In these distinct rhetorical situations, King's capacity to tune his message to various audiences is evident. The narrative in the book, geared toward a mixed-race audience of non-religious and religious folk, contains only a small dose of racial tension. Furthermore, King tempers the overt spirituality of the experience ("it seemed as though . . . ") and comes to a quick resolution of his inner conflict. In the sermon, he displays his vulnerability much more. Rieder shows that as the sermon reached its climax, King's voice wavered, re-creating the emotion that he felt on the evening of the phone call. The expanded story in the sermon often evokes the dynamics of racism and its devastating effects. The sermon, in other words, is pointedly directed toward the black community and evokes in the audience feelings of sympathy and empathy.

King seems to live the experience of St. Paul, who described his own task—which, like King's, centered upon proclamation as follows: "I have become all things to all people, that I might by all means save some. I do it all for the sake of the gospel, so that I may share in its blessings." Neither King nor Rieder quotes this passage from 1 Corinthians, but it captures the heart of the "righteous performances" of the book's title. Rieder presents a portrait of a man committed to an ideology but determined not to project himself as an ideologue. In almost every situation, King displayed pragmatism without cheapening his core beliefs.

On a superficial level, the main thesis of Rieder's work is not surprising. King spoke in different modes to different audiences, but every public figure at least attempts to adapt his or her rhetoric to the situation. The great value of this book lies in the analysis of how King executed these modulations and his uncanny success in doing so. Rieder presents King almost as a classical orator in the tradition of Cicero or Quintilian, a person so aware of the dynamics between audience and message that he can blend the two. So, for example, Rieder recounts the story of Willie Bolden, a convert to the civil rights struggle whom King first met at a Savannah pool hall. King could both talk tough with Bolden and preach gently to him. To cite another of Rieder's examples, King became close to Abraham Joshua Heschel, a Polish Jew who became one of the most influential religious leaders in the United States. King drew on their shared commitment to the Hebrew prophets to forge a relationship that eventually led to Heschel taking part in the Selma marches.

In forging relationships with different individuals, King employed rhetoric that crossed boundaries and built bridges. Throughout Rieder's work, one gains the sense that King's goal in speech was twofold: to connect to his audience and then to make them consider a position opposed to their own. To his church congregations, King admitted that it was hard to love white people (thereby emphathizing with his listeners) and then he would point out faults in the black community (thereby challenging them). To an uneducated audience in a mass meeting, he would lapse into unschooled dialect and then spring a quote from an intellectual such as Søren Kierkegaard. King fulfills the role of a prophet, a person very much a part of a community whose goal is to critique it from within. The different situations in the book show that King was a prophet to a variety of communities, from Dexter Avenue Baptist Church in Montgomery to the United States itself.

Although Rieder's book is not explicitly biographical, it is easy to see that King's own life mirrored his rhetorical personae. Three influences combined to shape King—the black church, the racist South, and liberal Protestantism—and he drew from all three of these formative influences. Many Southerners who move North renounce their Southern roots or, alternatively, dig them deeper. Religious students who attend academic seminaries shun their formative spirituality or reject the more liberal teaching they encounter in their studies. King never settled for seeing himself on one side of a binary opposition. He much preferred "both/and" to "either/or." Many of Rieder's chapters highlight King's willingness to straddle oppositions such as secular/sacred, intellectual/emotional, white/black, raw/refined. This allowed him to speak movingly to so many audiences and to encourage them to widen their horizons. It sounds simple enough, but it is difficult to think of another figure who has embraced the tensions of modern America the way King did. To use Rieder's words, King had a remarkable "forte for translation," and this book admirably shows what a great and difficult feat translation can be.

Kyle Keefer

Review Sources

Booklist 104, no. 11 (February 1, 2008): 22.
Library Journal 133, no. 6 (April 1, 2008): 88.
Los Angeles Times, April 6, 2008, p. R3.
The Nation 286, no. 19 (May 19, 2008): 36-41.
The New York Times Book Review, April 27, 2008, p. 17.
Publishers Weekly 255, no. 5 (February 4, 2008): 49-50.
The Washington Post Book World, April 6, 2008, p. BW05.

THE WORLD IS WHAT IT IS
The Authorized Biography of V. S. Naipaul

Author: Patrick French (1966-   )
Publisher: Alfred A. Knopf (New York). 487 pp. Illustrated. $30.00
Type of work: Literary biography
Time: 1498-2001, particularly 1932-1996
Locale: The Caribbean islands (Trinidad in particular), England, Scotland, Argentina, India, Pakistan, Uganda, Zimbabwe, and more

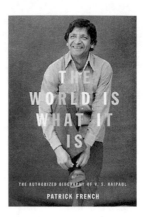

This authorized biography of Naipaul—an East Indian, West Indian Trinidadian turned British citizen of the world—examines his life and canon set against the history of colonialism as he moved from island scholarship lad to Oxford graduate to controversial author and Nobel Prize winner

Principal personages:
> V. S. NAIPAUL, author and winner of many prizes, including the Booker Prize and the Nobel Prize in Literature
> KAMLA NAIPAUL, his elder sister, a scholarship student at Benares Hindu University, her brother's primary family link, adviser, confidant, and critic with free access to his inner self
> SHIVA NAIPAUL, his younger brother, a successful writer of whom Naipaul felt protective, mourning his early death greatly
> MARGARET GOODING, Naipaul's Argentine mistress, who reveled in their sadomasochistic relationship
> DROAPATIE "MA" CAPILDEO NAIPAUL, his mother, from whom he inherited his strength and tenacity, although they drifted apart over his relationship with Margaret
> SEEPERSAD NAIPAUL, his father, his favorite author, and a lasting influence, who spurred his love of literature, taught him the art of precision (a stylistic feature of Naipaul's writing) and of Brahmin values (vegetarianism), and influenced his belief that women should serve men but sexual desire should be quashed
> SOOGEE "NANIE" CAPILDEO, his grandmother and ruling matriarch of his extended family
> PETER BAYLEY, a Fellow of English at University College, who assured Naipaul's admittance to the university and who guided his scholastic career
> PATRICIA "PAT" HALE NAIPAUL, Naipaul's first wife from 1955 until her death in 1996, who thwarted her family to marry an impoverished outsider in whose potential she believed; Pat's diaries provide one of the most complete records of Naipaul's

life and show how affected she was by his manner, his temperament,
  and his personal drive to succeed at all costs
HUGH and ANTONIA FRASER, friends originally introduced to Naipaul by
  long-term supporter Francis Wyndham and who offered him largesse,
  hospitality, and social connections
ANDRE DEUTSCH, publisher who printed most of Naipaul's works
  despite constant confrontations with the writer
DIANA ATHILL, Naipaul's attentive editor at Andre Deutsch, one of the
  first to recognize his publishable material
ANTHONY POWELL, an early patron and friend, whose writing Naipaul
  later attacked viciously
SAMUEL SELVON, a black Trinidadian writer who had an affair with
  Kamla Naipaul
HENRY SWANZY, Irish editor of "Caribbean Voices" in the early 1950's
PAUL THEROUX, American author of *Sir Vidia's Shadow* (2001) and of
  Patricia Naipaul's obituary, a longtime would-be friend
DEREK WALCOTT, a Caribbean intellectual and rival, whom Naipaul has
  debated since the 1930's and who once dubbed him V. S. Nightfall

Patrick French's *The World Is What It Is* indirectly links V. S. Naipaul's canon
(style, themes, characters) to his personal and familial history, showing readers how
Naipaul has infused his art with his special vision of reality as a displaced, Oxford-
educated East Indian, West Indian, Trinidadian and world wanderer. However, French
does not read Naipaul's works as biographical projections but instead, through discerning, intuitive discussions, confirms Naipaul's enormous creative output, as he al-
ternated fiction and nonfiction and turned from Trinidadian themes to close observation of the cultural and political realities of Argentina, India, the Caribbean, Central
Africa, the Muslim world, the American South, and the English countryside. French's
title reflects his approach to biography, an open look at an outrageous and controversial
figure, probing his fears, his self-doubts, his genius, his disturbing personal life, and
his character flaws. This is Naipaul as he is: troubled, paradoxical, controlling, needy,
brilliant, selfish, exploitive, patronizing, yet
solicitous of patronage, an impish and often
vicious masquerader whose insights shock and   ∽
compel, a cruel taskmaster, and an enigmatic   *English journalist Patrick French met*
narcissist.   *Naipaul while working for* The New
    Fully committed to taking a cold, objective   Yorker. *He wrote* Younghusband: The
look at unpleasant realities, Naipaul provided   Last Great Imperial Adventurer *(1995),*
French unrestricted access to his carefully pre-   Liberty or Death: India's Journey to
served wealth of personal papers (fifty thou-   Independence and Division *(1997), and*
sand documents in the University of Tulsa,   Tibet, Tibet: A Personal History of a
Oklahoma, collection, including his wife Pat's   Lost Land *(2003). French won the*
diary), introductions to important figures in   Sunday Times *Young Writer of the*
his life, and no-holds-barred, candid, face-to-   *Year Award, the Royal Society of*
face interviews. He did so without reserva-   *Literature Heinemann Prize, and the*
tion, but requested that the book end abruptly,   *Somerset Maugham Award.*
                                                                 ∽

with Pat's death and his second marriage. The biographer concurred that the years thereafter need distance to evaluate.

French provides an uncompromising yet empathetic portrait of the struggling writer, even at the top of his form methodically and obsessively controlling his art, producing twenty-nine books (history, linked stories, literary criticism, novels, travel writing, fused autobiography-fiction) while his personal life deteriorates, with friendships destroyed and enemies cultivated. In the main, French lets words and deeds speak for themselves, recording evidence gleaned from numerous interviews, direct quotations, and carefully cited sources while mostly avoiding psychological analysis and personal opinion.

French's title is from Naipaul's powerful 1979 novel *A Bend in the River*, written in the style of Joseph Conrad: "The world is what it is. Men who are nothing, who allow themselves to become nothing, have no place in it." The title reflects the biographer's thesis that, in the world's view, the young Naipaul was a "nothing" who chose, with sheer determination, struggle, and self-assertion, to become something: a much declaimed and proclaimed author, a British knight, and a Nobel Prize winner. The chapter headings trace the movement: the young Trinidadian Vido suffers "Like Oliver Twist in the Workhouse," copes with racism ("They Want Me to Know My Place") and being undervalued and underpaid ("He Asked for 10 Gns!!"), but transforms himself into the noted, accomplished literary figure V. S. Naipaul, using clear, powerful but progressively elliptical prose ("The Schintsky Method"), highly concrete detail, and a sharp, biting wit ("There Wasn't Any Kind Remark"). As V. S. Naipaul he challenged the literary dominance of dead white males and modernists with an exacting, excoriating global view eventually at odds with even the developing post-colonialists ("With the Aid of a Cutlass Blade"). He ends as he vowed he would, transformed into an Englishman, in 1990 knighted by the queen as Sir Vidia Naipaul ("Arise, Sir Vidia"), a contrarian praising the virtues of rural England while capturing the zeitgeist of former colonies and beating the English at their own language.

French takes almost half the book to reach Naipaul's thirtieth birthday, studying Naipaul's journey from "nowhere" to the literary center, suggesting that the writer's Trinidadian childhood—its quarrels, deprivations, and intrigues—informed his fiction lifelong. After quickly sketching Europe's role in the Caribbean, he concentrates on Naipaul's family heritage: his grandfather transported as an indentured cane-cutter; his Catholic grandmother producing a dynasty of strong, domineering women; the family mythology of Brahmin caste origins; his father's struggles to succeed as an enlightened journalist and novelist, psychologically and professionally ruined by forced bloodletting to appease Hindu gods. Perhaps Naipaul's finest achievement, *A House for Mr. Biswas* (1961) pays tribute to a father whose own writing shaped Naipaul's literary style and whose loving concern stayed in his memory despite difficulties reconciling with his family's past. According to Naipaul, says French, growing up in Trinidad taught the youth the ease with which civilization could be destroyed and drove him to excel at Queen's Royal College, Trinidad, and, as a depressed, half-starved scholarship student, to earn a bachelor's degree from University College, Oxford, England, in defiance of the prevailing attitude toward "wogs" from abroad. Oxford taught the small, dark, asthmatic Naipaul a disdainful, snobbish pose, and working with talented colleagues for the radio program "Caribbean Voices" taught him a writing voice and honed his literary skills.

Despite successful publications and literary awards, Naipaul and his wife were impoverished, dependent on Pat's teaching salary and on generous upper-class patrons such as Hugh and Antonia Frasier. French delineates Naipaul's relationship with his patrons and with editors: his ability to charm upper-class liberals and ordinary folk whose assistance he needed, the parsimony of Andre Deutsch and Diana Athill at keeping publications payments low, the skill of agent Gillon Aitken at negotiating staggeringly high advances for manuscripts and repeated *New York Review of Books* assignments. French's Naipaul is both the victim of racial prejudice and the victimizer, a ruthlessly objective critic of mankind's heart of darkness but privately fascinated by it. He tested the limits of the novel, merging genres, intertwining fact and fiction, to explore the unfamiliar and shatter easy complacencies. French notes Naipaul's careful observations and insightful conclusions: his criticism of Indian latrines led to hygiene reforms and prophetic warnings about Islamic threats.

French's most shocking revelations concern Naipaul's personal life. The biographer describes Naipaul's complicated relationships with women, beginning in his childhood when the matriarch "Nanie" reigned over a shared household where all women, including his mother, forbade any budding sexuality, leaving him an emotionally and sexually immature but pampered male. This upbringing directly affected his 1955 marriage to Pat Hale at age twenty-two, a "pure" love. Naipaul treated Pat as personal servant and editor throughout their marriage. She helped him through nervous anxiety and attempted suicide, supported him financially, prepared his special diet, organized his daily life, admired, advised, weathered all of his mannerisms, and recorded their experiences in her diary. His abusive insults, however, cut to the core of her self-esteem. She became increasingly apologetic and unsure of her own worth as he cheated on her with prostitutes and took as his mistress of twenty-four years an Argentine mother of three, Margaret Gooding. Although Pat desired children, she never conceived, while Margaret aborted three of Naipaul's children. Margaret endured ferocious beatings, sadomasochistic sex, and humiliating insults, only to be paid off with a large severance check in her old age. French purposefully elicits sympathy for Pat over Margaret (describing Naipaul cajoling her to listen to his work in progress as she lay on her deathbed), though he recognizes that both women contributed to Naipaul's writing: stability and editing skill versus passion and inspiration. French suggests that perhaps Pat's greatest horror was to find elements of herself in both the murder victim and the avenger in *A Bend in the River*. As Pat was dying of cancer in 1996, Naipaul began an affair with Kenyan-Pakistani journalist Nadira Khannum Alvi, twenty years his junior, and he married her shortly after Pat's lonely death (possibly hastened by his betrayals). Pat sacrificed herself and her self-respect to his "genius," loyally providing Naipaul stability and a trusted amanuensis, only to be publicly embarrassed, snubbed, and ultimately rejected at her time of greatest need. French ends with Naipaul's new bride scattering Pat's ashes and blessing them with a passage from the Qurʾān and a children's verse, with Naipaul too emotionally distraught to assist.

French suggests that Naipaul's patrician attitudes, his lifetime dependence on others to carry out the daily concerns of life (food, shelter, transportation, travel, interview preparation, editing), his thematic concerns, his basic literary style, and his pleasure in the stinging bon mot all have their roots in his Trinidadian youth. French shows us the human side of a challenging writer, one able to win the confidence and assistance of strangers but loyal only to his art, enigmatic, driven, wickedly funny, and irredeemably flawed.

Gina Macdonald and Elizabeth Sanders

Review Sources

The Atlantic Monthly 302, no. 4 (November, 2008): 134-139.
Booklist 105, no. 4 (October 15, 2008): 13.
Kirkus Reviews 76, no. 17 (September 1, 2008): 926-927.
Library Journal 133, no. 17 (October 13, 2008): 69-70.
Los Angeles Times, November 11, 2008, p. E6.
The Nation 287, no. 19 (December 8, 2008): 30-36.
The New York Review of Books 55, no. 18 (November 20, 2008): 22-28.
The New York Times Book Review, November 23, 2008, p. 1.
The Observer, April 13, 2008, p. 23.
Publishers Weekly 255, no. 36 (September 8, 2008): 44.
Quadrant 52 (September, 2008): 58-63.
The Spectator 306 (April 5, 2008): 32-33.
Sunday Times, March 30, 2008, p. 39.
The Washington Post Book World, November 16, 2008, p. BW10.

WORLD WAR I
The African Front—An Imperial War on the African Continent

Author: Edward Paice
First published: Tip and Run: The Untold Tragedy of the
Great War in Africa, 2007, in Great Britain
Publisher: Pegasus (New York). 488 pp. $35.00
Type of work: History
Time: 1914-1918
Locale: Africa, principally German East Africa and British East Africa

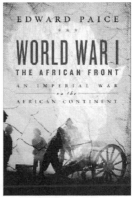

Paice describes a grueling campaign of World War I on a nearly forgotten front, East Africa

Principal personages:
COLONEL (later GENERAL) PAUL VON
    LETTOW-VORBECK, commander-in-chief of German forces in East
    Africa, 1914-1918
HEINRICH SCHNEE, governor of German East Africa, 1912-1919
GENERAL JAN SMUTS, commander-in-chief of British and South African
    forces, 1916-1917
WINSTON CHURCHILL, First Lord of the British Admiralty, 1911-1915
CAPTAIN MAX LOOFF, captain of the SMS *Königsberg* and colonial
    troop detachment commander
LIEUTENANT-COMMANDER GEOFFREY BASIL SPICER-SIMSON, senior
    naval officer, Lake Tanganyika Expedition

The first shots by British troops during World War I were fired in a pestilential, little-known German colony in West Africa. Most readers—indeed most history buffs—will be surprised to learn that Africa played a role in that great conflict. However, anyone familiar with *The African Queen* (1935) by British novelist C. S. Forester or the classic 1951 film version is at least marginally aware that the British and the Germans were facing each other down on what was then still known as the Dark Continent.

At the opening of hostilities in mid-1914, almost all of Africa was under the control, real or nominal, of one European country or another. Germany possessed four colonies on the continent: Togo, Cameroons, German South-West Africa, and (largest of all, at 384,170 square miles) German East Africa. Together their area was five times the size of the mother country itself.

Opposing Germany and its allies were the Entente Powers, whose combined holdings in Africa were immense. As a result, Germany's African colonies were surrounded by immediate and potential enemies, and most had little chance of resistance. Tiny Togo in West Africa—the site of those first British shots—surrendered during the first month of the war to a combined Anglo-French force. Its fall was followed by

~

Edward Paice studied history at
Cambridge University and spent
several years in East Africa before
returning to live in England. He is the
author of Lost Lion of Empire: The
Life of "Cape to Cairo" Grogan *(2001)*
and a Fellow of the Royal
Geographical Society.

~

that of German South-West Africa, which surrendered to South African forces in July, 1915. Britain had only recently concluded peace with South Africa's Boer (Dutch) settlers after two bitter wars, and there had been concern about the Boers' sympathies, but they proved loyal to the British crown. Germany's other West African colony, Cameroons, capitulated in February of the following year. This left only German East (as English speakers routinely referred to the territory), but that colony was destined to consume the efforts of combined British and Indian forces (with some help from Belgian and Portuguese troops) for four years.

Besides their ostensible foes, troops faced a daunting array of "natural" enemies in Africa—cruel terrain, a debilitating climate, and a variety of vexatious and often dangerous animals. (On more than one occasion, swarms of angry bees joined in the melee, attacking both sides indiscriminately.) Endemic diseases included malaria, blackwater fever, dysentery, smallpox, and meningitis. The great pandemic of "Spanish" influenza reached sub-Saharan Africa in late 1918. The European participants were also constrained by a crucial psychosocial factor, the fear that their African subjects, whom they reflexively treated as inferiors, would come to see the Europeans as just another collection of warring tribes—more powerful, certainly, but otherwise no better than themselves. In any case, the colonizers were not constrained for long, using (and ruthlessly sacrificing) native Africans in virtually every capacity.

That German East resisted as long as it did was due largely to a single individual— Paul von Lettow-Vorbeck, who became commander-in-chief of German forces in East Africa in 1914. A veteran of brutal colonial wars in South-West Africa that would today be classified as genocidal, von Lettow-Vorbeck had developed into a skilled, ruthless guerrilla leader determined to win at any cost. He quickly put German East on a war footing, overriding the concerns of timid Governor Heinrich Schnee and in effect assuming control of the colony.

On the map, German East's predicament appeared dire. To the north lay British East Africa (Kenya) and Uganda, while to the southwest were two more British territories, Northern Rhodesia and Nyasaland. Off the coast lay the British protectorate of Zanzibar and its sister island Pemba. On the west was the vast Belgian Congo, while to the south was Portuguese East Africa (Mozambique). However, the situation was not as one-sided as it might appear. Although Belgium had been invaded by Germany in early August of 1914, cooperation between its commanders in Africa and their British counterparts left much to be desired. Portugal entered the war on the Allied side only in 1916, but its efforts in Africa proved inept at nearly every turn. Over the next four years the resourceful von Lettow-Vorbeck ranged with remarkable speed over the region, waging a brilliant campaign against forces ten times the size of his own. His primary opponent was General Jan Smuts, a veteran of the Second Boer War and the German South-West campaign who was appointed commander-in-chief of British and South African forces in East Africa in 1916.

Britain's war in East Africa got off to a bad start with the battle for Tanga, a port in German East and the terminus of one of the region's few rail lines. Under the inept command of the hapless Major-General Arthur Aitken, who neglected to reconnoiter the area in which he landed his troops, the British suffered an ignominious defeat. Subsequently the British fared better, but the loss of the battle was a severe blow to morale in Britain as well as in British Africa.

Both sides expended much of their energy during the opening months of conflict on SMS *Königsberg*, a German light cruiser responsible for the first loss of merchant shipping in the war. Under the command of Captain Max Looff, the *Königsberg* captured the SS *City of Winchester*, a British cargo ship heading for Britain with a load of Indian tea, on August 6, 1914. Afterward, however, the *Königsberg*, running short of coal and supplies, sought a safe haven in the vast delta of the Rufiji River, one of the German colony's major water courses. It slipped out in September to shell and destroy the British cruiser HMS *Pegasus*, which was laid up in the harbor at Zanzibar, before returning to the delta. The fear of mines kept British ships from following it upstream. Winston Churchill (then First Lord of the Admiralty) became obsessed with the ship, and Britain spent vast sums of money to destroy it. Both sides endured extremes of heat, humidity, and boredom (not to mention the predations of mosquitoes) before the issue was finally resolved. It was thanks to two British monitors, or shallow-draft gunboats, towed from the Mediterranean that the cruiser was blown up. The British also used small planes to direct the attack, the first such use of planes to destroy a warship. However, the Germans managed to salvage ten of the ship's guns, which they used against the British for the duration of the conflict. In a fitting end, the wreck of the *Königsberg* was eventually sold for two hundred pounds to the captain of the *Pegasus*.

Several enormous bodies of water lying along German East Africa's western borders—Victoria Nyanza, Lake Tanganyika, and Lake Nyasa—played key roles in the fighting. Two German craft, the gunboat *Hedwig von Wissmann* and the tug *Kingani*, held sway over the waters of Lake Tanganyika during the early months of the war, sinking a Belgian steamer and two British steamers in 1914. The following year they were joined by the *Goetzen*. This huge steamer had been built in Germany, disassembled, shipped to Dar-es-Salaam on the coast of German East, and then carried by train and porter to the lake, where it was reassembled. One of the *Königsberg*'s salvaged guns made the ship especially dangerous. In an even more astonishing feat, however, Lieutenant-Commander Geoffrey Basil Spicer-Simpson oversaw the transport of the bizarrely named motorboats *Mimi* and *Toutou* on cradles from South Africa to the lake and, with the help of two small Belgian craft, sank the *Hedwig von Wissmann* and captured the *Kingani*. With the aid of planes, the smaller, faster Allied craft were able to keep *Goetzen* at bay in the port of Kigoma, and it was eventually scuttled by its crew. These events inspired Forester to write his famous adventure novel.

The armistice ending Germany's involvement in the war was signed November 18, 1918, yet von Lettow-Vorbeck—who by then commanded only 153 German troops—did not immediately learn of his country's defeat or even believe the news. He clearly would have fought to the last man. After the war he crusaded with Schnee for the return of Germany's colonies and took part in an unsuccessful 1920 putsch to impose a military dictatorship on Germany. Adolf Hitler decorated him in 1939, and he lived well into the 1960's. It is possible that, if other Germans had fought with the same determination (or fanaticism, depending on one's point of view), the outcome of the war might have been different.

The campaign in Africa has routinely been dismissed as a "sideshow," but for a sideshow it was immensely costly. Britain's bill alone ran to more than four billion dollars in today's money, and when the cost to India and Britain's other African colonies is included, the amount was far greater. The war was even costlier in lives. The official death toll among those fighting on the British side in East Africa was one hundred thousand, but the actual number was probably twice that. At least one-eighth of British East Africa's male population died. German brutality resulted in the death of as many as three hundred thousand African civilians in German East alone.

There have been several books in English about World War I in East Africa, including Ross Anderson's well-received 2004 study *The Forgotten Front, 1914-1918: The East African Campaign.* However, Paice's exhaustive history is likely to remain the standard work for the foreseeable future. He has consulted not only printed sources (as his lengthy bibliography attests) but also archives in eight countries. His command of detail is extraordinary, although he suffers from a desire to share everything he knows about his subject. Long, ambitious sentences constructed of multiple clauses and bristling with military abbreviations and references to commanders, armament types, troop strength, and unfamiliar place names may overwhelm all but the most determined reader. Here the book's glossary, dramatis personae, and maps are a great help, as are the eight appendixes summarizing orders of battle.

It is unfortunate, however, that Paice's editors have not attended to the minor details of their production. The map of colonial Africa at the outbreak of the war incorrectly shows French Morocco, Algeria, and Tunisia as parts of French West Africa. The index is incomplete, and there are several incorrect references; an entry for "Somaliland" contains "see also" references to "French Somaliland" and "Italian Somaliland," but those entries are nowhere to be found. Finally, Paice's title itself is somewhat misleading, as his book is devoted almost entirely to the campaign in East Africa and neglects the fighting in German Southwest Africa and Cameroons. Thus the definitive history of the African front in World War I remains to be written.

Grove Koger

Review Sources

Booklist 104, no. 22 (August 1, 2008): 32.
Contemporary Review 289 (Winter, 2007): 529.
The Economist 382 (February 17, 2007): 87.
Journal of Military History 71, no. 2 (April, 2007): 545-546.
Kirkus Reviews 76, no. 12 (June 15, 2008): 90.
Library Journal 133, no. 11 (June 15, 2008): 81.
Publishers Weekly 255, no. 22 (June 2, 2008): 38.
The Times Literary Supplement, April 20, 2007, p. 8.
The Wall Street Journal 252, no. 34 (August 9, 2008): W8.

WORLDS BEFORE ADAM
The Reconstruction of Geohistory in the Age of Reform

Author: Martin J. S. Rudwick (1932-)
Publisher: University of Chicago Press (Chicago). 614
pp. $49.00
Type of work: History of science, natural history, science
Time: 1817-1845
Locale: Europe

Through an analysis of the work of such scientists as Charles Lyell, Rudwick shows how geologists, through their discoveries and search for causes, constructed an accurate, consistent, and enlightening history of the earth with a periodization and directional sweep characteristic of the reconstructive histories of ancient Greece and Rome

> *Principal personages:*
> CHARLES LYELL (1797-1875), Scottish geologist, author of *Principles of Geology* (1830-1833), and proponent of the uniformitarian theory
> GEORGES CUVIER (1769-1832), French comparative anatomist, classifier of fossil animals, and proponent of the catastrophist theory
> WILLIAM BUCKLAND (1784-1856), English geologist whose theory of a great deluge was compatible with the biblical flood of Noah
> LOUIS AGASSIZ (1807-1873), Swiss paleontologist and geologist most famous for his theory of an Ice Age
> CHARLES DARWIN (1809-1882), English naturalist whose early work as a geologist was influenced by Lyell

Books have histories, just as the human race and the earth itself. In the past, Martin J. S. Rudwick devoted much of his career to the history of the natural sciences, through a study of a historical debate, *The Great Devonian Controversy: The Shaping of Scientific Knowledge Among Gentlemanly Specialists* (1985); a biography, *Georges Cuvier, Fossil Bones, and Geological Catastrophes* (1997); and an investigation of a specific period, *Bursting the Limits of Time: The Reconstruction of Geohistory in the Age of Revolution* (2005). The last book is the prequel to *Worlds Before Adam.* Indeed, *Bursting the Limits of Time* is the first volume and *Worlds Before Adam* is the second of an exploration of how a new field, geohistory, originated and developed. In the first volume, Rudwick concentrated on how scientists discovered that the earth had an immensely long history and that its "deep time" could be reconstructed just as historians had been reconstructing the "shallow time" of recorded human history. In this second volume, which can be read independently of the first, Rudwick focuses on how geologists attempted to discover the causes of the principal events of geohistory. He has chosen to study the accomplishments of important geologists, paleontologists, and glaciologists within the historical period after Waterloo (1815) and before the

1848 revolutions, hoping that they will epito-
mize pivotal historical trends, such as how a
scientific approach to history was central and
constitutive for the human as well as the earth
sciences. He opposes this approach to certain
traditional treatments that erroneously emphasized the conflict between science and religion, Genesis and geology.

Rudwick structures his book in roughly
chronological order, though his thematic chapters often contain temporal overlaps. Each
of the book's four parts centers on the work
of individuals whose discoveries or theories

~

Martin J. S. Rudwick has had a
distinguished career at the University
of California, San Diego, and at
Cambridge University. Between 1970
and 2008, he published nine books. In
1988, he received the Sue Tyler
Friedman Medal, and in 2007 he was
the recipient of the George Sarton
Medal from the History of Science
Society.

~

helped to clarify the long and complex history of the earth. Part 1 focuses on Cuvier,
who wanted to "burst the limits of time" the way astronomers had "burst the limits of
space." Part 2 deals with those French and English geologists and paleontologists who
developed ways of reading the story of the earth through its rock layers and the fossils
they contained. Part 3 uses the life and achievements of Charles Lyell to illuminate
both the strengths and the weaknesses of his uniformitarian system. Part 4 concludes
with an account of how Louis Agassiz's Ice Age theory presented a challenge to both
uniformitarians and catastrophists, and how Charles Darwin was working on a theory
of "descent with modification" that would provide a mechanism—natural selection—
to explain the origin and development of all species of plants and animals.

A major theme of Rudwick's book is the corrigibility of those observations, ideas,
and explanations that are at the heart of the scientific enterprise. He realizes that there
are no such things as theory-free facts. For example, Cuvier interpreted extinct creatures, which he had adeptly reconstructed from a paucity of fossil remains, in terms of
his catastrophist theory, according to which the earth had, at times, experienced cataclysmic events that had caused mass extinctions and left behind misshapen and shattered strata. However, Cuvier recognized that the rock layers also told a story of long
periods of relative tranquillity and of an age of reptiles that had preceded the age of
mammals. Cuvier made use of the data gathered by such stratigraphers as William
Smith, who saw his task as describing fossils that characterized certain strata, but he
did not try to explain their causal origin or their place in geohistory.

Unlike early historians of the earth sciences, Rudwick understands that it is his
duty to reconstruct the past on its own terms and not through the eyes of a twenty-first
century geologist. So-called Whig historians evaluate the past through the present
state of scientific knowledge, while dividing early scientists into heroes or villains,
depending on how close their ideas mesh with accepted ones in the present. Rudwick
will have none of this. Consequently, he treats William Buckland's views of a worldwide deluge with the respect and the criticism that it garnered during his time. For instance, Cuvier visited Buckland in England where he interpreted a fossil of a lower
jaw bone as coming from an extinct giant lizard, or megalosaurus. Unlike scriptural
literalists, Buckland, like Cuvier, accepted a very long chronology for the earth before

Adam. On the other hand, some of Buckland's critics accepted a geological deluge but not his identification of it with the Noachian Flood. Other critics, who doubted the reality of the deluge and mass extinctions, deplored Buckland for mixing the immiscibles of science and religion.

Although scientists with different ideas about the earth's past agreed that the "actualistic method" of using well-understood present forces was the best way to explain the data gathered from fossil-filled rock layers, some, such as Cuvier, emphasized that this method had limitations, because present causes were unable to account for the worldwide revolutionary events that had punctuated the earth's past. Lyell, on the other hand, based his geology on the principle that ancient causes were the same as present ones. He applied this uniformitarian principle not only to the gradual changes that characterized long periods of geological history but also to crustal movements, volcanic eruptions, and tsunamis that, according to the catastrophists, had had devastating effects on prehistoric plant and animal life. Lyell was certain that the earth had never experienced events more sudden, violent, massive, or violent than the ones that humans had witnessed in recorded history. Furthermore, Lyell contended that the earth, in the present as in the past, existed in a steady state of dynamic equilibrium in which geological and biological changes were cyclic rather than directional.

Lyell had critics as well as supporters, though more common were geologists who had mixed feelings about the ideas in the three volumes of his *Principles of Geology*. While agreeing with Lyell that the basic laws of physics and chemistry had not changed throughout the history of the universe, some critics did not agree that this uniformity meant that the forces that had shaped the earth and influenced its forms of life had always been the same. In fact, evidence from physics and chemistry, as analyzed by Joseph Fourier, showed that the earth had originated in a very hot state and had been cooling ever since. Lyell, to the contrary, believed that cyclic climatic changes had characterized the earth's history, rather than a consistently downward trend in temperature. Similarly, by studying the increasingly more detailed fossil record, paleozoologists had become convinced that life in the deep past had been vastly different from life in the present. Furthermore, a directionality characterized the progression from the age of fish through the age of reptiles to the age of mammals. Even within the Tertiary period, mammalian fossils exhibited wide variability and stages of development. Lyell, during the time covered by Rudwick, was vigorously opposed to any theory of the transmutation of organisms.

Even though Lyell tried to keep his *Principles of Geology* up-to-date in later editions, by the 1840's new observations and systems of explanation made his form of uniformitarianism seem outmoded. He had clearly misinterpreted Primary rocks, such as granite and gneiss, and his view that human rationality set *Homo sapiens* apart from the primates became increasingly untenable when bones of humans contemporary with extinct mammals were uncovered and when the first fossil primates were found. Even Buckland was forced to adjust his views to the new evidence, abandoning his claim that the Noachian Flood should be identified with the geological evidence for a primeval deluge. Just as the history of the earth had its unexpected developments, so, too, did the history of ideas about geohistory. Louis Agassiz was responsible for just such an unexpected development. He had begun his career conventionally with a study of fossil fish, proving that an age of fish had antedated the earliest reptiles. However, Agassiz became most famous for his theory of an Ice Age, which he formulated based on the observations of other glaciologists and his own studies of Alpine glaciers. His theory was unexpected because of the nearly total agreement among scientists about the cooling-earth theory. Surprisingly, Agassiz insisted that the evidence revealed that, in the past, the earth had been much colder than at present. Soon evidence accumulated, not only in Europe but also in North America, that supported his contention that much of Europe and North America had been once covered by a thick sheet of ice. Neither the uniformitarians nor the catastrophists had a place for ice ages in their systems. Uniformitarians now had to accept nonuniform, violently cold events and catastrophists had to add gigantic ice sheets to their array of cataclysmic causes of mass extinctions.

The reader may also find unexpected the way that Rudwick abruptly ends his book with the controversy over the Ice Age. Agassiz's theory raised as many questions as it answered, and the major systems of geohistorical explanation, both uniformitarian and catastrophist, had been found wanting. Nevertheless, the geologists by this time had worked out a periodization of geohistory that, by and large, became the framework for future discoveries and theories. Most of the discoverers and theoreticians of this geohistory had been religious, and they had found ways to accommodate their scientific and religious beliefs. Interestingly, Rudwick sees the contingent world of the past that geohistorians created as supportive of a religious view of the universe. Natural theologians had used the world's contingency as a proof of God's existence and sovereignty. For Rudwick, the historian, atheist or theist, has the obligation to reveal the connections between the creators of history and what they created, in this case, the vast richness of a "world before Adam."

Appended to Rudwick's account of early nineteenth century geohistory is a "Concluding (Un)Scientific Postscript," in which he tries to anticipate and respond to possible criticisms of his book. To those critics who object to any "great persons" approach to history, he responds by stating that his great scientists also serve as exemplars for other, lesser scientists, their social interactions, and the fields that they helped to create. To those who say that he has neglected mineralogy, petrology, economic geology, and other significant fields, Rudwick responds that his approach was never intended to be comprehensive. To those critics who believe that histories of geology have tended to overemphasize British contributions, and *Worlds Before Adam* is no exception, he points out that, in addition, he deals extensively with the geologists of France, Germany, and several other countries. To those who say that he has downplayed the roles of scientific societies, journals, and cultural as well as historical forces, he responds that he has treated these in the contexts of the individual lives and works he covers. He also admits that other geohistories can be written by using viewpoints different from his own, and that is fine. Just as there is no end to geohistory, there is no end to writing books about geohistory.

Robert J. Paradowski

Review Sources

History Today 58, no. 11 (November, 2008): 63.
Nature 454 (July 24, 2008): 406-407.
New Scientist 198 (June 21, 2008): 55.
Science 321 (September 12, 2008): 1447-1448.
The Times Literary Supplement, October 17, 2008, pp. 26-27.

THE WRITER AS MIGRANT

Author: Ha Jin (1956-   )
Publisher: University of Chicago Press (Chicago). 112
  pp. $14.00
Type of work: Literary criticism

  A collection of three essays, originally delivered as lectures, by Ha Jin, who is an eminent immigrant translingual writer, on writers like himself who have moved between countries and languages

  Like Ovid, Dante, and Heinrich Heine, Ha Jin writes in exile. Like Joseph Conrad, Samuel Beckett, and Aleksandar Hemon, he writes in a language other than his native one. What distinguishes Ha Jin from other prominent Chinese American authors such as Maxine Hong Kingston, Amy Tan, and Gish Jen is the fact that he was born in China and emigrated to the United States as an adult. Though he arrived without fluency in English, he has chosen to make his career in that language, not Chinese. That career was confirmed when, ten years after his decision to settle in the United States, he won both the National Book Award and the PEN/Faulkner Award for his 1999 novel *Waiting.*

  Invited to serve as guest speaker for the Campbell Lecture Series at Rice University, Ha Jin addressed the challenges faced by writers who live outside their native lands and who, as translinguals, write in adopted languages. Speaking on three successive days in October, 2006, he drew from his own experience and from the lives and works of kindred writers he admires. *The Writer as Migrant* is a transcript of those three overlapping lectures, titled in turn "The Spokesman and the Tribe," "The Language of Betrayal," and "An Individual's Homeland."

  Expatriation is nothing new in world literature. The "Lost Generation" of American writers, including Ernest Hemingway, F. Scott Fitzgerald, and John Dos Passos, made its home, temporarily, in Paris. Much earlier, Rome drew Seneca from Iberia and Apuleius from North Africa, and Latin literature is said to have begun with Livius Andronicus, a Greek slave who wrote a Latin version of Homer's *Odyssey* (725 B.C.E.). However, with increased mobility and the globalization of cultures, the phenomenon of the writer as migrant has become more common. Written in lucid, engaging English, Ha Jin's short book offers a cogent discussion of literary figures who, like its author, find themselves situated between countries and languages.

  In his opening essay, "The Spokesman and the Tribe," Ha Jin recalls how, with his first book of poetry, his ambition, despite writing in English in the United States, was to give voice to the voiceless Chinese people. He contrasts his situation to that of Aleksandr Solzhenitsyn, who, throughout the eighteen years he spent in exile in rural Vermont, continued to write in Russian for the Russian people. He attributes Solzhenitsyn's ability to work in stubborn isolation to his Christian faith in an afterlife

Ha Jin obtained English degrees at Chinese universities. He was studying at Brandeis during the Tiananmen Square massacre and decided not to return to China. His first book was the poetry volume Between Silences *(1990). His novel* In the Pond *(1998) was followed by* Waiting *(1999), which received the National Book Award and the PEN/Faulkner Award. His short-story collections have won the PEN/ Hemingway Award and the Flannery O'Connor Award.*

but, turning to the case of Lin Yutang, notes that Chinese writers crave community. Ha Jin describes Lin Yutang's role as cultural ambassador in two directions, from China to the West and from the West to China, and he praises his *My Country and My People* (1935) as still the best book about its subject, China. However, Ha Jin faults Lin Yutang's fiction for being too general and didactic; subsuming his individual vision under that of the communities he tried to represent, Lin Yutang, Ha Jin contends, forgot the lesson that "great literature has never been produced by collectives."

Encouraged by the way Salman Rushdie's novel *Shame* (1983) subverts the clichéd analogy between human beings and trees, as if human "roots" were anything but a hackneyed metaphor, Ha Jin states: "The debunking of the tree metaphor makes it clear that human beings are different from trees and should be rootless and entirely mobile." He contends that, unlike Solzhenitsyn and Lin Yutang, who were established authors before they departed their native lands, most migrant writers must accept the fact that they are more like V. S. Naipaul, fundamentally rootless. They must establish new identities within alien cultures. By the conclusion of the first chapter of *The Writer as Migrant*, Ha Jin recognizes the naiveté of his earlier aim of speaking on behalf of the downtrodden Chinese. While conceding the obligation to take a stand against injustice, he insists that the writer serves society best by pursuing his art: "He must serve on his own terms, in the manner and at the time and place of his own choosing. Whatever role he plays, he must keep in mind that his success or failure as a writer will be determined only on the page. That is the space where he should strive to exist." Proclaiming the independence of the artist, Ha Jin thus rejects his early aspiration to write—albeit in English—on behalf of the Chinese masses.

In the second essay in the book, "The Language of Betrayal," Ha Jin examines the phenomenon of translingualism, of writing in an adopted language. Contending that the motives for switching languages are often mixed, he attributes his own use of English, rather than Chinese, to the demands of survival—not only the need to earn a livelihood but also the desire to make the best possible use of his talents in the circumstances in which he found himself. Although many of the classic Latin writers adopted the language of Rome instead of their native tongues, he hails Joseph Conrad—who was born Józef Teodor Konrad Korzeniowski in Poland but became a major novelist in English, a language he did not learn until he was in his twenties—as a pioneer of translingual literature. While noting that betrayal is in fact a theme within Conrad's fiction, he defends him against charges of cultural treason leveled by champions of Polish. In addition, he discusses the anxiety that Vladimir Nabokov felt about differentiating himself from Conrad. Nabokov, who wrote in Russian, French, and English, was intent on demonstrating greater stylistic virtuosity in English, the language he wrote in after Russian and French.

Ha Jin notes the linguistic playfulness that characterizes much of Nabokov's English fiction, particularly the 1957 novel *Pnin*, but he maintains that Nabokov's use of English rather than his native Russian crippled him as a poet. However, he proclaims Nabokov the prose artist "a supreme example of how to adapt writing to the circumstances of displacement, how to imagine and attain a place in the adopted language while still maintaining an intimate relationship with his mother tongue, and how to face an oppressive regime with contempt, artistic integrity, and individual dignity." Ha Jin identifies the humor in *Pnin*, based on a disproportionate attention to trivial matters, as Gogolian and praises it as "completely translatable." In fact, uncomfortable with word play, which is unique to each language, he insists that translatability is the hallmark of successful literature. While mastering the unique idiosyncrasies of a new language, the writer should, according to Ha Jin, strive to create a text that is not dependent upon or limited to those idiosyncrasies. "Therefore," he claims, "the writer who adopts English, while striving to seek a place in this idiom, should also imagine ways to transcend any language."

However, Nabokov was himself a translator, from Russian to English and from English to Russian. In elaborate commentary he appended to his 1964 four-volume translation of Alexander Pushkin's *Evgeny Onegin* (1825-1832, 1833; *Eugene Onegin*, 1881), Nabokov insisted both on the incommensurability of Pushkin's narrative poem and any English facsimile and on the principle that all translation ought to embody acknowledgment that it is derivative. Addressing Pushkin in his poem "On Translating *Eugene Onegin*," Nabokov belittles his own arduous effort as "Dove-droppings on your monument." Because Nabokov's *Pale Fire* (1962), a novel constructed around a poem and its commentary, makes elaborate use of linguistic play, it resists translation. It is Nabokov's greatest literary achievement, precisely because it is a consummate marriage of specific words and theme. It is what it is, which it would cease to be if rendered into anything else. It is likely that Nabokov himself would reverse Ha Jin's contention and insist that a text approaches perfection as it approaches untranslatability.

"An Individual's Homeland," the third and final chapter in *The Writer as Migrant*, is largely a meditation on the archetypal wanderer Odysseus. Contending that all of us, migrants or not, seek an Ithaca, Ha Jin begins with a few comments on C. P. Cavafy's "Ithaka" (1911), a poem in which the Greek island-state functions as a symbol of arrival, not, as in the *Odyssey*, of return. He notes that Mr. Shimerda in Willa Cather's *My Ántonia* (1918), Albert Schearl in Henry Roth's *Call It Sleep* (1934), and Carlos Chang in Sigrid Nunez's *A Feather on the Breath of God* (1995) are all broken by the pain of displacement. He contrasts them with Bertha in *Call It Sleep* and Stephen Dedalus in James Joyce's *A Portrait of the Artist as a Young Man* (1916), who are both invigorated by exile. He ponders the ambiguity of the word "homeland," which can refer either to the land of one's birth or to the land in which one has established residence. Like Thomas Wolfe, who titled his 1940 novel *You Can't Go Home Again*, he notes that, for all of Odysseus's longing to return, he can never go back to the same place as the same person. Things change, and, inevitably, so do people.

Ha Jin examines the two most famous accounts of Odysseus's life after he comes back from the Trojan War, twenty years after departing his native island. In the *Inferno* from *La divina commedia* (c. 1320; *The Divine Comedy*, 1802), Dante places the Greek hero in the eighth circle of hell, punished as an evil counselor for the sin of pride in his refusal to accept God's order and his deceit in persuading others to set out again from Ithaca to sail with him beyond mortal limits. Ha Jin reads Alfred, Lord Tennyson's 1842 poem "Ulysses" not, conventionally, as the celebration of a hero determined "[t]o strive, to seek, to find, and not to yield," but rather as the portrait of an egotist indifferent to the harm he is causing the mariners he coaxes into joining him for a final, suicidal voyage westward. He also discusses the search for home in Naipaul's *A Bend in the River* (1979) and the strategy for artistic survival in exile portrayed in W. G. Sebald's *Ausgewanderten* (1992; *The Emigrants*, 1996). Since global migration is continuous and irreversible, any conclusion to a book called *The Writer as Migrant* will be abrupt and arbitrary. Ha Jin gains enough trust through his unpretentious style that he can be forgiven for the banality of his pious parting words: "no matter where we go, we cannot shed our past completely—so we must strive to use parts of our past to facilitate our journeys. As we travel along, we should also imagine how to rearrange the landscapes of our envisioned homelands."

Steven G. Kellman

Review Sources

The Guardian, December 6, 2008, p. 7.
The New Republic 239, no. 11 (December 24, 2008): 40-43.
San Francisco Chronicle, November 9, 2008, p. M5.
The Spectator 309 (January 24, 2009): 41.

YOUR INNER FISH
A Journey into the 3.5-Billion-Year History of the Human Body

Author: Neil Shubin (1960-   )
Publisher: Pantheon Books (New York). Illustrated. 229 pp. $24.00
Type of work: Natural history, science
Time: From the Devonian Period to the present
Locale: Worldwide

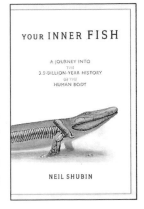

Retracing studies in paleontology, genetics, and cellular and molecular biology, Shubin draws upon his own experiences and the history of seminal experiments to demonstrate how mammalian anatomy can be traced back to the anatomy of fishes living between three and four billion years ago

Where many popular books about the animal kingdom focus on the differences between, for instance, types of primate behavior, or breeds of dogs, or variations in animal psychology and morphology because of ecological habitat, and so forth, Neil Shubin's *Your Inner Fish* focuses on the underlying similarities. As he writes, "When you look into eyes, forget about romance, creation, and the windows into the soul. With their molecules, genes, and tissues derived from microbes, jellyfish, worms, and flies, you see an entire menagerie."

Shubin is an authority on reconstructing the relationships among prehistoric creatures and those living today. In 2004 he discovered a famous "missing link," a fossil called *Tiktaalik roseae*, which excited the worlds of both science and the public upon publication of its description in 2006. This creature is a remarkable intermediate between fishes and land-living animals: Though a fish, living in shallow streams and mud-flats, it had arm and leg bones similar to those of a mammal; it was able to do push-ups.

While Shubin's autobiographical anecdotes (chiefly about his work as a paleontologist on site) appear in nonlinear order throughout his text, the book is astutely organized. In the first four chapters he shows how various branches of science prove that various organs within various creatures, ancient or extant, are profoundly related. The following chapters enumerate the resemblances between the designs of bodies, heads, hands, noses, eyes, and ears belonging to most of the denizens of the animal kingdom. "There isn't just a single fish inside of our limbs; there is a whole aquarium."

Most of the text expounds upon the relationships between unicellular creatures and invertebrates on the one hand and far more complex living forms on the other.

His discussion of the hand (or fin or paw) is exemplary, describing experiments by various genetic researchers who tinkered with a gene (which they comically named *Sonic hedgehog* after a computer game character) in creatures as different as sharks, chickens, and flies. They discovered that *Sonic hedgehog* is responsible for shaping ap-

Neil Shubin, an evolutionary biologist, holds the titles of Robert R. Bensley Professor at the University of Chicago's Department of Organismal Biology and Anatomy as well as Provost of the Field Museum of Natural History. He rose to fame with his 2004 discovery of a 375-million-year-old transitional fossil called Tiktaalik roseae

pendages, whether shark fins or human hands, and that if its normal function is interfered with, in the laboratory, the result is a surprising reduplication of digits, such as changing a thumb into a pinkie finger or vice versa. The importance of this finding is that the evolution of fish fins into land-based limbs was not based on the emergence of new kinds of DNA, but, rather, that ancient genes merely recombined in new ways.

Shubin's recollections of his first investigations in the world of fossil-finding under the tutelage of colleague Dr. Farish A. Jenkins are delightful. He jests about his beginner's inability to distinguish among tooth, bone, and sandy rocks in the Arizona desert. He recalls the electrifying jolt he felt when he first spotted a tiny tooth, "as glorious as the biggest dinosaur in the halls of any museum." On a 1984 excursion to Nova Scotia, Shubin felt disappointed by his team's tiny haul, only to find later that he had brought home a rare specimen: a tooth from a fossilized tritheledont, a remarkable creature that is part mammal and part reptile; it might have resembled a mouse with crocodile teeth or, more precisely, a furry lizard with mammalian carnivorous teeth.

Recognizing that his subjects under discussion may be abstruse for some readers, he leavens his scientific jargon with wit, as for instance in his amusing instructions on how to extract DNA in the kitchen, using a piece of steak, salted water, soap, and a few other ingredients. Elsewhere, he remarks jocularly, "The job of teeth is to make bigger creatures into smaller pieces." Such enjoyable tidbits abound in his book.

Shubin references popular culture frequently for clarity. "For those who believed that skeletons began with jaws, backbones, or body armor, conodonts [extinct animals similar to eels] provide an 'inconvenient tooth,' if you will"—an allusion to the film *An Inconvenient Truth* (2006), a documentary about Vice President and Nobel Peace Prize winner Al Gore's attempts to educate the public about the issue of global warming. In another allusion, he writes: "The only thing we can compare it with is the alien creature in the Steve McQueen [1958] film *The Blob*." He also writes that, "If we were like sponges, then the Steve Buscemi character who gets minced in the woodchipper in the Coen brothers' [1996] film *Fargo* would have been just fine." In another allusion, "It may have taken the paleontological equivalent of a perfect storm to bring about bodies"—a reference to the book *The Perfect Storm* (1997) by historian and journalist Sebastian Junger and the 2000 film adaptation of that title.

He uses an ingenious array of analogies: the skeleton is like a bridge; molecules may act like rivets, or glue, or like telegraphs sent from one cell to another; genes that fall into disuse do so in the way that photocopies lose their fidelity with repeated copyings; the evolution of the human eye is much like the evolution of a Chevrolet Corvette through decades of variation in model design; equilibrioception (or sense of balance) is compared with the movement of white particles within a snow globe; examining "descent with modification" is like opening a time capsule.

One problem with simplification for the lay reader in popular science texts—and one that has been frequently commented upon—is that scientific precision may be lost and may suggest that evolution is goal-oriented, whereas evolution actually proceeds entirely by random occurrences and has no "end" in mind. To put it in other words, there is no Mother Nature trying a design, then discarding it for another design, always seeking some final sort of "perfect" design. When Shubin writes, "The new ability came about by modifying the upper jawbone of a fish," it would be more accurate to state the case otherwise, by writing "came about by gradual modifications over millennia" or something of the sort. Fortunately, Shubin rarely uses phraseology that suggests any ideological determination to explain phenomena by final causes, as he is so much more interested in true causality.

Shubin's method of creating narrative suspense is rather like that of a mystery novelist: He poses a question, recounts an investigation by himself or other scientists, then provides the solution, one that might lead to further questions. For the second step, investigation, Shubin describes many of the seminal experiments in biology that have led to important, ongoing, and sometimes interdisciplinary projects. For example, a question is offered: How and why did vertebrate bodies arise? Shubin explains that biologist Martin E. Boraas showed how a single-celled alga could turn into a colony of bodies (by introducing a predator into the habitat). The significance of this result rests on the fact that for the first 3.5 billion years of the history of Earth, there is no evidence of any kind of life except for micro-organisms. Then the fossil record begins to teem for many millions of years. As Shubin remarks, "If an experiment can produce a simple body-like organization from a no-body in several years, imagine what could happen in billions of years. The question then becomes not how could bodies arise, but why didn't they arise sooner?" Shubin then proceeds to explain a probable solution to this follow-up riddle (an increase of oxygen in Earth's atmosphere).

In another example, he reveals that fully 3 percent of the human genome is devoted to the sense of smell, and he questions why humans need so many genes for odor detection. A related question notes that hundreds of these genes actually do not function at all, so why are they present in the body? The investigation into this mystery comes through study of what is called nasal drift in dolphins and whales: Unlike fishes, who have specialized genes for smelling in water, dolphins and whales have specialized genes for smelling scents in air. The nostrils of ancient cetaceans were located at the front of the face, as with other mammals, but through millennia the nasal passages migrated upward to the top of the head, becoming the blowhole, through which breathing is done, but not smelling. In other words, cetaceans have the full array of olfactory genes, but do not use a single one. The puzzle is solved, then, with the understanding that humans do not need every single olfactory gene, either. Genes for vision have supplanted them.

While finding beauty in the great diversity of the animal kingdom and its earliest citizens, Shubin also acknowledges pitfalls:

Our humanity comes at a cost. For the exceptional combination of things we do— talk, think, grasp, and walk on two legs—we pay a price . . . .Take the body plan of a fish, dress it up to be a mammal, then tweak and twist that mammal until it walks on two legs, talks, thinks, and has superfine control of its fingers—and you have a recipe for problems . . . . In a perfectly designed world—one with no history—we would not have to suffer everything from hemorrhoids to cancer . . . we were not designed to live past the age of eighty, sit on our keisters for ten hours a day, and eat Hostess Twinkies, nor were we designed to play football. This disconnect between our past and our human present means that our bodies fall apart in certain predictable ways. Virtually every illness we suffer has some historical component.

He continues to explain some of these problems: the design of the throat (modified from fishes' gills) that allows humans to speak also allows them to suffer sleep apnea and choking. Tadpoles use both lungs and gills to breathe, but modifications over the millennia have led to the horridness called hiccups. The gonads of most fishes are located near their hearts, but complications arising from the gradual descent of gonads into human testes make men vulnerable to hernias. However, Shubin ends on a positive note: "I can imagine few things more beautiful or intellectually profound than finding the basis for our humanity, and remedies for many of the ills we suffer, nestled inside some of the most humble creatures that have ever lived on our planet."

Shubin's gift is for sharing his sense of wonder and beauty with readers who may never have given much thought to worms, jellyfish, or flies, but who will henceforth look upon such so-called lowly animals with new respect for the interconnectedness of all living things. This book is best suited to readers interested in paleontology, biology, and physical anatomy, with some understanding of the basics of these subjects. It assuredly belongs in most libraries.

Fiona Kelleghan

Review Sources

American Scientist 96, no. 3 (May/June, 2008): 257-258.
Booklist 104, nos. 9/10 (January 1, 2008): 31.
Chicago Tribune, February 18, 2008, p. 1.
The Chronicle of Higher Education 54, no. 27 (March 14, 2008): B27.
Discover 29, no. 2 (February, 2008): 72.
The Globe and Mail, March 29, 2008, p. D5.
Kirkus Reviews 75, no. 22 (November 15, 2007): 1196.
Library Journal 133, no. 1 (January 1, 2008): 129.
Los Angeles Times, January 13, 2008, p. R6.
Nature 451 (January 17, 2008): 245.
New Scientist 197 (January 19, 2008): 45.
Publishers Weekly 254, no. 43 (October 29, 2007): 41.
The Washington Post, February 17, 2008, p. T6.

MAGILL'S
LITERARY ANNUAL
2009

BIOGRAPHICAL WORKS BY SUBJECT

2009

ADORNO, THEODOR W.
   Theodor W. Adorno (Claussen), 788

BARNES, JULIAN
   Nothing to Be Frightened Of (Barnes),
   591
BIN LADEN, OSAMA
   Bin Ladens, The (Coll), 83
BOYLAN, JENNIFER FINNEY
   I'm Looking Through You (Boylan),
   392
BROTTMAN, MIKITA
   Solitary Vice, The (Brottman), 738
BUCKLEY, WILLIAM F., JR.
   Flying High (Buckley), 269

DALAI LAMA
   Open Road, The (Iyer), 609
DAWIDOFF, NICHOLAS
   Crowd Sounds Happy, The (Dawidoff),
   166
DICKINSON, EMILY
   Summer of Hummingbirds, A (Benfey),
   764
   White Heat (Wineapple), 843
DOUGLAS, SCOTT
   Quiet, Please (Douglas), 671
DOUGLAS, STEPHEN
   Lincoln and Douglas (Guelzo), 474

FILKINS, DEXTER
   Forever War, The (Filkins), 273

GODARD, JEAN-LUC
   Everything Is Cinema (Brody), 238
GOLDWATER, BARRY
   Flying High (Buckley), 269

HEADE, MARTIN
   Summer of Hummingbirds, A (Benfey),
   764
HEMINGS, SALLY
   Hemingses of Monticello, The
   (Gordon-Reed), 344
HIGGINSON, THOMAS WENTWORTH
   White Heat (Wineapple), 843
HITLER, ADOLF
   Hitler's Private Library (Ryback), 358
HOPKINS, GERARD MANLEY
   Gerard Manley Hopkins (Mariani), 301
HULL, AGRIPPA
   Friends of Liberty (Nash and Hodges),
   292

JACKSON, ANDREW
   American Lion (Meacham), 43
JEFFERSON, THOMAS
   Friends of Liberty (Nash and Hodges),
   292
   Hemingses of Monticello, The
   (Gordon-Reed), 344

KAZIN, ALFRED
   Alfred Kazin (Cook), 14
KEATS, JOHN
   Posthumous Keats (Plumly), 653
KEENE, DONALD
   Chronicles of My Life (Keene), 129
KING, MARTIN LUTHER, JR.
   Word of the Lord Is upon Me, The
   (Rieder), 874
KOŚCIUSZKO, TADEUSCZ
   Friends of Liberty (Nash and Hodges),
   292

CATEGORY INDEX

2009

ANTHROPOLOGY. *See* SOCIOLOGY,
ARCHAEOLOGY, and
ANTHROPOLOGY

ARCHAEOLOGY. *See* SOCIOLOGY,
ARCHAEOLOGY, and
ANTHROPOLOGY

AUTOBIOGRAPHY, MEMOIRS,
DIARIES, and LETTERS
Acedia and Me (Norris), 1
Armageddon in Retrospect (Vonnegut), 56
Bishop's Daughter, The (Moore), 88
Books (McMurtry), 103
Called Out of Darkness (Rice), 120
Chronicles of My Life (Keene), 129
Crowd Sounds Happy, The (Dawidoff),
166
Flying High (Buckley), 269
Forever War, The (Filkins), 273
Freewheelin' Time, A (Rotolo), 288
I'm Looking Through You (Boylan), 392
Last Days of Old Beijing, The (Meyer), 437
Nothing to Be Frightened Of (Barnes), 591
Quiet, Please (Douglas), 671

Solitary Vice, The (Brottman), 738
Step from Death, A (Woiwode), 751
What I Talk About When I Talk About
Running (Murakami), 831
When You Are Engulfed in Flames
(Sedaris), 835

BIOGRAPHY. *See also* LITERARY
BIOGRAPHY
American Lion (Meacham), 43
Beautiful Soul of John Woolman, The
(Slaughter), 74
Bin Ladens, The (Coll), 83
Did Lincoln Own Slaves? (Prokopowicz),
225
Everything Is Cinema (Brody), 238
Friends of Liberty (Nash and Hodges), 292
Gustav Mahler, 1907-1911 (La Grange), 325
Hemingses of Monticello, The (Gordon-
Reed), 344
Ida, A Sword Among Lions (Giddings),
387
Man Who Loved China, The (Winchester),
518
Man Who Made Lists, The (Kendall), 523

TITLE INDEX

2009

AUTHOR INDEX

2009